Henry Green

Shakespeare and the emblem writers

Henry Green

Shakespeare and the emblem writers

ISBN/EAN: 9783742858757

Manufactured in Europe, USA, Canada, Australia, Japa

Cover: Foto ©Thomas Meinert / pixelio.de

Manufactured and distributed by brebook publishing software
(www.brebook.com)

Henry Green

Shakespeare and the emblem writers

SHAKESPEARE

AND

THE EMBLEM WRITERS.

PORTRAITS FROM ORIGINAL PLATES.—*Bocchius by Bonasone*, A.D. 1555; *the others by Theodore de Bry*, A.D. 1598.

SHAKESPEARE

AND

THE EMBLEM WRITERS;

AN EXPOSITION OF THEIR

SIMILARITIES OF THOUGHT AND EXPRESSION.

PRECEDED BY A VIEW OF EMBLEM-LITERATURE DOWN TO A.D. 1616.

BY HENRY GREEN, M.A.

With numerous Illustrative Devices from the Original Authors.

Portrait of Shakespeare.
From the Oil Painting in the possession of Dr. [illegible]

LONDON: TRÜBNER & CO., 60, PATERNOSTER ROW.
1870.

Preface.

FEW only are the remarks absolutely needed by way of introduction to a work which within itself sufficiently explains and carries out a new method of illustration for the dramas of Shakespeare. As author, I commenced this volume because of various observations which, while reading several of the early Emblem writers, I had made on similarities of thought and expression between themselves and the great Poet; and I had sketched the whole outline, and had nearly filled it in, without knowing that the path pursued by me had in any instance been trodden by other amateurs and critics. From the writings of the profoundly learned Francis Douce, whose name ought never to be uttered without deep respect for his rare scholarship and generous regard to its interests, I first became aware that Shakespeare's direct quotation of Emblem mottoes, and direct description of Emblem devices, had in some degree been already pointed out to the attention of the literary public.

And right glad am I to observe that I have had precursors in my labours, and companions in my researches; and that, in addition to Francis Douce, writers of such repute as Langlois of Rouen, Charles Knight, Noel Humphreys, and Dr. Alfred Woltmann, of Berlin, have, each by an example or two, shown how, with admirable skill and yet with evident appropriation, our great Dramatist has interwoven among his own the materials which he had gathered from Emblem writers as their source.

To myself the fact is an assurance that neither from aiming at singularity of conjecture, nor from pretending to a more penetrating insight into Shakespeare's methods of composition, have I put before the world the following pages for judgment. Those pages are the results of genuine study,—a study I could not have so well pursued had not liberal-minded friends freely entrusted to my use the book-treasures which countervailed my own deficiencies. The results arrived at, though imperfect, are also, I believe, grounded on real similitudes between Shakespeare and his predecessors and contemporaries; and those similitudes, parallelisms, or adaptations of thought, by whichever name distinguished, often arose from the actual impression made on his mind and memory by the Emblematists whose works he had seen, read, and used.

As a suitable Frontispiece the portraits are presented of five celebrated authors of the fifteenth and sixteenth centuries: one a German—Sebastian Brandt; three Italian—Andrew Alciat, Paolo Giovio, and Achilles Bocchius; and one from Hungary—John Sambucus. They were all men of learning and renown, whom kings and emperors honoured, and whom the foremost of their age admired. The central portrait, that of Bocchius of Bologna, is from the famous artist Giulio Bonasone, and the original engraving was retouched by Augustino Caracci. The other portraits have been reduced from the "ICONES," or *Figures of Fifty Illustrious Men*, which Theodore de Bry executed and published during Shakespeare's prime, in 1597. In their own day they were regarded as correct delineations and likenesses, and are said to be authentic copies.

The vignette of Shakespeare on the title-page is now

engraved for the first time. The original is an oil-painting, a head of the life size, and possessing considerable animation and evidences of power. It is the property of Charles Clay, Esq., M.D., Manchester. Without vouching for its authenticity, we are justified in saying, when it is compared with some other portraits, that it offers equal, if not superior, claims to genuineness. To discuss the question does not belong to these pages, but simply and cordially to acknowledge the courtesy with which the oil-painting was offered for use and allowed to be copied, and to say that our woodcut is an accurate and well-executed representation of the original picture.

Of the ornamental capitals at the head of the chapters, and of the little embellishments at their end, it may be remarked that, with scarcely an exception, there are none later than our Poet's day, and but few that do not belong to Emblem books: they are forty-eight in number. The illustrative woodcuts and photolith plates, of which there are one hundred and fifty-three of the former and nineteen of the latter, partake of the variety, and, it may be said, apologetically, of the defects of the works from which they have been taken. However fanciful in themselves, they are realities,—true exponents of the Emblem art of their day; so that, within the compass of our volume, containing above two hundred examples of emblematic devices and designs, is exhibited a very full representation of the various styles of the original works, and which, in the absence of the works themselves, may serve to show their chief characteristics. The Photoliths, I may add, have been executed by Mr. A. Brothers, of Manchester.

Doubtless both the woodcuts and the plates are very unequal in their execution; but to have aimed at a uniformity even of high excellence would have been to sacrifice truth to mere embellishment. It should be borne in mind what one of our objects has been, — namely, to place before the reader examples of the Emblem devices themselves, very nearly as they existed in their own day, and not to attempt the ideal perfection to which modern art rightly aspires.

The Edition of Shakespeare from which the extracts are taken is the very excellent one, in nine volumes, issued from Cambridge, 1863—1866. Its numbering of the lines for purposes of reference is most valuable.

Our work offers information, and consequently advantage, to three classes of the literary public :—

1st. To the Book Agent and Book Antiquarian, so far as relates to books of Emblems previous to the early part of the seventeenth century, A. D. 1616. In a collected and methodical form, aided not a little by the General Index, the first chapters and sections of our volume supply information that is widely scattered, and not to be obtained without considerable trouble and search. The authors, titles, and dates of the *chief* editions of Emblem books within the period treated of, are clearly though briefly given, arranged according to the languages in which the books were printed, and accompanied where requisite by notices and remarks. There is not to be found, I believe, in any other work so much information about the early Emblem books, gathered together in so compendious and orderly a manner.

2nd. To the Students and Scholars of Shakespeare, — a widely-extended and ever-increasing community. Another aspect of the Master's reading and attainments is opened to them ; and into the yet unquarried illustrations of which his marvellous writings are susceptible, another adit is driven. We may have followed him through Histories and Legends, through the Epic and the Ballad, through Popular Tales and Philosophic

Treatises,—from the forest glade to the halls and gardens of palaces,—across the wild moor where the weird sisters muttered and prophesied, and to that moon-lighted bank where the sweet Jessica was sitting in all maiden loveliness;—but if only for variety's sake it may interest us, even if it does not impart pleasure, to mark how much his mind was in accord with the once popular Emblem literature, which now perchance awakens scarcely a thought or a regret, though great scholars and men of genius devoted themselves to it; and how from that literature, imbued with its spirit and heightening its power, even he—the self-reliant one—borrowed help and imagery, and made his own creations more his own than otherwise they would have been.

And 3rd. To the great Brotherhood of nations among the Teutonic race, to whom Shakespeare is known as a chieftain among the Lares,—the heroes and guardians of their households. In him they recognise an impersonation of high poetic Art, and they desire to see unrolled from the treasures of the past whatever course his genius pursued to elevate and refine its powers;—persuaded that out of the elevation and refinement ever is springing something of his own inspiration to improve and ennoble mankind.

A word or two may be allowed respecting the translations into English which are offered of the Emblem writers' verses occurring in the quotations. An accurate rendering of the original was desirable; and, therefore, in many instances, rhymes and strictly measured lines have been abjured, and cadence trusted rather than metre; the defect of the plan, perhaps, is that cadence varies with the peculiar pitch and intonation of each person's voice. Nevertheless, among rhymes the *Oarsman's Cry* (p. 61) might find a place on Cam, or Isis, and the *Wolf and the Ass* (p. 54) be entitled to abide in a book of fables.

In behalf of quotations from the original, it is to be urged that, to defamiliarise the minds of the public, so much as is now the custom, from the sight of other languages than their own, is injurious to the maintenance of scholarship; and were it not so, the works quoted from are many of them not in general use, and some are of highest rarity;—it is, therefore, only simple justice to the reader to place before him the original on the very page he is reading.

The value of the work will doubtless be increased by the Appendices and the very full Index which have been added. These will enable such as are inclined more thoroughly to compare together the different parts of the work, and better to judge of it, and to pursue its subjects elsewhere.

My offering I hang up where many brighter garlands have been placed,—and where, as generations pass away, many more will be brought; it is at his shrine whose genius consecrated the English tongue to some of the highest purposes of which speech is capable. For Humanity itself he rendered his Service of Song a guidance to that which is noble as well as beautiful,—a sympathy with our nature as well as a truth for our souls. God's benison rest upon his memory!

Knutsford,

August 10, 1869.

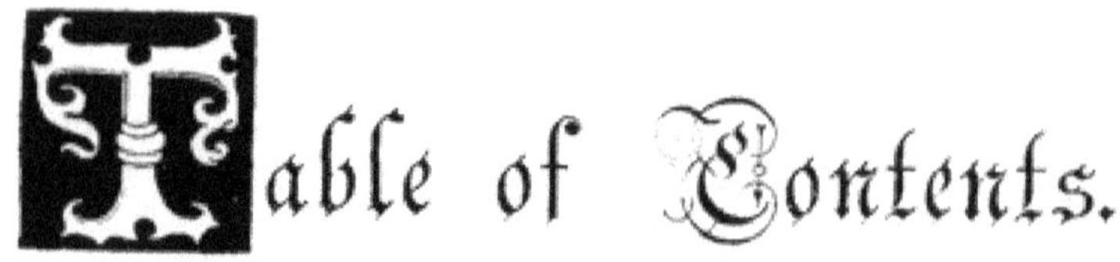

Table of Contents.

CHAPTER II.—(*continued*).

CHAPTER III.

CHAPTER IV.

CHAPTER V.

CHAPTER VI.

CHAPTER VII.

APPENDICES.

PHOTO-LITH PLATES.

Hesius, 1636.

Stans vno capit omnia puncto.

In Remembrance
JOSEPH BROOKS YATES
LIVERPOOL,
BOOKS OF EMBLEMS
AUTHOR

SHAKESPEARE

AND THE

EMBLEM-WRITERS OF HIS AGE.

CHAPTER I.

EMBLEMS, AND THEIR VARIETIES, WITH SOME EARLY EXAMPLES.

HAT Emblems are, in the general acceptation of the word in modern times, is well set forth in Cotgrave's *Dictionary*, Art. EMBLEMA, where he defines an emblem to be, "a picture and short posie, expressing some particular conceit;" and very pithily by Francis Quarles, when he says,—"an Emblem is but a silent Parable." Though less terse and clear than either of these, we may also take Bacon's description, in his *Advancement of Learning*, bk. v. chap. 5;—"*Embleme* deduceth conceptions intellectuall to images sensible, and that which is sensible more forcibly strikes the memory, and is more easily imprinted than that which is intellectual."

By many writers of Emblem books, perhaps by the majority in their practice if not in their theories, there is very little difference of meaning observed between Symbols and Emblems. We find, however, in other Authors a more exact usage of the word Symbol. The Greek poet Pindar* speaks of "a trustworthy symbol, or sign, concerning a future action," or from which the future can be conjectured; Iago, recounting the power of Desdemona over Othello, act ii. scene 3, l. 326, declares it were easy

"for her
To win the Moor, were't to renounce his baptism,
All seals and symbols of redeemed sin;"

and Cudworth, in his *True Intellectual System of the Universe*, ed. 1678, p. 388, after giving Aristotle's assertion "*that Numbers were the Causes of the Essence of other things*," adds, "though we are not ignorant, how the Pythagoreans made also the Numbers within the Decad, to be Symbols of things."

Claude Mignault, or Minōs, the famous commentator on the Emblems of Andreas Alciatus, in his Tract, *Concerning Symbols, Coats of Arms, and Emblems*,—eds. 1581, or 1608, or 1614,—maintains there is a clear distinction between emblems and symbols, which, as he affirms, "many persons rashly and ignorantly confound together." † "We confess," he adds, "that the force of the Emblem depends upon the Symbol: but they differ, I say, as Man and Animal; for people who have any judgment at all know, that here of a certainty the latter is taken more generally, the former more specially." Mignault's meaning may be carried out by saying, that all men are animals,—but all animals are not men; so all emblems are symbols, tokens, or signs, but all symbols are not emblems;—the two

* See the *Olympica*, 12. 10: "σύμβολον πιστὸν ἀμφὶ πράξιος ἐσσομένης." Also Æschylus, *Agamemnon*, 8: "καὶ νῦν φυλάσσω λαμπάδος τὸ σύμβολον."

† *Syntagma De Symbolis, &c.*, per Clavdivm Minoem, Lvgdvni, M.DC.XIII. p. 13: "Plerique sunt non satis acuti, qui Emblema cum Symbolo, cum Ænigmate, cum Sententia, cum Adagio, temerè & imperitè confundunt. Fatemur Emblematis quidem vim in symbolo sitam esse; sed differunt, inquam, vt Homo & Animal: alterum enim hîc maximè generaliùs accipi, specialiùs verò alterum norũt omnes qui aliquid indicii habeant."

possess affinity but not identity,—they have no absolute convertibility of the one for the other.

An example of Emblem and Symbol united occurs in Symeoni's Dedication * "To Madame Diana of Poitiers, Dutchess of Valentinois;" for Emblem, there are "picture and short posie" expressing the particular conceit, "Quodcunque petit, consequitur,"— *She attains whatever she seeks;* and for Symbols, or signs, the sun, the temple, the dogs, the arrow, and the stag; and for exposition, the stanza;

Symeoni, 1559.

> "*Sante le Muse son, santa è Diana,*
> *Caste son quelle, et casta è questa anchora.*
> *Dalle Muse il Sol mai non s' allontana,*
> *Et d' Apollo Diana unica è suora.*
> *Nelle Muse è d' Amore ogni arte vana,*
> *Et de i lacci d' Amor Diana è fuora.*
> *Chi fia Diana quel dunque che dica,*
> *Che voi non siete delle Muse amica?*"

Thus metrically rendered,

> "Holy the Muses are, holy is Diana,
> Chaste are they, and chaste also is she.
> From the Muses the Sun indeed moves not afar,
> And alone of Apollo Diana is sister.
> Against the Muses Love's every art is vain,
> And free is Diana from all snares of Love.
> Who then is the Diana that says,
> That you are not a friend of the Muses?"

* "LA VITA ET METAMORFOSEO:" "A Lione, per Giouanni di Tornes," 8vo, 1559, pp. 2, 3.

The word emblem, ἔμβλημα, is one that has strayed very widely from its first meaning, and yet by a sort of natural process, as the apple grows out of the crab, its signification now is akin to what it was in distant ages. It then denoted the thing, whether implement or ornament, placed in, or thrown on, and so joined to, some other thing. Thus a word of cognate origin, *Epiblēs*, in the *Iliad*, bk. xxiv. l. 453,* denoted the bolt of fir that held fast the door;—it was something put against the door,—the peg or bar that kept it from opening. So in the *Odyssey*, bk. ii. l. 37,† the sceptre, the emblem of command, was the baton which the herald Peisēnor *placed in* the hand of the son of Ulysses; and again in the *Iliad*, bk. xiii. l. 319, 20,‡ the flaming torch was the implement which the son of Kronos might *throw on* the swift ships.

Of the changes through which a word may pass, "the word Emblem presents one of the most remarkable instances." They cannot be better given than in the "*Sketch of that branch of Literature called* BOOKS OF EMBLEMS," read in 1848 before the Literary and Philosophical Society of Liverpool, by the late Joseph Brooks Yates, Esq. He says of the word EMBLEM, pp. 8, 9,—"its present signification, 'Type or allusive representation,' is of comparatively modern use, while its original meaning is become obsolete. Among the Greeks an Emblem (εμβλημα), derived from εμβαλλειν, meant something thrown in or inserted after the fashion of what we now call Marquetry and Mosaic work, or in the form of a detached ornament to be affixed to a pillar, a tablet, or a vase, and put off or on, as there might be occasion. Pliny, in his *Natural History*," bk. xxxiii. c. 12,

* . . . . "θύρην δ' ἔχε μοῦνος ἐπιβλὴς Εἰλάτινος."

† . . . . "σκῆπτρον δέ οἱ ἔμβαλε χειρὶ Κῆρυξ Πεισήνωρ."

‡ "Νῆας ἐνεπρῆσαι, ὅτε μὴ αὐτός γε Κρονίων
Ἐμβάλοι αἰθόμενον δαλὸν νήεσσι θοῇσιν.

"mentions an artist called Pytheus, who executed works of this last description in silver, one of which, intended to be attached to a jar (in phialæ emblemate), represented Ulysses and Diomed carrying off the Palladium.* It weighed two ounces, and sold for 10,000 sesterces = 80*l.* 14*s.* 7*d.* of our money. According to one ancient manuscript of Pliny, it sold for double that amount. Marcus Curtius leaping into the gulph forms the subject of a beautiful silver Emblem, in the possession of the writer.† When the arts of Greece were transplanted into Italy and Sicily, the word *Emblema* became naturalised in the Latin tongue, though not without some resistance on the part of the reigning prince Tiberius. That emperor is reported by Suetonius," *Tiber. Cæsar Vita*, c. 71, "to have found fault with the introduction of the word into a Decree of the Senate, as being of foreign growth. Cicero, however, had used it in his orations against Verres, where he accuses that rapacious governor (amongst other crimes) of having compelled the people of Haluntium to bring to him their vases, from which he carefully abstracted the valuable Emblems and inserted them upon his own golden vessels. Quintilian," lib. 2, cap. 4, "soon after this period, in enumerating the arts of oratory used by the pleaders of his day, describes some of them as in the habit of preparing and committing to memory certain highly finished clauses, to be inserted (as occasion might arise) *like Emblems* in the body of their orations." ‡

"Such was the meaning of the term in the classical ages of Greece and Rome; nor was its signification altered until some time after the revival of literature in the fifteenth century."

Our own Geoffrey Whitney, deriving, as he does the other

* Philemon Holland names the work of art, "A broad goblet or standing piece," —"*with a device appendant to it*, for to be set on and taken off with a vice."

† Now the property of his grandson, Mr. Henry Yates Thompson, of Thingwall, near Liverpool.

‡ Quidam . . . . scriptos eos (scilicet locos) memoriæque diligentissime mandatos, inpromptu habuerent, ut quoties esset occasio, extemporales eorum dictiones, his, velut Emblematibus exornarentur."—*Quint. Lib.* 2, *cap.* 4.

parts of his *Choice of Emblemes* from the writers on the subject that preceded him, gives very exactly the same explanation as Mr. Yates. In his address "To the Reader" (p. 2) he says;—"It resteth now to shewe breeflie what this worde Embleme signifieth, and whereof it commeth, which thoughe it be borrowed of others, & not proper in the Englishe tonge, yet that which it signifieth: Is, and hathe bin alwaies in vse amongst vs, which worde being in Greek ἐμβάλλεσθαι, vel ἐπεμβλῆσθαι is as muche to saye in Englishe as *To set in, or to put in:* properlie ment by suche figures, or workes; as are wroughte in plate, or in stones in the pauementes, or on the waules, or suche like, for the adorning of the place: hauinge some wittie deuise expressed with cunning woorkemanship, somethinge obscure to be perceiued at the first, whereby, when with further consideration it is vnderstood, it maie the greater delighte the behoulder. And althoughe the worde dothe comprehende manie thinges, and diuers matters maie be therein contained; yet all Emblemes for the most parte, maie be reduced into these three kindes, which is *Historicall*, *Naturall*, & *Morall*. *Historicall*, as representing the actes of some noble persons, being matter of historie. *Naturall*, as in expressing the natures of creatures, for example, the loue of the yonge Storkes, to the oulde, or of suche like. *Morall*, pertaining to vertue and instruction of life, which is the chiefe of the three, and the other two maye bee in some sorte drawen into this head. For, all doe tende vnto discipline, and morall preceptes of liuing. I mighte write more at large hereof, and of the difference of *Emblema*, *Symbolum*, *&* *Ænigma*, hauinge all (as it weare) some affinitie one with the other. But bicause my meaning is to write as briefely as I maie, for the auoiding of tediousnes, I referre them that would further inquire therof, to *And. Alciatus*, *Guiliel. Perrerius*, *Achilles Bocchius* & to diuers others that haue written thereof, wel knowne to the learned. For I purpose at this present, to write onelie of this worde Embleme:

Bicause it chieflie doth pertaine vnto the matter I haue in hande, whereof I hope this muche, shall giue them some taste that weare ignoraunt of the same."

Whitney's namesake, to whom flattering friendship compared him, Geoffrey Chaucer, gives us more than the touch of an Emblem, when he describes, in the *Canterbury Tales*, l. 159-63, the dress of "a Nonne, a Prioresse,"—

"Of smale corall aboute hire arm she bare
A pair of bedes, gauded all with grene;
And theron heng a broche of gold ful shene,
On whiche was first ywritten a crouned A,
And after, *Amor vincit omnia*."*

So the "Cristofre," which the Yeoman wore, l. 115,

"A Cristofre on his brest of silver shene,"

was doubtless a true Emblem, to be put on, and taken off, as occasion served,—and was probably a cross with the image of Christ upon it: and if pictured forth according to the description in *The Legend of Good Women*, l. 1196-8, an emblematical device was exhibited, where

"With saddle redde, embrouded with delite
Of gold the barres, up enbossed high,
Sate Dido, all in gold and perrie wrigh."

This form, the natural form of the Emblem, we may illustrate from a Greek coin, figured in Eschenburg's *Manual of Classical Literature*, by Fisk, ed. 1844, pl. xl. p. 351.

The Flying Horse and other ornaments of this coin on the helmet of Minerva are Emblems,—and so are the owl, the olive wreath, and the amphora, or two-handled vase. Were these

---

* So the note in illustration quotes from Gower, *Conf. Am.* f. 190,

"Upon *the gaudees* all without
Was wryte of gold, *pur reposer*."

independent castings or mouldings, to be put on or taken off, they would be veritable emblems in the strict literal sense of the word.

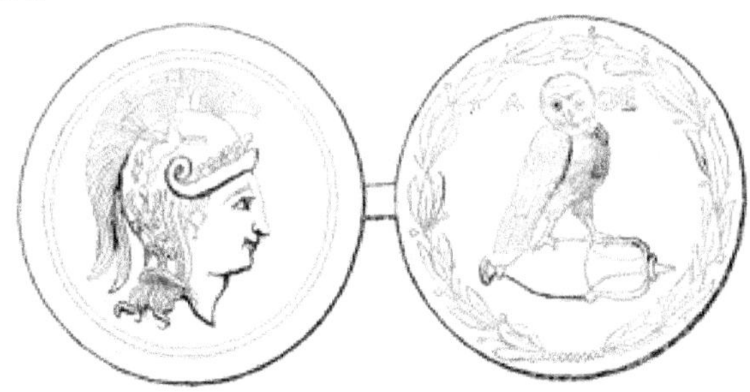

Spenser's ideas of devices and ornaments correspond to this meaning. Mercilla, the allegorical representation of the sovereign Elizabeth, is described as

"that gratious Queene:
Who sate on high, that she might all men see
And might of all men royally be seene,
Upon a throne of gold full bright and sheene,
Adorned all with gemmes of endless price,
As either might for wealth have gotten beene,
Or could be fram'd by workman's rare device
And all embost with lyons and with flour de lice."

Faerie Queene, v. 9. 27.

In *Cymbeline*, Shakespeare represents Iachimo, act i. sc. 6, l. 188, 9, describing "a present for the emperor;"

"'Tis plate, of rare device; and jewels
Of rich and exquisite form; their values great."

So Spenser, *Faerie Queene*, iv. 4. 15, sets forth, "a precious rebeke in an arke of gold," as

"A gorgeous Girdle, curiously embost
With pearle and precious stone, worth many a marke;
Yet did the workmanship farre passe the cost."

In the literal use of the word emblem Shakespeare is very exact. Parolles, *All's Well*, act ii. sc. 1, l. 40, charges the young lords of the French court, as

"Noble heroes, my sword and yours are kin;" and adds, "Good sparks and lustrous, a word, good metals: you shall find in the regiment of the Spinii one Captain Spurio, with his cicatrice, an emblem of war, here on his sinister cheek; it was this very sword entrenched it."

The Coronation Scene in *Henry VIII.*, act iv. sc. 1, l. 81—92, describes the solemnities, when Anne Bullen, "the goodliest woman that ever lay by man,"

> "with modest paces
> Came to the altar; where she kneel'd, and saint-like
> Cast her fair eyes to heaven, and pray'd devoutly:"

Each sacred rite is then observed towards her;—

> "She had all the royal makings of a queen;
> As holy oil, Edward Confessor's crown,
> The rod, and bird of peace, and all such emblems
> Lay'd nobly on her."

And down to Milton's time the original meaning of the word Emblem was still retained, though widely departed from as used by some of the Emblem writers. Thus he pictures the "blissful bower" of Eden, bk. iv. l. 697—703, *Paradise Lost*,

> "each beauteous flower,
> Iris all hues, roses, and jessamin,
> Rear'd high their flourish'd heads between, and wrought
> Mosaic: underfoot the violet,
> Crocus, and hyacinth, with rich inlay
> Broider'd the ground, more colour'd than with stone
> Of costliest emblem."

Thus, in their origin, Emblems were the figures or ornaments fashioned by the tools of the artists, in metal or wood, independent of the vase, or the column, or the furniture, they were intended to adorn; they might be affixed or detached at the promptings of the owner's fancy. Then they were formed, as in mosaic, by placing side by side little blocks of coloured stone, or tiles, or small sections of variegated wood. Raised or carved figures, however produced, came next to be considered as Emblems; and afterwards any kind of figured ornament, or device, whether carved or engraved, or simply traced, on the walls and floors of houses or on vessels of wood, clay, stone, or metal. These ornaments were sometimes like the raised work on the Warwick and other vases, and formed a *crust* which made a part of the vessel which they embellished; but at other times they were devices, drawings and carvings on a *framework* which might be detached from the cup or goblet on which the owner had placed them, and be applied to other uses.*

We may here remark, since embossed ornaments and sculptured figures on any plain surface are essentially Emblems, the sculptor, the engraver, the statuary and the architect, indeed all workers in wood, metal, or stone, who embellish with device or symbol the simplicity of nature's materials, are especially entitled to take rank in the fraternity of the Emblematists. They and their patrons, the whole world of the civilized and the intellectual, are not content with the beam out of the forest, or with the marble from the quarry, or with even the gold from the mine. In themselves cedar, marble and gold are only forms of brute and unintelligent nature,—and therefore we impose upon them signs of deep-seated thoughts of the heart and devices of wondrous meaning, and out of the rocks call forth sermons, and lessons and parables, and highly spiritual suggestions. On the very shrines of God we place our images of corruptible things,—but then the soul that rightly reads the images lifts them out of their corruptibility and makes them the teachers of eternal truths.

---

* See Smith's *Dictionary of Gk. and Rom. Ant.*, p. 377 *b*, article EMBLEMA.

The domains of the statuary and of the architect are however too vast to be entered upon by us, except with a passing glance; they are like Philosophy; it is all *Natural,*—and yet wisely men map it out into kingdoms and divisions, and pursue each his selected work.

So we remember it is not the Universe of Emblematism we must attempt, even though Shakespeare should lend us

> "The poet's eye, in a fine frenzy rolling,
> *To* glance from heaven to earth, from earth to heaven;
> And as imagination bodies forth
> The forms of things unknown,"

should add the gift of "the poet's pen," so that we might

> "Turn them to shapes, and give to airy nothing
> A local habitation and a name."
> *Midsummer Night's Dream,* act v. sc. 1. l. 12–17.

Our business is only with that comparatively small section of the Emblem-World, which, "like mummies in their cerements," is wrapped up within the covers of the so called Emblem-books. Whether, when they are unrolled, they are worth the search and the labour, some may doubt;—but perchance a scarabæus, or an emerald, with an ancient harp upon it, may reward our patience.

By a very easy and natural step, figures and ornaments of many kinds, when placed on smooth surfaces, were named emblems; and as these figures and ornaments were very often symbolical, *i. e.*, signs, or tokens of a thought, a sentiment, a saying, or an event, the term emblem was applied to any painting, drawing, or print that was representative of an action, of a quality of the mind, or of any peculiarity or attribute of character.* "Emblems in fact were, and are, a species of hiero-

* See the Author's *Introductory Dissertation*, p. x, to the Fac-simile Reprint of Whitney's *Emblems*.

glyphics, in which the figures or pictures, besides denoting the natural objects to which they bear resemblances, were employed to express properties of the mind, virtues and abstract ideas, and all the operations of the soul."

Thus, the *Tablet of Cebes*, a work by one of the disciples of Socrates, about B.C. 390, is an explanation, in the form of a Dialogue, of a picture, said to have been set up in the temple

Tabula Cebetis philosophi so=
cratici-cū Iohānis Aeſticāpiani Epiſtola.

Tab. Cebetis, 1507.

Tableau of Human Life from Cebes B. C. 390

of Kronos at Athens or at Thebes, and which was declared to be emblematical of Human Life.

One of the older Latin versions, printed in 1507, presents the foregoing illustrative frontispiece.

As the book has come down to modern times it is, generally, what has sometimes been named, *nudum Emblema*, a naked Emblem, because it has neither device nor artistic drawing, but, like Shakespeare's comparison of all the world to a stage in which man plays many parts, the course of Life, with its discipline, false hopes and false pleasures, is in the Tablet so described,—in fact so delineated,* as to have enabled the Dutch designer and engraver, Romyn de Hooghe, in 1670, to have pictured "the whole story of Human Life as narrated to the Grecian sage."

The Moral of the Allegory may not be set forth with entire clearness in the picture, but it can be given in the words of one of the *Golden Sentences* of Democritus,—see Gale's *Opus. Mythol.*:—

> "That human happiness does not result from bodily excellencies nor from riches, but is founded on uprightness of mind and on righteousness of conduct."

Coins and medals furnish most valuable examples of emblematical figures; indeed some of the Emblem writers, as Sambucus in 1564, were among the earliest to publish impressions or engravings of ancient Roman money, on which are frequently given very interesting representations of customs and symbolical acts. On Grecian coins, which Priestley, in his *Lectures on History*, vol. i. p. 126,—highly praises for "a design, an attitude, a force, and a delicacy, in the expression even of the muscles and veins of human figures,"—we find, to use heraldic language, that the owl is the crest of Athens,—a wolf's head, that of Argos,—and a tortoise the badge of the Peloponnesus. The whole history of Louis XIV. and that of his great adversary,

* See Plate I., containing De Hooghe's engraving, reproduced on a smaller scale.

William III., are represented in volumes containing the medals that were struck to commemorate the leading events of their reigns, and though outrageously untrue to nature and reality by the adoption of Roman costumes and classic symbols, they serve as records of remarkable occurrences.

Heraldry throughout employs the language of Emblems;—it is the picture-history of families, of tribes and of nations, of princes and emperors. Many a legend and many a strange fancy may be mixed up with it and demand almost the credulity of simplest childhood in order to obtain our credence; yet in the literature of Chivalry and Honours there are enshrined abundant records of the glory that belonged to mighty names. I recall now but one instance. In the fine folio lately emblazoned with the well-known motto "GANG FORWARD," "I AM READY," what volumes, to those who can interpret each mark and sign and tutored symbol, are wrapped up in the *Examples of the ornamental Heraldry of the sixteenth Century:* London, 1867, 1868.

The custom of taking a device or badge, if not a motto, is traced by Paolo Giovio, in his *Dialogo dell' Imprese militari et amorose*, ed. 1574, p. 9,* to the earliest times of history. He writes,

> "To bear these emblems was an ancient usage." GIO. "It is a point not to be doubted, that the ancients used to bear crests and ornaments on the helmets and on the shields: for we see this clearly in Virgil, when he made the catalogue of the nations which came in favour of Turnus against the Trojans, in the eighth book of the Æneid; Amphiaraus then (as Pindar says) at the war of Thebes bore a dragon on his shield. Similarly Statius writes of Capaneus and of Polinices, that the one bore the Hydra, and the other the Sphynx," &c.

* "*Il portar queste imprese fu costume antico.* GIO. *Non è punto da dubitare, che gli antichi usassero di portar Cimieri & ornamenti ne gli elmetti e ne gli scudi: perche si vede chiaramēte in Vergil. quādo fà il Catalogo delli genti, che vēnero in fauore di Turno contra i Troiani, nell' ottauo dell' Eneida; Anfiarao ancora (come dice Pindaro) alla guerra di Thebe portò vn dragone nello scudo. Statio scriue similmente di Capaneo & di Polinice; che quelli portò l' Hidra, e queste la Sfinge,"* &c.

But these were simple emblems, without motto inscribed. The same Paolo Giovio, and other writers after him,* assign both "picture and short posie," to two of the early Emperors of Rome.

"Augustus, wishing to show how self-governed and moderate he was in all his affairs, never rash and hasty to believe the first reports and informations of his servants, caused to be struck, among several others, on a gold medal of his own, a Butterfly and a Crab, signifying quickness by the Butterfly, and by the Crab slowness, the two things which constitute a temperament necessary for a Prince."

The motto, as figured below,—"MAKE HASTE LEISURELY."

AVGVSTE.

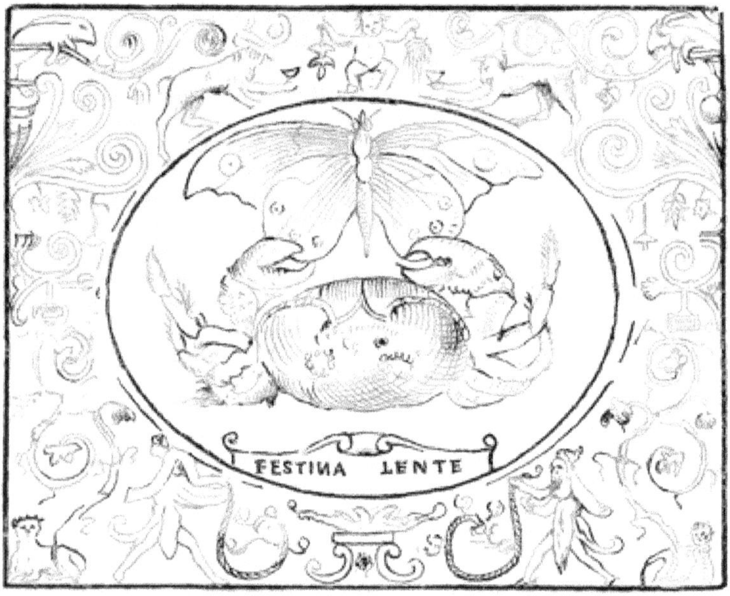

FESTINA LENTE

Symeon, Dev. Her. 1561.

The Device is thus applied in Whitney's *Emblems*, p. 121, and dedicated to two eminent judges of Elizabeth's reign;

---

* See Gabriel Symeon's *Devises ov Emblemes Heroiques et Morales*, ed. à Lyon, 1561, pp. 218, 219, 220.

"This figure, lo, AVGVSTVS did deuise,
A mirror good, for Iudges iuste to see,
And alwayes fitte, to bee before their eies,
When sentence they, of life, and deathe decree :
Then muste they haste, but verie slowe awaie,
Like butterflie, whome creepinge crabbe dothe staie.

"The Prince, or Judge, maie not with lighte reporte,
In doubtfull thinges, giue iudgement touching life :
But trie, and learne the truthe in euerie sorte,
And mercie ioyne, with iustice bloodie knife :
This pleased well AVGVSTVS noble grace,
And Iudges all, within this tracke shoulde trace."

The other is the device which the Aldi, celebrated printers of Venice, from A.D. 1490 to 1563, assumed, of the dolphin and

Symeoni.

anchor, but which Titus, son of Vespasian, had long before adopted, with the motto "PROPERA TARDE,"* *Hasten slowly:* "*facendo*," says Symeoni, "*vna figura moderata della velocità di questo, e della grauezza di quell' altra, nel modo che noi veggiamo dinanzi à i libri d' Aldo.*"

* See Paolo Giovio's *Dialogo*, p. 10, and Symeon's *Devises Heroïques*, p. 220. Also *Le Imprese del. S. Gab. Symeoni*, ed. in Lyone 1574; from which, p. 175, the above device is figured.

But the heraldry of mankind is a boundless theme, and we might by simple beat of drum heraldic collect almost a countless host of crests, badges, and quarterings truly emblematical, and adopted and intended to point out peculiarities or remarkable events and fancies in the histories of the coat-armour families of the world.

The emblematism of bodily sign or action constitutes the language of the dumb. An amusing instance occurs in the Abbé Blanchet's "APOLOGUES ORIENTAUX," in his description of "*The Silent Academy, or the Emblems:*"—

"There was at Hamadan, a city of Persia, a celebrated academy, of which the first statute was conceived in these terms; *The academicians shall think much, write little, and speak the very least that is possible.* It was named *the silent Academy;* and there was not in Persia any truly learned man who had not the ambition of being admitted to it. Dr. Zeb, an imaginary person, author of an excellent little work, THE GAG, learned, in the retirement of the province where he was born, there was one place vacant in the silent Academy. He sets out immediately; he arrives at Hamadan, and presenting himself at the door of the hall where the academicians are assembled, he prays the servant to give this billet to the president: *Dr. Zeb asks humbly the vacant place.* The servant immediately executed the commission, but the Doctor and his billet arrived too late,—the place was already filled.

"The Academy was deeply grieved at this disappointment; it had admitted, a little against its wish, a wit from the court, whose lively light eloquence formed the admiration of all *ruelles.** The Academy saw itself reduced to refuse Doctor Zeb, the scourge of praters, with a head so well formed and so well furnished! The president, charged to announce to the Doctor the disagreeable news, could scarcely bring himself to it, and knew not how to do it. After having thought a little, he filled a large cup with water, but so well filled it, that one drop more would have made the liquid overflow; then he made sign that the candidate should be introduced. He appeared with that simple and modest air which almost always announces true merit. The president arose and, without offering a single word, showed, with an appearance of deep sorrow, the emblematic cup, this cup so exactly filled. The Doctor understood that there was no more

* *i.e.*, the space left between one of the sides of a bed and the wall. Employed figuratively, this word relates to a custom which has passed away, when people betook themselves to the alcove or sleeping room of their friends to enjoy the pleasure of conversation.

room in the Academy; but without losing courage, he thought how to make it understood that one supernumerary academician would disarrange nothing. He sees at his feet a roseleaf, he picks it up, he places it gently on the surface of the water, and did it so well that not a single drop escaped.

"At this ingenious answer everybody clapped hands; the rules were allowed to sleep for this day, and Doctor Zeb was received by acclamation. The register of the Academy was immediately presented to him, where the new members must inscribe themselves. He then inscribed himself in it; and there remained for him no more than to pronounce, according to custom, a phrase of thanks. But as a truly silent academician, Doctor Zeb returned thanks without saying a word. He wrote in the margin the number 100,—it was that of his new brethren; then, by putting a 0 before the figures, 0100, he wrote below, *they are worth neither less nor more*. The president answered the modest Doctor with as much politeness as presence of mind. He placed the figure 1 before the number 100, *i.e.* 1100; and he wrote, *they will be worth eleven times more*."

The varieties in the Emblems which exist might be pursued from "the bird, the mouse, the frog, and the four arrows," which, the Father of history tells us,* the Scythians sent to Darius, the invader of their country,—through all the ingenious devices by which the initiated in secret societies, whether political, social, or religious, seek to guard their mysteries from general knowledge and observation,—until we come to the flower-language of the affections, and learn to read, as Hindoo and Persian maidens can, the telegrams of buds and blossoms,† and to interpret the flashing of colours, either simple or combined. We should have to name the Picture writing of the Mexicans, and to declare what meanings lie concealed in the signs and imagery which

* Herodotus, in the *Melpomene*, bk. iv. c. 131.

† So in the autumn and winter which preceded Napoleon's return from Elba, the question was often asked in France by his adherents,—"Do you like the violet?" and if the answer was,—"The violet will return in the spring," the answer became a sure revelation of attachment to the Emperor's cause. For full information on *Flower signs* see Casimir Magnat's *Traité du Langage symbolique, emblématique et religieux des Fleurs*. 8vo: A. Touzet, Paris, 1855. In illustration take the lines from Dr. Donne, at one time secretary to the lord keeper Egerton:—

> "I had not taught thee then the alphabet
> Of flowers, how they devisefully being set
> And bound up, might with speechless secresy
> Deliver errands mutely and mutually." *Elegy 7.*

adorn tomb and monument,—or peradventure to set forth the art by which, on so simple a material as the bark of a birch-tree, some Indians, on their journey, emblematized a troop with attendants that had lost their way. "In the party there was a military officer, a person whom the Indians understood to be an attorney, and a mineralogist; eight were armed: when they halted they made three encampments." With their knives the Indians traced these particulars on the bark by means of certain signs, or, rather, hieroglyphical marks;—"a man with a sword," they fashioned "for the officer; another with a book for the lawyer, and a third with a hammer for the mineralogist; three ascending columns of smoke denoted the three encampments, and eight muskets the number of armed men." So, without paper or print, a not unintelligible memorial was left of the company that were travelling together.

And so we come to the very Early Examples—if not the earliest—of Emblematical Representation, as exhibited in fictile remains, in the workmanship of the silversmith, and of those by whom the various metals and precious stones have been wrought and moulded; and especially in the numerous specimens of the skill or of the fancy which the glyptic and other artizans of ancient Egypt have left for modern times.

For the nature of Fictile ornamentation it were sufficient to refer to the recently published *Life of Josiah Wedgwood*;* but in the *antefixæ*, or terra cotta ornaments, derived from the old Etruscan civilisation, we possess true and literal Emblems. As the name implies, these ornaments "were *fixed before the buildings*," often on the friezes "which they adorned," and were

* See also "REAL MUSEO BORBONICO," *Napoli Dalla Stamperia Reale*, 1824. Vol. i. tavola viii. e ix. Avventura e Imprese di Ercoli. Vol. ii. tav. xxviii. Dedalo e Icaro. Vol. iii. tav. xlvi. Vaso Italo-Greco depinto. Vol. v. tav. li. Vaso Italo-Greco,—a very fine example of emblem ornaments in the literal sense.

fastened to them by leaden nails. For examples, easy of access, we refer to the sketches supplied by James Yates, Esq., of Highgate; to the *Dictionary of Gk. and Rom. Antiquities*, p. 51; and especially to that antefixa which represents Minerva superintending the construction of the ship Argo. The man with the hammer and chisel is Argus, who built the vessel under her direction. The pilot Tiphys is assisted by her in attaching the sail to the yard. The borders at the top and bottom are in the Greek style, and are extremely elegant."

And the pressing of clay into a matrix or mould, from which the form is taken, appears to be of very ancient date. The book of Job xxxviii. 14, alludes to the practice in the words, "it is turned as clay to the seal." Of similar or of higher antiquity is "the work of an engraver in stone, *like* the engravings of a signet," Exodus xxviii. 11. And "the breastplate of judgment, the Urim and the Thummim," v. 30, worn "upon Aaron's heart," was probably a similar emblematical ornament to that which Diodorus Siculus, in his *History*, bk. i. chap. 75, tells us was put on by the president of the Egyptian courts of justice: "He bore about his neck a golden chain, at which hung an image, set about, or composed of precious stones, which was called TRUTH."*

Among instances of emblematical workmanship by the silversmith and his confabricators of similar crafts, we may name that shield of Achilles which Homer so graphically describes,† "solid and large," "decorated with numerous figures of most skilful art;"— or the shields of Hercules and of Æneas, with which Hesiod, *Eoœ*, iv. 141—317, and Virgil, *Æneid*, viii. 615-73, might make us familiar. Or to come to modern times,—to days

* "Εφορει δ' αυτος περι τον τραχηλον εκ χρυσης ἁλυσεως ηρτημενον ζωδιον των πολυτελων λιθων, ὁ προσηγορευον ΑΛΗΘΕΙΑΝ."

† *Iliad*, xviii. 478, "Ποίει δὲ πρώτιστα σάκος μέγα τε στιβαρόντε,—"

,, ,, 482, "Ποίει δαίδαλα πολλὰ ἰδυίῃσι πραπίδεσσιν."

our very own,—there is the still more precious, the matchless shield by Vehm, whereon, in most expressive imagery, are hammered out the discoveries of Newton, Milton's noble epics, and Shakespeare's dramatic wonders. We may, too, in passing, allude to the richly-embossed and ornamented cups for which our swift racers and grey-hounds, and those "dogs of war," our volunteers, contend; and the almost imperial pieces of plate, such as the Cæsars never beheld, in which genius and the highest art combine, by their "cunning work," to carve the deeds and enhance the renown of some of our great Indian administrators and illustrious generals; these all, truly "choice emblemes," intimate the extent to which our subject might lead. But I forbear to pursue it, though scarcely any path offers greater temptations for wandering abroad amid the marvels of human skill, and for considering reverently and gladly how men have been "filled with the spirit of God, in wisdom, and in understanding, and in knowledge, and in all manner of workmanship." Exodus xxxi. 3.

Of glyptic art the most ancient, as well as the most ample, remains are found in the temples and the other monuments of Egypt. Various modern explorers and writers have given very elaborate accounts of those remains, and still are carrying on their researches; but of old writers only Clemens, of Alexandria, who flourished "towards the end of the second century after Christ," "has left us a full and correct account of the principle of the Egyptian writing,"* and has declared what the subjects were which were included in the word hieroglyphics; † and as

* See Kenrick's *Ancient Egypt under the Pharaohs*, vol. i. p. 291.

† See the *Stromata* of Clemens, vi. 633,—where we learn that it was the duty of the Hierogrammateis, or Sacred Scribe, to gain a knowledge of "what are named Hieroglyphics, which relate to cosmography, geography, the action of the sun and moon, to the five planets, to the topography of Egypt, and to the neighbourhood of the Nile, to a record of the attire of the priests and of the estates belonging to them, and to other things serviceable to the priests."

far as is known, no other early author, except Horapollo of the Nile, has written expressly on the Hieroglyphics of Egypt, and declared that his work—which was probably translated into Greek in the reign of the emperor Zeno, or even later—was derived from Egyptian sources: indeed, was a book in the language of Egypt.

Probably the best account we have of the author and of the translator, is given by Alexander Turner Cory, in the Preface to his edition of Horapollo. He says, pp. viii. and ix.,—

> "At the beginning of the fifth century, Horapollo, a scribe of the Egyptian race, and a native of Phoenebythis, attempted to collect and perpetuate in the volume before us, the then remaining, but fast fading knowledge of the symbols inscribed upon the monuments, which attested the ancient grandeur of his country. This compilation was originally made in the Egyptian language; but a translation of it into Greek by Philip has alone come down to us, and in a condition very far from satisfactory. From the internal evidence of the work, we should judge Philip to have lived a century or two later than Horapollo; and at a time when every remnant of actual knowledge of the subject must have vanished."

However this may be, it is certainly a book of Emblems, and just previous to Shakespeare's age, and during its continuance was regarded as a high authority. Within that time there were at least five editions of the work,—and it was certainly the mine in which the writers of Emblem books generally sought for what were to them valuable suggestions. The edition we have used is the small octavo of 1551,* with many woodcuts, imaginative indeed, but designed in accordance with the original text. J. Mercier, a distinguished scholar, who died in 1562, was the editor. In 1547 he was professor of Hebrew at the Royal

* "ORI APOLLINIS NILIACI, De Sacris notis et sculpturis libri duo," &c. "Parisiis: apud Jacobum Keruer, via Jacobæa, sub duobus Gallis, M.D.LI." Also, *Martin's* "Orus Apollo de Ægypte de la sygnification des notes hieroglyphiques des Ægyptiens: Paris, Keruer, sm. 8vo, 1543."

College of Paris, and in 1548 edited the quarto edition of Horapollo's *Hieroglyphics.*

From the edition of 1551, p. 52, we take a very popular illustration; it is the Phœnix, and may serve to show the nature of Horapollo's work.

Horapollo, 1551.

"How," he asks, "do the Egyptians represent a soul passing a long time here?" "They paint a bird—the Phœnix; for of all creatures in the world this bird has by far the longest life."

Again, bk. i. 37, or p. 53, "How do they denote the man who after long absence will return to his friends from abroad?" By the Phœnix; "for this bird, after five hundred years, when the death hour is about to seize it, returns to Egypt, and in Egypt, paying the debt of nature, is burned with great solemnity. And whatever sacred rites the Egyptians observe towards their other sacred animals, these they observe towards the Phœnix."

And bk. ii. 57,—"The lasting restoration which shall take place after long ages, when they wish to signify it, they paint the bird Phœnix. For when it is born this bird obtains the restoration of its properties. And its birth is in this manner: the Phœnix being about to die, dashes itself upon the ground, and receiving a wound, ichor flows from it, and through the opening another Phœnix is born. And when its wings are fledged, this other sets out with its father to the city of the Sun in Egypt, and on arriving there, at the rising of the Sun, the parent dies; and after the death of the father, the young one sets out again for its own country. And the dead Phœnix do the priests of Egypt bury."

But the drawings, which in the old editions of Horapollo were fancy-made, have, through the researches of a succession of Egyptian antiquaries, assumed reality, and may be appealed to for proof that Horapollo described the very things which he had seen, though occasionally he, or his translator Philip, attributes to them an imaginative or highly mythical meaning. The results of those researches we witness in the editions of Horapollo, first by the celebrated Dr. Conrad Leemans, of Leyden, in 1835,* and second, by Alexander Turner Cory, Fellow of Pembroke College, Cambridge, in 1840;† both of which editions, by their illustrative plates, taken from correct drawings of the originals, present Horapollo with an accuracy that could not have been approached in the sixteenth century. We have indeed of that age the great work of Pierius Valerian (ed. folio, Bâle, 1556, leaves 449), the *Hieroglyphica*, dedicated to Cosmo de' Medici, with almost innumerable emblems, in fifty-eight books, and with about 365 devices. But it cannot be regarded as an exposition of the Egyptian art, and labours under the same defect as the early editions of Horapollo,—the illustrations are not taken from existing monuments.

An example or two from Leemans and Cory will supply sufficient information to enable the reader to understand something of the nature of Horapollo's work, and of the actual Hieroglyphics from which that work has in great part been verified.

The following is the 31st figure in the plates which Leemans gives; it is the pictorial representation to explain "What

* *Horapollinis Niloi Hieroglyphica*, 8vo, pp. xxxvi. and 446: "Amstelodami, apud J. Muller et Socios, MDCCCXXXV."

† *The Hieroglyphics of Horapollo Nilous*, sm. 8vo, pp. xii. and 174: "London, William Pickering, MDCCCXL."

the Egyptians mean when they engrave or paint a star." * "Would they signify the God who sets in order the world, or destiny, or the number five, they paint a star; God, indeed, because the providence of God, to which the motion of the stars and of all the world is subject, determines the victory; for it seems to them that, apart from God, nothing whatever could endure; and destiny *they signify*, since this also is regulated by stellar management,—and the number five, because out of the multitude which is in heaven, five only, by motion originating from themselves, make perfect the management of the world."

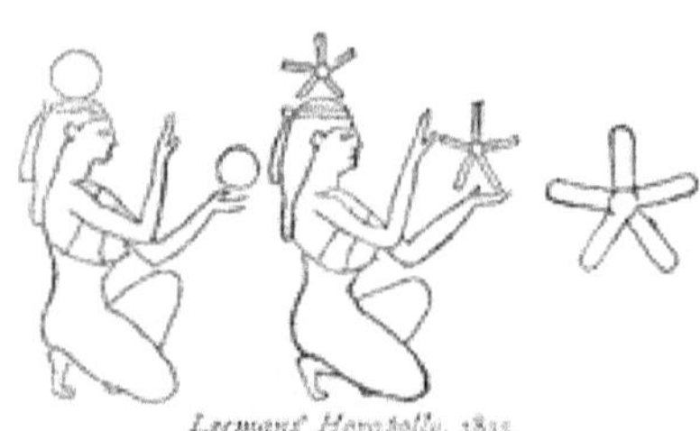

Leemans' Horapollo, 1835.

Of the three figures which are delineated above, the one to the left hand symbolizes God, that in the middle destiny, and the third, the number 5, from five rays being used to indicate a star.

The same subjects are thus represented in Cory's Horapollo.

Cory's Horapollo, bk. i. c. 8, p. 15, also illustrates the question, "How do they indicate the soul?" by the accompanying symbols; of which

* Horapollo's *Hieroglyphica*, by Conrad Leemans, bk. i. c. 13, p. 20:—Τί ἀστέρα γράφοντες δηλοῦσι. Θεὸν δὲ ἐγκόσμιον σημαίνοντες, ἢ εἱμαρμένην, ἢ τὸν πέντε ἀριθμὸν, ἀστέρα ζωγραφοῦσι· θεὸν μὲν, ἐπειδὴ πρόνοια θεοῦ τὴν νίκην προστάσσει, ᾗ τῶν ἀστέρων καὶ τοῦ παντὸς κόσμου κίνησις ἐκτελεῖται· δοκεῖ γὰρ αὐτοῖς δίχα θεοῦ, μηδὲν ὅλως συνεστάναι· εἱμαρμένην δέ, ἐπεὶ καὶ αὕτη ἐξ ἀστρικῆς οἰκονομίας συνίσταται· τὸν δὲ πέντε ἀριθμὸν, ἐπειδὴ πλήθους ὄντος ἐν οὐρανῷ, πέντε μόνοι ἐξ αὐτῶν κινούμενοι, τὴν τοῦ κόσμου οἰκονομίαν ἐκτελοῦσι.

I. represents the mummy and the departing soul, II. the hawk found sitting on the mummy, and III. the external mummy case. The answer to the question is:—

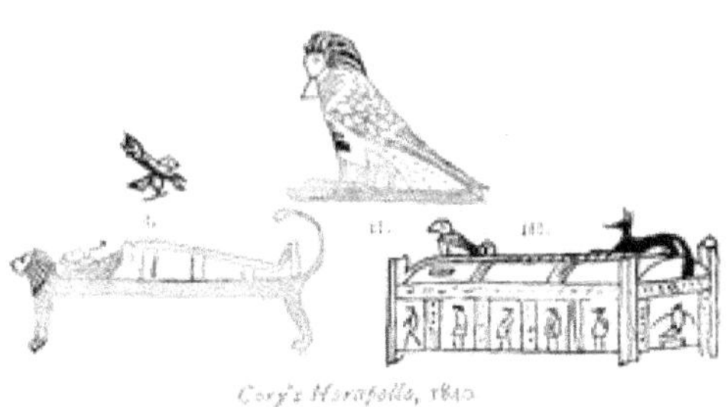

Cory's Horapollo, 1840.

"Moreover, the HAWK is put for the soul, from the signification of its name; for among the Egyptians the hawk is called BAIETH: and this name in decomposition signifies soul and heart; for the word BAI is the soul, and ETH the heart: and the heart according to the Egyptians is the shrine of the soul; so that in its composition the name signifies 'soul enshrined in heart.' Whence also the hawk, from its correspondence with the soul, never drinks water, but blood, by which, also, the soul is sustained."

And in a similar way many of the sacred engravings or drawings are interpreted. A serpent with its tail covered by the rest of its body, "depicts Eternity;"* "to denote an *only begotten*, or *generation*, or a *father*, or the *world*, or a *man*, they delineate a SCARABÆUS;" † a LION symbolises *intrepidity*,—its FOREPARTS, *strength*, and its HEAD, *watchfulness*; ‡ the STORK denotes *filial affection*, the CRANE on the watch, a man on guard against his enemies, and the FEATHER of an Ostrich, *impartial justice*,—for, adds the author, "this animal, beyond other animals, has the wing feathers equal on every side." §

Christian Art, like the Religious Art of the world in general, —from the *thou* and *thee* of simplest Quakerism, outward and audible sounds of an inward and silent spirit, up to the profoundest mystic ritualism of the Buddhist,—Christian Art

* Horapollo, bk. i. c. 1.
† Bk. i. c. 10.
‡ Bk. i. c. 17-19.
§ Bk. ii. c. 58, 94, 118.

abounds in Emblems; gems and colours, genuflexions and other bodily postures supply them; they are gathered from the mineral, animal, and vegetable kingdoms, and besides are enriched from the whole domain of imaginary devices and creatures. Does the emerald flash in its mild lustre?—it is of "victory and hope, of immortality, of faith, and of reciprocal love," that it gives forth light. Is blue, the colour of heaven, worn in some religious ceremony?—it betokens "piety, sincerity, godliness, contemplation, expectation, love of heavenly things." Do Christian men bare the head in worship?—it is out of reverence for the living God, whose earthly temples they have entered. The badge of St. John the Baptist, is a lamb on a book,—that of St. John the Evangelist is a cup of gold with a serpent issuing from it. The Pomegranate, "showing its fulness of seed and now bursting," typifies the hope of immortality;—and a Fleur-de-lys, or the Rose of Sharon, embroidered or painted on a robe,—it marks the Blessed Virgin. With more intricate symbolism the Greek Church represents the Saviour's name **IHCOYC XPICTOC**,—IesuS CHristuS. The first finger of the hand extended is for **I**, the second bent for **C** or s, the thumb crossed upon the third finger for **X** or Ch, and the fourth finger curved for **C** or s. Thus are given the initial and final letters of that Holy Name, the Saviour, the Christ.*

Of early Emblems examples enough have now been given to indicate their nature. Whether in closing this part of the subject we should name a work of more ancient date even than the Greek version of Horapollo would admit of doubt, were it not that every work partakes of an emblematical character, when the descriptions given or the instances taken pertain, as

* For a further and very interesting account of the Emblems of Christian Art, reference may be made to a work full of information,—too brief it may be for all that is desirable,—but to be relied on for its accuracy, and to be imitated for its candid and charitable spirit:—*Sacred Archæology*, by Mackenzie E. C. Walcott, B.D., 8vo, pp. 640: London, Reeve & Co. 1868.

Whitney says, "to vertue and instruction of life," or "doe tende vnto discipline, and morall preceptes of living."

Under this rule we hesitate not to admit into the wide category of Emblem writers, EPIPHANIUS, who was chosen bishop of Constantia in Cyprus, A.D. 367, and who died in 402. His *Physiologist*, published with his sermon on the Feast of Palms, is, like many writings of the Fathers, remarkable for highly allegorical interpretations. An edition, by Ponce de Leon, a Spaniard of Seville, was printed at Rome in 1587, and repeated at Antwerp* in 1588. It relates to the real and imaginary qualities of animals, and to certain precepts and doctrines of which those qualities are supposed to be symbolical. As an example we give here an extract from chapter XXV. p. 106, "*Concerning the Stork.*"

Epiphanius, 1588.

* "Ex Officina Christophori Plantini, Architypographi Regij, 1588."

The Stork is described as a bird of extreme purity; and as nourishing, with wonderful affection, father and mother in their old age. The "interpretation" or application of the fact is;—"So also it behoves us to observe these two divine commands, that is to turn aside from evil and to do good, as the kingly prophet wrote; and likewise in the decalogue the Lord commands, thus saying;—Honour thy father and thy mother."

In a similar way the properties and habits of various animals,—of the lion, the elephant, the stag, the eagle, the pelican, the partridge, the peacock, &c., are adduced to enforce or symbolize virtues of the heart and life, and to set forth the doctrines of the writer's creed.

To illustrate the Emblem side of Christian Art a great variety of information exists in *Sketches of the History of Christian Art*, by Lord Lindsay (3 vols. 8vo: Murray, London, 1847); and Northcote and Brownlow's *Roma Sotterranea*, compiled from De Rossi (8vo: Longmans, London, 1869) promises to supply many a symbol and type of a remote age fully to set forth the same subject.

Giovio, 1556.

CHAPTER II.

SKETCH OF EMBLEM-BOOK LITERATURE PREVIOUS TO A.D. 1616.

SECTION I.

EXTENT OF THE EMBLEM LITERATURE TO WHICH SHAKESPEARE MIGHT HAVE HAD ACCESS.

N the use of the word Emblem there is seldom a strict adherence observed to an exact definition,—so, when Emblem Literature is spoken of, considerable latitude is taken and allowed as to the kind of works which the terms shall embrace. In one sense every book which has a picture set in it, or on it, is an emblem-book,—the diagrams in a mathematical treatise or in an exposition of science, inasmuch as they may be, and often are, detached from the text, are emblems: and when to Tennyson's exquisite poem of "ELAINE," Gustave Doré conjoins those wonderful drawings which are themselves poetic, he gives us a book of emblems;—Tennyson is the one artist that out of the gold of his own soul fashioned a vase incorruptible,—and Doré is that second artist who placed about it ornaments of beauty, fashioned also out of the riches of his mind.

Yet by universal consent, these and countless other works, scientific, historical, poetic, and religious, which artistic skill has embellished, are never regarded as emblematical in their character. The "picture and short posie, expressing some particular conceit," seem almost essential for bringing any work within the province of the Emblem Literature;—but the practical application of the test is conceived in a very liberal spirit, so that while the small fish sail through, the shark and the sea-dog rend the meshes to tatters.

A proverb or witty saying, as, in Don Sebastian Orozco's "EMBLEMAS MORALES" (Madrid 1610), "Divesqve miserqve," *both rich and wretched*, may be pictured by king Midas at the table where everything is turned to gold, and may be set forth in an eight-lined stanza, to declare how the master of millions was famishing though surrounded by abundance;—and these things constitute the Emblem. Some scene from Bible History shall be taken, as, in **"Les figures du vieil Testament, & du nouuel"** (at Paris, about 1503), *Moses at the burning bush;* where are printed, as if an Emblem text, the passage from Exodus iii. 2—4, and by its side the portraits of David and Esaias; across the page is a triplet woodcut, representing Moses at the bush, and Mary in the stable at Bethlehem with Christ in the manger-cradle; various scrolls with sentences from the Scriptures adorn the page:—such representations claim a place in the Emblem Literature. Boissard's *Theatrum Vitæ Humanæ* (Metz, 1596) shall mingle, in curious continuity, the Creation and Fall of Man, Ninus king of the Assyrians, Pandora and Prometheus, the Gods of Egypt, the Death of Seneca, Naboth and Jezabel, the Advent of Christ and the Last Judgment;—yet they are all Emblems,—because each has a "picture and a short posie" setting forth its "conceit." To be sure there are some pages of Latin prose serving to explain or confuse, as the case may be, each particular imagination; but the text constitutes the emblem, and however long and tedious the comment, it is from the text the composition derives its name.

"Stam und Wapenbuch hochs und nidern Stands,"—*A stem and armorial Bearings-book of high and of low Station,*

—printed at Frankfort-on-Mayne, 1579, presents above 270 woodcuts of the badges, shields and helmets, with appropriate symbols and rhymes, belonging as well to the humblest who can claim to be "vom gutem Geschlecht," *of good race*, as to the Electoral Princes and to the Cæsarean Majesty of the Holy Roman Empire. Most of the figures are illustrated by Latin and German verses, and again "picture and short posie" vindicate the title,—book of Emblems.

And of the same character is a most artistic work by Theodore de Bry, lately added to the treasure-house at Keir: it is also a *Stam und Wapenbuch*, issued at Frankfort in 1593, with ninety-four plates all within most beautiful and elaborate borders. Its Latin title, *Emblema Nobilitate et Vulgo scitu digna, &c.*, declares that these Emblems are "worthy to be known both by nobles and commons."

And so when an Emperor is married, or the funeral rites of a Sovereign Prince celebrated, or a new saint canonized, or perchance some proud cardinal or noble to be glorified, whatever Art can accomplish by symbol and song is devoted to the emblem-book pageantry,—and the graving tool and the printing press accomplish as enduring and wide-spread a splendour as even Titian's Triumphs of Faith and Fame.

Devotion that seeks wisdom from the skies, and Satire that laughs at follies upon the earth, both have claimed and used emblems as the exponents of their aims and purposes.

With what surpassing beauty and nobleness both of expression and of sentiment does Otho Vænius in his "AMORIS DIVINI EMBLEMATA," Antwerp, 1615, represent to the mind as well as to the eye the blessed Saviour's adoption of a human soul, and the effulgence of love with which it is filled! (See Plate II.) They are indeed divine Images portrayed for us, and the great word is added from the beloved disciple,—"Behold, what manner of love the Father hath bestowed upon us, that

Christ's adoption of the Human Soul   Otho Venius 1615

we should be called the sons of God." And the simple *Refrain* follows,—

> *"C'est par cet Amour que les hommes*
> *Sont esleuez de ce bas lieu;*
> *C'est par cet Amour que nous sommes*
> *Enfans legitimes de Dieu:*
> *Car l'Ame qui garde en la vie*
> *De son Pere la volonté,*
> *Doit au Pere ès cieux estre unie*
> *(Comme fille) en eternité."*

And that clever imitation of the "**Stultifera Nauis**," *the Fool-freighted Ship*, of the fifteenth century, namely, the "CENTIFOLIUM STULTORUM," edition 1707, or *Hundred-leaved Book of Fools* of the eighteenth, proves how the Satirical may symbolize and fraternize with the Emblematical. The title of the book alone is sufficient to show what a vehicle for lashing men's faults the device with its stanzas and comment may be made; it is, "A hundred-leaved book of Fools, in Quarto; or an hundred exquisite Fools newly warmed up, in Folio,—in an Alapatrit-Pasty for the show-dish; with a hundred fine copper engravings, for honest pleasure and useful pastime, intended as well for frolicsome as for melancholy minds; enriched moreover with a delicate sauce of many Natural Histories, gay Fables, short Discourses, and edifying Moral Lessons."

Among the one hundred *distinguished* characters, we might select, were it only in self-condemnation, the Glass and Porcelain dupe, the Antiquity and Coin-hunting dupe, and especially the Book-collecting dupe. These are among the best of the devices, and the stanzas, and the expositions. Dupes of every kind, however, may find their reproof in the six simple German lines,—p. 171,

> "Wer Narren offt viel predigen will,
> Bey ihnen nicht wird schaffen viel.
> Dann all's was man am besten redt,
> Der Narr zum ärgsten falsch versteht,

Ein Narr, ein Narr, bleibt ungelehrt,
Wann man ihn hundert Jahr schon lehrt."

meaning pretty nearly in our vernacular English,

"Whoso to fools will much and oft be preaching,
By them not much will make by all his teaching,
For though we of our very best be speaking,
Falsely the fool the very worst is seeking.
Therefore the fool, a fool untaught, remains,
Though five score years we give him all our pains."

But Politics also have the bright, if not the dark, side of their nature presented to the world in Emblems. Giulio Capaccio, Venetia, 1620, derives "IL PRINCIPE," *The Prince*, from the Emblems of Alciatus, "with two hundred and more Political and Moral Admonitions," "useful," he declares, "to every gentleman, by reason of its excellent knowledge of the customs, economy, and government of States." Jacobus à Bruck, of Angermunt, in his "EMBLEMATA POLITICA," A.D. 1618, briefly demonstrates those things which concern government; but Don Diego Saavedra Faxardo, who died in 1648, in a work of considerable repute,—"IDEA de vn Principe Politico-Christiano, representada EN CIEN EMPRESAS,"—*Idea of a Politic-Christian Prince, represented in one hundred Emblems* (edition, Valencia, 1655), so accompanies his Model Ruler from the cradle to maturity as almost to make us think, that could we find the bee-bread on which Kings should be nourished, it would be no more difficult a task for a nation to fashion a perfect Emperor than it is for a hive to educate their divine-right ruling Queen.

But, so great is the variety of subjects to which the illustrations from Emblems are applied, that we shall content ourselves with mentioning one more, taking out the arguments, as they are named, from celebrated classic poets, and converting them into occasions for pictures and short posies. Thus, like the dust of Alexander, the remains of the mighty dead, of

La Creatione & confusione del Mondo. I

Prima ch' il gran fattor dell' Vniuerso
Con pietà gli ponesse intorno mente,
Era cieco nel Mar l' Aer sommerso,
Nel centro il Fuoco, e'l tutto era niente,
Ch' ogni Elemento, di virtù diuersi,
Non hauea luogo à lui conueniente:
Ma del verbo diuin l' amor profondo
D'vn CAOS ordinò si bello il Mondo.

Create. Symeone 1559

Homer and Virgil, of Ovid and Horace, have served the base uses of Emblem-effervescence, and in nearly all the languages of Europe have been forced to misrepresent the noble utterances of Greece and Rome. Many of the pictures, however, are very beautiful, finely conceived, and skilfully executed;—we blame not the artists, but the false taste which must make little bits of verses where the originals existed as mighty poems.

Generally it is considered that the Ovids of the fifteenth century were without pictorial illustrations, and could not, therefore, be classed among books of Emblems; but the Blandford Catalogue, p. 21, records an edition, "Venetia, 1497," "*cum figuris depictis*,"— with figures portrayed. Without discussing the point, we will refer to an undoubted emblematized edition of the *Metamorphoses* of Ovid, "Figurato & abbreviato in forma d'Epigrammi da M. Gabriello Symeoni,"—*figured and abbreviated in form of Epigrams by M. Gabriel Symeoni.* The volume is a small 4to of 245 pages, of which 187 have each a title and device and Italian stanza, the whole surrounded by a richly figured border. The volume, dedicated to the celebrated "Diana di Poitiers, Dvchessa di Valentinois," was published "A Lione per Giouanni di Tornes nella via Resina, 1559." An Example, p. 13, (see Plate III.,) will show the character of the work, of which another edition was issued in 1584. The Italian stanzas are all of eight lines each, and the passages of the original Latin on which they are founded are collected at the end of the volume. Thus, for "La Creatione & confusione del Mondo," the Latin lines are,

> "*Ante mare & terras & quod tegit omnia, cœlum.*
> . . . . *Nulli sua forma manebat.*
> *Hanc Deus, & melior litem natura diremit.*"

Of the devices several are very closely imitated in the woodcuts of Reusner's Emblems, published at Frankfort, in 1581.

The engravings in Symeoni's Ovid are the work of Solomon Bernard, "the little Bernard," a celebrated artist born at Lyons in 1512; who also produced a set of vignettes for a French translation of Virgil, *L'Eneide de Virgile, Prince des Poetes latins*, printed at Lyons in 1560.

"QVINTI HORATII FLACCI EMBLEMATA," as Otho Vænius names one of his choicest works, first published in 1607, is a similar adaptation of a classic author to the prevailing taste of the age for emblematical representation. The volume is a very fine 4to of 214 pages, of which 103 are plates; and a corresponding 103 contain extracts from Horace and other Latin authors, followed, in the edition of 1612, by stanzas in Spanish, Italian, French and Flemish. An example of the execution of the work will be found as a Photolith, Plate XVII., near the end of our volume: it is the "VOLAT IRREVOCABILE TEMPUS,"—*Irrevocable time is flying*,—so full of emblematical meaning.

From the office of the no less celebrated Crispin de Passe, at Utrecht, in 1613, issued, in Latin and French verse, "SPECVLVM HEROICVM Principis omnium temporum Poetarum HOMERI,"—*The Heroic Mirror of Homer, the Prince of the Poets of all times.* The various arguments of the twenty-four books of the *Iliad* have been taken and made the groundwork of twenty-four Emblems, with their devices most admirably executed. The Latin and French verses beneath each device unmistakeably impress a true emblem-character on the work. The author, "le Sieur J. Hillaire," appends to the Emblems, pp. 69—75, "Epitaphs on the Heroes who perished in the Trojan War," and also "La course d'Vlisses, son tragitte retour, & deffaicte des amans qui poursuivoient la chaste & vertueuse Penelope."

What might not in this way be included within the wide-encompassing grasp of the determined Emblematist it is almost impossible to say; and therefore it ought to be no matter of surprise to find there is practically a greater extent given to the Literature of Emblems than of absolute right belongs to it. We shall not go much astray if we take Custom for our guide, and keep to its decisions as recorded in the chief catalogues of Emblem works.

Horapollo, 1551.

SECTION II.

EMBLEM WORKS AND EDITIONS DOWN TO THE END OF THE FIFTEENTH CENTURY.

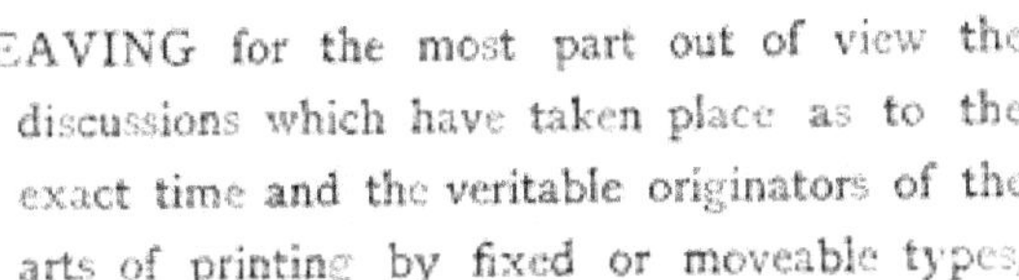

LEAVING for the most part out of view the discussions which have taken place as to the exact time and the veritable originators of the arts of printing by fixed or moveable types, and of the embellishing of books by engravings on blocks of wood or plates of copper, we are yet—for the full development of the condition and extent of the Emblem Literature in the age of Shakespeare—required to notice the growth of that species of ornamental device in books which depends upon Emblems for its force and meaning. We say advisedly "ornamental device in books," for infinite almost are the applications of Symbol and Emblem to Architecture, Sculpture, and Painting, as is testified by the Remains of Antiquity in all parts of the world, by the Pagan tombs and Christian catacombs of ancient Rome, by nearly every temple and church and stately building in the empires of the earth, and especially in those wonderful creations of human skill in which form and colour bring forth to sight nearly every thought and fancy of our souls.

Long before either block-printing or type-printing was practised, it is well known how extensively the limner's art was employed "to illuminate," as it is called, the Manuscripts that were to be found in the rich abbeys or convents, and in the mansions of the great and noble. For instance, the devices

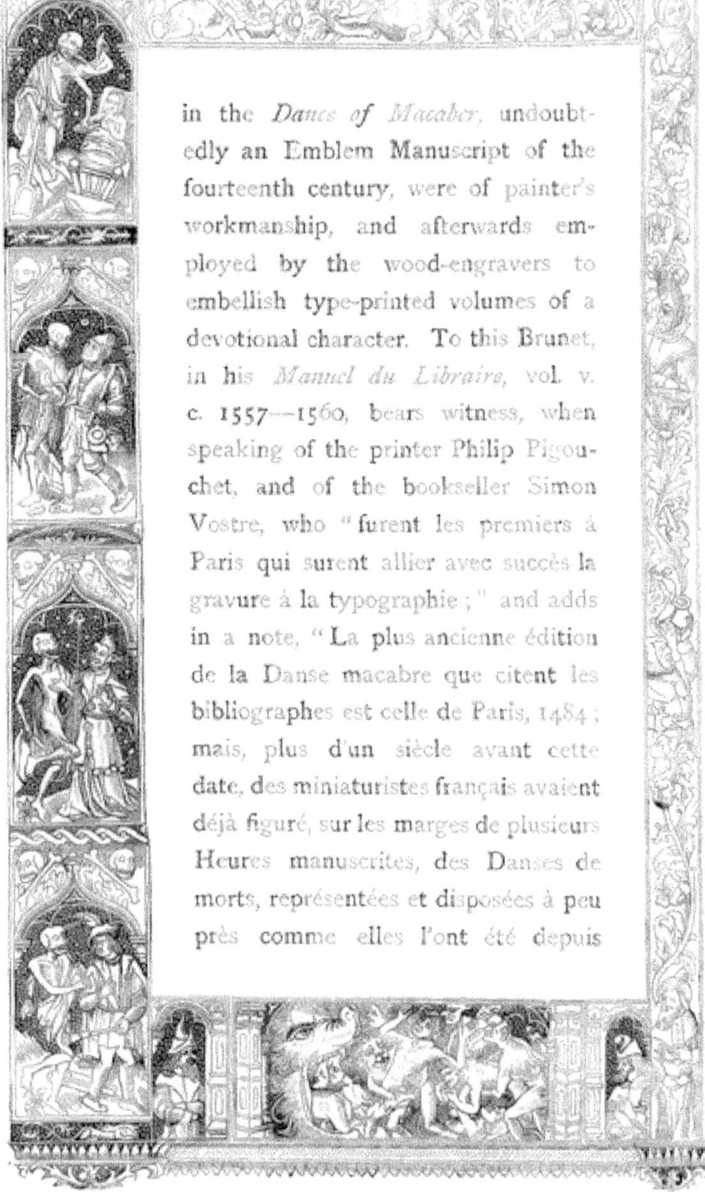

in the *Dance of Macaber,* undoubtedly an Emblem Manuscript of the fourteenth century, were of painter's workmanship, and afterwards employed by the wood-engravers to embellish type-printed volumes of a devotional character. To this Brunet, in his *Manuel du Libraire,* vol. v. c. 1557—1560, bears witness, when speaking of the printer Philip Pigouchet, and of the bookseller Simon Vostre, who "furent les premiers à Paris qui surent allier avec succès la gravure à la typographie;" and adds in a note, "La plus ancienne édition de la Danse macabre que citent les bibliographes est celle de Paris, 1484; mais, plus d'un siècle avant cette date, des miniaturistes français avaient déjà figuré, sur les marges de plusieurs Heures manuscrites, des Danses de morts, représentées et disposées à peu près comme elles l'ont été depuis

From Brunet, v. 1559.

dans les livres de Simon Vostre ; c'est ce que nous avons pu remarquer dans un magnifique manuscrit de la seconde moitié du quatorzième siècle, enrichi de nombreuses et admirables miniatures qui, après avoir été conservé en Angleterre dans le cabinet du docteur Mead, à qui le roi Louis XV. en avait fait présent, est venu prendre place parmi les curiosités de premier ordre réunies dans celui de M. Ambr. Firmin Didot."

A strictly emblematical work in English is the following, "from a finely written and illuminated parchment roll, in perfect

Five wounds of Christ, 1400—1430.

preservation, about two yards and three quarters in length," "**The Fyve Woundys of Christ.**" "**By William Billyng;**" "Manchester: Printed by R. and W. Dean, 4to, 1814." The date is fixed by the editor, William Bateman, "between the years 1400 and 1430;" and the poem contains about 120 lines, with six illuminated devices. We give here, on page 40, in outline, the DEVICE of "*The Heart of Jesus the Well of everlasting Lyfe.*"

There follows, as to each of the Emblems, a Prayer, or Invocation; the Device in question has these lines,—

> "Hayle welle and cōdyte of eu'lastyng lyffe
> Thorow launced so ferre wtyn my lordes syde
> The flodys owt traylyng most aromatyf
> Hayle pcious ♥ wounded so large and wyde
> Hayle trusty tresoure our joy to provide
> Hayle porte of glorie wt paynes alle embrued
> On alle ẏ sprynglyde lyke purpul dew enhuede."

An Astronomical Manuscript in the Chetham Library, Manchester, the eclipses in which are calculated from A.D. 1330 to A.D. 1462, contains emblematical devices for the months of the year, and the signs of the zodiac; these are painted medallions at the beginning of each month; and to each of the months is attached a metrical line explanatory of the device.

Januarius.	Ouer yis feer I warme myn handes.
Februarius.	Wyth yis spade I delve my londes.
Martius.	Here knitte I my vynes in springe.
Aprilis.	So merie I here yese foules singe.
Mayus.	I am as Joly as brid on bouz.
Junius.	Here wede I my corn, clene I houz.
Julius.	Wyth yis sythe my medis I mowe.
Augustus.	Here repe I my corn so lowe.
September.	Wyth ys flayll I yresche my bred.
October.	Here sowe I my Whete so reed.
Nobember.	Wyth ys knyf I steke my swyn.
December.	Welcome cristemasse Wyth ale and Wyn.

This manuscript contains, as J. O. Halliwell says of it, "an astrological volvelle—an instrument mentioned by Chaucer: it is the only specimen, I believe, now remaining in which the steel stylus or index has been preserved in its original state."

Doubtless it is a copy of the *Kalendrier des Bergers*, which with the *Compost des Bergers*, has in various forms been circulated in France from the fourteenth century almost, if not quite, to the present day. An edition in 4to, of 144 pages, printed at Troyes, in 1705, bears the title, *Le Grand Calendrier et Compost des Bergers; composé par le Berger de la grand Montagne.*

Kindred works issued from the presses of Venice, of Nuremberg, and of Augsburg, between 1475 and 1478, in Latin, Italian, and German, and are ascribed to John Muller, more known under the name of Regiomontanus, a celebrated astronomer, born in 1436, at Koningshaven, in Franconia, and who died at Rome in 1476. One of these editions, in folio, was printed at Augsburg in 1476 by Erhard Ratdolt, being the first work he sent forth after his establishment in that city. (See *Biog. Univ.*, vol. xxx. p. 381, and vol. xxxvii. p. 25.) But the most thoroughly emblematical work from Ratdolt's press was an "**Astrolabium planũ in tabulis,**" "wrought out anew by John Angeli, master of liberal arts, MCCCCLXXXVIII." There are 414 woodcuts, and all of them emblematical. The library at Keir contains a perfect copy, 4to, in most admirable condition. Brunet, i. c. 290, names a Venice edition in 1494, and refers to other astronomical works by the same author.

In its manuscript form, too, the celebrated "SPECULUM HUMANÆ SALVATIONIS," *Mirror of Human Salvation*, exhibits throughout the emblem characteristics. Of this work, both as it exists in manuscript and in the earliest printed form by Koster of Haarlem, about 1430, specimens are given in "A History of the Art of Printing from its invention to its wide spread developement in the middle of the sixteenth century;" "by H. NOEL HUMPHREYS," "with one hundred illustrations produced in Photo-lithography:" folio: Quaritch, London, 1867. Pl. 8 of Humphreys' learned and magnificent volume exhibits "a page from a manuscript copy of the *Speculum Humanæ Salvationis*, executed previous to the printed edition attributed to Koster;" and pl. 10, "A page from the *Speculum Humanæ Salvationis* attributed to Koster of Haarlem, in which the text is printed from moveable types."

The inspection of these plates, and the assurance by Humphreys, p. 60, that "the illustrations, though inferior to Koster's woodcuts, are of similar arrangement," may satisfy us that the *Speculum Humanæ Salvationis*, and all its kindred works, in German, Dutch, and French, amounting to many editions previous to the year 1500,* are truly books that belong to the Emblem literature. Thus pl. 8, "though without the decorative Gothic framework which separates, and, at the same time, binds together the double illustrations of the xylographic artist," exhibits to us the exact character of "the double pictures of the *Speculum*." "These double pictures," p. 60 of Humphreys, "illustrate first a passage in the New Testament, and secondly the corresponding subject of the Old, of which it is the antitype. In the present page we have Christ bearing His cross (Christus bajulat crucem) typified by Isaac carrying the wood for his own sacrifice (Isaac portat ligna sua)." "The engravings," p. 58, "*i.e.*, of Koster's first great effort, occur at the top of each leaf, and the rest of the page is filled with two columns of text, which, in the supposed first edition, is composed of Latin verse

* See Brunet's *Manuel du Libraire*, vol. v. col. 476–483, and col. 489; also vol. iv. col. 1343-46.

(or, rather, Latin prose with rhymed terminations to the lines, as the lines do not scan); and in later editions, in Dutch prose." "This specimen," pl. 8, p. 60, "will enable the student to understand precisely the kind of manuscript book which Koster reproduced in a cheaper form by xylography, to which he eventually allied the still more important invention of moveable types."

From a very fine MS. copy of the *Speculum Humanæ Salvationis*, belonging to Mr. Henry Yates Thompson, our fac-simile Plates IV. and V., though on a smaller scale, present the Title and the first Pair of devices with their text. The work is in twenty-nine chapters, and to each there are four devices in four columns, with appropriate explanations in Latin verse, and at the foot of the columns are the references to the Old or the New Testament.

The manuscript entitled "**De Volucribus, sive de tribus Columbis**,"—*Concerning Birds, or the Three Doves*, in the library "du Grand Seminaire," at Bruges, is also an emblem-book. It is excellently illuminated, and the workmanship is probably of the thirteenth century. (See the Whitney Reprint, p. xxxii.)

The illuminated *Missal*, executed in 1425 for John, Duke of Bedford and regent of France, according to the account published of it by Richard Gough, 4to, London, 1794, and by others, abounds in emblem devices. It contains "fifty-nine large miniatures, which nearly occupy the page, and above a thousand small ones in circles of about an inch and half diameter, displayed in brilliant borders of golden foliage, with variegated flowers, &c. At the bottom of every page are two lines in blue and gold letters, which explain the subject of each

* Sold at the Duchess of Portland's sale in 1789 to Mr. Edwards for £215,—and at his sale in 1815 to the Duke of Marlborough for £637 15s. See Dibdin's "*Bibliomania*," ed. 1811, p. 253; and Timperley's *Dictionary of Printers and Printing*, ed. 1839, p. 93.

Plate 4

Title Page from a M.S. Speculum Humanæ Salvationis

Cristus manducat pascha cū discipulis suis

Manna datur filijs isrl' in deserto

In precedenti audivimus de palmarum die
Nunc audiamus de cena i sacramento eukaristie
Appropinquante tpe q xps voluit subire passioēz
decrevit p memoriali ppetuo instituere sacramentum
Vt a nob suam dulcissimā dileccōnē d'nob recol
Placuit ipi ut seipm nobis in cibū daret
Qd olim in manna celi fuit prefiguratum
Qd filijs israhel in deserto erat donatum
Magnā dileccionem dns iudeis videt exhibuisse
Sz i fortiores magis phibet nobis contulisse
Dedit iudeis panē manne sz tpale z mortale
Nobis aūt otulit panem sup sbalē z eternalē
Manna dicebat panis celi nūqz tn fuit i celo vero
Sz creatū fuit i aere tunc i celo aereo
Xps salvator nr ē panis verus z vivus
Qui de celo vero descēdens factus ē nr cibus
Iudeis ergo dedit solū mō figurā vel panis c'p'ual
Nobis aūt figurā sz veritatem dei panis otulit
Nolidū qz mlta fuerūt i manna figurā demostrā
Que i sacra heukaristia sūt veracie cōsumata
Manna celi valde mirabil nature eē videbat
Quia i radio sol' liqfiebat et ad igne idurabat
Ita eukaristia i cordibus vas liqfacit z remollescit
In cordib' ignitis ponitur z abcedere nescit
Malis ecia sumentes eukaristiā ad sui dāpnacione
Marci xiiii° caplo

Bonis aūt ad divinam z ppetuā consolacionem
Cūqz descēderet manna descēdebat sil z ros celi
p quē innuit q dignus cū eukaristia sil cōfert graciā
Manna erat albū z ad modū nivis candidum
p qd innuit cōsciēcia dz hre cor purū z mūdum
Manna habebat in se oē delectamentū cibi celestis
Sz eukaristia hz i se oē delectamētū cibi celestis
Iz delectamentū nō sentit i sacramenti manducacōe
Sz i sciis meditacionibz z celestiū cōtēplacōe
Gust' manne i oēz saporē u' quisqz volebat gustabat
Sz dulcedō xpi null' sapor h' mūdi assilat
Qm de hac dulcedie semel gustaverit
Oē delectamentum h' scl' ad nichilū reputavit
Petr' de hac dulcedine i monte tabor gustabat
Sicut ibi tabernaculū facē z semp manē affectabat
Precepit moyses pplo ut mane añ sol' ortū exirent
et singli p illo die sibi unū gomor colligerent
Contigit miraculose q viatores q pl' collegerāt
Qū ad ppia redibāt nō pl' gomor habuerunt
Silr z illi q ad plenā mēsā colligē nō poterāt
Cū ad ppia redierūt plenā mensurā invenerunt
Sic cōmunicās q plures hostias recepit
Nō pl' hz qm ille q tm unā accipit
Silr z illi qui particulā hostie sumpserunt
Nō hnt minus qm illi q integrā vl plures sumpserunt
Exodi xvi° caplo

Leaf 31 from a M.S. "Speculum Humanae Salvationis"

miniature." "The Missal," says Dibdin, "frequently displays the arms of these noble personages," (John, Duke of Bedford, and of his wife Jane, daughter of the Duke of Burgundy,) "and also affords a pleasing testimony of the affectionate gallantry of the pair: the motto of the former being 'A VOUS ENTIER;' that of the latter, 'J'EN SUIS CONTENTE.'" Among its ornaments are emblems or symbols of the twelve months, and a large variety of paintings derived from the Sacred Scriptures, many of which possess an emblematical meaning.

Not aiming at any exhaustive method in the information we gather and impart respecting Emblem works and editions previous to the year A.D. 1500, we pass by the very numerous other instances in support of our theme which a search into manuscripts would supply. The "Block-Books," which, in the main, are especially emblematical, we next consider. We select two instances as representative of the whole set;—namely, the "BIBLIA PAUPERUM," *Bibles of the Poor*, and the "ARS MEMORANDI," *The Art of Remembering*.

In his "BIBLIOGRAPHICAL DECAMERON," vol. i. p. 160, Dibdin tells us, "The earliest printed book, containing *text* and *engravings* illustrative of scriptural subjects, is called the *Histories of Joseph, Daniel, Judith, and Esther*. This was executed in the German language, and was printed by Pfister at Bamberg in 1462. It is among the rarest of typographical curiosities in existence." Dibdin's dictum is considerably modified, if not set aside, by Noel Humphreys; who, though affirming, p. 41, that "a late German edition of the *Biblia Pauperum* has the date 1475, but that before that period editions had been printed at

* One of the earliest and most curious of the Block-books, *Biblia Pauperum*, has been reproduced in fac-simile by Mr. J. Ph. Berjeau, from a copy in the British Museum.

the regular press with moveable types, as, for instance, that of Pfister, printed at Bamberg in 1462,"—yet had previously declared, p. 39, "many suppose that Laurens Koster, of Haarlem, who afterwards invented moveable types, was one of the earliest engravers of Block-books, and that in fact the *Biblia Pauperum* was actually his work." "The period of its execution may probably be estimated as lying between 1410 and 1420: probably earlier, but certainly not later."

The earliest editions of these *Biblia Pauperum* contain forty leaves, the later editions fifty, printed only on one side. Opposite to p. 40, Noel Humphreys gives, pl. 2, "A Page from the Biblia Pauperum generally supposed to be one of the earliest block-books."

Availing ourselves of the Author's remarks, p. 40, we yet prefer, on account of some inaccuracies in his decyphering the Latin contractions, giving our own description of this plate. The page is in *three* divisions, all in the Gothic decorative style, with separating archways between the subjects. In the *upper* division, in the centre, are seated, each in his niche, "Isaya" and "Dauid." (See Plate VI.) In the upper corners, on the right hand of the first, and on the left hand of the second, are Latin inscriptions,—the former relating to Eve's seed bruising the serpent's head, Genesis iii. c., and the latter to Gideon's fleece saturated with dew, Judges vi. c. The *middle* compartment is a triptych, consisting of Eve's Temptation, the Annunciation by the Angel to the Blessed Virgin; and Gideon in his armour, on his knees, with his shield on the ground, watching the fleece. Over Eve's Temptation there is a scroll issuing from Isaiah's niche, and having this inscription: "**Ecce virgo concipiet et pariet filium,**"—*Behold a virgin shall conceive and bear a son*, Is. vii. 14; Eve stands near the tree of life, emblematized by God the Father among the branches,—and erect before her is the serpent, almost on the tip of its tail, with its body slightly curved. In

Plate 6

A Page from the "Biblia Pauperum" generally supposed one of the earliest Block Books

the Annunciation appears a ray of light breathed upon the Virgin from God the Father seated in the clouds, and in the ray are the dove, the emblem of the Holy Spirit, descending, and an infant Christ bearing his cross; the Angel stands before Mary addressing to her the salutation, "**Ave gratiâ plena, dominus tecum,**"—*Hail full of grace, the Lord is with thee,* Luke i. 28; and Mary, seated with a book on her knees, and her hands devoutly crossed on her breast, replies, "**Ecce, ancilla domini, fiat mihi,**"—*Behold, the handmaid of the Lord, be it unto me,* Luke i. 38. Of Gideon and the fleece little needs be said, except that over him from the niche of David issues a scroll with the words "**Descendet dominus sicut pluvia in vellus,**" in the Latin Vulgate, Ps. lxxi. 6, *i.e. The Lord shall descend as rain upon the fleece;* but in the English version, Ps. lxxii. 6, *He shall come down like rain upon the mown grass.* The Angel also addressing Gideon bears a scroll, not quite legible, but evidently meaning, "**Dominus tecum virorum fortissime,**" Judges vi. 12,—English version, *The Lord is with thee, thou mighty man of valour.* The *lower* compartment, like the upper, has in the centre two arched niches, which contain, the one Ezekiel, the other Jeremiah; beneath Eve's temptation and Gideon's omen are the alliterative and rhyming couplets

"**Vipera vim perdet,** and "**Rore madet vellus**
Sine vi pariente puella." **Permansit arida tellus;**" *

and beneath the Annunciation, "**Virgo salutatur, Innupta manens gravidatur.**"

From Ezekiel's niche issues the scroll, Ez. xliv. 2, "**Porta hæc**

* Mr. Humphreys reads "Pluviam sicut arida tellus;" but in this, as in two or three other instances in this pl. 2, and p. 40, a botanical lens will show that the readings are those which I have given. I desire here to express to him my obligation for the courteous permission to make use of pl. 2, p. 40, of his work, for a photolith (see Plate VI.), to illustrate my remarks.

clausa erit, et non aperietur;" and from Jeremiah's, xxxi. 22, "Creabit dominus nobum super terram, femina circumdabit birum."

It requires no argument to prove the emblematical nature of the *middle* compartment of this page from the *Biblia Pauperum;* and the texts on scrolls are but the accessories to the devices, and serve only the more clearly to mark this Block-book as an Emblem-book.

Passing by similar Block-books, as *The Book of Canticles*, and *The Apocalypse of St. John*, we will conclude the subject with a notice of Humphreys' pl. 5, following p. 42 of his text; it is "A Subject from the Block-book entitled 'Ars memorandi,' executed probably at the beginning of the fifteenth century."

"The entire work," we are informed, p. 42, "consists of the symbols of the four evangelists, each occupying a page, and being most grotesquely treated, the bull of St. Luke and the lion of St. Mark standing upright on their hind legs. These symbols are surrounded with various objects, calculated to recall the leading events in their respective Gospels."

But the whole passage in explanation of the Plate is so much to our purpose, that we ask pardon of the author for inserting it entire. He says :—

"The page I have selected for reproduction is the fourth 'image or symbol' of St. Matthew—the Angel. The objects grouped around are many of them very curious, and, without the assistance of the accompanying explanations, would certainly not serve to aid the memory of the modern Biblical students. The symbolic Angel holds in the left hand objects numbered 18, which by the explanation we learn to be the sun and moon, accompanied by an unusual arrangement of stars and planets; intended to recall the passage, 'there were signs in the sun and moon'—*erant signa in sole et luna.* I give the text of monkish explanation in MS. No. 19, the clasped hands, represents marriage, in reference to the generations of the Ancestors of Christ as enumerated by St. Matthew. No. 20, the cockle

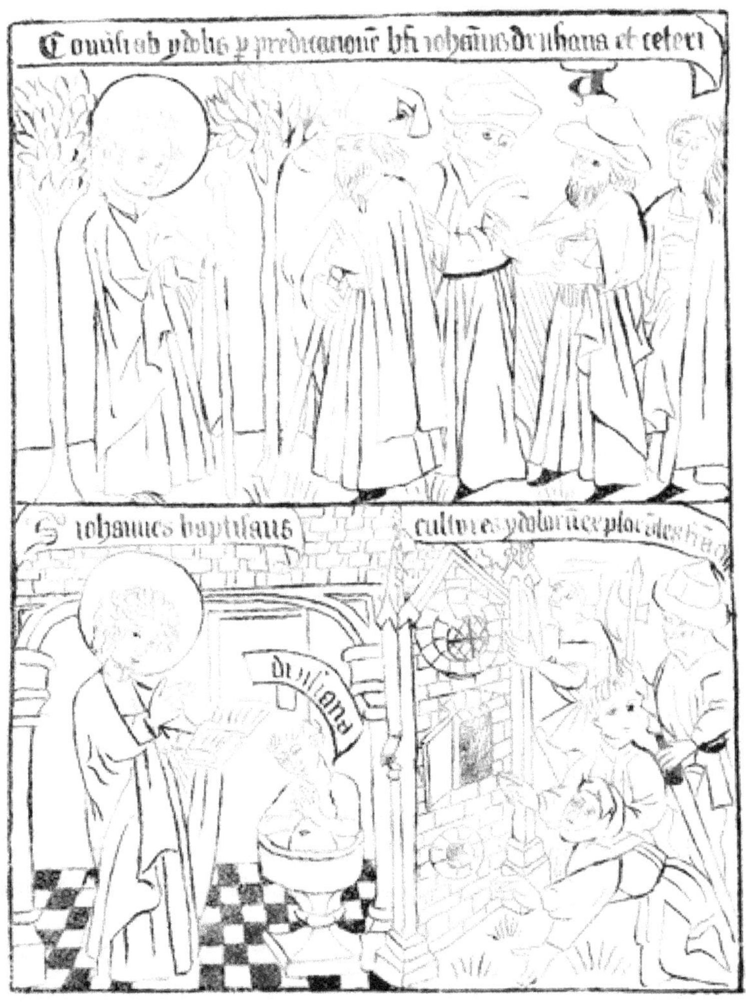

S. John the Evangelist. 1st edition Block Book from the Corser Collection

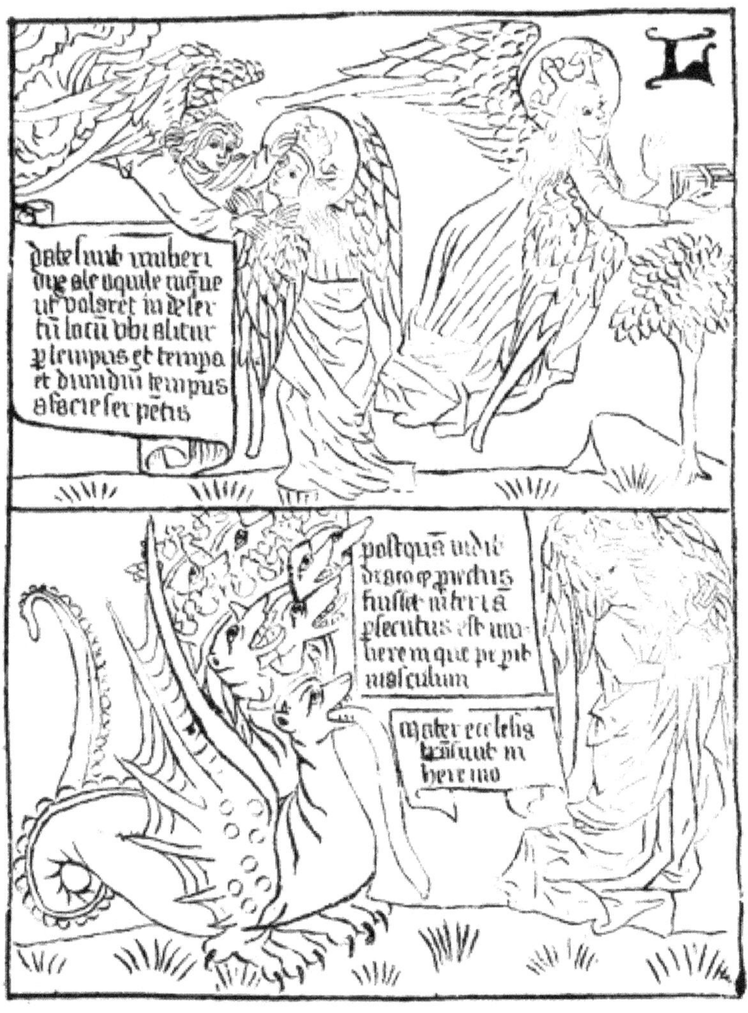

A Page of the Apocalypse from Block Book in the Cracow Collection

shell and the bunch of grapes are emblems of travelling and pilgrimage, and appear to represent the flight into Egypt; 21, the head of an ass, is intended to recall the entrance of Christ into Jerusalem riding on an ass; 22, a table, with bread-knife and drinking cup, recalls the Last Supper (*Cœna magna*): and the accompanying symbol, without a number, represents the census rendered to Cæsar."*

With great kindness Mr. Corser, of Stand, offered me, in the spring of 1868, the use of a very choice Block-book, soon after sold for £415, entitled *Historia S. Joan. Euangelist. per Figuras*, and which is, I believe, the very copy from which Sotheby's specimens of the work are taken. Whether it be the "*editio princeps*," as a former owner claimed it to be, is doubted on merely conjectural grounds; but a most precious copy it is, internally vindicating its claim to priority. The volume measures 2·82 decimetres by 2·14; or 11 inches by 8·42. There are forty-eight leaves, in perfect preservation, printed on one side. The figures, all coloured, relate either to the traditions and legends of the Evangelist, or to the visions of the Apocalypse, the former being simply pictorial, the latter emblematical.

The two Plates uncoloured (Plate VII. and Plate VIII.) very clearly show the difference between the mere drawing and the device. The pictures of the Evangelist preaching, of Drusiana being baptized, and of the search after John, have no meaning beyond the historical or legendary event;—but the two wings of an eagle given to the woman, of the angel flying with a book above the tree of life, of the dragon persecuting the woman, and of the mother-church passing into the desert: these have a meaning beyond that of the

* To follow out the subject of the *Biblia Pauperum*, or of Block-books in general, the Reader may consult Sotheby's *Principia typographica, The Block-Books*, &c., 3 vols. 4to, London, 1858; Dibdin's *Bibliotheca Spenseriana*, 4 vols. London, 1814, 1815; or Berjeau's *Biblia Pauperum*, a fac-simile with an historical introduction, 4to: Trubner, London, 1859.

figures delineated;—they are emblematical of hidden truths;—so are all the other plates of this Block-book which represent the visions of the Apocalypse. The date is probably 1420 to 1425.

The Bodleian Library at Oxford is very rich in this particular Block-book, possessing no fewer than *three* copies of the *History of S. John the Evangelist.* Among its treasures, however, is a MS. on the same subject, worth them all by reason of its beauty and exquisite finish, which the Block-books certainly do not claim. This MS., on fine vellum and finely drawn and illuminated, is said to have been written in the twelfth century, and to have belonged to Henry II.

But the printing with moveable types is firmly established, and Emblem-books are among its earliest productions. At Bamberg, a city on the Regnitz, near its influx into the Main, the first purely German book was printed in 1461, by the same Pfister who published an edition of the *Biblia Pauperum,* and who probably learned his art at Mayence with Guttenberg himself. The work in question was a Collection of eighty-five Fables in German, with 101 vignettes cut on wood, each accompanied by a German text of rhyming verses. The first device, says Brunet, vol. i. p. 1096, represents three apes and a tree, and the verses begin with—

"Once on a time came an ape (*gerãt*) upright."

The colophon, or subscription, at the end informs us,

"At Bamberg this little book ended is
After the birth of our Lord Jesus Christ,
When one counts a thousand four hundred year,
And to it, as truth, one and sixty more,
On the day of holy Valentine;
God shield us from the wrath divine. Amen.

The fables were collected by Ulric Boner, a Dominican friar

of Bonn, in the thirteenth or at the beginning of the fourteenth century. Their chief value is that they present the most precious remains of the Minnesingers, or German Troubadours, and possess much grace, and "une moralité piquante." See *Biographie Universelle,* vol. v. pp. 97, 98: Paris, 1812; and vol. xxxiii. p. 584: Paris, 1823.

Of Æsop's *Fables* in Greek, the Milan edition, about A.D. 1480, was the earliest. There had been Latin versions, previously at Rome in 1473, at Bologna and Antwerp in 1486, and elsewhere. The German translation appeared in 1473, the Italian in 1479, the French and the English in 1484, and the Spanish in 1489. Besides these there were at least thirty other editions previous to the year 1500.

It has been doubted if Fables should be classed among the Emblem Literature,—but whether *nude,* as other emblems have been named when unclothed in the ornaments of wood or copper engravings, or *adorned* with richly embellished devices, they are, as Whitney would name them, *naturally* emblematical. Apart from whatever artistic skill can effect for them, they have in themselves meanings to be evolved different from those which the words convey. The Lion, the Fox, and the Ass are not simply names for the veritable animals, but emblems of different characters and qualities among the human race; they symbolize moral sentiments and actions, and when we add the figures of the creatures, though we may make pleasing and significant pictures, we do little for the real development of the emblems.

Books of Fables, however, are so numerous that they and their editors may be counted by hundreds; and as Dibdin intimates, the Bibliomaniac who had gathered up all the editions of Æsop in nearly all the languages of the civilized world, would have formed a very considerable library. Only on a few occasions therefore shall we make mention of books of Fables in our present inquiries.

We shall not however pass unnoticed, since it belongs especially to this period, the "**Dyalogus Creaturarum,**" or, *Dialogues of the Creatures*, a collection of Latin Fables, attributed in the fourteenth century to Nicolas Pergaminus, first printed at Gouda in Holland by Gerard Leeu in 1480, and at Stockholm by John Snell in 1483. (See Brunet, vol. ii. p. 674.) A French version, by Colard Mansion, was issued at Lyons in 1482, *Dialogue des Creatures moralizie*; and an English version, about 1520, by J. Rastall, "Powly's Churche," London, namely, "The Dialogue of Creatures moralyzed, of late translated out of latyn in to our English tonge."

There were various editions and modifications of the work,* but perhaps the contrast between them cannot be better pointed out than by selecting the Fable of the Wolf and the Ass from the Gouda edition of 1480, and also from the Antwerp edition of 1584. The original edition, with the woodcut on the next page in mere outline, tells in simple Latin prose how a wolf and an ass were sawing a log of wood together. From good nature

* As in Nourry's Lyons editions of 1509 and 1511, where the title given is, "**Destructoriū vitiorum ex similitudinū creaturarum exemplorū appropriatiōe per modum dialogi,**" &c.; lge. 4to, in the Corser Library, from which we take—**De Sole et Luna.**

Lyons ed. 1511.

the ass worked up above, the wolf through maliciousness down below, desiring to find an opportunity for devouring the ass; therefore he complained that the ass was sending the

Dyalogus Creat., ed. 14[illegible]

sawdust into his eyes. The ass replied, "It is not I who am doing this,—I only guide the saw. If you wish to saw up above I am content,—I will work faithfully down below." And so they talked on, until the wolf threatening revenge drew back, and the fissure in the beam being suddenly widened, the wedge fell upon the wolf's head, and the wolf himself was killed.

The Antwerp edition of 1584* changes the simple Latin prose into the elegant Latin elegiacs of John Moerman, and the outline woodcuts of an unknown artist into the copperplate engravings of Gerard de Jode, the eldest of four generations of engravers. THE WOLF and THE ASS are made to emblematize, "scelesti hominis imago et exitus,"—*the image and end of a wicked man.* Moerman's Latin may thus be rendered, from leaf 54, ed. 1584:—

"The Wolf and careless Ass a treaty made,
 Both studious with a saw a beam to rive;—
The ready Ass above directs the blade,
 The Wolf doth down below deceit contrive.
He seeks for cause the wretched Ass to slay,
 And cries,—'With sawdust much thou troublest me,
The trouble check, or with these teeth, I say,
 My spoil to be devoured thou straight shalt be.'
To this the Ass,—'Friend Wolf, be not annoyed;
 Guileless the saw I guide with might and main.'
But soon the long-eared brute would be destroyed,
 When falls the wedge;—ah! 'tis the Wolf is slain."

Apologi Creaturarum, 1584.

* The Title is "APOLOGI CREATVRARVM;" "Vtilia prudenti, imprudenti futilia. *G. de Jode excu.* 1584."

MORAL.

"Insonti qui insidias struit, ipse perit."

"Who for the innocent spreads snares,
Himself shall perish unawares."

"*The wicked man his nets doth spread
The innocent to take the while;
But who would harm his brother's head
Doth perish from his selfish guile.
God will not deem him innocent,
Nor raise him to the stars above,
Who on unrighteous thoughts is bent,
Or neighbours serves with feigned love.
But after death to the fiery marsh
Of Phlegethon shall he be hurled,
Where Tartaræan Pluto harsh
With hated sceptres rules a world.*"

As in the Blandford Catalogue, it has been usual to count among Emblem-books the "ECATONPHYLA," printed at Venice in 1491. The French translation of 1536 describes the title as, "signifiãt centiesme amour, sciemment appropriees a la dame ayãt en elle autant damour que cent aultres dames en pouroient comprendre," *signifying a hundredth love, knowingly appropriated to the lady having in her as much love as a hundred other ladies could possibly comprehend.* (Brunet's *Manuel*, i. c. 131, 132.) The author of this work, of which there are several editions, was the celebrated Italian architect, Leoni-Baptista Alberti, born of a noble family of Florence in 1398, and living as some suppose up to 1480. He was a universal scholar, a doctor of laws, a priest, a painter, and a good mechanic.

We are inclined to ask whether *Gli Trionfi del Petrarcha*, printed at Bologna in 1475,—especially, when as in the Venice editions of 1500 and 1523 they were adorned by the vignettes and wood engravings of Zoan Andrea Veneziano,—whether these "Triumphs of Love, Chastity, and Death" may not, from their highly allegorical character, be included among the Emblem-books of this age?* The same question we might ask respecting "**Das Heldenbuch**,"—*The Book of Heroes*,—printed at Augsburg, in 1477, by Gunther Zainer, who had first been a printer at Cracow about 1465: and also concerning the "**Libri Cronicarum cũ figuris et imaginibus ab inicio mũdi**," a large folio known as the *Chronicles of Nuremberg*, which with its 2000 fine wood engravings, attributed to Michael Wohlgemuth, was published in that city in 1493.†

The original "**Todtentanz**," or *Dance of Death*, painted as a memorial of the plague which raged during the Council of Bâle, held between 1431 and 1446 (Bryan, p. 335), certainly was not the work of either of the Holbeins. There are several representations of a Death-dance in the fifteenth century, between 1485 and 1496 (Brunet, v. 873, 874); and there can be little doubt of their emblematical character. The renowned *Dance of Death* by Hans Holbein the younger we will reserve for its proper place in the next section.

We must not however leave unmentioned *The Dance of Macaber*, especially as it is presented to us in an English form by John Lydgate, a monk of the Benedictine abbey of Bury St. Edmunds, who was born about 1375, and attained his greatest eminence about 1430. His own power for supplying the materials for an Emblem-device we observe in the lines on "*God's Providence*."

"God hath a thousand handés to chastise;
A thousand dartés of punicion;
A thousand bowés made in divers wise;
A thousand arlblasts bent in his dongèon."

* An English translation, with wood engravings, appeared about the time of Shakespeare's birth, it may be a few years earlier:—*The Trynmphes of Fraunces Petrarcke*, "translated out of Italian into English by Hẽrye Parker knyght, lorde Morley," sm. 4to.

† See Brunet's *Manuel*, iii. c. 85, and i. c. 1860; *Biog. Universelle*, "Zainer;" Timperley's *Dictionary of Printers*, p. 197; and Bryan's *Dict. of Engravers*, p. 918.

Stultifera Nauis.

Narragonice pfectionis nunq̄

satis laudata Nauis: per Sebastianū Brant: vernaculo vulgariq; sermone & rhythmo/ p cūctoꝝ mortaliū fatuitatis semitas effugere cupiētiū directione/speculo/cōmodoq; & salute: proq; inertis ignaueq; stultitię ppetua infamia/execratione/& confutatione/nup fabricata: Atq; iampridem per Iacobum Locher/cognomēto Philomusum: Sueuū: in latinū traducta eloquiū: & per Sebastianū Brant denuo seduloq; reuisa/& noua q̄dā exactaq; emendatōe elimata: atq; supadditis qbusdā nouis/admirādisq; fatuoꝝ generibus suppleta: fœlici exorditur principio.

·1497·

Nihil sine causa.

Io. de. Olpe.

For an account of Lydgate's *Dance of Macaber*, and indeed for his version in English, we should do well to consult the remarks by Francis Douce, in Wenceslaus Hollar's *Dance of Death*, published about the year 1790, and more particularly the remarks in Douce's Dissertation, edition 1833.

The earliest known edition of *La Danse Macabre*, originally composed in German, is dated at Paris, 1484, but before the completion of the century there were seven or eight other reprints, some with alterations and others with additions. It was a most popular work, issued at least eight or ten times during the sixteenth century, and still exciting interest.[*] At p. 39 may be seen copies of some of the devices as used by Verard.

The chief Emblem deviser and writer towards the end of the century was Sebastian Brandt, born at Strasburg in 1458, and after a life of great usefulness and honour dying at Bâle in 1520. The publication in German Iambic verse of his "**Narren Schyff**," Bâle, Nuremberg, Ruttlingen, and Augsburg, A.D. 1494, forms quite an epoch in Emblem-book literature. Previous to A.D. 1500, *Locher*, crowned poet laureate by the Emperor Maximilian I., translated the German into Latin verse, with the title "**Stultifera Nauis**" (see Plate IX.); *Riviere* of Poitiers, the Latin into French verse, "**La Nef des Folz du Monde;**" and *Droyn* of Amiens, into French prose, "**La grāt Nef des Folz du Monde.**" Early in the next century, 1504, or even in 1500, there was a Flemish version; and in 1509 two English versions, —*one* translated out of French, "THE SHYPPE OF FOOLES," by Henry Watson, and printed by "Wynkyn de Worde, MCCCCCIX." (see Dibdin's *Tour*, ii. p. 103); *the other*, — "STULTIFERA NAUIS," or "**The Shyp of Folys of the Worlde:**" "Inprentyd in the Cyte of London, by Richard Pynson, M.D.IX." (Dibdin's

[*] Langlois in his *Essai*, pp. 331—340, names thirty-two editions previous to A.D. 1730.

Typ. Ant. ii. p. 431.) This latter was "*translated out of Latin, French, and Duch into Englishe*, by Alexander Barclay, *Priest*;" and reprinted in 1570, during Shakespeare's childhood by the "Printer to the Queenes Maiestie." At the same time, 1570, another work by Barclay was published, which, although without devices, partakes of an allegorical or even of an emblematical character; it is *The Mirrour of good Maners*; "conteining the foure Cardinal Vertues."

Dibdin, in his *Bibliographical Antiquarian*, iii. p. 101, mentions "a pretty little volume—'as fresh as a daisy,' the *Hortulus Rosarum de Valle Lachrymarum*, 'A little Garden of Roses from the Valley of Tears' (to which a Latin ode by S. Brandt is prefixed), printed by J. de Olpe in 1499,"—but he gives no intimation of its character; conjecturing from its title and from the woodcuts with which it is adorned, it will probably on further inquiry be found to bear an emblematical meaning.

Dibdin also, in the same work, iii. p. 294, names "a German version of the 'HORTULUS ANIMÆ' of S. Brant," in manuscript; "undoubtedly," he says, "among the loveliest books in the Imperial Library." The Latin edition was printed at Strasburg in 1498, and is ornamented with figures on wood; many of these are mere pictures, without any symbolical meaning,—but it often is the case that the illuminated manuscripts, especially if devotional, and the early printed books of every kind that have pictorial illustrations in them, present various examples of symbolical and emblematical devices.

The last works we shall name of the period antecedent to A.D. 1501, are due to the industry and skill of John Sicile, herald at arms to Alphonso King of Aragon, who died in 1458. Sicile, it seems, prepared two manuscripts, *one* the Blazonry of Arms,—the *other*, the Blazonry of Colours. Of the former there was an edition printed at Paris in 1495, *Le* BLASON *de toutes*

Armes et Ecutz, &c.—and of the latter at Lyons early in the sixteenth century, *Le Blason des Couleurs en Armes, Liurees et deuises.* Within an hundred years, ending with 1595, above sixteen editions of the two works were issued.

Several other authors there are belonging to the period of which we treat,—but enough have been named to show to what an extent Emblem devices and Emblem-books had been adopted, and with what an impetus the invention of moveable types and greater skill in engraving had acted to multiply the departments of the Emblem Literature. It was an impetus which gathered new strength in its course, and which, previous to Shakespeare's youth and maturity, had made an entrance into almost every European nation. Already in 1500, from Sweden to Italy and from Poland to Spain, the touch was felt which was to awaken nearly every city to the west of Constantinople, to share in the supposed honours of adding to the number of Emblem volumes.

Section III.

Other Emblem Works and Editions between A.D. 1500 and 1564.

LABORIOUS in some degree is the enterprise which the title of this Section will indicate before it shall be ended. Perchance we shall have no myths to perplex us, but the demands of sober history are often more inexorable than those flexible boundaries within which the imagination may disport amid facts and fictions.

Better, as I trust, to set this period of *sixty-three* years before the mind, it may be well to take it in three divisions: 1st, the twenty-one years before Alciatus appeared, to conquer for himself a kingdom, and to reign king of Emblematists for about a century and a half; 2nd, the twenty-one years from the appearance of the first edition of Alciat's *Emblems* in 1522 at Milan, until Hans Holbein the younger had introduced the *Images and Epigrams of Death*, and La Perriere and Corrozet, the one his *Theatre of good Contrivances in one hundred Emblems*, and the other his *Hecatomgraphie*, or descriptions of one hundred figures; 3rd, the twenty-one years up to Shakespeare's birth, distinguished towards its close chiefly by the Italian writers on *Imprese*, Paolo Giovio, Vincenzo Cartari, Girolamo Ruscelli, and Gabriel Symeoni.

I.—*A Fool-freighted Ship* was the title of almost the last book of the fifteenth century,—by a similar title is the Emblem-book called which was launched at the beginning of the sixteenth century; it is, "**Jodoci Badii ascēsii** Stultiferę nauiculę seu scaphę Fatuarum mulierum: circa sensus quinq̄ exteriores fraude nauigantium,"—*The Fool-freighted little ships of Josse Badius ascensius, or the skiffs of Silly women in delusion sailing about the five outward senses,*—"printed by honest John Prusz, a citizen of Strasburg, in the year of Salvation M.CCCCC.II." There was an earlier edition in 1500,—but almost exactly the same. From that before us we give a specimen of the work, *The Skiff*

Stultę gustationis scapha.

Badius, 1502.

of Foolish Tasting. A discourse follows, with quotations from Aulus Gellius, Saint Jerome, Virgil, Ezekiel, Epicurus, Seneca, Horace, and Juvenal: and the discourse is crowned by twenty-four lines of Latin elegiacs, entitled "**Celeusma Gustationis fatuę,**"—*The Oarsman's cry for silly Tasting,*—thus exhorting—

"Slothful chieftains of the gullet!
  Offspring of Sardanapálus!
In sweet sleep no longer lull it,—
  Rouse ye, lest good cheer should fail us.
Gentle winds to pleasures calling
  Waft to regions soft and slow;
On a thousand dishes falling,
  How our palates burn and glow!
Suppers of Lucillus name not,
  Ancient faith! nor plate of veal;
Ancient faith to luncheon came not
  Crowned with flowers that age conceal.
Let none boast of pontiff's dishes,—
  Nor Mars' priests their suppers spread;
Alban banquets bless our wishes,—
  Cæsar's garlands deck our head.
Now the dish of Æsop yielding,
  Apicius all his luxuries pours;
And Ptolomies the sceptres wielding
  Richest viands give in showers."

And so on, until in the concluding stanza Badius declares—

"If great Jove himself invited
  At our feasting takes his seat,
Jove would say, 'I am delighted,
  Not in heaven have I such meat.'
Therefore, stupids! what of summer
  Enters now our pinnace gay,—
Onward in three hours 'twill bear us
  Where kingdoms blessed bid us stay." *

The same work was published in another form, "La nef des folles, selon les cinq sens de nature, composé selon levangile de monseigneur saint Mathieu, des cinq vierges qui ne prindrent point duylle avec eulx pour mectre en leurs lampes:" Paris 4to, about 1501.

* Be lenient, gentle Reader, if you chance to compare the above translation with the original; for even should you have learned by heart the two very large 4to volumes of Forcellini's *Lexicon of all Latinity*, I believe you will find some nuts you cannot crack in the Latin verses of Jodocus Badius.

Of Badius himself, born in 1462 and dying in 1535, it is to be said that he was a man of very considerable learning, professor of "belles lettres" at Lyons from 1491 to 1511, when he was tempted to settle in Paris. There he established the famous Ascensian Printing Press,—and like Plantin of Antwerp, gave his three daughters in marriage to three very celebrated printers: Michel Vascosan, Robert Etienne, and Jean de Poigny. He was the author of several works besides those that have been mentioned. (*Biog. Univ.* vol. iii. p. 201.)

Symphorien Champier, Doctor in Theology and Medicine, a native of Lyons, who was physician to Anthony Duke of Lorraine when he accompanied Louis XII. to the Italian war, graduated at Pavia in 1515, and, after laying the foundations of the Lyons College of Physicians, and enjoying the highest honours of his native city, died about 1540. (Aikin's *Biog.* ii. 579.) His medical and other works are of little repute, but among them are two or three which may be regarded as imitations of Emblem-books. We will just name,—Balsat's work with Champier's additions, *La Nef des Princes et des Batailles de Noblesse, &c.* (Lyons, 4to goth. with woodcuts, A.D. 1502.); also, *La Nef des Dames vertueuses cõposee par Maistre Simphoriẽ Champier, &c.* (Lyons, 4to goth. with woodcuts, A.D. 1503.)

"Bible figures," too, again have a claim to notice. A very fine copy of "**Les figures du vieil Testament, & du nouuel,**" which belonged to the Rev. T. Corser, Rector of Stand, near Manchester, supplies the opportunity of noticing that it is decidedly an Emblem work. It is a folio, of 100 leaves, containing forty-one plates, of which one is introductory, and forty are on Scriptural subjects, unarranged in order either of time or place. The work was published in Paris in 1503 by Anthoine Verard, and is certainly, as Brunet declares, ii. c. 1254, "une imitation de l'ouvrage connu sous le nom de *Biblia Pauperum.*" There are forty sets of figures in triptychs, the wood engravings being very bold and good. Each is preceded or followed by a French stanza of eight lines, declaring the subject; and has appended two or three pages of Exposition, also in French. The Device pages, each in three compartments, are in Latin, and may thus be described. At the top to the left hand, a quotation from the Vulgate appropriate to the pictorial representation beneath it: in the centre two niches, of which David always occupies one, and some writer of the Old Testament the other, a scroll issuing from each niche. The middle compartment is filled by a triptych, the centre subject from the New Testament, the right and left from the Old. At the bottom are Latin verses to the right and left, with two niches in the centre occupied by biblical writers. The Latin verses are rhyming couplets, as on fol. a. iiij, beneath Moses at the burning bush, "**Lucet et ignescit, sed non rubus igne calescit,**"—*It shines and flames, but the bush is not heated by the fire.* In triptych, on p. i. *rev.* are, Enoch's Translation, Christ's Ascension, and the Translation of Elijah.

The Aldine press at Venice, A.D. 1505, gave the world the first printed edition of the "HIEROGLYPHICA" of Horapollo. It was in folio, having in the same volume the Fables of Æsop, of Gabrias, &c. See Leemans' *Horapollo*, pp. xxix—xxxv. A Latin version by Bernard Trebatius was published at Augsburg in 1515, at Bâle in 1518, and at Paris in 1521; and another Latin version by Phil. Phasianinus, at Bologna in 1517. Previous to Shakespeare's birth there were translations into French in 1543, into Italian in 1548, and into German in 1554,—and down to 1616 sixteen other editions may readily be counted up.

John Haller, who had introduced printing into Cracow in 1500, published in 1507 the first attempt to teach logic by means of a game of cards; it was in Murner's quarto entitled, "CHARTILUDIUM logicę seu Logica poetica vel memorativa cum jocundo Pictasmatis Exercimento,"—*A Card-game of Logic, or Logic poetical or memorial, with the pleasant Exercise of pictured Representation.* It is a curious and ingenious work, and reprints of it appeared at Strasburg in 1509 and 1518: at Paris, by Balesdens, in 1629; and again in 1650, 4to, by Peter Guischet. As an imitation of Brandt's *Ship of Fools,* so far as it relates to the follies and caprices of mankind, mention should also be made of Murner's "**Narren Beschwörung,**"—*Exorcism of Fools,*—Strasburg, 4to, 1512 and 1518; which certainly at Francfort, in 1620, gave origin to Flitner's "NEBVLO NEBVLONVM,"—or, *Rascal of Rascals.*

"**Speculū Pacietiecum** theologycis Consolationibus Fratris Ioannis de Tambaco,"—*The Mirror of Patience with the theological Consolations of Brother John Tambaco,*—Nuremberg, MCCCCCIX., 4to, is a work of much curiousness. On the reverse of the title is an Emblematical device of Job, Job's wife, and the Devil, followed by exhortations to patience; and on the reverse of the introduction to the second part, also an Emblematical device,—the Queen of Consolation, with her four maidens by her side, and two men kneeling before her. The chapters on consolation are generally in the form of *sermonettes,* in which the maidens, three or four, or even a dozen, expatiate on different subjects proper for reproof, exhortation, and comfort. The devices in this volume are understood to be from the pencil of Albert Durer.

This same year, 1509, witnessed two English translations, or paraphrases, of Brandt's "**Narren Schif,**"—the one *The Shyppe of Fooles,* taken from the French by Henry Watson, and printed by De Worde;—the other rendered out of Latin, German, and French, *The Ship of Fooles,* by Alexander Barclay, and printed by Pinson. Of Watson little, if anything, is known, but Barclay is regarded as one of the improvers of the English tongue, and to him it is chiefly owing that a true Emblem-book was made popular in England.

Of the "Dyalogus Creaturarum," written in the fourteenth century by Nicolas Pergaminus, and printed by Gerard Leeu, at Gouda, in 1480, an English version appeared about 1520,—"The dialogue of Creatures moralyzed, of late translated out of Latyn in to our English tonge."

The famous preacher and the founder of the first public school in Strasburg was John Geyler, born in 1445. He was highly esteemed by the Emperor Maximilian, and after a ministry of about thirty years, died in 1510. Two Emblem-books were left by him, both published in 1511 by James Other;—the one "Nabicula sive Speculū Fatuorum,"—*The little Ship or Mirror of Fools;* the other, "Nabicula Penitentie,"—*The little Ship of Penitence.* To the first there are 110 emblems and 112 devices, each having a discourse delivered on one of the Sabbaths or festivals of the Catholic Church—the text always being, *Stultorum infinitus est,*—"Infinite is the number of fools." The second, not strictly an Emblem-book, is devoted "to the praise of God and the salvation of souls in Strasburg," and consists really of a series of sermons for Lent and other seasons of the year, but all having the same text, *Ecce ascendimus Hierosolimam,*—"Behold we go up to Jerusalem." There were several reprints of both the works, and two German translations; and the edition of 1520, folio, with wood engravings, is remarkable for being the first book to which was granted the "Imperial privilege." It is said that the rhymes of Brandt's *Ship of Fools* which Geyler had translated into Latin in 1498, not unfrequently served him for texts and quotations for his sermons. Alas! we have no such lively preachers in these sleepy days of perfect propriety of phrase and person. Our prophets, in putting away "locusts and wild honey," too often forget to cry, "Repent, for the kingdom of heaven is at hand."

Next, however, to the famous preacher, we name a notorious prophet, the Abbot Joachim, who died between the years 1201 and 1202, but whose works, if they really were his, did not appear in print, until the folio edition was issued about 1475,—*Revelations concerning the State of the chief Pontiffs.* An Italian version, "PROPHETIA dello Abbate Joachimo circa li Pontefici & Re," appeared in 1515: and another Latin edition, with wood engravings, by Marc-Antoine Raimondi, in 1516.* Many tales are related of the Abbot and of his followers; suffice it to say, that they maintained the Gospel of Christ would be abolished A.D. 1260; and thenceforward Joachim's "true and everlasting Gospel" was to be prevalent in the world.

According to the Blandford *Catalogue*, p. 6, we should here insert P. Dupont's *Satyriques Grotesques* (Desseins Orig.), 8vo, Paris, 1513; but it may be passed over with the simplest notice.

If we judge from the wonderfully beautiful copy on finest vellum in the Hunterian Museum at Glasgow, the next Emblem-book surpasses all others we have named; it is the "**Tewrdannckh**"—or, *Dear-thought*,—usually attributed to Melchior Pfintzing, a German poet, born at Nuremberg in 1481, and who at one time was secretary to the Emperor Maximilian. The poem is allegorical and chivalric, and adorned with 118 plates, some of which are considered the workmanship of Albert Durer.†

The *Tewrdanck* was intended to set forth the dangers and love adventures of the emperor himself on occasion of his

* For a very good account of Joachim's supposed works, consult a paper in *Notes and Queries*, September, 1862, pp. 181-3, by Mr. Jones, the excellent Librarian of the Chetham Library, Manchester; and for an account of the man, Aikin's *General Biography*, v. pp. 478-80.

† The "Ehrenpforte," or *Triumphal Arch*, about 1515, and the "Triumphwagen," or *Triumphal Car*, A.D. 1522, both in honour of Maximilian I., are among the noblest of Durer's engravings; but the *Biographie Universelle*, t. 33, p. 582, attributes the engravings in the "Tewrdannckh" to Hans Shaeufflein the younger, who was born at Nuremberg about 1487; and with this agrees Stanley's *Dict. of Engravers*, ed. 1849, p. 705. There are other works by Durer which, it may be, should be ranked among the Emblematical, as *Apocalypsis cum Figuris*, Nuremberg, 1498; and *Passio Domini nostri Jesu*, 1509 and 1511. It is, however, now generally agreed that Durer designed, but did not engrave, on wood. See Stanley, p. 224.

marriage to the great heiress of that day, Mary of Burgundy. There are some who believe that Maximilian was the author, or at least that he sketched out the plan which Pfintzing executed. As, however, the espousals took place in 1479, before the poet was born, and Mary had early lost her life from a fall,—the probability is that the emperor supplied some of the incidents and suggestions, and that his secretary completed the work. The splendid volume was dedicated to Charles V. in 1517, and published the same year, a noble monument of typographic art.

Of a later work known under the name of "**Turnierbuch**,"—*The Tournament-book*,—by George Ruxner, namely, *Beginning, Source, and Progress of Tournaments in the German nation* (Siemern, S. Rodler, 1530, folio, pp. 402), Brunet informs us (*Manuel*, vol. iv. c. 1471), "There are found for the most part in this edition printed at the castle of Simmern" (about twenty-five miles south of Coblentz) "in 1530, the characters already employed in the two editions of the *Tewrdannckh* of 1517 and 1519; there may also be remarked numerous engravings on wood of the same kind as those of the romance in verse we have just cited." The edition of 1532 "printed at the same castle," is not in the same characters as that of 1530.

CEBES, the Theban, the disciple of Socrates, though mentioned at pp. 12, 13, must again be introduced, for an edition of his little work in Latin had appeared at Boulogne in 1497, and at Venice in 1500; also at Francfort, "by the honest men Lamperter and Murrer," in 1507, with the letter of John Æsticampianus; the Greek was printed by Aldus in 1503, and several other editions followed up to the end of the century; —indeed there were translations into Arabic, French, Italian, German, and English.*

* Belonging to one of the earlier editions, or else as an Imagination of the Tablet itself, is a wonderfully curious woodcut, in folio, of which our Plate I. *b* is a smaller fac-simile.

Plate I[b]

Tableau of Human Life from Cebes. B C 390

II.—ANDREW ALCIAT, the celebrated jurisconsult, remarkable, as some testify, for serious defects, as for his surpassing knowledge and power of mind, is characterized by Erasmus as "the orator best skilled in law," and "the lawyer most eloquent of speech;"—of his composition there was published in 1522, at Milan, an *Emblematum Libellus*, or "Little Book of Emblems."* It established, if it did not introduce, a new style for Emblem Literature, the classical in the place of the simply grotesque and humorous, or of the heraldic and mythic. It is by no means certain that the change should be named an unmixed gain. Stately and artificial, the school of Alciat and his followers indicates at every stanza its full acquaintance with mythologies Greek and Roman, but it is deficient in the easy expression which distinguishes the poet of nature above him whom learning chiefly guides: it seldom betrays either enthusiasm of genius or depth of imaginative power.

Nevertheless the style chimed in with the taste of the age, and the little book,—at least that edition of it which is the earliest we have seen, Augsburg, A.D. 1531,† contained in eighty-eight pages, small 8vo, with ninety-seven Emblems and as many woodcuts,—won its way from being a tiny volume of 11·5 square inches of letterpress on each of eighty-eight pages, until with notes and comments it was comprised only in a large 4to of 1004 pages with thirty-seven square inches of letterpress on each page. Thus the little one that had in it only 1012 square inches of text and picture became a mountain, a

* The title is rather conjectured than ascertained, for owing, as it is said, to Alciat's dissatisfaction with the work, or from some other cause, he destroyed what copies he could, and not one is now of a certainty known to exist. For solving the doubt, the Editor of the Holbein Society of Manchester has just issued a note of inquiry to the chief libraries of Europe, *Enquête pour découvrir la première Edition des Emblêmes d'André Alciat, illustre Jurisconsulte Italien.* Milan, A.D. 1522.

† A copy was in the possession of the Rev. Thos. Corser, and has passed through the hands of Dr. Dibdin and Sir Francis Freeling; also another copy is at Keir, Sir William Stirling Maxwell's; both in admirable condition.

monument in Alciat's honour, numbering up 37,128 square inches of text, picture, and comment. The *little* book of Augsburg, 1531, may be read and digested, but only an immortal patience could labour through the entire of the *great* book of Padua, 1621. In that interval of ninety years, however, edition after edition of the favourite emblematist appeared: with translations into French 1536, into German 1542, into Spanish and Italian in 1549, and, if we may credit Ames' *Antiquities of Printing*, Herbert's edition, p. 1570, into English in 1551. The total number of the editions during that period was certainly not less than 130, of seventy of which a pretty close examination has been made by the writer of this sketch. The list of editions, as far as completed, numbers up about 150, and manifests a persistence in popularity that has seldom been attained.

The earliest French translator was John Lefevre, an ecclesiastic, born at Dijon in 1493,—*Les Emblemes de Maistre Andre Alciat:* Paris, 1536. He was secretary to Cardinal Givry, whose protection he enjoyed, and died in 1565. Bartholomew Aneau, himself an emblematist, was the next translator into French, 1549; and a third, Claude Mignault, appeared in 1583. Wolfgang Hunger, a Bavarian, in 1542,* and Jeremiah Held of Nordlingen, were the German translators; Bernardino Daza Pinciano, in 1549, *Los Emblemas de Alciato,* was the Spanish; and Giovanni Marquale, in 1547, the Italian,—*Diverse Imprese.*

The notes and comments upon Alciat's Emblems manifest great research and very extensive learning. Sebastian Stockhamer supplied *commentariola*, short comments, to the Lyons edition of 1556. Francis Sanctius, or Sanchez, one of the restorers of literature in Spain, born in 1523, also added *commentaria* to the Lyons edition of 1573. Above all we must

* CLARISSIMI VIRI D. ANDREÆ ALciati *Emblematum libellus, vigilanter recognitus, et iã recens per Wolphgangum Hungerum Bavarum, rhythmis Germanicis uersus.* PARISIIS, *apud Christianum Wechelum, &c., Anno* M.D.XLII.

name Claude Mignault, whose praise is that "to a varied learning he joined a rare integrity." He was born near Dijon about 1536, and died in 1606. His comments in full appeared in Plantin's * Antwerp edition, 8vo, of 1573, and may be appealed to in proof of much patient research and extensive erudition. Lorenzo Pignoria, born at Padua in 1571, and celebrated for his study of Egyptian antiquities, also compiled notes on Alciat's Emblems in MDCXIIX.† The results of the labours of the three, Sanchez, Mignault, and Pignorius, were collected in the Padua editions of 1621 and 1661. It is scarcely possible that so many editions should have issued from the press, and so much learning have been bestowed, without the knowledge of Alciat's Emblems having penetrated every nook and corner of the literary world.

With a glance only at the "PROGNOSTICATIO," of Theophrastus Paracelsus, the alchemist and enthusiast, written in 1536, and expressed in thirty-two copperplates, we pass at once to the *Dance of Death*, by Hans Holbein, which Bewick, 1789, and Douce, 1833, in London, and Schlotthauer and Fortoul, 1832, in Munich and Paris, have made familiar to English, German, and French readers. Of Holbein himself, it is sufficient here to say that he was born at Bale in 1495, and died in London in 1543.

Mr. Corser's copy of the first edition of the *Dance of Death*, and which was the gift of Francis Douce, Esq., to Edward Vernon Utterson, supplies the following title, "LES SIMULACHRES & HISTORIEES FACES DE LA MORT, avtant elegamm̄et pourtraictes, que artificiellement imaginées: A Lyon, soubz

* "OMNIA ANDREÆ ALCIATI V. C. EMBLEMATA. Adiectis commentariis, &c. Per Clavdivm Minoim Diuionesem. ANTVERPLÆ, Ex officina Christophori Plantini, Architypographi Regij, M.D.LXXIII.;" also, "Editio tertia multo locupletior," M.D.LXXXI.

† "Emblemata v. Cl. Andreæ Alciati—*notulis extemporarijs Laurentij Pignorij Patauini. Patauij, apud Pet. Paulum Tozzium*, M.DCXIIX," sm. 8vo."

l'escu de Coloigne, M.D.XXXVIII." The volume is a small quarto of 104 pages, unnumbered, dedicated to Madame Johanna de Touszele, the Reverend Abbess of the convent of Saint Peter at Lyons. There are forty-one emblems, each headed by a text of scripture from the Latin version; the devices follow, with a French stanza of four lines to each; and there are sundry Dissertations by Jean de Vauzelles, an eminent divine and scholar of the same city. But who can speak of the beauty of the work? The designs by Holbein are many of them wonderfully conceived, — the engravings by Hans Lützenberge, or Leutzelburger, as admirably executed.[*]

Rapidly was the work transferred into Latin and Italian, and before the end of the century at least fifteen editions had issued from the presses of Lyons, Bâle, and Cologne.

Scarcely less celebrated are Holbein's *Historical Figures of the Old Testament*, which Sibald Beham's had preceded in Francfort by only two years. Beham's whole series of Bible Figures are contained in 348 prints, and were published between 1536 and 1540. Dibdin's *Decameron*, vol. i. pp. 176, 177, will supply a full account of Holbein's "Historiarum Veteris Instrumenti icones ad vivum expressæ una cum brevi, sed quoad fieri potuit, dilucida earundem expositione:" Lyons, small 4to, 1538. The edition of Frellonius, Lyons, 1547, is a very close reprint of the second edition, and from this it appears that the work is contained in fifty-two leaves, unnumbered, and that there are ninety-four devices, which are admirable specimens of wood-engraving. The first four are from the *Dance of Death*, but the others appropriate to the subjects, each being accompanied by a French stanza of four lines.

A Spanish translation was issued in 1543; and in 1549, at

---

* The Holbein Society of Manchester have just completed, May, 1869, a Photo-lithographic Reprint of the whole work, with an English Translation, Notes, &c., by the Editor, Henry Green, M.A.

Lyons, an English version, "The Images of the Old Testament, lately expressed, set forthe in Ynglishe and Frenche, vuith a playn and brief exposition." All the editions of the century were about twelve.

Hans Brosamer, of Fulda, laboured in the same mine, and between 1551 and 1553, copying chiefly from Holbein and Albert Durer, produced at Francfort his "**Biblische Historien kunstlich fürgemalet,**"—*Bible Histories artistically pictured* (3 vols. in 1).

We will, though somewhat earlier than the exact date, continue the subject of Bible-Figure Emblem-books by alluding to the *Quadrins historiques de la Bible,*—"Historic Picture-frames of the Bible,"—for the most part engraved by "Le Petit Bernard," *alias* Solomon Bernard, who was born at Lyons in 1512. Of these works in French, English, Spanish, Italian, Latin, Flemish, and German, there were twenty-two editions printed between 1553 and 1583. Their general nature may be known from the fact that to each Scripture subject there is a device, in design and execution equally good, and that it is followed or accompanied by a Latin, Italian, &c. stanza, as the case may be. In the Italian version, Lyons, 1554, the Old Testament is illustrated by 222 engravings, and the New by ninety-five.

The first of the series appears to be *Quadrins historiques du Genèse,* Lyons, 1553; followed in the same year by *Quadrins historiques de l'Exode.* There is also of the same date (see Brunet, iv. c. 996), "The true and lyuely historyke Pvrtreatures of the woll Bible (with the arguments of eache figure, translated into english metre by Peter Derendel): Lyons; by Jean of Tournes."

To conclude, there were *Figures of the Bible,* illustrated by French stanzas, and also by Italian and by German; published at Lyons and at Venice between 1564 and 1582. (See Brunet's

Manuel, ii. c. 1255.) Also Jost Amman, at Francfort, in 1564: and Virgil Solis, from 1560 to 1568, contributed to German works of the same character.

Two names of note among emblematists crown the years 1539 and 1540, both in Paris: they are William de la Perrière, and Giles Corrozet; of the former we know little more than that he was a native of Toulouse, and dedicated his chief work to "Margaret of France, Queen of Navarre, the only sister of the very Christian King of France:" and of the latter, that, born in Paris in 1510, and dying there in 1568, he was a successful printer and bookseller, and distinguished (see Brunet's *Manuel*, ii. cc. 299—308) for a large number of works on History, Antiquities, and kindred subjects.

La Perrière's chief Emblem-work is *Le Theatre des bons Engins, auquel sont contenus cent Emblemes*: Paris, 8vo, 1539. There are 110 leaves and really 101 emblems, each device having a pretty border. His other Emblem-works are—*The Hundred Thoughts of Love*, 1543, with woodcuts to each page; *Thoughts on the Four Worlds*, "namely, the divine, the angelic, the heavenly, and the sensible," Lyons, 1552; and "LA MOROSOPHIE,"—*The Wisdom of Folly*,—containing a hundred moral emblems, illustrated by a hundred stanzas of four lines, both in Latin and in French.

Corrozet's "HECATOMGRAPHIE," Paris, 1540, is a description of a hundred figures and histories, and contains Apophthegms, Proverbs, Sentences, and Sayings, as well ancient as modern. Each page of the 100 emblems is surrounded by a beautiful border, the devices are neat woodcuts, having the same borders with La Perrière's *Theatre of good Contrivances*. There is also to each a page of explanatory French verses.

It requires a stricter inquiry than I have yet been able to make in order to determine if Corrozet's *Blasons domestiques*; *Blason du Moys de May*; and *Tapisserie de l'Eglise chrestienne*

& catholique, bear a decided emblematical character; the titles have a taste of emblematism, but are by no means decisive of the fact.

III.—Maurice Sceve's *Delie, Object de plus haulte Vertu*, Lyons, 1544, with woodcuts, and 458 ten-lined stanzas on love, is included in the Blandford *Catalogue;* and in the Keir Collection are both *The very admirable, very magnificent and triumphant Entry of Prince Philip of Spain into Antwerp in* 1549,* by Grapheus, *alias* Scribonius; edition 1550: and Gueroult's *Premier Livre des Emblemes;* Lyons, 1550. The same year, 1550, at Augsburg, has marked against it "Geschlechtes Buch,"—*Pedigree-book*,—which recurs in 1580.

Claude Paradin, the canon of Beaujeu, a small town on the Ardiere, in the department of the Rhone, published the first edition of his simple but very interesting *Devises heroiques*, with 180 woodcuts, at Lyons in 1557. It was afterwards enlarged by gatherings from Gabriel Symeoni and other writers; but, either under its own name or that of *Symbola heroica* (edition 1567) was very popular, and before 1600 was printed at Lyons, Antwerp, Douay, and Leyden, not fewer than twelve times. The English translation, with which it is generally admitted that Shakespeare was acquainted, was printed in London, in 12mo, in 1591, and bears the title, *The Heroicall Devises of M. Claudius Paradin, Canon of Beaujeu*, "Whereunto are added the Lord Gabriel Symeons and others. Translated out of Latin into English by P. S."

To another Paradin are assigned *Quadrins historiques de la Bible*, published at Lyons by Jean de Tournes, 1555; and of which the same publisher issued Spanish, English, Italian, German, and Flemish versions.

* *La tres admirable, &c., entrée du Prince Philipe d'Espaignes—en la ville d'Anvers, anno* 1549. 4to, Anvers, 1550.

The rich Emblem Collection at Keir furnishes the first edition of each of Doni's three Emblem-works, in 4to, printed by Antonio Francesco Marcolini at Venice in 1552-53; they are: 1. "I MONDI,"—*i.e., The Worlds, celestial, terrestrial, and infernal*,—2 parts in 1, with woodcuts. 2. "I MARMI,"—*The Marbles*,—4 parts in 1, a collection of pleasant little tales and interesting notices, with woodcuts by the printer: who also, according to Bryan, was an engraver of "considerable merit." 3. "LA MORAL FILOSOFIA,"—*Moral Philosophy drawn from the ancient Writers*,—2 parts in 1, with woodcuts. In it are abundant extracts from the ancient fabulists, as Lokman and Bidpai, and a variety of little narrative tales and allegories.

Of an English translation, two editions appeared in London in 1570 and 1601, during Shakespeare's lifetime; namely, "The Morall Philosophie of Doni, englished out of italien by sir Th. North,"* 4to, with engravings on wood.

Under the two titles of "PICTA POESIS," and "LIMAGINATION POETIQUE," Bartholomew Aneau, or Anulus, published his "exquisite little gem," as Mr. Atkinson, a former owner of the copy which is now before me, describes the work. It appeared at Lyons in 1552, and contains 106 emblems, the stanzas to which, in the Latin edition, are occasionally in Greek, but in the French edition, "vers François des Latins et Grecz, par l'auteur mesme d'iceux."

Achille Bocchi, a celebrated Italian scholar, the founder, in 1546, of the Academy of Bologna, Virgil Solis, of Nuremberg, an artist of considerable repute, Pierre Cousteau, or Costalius, of Lyons, and Paolo Giovio, an accomplished writer, Bishop of Nocera, give name to four of the Emblem-books which were

* North's translation of Plutarch's *Lives*, we may remark, was the great treasury to which Shakespeare often applied in some of his Historical Dramas; and we may assume that other productions from the same pen would not be unknown to him.

issued in the year 1555. That of Bocchius is entitled "SYMBOLICARVM QVAESTIONVM, LIBRI QVINQVE," Bononiæ, 1555, 4to; and numbers up 146, or, more correctly, 150 emblems in 340 pages: the devices are the work of Giulio Bonasone, from copper-plates of great excellence. In 1556, *Bononiæ* Sambigucius put forth *In Hermathenam Bocchiam Interpretatio*, which is simply a comment on the 102nd emblem of Bocchius. Virgil Solis published in 4to, at Nuremberg, the same year, "LIBELLUS Sartorum, seu Signorum publicorum,"—*A little Book of Cobblers, or of public Signs.* Cousteau's "PEGMA,"* which some say appeared first in 1552, is, as the name denotes, a *Structure* of emblems, ninety-five in number, with *philosophical narratives*,—each page being surrounded by a pretty border. And Giovio's "DIALOGO dell' Imprese Militari et Amore,"—*Dialogue of Emblems of War and of Love;* or, as it is sometimes named, "RAGIONAMENTO, *Discourse concerning the words and devices of arms and of love, which are commonly named Emblems,*"—is probably the first regular treatise on the subject which had yet appeared, and which attained high popularity.

Its estimation in England is shown by the translation which was issued in London in 1585, entitled, "THE Worthy tract of Paulus Iouius, contayning a Discourse of rare inuentions, both Militarie and Amorous, *called Imprese. Whereunto is added* a Pre*face contay*-ning the Arte of composing them, with *many other notable deuises. By Samuell Daniell late Student* in Oxenforde."

Intimately connected with Giovio's little work, indeed often constituting parts of the same volume, were Ruscelli's "DISCORSO" on the same subject, Venice, 1556; and Domenichi's "RAGIONAMENTO," also at Venice, in 1556. From the testi-

* "PETRI COSTALII PEGMA *Cum narrationibus philosophicis.*" 8vo, LVGDVNI, 1555.

"LE PEGME DE PIERRE COVSTAV auec les Narr. philosophiqves." 8vo, A Lyon, M.D.LX.

mony of Sir Egerton Brydges (*Res Lit.*), "Ruscelli was one of the first literati of his time, and was held in esteem by princes and all ranks of people."

Very frequently, too, in combination with Giovio's Dialogue on Emblems, are to be found Ruscelli's "IMPRESE ILLVSTRI," Venice, 1566; or Symeoni's "IMPRESE HEROICHE ET MORALI," Lyons, 1559: and "SENTENTIOSE IMPRESE," Lyons, 1562.

Roville's Lyons edition, of 1574, thus unites in one title-page Giovio, Symeoni, and Domenichi, "DIALOGO DELL'IMPRESE MILITARI ET AMOROSE, De Monsignor Giouio Vescouo di Nocera *Et del S. Gabriel Symeoni Fiorentino,* Con vn ragionamento di M. Lodouico Domenichi, nel medesimo soggetto."

Taking together all the editions in Italian, French, and Spanish, of these four authors, single or combined, which I have had the opportunity of examining, there are no less than *twenty-two* between 1555 and 1585, besides five or six other editions named by Brunet in his *Manuel du Libraire.* Roville's French edition, 4to, Lyons, 1561, is by Vasquin Philieul, "Dialogve des Devises d'Armes et d'Amovrs dv S. Pavlo Iovio, *Auec vn Discours de M. Loys Dominique*—et *les Deuises Heroiques et Morales du Seigneur Gabriel Symeon.*"

At this epoch we enter upon ground which has been skilfully upturned and cultivated by Claude Francis Menestrier, born at Lyons in 1631, and "distinguished by his various works on heraldry, decorations, public ceremonials, &c." (Aikin's *Gen. Biog.* vii. p. 41.) In his "PHILOSOPHIA IMAGINUM,"—*Philosophy of Images,*—an octavo volume of 860 pages, published at Amsterdam, 1695, he gives, in ninety-four pages, a "JUDICIUM," *i.e., a judgment respecting all authors who have written on Symbolic Art*; and of those Authors whom we have named, or may be about to name, within the Period to which our Sketch extends, he mentions that he has examined the works of

A.D.		A.D.	
1555.*	*Paulus Jovius*, p. 1.	1580.	*Franciscus Caburaccius*, p. 12.
1556.	*Ludovicus Dominicus*, p. 3.	1588.	*Abrahamus Fransius*, p. 15.
„	*Hieronymus Ruscellius*, p. 4.	1591.	*Julius Cæsar Capacius*, ibid.
1561.	*Alphonsus Ulloa*, ibid.	„	*D. Albertus Bernardetti*, p. 17.
1562.	*Scipio Amiratus*, p. 5.	1594.	*Torquatus Tassus*, p. 14.
1571.	*Alexander Farra*, p. 6.	1600.	*Jacobus Sassus*, p. 18.
„	*Bartholomæus Taegius*, p. 7.	1601.	*Andreas Chioccus*, ibid.
1574.	*Lucas Contile*, p. 9.	1612.	*Hercules Tassus*, p. 19.
1577.	*Johannes Andreas Palatius*, p. 10.	„	*P. Horatius Montalde*, p. 23.
		„	*Johannes Baptista Personé*, ib.
1578.	*Scipio Bergalius*, p. 12.	1620.	*Franciscus d'Amboise*, ibid.

It may also be gathered from the "JUDICIUM" that Menestrier had read with care what had been written on Emblems by the following authors :—

A.D.		A.D.	
1551.	*Gabriel Simeoni*, p. 63.	1588.	*Bernardinus Percivalle*, p. 64.
1557.	*Claudius Paradinus*, p. 68.	„	*Principius Fabricius*, p. 76.
1562.	*Mauritius Sevus*, p. 55.	1600.	*Johannes Pinedi*, p. 60.
1565.	*J. Baptista Pittonius*, p. 70.	1609.	*Jacobus Le Vasseur*, p. 91.
1573.	*Claudius Minos*, p. 54.	1613.	*J. Franciscus de Villava*, p. 55.

Excluding the editions before enumerated, the books of emblems which I have noted from various sources as assigned to the authors in the above lists from Menestrier, amount to from *twenty-five* to *thirty*, with the titles of which there is no occasion to trouble the reader.

Returning from this digression, Vincenzo Cartari should next be named in order of time. At Venice, in 1556, appeared his "IMAGINI DEI *Dei degli Antichi*,"—*Images of the Gods of the Ancients*,—4to, of above 500 pages. It contains an account of the Idols, Rites, Ceremonies, and other things appertaining to

* The dates have been added to Menestrier's list.

the old Religions. It was a work often reprinted, and in 1581 translated into French by Antoine du Verdier, the same who, in 1585, gave in folio a Catalogue of all who have written or translated into French up to that time.

A folio of 1100 pages, which within the period of our sketch was reprinted four times, issued from Bâle in 1556; it is, "HIEROGLYPHICA," — *Hieroglyphics*, or, *Commentaries on the Sacred Literature of the Egyptians*,—by John Pierius Valerian, a man of letters, born in extreme poverty at Belluno in 1477, and untaught the very elements of learning until he was fifteen. (Aikin's *Gen. Biog.* ix. 537.) He died in 1558. As an exposition of the Egyptian hieroglyphics, his very learned work is little esteemed; but it contains emblems innumerable, comprised in fifty-eight books, each book dedicated to a person of note, and treating one class of objects. The devices—small woodcuts—amount to 365.

Etienne Jodelle, a poet, equally versatile whether in Latin or in French, was skilled in the ancient languages, and acquainted with the arts of painting, sculpture, and architecture, as well as dexterous in the use of arms. He published, in 1558, a thin quarto "RECUEIL," or *Collection* of the inscriptions, figures, devices, and masks ordained in Paris at the Hôtel de Ville. The same year, and again in 1569 and 1573, appeared the large folio volume, in five parts, "AUSTRIACIS GENTIS IMAGINES,"—*Portraits of the Austrian family*,—full lengths, engraved by Gaspar ab Avibus, of Padua. At the foot of each portrait are a four-lined stanza, a brief biographical notice, and some emblematical figure. Of similar character, though much inferior as a work of art, is Jean Nestor's HISTOIRE *des Hommes illustres de la Maison de Medici*; a quarto of about 240 leaves, printed at Paris in 1564. (See the Keir *Catalogue*, p. 143.) It contains "twelve woodcuts of the emblems of the different members of the House of Medici."

Hoffer's "ICONES CATECHESEOS," or *Pictures of instruction*, and of virtues and vices, illustrated by verses, and also by seventy-eight figures or woodcuts, was printed at Wittenberg in 1560. The next year, 1561—if not in 1556 (see Brunet's *Manuel*, vol. ii. cc. 930, 931)—John Duvet, one of the earliest engravers on copper in France, at Lyons, published in twenty-four plates, folio, his chief work, "LAPOCALYPSE FIGUREE;" and in 1562, at Naples, the Historian of Florence, Scipione Ammirato, gave to the world "IL ROTA OVERO DELL' IMPRESE," or, *Dialogue of the Sig. Scipione Ammirato*, in which he discourses of many emblems of divers excellent authors, and of some rules and admonitions concerning this subject written to the Sig. Vincenzo Carrafa.

Were it less a subject of debate between Dutch and German critics as to the exact character of the "SPELEN VAN SINNE," which were published by the Chambers of Rhetoric at Ghent in 1539, and by those of Antwerp in 1561 and 1562 (see Brunet's *Manuel*, vol. v. c. 484), we should claim these works for our Emblem domain. But whether claimed or not, the exhibitions and amusements of the Chambers of Rhetoric, especially at their great gatherings in the chief cities of the Netherlands, were often very lively representations by action and accessory devices of dramatic thought and sentiment, from "King Herod and his Deeds," "enacted in the Cathedral of Utrecht in 1418," to what Motley, in his *Dutch Republic*, vol. i. p. 80, terms the "magnificent processions, brilliant costumes, living pictures, charades, and other animated, glittering groups,"—"trials of dramatic and poetic skill, all arranged under the superintendence of the

* A friend, Mr. Jan Hendrik Hessells, now of Cambridge, well acquainted with his native Dutch literature, informs me the "*Spelen van Sinnen* (Sinnespelen, Zinnespelen) were thus called because allegorical personifications, *Zinnebeeldige personen* (in old Dutch, *Sinnekens*), for instance reason, religion, virtue, were introduced." They were, in fact, "allegorical plays," similar to the "Interludes" of England in former times.

particular association which in the preceding year had borne away the prize."

"The Rhetorical Chambers existed in the most obscure villages" (Motley, i. p. 79); and had regular constitutions, being presided over by officers with high-sounding titles, as kings, princes, captains, and archdeacons,—and each having "its peculiar title or blazon, as the Lily, the Marigold, or the Violet, with an appropriate motto." After 1493 they were "incorporated under the general supervision of an upper or mother-society of Rhetoric, consisting of fifteen members, and called by the title of 'Jesus with the balsam flower.'"

As I have been informed by Mr. Hessells, Siegenbeek, in his *Geschiedenis der Nederlandsche Letterkunde*, says,—"Besides the ordinary meetings of the Chambers, certain poetical feasts were in vogue among the Rhetor-gevers, whereby one or other subject, to be responded to in burdens or short songs (*liedekens*), according to the contents of the card, was announced, with the promise of prizes to those who would best answer the proposed question. But the so-called *Entries* deserve for their magnificence, and the diversity of poetical productions which they give rise to, especially our attention.

"It happened from time to time that one or other of the most important Chambers sent a card in rhyme to the other Chambers of the same province, whereby they were invited to be at a given time in the town where the senders of the card were established, for the sake of the celebration of a poetical feast. This card contained further everything by which it was desired that the Chambers, which were to make their appearance, should illustrate this feast, viz., the performance of an allegorical play (*sinnespel*) in response to some given question;* the preparation of *esbatementez* (drawings), *faceties* (jests), prologues; the

* As "Wat den mensch aldermeest tot' conste verweet?"—*What most of all stirs man to art?*

execution of splendid entries and processions; the exhibitions of beautifully painted coats of arms, &c. These entries were of two kinds, *landiuweelen*, and *haagspelen*;—the *landjewels* were the most splendid, and were performed in towns; the *hedge-plays* belonged properly to villages, though sometimes in towns these followed the performance of a landjewel." Originally, *landjewel* meant a prize of honour of the land; called also *landprys* (land-prize).

Such were the periodic jubilees of a neighbouring people, their "land-jewels," as they were termed, when the birthtime of our greatest English dramatist arrived. And as we mark the wide and increasing streams of the Emblem Literature flowing over every European land, and how the common tongue of Rome gave one language to all Christendom, can we deem it probable that any man of genius, of discernment, and of only the usual attainments of his compeers, would live by the side of these streams and never dip his finger into the waters, nor wet even the soles of his feet where the babbling emblems flowed?

Some there have been to maintain that Shakespeare had visited the Netherlands, or even resided there; and it is consequently within the limits of no unreasonable conjecture that he had seen the *landjewels* distributed, and at the sight felt himself inspirited to win a nobler fame.

Whitney, 1586.

SECTION IV.

EMBLEM WORKS AND EDITIONS BETWEEN A.D. 1564 *AND A.D.* 1616.

N the year at which this Section begins, Shakespeare was born, and for a whole century the Emblem tide never ebbed. There was an uninterrupted succession of new writers and of new editions. Many eminent names have appeared in the past, and names as eminent will adorn the future.

The fifty years which remain to the period comprised within the limits of this Sketch of Emblem Literature we divide into two portions of twenty-five years each: 1st, up to 1590, when Shakespeare had fairly entered on his dramatic career: and 2nd, from 1590 to 1615, when, according to Steevens (edition 1785, vol. i. p. 354), his labours had ended with *The Twelfth Night, or, What You Will.* As far as actual correspondences between Shakespeare and the Emblem Writers demand, our Sketch might finish with 1610, or even earlier: for some time will of necessity intervene, after a work has been issued, before it will modify the thoughts of others, or enter into the phrases which they employ. However, there is nothing very incongruous in making this Sketch and the last of Shakespeare's dramas terminate with the same date.

I.—In 1564, at Rome, in 4to, the distinguished Latinist, Gabriel Faerno's Fables were first printed, 100 in number;—it was three years after his death. The plates are from designs which Titian is said to have drawn. Our English Whitney adopts several of Faerno's Fables among his Emblems, and on this authority we class them with books of Emblems. From time to time, as late as to 1796, new editions and translations of the Fables have been issued. A copy in the Free Library, Manchester, "Romæ Vincentius Luchinus, 1565," bears the title, *Fabvlae Centvm ex antiqvis avctoribvs delectae, et a Gabriele Faerno, Cremonensi carminibvs explicatae.*

Virgil Solis, a native of Nuremberg, where he was born in 1514, and where he died in 1570; and Jost Amman, who was born at Zurich in 1539, but passed his life at Nuremberg, and died there in 1591, were both artists of high repute, and contributed to the illustration of Emblem-works. The former, between 1560 and 1568, produced 125 *New Figures for the New Testament,* and *An Artistic little Book of Animals:* and the latter, from 1564 to 1586, contributed very largely to books of *Biblical Figures,* of "Animals," of "Genealogies," of "Heraldry," and of the *Habits* and *Costumes* of All Ranks of the *Clergy of the Roman Church,* and of *Women* of every "Condition, profession, *and age,*" throughout the nations of Europe.

From the press of Christopher Plantin, of Antwerp, there issued nearly fifty editions of Emblem-books between 1564 and 1590. Of these, one of the earliest was, "EMBLEMATA CVM ALIQVOT NVMMIS ANTIQVIS,"—*Emblems with some ancient Coins,*—4to, 1564, by the Hungarian, John Sambucus, born at Tornau in 1531. A French version, *Les Emblemes de Jehan Sambucus,* issued from the same press in 1567. Among Emblematists, none bears a fairer name as "physician, antiquary, and poet." According to De Bry's *Icones,* pt. iii., ed. 1598, pp. 76—83, he obtained the patronage of two emperors, Maximilian II. and Rudolph II., under whom he held the offices of counsellor of state and historian of the empire. To him also belonged the rare honour of having his work commented on by one of the great heroes of Christendom, Don John of Austria, in 1572.

Les Songes drolatiques de Pantagruel, by Rabelais, appeared at Paris in 1565, but its emblematical character has been doubted. Not so, however, the ten editions of the "EMBLEMATA" of *Hadrian Junius*, a celebrated Dutch physician, of which the first edition appeared in 1565, and justly claims to be "the most elegant which the presses of Plantin had produced at this period."

We may now begin to chronicle a considerable number of works and editions of Emblems by ITALIAN writers, which, to avoid prolixity and yet to point out, we present in a tabulated form, giving only the earliest editions :—

Pittoni's .	. *Imprese di diversi principi, duchi, &c.*	sm. fol.	Venice	. 1566 *k.**
Troiano's	. *Discorsi delli triomfi, giostre, &c.* .	4to	Monica	. 1568 *k.*
Rime .	. *Rime de gli Academici occulti, &c.* .	4to	Brescia	. 1568 *k.*
Farra's .	. *Settenario dell' humana riduttione* .	...	...	1571 *v.*
Dolce's .	. *Le prime imprese del conte Orlando*	4to	Venice	. 1572 *v.*
" .	. *Dialogo*	8vo	Venice	. 1575 *k.*
Contile's .	. *Ragionamento—sopra la proprieta delle Imprese, &c.*	Fol.	Pavia	. 1574 *k.*
Fiorino's	. *Opera nuova, &c.* .	4to	Lyons	. 1577 *k.*
Palazza's	. *I Discorsi—Imprese, &c.* . . .	8vo	Bologna	1577 *k.*
Caburacci's .	*Trattato,—dove si dimostra il vero e novo modo di fare le Imprese.*	4to	Bologna	1580 *k.*

* The works to which a *k* is appended are all in the very choice and yet most extensive collection of Emblem-books at Keir, made by the Author of *The Cloister Life of Charles V.*, Sir William Stirling Maxwell, Bart. ; *c*, in the Library formed by the Rev. Thomas Corser, Rector of Stand, near Manchester ; *t*, in that of Henry Yates Thompson, Esq., of Thingwall, near Liverpool. I have had the opportunity, most kindly given, of examining very many of the Emblem-works at Keir, and nearly all of those at Stand and Thingwall. The three collections contained at the time of my examination of them 934, 204, and 248 volumes, in the whole 1386 volumes. Deducting duplicates, the number of distinct editions in the three libraries is above 900. Where I have placed a *v*, it denotes that the sources of information are various, but those sources I possess the means of verifying. I name these things that it may be seen I have not lightly nor idly undertaken the sketch which I present in these pages.

Guazzo's	. *Dialoghi piacevoli*	4to	Venice .	1585 *k*.
Camilli's .	. *Imprese—co i discorsi, et con le figure*	4to	Venice .	1586 *k*.
Cimolotti's	. *Il superbi*	4to	Pavia .	1587 *k*.
Fabrici's .	. *Delle allusioni, imprese & emblemi sopra la vita, &c., di Gregorio XIII.*	4to	Roma .	1588 *k*.
Rinaldi's	. *Il mostruosissimo*	8vo	Ferrara .	1588 *k*.
Porro's .	. *Il primo libro*	4to	Milano .	1589 *k*.
Pezzi's .	. *La Vigna del Signore—Sacramenti, Paradiso, Limbo, &c.*	4to	Venetia .	1589 *t*.
Bargagli's	. *Dell' Imprese* . .	4to	Venetia .	1589 *v*.

So, briefly, in the order of time, may we name several of the French, Latin, and German Emblem-writers of this period, together with the Spanish and English :—

FRENCH.

Grevin's .	. *Emblemes d'Adrian La Jeune* .	16mo	Anvers .	1568 *v*.
Vander Noot's	*Theatre . . . les inconueniens et miseres qui suiuent les mondains et vicieux, &c.*	8vo	Londres.	1568 *v*.
De Montenay's	*Emblêmes ou devises chrestiennes* .	4to	Lyon .	1571 *k*.
Chartier's .	. *Les Blasons de vertu par vertu* .	4to	Aureliæ .	1574 *v*.
Droyn's* .	. *La Grand nef des fols du monde* .	fol.	à Lyon .	1579 *c*.
Goulart's .	. *Les Vrais Pourtraits des Hommes illustres.*	4to	Genue .	1581 *k*.
Verdier's .	. *Les images des anciens dieux* (par V. Cartari).	4to	Lyon .	1581 *v*.
Anjou . .	. *La joyeuse et magnif. entrée de Mons. Françoys, duc de Brabant, Anjou, &c., en ville d'Anvers.*	fol.	à Anvers	1582 *k*.
L'Anglois .	. *Discours des hierog. égyptiens, emblêmes, &c.*	4to	Paris .	1583 *k*.
Messin . .	. *Emblêmes latins de J. J. Boissard, avec l'interpretation françoise.*	4to	Metis .	1588 *c*.

Of these works, Vander Noot's was translated into English, says Brunet, (v. c. 1072,) by Henry Bynneman, 1569, and is remarkable for containing (see *Ath. Cantab.* ii. p. 258) certain

* First printed at Lyons in 1498.

poems, termed sonnets, and epigrams, which Spenser wrote before his sixteenth year. Mademoiselle Georgette de Montenay was a French lady of noble birth, and dedicated her 100 Emblems "to the very illustrious and virtuous Princesse, Madame Jane D'Albret, Queen of Navarre." Chartier, a painter and engraver, flourished about 1574; L'Anglois is not mentioned in the *Hieroglyphics* of Dr. Leemans, nor do I find any notice of Messin.

LATIN.

Schopperus	Πανοπλία, *omnium illiberalium mechanicarum, &c.*	8vo Francof.	1568 *v.*
,,	*De omnibus illiberalibus sive mechanicis artibus.*	8vo Francof.	1574 *t.*
Arias Montanus	*Humanæ salutis monumenta, &c.*	4to Antverpiæ	1572 *k.*
Sanctius	*Commentaria in A. Alciati Emblemata.*	8vo Lugduni	1573 *k.*
Furmerus	*De rerum usu et abusu*	4to Antverpiæ	1575 *t.*
Lonicer, Ph.	*Insignia sacræ Cæsareæ, maj. &c.*	4to Francof.	1579 *k.*
Estienne, Henri	*Anthologia gnomica*	8vo Francof.	1579 *k.*
Freitag	*Mythologia ethica*	4to Antverpiæ	1579 *t.*
Microcosm.	Μικρόκοσμος, *parvus mundus, &c.*	4to	1579 *v.*
ΜΙΚΡΟΚΟΣΜΟΣ	*Parvus Mundus*	4to Antverpiæ	1592 *k.*
Beza	*Icones—accedunt emblemata*	4to Genevæ	1581 *c.*
Hesius, G.	*Emblemata sacra*	4to Francof.	1581 *v.*
Reusner	*Emblemata—partim ethica et physica, &c.*	4to Francof.	1581 *k.*
,,	*Aureolorum Emblem. liber singularis.*	8vo Argentor	1591 *t.*
Lonicer, J. A.	*Venatus et Aucupium Iconibus artif.*	4to Francof.	1582 *c.*
Moherman	*Apologi Creaturarum*	4to Antverpiæ	1584 *t.*
Emblemata	*Emblemata Evangelica ad XII. signa, &c.*	fol.	1585 *k.*
Bol.	*Emblemata Evang. ad. XII. Signa cœlestia.*	4to Francof.	1585 *v.*
Hortinus	*Icones operum, &c.*	4to Romæ	1585 *k.*
Modius	*Liber—ordinis Ecclesiastici origo, &c.*	8vo Francof.	1585 *t.*

Modius	. *Pandectæ triumphales, &c.* .	fol.	Francof.	. 1586 *k.*
Fraunce	. *Insignium, Armorum, Emblematum, Hierogl., &c.*	4to	Londini	. 1588 *t.*
Zuingerus .	. *Icones aliquot clarorum Virorum, &c.*	8vo	Basileæ	. 1589 *t.*
Cælius (S. S.)	. *Emblemata Sacra*	8vo	Romæ	. 1589 *v.*
Hortinus .	. *Emblemata Sacra* . . .	4to	Trajecti	. 1589 *v.*
Camerarius	. *Symbolorum et Emblematum, &c.*	4to	Norimberg	. 1590 *k.*

Arias Montanus, born in Estremadura in 1527, was one of the very eminent scholars of Spain; Furmerus, a Frieslander, flourished during the latter half of the sixteenth century, and his work was translated into Dutch by Coörnhert in 1585; Henri Estienne, one of the celebrated printers of that name, was born in Paris in 1528, and died at Lyons in 1598; a list of his works, many of them of high scholarship, occupies eight pages in Brunet's *Manuel du Libraire.* The name of Beza is of similar renown;—both Etienne and he had to seek safety from persecution; and when Etienne's effigy was being burnt, he pleasantly said "that he had never felt so cold as on the day when he was burning." Laurence Haechtanus was the author of the *Parvus Mundus,* 1579, which Gerardt de Jode *den liefhebbers der consten,* the lover of art, has so admirably adorned. Nicolas Reusner was a man of extensive learning, to whom the emperor Rudolph II. decreed the poetic crown. Francis Modius was a Fleming, a learned jurisconsult and Latinist, who died at Aire in Artois, in 1597, at the age of sixty-one; Theodore Zuinger was a celebrated physician of Bâle; and Joachim Camerarius, born at Nuremberg in 1534, also a celebrated physician, one of the first to form a botanical garden, "attained high reputation in his profession, and was consulted for princes and persons of rank throughout Germany."

An edition of a work reputed to be emblematic belongs to this period—to 1587; it is the *Physiologist,* by S. Epiphanius, to whom allusion has been made at p. 28.

GERMAN.

Stimmer	*Neue Kunstliche Figuren Biblischen, &c.*	4to	Besel	1576 *t.*
Feyrabend	*Stam und Wapenbuch*	4to	Franckfurt	1579 *k.*
Schrot	*Wappenbuch*	8vo	Munich	1581 *k.*
Lonicer, J. A.	*Stand und Orden der heiligen Romischen Catholischen Kirchen.*	4to	Francfurt	1585 *v.*
Clamorinus	*Thurnier-buch*	4to	Dresden	1590 *k.*

Tobias Stimmer was an artist, born at Schaffhausen in 1544, and in conjunction with his younger brother, John Christopher Stimmer, executed part of the woodcuts in the Bible of Basle, 1576 and 1586. The younger brother also prepared the prints for a set of Emblems, *Icones Affabræ*, published at Strasburg in 1591. Sigismund Feyrabend is a name of great note as a designer, engraver on wood, and bookseller, at Francfort, towards the end of the sixteenth century. Who Martin Schrot was, does not appear from the *Biographie Universelle;* and Clamorinus may probably be regarded as only the editor of a republication of Ruxner's *Book of Tournaments* that was printed in 1530.

DUTCH OR FLEMISH.

Van Ghelen	Flemish translation, *Navis stultorum.*		Anvers	1584 *v.*
Coörnhert	*Recht Ghebruyck ende Misbruyck van tydlycke Have.*	4to	Leyden	1585 *v.*

SPANISH.

Manuel	*El conde Lucanor* (apologues & fables).	4to	Sevilla	1575 *v.*
Boria	*Empresa Morales*	4to	Praga	1581 *k.*
Guzman	*Triumphas morales* (nueuamente corregidos).	8vo	Medina	1587 *t.*
Horozco	*Emblemas Morales*	8vo	Segovia	1589 *t.*

Don Juan Manuel was a descendant of the famous Alphonso V. His work consists of forty-nine little tales, with a moral in verse to each. It is regarded, says the *Biog. Univ.*

vol. xxvi. p. 541, "as the finest monument of Spanish literature in the sixteenth century." There are earlier editions of Francisco de Guzman's *Moral Triumphs*, as at Antwerp in 1557, but the edition above named claims to be more perfect than the others. Horozco y Covaruvias was a native of Toledo, and died in 1608; one of his offices was that of Bishop of Girgenti in Sicily. In 1601 he translated his Emblems into Latin, and printed it under the title of *Symbolæ Sacræ*.

ENGLISH.

Bynneman's	*Translation of Vander Noot's Theatre.*	8vo	London	1569 *v.*
North	*The Morall Philosophie of Doni*	4to	London	1570 *v.*
Daniell	*The worthy tract of Paulus Jovius, &c.*	8vo	London	1585 *k.*
Whitney	*A Choice of Emblemes, &c.*	4to	Leyden	1586 *k.*

Henry Bynneman, whose name is placed before the version of Vander Noot's *Theatre*, is not known with any certainty to have been the translator. He was a celebrated printer in London from about 1566 to 1583. Sir Thomas North, to whose translation of Plutarch, Shakespeare was largely indebted, was probably an ancestor of the Lord Keeper of the Great Seal under Charles II. Samuel Daniell enjoyed considerable reputation as a poet, and on Spenser's death in 1598, was appointed poet-laureate to the Queen. Of Whitney it is known that he was a scholar of Oxford and of Cambridge, and that his name appears on the roll of the university of Leyden. He was a native of Cheshire, and died there in 1601. It may be added that an edition of Barclay's *Ship of Fooles* was in 1570 "Imprinted at London in Paules Churchyarde by John Cawood Printer to the Queenes Maiestie."

Thus, in the period between Shakespeare's birth and his full entry on his dramatic career, we have named above sixty persons, many of great eminence, who amused their leisure, or indulged their taste, by composing books of Emblems; had we named also the editions of the same authors, within these twenty-five years, they would have amounted to 156, exclusive of many reprints from other authors who wrote Emblems between A.D. 1500 and A.D. 1564.

II. — Shakespeare's Dramatic Career comprises another period of twenty-five years,—from 1590 to 1615. From the necessity of the case, indeed, few, if any of the Emblem writers and compilers towards the end of the time could be known to him, and any correspondence between them in thoughts or expressions must have been purely accidental. For the completion of our Sketch, however, we proceed to the end of the period we had marked out. And to save space, and, we hope, to avoid tediousness, we will continue the tabulated form adopted in the last Section.

ITALIAN.

Bernardetti .	*Giornata prima dell' Imprese* .	...	...	about 1592 *v.*
Capaccio .	*Delle Imprese trattato, in tre libri diviso,*	4to	Napoli .	. 1594 *k.*
Tasso .	*Discorsi del Poeme* . . .	4to	Napoli .	. 1594 *k.*
Porri . .	*Vaso di verita . . dell' antichristo*	4to	Venetia	1597 *v.*
Dalla Torre	*Dialogo*	4to	Trivegi .	. 1598 *k.*
Caputi .	*La Pompa* .	4to	Napoli .	. 1599 *k.*
Zoppio	*La Montagna*	4to	Bologna	. 1600 *k.*
Belloni .	*Discorso* . .	4to	Padova	. 1601 *k.*
Chiocci . .	*Delle imprese, e del vero modo di formarle.*			1601 *v.*
Pittoni .	*Imprese di diversi principi, &c.* (reprint).	fol.	Venezia	. 1602 *v.*
Ripa .	*Iconologia, &c., Concetti, Emblemi, ed Imprese.*	4to	Roma .	. 1603 *k.*
,,	,, ,, ,, ,,	4to	Siena .	1613 *t.*
Vænius .	. *Amorum Emblemata,* in Latin, English, and Italian.	obl. 4to	Antverp.	. 1608 *k. t.*
Glissenti	*Discorsi morali . . contra il dispiacer del morire, &c.*	4to	Venetia	1609 *v.*

Giulio Cesare Capaccio, besides his Neapolitan History, and one or two other works, is also the author of *Il Principe*, Venetia, 1620, a treatise on the Emblems of Alciatus, with more than 200 political and moral notices. Torquato Tasso is a name that needs no praise here. Of Alessio Porri I have found no other mention; and I may say the same of Gio. Dalla Torre, of Ottavio Caputi, and of Gio. Belloni. Melchior Zoppio, born in 1544 at Bologna (*Biog. Univ.* vol. lii. p. 430), was one of the founders of the Academia di Gelati, in his native town. Battisti Pittoni was a painter and engraver, who flourished between 1561 and 1585. The extensive work of Cesare Ripa of Perugia, which has passed through about twenty editions in Italian, Latin, Dutch, Spanish, German, and English, is alphabetically arranged, and treats of nearly 800 different subjects, with about 200 devices. Otho van Veen, or Vænius, belongs to Holland, not to Italy,—and his name appears here simply because his *Emblems of Love* were translated into Italian. Fabio Glissenti in 1609 introduced into his work (Brunet, iii. c. 256, 7) twenty-four of the plates out of the forty-one which adorned an Italian edition of the *Images of Death* in 1545.

FRENCH.

Desprez . .	*Théatre des animaux . . . actions de la vie humaine.*	4to	Paris .	1595 *v.*
Boissart . .	*Mascarades recueillies,* Geyn (J. de) Opera.	4to		1597 *v.*
Emblesmes.	*Emblesmes sus les Actions—du Segnor Espagnol.*	12mo	Mildelbourg .	1605 *k.*
Hymnes .	*Hymnes des vertus . . . par belles et délicates figures.*	8vo	Lyon .	1605 *v.*
Vænius . .	*Amorum Emblemata* (Latin, Italian, and French).	4to	Antverpiæ .	1608 *v.*
Vasseur . .	*Les Devises des Empereurs Romains, &c.*	8vo	Paris	1608 *t.*
,,	*Les Devises des Rois de France .*	...	Paris	1609 *v.*
Valence . .	*Emblesmes sur les Actions—du Segnor Espagnol.*	8vo	.	1608 *k.*

Rollenhagen	*Les Emblemes . . . mis en vers françois.*	4to	Coloniæ . .	1611 *v.*
Dinet . .	*Les cinq Livres des Hiéroglyphiques.*	4to	Paris . .	1614 *v.*
De Bry . .	*Pourtraict de la Cosmographie morale.*	4to	Francfort .	1614 *v.*

Robert Boissart, a French engraver (Bryan, p. 90) flourished about 1590, and is said to have resided some time in England. Of Vænius, so well known, there is no occasion to speak here. Jacques de Vasseur was archdeacon of Noyon, celebrated as the birth-place of Calvin, and in 1608 also published another work in French verse, *Antithises, ou Contrepointes du Ciel & de la Terre.* Desprez and Valence are unknown save by their books of Emblems. Pierre Dinet is very briefly named in *Biog. Univ.* vol. ii. p. 371; and Rollenhagen and De Bry will be mentioned presently.

LATIN.

Callia . .	*Emblemata sacra, e libris Mosis excerpta.*	32mo	Heidelbergæ	1591 *k.*
Borcht . .	*P. Ovidii Nasonis Metamorphoses.*	obl. 16mo	Antverpiæ .	1591 *t.*
Stimmer . .	*Icones Affabræ*	. . .	Strasburg .	1591 *v.*
Mercerius .	*Emblemata . . . . .*	4to	Bourges . .	1592 *t.*
De Bry . .	*Emblemata nobilitate et vulgo scitu digna.*	obl. 4to	Francof. .	1592 *v.*
„ . .	*Emblemata secularia . .*	4to	„	1593 *v.*
Freitag . .	*Viridiarium Moralis Phil. per fabulas, &c.*	4to	Coloniæ . .	1594 *k.*
Taurellius .	*Emblema physico-ethica, &c.*	8vo	Norimbergæ	1595 *k.*
Boissard .	*Theatrum vitæ Humanæ .*	4to	Metz . . .	1596 *t.*
Franceschino	*Hori Apollinis selecta hieroglyphica.*	16mo	Romæ .	1597 *v.*
Le Bey de Batilly.	*Emb. a J. Boissard delineata, &c.*	4to	Francof. . .	1596 *t. k.*
Altorfinæ .	*Emb. anniversaria Academiæ Altorfinæ.*	4to	Norimbergæ	1597 *k.c.t.*
David . . .	*Virtutis spectaculum .*	4to	Francof. . .	1597 *v.*
„	*Veridicus christianus .*	4to	Antverpiæ .	1601 *t. k.*

David	. *Occasio arrepta, neglecta, &c.*	4to	Antverpiæ	. 1605 *c. t.*
"	. *Pancarpium Marianum* .	8vo	"	1607 *t.*
"	. *Messis myrrhæ et aromatum, &c.*	8vo	"	1607 *v.*
" . .	. *Paradisus sponsi et sponsæ, &c.*	8vo	"	1607 *k.*
" . .	. *Dvodecim Specvla, &c.* .	8vo	"	1610 *t. k.*
Sadeler, Æg.	*Symbola Divina et Humana Pontif. Imper., &c.*	fol.	Prague .	. 1600 *k.*
"	*Symb. Div. et. Hum., &c.; Isagoge Jac. Typotii.*	fol.	Francof. .	. 1601, 2, 3 *k.*
Passæus	. *Metamorphoseωn Ouidianarum typi, &c.*	obl. 4to		1602 *t.*
Epidigma	. *Emblematum Philomilæ Thiloniæ Epidigma.*	4to		1603 *v.*
Vænius .	. *Horatii Emblemata, imaginibus* (ciii.) *in æs incisis.*	4to	Antuerp .	. 1607 *k.*
" . .	. *Amorvm Emblemata, Figvris æneis incisa.*	4to	Antuerpiæ	. 1608 *t. k.*
" . .	. *Amoris Divini Emblemata*	4to	Antuerpiæ	. 1615 *t.*
Pignorius	. *Vetustissimæ tabulæ æneæ sacris Ægyptiorum simulacris cælatæ explicatio.*	4to	Venetia .	. 1605 *v.*
"	. *Characteres Ægyptii . . per Jo. Th. et Io. Isr. de Bry.*	4to	Francofurti	1608 *v.*
Sadeler, Æg.	*Theatrum morum. Artliche gespräch der Thier met wahren Historien, &c.*	4to	Pragæ	. 1608.
Broecmer	. *Emblemata moralia et æconomica.*	4to	Arnhemi .	. 1609 *t.*
Aleander	. *Explicatio antiquæ Fabulæ marmoreæ Solis effigie, symbolisque exsculptæ, &c.*	4to	Romæ .	. 1611 *k.*
Rollenhagen	*Nvclevs Emblematum selectissimorum.*	4to	Coloniæ .	. 1611–13 *c. t.*
"	" " "	4to	Arnhemi	. 1615 *k.*
Hillaire .	. *Specvlvm Heroicvm—Homeri—Iliados.*	4to	Traject. Bat.	1613 *c.*
À Bruck	. *Emblemata moralia et bellica*	4to	Argentinæ	. 1615 *v.*

Peter Vander Borcht, born at Brussels about A.D. 1540, engraved numerous works, and among them 178 prints for this edition of Ovid. The Stimmers have been mentioned before, p. 90. Jean Mercier, born at Uzès in Languedoc, wrote the Latin version of the *Hieroglyphics* of Horapollo, Paris, 1548,—but probably it was his son Josias whose Emblems are mentioned under the year 1592, and who dates them from Bruges. Theodore De Bry, born at Liege in 1528 (Bryan, p. 119), carried on the business of an engraver and bookseller in Francfort, where he died in 1598. He was greatly assisted by his sons John Theodore and John Israel. *The Procession of the Knights of the Garter in* 1566, and that at the *Funeral of Sir Philip Sidney*, are his workmanship. Nicolas Taurellius was a student, and afterwards professor of Physic and Medicine in the University of Altorf in Franconia. An oration of his appears in the *Emblemata Anniversaria* of that institution. He was named "the German Philosopher." Denis le Bey de Batilly appears to have been royal president of the Consistory of Metz. John David, born at Courtray in Flanders, in 1546, entered the Society of the Jesuits, and was rector of the colleges of Courtray, Brussels, and Ghent: he died in 1613. Ægidius Sadeler, known as the Phœnix of engravers, was a native of Antwerp, born in 1570, the nephew and disciple of the two eminent engravers John and Raphael Sadeler. He enjoyed a pension from three successive emperors, Rodolphus II., Matthias, and Ferdinand II. Of Crispin de Passe, born at Utrecht about 1560, Bryan (p. 548) says, "He was a man of letters, and not only industrious to perfect himself in his art, but fond of promoting it." His works were numerous, and have examples in the Emblem-books of his day. Otho van Veen, of a distinguished family, was born at Leyden in 1556. After a residence of seven years in Italy, he established himself at Antwerp, and had the rare claim to celebrity that Rubens became his disciple. In his Emblem-works the designs were by himself, but the engravings by his brother Gilbert van Veen. (Bryan, p. 853, 4.) Lawrence

Pignorius, born at Padua, 1571, and educated at the Jesuits' school and the university of that city, gained a high reputation by several learned works, and especially by those on Egyptian antiquities. He died of the plague in 1631. The work of Richard Lubbæus Broecmer, is little more than a reprint of one by Bernard Furmer, in 1575, *On the Use and Abuse of Wealth.* Jerome Aleander, nephew of one of Luther's stoutest opponents, the Cardinal Aleander, was of considerable literary reputation at Rome, being a member of the society of Humourists, established in that city,—his death was in 1631. According to Oetlinger's brief notice, *Bibliog. Biograph. Univ.*, Gabriel Rollenhagen, of Magdeburg, was a German schoolmaster, born in 1542, and dying in 1609; his *Kernel of Emblems* is well illustrated by Crispin de Passe. The same "excellent engraver" adorned *The Mirror of Heroes,* founded on Homer's *Iliad* by "le sieur de la Rivière, Isaac Hillaire." Both Latin and French verses are appended to the Emblems, and at their end are curious "Epitaphs on the Heroes who fell in the Trojan war," too late, it is to be feared, to afford any gratification to their immediate friends. To Jacobus à Bruck, surnamed of Angermunde, a town of Brandenberg, there belongs another Emblem-book, *Emblemata Politica,* Cologne, 1618. In it are briefly demonstrated the duties which belong to princes; it is dedicated "to his most merciful Prince and Lord, the Emperor Matthias I., 'semper Augusto.'"

GERMAN.

De Bry .	. *Emblemata Secularia—rhythmis Germanicis, &c.*	4to	Francofurti	. 1596 *v.*
„ . .	. „ „ „ „	4to	Oppenhemii	. 1611 *t.*
Boissard	. *Shawspiel Menschliches Lebens*	4to	Franckf.	. 1597 *v.*
Sadeler .	. *Theatrum morum. Artliche gesprach der Thier, &c.*	4to	Praga	1608 *v.*

DUTCH OR FLEMISH.

David .	. *Christelucke*	4to	Antuerp	. 1603 *k.*

Vænius . .	*Zinnebeelden der Wereldtsche Liefde.*	4to	Amstel. . .	1603 *v.*
À Ganda .	*Spiegel van de doorluchtige, &c., Vrouwen.*	obl. 4to	Amsterod. .	1606 *t.*
" . .	*Emblemata Amatoria Nova* .	obl. 4to	Lugd. Bat. .	1613 *k.*
Moerman .	*De Cleyn Werelt . . . met-over schoone Const-platen.*	4to	Amstelred. .	1608 *k.*
Ieucht. . .	*Den nieuwen Ieucht spieghel . . . C. de Passe.*	obl. 4to		1610 *t.*
Embl. Amat.	*Afbeeldinghen, &c.* . .	obl. 4to	Amsterd. .	1611 *k.*
Gulden . .	*Den Gulden Winckel der Konstliev ende Nederlanders Gestoffeert.*	4to	Amsterdam.	1613 *k.*
Bellerophon	*Bellerophon, of Lust tot Wyskeyd.*	4to	Amsterdam.	1614 *k.*
Visscher .	*Sinnepoppen* (or Emblem Play) *van Roemer Visscher.*	12mo	Amsterdam.	1614 *k.*

De Bry, Sadeler, David, and Vænius have been mentioned in page 96. Theocritus à Ganda is known for this work, *The Mirror of virtuous Women*, for which Jost de Hondt executed the fine copper-plates that accompany it: and also for *Emblemata Amatoria Nova*, published at Amsterdam in 1608, and at Leyden in 1613. *The Little World*, by Jan Moerman, is of the same class with *Le Microcosme*, Lyons, 1562, by Maurice de Sceve; or with "ΜΙΚΡΟΚΟΣΜΟΣ," Antwerp, 1584 and 1594, and which Sir Wm. Stirling-Maxwell attributes to Henricus Costerius of Antwerp. *The New Mirror of Youth*, 1610; *The Delineations*, 1611; *The golden Ship of the Art-loving Netherlander finished*, 1613; and *Bellerophon, or Pleasure of Wisdom*, 1614; are all anonymous. Roemer van Visscher, born at Amsterdam in 1547 (*Biog. Univ.* vol. xlix. p. 276), is of high celebrity as a Dutch poet,—with Spiegel and Coörnhert, he was one of the chief restorers of the Dutch language, and an immediate predecessor of the two illustrious poets of Holland, Cornelius van Hooft and Josse du Vondel.

SPANISH.

De Soto	. *Emblemas Moralizadas* . . .	8vo	Madrid .	. 1599 *t. k.*
Vænius	. *Amorum emblemata.* (Latin and Spanish verses).	4to	Antuerpiæ	. 1608 *v.*
„	. *Amoris divini Emb....hispanicè,* &c.	4to	„	1615 *t.*
Orozco	. *Emblemas Morales*	4to	Madrid .	. 1610 *t. k.*
Villava	. *Empresas Espirituales y Morales* .	4to	Baeça	. 1613 *k.*

Hernando de Soto was auditor and comptroller for the King of Spain in his house of Castile. At the end are stanzas of three verses each, in Latin and Spanish on alternate pages, "to our Lady the Virgin." Don Sebastian de Couarrubias Orozco was chaplain to the King of Spain, schoolmaster and canon of Cuenca, and adviser of the Holy Office. Both Soto and Orozco dedicate their works to Don Francisco Gomez de Sandoual, Duke of Lerma. Juan Francisco de Villava dedicates his first Emblem "to the Holy and General Inquisition of Spain." Neither of the three names occurs in the Biographies to which I have access.

ENGLISH.

P. S. .	. *The Heroicall Devises of M. Clavdivs Paradin.*	8vo	London .	. 1591 *c.*
Wyrley .	. *The true use of Armorie, shewed by historie, and plainly proved by example.*	4to	London .	. 1592 *v.*
Willet	. *Sacrorvm Emblematvm Centvria vna,* &c. *A Century of Sacred Emblems.*	4to	Cambridge .	1598 *v.*
Crosse .	. *Crose his Covert, or a Prosopopœicall Treatise.*	MS. .		About 1600 *c.*
Vænius .	. *Amorum Emblemata* (Latin, English, and Italian).	4to	Antverpiæ	. 1608 *k. t.*
Guillim .	. *A Display of Heraldry* . .	fol.	London .	. 1611 *k.*
Peacham	. *Minerva Britanna, or a Garden of Heroical Deuises,* &c.	4to	London .	. 1612 *c. t. k.*
Yates, MS.	. *The Emblems of Alciatus in English verse.*	MS. .		About 1610 *t.*

William Wyrley's *True use of Arms*, was reprinted in 1853. In *Censura Lit.*, i. p. 313, Samuel Egerton Brydges gives a pleasing account of the character of Andrew Willet, whom Fuller ranks among England's worthies (vol. i. p. 238). Of John Crosse himself, nothing is known, but his MS. is certainly not later than Elizabeth's reign, for the royal arms, at p. 33, are of earlier date than the accession of the Stuarts; and the allusion to the Belgian dames, pp. 2—6, agrees with her times. The work contains 120 shields and devices, and was lent me by my very steadfast friend in Emblem lore, Mr. Corser of Stand. At pp. 10 and 37, it is said,—

> "In Troynovant a famous schoole was founde
> By famous Citizens; whilome the grounde
> Of noble Boone;"—

and

> "To traine vp youth in tongues fewe might compare
> With Mulcaster, whose fame shall never fade."

Now it was in 1561 Richard Mulcaster, of King's College, Cambridge, and of Christchurch, Oxford, was appointed head master of Merchant-Taylor's School in London, then just founded. (Warton, iii. 282.) Thus it is shown to be very probable that *Crosse his Covert* may take date not later than A.D. 1600. It may be added that at the end of the MS. the figure of Fortune, or Occasion, on a wheel, is almost a fac-simile from Whitney's Device, p. 181, which was itself struck from the block (Emb. 121. p. 438) of Plantin's edition of Alciatus, MDLXXXI. John Guillim's work on *Heraldry* passed through five editions previous to that of Capt. John Logan, in 1724; the original folio is one of the book-treasures at Keir. Henry Peacham, *Mr. of Artes*, as he terms himself, was a native of Leverton in Holland, in the county of Lincoln, and a student under "the right worshipfull Mr. D. Laifeild," in Trinity College, Cambridge. He has dedicated his work "to the Right High and Mightie Henrie, Eldest Sonne of our Soveraigne Lord the King."

Singular it is, that except the MS. which belonged to the late Joseph B. Yates, of Liverpool, there is not known to exist any translation into English of the once famous *Emblems of Alciatus.* That MS. (see *Transact. Liverpool L. and P. Society, Nov.* 5, 1849) "appears to be of the time of James the First." The Devices are drawn and coloured, and have considerable resemblance to those in Rapheleng's edition of Alciatus, 1608. As a specimen we add the translation of Emblem XXXIII. p. 39, "Signa fortium."

"O Saturn's birde! what cause doth thee incyte
Upon Aristom's tombe so highe to sitt?
'As I all other birds excell in mighte—
So doth Aristom, Lords, in strength and witt.
Let fearful Doves on cowards' tombs take rest—
We Eagles stoute to stoute men give a crest.'"

How pleasant to feel that this Sketch of Emblem-books and their authors, previous to and during the times of Shakespeare, has been brought to an end. "Vina coronant," *fill a bumper,* "let the sparkling glass go round."

The difficulty really has been to compress. The materials collected were most abundant. From curiously or artistically arranged title pages,—from various dedications,—from devices admirably designed or of wondrous oddity,—and from the countless collateral subjects among which the Emblem writers and their commentators disported themselves, the temptations were so rich to wander off here and there, that it was necessary continually to remember that it was a veritable sketch I was engaged on and not a universal history. I lashed myself therefore to the mast and sailed through a whole sea of syrens, deaf, though they charmed ever so sweetly to make me sing with them of emperors and kings, of popes and cardinals, of the learned and the gay, who appeared to believe that everyone's literary salvation depended on the contrivance of a device and the interpretation of an emblem.

Had I known where to refer my readers for a general view of my subject, either brief or prolix, I should have spared myself the labour of compiling one. The results are, that, previous to the year 1616, the Emblem Literature of Europe could claim for its own at least 200 authors, not including translators, and that above 770 editions of original texts and of versions had issued from the press.*

If Shakespeare knew nothing of so wide-spread a literature it is very wonderful; and more wondrous far, if knowing, he did not inweave some of the threads into the very texture of his thoughts.

In this Sketch of Emblem writers, it will be perceived, though their names are seldom heard of except among the antiquaries of letters, that, as a class, they were men of deep erudition, of considerable natural power, and of large attainments. To the literature of their age they were as much ornaments as to the literature of our modern times are the works, illustrated or otherwise, with which our hours of leisure are wont to be both amused and instructed. No one who is ignorant of them can possess a full idea of the intellectual treasures of the more cultivated nations of Europe about the period of which the works of Alciatus and of Giovio are the types. We may be learned in its controversies, well read in its ecclesiastical and political history, intimate even with the characters and pursuits of its great statesmen and sovereigns, and strong as well as enlightened in our admiration of its

* Since the above was written I have good reasons for concluding that the fact is very much understated. I am now employed, as time allows, in forming an Index to my various notes and references to Emblem writers and their works; the Index so far made comprises the letters A, B, C, D (very prolific letters indeed), and they present 330 writers and translators, and above 900 editions.

painters, statuaries, poets, and other artistic celebrities, but we are not baptized into its perfect spirit unless we know what entertainment and refreshing there were for men's minds when serious studies were intermitted and the weighty cares and business of life for a while laid aside.

Take up these Emblem writers as great statesmen and victorious commanders did; read them as did the recluse in his study and the man of the world at his recreation; search into them as some did for good morals suitable to the guidance of their lives, and as others did for snatches of wit and learning fitted to call forth their merriment; and see, amid divers conceits and many quaintnesses, and not a few inanities and vanities, how richly the fancy was indulged, and how freely the play of genius was allowed; and then will you be better prepared to estimate the whole literature of the nations of that busy, stirring time, when authorities were questioned that had reigned unchallenged for centuries, and men's minds were awakened to all the advantages of learning, and their tastes formed for admiring the continually varying charms of the poet's song and the artist's skill.

True; those strange turns of thought, those playings upon mere words, those fançiful dreamings, those huntings up and down of some unfortunate idea through all possible and impossible doublings and windings, are not approved either by a purer taste, or by a better-trained judgment. We have outgrown the customs of those logo-maniacs, or word-worshippers, whom old Ralph Cudworth, in his *True Intellectual System of the Universe*, p. 67, seems to have had in view, when he affirms, "that they could not make a Rational Discourse of anything, though never so small, but they must stuff it with their Quiddities, Entities, Essences, Hæcceities, and the like."

But at the revival of literature, when the ancient learning was devoured without being digested, and the modern investigations were not always controlled by sound discretion,—when the child was as a giant, and the giant disported himself in fantastic gambols,—we must not wonder that compositions, both prose and poetic, were perpetrated which receive unhesitatingly from the higher criticism the sentence of condemnation. But in condemning let not the folly be committed of despising and undervaluing. We may devotedly love our more advanced civilization, our finer sensibilities, and our juster estimate of what true taste for the beautiful demands, and yet we may accord to our leaders and fathers in learning and refinement the no unworthy commendation, that, with their means and in their day, they gave a mighty onward movement to those literary pursuits and pleasures in which the powers of the fancy heighten the glow of our joy, and the resources of accurate knowledge bestow an abiding worth upon our intellectual labours.

Sambucus, 1564.

CHAPTER III.

SHAKESPEARE'S ATTAINMENTS AND OPPORTUNITIES WITH RESPECT TO THE FINE ARTS.

MONG some warm admirers of Shakespeare it has not been unusual to depreciate his learning for the purpose of exalting his genius. It is thought that intuition and inborn power of mind accomplished for him what others, less favoured by the inspiration of the all-directing Wisdom, could scarcely effect by their utmost and life-patient labours. The worlds of nature and of art were spread before him, and out of the materials, with perfect ease, he fashioned new creations, calling into existence forms of beauty and grace, and investing them at will with the rare attributes of poetic fancy.

On the very surface, however, of Shakespeare's writings, in the subjects of his dramas and in the structure of their respective plots, though we may not find a perfectly accurate scholarship, we have ample evidence that the choicest literature of his native land, and, through translations at least, the ample stores of Greece and of Italy were open to his mind. Whether his scenes be the plains of Troy, the river of Egypt, the walls of Athens, or the capitol of Rome, his learning is amply sufficient for the occasion; and though the critic may detect incongruities and errors,* they are probably not greater than those which many a finished scholar falls into when he ventures to describe the features of countries and cities which he has not actually visited. The heroes and heroines of pagan mythology and pagan history, the veritable actors in ancient times of the world's great drama,—or the more unreal characters of fairy land, of the weird sisterhood, and of the wizard fraternity,—these all stand before us instinct with life.† And from the old legends of Venice, of Padua and Verona,—from the traditionary lore of England, of Denmark, and of Scotland,—or from the more truth-like delineations of his strictly historical plays, we may of a certainty gather, that his reading was of wide extent, and that with a student's industry he made it subservient to the illustration and faithfulness of poetic thought.

Trusting, as we may do in a very high degree, to Douce's *Illustrations of Shakspeare and of Ancient Manners* (2 vols., London, 1807), or to the still more elaborate and erudite work of Dr. Nathan Drake, *Shakspeare and his Times* (2 vols., 4to, London, 1817), we need not hesitate at resting on Mr. Capel Lofft's conclusion, that Shakespeare possessed "a very reasonable portion of Latin; he was not wholly ignorant of Greek; he

---

* We select an instance common to both Holbein and Shakespeare; it is pointed out by Woltmann, in his *Holbein and his Time*, vol. ii. p. 23, where, speaking of the Holbein painting, *The Death of Lucretia*, the writer says,—"The costume is here, as ever, that of Holbein's own time. The painter reminds us of Shakespeare, who also conceived the heroes of classic antiquity in the costume of his own days; in the *Julius Cæsar* the troops are drawn up by beat of drum, and Coriolanus comes forth like an English lord: but the historical signification of the subject nevertheless does in a degree become understood, which the later poetry, with every instrument of archæological learning, troubles itself in vain to reach."

It may be noted that in other instances both Wornum, the English biographer of Holbein, and Woltmann, the German, compare Holbein and Shakespeare, or, rather, illustrate the one by the other.

† As when Cooper, at the tomb of Shakespeare, describes it,—

"The scene then chang'd from this romantic land,
To a bleak waste by bound'ry unconfin'd,
Where three swart sisters of the weird band
Were mutt'ring curses to the troublous wind."

had a knowledge of French, so as to read it with ease; and I believe not less of the Italian. He was habitually conversant with the chronicles of his country. He lived with wise and highly cultivated men, with Jonson, Essex, and Southampton, in familiar friendship." (See Drake, vol. i. pp. 32, 33, *note*.) And again, "It is not easy, with due attention to his poems, to doubt of his having acquired, when a boy, no ordinary facility in the *classic* language of Rome; though his knowledge of it might be small, comparatively, to the knowledge of that great and indefatigable scholar, Ben Jonson."

Dr. Drake and Mr. Capel Lofft differ in opinion, though not very widely, as to the extent of Shakespeare's knowledge of Italian literature. The latter declares, "My impression is, that Shakespeare was not unacquainted with the most popular authors in *Italian prose*, and that his ear had listened to the enchanting tones of *Petrarca*, and some others of their great poets." And the former affirms, that "From the evidence which his genius and his works afford, his acquaintance with the French and Italian languages was not merely confined to the picking up *a familiar phrase or two* from the conversation or writings of others, but that he had actually commenced, and at an early period too, the study of these languages, though, from his situation, and the circumstances of his life, he had neither the means, nor the opportunity, of cultivating them to any considerable extent." (See Drake, vol. i. pp. 54, *note*, and 57, 58.)

Now the Emblem-writers of the sixteenth century, and previously, made use chiefly of the Latin, Italian, and French languages. Of the Emblem-books in Spanish, German, Flemish, Dutch, and English, only the last would be available for Shakespeare's benefit, except for the suggestions which the engravings and woodcuts might supply. It is then well for us to understand that his attainments with respect to language were sufficient to enable him to study this branch of literature, which before his day, and in his day, was so widely spread through all the more civilized countries of Europe. He possessed the mental apparatus which gave him power, should inclination or fortune lead him there, to cultivate the *viridiaria*, the pleasant blooming gardens of emblem, device, and symbol.

Even if he had not been able to read the Emblem writers in their original languages, undoubtedly he would meet with their works in the society in which he moved and among the learned of his native land. As we have seen, he was in familiar friendship with the Earl of Essex. To that nobleman Willet, in 1598, had dedicated his *Sacred Emblems*. Of men of Devereux's stamp, several had become acquainted with the Emblem Literature. To his rival, Robert Dudley, the Earl of Leicester, Whitney devoted the *Choice of Emblemes*, 1586; in 1580, Beza had honoured the young James of Scotland with the foremost place in his *Portraits of Illustrious Men*, to which a set of Emblems were appended; Sir Philip Sidney, during his journey on the continent, 1571—1575, became acquainted with the works of the Italian emblematist, Ruscelli; and as early as 1549, it was "to the very illustrious Prince James earl of Arran in Scotland," that "Barptolemy Aneau" commended his French version of Alciat's classic stanzas.

And were it not a fact, as we can show it to be, that Shakespeare quotes the very mottoes and describes the very drawings which the Emblem-books contain, we might, from his highly cultivated taste in other respects, not unreasonably conclude that he must both have known them and have used them. His information and exquisite judgment extended to works of highest art,—to sculpture, painting, and music, as well as to literature. There is, perhaps, no description of statuary extant so admirable for its truth and beauty as the lines quoted by

Drake, p. 617, from the *Winter's Tale*,* "where Paulina unveils to Leontes the supposed statue of Hermione."

"*Paulina.* As she lived peerless,
So her dead likeness, I do well believe,
Excels whatever yet you look'd upon,
Or hand of man hath done; therefore I keep it
Lonely, apart. But here it is: prepare
To see the life as lively mock'd as ever
Still sleep mock'd death: behold, and say 'tis well.
[PAULINA *draws a curtain, and discovers* HERMIONE *standing like a statue.*
I like your silence, it the more shows off
Your wonder: but yet speak; first, you, my liege.
Comes it not something near?
Leontes. Her natural posture!
Chide me, dear stone, that I may say indeed
Thou art Hermione. . . . .
O, thus she stood,†
Even with such life of majesty, warm life,
As now it coldly stands, when first I woo'd her!
I am ashamed: does not the stone rebuke me
For being more stone than it?
. . . .
Paul. No longer shall you gaze on't, lest your fancy
May think anon it moves.
Leon. Let be, let be.
Would I were dead, but that, methinks, already—
What was he that did make it? See, my lord,
Would you not deem it breathed? and that those veins
Did verily bear blood?
Paul. Masterly done:
The very life seems warm upon her lip.
Leon. The fixure of her eye has motion in't,
As we are mock'd with art . . . . .
Still, methinks

* Act v. sc. 3. lines 14—84, Cambridge edition, vol. iii. pp. 422-25.

† The ivory statue changed into a woman, which Ovid describes, *Metamorphoses*, bk. x. fab. viii. 12–16, is a description of kindred excellence to that of Shakespeare:

"Sæpe manus operi tentantes admovet, an sit
Corpus, an illud ebur: nec ebur tamen esse fatetur.
Oscula dat, reddique putat; loquiturque, tenetque:
Et credit tactis digitos insidere membris:
Et metuit, pressos veniat ne livor in artus."

There is an air comes from her: what fine chisel
Could ever yet cut breath? Let no man mock me,
For I will kiss her.
  Paul. Good my lord, forbear:
The ruddiness upon her lip is wet;
You'll mar it if you kiss it; stain your own
With oily painting. Shall I draw the curtain?
  Leon. No, not these twenty years.
  Perdita. So long could I
Stand by, a looker on."

This exquisite piece of statuary is ascribed by Shakespeare (*Winter's Tale*, act v. sc. 2, l. 8, vol. iii. p. 420) to "that rare Italian master Julio Romano, who, had he himself eternity, and could put breath into his work, would beguile Nature of her custom, so perfectly is he her ape: he so near to Hermione hath done Hermione, that they say one would speak to her, and stand in hope of answer."

According to Kugler's "GESCHICHTE DER MALEREI,"—*History of Painting* (Berlin, 1847, vol. i. p. 641),—Julio Romano was one of the most renowned of Raphael's scholars, born about 1492, and dying in 1546. "Giulio war ein Kunstler von rustigem, lebendig, bewegtem, keckem Geiste, begabt mit einer Leichtigkeit der Hand, welche den kuhnen und rastlosen Bildern seiner Phantasie überall Leben und Dasein zu geben wusste."*

His earlier works are to be found at Rome, Genoa, and Dresden. Soon after Raphael's death he was employed in Mantua both as an architect and a painter; and here exist some of his choice productions, as the Hunting by Diana, the frescoes of the Trojan War, the histories of Psyche, and other Love-tales of the gods. Pictures by him are scattered over Europe,—some at Venice, some in the sacristy of St. Peter's, and in other places in

* "Julio was an artist of vigorous, lively, active, fearless spirit, gifted with a lightness of hand which knew how to impart life and being to the bold and restless images of his fancy." The same volume, pp. 641-5, continues the account of Romano.

Rome; some in the Louvre, and some in the different collections of England,* as the Jupiter among the Nymphs and Corybantes.

Whether any of his works were in England during the reign of Elizabeth, we cannot affirm positively; but as there were "sixteen by Julio Romano" in the fine collection of paintings at Whitehall, made, or, rather, increased by Charles I., of which Henry VIII. had formed the nucleus, it is very probable there were in England some by that master so early as the writing of the *Winter's Tale*, or even before, in which, as we have seen, he is expressly named. It may therefore be reasonably conjectured that in the statue of Hermione Shakespeare has accurately described some figure which he had seen in one of Julio Romano's paintings.

The same rare appreciation of the beautiful appears in the *Cymbeline*, act ii. sc. 4, lines 68—74, 81—85, 87—91, vol. ix. pp. 207, 208, where the poet describes the adornments of Imogen's chamber:—

"It was hang'd
With tapestry of silk and silver; the story
Proud Cleopatra, when she met her Roman,
And Cydnus swell'd above the banks, or for
The press of boats, or pride: a piece of work
So bravely done, so rich, that it did strive
In workmanship and value. . . . .
And the chimney-piece
Chaste Dian, bathing:† never saw I figures
So likely to report themselves: the cutter
Was as another nature, dumb; outwent her,
Motion and breath left out. . . . . . .
The roof o' the chamber
With golden cherubins is fretted: her andirons—
I had forgot them—were two winking Cupids
Of silver, each on one foot standing, nicely
Depending on their brands."

* "An important one," says Kugler, "at Lord Northwick's, in London."

† Two of Titian's large paintings, now in the Bridgewater Gallery, represent "Diana and her Nymphs bathing." (See Kugler, vol. ii. p. 44.)

So, in the *Taming of the Shrew*, act ii. sc. 1, lines 338—348, vol. iii. p. 45, Gremio enumerates the furniture of his house in Padua :—

"First, as you know, my house within the city
Is richly furnished with plate and gold;
Basins and ewers to lave her dainty hands;
My hangings all of Tyrian tapestry;
In ivory coffers I have stuff'd my crowns;
In cypress chests my arras counterpoints,
Costly apparel, tents, and canopies,
Fine linen, Turkey cushions boss'd with pearl,
Valance of Venice gold in needlework,
Pewter and brass and all things that belong
To house or housekeeping."

And Hamlet, when he contrasts his father and his uncle, act iii. sc. 4, lines 55—62, vol. viii. p. 111, what a force of artistic skill does he not display! It is indeed a poet's description, but it has all the power and reality of a most finished picture. The very form and features are presented, as if some limner, a perfect master of his pencil, had portrayed and coloured them:—

"See what a grace was seated on this brow;
Hyperion's curls, the front of Jove himself,
An eye like Mars, to threaten and command;
A station like the herald Mercury
New lighted on a heaven-kissing hill;
A combination and a form indeed,
Where every god did seem to set his seal
To give the world assurance of a man."

In the *Merchant of Venice*, too, act iii. sc. 2, lines 115—128, vol. ii. p. 328, when Bassanio opens the leaden casket and discovers the portrait of Portia, who but one endowed with a painter's inspiration could speak of it as Shakespeare does!—

"Fair Portia's counterfeit! What demi-god
Hath come so near creation? Move these eyes?
Or whether, riding on the balls of mine,

Seem they in motion? Here are sever'd lips,
Parted with sugar breath: so sweet a bar
Should sunder such sweet friends. Here in her hairs
The painter plays the spider, and hath woven
A golden mesh to entrap the hearts of men,
Faster than gnats in cobwebs; but her eyes,—
How could he see to do them? Having made one,
Methinks it should have power to steal both his
And leave itself unfurnish'd."

Such power of estimating artistic skill authorises the supposition that Shakespeare himself had made the painter's art a subject of more than accidental study; else whence such expressions as those which in the *Antony*, act ii. sc. 2, lines 201—209, vol. ix. p. 38, are applied to Cleopatra?—

"For her own person,
It beggar'd all description: she did lie
In her pavilion, cloth-of-gold of tissue,
O'er-picturing that Venus where we see
The fancy outwork nature: on each side her
Stood pretty dimpled boys, like smiling Cupids,
With divers-colour'd fans, whose wind did seem
To glow the delicate cheeks which they did cool,
And what they undid did."

Or, even when sportively, in *Twelfth Night*, act i. sc. 5, lines 214—230, vol. iii. p. 240, Olivia replies to Viola's request, "Good Madam, let me see your face,"—is it not quite in an artist's or an amateur's style that the answer is given? "We will draw the curtain and show you the picture. Look you, sir, such a one I was this present: is't not well done?" [*Unveiling.*

"*Viol.* Excellently done, if God did all.
Oli. 'Tis in grain, sir; 'twill endure wind and weather.
Vio. 'Tis beauty truly blent, whose red and white
Nature's own sweet and cunning hand laid on:
Lady, you are the cruel'st she alive,
If you will lead these graces to the grave
And leave the world no copy.

Oli. O, sir, I will not be so hard-hearted; I will give out divers schedules of my beauty: it shall be inventoried, and every particle and utensil labelled to my will: as, item, two lips, indifferent red; item, two grey eyes, with lids to them; item, one neck, one chin, and so forth."

But from certain lines in the *Taming of the Shrew* (Induction, sc. 2, lines 47—58), it is evident that Shakespeare had seen either some of the mythological pictures by Titian, or engravings from them, or from similar subjects. Born in 1477, and dying in 1576, in his ninety-ninth year, the great Italian artist was contemporary with a long series of illustrious men, and his fame and works had shone far beyond their native sky. Our distant and then but partially civilised England awoke to a perception of their beauties, and though few—if any—of Titian's paintings so early found a domicile in this country, yet pictures were, we are assured,* "a frequent decoration in the rooms of the wealthy." Shakespeare even represents the Countess of Auvergne, 1 *Henry VI.*, act ii. sc. 3, lines 36, 37, vol. v. p. 33, as saying to Talbot,—

"Long time thy shadow hath been thrall to me,
For in my gallery thy picture hangs."

The formation of a royal gallery, or collection of paintings, had engaged the care of Henry VIII.; and the British nobility at the time of his daughter Elizabeth's reign, "deeply read in classical learning, familiar with the literature of Italy, and polished by foreign travel," "were well qualified to appreciate and cultivate the true principles of taste."

Titian, as is well known, "displayed a singular mastery in the representation of nude womanly forms, and in this the witchery of his colouring is manifested with fullest power."† Many instances of this are to be found in his works. Two are

* See Drake's *Shakspeare and his Times*, vol. ii. p. 119.

† See D. Franz Kugler's *Handbuch der Geschichte der Malerei*, vol. ii. pp. 44-6.

presented by the renowned Venus-figures at Florence, and by the beautiful Danae at Naples. The Cambridge gallery contains the Venus in whose form the Princess Eboli is said to have been portrayed, playing the lute, and having Philip of Spain seated at her side. In the Bridgewater gallery are two representations of Diana in the bath,—the one having the story of Actæon, and the other discovering the guilt of Calisto; and in the National Gallery are a Bacchus and Ariadne, and also a good copy, from the original at Madrid, of Venus striving to hold back Adonis from the chase. To these we may add the Arming of Cupid, in the Borghese palace at Rome, in which he quietly permits Venus to bind his eyes, while another Cupid whispering leans on her shoulder, and two Graces bring forward quivers and bows.

It is to such a School of Painting, or to such a master of his art, that Shakespeare alludes, when, in the Induction scene to the *Taming of the Shrew*, Christopher Sly is served and waited on as a lord:—

> "*Sec. Serv.* Dost thou love pictures? we will fetch thee straight
> Adonis painted by a running brook,
> And Cytherea all in sedges hid,
> Which seem to move and wanton with her breath,
> Even as the waving sedges play with wind.
> *Lord.* We'll show thee Io as she was a maid,
> And how she was beguiled and surprised,
> As lively painted as the deed was done.
> *Third Serv.* Or Daphne roaming through a thorny wood,
> Scratching her legs that one shall swear she bleeds,
> And at that sight shall sad Apollo weep,
> So workmanly the blood and tears are drawn."

Among Shakespeare's gifts was also the power to appreciate the charms of melody and song. Their influence he felt, and their effect he most eloquently describes. He speaks of them with a sweetness, a gentleness, and force which must have had counterparts in his own nature. As in the *Midsummer Night's Dream*, act ii. sc. 1, line 148, vol. ii. p. 215, when Oberon bids Puck to come to her,—

> "Thou rememberest
> Since once I sat upon a promontory,
> And heard a mermaid, on a dolphin's back,
> Uttering such dulcet and harmonious breath,
> That the rude sea grew civil at her song,
> And certain stars shot madly from their spheres
> To hear the sea-maid's music."

And again, in the *Merchant of Venice*, act v. sc. 1, lines 2 and 54, vol. ii. p. 360, how exquisite the description!—

> "When the sweet wind did gently kiss the trees,
> And they did make no noise."

Lorenzo's discourse to Jessica is such as only a passion-warmed genius could conceive and utter:—

> "How sweet the moonlight sleeps upon this bank!
> Here will we sit, and let the sounds of music
> Creep in our ears: soft stillness and the night
> Become the touches of sweet harmony.
> Sit, Jessica. Look how the floor of heaven
> Is thick inlaid with patines of bright gold:
> There's not the smallest orb which thou behold'st
> But in his motion like an angel sings,
> Still quiring to the young-eyed cherubins;
> Such harmony is in immortal souls."

And Ferdinand, in the *Tempest*, act i. sc. 2, l. 387, vol. i. p. 20, after listening to Ariel's song, "Come unto these yellow sands," thus testifies to its power:—

> "Where should this music be? i' th' air, or th' earth?
> It sounds no more: and sure it waits upon
> Some god o' th' island. Sitting on a bank,
> Weeping again the king my father's wreck,
> This music crept by me upon the waters

> Allaying both their fury and my passion
> With its sweet air: thence have I follow'd it,
> Or it hath drawn me rather."

Thus, from his sufficient command over the requisite languages, from his diligent reading in the literature of his country, translated as well as original, from his opportunities of frequent converse with the cultivated minds of his age, and still more from what we have shown him to have possessed,—accurate taste and both an intelligent and a warm appreciation of the principles and beauties of Imitative Art,—we conclude that Shakespeare found it a study congenial to his spirit and powers, to examine and apply, what was both popular and learned in its day,—the illustrations, by the graver's art and the poet's pen, of the proverbial wisdom which constitutes almost the essence of the Emblematical writers of the sixteenth century. To him, as to others, their works would be sources of interest and amusement; and even in hours of idleness many a sentiment would be gathered up to be afterwards almost unconsciously assimilated for the mind's nurture and growth.

When we maintain that Shakespeare not unfrequently made use of the Emblem writers, we do not mean to imply that he was generally a direct copyist from them. This is seldom the case. But a word, a phrase, or an allusion, sufficiently demonstrates whence particular thoughts have been derived, and how they have been coloured and clothed. They have been gathered as flowers in a country-walk are gathered—one from this hedge-side, another from that, and a third from among the standing corn, and others from the margin of some murmuring stream; but all have their natural beauty heightened by the skill with which they are blended so as to impart gracefulness to the whole. Flora's gems they may be, but the enwoven coronal borrows its chief charm from the artistic power and fitness with which its parts are arranged: break the thread, or cut the string with which Genius has bound them together, and they fall into inextricable confusion—a mass of disorder—no longer a pride and a joy: but let them remain, as a most excellent skill has placed them, and for ever could we gaze on their loveliness. A matchless beauty has been achieved, and all the more do we value it, because upon it there is also stamped eternal youth.

CHAPTER IV.

THE KNOWLEDGE OF EMBLEM-BOOKS IN BRITAIN, AND GENERAL INDICATIONS THAT SHAKESPEARE WAS ACQUAINTED WITH THEM.

ONUMENTS, or memorial stones, with emblematical figures and characters carved upon them, are of ancient date in Britain as elsewhere—probably antecedent even to Christianity itself. Manuscripts, too, ornamented with many a symbolical device, carry us back several hundred years. These we may dismiss from consideration at the present moment, and simply take up printed books devoted chiefly or entirely to Emblems.

I.—Of printed Emblem-books in the earlier time down to 1598, when Willet's *Century of Sacred Emblems* appeared, though there were several in the English language, there were only few of pure English origin. Watson and Barclay, in 1509, gave English versions of Sebastian Brant's *Fool-freighted Ship*. Not later than 1536, nor earlier than 1517, *The Dialogue of Creatures moralysed* was translated "out of latyn in to our English tonge." In 1549, at Lyons, *The Images of the Old Testament, &c.*, were "set forthe in Ynglishe and Frenche;" and in 1553, from the same city, Peter Derendel gave in English metre *The true and lyvely historyke Portreatures of the woll Bible.*

The Workes of Sir Thomas More Knyght, sometyme Lorde

Chauncellour of England, were published in small folio, London, 1557, and in them at the beginning (signature C ij:o—C iiij) are inserted what the author names "nyne pageauntes," which, as they existed in his father's house about A.D. 1496, were certainly Emblems. To this list Sir Thomas North, in London, 1570, added *The Morall Philosophie of Doni*, "out of Italien;" Daniell, in 1585, *The worthy Tract of Paulus Jovius*, which Whitney, in 1586, followed up by *A Choice of Emblemes*, "Englished and moralized;" and Paradin's *Heroicall Devises* were "Translated out of Latin into English," London, 1591.

To vindicate something of an English origin for a few emblems at least, reference may again be made to the fact that about the year 1495 or 6, "Mayster Thomas More in his youth deuysed in hys fathers house in London, a goodly hangyng of fyne paynted clothe, with nyne pageauntes,* and verses ouer of euery of those pageauntes: which verses expressed and declared, what the ymages in those pageauntes represented: and also in those pageauntes were paynted, the thynges that the verses ouer them dyd (in effecte) declare." In 1592, Wyrley published at London *The true use of Armories, &c.*: soon after appeared Emblems by Thomas Combe, which, however, are no longer known to be in existence; and then, in 1598, Andrew Willet's *Sacrorum Emblematum Centuria vna, &c.*,—"A Century of Sacred Emblems." Guillim, in 1611, supplied *A Display of Heraldry;* and Peacham, in 1612, *A Garden of Heroical Devices.* There were, too, in MSS., several Emblem-works in English, some of which have since been edited and made known.

Yet we must not suppose that the knowledge of Emblem-books in Britain depended on those only of which an English

* The subjects of the "nyne pageauntes," and of their verses, are—"Chyldhod, Manhod, Venus and Cupyde, Age, Deth, Fame, Tyme, Eterniter," in English; and "The Poet" in Latin.

version had been achieved. To men of culture, the whole series was open in almost its entire extent. James Hamilton, Earl of Arran, had resided in France, and in 1555, being high in the favour of Henry II., "was made captain of his Scotch life-guards." A few years before, namely, in 1549, as we have mentioned, p. 108, Aneau's French translation of Alciat's *Emblems* had been dedicated to him as, "filz de tres noble Prince Jacque Duc de Chastel le herault, Prince Gouverneur du Royaume d'Escoce."

Among the rare books in the British Museum is Marquale's Italian Version of Alciat's *Emblems*, printed at Lyons in 1549; a copy of it, a very lovely book, in the original binding, bears on the back the royal crown, and at the foot the letters "E. VI. R.," —*Edwardus Sextus Rex;* and, as he died in 1553, we thus have evidence at how early a date the work was known in England. To the young king it would doubtless be a book "for delight and for ornament."

Of Holbein's *Imagines Mortis*, Lyons, 1545, by George Æmylius, Luther's brother-in-law, a copy now in the British Museum "was presented to Prince Edward by Dr. William Bill, accompanied with a Latin dedication, dated from Cambridge, 19th July, 1546, wherein he recommends the prince's attention to the figures in the book, in order to remind him that all must die to obtain immortality; and enlarges on the necessity of living well. He concludes with a wish that the Lord will long and happily preserve his life, and that he may finally reign to all eternity with his *most Christian father*. Bill was appointed one of the king's chaplains in ordinary, 1551, and was made the first Dean of Westminster in the reign of Elizabeth."—Douce's *Holbein*, Bohn's ed., 1858, pp. 93, 94.

In 1548, Mary of Scotland was sent into France for her education (Rapin, ed. 1724, vol. vi. p. 30), and here imbibed the taste for, or rather knowledge of, Emblems, which afterwards she put into practice. To her son, in his fourteenth year, emblems were introduced by no less an authority than that of Theodore Beza. A copy indeed of the works of Alciatus was bound for him when he became King of England,—it is a folio edition, in six volumes or parts, and is still preserved in the British Museum; the royal arms are on the cover, front and back, and fleurs-de-lis in the corners. It was printed at Lyons in 1560, and possibly the Emblems in vol. vi., leaves 334—354, with their very beautiful devices, may have been the companions of his boyhood and early years. By the Emblem-works of Beza and of Alciat probably was laid the foundation of the king's love for allegorical representations, which, under the name of masques, were provided by Jonson for the Court's amusement. The king's weakness in this respect is wittily set forth in the French epigram soon after his death (Rapin's *History*, 4to, vol. vii. p. 259):—

> "*Tandis qu' Elisabeth fut Roi,*
> *L'Anglois fut d'Espagne l'effroi;*
> *Maintenant, dévise & caquette,*
> *Régi par la Reine Jaquette.*" *

To English noblemen, in 1608, Otho van Veen, from Antwerp, commends his *Amorum Emblemata*,—"Emblems of the Loves,"—with 124 excellent devices. Thus the dedication runs: "To the moste honorable and woerthie brothers, *William* Earle of *Pembroke*, and *Philip* Earle of *Mountgomerie*, patrons of learning and cheualrie." In England, therefore, as in Scotland, there were eminent lovers of the Emblem literature.

But an acquaintance with that literature may be regarded as more spread abroad and increased when Emblem-books became

---

* Thus to be rendered—

> While Elizabeth, as king, did reign,
> England the terror was of Spain;
> Now, chitter-chatter and Emblemes
> Rule, through our queen, the little James.

the sources of ornamentation for articles of household furniture, and for the embellishment of country mansions. A remarkable instance is supplied from *The History of Scotland,* edition London, 1655, "By William Drummond of Hauthornden." It is in a letter "*To his worthy Friend* Master Benjamin Johnson," dated July 1, 1619, respecting some needle-work by Mary Queen of Scots, and shows how intimately she was acquainted with several of the Emblem-books of her day, or had herself attained the art of making devices. The whole letter, except a few lines at the beginning, is most interesting to the admirers of Emblems. Drummond thus writes :—

"I have been curious to find out for you the *Impresaes* and Emblemes on a Bed of State * wrought and embroidered all with gold and silk by the late Queen *Mary*, mother to our sacred Soveraign, which will embellish greatly some pages of your Book, and is worthy your remembrance ; the first is the Loadstone turning towards the pole, the word her Majesties name turned on an Anagram, *Maria Stuart, sa virtu, m'attire,* which is not much inferiour to *Veritas armata.* This hath reference to a Crucifix, before which with all her Royall Ornaments she is humbled on her knees most liuely, with the word, *undique;* an *Impresa* of *Mary* of *Lorrain*, her Mother, a *Phœnix* in flames, the word,† *en ma fin git mon commencement.* The *Impressa* of an Apple-Tree growing in a Thorn, the word, *Per vincula crescit.* The *Impressa* of *Henry* the second, the *French King*, a *Cressant*, the word, *Donec totum impleat orbem.* The *Impressa* of King *Francis* the first, a *Salamander* crowned in the midst of Flames, the word, *Nutrisco et extinguo.* The *Impressa* of *Godfrey* of *Bullogne*, an arrow passing through three birds, the word, *Dederit ne viam Casusve Deusve.* That of *Mercurius* charming *Argos*, with his hundred eyes, expressed by his *Caduceus*, two *Flutes*, and a Peacock, the word, *Eloquium tot lumina clausit.* Two Women upon the Wheels of

---

* Through Mr. Jones, of the Chetham Library, Manchester, I applied to D. Laing, Esq., of the Signet Library, Edinburgh, to inquire if the bed of state is known still to exist. The reply, Dec. 31st, 1867, is—

"In regard to Queen Mary's bed at Holyrood, there is one which is shown to visitors, but I am quite satisfied that it does not correspond with Drummond's description, as 'wrought in silk and gold.' There are some hangings of old tapestry, but in a very bad state of preservation. Yesterday afternoon I went down to take another look at it, but found, as it was getting dark, some of the rooms locked up, and no person present. Should, however, I find anything further on the subject, I will let you know, but I do not expect it."

† This mode of naming the motto appears taken from Shakespeare's *Pericles*, as—

"A black Æthiop, reaching at the sun :
The word, *Lux tua vita mihi.*"

Fortune, the one holding a Lance, the other a *Cornucopia;* which *Impressa* seemeth to glaunce at Queen *Elizabeth* and herself, the word, *Fortunæ Comites.* The *Impressa* of the Cardinal of *Lorrain* her Uncle, a *Pyramid* overgrown with ivy, the vulgar word, *Te stante virebo;* a Ship with her Mast broken and fallen in the Sea, the word, *Nusquam nisi rectum.* This is for herself and her Son, a Big *Lyon* and a young Whelp beside her, the word, *Unum quidem, sed Leonem.* An embleme of a *Lyon* taken in a Net, and Hares wantonly passing over him, the word, *Et lepores devicto insultant Leone. Cammomel* in a garden, the word, *Fructus calcata dat amplos.* A Palm Tree, the word, *Ponderibus virtus innata resistit.* A Bird in a *Cage*, and a *Hawk* flying above, with the word, *Il mal me preme et me spaventa a Peggio.* A triangle with a Sun in the middle of a Circle, the word, *Trino non convenit orbis.* A Porcupine amongst Sea Rocks, the word, *Ne volutetur.* The *Impressa* of king Henry the eight, a *Portculles*, the word, *altera securitas.* The *Impressa* of the Duke of *Savoy*, the annunciation of the Virgin *Mary*, the word, *Fortitudo ejus* Rhodum *tenuit.* He had kept the Isle of *Rhodes.* Flourishes of Armes, as Helms, Launces, Corslets, Pikes, Muskets, Canons, the word, *Dabit Deus his quoque finem.* A Tree planted in a Church-yard environed with dead men's bones, the word, *Pietas revocabit ab orco.* Ecclipses of the Sun and the Moon, the word, *Ipsa sibi lumen quod invidet aufert*, glauncing, as may appear, at Queen *Elizabeth. Brennus* Ballances, a sword cast in to weigh Gold, the word, *Quid nisi Victis dolor!* A Vine tree watred with Wine, which instead to make it spring and grow, maketh it fade, the word, *Mea sic mihi prosunt.* A wheel rolled from a Mountain in the Sea, the word, *Piena di dolor voda de Sperenza.* Which appeareth to be her own, and it should be, *Precipitio senza speranza.* A heap of Wings and Feathers dispersed, the word, *Magnatum Vicinitas.* A Trophie upon a Tree, with Mytres, Crowns, Hats, Masks, Swords, Books, and a Woman with a Vail about her eyes or muffled, pointing to some about her, with this word, *Ut casus dederit.* Three crowns, two opposite and another above in the Sea, the word, *Aliamque moratur.* The Sun in an Ecclipse, the word, *Medio occidet Die.*"

"I omit the Arms of *Scotland*, *England*, and *France* severally by themselves, and all quartered in many places of this Bed. The workmanship is curiously done, and above all value, and truely it may be of this Piece said, *Materiam superabat opus.*"*

* In two other Letters Drummond makes mention of Devices or Emblems. Writing from Paris, p. 249, he describes "the Fair of St. Germain:"—

"The diverse Merchandize and Wares of the many nations at that Mart;" and adds, "Scarce could the wandering thought light upon any Storie, Fable, Gayetie, which was not here represented to view."

A letter to the Earl of Perth, p. 256, tells of various Emblems:

"My noble Lord,—After a long inquiry about the Arms of your Lordships antient House, and the turning of sundry Books of *Impresaes* and Herauldry, I found your V N D E S. famous and very honourable."

"In our neighbour Countrey of *England* they are born, but inversed upside down and diversified.

It would be tedious to verify, as might be done in nearly every instance, the original authors of these twenty-nine *Impreses* and Emblems. Several of them are in our own Whitney, several in Paradin's *Devises heroiques*, and several in *Dialogue des Devises d'armes et d'amovrs dv S. Pavlo Jovio, &c.*, 4to, A Lyon, 1561.

From the last named author we select as specimens two of the Emblems with which Queen Mary embellished the bed for her son;—the first is "the *Impressa* of King *Francis* the First," who, as the *Dialogue*, p. 24, affirms, "*changea la fierté des deuises de guerre en la douceur & ioyeuseté amoureuse*,"—"And to signify that he was glowing with the passions of love,—and so pleasing were they to him, that he had the boldness to say that he found nourishment in them;—for this reason he chose the Salamander, which dwelling in the flames is not consumed." (See woodcut next page.) The second, p. 25, is "the *Impressa* of *Henry* the second, the *French King*," the son and successor of Francis in 1547. (See woodcut, p. 127.)

He had adopted the motto and device when he was Dauphin, and continued to bear them on his succession to the throne;—in the one case to signify that he could not show his entire worth until he arrived at the heritage of the kingdom: and in the other that he must recover for his kingdom what had been lost to it, and so complete its whole orb.

It may appear almost impossible, even on a "Bed of State," to work twenty-nine Emblems and the arms of Scotland, England, and France, "severally by themselves and all quartered in many places of the bed,"—but a bed, probably of equal

Torquato Tasso in his *Rinaldo* maketh mention of a Knight who had a Rock placed in the Waves, with the Worde *Rompe ch'il percote*. And others hath the Seas waves with a Syren rising out of them, the word *Bella Maria*, which is the name of some Courteran. *Antonio Perenotto, Cardinal Granvella*, had for an *Impresa* the sea, a Ship on it, the word *Durate* out of the first of the Æneades, *Durate et vosmet rebus servate secundis*. *Tomaso de Marini*, Duca di terra nova, had for his *Impresa* the Waves with a sun over them, the word, *Nunquam siccabitur æstu*. The Prince of Orange used for his *Impresa* the *Waves* with an *Halcyon* in the midst of them, the word, *Medijs tranquillus in undis*, which is rather an *Embleme* than *Impresa*, because the figure is in the word."

antiquity, was a few years since, if not now, existing at Hinckley in Leicestershire, on which the same number "of emblematical devices, and Latin mottoes in capital letters conspicuously introduced," had found space and to spare. All these emblems are, I believe, taken from books of Shakespeare's time, or before

Paolo Jovio, 1562.

him; as, "An ostrich with a horseshoe in the beak," the word, *Spiritus durissima coquit;* "a cross-bow at full stretch," the word, *Ingenio superat vires.* "A hand playing with a serpent," the word, *Quis contra nos?* "The tree of life springing from the cross on an altar," the word, *Sola vivit in illo.* (See *Gentleman's Magazine*, vol. lxxxi. pt. 2, p. 416, Nov. 1811.)

Of the use of Emblematical devices in the ornamenting of houses, it will be sufficient to give the instance recorded in

See device at a later part of our volume.

"The History and Antiquities of Hawsted and Hardwick, in the county of Suffolk, by the Rev. Sir John Cullum, Bart:" the 2nd edition, royal 4to, London, 1813, pp. 159—165. This History makes it evident that in the reign of James I., if not earlier, Emblems were so known and admired as to have been freely

Paolo Jovio, 1561.

employed in adorning a closet for the last Lady Drury. "They mark the taste of an age that delighted in quaint wit, and laboured conceits of a thousand kinds," says Sir John; nevertheless, there were *forty-one* of them in "the painted closet" at Hawsted, and which, at the time of his writing, were put up in a small apartment at Hardwick. To all of them, as for King James's bed, and for the "very antient oak wooden bedstead, much gilt and ornamented," at Hinckley, there were a Latin motto and a device. Some of them we now present to the reader, adding occasionally to our author's account a further notice of the sources whence they were taken:

Emblem 1. *Ut parta labuntur*,—"As procured they are slipping away." "A monkey, sitting in a window and scattering money into the streets, is among the emblems of Gabriel Simeon:" it is also in our own English Whitney, p. 169, with the word, *Malè parta malè delabuntur*,—"Badly gotten, badly scattered."

Emblem 5. *Quò tendis?*—"Whither art thou going?" "A human tongue with bats' wings, and a scaly contorted tail, mounting into the air," "is among the *Heroical Devises of Paradin*:" leaf 65 of edition Anvers, 1562.

Emblem 8. *Jam satis*,—"Already enough." "Some trees, leafless, and torn up by the roots; with a confused landscape. Above, the sun, and a rainbow;" a note adds, "the most faire and bountiful queen of France Katherine used the sign of the rainbow for her armes, which is an infallible sign of peaceable calmeness and tranquillitie."—Paradin. Paradin's words, ed. 1562, leaf 38, are "*Madame Catherine, treschretienne Reine de France, a pour Deuise l'Arc celeste, ou Arc en ciel: qui est le vrai signe de clere serenité & tranquilité de Paix.*"

Emblem 20. *Dum transis, time*,—"While thou art crossing, fear." "A pilgrim traversing the earth: with a staff, and a light coloured hat, with a cockle shell in it." In *Hamlet*, act iv. sc. 5, l. 23, vol. viii. p. 129,—

> "How should I your true love know
> From another one?
> By his cockle hat and staff,
> And his sandal shoon."

"Or," remarks Sir John Cullum, "as he is described in Greene's *Never too Late*, 1610;"—

> "With *Hat of straw*, like to a swain,
> Shelter for the sun and rain,
> With scallop-shell before."

Emblem 24. *Fronte nulla fides*,—"No trustworthiness on the brow." The motto with a different device occurs in Whitney's *Emblems*, p. 100, and was adopted by him from the Emblems of John Sambucus; edition Antwerp, 1564, p. 177. The device, however, in "the painted closet" was "a man taking the dimensions of his own forehead with a pair of compasses;" "a contradiction," inaptly remarks Sir J. Cullum, "to a fancy of Aristotle's that the shape and several other circumstances, relative to a man's forehead, are expressive of his temper and inclination.

POVR CONGNOISTRE
VN HOMME.

Symeoni, 1561

Upon this supposition Symeon,* before mentioned, has invented an Emblem, representing a human head and a hand issuing out of a cloud, and pointing to it, with this motto, *Frons hominem præfert*,—"The forehead shows the man."

* See Symeon's *Devises Heroiques & Morales*, edition, 4to, Lyons, 1561, p. 246, where the motto and device occur, followed by the explanation, "*Ceux qui ont escrit de la Physiognomie, & mesme Aristote, disent parmy d'autres choses que le front de l'homme est celuy, par lequel on peut facilement cognoistre la qualité de ses mœurs, & la complexion de sa nature*," &c.

Emblem 33. *Speravi et perii*,—"I hoped and perished;"—the device, "A bird thrusting its head into an oyster partly open." A very similar sentiment is rather differently expressed by Whitney, p. 128, by Freitag, p. 169, and by Alciat, edition Paris, 1602, emb. 94, p. 437, from whom it was borrowed. Here the device is a mouse invading the domicile of an oyster, the motto, *Captivus ob gulam*,—"A prisoner through gluttony:" and the poor little mouse—

"That longe did feede on daintie crommes,
And safelie search'd the cupborde and the shelfe:
At lengthe for chaunge, vnto an Oyster commes,
Where of his deathe, he guiltie was him selfe:
The Oyster gap'd, the Mouse put in his head,
Where he was catch'd, and crush'd till he was dead."

Now, since so many Emblems from various authors were gathered to adorn a royal bed,* "a very antient oak wooden bed," and "a lady's closet," in widely distant parts of Britain, the supposition is most reasonable that the knowledge of them pervaded the cultivated and literary society of England and Scotland; and that Shakespeare, as a member of such society, would also be acquainted with them. The facts themselves are testimonies of a generally diffused judgment and taste, by which Emblematic devices for ornaments would be understood and appreciated.

And the facts we have mentioned are not solitary. About the period in question, in various mansions of the two kingdoms,

* It may be named as a curious fact that a copy of Alciat's *Emblemes en Latin et en Francois Vers pour Vers*, 16mo, Paris, 1561, contains the autograph of the Prolocutor against Mary Queen of Scots, W. PYKERYNGE, 1561, which would be about *five* years before Mary's son was born, for whom she wrought a bed of state. The edition of Paradin, a copy of which bears Geffrey Whitney's autograph, was printed at Antwerp in 1562; and one at least of his Emblems to the motto, *Video et taceo*, was written as early as 1568.

Device and Emblem were employed for their adorning. In 1619, close upon Shakespeare's time, and most likely influenced by his writings, there was set up in the Ancient Hall of the Leycesters of Lower Tabley, Cheshire, a richly carved and very curious chimney-piece, which may be briefly described as emblematizing country pursuits in connection with those of heraldry, literature, and the drama. In high relief, on one of the upright slabs, is a Lucrece, as the poet represents the deed, line 1723,—

> "Even here she sheathed in her harmless breast
> A harmful knife, that thence her soul unsheathed."

On the other slab is a Cleopatra, with the deadly creature in her hand, though not at the very moment when she addressed the asp;—act. v. sc. 2, l. 305, vol. ix. p. 151,—

> "Peace, peace!
> Dost thou not see my baby at my breast,
> That sucks the nurse asleep?"

The cross slab represents the hunting of stag and hare, which with the hounds have wonderfully human faces. Here might the words of Titus Andronicus, act. ii. sc. 2, l. 1, vol. vii. p. 456, be applied,—

> "The hunt is up, the moon is bright and gray,
> The fields are fragrant, and the woods are green;
> Uncouple here, and let us make a bay,
> And wake the emperor and his lovely bride,
> And rouse the prince, and ring a hunter's peal
> That all the court may echo with the noise."

The heraldic insignia of the Leycesters surmount the whole, but just below them, in a large medallion, is an undeniable Emblem, similar to one which in 1624 appeared in Hermann Hugo's *Pia Desideria*, bk. i. emb. xv. p. 117; *Defecit in dolore vita mea et anni mei in gemitibus* (*Psal.* xxx. or rather *Psal.* xxxi. 10),—"My life is spent with grief, and my years with sighing." Appended to Hugo's device are seventy-six lines of

Latin elegiac verses, and five pages of illustrative quotations from the Fathers; but the character of the Emblem will be seen from the device presented.

Drayton in his *Barons' Wars*, bk. vi., published in 1598, shows how the knowledge of our subject had spread and was spreading; as when he says of certain ornaments,—

> "About the border, in a curious fret,
> Emblems, impressas, hieroglyphics set."

There is, however, no occasion to pursue any further this branch of our theme, except it may be by a short continuation or extension of our Period of time, to show how Milton's greater Epic most curiously corresponds with the title-page of a Dutch Emblem-book, which appeared in 1642, several years before *Paradise Lost* was written. (See Plate X.) The book is, *Jan Vander Veens Zinne-beelden, oft Adams Appel*,—"John Vander Veen's Emblems, or Adam's Apple,"—presenting some Dutch doggerel lines, of which this English doggerel contains the meaning,—

> "When wounded Adam lay from the sin and the fall,
> Out of the accursed wound flowed corruption and gall;
> Hence is all wickedness and evil bred,
> As here in print ye see the Devil fashioned."

And again,—

> "Out of Adam's Apple springs
> Misery, Sin, and deadly things."

Singularly like to Milton's Introduction (bk. i. lines 1—4),—

> "Of Man's first disobedience, and the fruit
> Of that forbidden tree, whose mortal taste
> Brought death into the world, and all our woe,
> With loss of Eden."

With equal singularity appears in Boissard's *Theatrum Vitæ Humanæ*,—"Theatre of Human Life,"—edition Metz, 1596, p. 19,

IAN VANDER VEENS

ZINNE-BEELDEN,

OFT

ADAMS APPEL.

Verciert met seer aerdige Const-Plaeten

Mitsgaders

Syne oude ende nieuwe ongemee[illegible]e Bruydt-lofs ende Zege-zangen.

[illegible]

[illegible]

Lapsus diaboli.

CAP. III.

LAPSVS SATANÆ.

Cælestes Genios perfecta luce creatos
Peccatum horrendo perdidit exitio.
Sub Phlegethonte Satan Cocyti mergitur undis:
Pœna eadem reliquis addita dæmonibus.

C 2

Fall of Satan from Boissards Theatrum Vitæ Humanæ, 1596

the coincidence with Milton's Fall of the rebel Angels. We have here pictured and described the Fall of Satan (see Plate XI.) almost as in modern days Turner depicted it, and as Milton has narrated the terrible overthrow (*Paradise Lost,* bk. vi.), when they were pursued

"With terrors, and with furies, to the bounds
And crystal wall of heaven; which, opening wide,
Roll'd inward, and a spacious gap disclosed
Into the wasteful deep: the monstrous sight
Struck them with horror backward, but far worse
Urged them behind: headlong themselves they threw
Down from the verge of heaven. . . . . .
Nine days they fell: confounded Chaos roar'd,
And felt tenfold confusion in their fall
Through his wild anarchy." *

That same *Theatre of Human Life,* p. 1 (see Plate XIV.), also contains a most apt picture of Shakespeare's lines, *As You Like It,* act. ii. sc. 7, l. 139, vol. ii. p. 409,—

"All the world's a stage,
And all the men and women merely players:
They have their exits and their entrances;
And one man in his time plays many parts,
His acts being seven ages."

The same notion is repeated in the *Merchant of Venice,* act. i. sc. 1, l. 77, vol. ii. p. 281, when Antonio says,—

"I hold the world but as the world, Gratiano;
A stage where every man must play a part,
And mine a sad one."

In England, as elsewhere, emblematical carvings and writings preceded books of Emblems, that is, books in which the art of

* In some of the more elaborate of Plantin's devices, the action of "the omnific word" seems pictured, though in very humble degree,—

"In his hand
He took the golden compasses, prepared
In God's eternal store, to circumscribe
This universe, and all created things:
One foot he centred, and the other turn'd
Round through the vast profundity obscure."—*Par. Lost,* bk. vii.

the engraver and the genius of the poet were both employed to illustrate one and the same motto, sentiment, or proverbial saying. Not to repeat what may be found in Chaucer and others, Spenser's *Visions of Bellay*,[1] alluded to in the fac-simile reprint of Whitney, pp. xvi & xvii, needed only the designer and engraver to make them as perfectly Emblem-books as were the publications of Brant, Alciatus and Perriere. Those visions portray in words what an artist might express by a picture. For example, in Moxon's edition, 1845, p. 438, iv.,—

> "I saw raisde vp on pillers of Iuorie,
> Wereof the bases were of richest golde,
> The chapters Alabaster, Christall frises,
> The double front of a triumphall arke.
> On eche side portraide was a Victorie,
> With golden wings, in habite of a nymph
> And set on hie vpon triumphing chaire;
> The auncient glorie of the Romane lordes.
> The worke did shew it selfe not wrought by man,
> But rather made by his owne skilfull hands
> That forgeth thunder dartes for Ioue his sire.
> Let me no more see faire thing vnder heauen,
> Sith I haue seene so faire a thing as this,
> With sodaine falling broken all to dust."

Now what artist's skill would not suffice from this description to delineate "the pillers of Iuorie," "the chapters of Alabaster," "a Victorie with golden wings," and "the triumphing chaire, the auncient glorie of the Romane lordes;" and to make the whole a lively and most cunning Emblem?

In his *Shephcards Calender*, indeed, to each of the months Spenser appends what he names an "Emblem;" it is a motto, or device, from Greek, Latin, Italian, French, or English, expressive of the supposed leading idea of each Eclogue, and forming

[1] Derived from Joachim du Bellay (who died in 1560 at the age of thirty-seven), the excellence of whose poetry entitled him to be named the Ovid of France. There is good evidence to show that Du Bellay was well acquainted with the Emblematists, who in his time were rising into fame.

a moral to it. The folio edition of Spenser's works, issued in 1616, gives woodcuts for each month, and so approaches very closely to the Emblematists of a former century. In the month "FEBRVARIE," there is introduced a veritable word-picture of "the Oake and the Brier," and also a pictorial illustration, with the sign of the Fishes in the clouds, to indicate the season of

FEBRVARIE.

Spenser, 1616.

the year. The oak is described as "broughten to miserie:" l. 213,—

> For nought mought they quitten him from decay,
> For fiercely the goodman at him did laye.
> The blocke oft groned under the blow,
> And sighed to see his neere overthrow.
> In fine, the steele had pierced his pith,
> Tho downe to the earth hee fell forthwith.'

The Brier, "puffed up with pryde," has his turn of adversity: l. 234,—

> "That nowe upright hee can stand no more;
> And, being downe, is trod in the durt
> Of cattel, and brouzed, and sorely hurt."

The whole Eclogue, or Fable, is rounded off by the curious Italian proverbs, to which Spenser gives the name of Emblems,—

THENOTS EMBLEME.
"Iddio, perche é vecchio,
Fa suoi al suo essempio.

CUDDIES EMBLEME.
"Niuno vecchio
Spavento Iddio.

i. e., "God, although he is very aged, makes his friends copies of himself," makes them aged too; but the biting satire is added, "No old man is ever terrified by Jove."

IVNE.

Spenser, 1579.

The Emblem for June represents a scene which the poet does not describe; it is the field of the haymakers, with the zodiacal sign of the Crab, and appropriate to the characters of Hobbinoll and Colin Clout,—but it certainly does not translate into pictures what the poet had delineated in words of great beauty:

"Lo! Colin, here the place whose plesaunt syte
From other shades hath weaned my wandring minde,
Tell mee, what wants mee here to worke delyte?
The simple ayre, the gentle warbling winde,
So calme, so coole, as nowhere else I finde;
The grassie grounde with daintie daysies dight,
The bramble bush, where byrdes of every kinde
To the waters fall their tunes attemper right."

No more needs be said respecting the knowledge of Emblem-books in Britain, unless it be to give the remarks of Tod, the learned editor of Spenser's works, edition 1845, p. x. "*The Visions* are little things, done probably when Spenser was *young*, according to the taste of the times for Emblems.* The *Theatre of Wordlings*, I must add, evidently presents a series of Emblems."

II. We will now state some of the general indications that Shakespeare was acquainted with Emblem-books, or at least had imbibed "the taste of the times."

Here and there in Shakespeare's works, even from the way in which sayings and mottoes, in Spanish, as well as in French and Latin, are employed, we have indications that he had seen and, it may be, had studied some of the Emblem-writers of his day, and participated of their spirit. Thus Falstaff's friend, the ancient Pistol, 2 *Henry IV.* act. ii. sc. 4, l. 165, vol. iv. p. 405, quotes the doggerel line, as given in the note, *Si fortuna me tormenta, il sperare me contenta,*—"If fortune torments me, hope contents me,"—which doubtless was the motto on his sword,

* Dibdin, in his *Bibliomania*, p. 331, adduces an instance; he says, "In the PRAYER-BOOK which goes by the name of QUEEN ELIZABETH'S, there is a portrait of her Majesty kneeling, upon a superb cushion, with elevated hands, in prayer. This book was first printed in 1575, and is decorated with woodcut borders of considerable spirit and beauty, representing, among other things, some of the subjects of Holbein's *Dance of Death*."

which he immediately lays down. As quoted, the line is Spanish; a slight alteration would make it Italian; but Douce's conjecture appears well founded, that as Pistol was preparing to lay aside his sword, he read off the motto which was upon it. Such mottoes were common as inscriptions upon swords; and Douce, vol. i. pp. 452, 3, gives the drawing of one with the French line, "Si fortune me tourmente, L'esperance me contente."

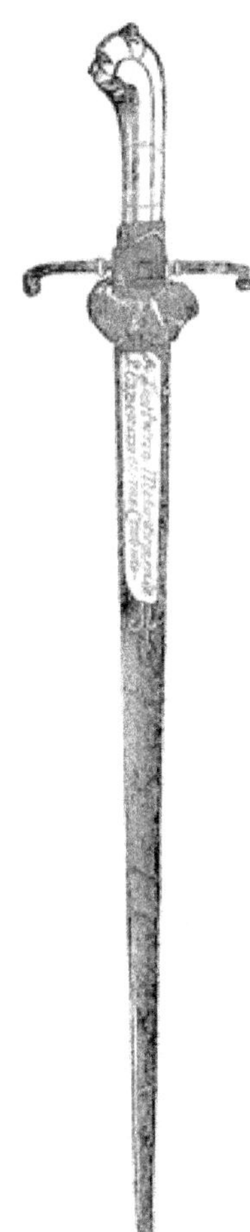

Douce, 1807.

He gives it, too, as a fact, that "Haniball Gonsaga being in the low-countries overthrowne from his horse by an English captaine and commanded to yeeld himselfe prisoner, *kist his sword*, and gave it to the Englishman, saying, '*Si fortuna me tormenta, il speranza me contenta.*'" Allow that Shakespeare served in the Netherlands, and we may readily suppose that he had heard the motto from the very Englishman to whom Gonsaga had surrendered.

The Clown in *Twelfth Night*, act. i. sc. 5, l. 50, vol. iii. p. 234, replies to the Lady Olivia ordering him as a fool to be taken away,—"Misprision in the highest degree! Lady, *cucullus non facit monachum*, [—it is not the hood that makes the monk,] —that's as much to say as I wear not motley in my brain." The saying is one which might appropriately adorn any Emblem-book of the day;—and the motley-wear receives a good illustration from a corresponding expression in Whitney, p. 81:

"The little childe, is pleas'de with cockhorse gaie,
Although he aske a courser of the beste:
The ideot likes, with bables for to plaie,
And is disgrac'de when he is brauelie dreste:
A motley coate, a cockescombe, or a bell,
Hee better likes, than Jewelles that excell."

So, during Cade's rebellion, when the phrase is applied by Lord Say, in answer to Dick the butcher's question, "What say you of Kent?" 2 *Henry VI.* act. iv. sc. 7, l. 49, vol. v. p. 197,—

"Nothing but this: 'Tis *bona terra, mala gens;*"

or when falling under the attack of York on the field of St. Alban's, Lord Clifford exclaims, *La fin couronne les œuvres* (2 *Henry VI.* act. v. sc. 2, l. 28, vol. v. p. 217); these again are instances after the methods of Emblem-writers; and if they were carried out, as might be done, would present all the characteristics of the Emblem, in motto, illustrative woodcut, and descriptive verses.

It is but an allusion, and yet the opening scene, act. i. sc. 1, l. 50, vol. ii. p. 280, of the *Merchant of Venice* might borrow that allusion from an expression of Alciatus, edition Antwerp, 1581, p. 92, *Jane bifrons,*—"two-headed Janus." (See woodcut, p. 140.)

IANE *bifrons, qui iam transacta futuraq̃ calles,*
Quiq̃ retro sannas, sicut & ante, vides;—

"Janus two-fronted, who things past and future well knowest,
And who mockings behind, as also before dost behold." *

* Amplified by Whitney, p. 108, *Respice, et prospice,* "Look back, and look forward."

"THE former parte, nowe paste, of this my booke,
The seconde parte in order doth insue:
Which, I beginne with IANVS double looke,
That as hee sees, the yeares both oulde, and newe,
So, with regarde, I may these partes behoulde,
Perusinge ofte, the newe, and eeke the oulde

And if, that faulte within vs doe appeare,
Within the yeare, that is alreadie donne,
As IANVS biddes vs alter with the yeare,
And make amendes, within the yeare begonne,
Euen so, my selfe suruayghinge what is past:
With greater heede, may take in hande the laste."

The friends of Antonio banter him for his sadness, and one of them avers,—

> "Now by two-headed Janus,
> Nature hath framed strange fellows in her time:
> Some that will evermore peep through their eyes,
> And laugh like parrots at a bag-piper;
> And other of such vinegar aspect
> That they'll not show their teeth in way of smile,
> Though Nestor swear the jest be laughable."

Even if Shakespeare understood no Latin, the picture itself, or a similar one, would be sufficient to give origin to the phrase "two-headed Janus." He adopts the picture, but not one of the sentiments; these, however, he did not need: it was only as a passing illustration that he named Janus, and how the author described the god's qualities was no part of his purpose.

Alciat, 1581.

Or if the source of the phrase be not in Alciatus, it may have been derived either from Whitney's *Choice of Emblemes*, p. 108, or from Perriere's *Theatre des Bons Engins*, Paris, 1539, emb. i., reproduced in 1866 to illustrate pl. 30 of the fac-simile reprint of Whitney. Perriere's French stanza is to this effect:—

> "In old times the god Janus with two faces
> Our ancients did delineate and portray,
> To demonstrate that counsels of wise races
> Look to a future, as well as the past day:
> In fact all time of deeds should leave the traces.

And of the past recordance ever have ;
The future should foresee like providence,
Following up virtue in each noble quality,
Seeking God's strength from sinfulness to save.
Who thus shall do will learn by evidence
That he has power to live in great tranquillity.*

Another instance of Emblem-like delineation, or description, we have in *King Henry V.* act iii. sc. 7, lines 10—17, vol. iv. p. 549. Louis the Dauphin, praising his own horse, as if bounding from the earth like a tennis ball (see woodcut on next page), exclaims,—

"I will not change my horse with any that treads but on four pasterns. Ça, ha! he bounds from the earth, as if his entrails were hairs; le cheval volant, the Pegasus, chez les narines de feu! When I bestride him, I soar, I am a hawk: he trots the air; the earth sings when he touches it; the basest horn of his hoof is more musical than the pipe of Hermes.†

Orl. He's of the colour of the nutmeg.

Dau. And of the heat of the ginger. It is a beast for Perseus: he is pure air and fire; and the dull elements of earth and water never appear in him, but only in patient stillness, while his rider mounts him: he is indeed a horse; and all other jades you may call beasts.

Con. Indeed, my lord, it is a most absolute and excellent horse.

Dau. It is the prince of palfreys; his neigh is like the bidding of a monarch, and his countenance enforces homage."

---

* We subjoin the old French,—

"LE Dieu Ianus iadis à deux visages,
Noz anciẽs ont pourtraict & trassé,
Pour demõstrer que l'aduis des gẽs sages
Visé au futur aussi bien qu' au passé,
Tout temps doibt estré en effect cõpassé
Et du passé auoir la recordance,
Pour au futur preueoir en prouidence,
Suyuant vertu en toute qualité,
Qui le fera verra par euidence,
Qu'il pourra viure en grãd tranquillité."

† The illustration we immediately choose is from Sym. cxxxvii. p. cccxiiii. of Achilles Bocchius, edition Bologna, 1555, with the motto—

"ARS RHETOR. TRIPLEX MOVET, IVVAT, DOCET,
SED PRÆPOTENS EST VERITAS DIVINITVS.
SIC MONSTRA VITIOR. DOMAT PRVDENTIA."

Rhetoric's art threefold, it moves, delights, instructs,
But powerful above all is truth of heaven inspired.
So the monsters of our vices doth wisdom's self subdue.

This lively description suits well the device of a Paris printer, Christian Wechel, who, in 1540,[1] dwelt "a l'enseigne du Cheval

volant;" or that of Claude Marnius of Francfort, who, before 1602, had a similar trade-mark. At least three of Reusner's *Emblems*, edition Francfort, 1581, have the same device; and the Dauphin's paragon answers exactly to a Pegasus in the first

[1] See *Les Emblemes de Maistre Andre Alciat, mis en rime francoyse*, Paris, 1540.

Emblem, dedicated to Rudolph II., who, on the death of his father, Maximilian, became Emperor of Germany.

ΣΥΝ ΑΥΩ ΕΡΧΟΜΕΝΩ.
Non abſque Theſeo.
EMBLEMA I.

Reusner, 1581.

Ad Diuum Rudolphum Secundum
Cæſarem Romanum.

Here * we have a Pegasus like that which Shakespeare praises; it has a warrior on its back, and bounds along, trotting the air. In other two of Reusner's *Emblems,* the Winged Horse is standing on the ground, with Perseus near him; and in a third, entitled *Principis boni imago,*—"Portrait of a good prince,"—St. George is represented on a flying steed † attacking the Dragon, and delivering from its fury the Maiden chained to a rock, that shadows forth a suffering and persecuted church. Shakespeare probably had seen these or similar drawings before

* The device, however, of this Emblem is copied from Symeoni's *Vita et Metamorfoseo d'Ouidio,* Lyons, 1559, p. 72; as also are some others used by Reusner.

† In *Troilus and Cressida,* act i. sc. 3, l. 39, vol. vi. p. 142, we read,—

"Anon beheld
The strong-ribb'd bark through liquid mountains cut,
Bounding between the two moist elements,
Like Perseus' horse."

he described Louis the Dauphin riding on a charger that had nostrils of fire.

The qualities of good horsemanship Shakespeare specially admired. Hence those lines in *Hamlet*, act iv. sc. 7, l. 84, vol. viii. p. 145,—

"I've seen myself, and served against, the French,
And they can well on horseback: but this gallant
Had witchcraft in't; he grew unto his seat,
And to such wondrous doing brought his horse,
As he had been incorpsed and demi-natured
With the brave beast."

An emblem in Alciatus, edition 1551, p. 20, also gives the mounted warrior on the winged horse;—it is Bellerophon in his contest with the Chimæra. The accompanying stanza has in it an expression like one which the dramatist uses,—

"Sic tu Pegaseis vectus petis æthera pennis,"—

"So thou being borne on the wings of Pegasus seekest the air."

Equally tasting of the Emblem-writers of Henry's and Elizabeth's reigns is that other proverb in French which Shakespeare places in the mouth of the Dauphin Louis. The subject is still his "paragon of animals," which he prefers even to his mistress. See *Henry V.* act iii. sc. 7, l. 54, vol iv. p. 550. "I had rather," he says, "have my horse to my mistress;" and the Constable replies, "I had as lief have my mistress a jade."

"*Dau.* I tell thee, constable, my mistress wears his own hair.

Con. I could make as true a boast as that, if I had a sow to my mistress.

Dau. Le chien est retourné à son propre vomissement, et la truie lavée au bourbier. Thou makest use of any thing." ["The dog has returned to his vomit, and the sow that had been washed, to her mire."]

Though the French is almost a literal rendering of the Latin Vulgate, 2 *Pet.* ii. 23, "Canis reversus ad suum vomitum: & sus lota in volutabro luti;" the whole conception is in the spirit of Freitag's *Mythologia Ethica*, Antwerp, 1579, in which there is appended to each emblem a text of Scripture. A subject is chosen, a description of it given, an engraving placed on the opposite page, and at the foot some passage from the Latin vulgate is applied.

It may indeed be objected that, if Shakespeare was well acquainted with the Emblem literature it is surprising he should pass over, almost in silence, some Devices which partake peculiarly of his general spirit, and which would furnish suggestions for very forcible and very appropriate descriptions. Were we to examine his works thoroughly, we should discover some very remarkable omissions of subjects that appear to be exactly after his own method and perfectly natural to certain parts of his dramas. We may instance the almost total want of commendation for the moral qualities of the dog, whether "mastiff, greyhound, mongrel grim, hound or spaniel, brach or lym, or bob-tail tike, or trundle-tail." The whole race is under a ban.

So industry, diligence, with their attendant advantages,—negligence, idleness, with their disadvantages, are scarcely alluded to, and but incidentally praised or blamed.

Perriere, 1539.

We may take one of Perriere's Emblems, the 101st of *Les Bons Engins*, as our example, to show rather divergence than agreement,—or, at any rate, a different way of treating the subject.

"En ce pourtraict pouuez veoir diligence,
Tenant en main le cornet de copie:
Elle triumphe en grand magnificence:
Car de paresse onc ne fut assoupie:

Dessoubz ses piedz tiẽt faminę acroupie
Et attachéę en grand captiuité :
Puis les formys par leur hastiuité
Diligemment tirent le tout ensemble :
Pour demonstrer qu' auec oysiuité,
Impossiblę est que grãdz biẽs l'õ assẽble."

"A portrait here you see of diligence
Bearing in hand full plenty's horn,
Triumphant in her great magnificence,
And ever holding laziness in scorn ;
Crouching beneath her feet famine forlorn
In fetters bound of strong captivity.
And then the ants with their activity
The whole most diligently along do draw,—
A demonstration clear that idleness
Finds it impossible by nature's law
With stores of goods her poverty to bless."

Under the motto, *Otiosi semper egentes*,—"The idle always destitute,"—Whitney, p. 175, describes the same conditions,—

"Here, Idlenes doth weepe amid her wantes,
Neare famished : whome, labour whippes for Ire :
Here, labour sittes in chariot drawen with antes :
And dothe abounde with all he can desire.
The grashopper, the toyling ante derides,
In Sommers heate, cause she for coulde prouides."

The idea is in some degree approached in the Chorus of *Henry V.* act i. l. 5, vol. iv. p. 491,—

"Then should the warlike Harry, like himself
Assume the port of Mars ; and at his heels,
Leash'd in like hounds, should famine, sword, and fire
Crouch for employment."

The triumph of industry may also be inferred from the marriage blessing which Ceres pronounces in the Masque of the *Tempest*, act iv. sc. 1, l. 110, vol. i. p. 57,—

"Earth's increase, foison plenty,
Barns and garners never empty ;

Vines with clustering bunches growing;
Plants with goodly burthen bowing;
Spring come to you at the farthest
In the very end of harvest!
Scarcity and want shall shun you,
Ceres' blessing so is on you."

Yet for labour, work, industry, diligence, or by whatever other name the virtue of steady exertion may be known, there is scarcely a word of praise in Shakespeare's abundant vocabulary, and of its effects no clear description. We are told in *Cymbeline*, act iii. sc. 6, l. 31, vol. ix. p. 240,—

"The sweat of industry would dry and die,
But for the end it works to. . . . . Weariness
Can snore upon the flint, when resty sloth
Finds the down pillow hard."

And in contrasting the cares of royalty with the sound sleep of the slave, Henry V. (act iv. sc. 1, l. 256, vol iv. p. 564) declares that the slave,—

"Never sees horrid night, the child of hell;
But like a lacquey, from the rise to set,
Sweats in the eye of Phœbus, and all night
Sleeps in Elysium; next day, after dawn,
Doth rise, and help Hyperion to his horse;
And follow so the ever running year
With profitable labour to his grave;"

but the subject is never entered upon in its moral and social aspects, unless the evils which are ascribed by the Duke of Burgundy (*Henry V.* act v. sc. 2, l. 48, vol. iv. p. 596) to war, are also to be attributed to the negligence which war creates,—

"The even mead, that erst brought sweetly forth
The freckled cowslip, burnet and green clover,
Wanting the scythe, all uncorrected, rank,
Conceives by idleness; and nothing teems
But hateful docks, rough thistles, kecksies, burs,
Losing both beauty and utility."

Another instance we may give of that Emblem spirit, which often occurs in Shakespeare, and at the same time we may supply an example of Freitag's method of illustrating a subject, and of appending to it a scriptural quotation. (See *Mythologia Ethica*, Antwerp, 1579, p. 29.) The instance is from *King Lear*, act ii. sc. 4, l. 61, vol. viii. p. 317, and the subject, *Contraria industriæ ac desidiæ præmia*—"The opposite rewards of industry and slothfulness."

When Lear had arrived at the Earl of Gloster's castle, Kent inquires,—

> "How chance the king comes with so small a train?
>
> *Fool.* An thou hadst been set i' the stocks for that question, thou hadst well deserv'd it.
>
> *Gent.* Why, fool?
>
> *Fool.* We'll set thee to school to an ant to teach thee there's no labouring in the winter."

That school we have presented to us in Freitag's engraving (see woodcut on next page), and in the stanzas of Whitney, p. 159. There are the ne'er-do-well grasshopper and the sage schoolmaster of an ant, propounding, we may suppose, the wise saying, *Dum ætatis ver agitur: consule brumæ*,—"While the spring of life is passing, consult for winter,"—and the poet moralizes thus:

> "IN winter coulde, when tree, and bushe, was bare,
> And frost had nip'd the rootes of tender grasse:
> The antes, with ioye did feede vpon their fare,
> Which they had stor'de, while sommers season was:
> To whome, for foode the grashopper did crie,
> And said she staru'd, if they did helpe denie.
>
> Whereat, an ante, with longe experience wise?
> And frost, and snowe, had manie winters seene:
> Inquired, what in sommer was her guise.
> Quoth she, I songe, and hop't in meadowes greene:
> Then quoth the ante, content thee with thy chaunce,
> For to thy songe, nowe art thou light to daunce?"

Contraria induſtriæ ac deſidiæ
præmia.

Freitag, 1579.

Propter frigus piger arare noluit: mendicabit ergo æſtate, & non dabitur illi.
Prouerb. 20, 4.

"The sluggard will not plow by reason of the cold; therefore shall he beg in harvest, and have nothing."

Freitag's representation makes indeed a change in the season at which the "ante, with longe experience wise," administers her reproof; but it is equally the school for learning in the time of youth and strength, to provide for the infirmities of age and the adversities of fortune.

And more than similar in spirit to the Emblem writers which preceded, almost emblems themselves, are the whole scenes from the *Merchant of Venice*, act ii. sc. 7 and 9, and act iii. sc. 2, where are introduced the three caskets of gold, of silver, and of lead, by the choice of which the fate of Portia is to be determined,*—

> "The first, of gold, who this inscription bears,
> 'Who chooseth me shall gain what many men desire;'
> The second, silver, which this promise carries,
> 'Who chooseth me shall get as much as he deserves;'
> This third, dull lead, with warning all as blunt,
> 'Who chooseth me must give and hazard all he hath.'"
>
> Act ii. sc. 7, lines 4—9.

And when the caskets are opened, the drawings and the inscriptions on the written scrolls, which are then taken out, examined and read, are exactly like the engravings and the verses by which emblems and their mottoes are set forth. Thus, on unlocking the golden casket, the Prince of Morocco exclaims,—

> "O hell! what have we here?
> A carrion Death, within whose empty eye
> There is a written scroll! I'll read the writing. [*Reads.*]
> All that glisters is not gold;
> Often have you heard that told:
> Many a man his life hath sold
> But my outside to behold:
> Gilded tombs do worms infold.
> Had you been as wise as bold,
> Young in limbs, in judgment old,
> Your answer had not been inscroll'd:
> Fare you well; your suit is cold.'
>
> Act ii. sc. 7, lines 62—73.

The Prince of Arragon, also, on opening the silver casket, receives not merely a written scroll, as is represented in Symeoni's "DISTICHI MORALI,"—*Moral Stanzas*,—but what corresponds to the device or woodcut of the Emblem-book;

* The description and quotations are almost identical with the Whitney *Dissertations*, pp. 294-6.

"The portrait of a blinking idiot," who presents to him "The schedule," or explanatory rhymes,—

> "The fire seven times tried this:
> Seven times tried that judgment is,
> That did never choose amiss.
> Some there be that shadows kiss;
> Such have but a shadow's bliss:
> There be fools alive, I wis,
> Silver'd o'er; and so was this.
> Take what wife you will to bed,
> I will ever be your head:
> So be gone: you are sped."
>
> Act ii. sc. 9, lines 63–72.

These Emblems of Shakespeare's are therefore complete in all their parts; the mottoes, the pictures, "a carrion Death" and "a blinking idiot," and the descriptive verses.

The words of Portia (act. ii. sc. 9, l. 79, vol. ii. p. 319), when the Prince of Arragon says,—

> "Sweet adieu, I'll keep my oath,
> Patiently to bear my wroth;"

Cosi viuo Piacer conduce à morte.

Paradin, 1562.

are moreover a direct reference to the Emblems which occur in various authors. *Les Devises Heroiques*, by Claude Paradin, Antwerp, 1562, contains the adjoining Emblem, *Too lively a pleasure conducts to death.*

And Giles Corrozet in his "HECATOMGRAPHIE, C'està dire, les descriptions de cent figures, &c.,"* adopting the motto, *War*

* See Whitney's *Fac-simile Reprint*, plate 32.

is sweet only to the inexperienced, presents, in illustration, a butterfly fluttering towards a candle.

La guerre doulce aux inexperimentez.

Corrozet, 1540.

Les Papillons se vont bruſler
A la chandelle qui reluyſt.
Tel veult à la bataille aller
Qui ne ſçaiſt combien guerre nuyſt.

"The Butterflies themselves are about to burn,
In the candle which still shines on and warms;
Such foolish, wish to battle fields to turn,
Who know not of the war, how much it harms."

This device, in fact, was one extremely popular with the Emblem literati. Boissard and Messin's *Emblems*, 1588, pp. 58, 59, present it to the mottoes, "Temerité dangereuse," or *Temere ac Periculose*,—"rashly and dangerously." Joachim Camerarius, in his Emblems *Ex Volatilibus et Insectis* (Nuremberg, 4to, 1596), uses it, with the motto, *Brevis et damnosa Voluptas*—"A short and destructive pleasure,"—and fortifies himself in adopting it by no less authorities than Æschylus and Aristotle. *Emblemes of Love, with Verses in Latin, English, and Italian*, by Otho Vænius, 4to, Antwerp, 1608, present Cupid to us, at p. 102, as watching the moths and the flames with great earnestness, the mottoes being, *Brevis et damnosa voluptas*,—"For one pleasure a thousand paynes,"—and *Breue gioia*,—"Brief the gladness."

There is, too, on the same subject, the elegant device which Symeoni gives at p. 25 of his "DISTICHI MORALI," and which we repeat on the next page.

The subject is, *Of Love too much;* and the motto, "Too much pleasure leads to death," is thus set forth, almost literally, by English rhymes:—

"In moderation Love is praised and prized,
Loss and dishonour in excess it brings:
In burning warmth how fail its boasted wings,
As simple butterflies in light chastised."

D'AMOR SO-
VERCHIO.

Giovio and Symeoni, 1561

Il moderato amor ſi loda & prezza,
Ma il troppo apporta danno & diſhonore,
Et ſpeſſo manca nel ſouerchio ardore,
Qual ſemplice farfalla al lume auuezza.

Coſi troppo piacer conduce à morte.

Now can there be unreasonableness in supposing that out of these many Emblem writers Shakespeare may have had some one in view when he ascribed to Portia the words,—

"Thus hath the candle singed the moth.
O, these deliberate fools! when they do choose,
They have the wisdom by their wit to lose."

Act ii. sc. 9, lines 79—81.

The opening of the third of the caskets (act. iii. sc. 2, l. 115, vol. ii. p. 328), that made of lead, is also as much an Emblem delineation as the other two, excelling them, indeed, in the beauty of the language as well as in the excellence of the device, a very paragon of gracefulness. "What find I here?" demands Bassanio: and himself replies,—

> "Fair Portia's counterfeit! What demi-god
> Hath come so near creation? Move these eyes?
> Or whether, riding on the balls of mine
> Seem they in motion? Here are sever'd lips,
> Parted with sugar breath: so sweet a bar
> Should sunder such sweet friends. Here in her hairs
> The painter plays the spider, and hath woven
> A golden mesh to entrap the hearts of men,
> Faster than gnats in cobwebs:* but her eyes,—
> How could he see to do them? Having made one,
> Methinks it should have power to steal both his,
> And leave itself unfurnish'd. Yet look, how far
> The substance of my praise doth wrong this shadow
> In underprizing it, so far this shadow
> Doth limp behind the substance. Here's a scroll,
> The continent and summary of my fortune.
> [*Reads*] You that choose not by the view,
> Chance as fair, and choose as true!
> Since this fortune falls to you,
> Be content and seek no new.
> If you will be pleased with this,
> And hold your fortune for your bliss,
> Turn you where your lady is,
> And claim her with a loving kiss."

In these scenes of the casket, Shakespeare himself, therefore, is undoubtedly an Emblem writer; and there needs only the

* In the work of Joachim Camerarius, just quoted, at p. 152, to the motto, "VIOLENTIOR EXIT,"—*The more violent escapes*, p. 99,—there is the device of Gnats and Wasps in a cobweb, with the stanza,—

> "*Innodat culicem, sed vespæ pervia tela est;*
> *Sic rumpit leges vis, quibus hæret inops.*"

> "The gnat the web entangles, but to the wasp
> Throughout is pervious: so force breaks laws,
> To which the helpless is held bound in chains."

woodcut, or the engraving, to render them as perfect examples of Emblem writing as any that issued from the pens of Alciatus, Symeoni, and Beza. The dramatist may have been sparing in his use of this tempting method of illustration, yet, with the instances before us, we arrive at the conclusion that Shakespeare knew well what Emblems were. And surely he had seen, and in some degree studied, various portions of the Emblem literature which was anterior to, or contemporary with himself.

C[illegible], ed. 1555. Motto from Plato.

CHAPTER V.

SIX DIRECT REFERENCES IN THE PERICLES TO BOOKS OF EMBLEMS, SOME OF THEIR DEVICES DESCRIBED, AND OF THEIR MOTTOES QUOTED.

SHAKESPEARE'S name, in three quarto editions, published during his lifetime, appears as author of the play of *Pericles, Prince of Tyre*; and if a decision be made that the authorship belongs to him, and that in the main the work was his composition, then our previous conjectures are changed into certainties, and we can confidently declare who were the Emblem writers he refers to, and can exhibit the very passages from their books which he has copied and adopted.

The early folio editions of the plays, those of 1623 and 1632, omit the *Pericles* altogether, but later editions restore it to a place among the works of Shakespeare. Dr. Farmer contends that the hand of the great dramatist is visible only in the last act; but others controvert this opinion, and maintain, though he was not the fabricator of the plot, nor the author of every dialogue and chorus, that his genius is evident in several passages.

In Knight's *Pictorial Shakspere*, supplemental volume, p. 13, we are informed: "The first edition of *Pericles* appeared in 1609," —several years before the dramatist's death,—"under the following title,—'The late and much admired play, called *Pericles, Prince of Tyre, &c.* By William Shakespeare: London, Glosson, 1609.'"

According to the Cambridge editors, vol. ix. p. i, Preface, "another edition was issued in the same year." The publication was repeated in 1611, 1619, 1630 and 1635, so that at the very time when Shakespeare was living, his authorship was set forth; and after his death, while his friends and contemporaries were alive, the opinion still prevailed.

The conclusion at which Knight arrives, sup. vol. pp. 118, 119, is thus stated by him: "We advocate the belief that *Pyrocles*, or *Pericles* was a very early work of Shakspere in some form, however different from that which we possess." And again, "We think that the *Pericles* of the beginning of the seventeenth century was the revival of a play written by Shakspere some twenty years earlier. . . . Let us accept Dryden's opinion, that

"'Shakespeare's own Muse his Pericles first bore.'"

The Cambridge editors, vol. ix. p. 10, ed. 1866, gave a firmer judgment:—"There can be no doubt that the hand of Shakespeare is traceable in many of the scenes, and that throughout the play he largely retouched, and even rewrote, the work of some inferior dramatist. But the text has come down to us in so maimed and imperfect a state that we can no more judge of what the play was when it left the master's hand than we should have been able to judge of *Romeo and Juliet*, if we had only had the first quarto as authority for the text."

Our own Hallam tells us,—"*Pericles* is generally reckoned to be in part, and only in part, the work of Shakespeare:" but with great confidence the critic Schlegel declares,—"This piece was acknowledged to be a work, but a youthful work of Shakespeare's. It is most undoubtedly his, and it has been admitted into several later editions of his works. The supposed imperfections originate in the circumstance that Shakespeare here handled a childish and extravagant romance of the old poet Gower, and was unwilling to drag the subject out of its proper sphere. Hence he even introduces Gower himself, and makes him deliver a prologue in his own antiquated language and versification. This power of assuming so foreign a manner is at least no proof of helplessness."

There are, then, strong probabilities that in the main the *Pericles* was Shakespeare's own composition, or at least was adopted by him; it belongs to his early dramatic life, and at any rate it may be taken as evidence to show that the Emblem writers were known and made use of between 1589 and 1609 by the dramatists of England.

Books of Emblems are not indeed mentioned by their titles, nor so quoted in the *Pericles* as we are accustomed to do, by making direct references; they were a kind of common property, on which everyone might pasture his Pegasus or his Mule without any obligation to tell where his charger had been grazing. The allusions, however, are so plain, the words so exactly alike, that they cannot be misunderstood. The author was of a certainty acquainted with more than one Emblem writer, in more than one language, and Paradin, Symeoni, and our own Whitney may be recognised in his pages. We conclude that he had them before him, and copied from them when he penned the second scene of the Second Act of *Pericles*.

The Dialogue is between Simonides, king of Pentapolis, and his daughter, Thaisa, on occasion of the "triumph," or festive pageantry, which was held in honour of her birthday. (*Pericles*, act. ii. sc. 2, lines 17—47, vol. ix. pp. 343, 344.)

"*Enter a* Knight; *he passes over, and his Squire presents his shield to the Princess.*

Sim. Who is the first that doth prefer himself?
Thai. A knight of Sparta, my renowned father:
And the device he bears upon his shield
Is a black Ethiope reaching at the sun:
The word, 'Lux tua vita mihi.'

Sim. He loves you well that holds his life of you.
[*The Second Knight passes.*
Who is the second that presents himself?
Thai. A prince of Macedon, my royal father;
And the device he bears upon his shield
Is an arm'd knight that's conquer'd by a lady;
The motto thus, in Spanish, 'Piu por dulzura que por fuerza.'
[*The Third Knight passes.*
Sim. And what's the third?
Thai. The third of Antioch;
And his device, a wreath of chivalry;
The word, 'Me pompæ provexit apex.'
[*The Fourth Knight passes.*
Sim. What is the fourth?
Thai. A burning torch that's turned upside down;
The word, 'Quod me alit, me extinguit.'
Sim. Which shows that beauty hath his power and will,
Which can as well inflame as it can kill.
[*The Fifth Knight passes.*
Thai. The fifth, an hand environed with clouds,
Holding out gold that's by the touchstone tried;
The motto thus, 'Sic spectanda fides.'
[*The Sixth Knight passes.*
Sim. And what's
The sixth and last, the which the knight himself
With such a graceful courtesy deliver'd?
Thai. He seems to be a stranger; but his present is
A wither'd branch, that's only green at top;
The motto, 'In hac spe vivo.'
Sim. A pretty moral;
From the dejected state wherein he is,
He hopes by you his fortunes yet may flourish."

As with the ornaments "in silk and gold," which Mary Queen of Scotland worked on the bed of her son James, or with those in "the lady's closet" at Hawsted, we trace them up to their originals, and pronounce them, however modified, to be derived from the Emblem-books of their age; so, with respect to the devices which the six knights bore on their shields, we conclude that these have their sources in books of the same character, or in the genius of the author who knew so well how to contrive and how to execute. Emblems beyond a doubt they are, though not engraved on our author's page, as they were on the escutcheons of the knightly company. Take the device and motto of the gnats or butterflies and the candle; we trace them from Vænius, Camerarius, and Whitney, to Paradin, from Paradin to Symeoni, and from Symeoni to Giles Corrozet,—at every step we pronounce them Emblems,—and should pass the same judgment, though we could not trace them at all. It is the same with these devices in the Triumph Scene of *Pericles*; we discover the origin of some of them in Emblem works of, or before Shakespeare's era,—and where we fail to discover, there we attribute invention, invention guided and perfected by masters in the art of fashioning pictures to portray thoughts by means of things. We will, however, in due order consider the devices and mottoes of these six knights who came to honour the king's daughter.

The first knight is the Knight of Sparta,—

> "And the device he bears upon his shield
> Is a black Ethiope reaching at the sun;
> The word, *Lux tua vita mihi.*"
>
> Act ii. sc. 2, lines 19—21.

A motto almost identical belongs to an old family of Worcestershire, the Blounts, of Soddington, of which Sir Edward Blount, Bart., is, or was the representative; their motto is, *Lux tua vita mea*,—"Thy light, my life;"—but their crest is an armed foot in the sun, not a black Ethiop reaching towards him. There was a Sir Walter Blount slain on the king's side at the battle of Shrewsbury, and whom, previous to the battle, Shakespeare represents as sent by Henry IV. with offers of pardon to Percy. (*Henry IV.* Pt. 1. act. iv. sc. 3, l. 30, vol. iv. p. 323.) A Sir James Blount is also briefly introduced in *Richard III.* act. v. sc. 2, l. 615. The name being familiar to Shakespeare, the motto also might be;—and by a very slight alteration he has ascribed it to the Knight of Sparta.

I have consulted a considerable number of books of Emblems published before the *Pericles* was written, but have not discovered either the device or "the word" exactly in the form given in the play. There is a near approach to the device in Reusner's *Emblems*, printed at Francfort in 1581 (Emb. 7, lib. i. p. 9). A man is represented stretching forth his hand towards the meridian sun, and the device is surmounted by the motto, *Sol animi virtus*,—"Virtue the sun of the soul." The elegiac verses which follow carry out the thought with considerable clearness,—

> "*Sol, oculus cæli, radijs illuminat orbem:*
> *Et Phœbe noctem disjicit alba nigram.*
> *Sol animi virtus sensus illuminat ægros:*
> *Et tenebras mentis discutit alma fides.*
> *Si menti virtus, virtuti prævia lucet*
> *Pura fides: nihil hoc clarius esse potest.*
> *Aurea virtutis species, fideiq., Philippe,*
> *Præradians, cælo sic tibi monstrat iter.*
> *Scilicet hic vitæ Sol est, & Lucifer vnus:*
> *Hæc Phœbe, noctem quæ fugat igne suo.*
> *Quæ dum mente vides correcta lumina; mundi*
> *Impauidus tenebras despicis, atq. metus.*
> *Sol magno Phœbeq. micent, & Lucifer orbi:*
> *Dum tibi sic virtus luceat, atq. fides.*"*

Among these lines is one to illustrate the first knight's motto;

> "*Scilicet hic vitæ Sol est, & Lucifer vnus,*"

> "This in truth is the Sun of life, and the one Light-bringer."

* Thus to be rendered into symmetrical lines of English,—

> "The Sun, the eye of heaven, with beams the world illumes,
> And the pale Moon afar scatters black night.
> So virtue, the soul's sun, our pining senses illumes,
> And genial faith dispels the darkness of the mind.
> If virtue to the mind,—so leading the way to virtue shines
> Faith in her purity: nothing can be brighter than this.
> The golden splendour of virtue and faith, O Philip,
> Throwing out beamings, shows to thee paths to the sky.
> This in truth is the Sun of life, and the one Light-bringer,
> This in truth the Moon which by shining drives away night.
> While in thy mind these lights thou seest on high,—of the world
> The darkness and terrors untrembling thou dost behold.
> Sun and Moon and the Light-bringer flash light to their orbs,
> And the while on thee shine, too, virtue and faith."

But Plautus, the celebrated comic poet of Rome, gives in his *Asinaria*, 3. 3. 24, almost the very words of the Spartan knight: *Certe tu vita es mihi*,—"Of a truth thou art life to me."

The introduction of an Ethiop was not unusual with Shakespeare. In the *Two Gentlemen of Verona* (act. ii. sc. 6. l. 25, vol. i. p. 112), Proteus avers,—

> "And Silvia,—witness Heaven that made her fair!—
> Shows Julia but a swarthy Ethiope;"

and in *Love's Labour's Lost* (act. iv. sc. 3, l. 111, vol. ii. p. 144), Dumain reads these verses,—

> "Do not call it sin in me,
> That I am forsworn for thee;
> Thou for whom Jove would swear
> Juno but an Ethiope were."

A genius so versatile as that of Shakespeare, and capable of creating almost a whole world of imagination out of a single hint, might very easily accommodate to his own idea Reusner's suggestive motto, and make it yield the light of love to the lover rather than to the reverend sage. Failing in identifying the exact source of the "black Ethiope reaching at the sun," we may then not unreasonably suppose that Shakespeare himself formed the device, and fitted the Latin to it.

In the Emblem-books of the sixteenth and seventeenth centuries, the Latin mottoes very greatly preponderated over those of other languages; and had Shakespeare confined himself to Latin, it might remain doubtful whether he knew anything of Emblem works beyond those of our own countrymen—Barclay and Whitney—and of the two or three translations into English from Latin, French, and Italian. But the quotation of a purely Spanish motto, that on the second knight's device, *Piu por dulzura que por fuerza*,—"More by gentleness than by force" (act ii. sc. 2, l. 27),—shows that his reading and observation extended beyond mere English sources, and that with other literary men of his day he had looked into, if he had not studied, the widely-known and very popular writings of Alciatus and Sambucus among Latinists, of Francisco Guzman and Hernando Soto among Spaniards, of Gabriel Faerni and Paolo Giovio among Italians, and of Bartholomew Aneau and Claude Paradin among the French.

Shakespeare gives several snatches of French, as in *Twelfth Night*, act iii. sc. 1, l. 68, vol. iii. p. 265,—

> "*Sir Andrew.* Dieu vous garde, monsieur,
> *Viola.* Et vous aussi; votre serviteur;"

and in *Henry V.* act iii. sc. 4; act iv. sc. 4 and 5; act v. sc. 2, vol. iv. pp. 538—540, 574—577, and 598—603: in the scenes between Katharine and Alice; Pistol and the French soldier taken prisoner; and Katharine and King Henry. Take the last instance,—

> "*K. Hen.* Fair Katharine, and most fair,
> Will you vouchsafe to teach a soldier terms
> Such as will enter at a lady's ear
> And plead his love-suit to her gentle heart?
>
> *Kath.* Your majesty shall mock at me; I cannot speak your England.
>
> *K. Hen.* O fair Katharine, if you will love me soundly with your French heart, I will be glad to hear you confess it brokenly with your English tongue. Do you like me, Kate?
>
> *Kath.* Pardonnez-moi, I cannot tell vat is 'like me.'
>
> *K. Hen.* An angel is like you, Kate, and you are like an angel.
>
> *Kath.* Que dit-il? que je suis semblable à les anges?
>
> *Alice.* Oui, vraiment, sauf votre grace, ainsi dit-il.
>
> *K. Hen.* I said so, dear Katharine; and I must not blush to affirm it.
>
> *Kath.* O bon Dieu! les langues des hommes sont pleines de tromperies."

Appropriately also to the locality of the *Taming of the Shrew* (act i. sc. 2, l. 24, vol. iii. p. 23), Hortensio's house in Padua, is the Italian quotation.

> "*Pet.* 'Con tutto il core ben trovato,' may I say.
> *Hor.* Alla nostra casa ben venuto, molto honorato, signor mio Petruchio.

We find only two Spanish sentences, those already quoted,—one being Pistol's motto on his sword, *Si fortuna me tormenta sperato me contenta*; the other, that of the Prince of Macedon, on his shield, *Piu por dulzura que por fuerza.*

Similar proverbs and sayings abound both in Cervantes, who died in 1616, the year of Shakespeare's death, and in the Spanish Emblem-books of an earlier date. I have very carefully examined the Emblems of Alciatus, translated into Spanish in 1549, but the nearest approach to the motto of the Prince of Macedon is, *Que mas puede la eloquençia que la fortaliza* (p. 124),—"Eloquence rather than force prevails,"—which may be taken from Alciat's 180th Emblem, *Eloquentia fortitudine præstantior.*

Other Spanish Emblem-books of that day are the *Moral Emblems* of Hernando de Soto, published at Madrid in 1599, and *Emblems Moralized*, of Don Sebastian Orozco, published in the year 1610, also at Madrid; but neither of these gives the words of the second knight's device. Nor are they contained in the *Moral Triumphs*, as they are entitled, of Francisco Guzman, published in 1587, the year after Whitney's work appeared. The *Moral Emblems*, too, of Juan de Horozco, are without them,—an octavo, published at Segovia in 1589.

But, although there has been no discovery of this Spanish motto in a Spanish Emblem-book, the exact literal expression of it is found in a French work of extreme rarity—Corrozet's "HECATOMGRAPHIE," Paris, 1540. There, at Emblem 28, *Plus par doulceur que par force*,[1]—"More by gentleness than by force,"—is the saying which introduces the old fable of the Sun and the Wind, and of their contest with the

[1] Of cognate meaning is Messin's motto in Boissard's *Emblems*, 1588, pp. 82-3, "Plvs par vertv qve par armes,"—*Plus virtute quàm armis*,—the device being a tyrant, with spearmen to guard him, but singeing his beard because he was afraid of his barber,—

"Et vuyde d'asseurance, il aymoit fier
La façon de son poil au charbon, qu'au barbier.
Tant l'injustice au cœur ente de meffiance."

travellers. Appended are a symbolical woodcut and a French stanza,

Plus par doulceur que par force.

Contre la froidure du vent,
L'homme ſe tient clos & ſe ſerre,
Mais le Soleil le plus ſouuent
Luy faict mettre ſa robę à terre.

Corrozet, 1540.

which may be pretty accurately rendered by the English quatrain,—

"Against the wind's cold blasts
Man draws his cloak around;
But while sweet sunshine lasts,
He leaves it on the ground."

This comment in verse follows Corrozet's Emblem,—

"Qvand le vent est fort & subit,
Violent pour robe emporter,
L'homme se serrę en son habit,
Affin qu'il ne luy puisse oster.
Mais quand le Soleil vient iecter
Sur luy ses rays clers & luysantz,
Le cauld le faict sans arrester
Despouiller ses habitz plaisantz.
* Ainsi ãmytié & doulceur
Faict plus que force & violence,
Doulceur est d'amour propre sœur,
Qui rend l'homme plein d'excellence.
Il ne fault doncq mettrę en silence
Ceste tres noble courtoisie,
Mais l'extoller en precellence;
Commę vne vertu bien choisie.
* Hommes, chassez de vous rigueur
Qui vostre grand beaulté efface,
Prenez de doulceur la vigueur,
Qui enrichera vostre face.
Doulceur ci bien meilleure grace,
Qui rend le visagę amoureux,
Que d'estre dict en toute place
L'oultre cuidé, fol, rigoureuz."

There is a brief allusion to this fable in *King John* (act iv. sc. 3, l. 155, vol. iv. p. 76), in the words of Philip, the half-brother of Faulconbridge,—

> "Now happy he whose cloak and cincture can
> Hold out this tempest."

The same fable is given in Freitag's "Mythologia Ethica," Antwerp, 1579, p. 27. It is to a very similar motto,—

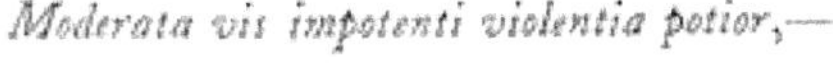

Moderata vis impotenti violentia potior,—

Freitag, 1579.

"Moderate force more powerful than impotent violence,"—to which are added, below the woodcut, two quotations from the Holy Scriptures,—

> "*Non quia dominamur fidei.*"—2 Cor. i. 24.
> "*Factus sum infirmis infirmus; vt infirmos lucrifacerem.*"—1 Cor. ix. 22.

> "Not that we have dominion over your faith;"
> "To the weak I became as weak, that I might gain the weak;

implying that not by the rigid exercise of authority, but by a sympathising spirit, the true faith will be carried onward unto victory.

Now, as the motto of the second knight existed in French, and, as we have seen, Emblem-books were translated into Spanish, the supposition is justifiable, though we have failed to trace out the very fact, that the author of the *Pericles*—Shakespeare, if you will—copied the words of the motto from some Spanish Emblem-book, or book of proverbs, that had come within his observation, and which applied the saying to woman's gentleness subduing man's harsher nature. Future inquirers will, perhaps, clear up this little mystery, and trace the very work in which the Spanish saying is original, *Piu por dulzura que por fuerza.*

We pass to the third, the fourth, and the fifth knights, with their "devices" and "words;" and to illustrate these we have almost a superabundant wealth of emblem-lore, from any portion of which Shakespeare may have made his choice. His materials may have come from some one of the various editions of Claude Paradin's, or of Gabriel Symeoni's "DEVISES HEROIQVES," which appeared at Lyons and Antwerp, in French and Italian, between the years 1557 and 1590; or, as the learned Francis Douce supposes, in his *Illustrations of Shakspere*, pp. 302, 393, the dramatist may have seen the English translation of these authors, which was published in London in 1591, or, with greater probability, as some are inclined to say, he may have used the emblems of our countryman, Geffrey Whitney. Were it not that Daniell's translation, in 1585, of *The Worthy Tract of Paulus Jovius* is without plates, we should include this in the number.

Of the devices in question, Whitney's volume contains two, and the other works the three; but between certain expressions of Whitney's and those of the *Pericles*, the similarity is so great, that the evidence of circumstance inclines, I may say decidedly inclines, to the conclusion that for two out of the three emblems referred to, Shakespeare was indebted to his fellow Elizabethan poet, and not to a foreign source.

From his use of Spanish and French mottoes, as well as Latin, it is evident that Shakespeare, no more than Spenser, needed the aid of translations to render the emblem treasures available to himself; and if, as some maintain,* the *Pericles* was in existence previous to the year 1591, it could not have been that use was made of the English translation of that date of the "Devises Heroiqves," by P. S.: it remains, therefore, that for two out of the three emblems he must either have employed one of the original editions of Lyons and of Antwerp, or have been acquainted with our Whitney's *Choice of Emblemes*, and have obtained help from them; and for the third emblem he must have gone to the French or Italian originals.

The third knight, named of Antioch, has for his device "a wreath of chivalry,"—

"The word, *Me pompæ provexit apex*;"—
(Act ii. sc. 2, l. 30,)

i. e., "The crown at the triumphal procession has carried me onward." On the 146th leaf of Paradin's "Devises Heroiqves," edition Antwerp, 1562, the wreath and the motto are exactly as Shakespeare describes them. But Paradin gives a long and

* See *Penny Cyclopædia*, vol. xxi. p. 343, where the *Pericles* and eight other plays are assigned "to the period from Shakspere's early manhood to 1591. Some of those dramas may possibly then have been created in an imperfect state, very different from that in which we have received them. If the *Titus Andronicus* and *Pericles* are Shakspere's, they belong to this epoch in their first state, whatever it might have been." See also Knight's *Pictorial Shakspere*, supplemental volume, p 119, where, as before mentioned, the opinion is laid down,—"We think that the *Pericles* of the beginning of the seventeenth century was the revival of a play written by Shakspere some twenty years earlier."

interesting account of the laurel-wreath, and of the high value accorded to it in Roman estimation. "It was," as that author remarks, "the grandest recompense, or the grandest reward which the ancient Romans could think of to offer to the Chieftains over armies, to Emperors, Captains, and victorious Knights."

Me pompæ prouexit apex.

Paradin, 1562.

To gratify the curiosity which some may feel respecting this subject, I add the whole of the original.

"*La plus grande recompense, ou plus grād loyer que les antiques Rommains estimassent faire aus Chefz d'armee, Empereurs, Capitaines, et Cheualiers victorieux, c'estoit de les gratifier & honnorer (selon toutefois leurs merites, estats, charges, & degrez) de certaines belles Couronnes: qui generalemēt (à cette cause) furent apellees Militaires. Desquelles (pour auoir estées indice & enseignes de prouesse & vertu) les figures des principales & plus nobles, sont ci tirees en deuises: tant a la louange & memoire de l'antique noblesse, que pareillement à la recreation, consolation, & esperance de la moderne, aspirāt & desirāt aussi de paruenir aus gages & loyers apartenās & dediez aus defenseurs de la recommendable Republique. La premiere donques mise en reng, representera la Trionfale: laquelle estant tissue du verd Laurier, auec ses bacques, estoit donnés au Trionfateur, auquel par decret du Senat, estoit licite de trionfer parmi la vile de Romme, sur chariot, comme victorieus de ses ennemis. Desquels neantmoins lui conuenoit deuant la pompe, faire aparoir de la deffaite, du nombre parfait de cinq mile, en vne seule bataille. La susdite Couronne trionfale, apres long trait de temps (declinant l'Empire) fut commēcee à estre meslee, & variée de Perles & pierrerie, & puis entierement changée de Laurier naturel en Laurier buriné, & enleué, sus vn cercle d'or: comme se void par les Medailles, de plusieurs monnoyes antiques.*"*

* It may be mentioned that Paradin describes five other Roman wreaths of honour.

Shakespeare does not add a single word of explanation, or of amplification, which he might be expected to have done, had he used an English translation; but simply, and without remark, he adopts the emblem and its motto, as is natural to anyone who, though not unskilled in the language by which they are expressed, is not perfectly at home in it.

Of chivalry, however, he often speaks, — "of chivalrous design of knightly trial." To Bolingbroke and Mowbray wager of battle is appointed to decide their differences (*Richard II.* act i. sc. 1, l. 202, vol. iv. p. 116), and the king says,—

> "Since we can not atone you, we shall see
> Justice design the victor's chivalry."

And (vol. iv. p. 137) John of Gaunt declares of England's kings; they were,—

> "Renowned for their deeds as far from home,
> In Christian service and true chivalry,
> As is the sepulchre in stubborn Jewry
> Of the world's ransom, blessed Mary's Son."

But in the case of the fourth and fifth knights, it is not the simple adoption of a device which we have to consider; the very ideas, almost the very phrases in which those ideas were clothed, have also been given, pointing out that the Dramatist had before him something more than explanations in an unfamiliar tongue.

The device of the fourth knight is both described and interpreted,—

> "A burning torch that's turned upside down;
> The word, *Quod me alit, me extinguit.*
> Which shows, that beauty hath this power and will,
> Which can as well inflame as it can kill."
>
> Act ii. sc. 2, lines 32—35.

Thus presented in Symeoni's "TETRASTICHI MORALI," edition Lyons, 1561, p. 35,—

SIGNOR DI S.
VALIER.

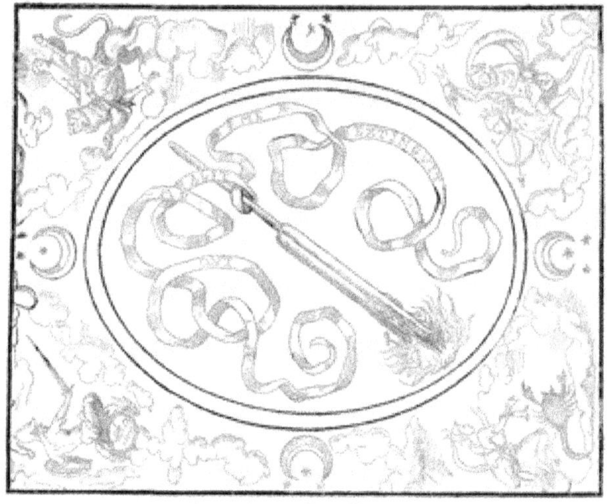

Symeoni, 1561 (diminished copy.

An Italian stanza explains the device,—

" Nutrisce il fuoco à lui la cera intorno,
Et la cera l'estingue. ò quanti sono,
Che dopo vn riceuuto & largo dono,
Dal donator riceuon danno & scorno."

" Qui me alit,
me extinguit."

The sense of which we now endeavour to give,—

" The wax here within nourishes the flames
And the wax stifles them ; how many names
Who after a large gift and kindness shown,
Get from the giver harm and scorn alone."

" Who nourishes me,
extinguishes me."

Symeoni (from edition Lyons, 1574, p. 200) adds this little piece of history :—

" In the battle of the Swiss, routed near Milan by King

Francis, M. de Saint Valier, the old man, father of Madame the Duchess de Valentinois,* and captain of a hundred gentlemen of the king's house, bore a standard, whereon was painted a lighted torch with the head downward, on which flowed so much wax as would extinguish it, with this motto 'QVI ME ALIT, ME EXTINGVIT,' imitating the emblem of the king his master; that is, 'NVTRISCO ET EXTINGVO.' It is the nature of the wax, which is the cause of the torch burning when held upright, that with the head downward it should be extinguished. Thus he wished to signify, that as the beauty of a lady whom he loved nourished all his thoughts, so she put him in peril of his life. See still this standard in the church of the Celestins at Lyons."†

Paradin, who confessedly copies from Symeoni, agrees very nearly with this account, but gives the name of the Duchess "Diane de Poitiers," and omits mentioning "the emblem of the king."

As stated in the *fac-simile Reprint* of Whitney's *Emblemes*, p. 302, Douce in his *Illustrations of Shakespeare*, pp. 302, 393, advances the opinion that the translation of Paradin into English, 1591, by P. S., was the source of Shakespeare's torch-emblem; "but it is very note-worthy that the torch in the English translation is not a torch 'that's turned upside down,' but one held uninverted, with the flame naturally ascending. This contrariety to Shakespeare's description seems fatal there-

* Symeoni, in 1559, dedicated "All' Illustrissima Signora Duchessa di Valentinois," his "VITA ET METAMORFOSEO D'OVIDIO," 8vo, containing 187 pages of devices, with beautiful borders.

† "*Nella giornata de Suizzeri, rotti presso à Milano dal Rè Francesco, Monsignor di San Valiere il Vecchio, padre di Madama la Duchessa di Valentinoys, e Capitano di cento Gentil'huomini della Casa del Rè, portò uno Stendardo, nel quale era dipinto un torchio acceso con la testa in giù, sulla quale colaua tanta cera, che quasi li spegneua, con queste parole,* QVI ME ALIT, ME EXTINGVIT, *imitando l'impresa del Rè suo Padrone: cio è,* NVTRISCO ET EXTINGVO. *È la natura della cera, la quale è cagione che 'l torchio abbrucia stando ritto, che col capo in giù si spegne: volendo per ciò significare, che come la bellezza d'una Donna, che egli amaua, nutriua tutti i suoi pensieri, così lo metteua in pericolo della vita. Vedesi anchora questo stendardo nella Chiesa de Celestini in Lyone.*"

fore to the translator's claim." P. S., however, renders the motto, "He that nourisheth me, killeth me;" and so may put in a claim to the sugges- tion of the line,—

> "Which can as well inflame as it can kill."

Qui me alit, me extinguit.

Paradin, 1562.

Let us next take Whitney's stanza of six lines to the same motto and the same device, p. 183; premising that the very same wood-block appears to have been used for the Paradin in 1562, and for the Whitney in 1586.

> "EVEN as the waxe dothe feede, and quenche the flame.
> So, loue giues life; and loue, dispaire doth giue:
> The godlie loue, doth louers croune with fame:
> The wicked loue, in shame dothe make them liue.
> Then leaue to loue, or loue as reason will,
> For, louers lewde doe vainlie languishe still."

Now, comparing together Symeoni, Paradin, Whitney, and Shakespeare, as explanatory of the fourth knight's emblem, we can scarcely fail to perceive in the *Pericles* a closer resemblance, both of thought and expression, to Whitney than to the other two. Whitney wrote,—

> "So, loue giues life; and loue, dispaire doth giue,"

which the *Pericles* thus amplifies:

> "Which shows, that beauty hath this power and will,
> Which can as well inflame as it can kill."

We conclude, therefore, from this instance, that Whitney's

Choice of Emblemes was known to the author of the *Pericles*, and that in this instance he has simply carried out the idea which was there suggested to him.

A slight allusion to this same device of the burning torch is made in 3 *Henry VI.* (act iii. sc. 2, l. 51, vol. v. p. 281), when Clarence remarks,—

"As red as fire! nay, then her wax must melt;"

but a very distinct one in Hamlet's words (act iii. sc. 4, l. 82, vol. viii. p. 112),—

"O shame! where is thy blush? Rebellious hell,
If thou canst mutine in a matron's bones,
To flaming youth let virtue be as wax
And melt in her own fire; proclaim no shame
When the compulsive ardour gives the charge,
Since frost itself as actively doth burn,
And reason panders will."

The "AMORVM EMBLEMATA,"—*Emblemes of Loue,—with verses in Latin, English, and Italian:* 4to, Antverpiæ, M.DC.IIX., gives the same variation in the reading of the motto as Shakespeare does, namely, "Quod" for "Qui;" and as Daniell had done in *The Worthy Tract of Paulus Jouius*, in 1585, by substituting "*Quod me alit*" for "*Qui me alit*."* The latter is the reading in Paulus Jovius himself,—and is also found in some of the early editions of this play. (See Cambridge *Shakespeare*, vol. ix. p. 343.) The *Amorum Emblemata*, by Otho Vænius, named above, and dated 1608—one year before "PERICLES, PRINCE OF TYRE," was first pulished, in quarto—has the Latin motto, "QVOD NVTRIT, EXTINGVIT," Englished and Italianised as follows:

* See *Essays Literary and Bibliographical*, pp. 301-2, and 311, in the Fac-simile Reprint of Whitney's *Emblemes*, 1866.

"*Loue killed by his owne nouriture.*"

"The torche is by the wax maintayned whyle it burnes,
But turned vpsyde-down it straight goes out & dyes,
Right so by Cupids heat the louer lyues lykewyse,
But thereby is hee kild, when it contrarie turnes."

"Quel che nutre, estingue."

"*Nutre la cera il foco, e ne lo priua
Quando è riuolto in giù: d'Amor l'ardore
Nutre e sfare l'Amante in vn calore,
Contrario effetto vn sol suggetto auiua.*"

At a much earlier date, 1540, Corrozet's *Hecatomgraphie* gives the inverted torch as a device, with the motto, "Mauluaise nourriture,"—

"Quelcun en prenant ses esbatz
M'ainsi mise contrebas
La cire le feu nourrissant
L'estainct & le faict perissant."

But the "device" and "the word" of the fifth knight,—

"An hand environed with clouds,
Holding out gold that's by the touchstone tried;
The motto thus, *Sic spectanda fides*,"
(Act ii. sc. 2, lines 36—38,)

DEVISES
Sic ſpectanda fides.

Paradin, 1562.

"So is fidelity to be proved," —occur most exactly in Paradin's "DEVISES HEROIQUES," edition 1562, leaf 100, *reverse*; they are here figured.

Paradin often presents an account of the origin and appropriation of his emblems, but, in this instance, he offers only an application. "If, in order to prove fine gold, or other metals, we bring them to the touch, without trusting to their glitter or their sound;—so, to recognise good people and persons of virtue, it is needful to observe the splendour of their deeds, without dwelling upon their mere talk." *

The narrative which Paradin neglects to give may be supplied from other sources. This Emblem or Symbol is, in fact, that which was appropriated to Francis I. and Francis II., kings of France from 1515 to 1560, and also to one of the Henries—probably Henry IV. The inscription on the coin, according to Paradin and Whitney's woodcut, is "FRANCISCVS DEI GRATIA FRAN. REX;" this is for Francis I.: but in the *Hierographia Regum Francorum* † (vol. i. pp. 87 and 88), the emblem is inscribed, "Franciscus II. Valesius Rex Francorum XXV. Christianissimus." A device similar to Paradin's then follows, and the comment, *Coronatum aureum nummum, ad Lydium lapidem dextra hæc explicat & sic, id est, duris in rebus fidem explorandam docet,*—"This right hand extends to the Lydian stone a coin of gold which is wreathed around, and so teaches that fidelity in times of difficulty is put to the proof." The coin applied to the touchstone bears the inscription, "FRANCISCVS II. FRANCORV. REX." An original drawing,‡ by Crispin de Passe, in the possession of Sir William Stirling Maxwell, Bart., of Keir, presents the inscription in another form, "HENRICVS, D. G. FRANCORV. REX." The first work of Crispin de Passe is dated 1589, and Henry IV. was recognised king of France in 1593. His portrait, and that of his queen, Mary of Medicis, were

* "*Si pour esprouuer le fin Or, ou autre metaus, lon les raporte sus la Touche, sans qu'on se confie de leurs tintemens, ou de leurs sons, aussi pour connoitre les gens de bien, & vertueus personnages, se faut prendre garde à la splendeur de leurs œuures, sans s'arrester au babil.*"

† See *Symbola Diuina & Humana Pontificum, Imperatorum, Regum*, 3 vols. folio in one, Franckfort, 1652.

‡ This original drawing, with thirty-four others by the same artist, first appeared in *Emblemata Selectiora*, 4to, Amsterdam, 1704; also in *Acht-en-Dertig Konstige Zinnebeelden*,—"Eight-and-thirty Artistic Emblems,"—4to, Amsterdam, 1737.

painted by De Passe; and so the Henry on the coin in the drawing above alluded to was Henry of Navarre.

The whole number of original drawings at Keir, by Crispin de Passe, is thirty-five, of the size of the following plate,—No 27 of the series.

*Crispin de Passe, about 1595.**

The mottoes in *Emblemata Selectiora* are,—

"PECUNIA SANGUIS ET ANIMA MORTALIUM.

Quidquid habet mundus, regina Pecunia vincit,
Fulmineoque ictu fortius una ferit."

"'T GELD VERMAG ALLES.

't Geld houd den krygsknecht in zyn plichten,
Kan meer dan't dondertuig uit richten."

---

* Or it may be a few years later. The drawings, however, are undoubted from which the above woodcut has been executed.

"MONEY THE BLOOD AND LIFE OF MEN.
Whatever the world possesses, money rules as queen,
And more strongly than by lightning's force smites together."

"MONEY CAN DO EVERYTHING.
To his duty the warrior, 'tis money can hold,—
Than the thunderbolt greater the influence of gold."

Very singular is the correspondence of the last two mottoes to a scene in *Timon of Athens* (act iv. sc. 3, lines 25, 377, vol. vii. pp. 269, 283). Timon digging in the wood finds gold, and asks,—

"What is here?
Gold! yellow, glittering, precious gold!"

and afterwards, when looking on the gold, he thus addresses it,—

"O thou sweet king-killer, and dear divorce
'Twixt natural son and sire! thou bright defiler
Of Hymen's purest bed! thou valiant Mars!
Thou ever young, fresh, loved, and delicate wooer,
Whose blush doth thaw the consecrated snow
That lies on Dian's lap! thou visible god,
That solder'st close impossibilities,
And makest them kiss! that speak'st with every tongue,
To every purpose! O thou touch of hearts!
Think, thy slave man rebels; and by thy virtue
Set them into confounding odds, that beasts
May have the world in empire!"

The Emblem which Shakespeare attributes to the fifth knight is fully described by Whitney (p. 139), with the same device and the same motto, *Sic spectanda fides*, —

"THE touche doth trye, the fine, and purest goulde:
And not the sound, or els the goodly showe.
So, if mennes wayes, and vertues, wee behoulde,
The worthy men, wee by their workes, shall knowe.
But gallant lookes, and outward showes beguile,
And ofte are clokes to cogitacions vile."

* This Emblem is dedicated to "GEORGE MANWARINGE *Esquier*," son of "Sir Arthvre Menwerynge," "of Ichtfeild," in Shropshire, from whom are directly descended the Mainwarings of Oteley Park, Ellesmere, and indirectly the Mainwarings of Over-Peover, Cheshire.

If, in the use of this device, and in their observations upon it, Paradin, either in the original or in the English version, and Whitney be compared with the lines on the subject in *Pericles*, it will be seen "that Shakespeare did not derive his fifth knight's device either from the French emblem or from its English translator, but from the English Whitney which had been lately published. Indeed, if *Pericles* were written, as Knight conjectures, in Shakespeare's early manhood, previous to the year 1591, it could not be the English translation of Paradin which furnished him with the three mottoes and devices of the Triumph Scene."

To the motto, "AMOR CERTVS IN RE INCERTA CERNITVR," —*Certain love is seen in an uncertain matter*,—Otho Vænius, in his *Amorum Emblemata*, 4to, Antwerp, 1608, represents two Cupids at work, one trying gold in the furnace, the other on the touchstone. His stanzas, published with an English translation, as if intended for circulation in England, may, as we have conjectured, have been seen by Shakespeare before 1609, when the *Pericles* was revived. They are to the above motto,—

> "*Nummi vt adulterium exploras priùs indice, quam sit*
> *Illo opus: haud aliter ritè probandus Amor.*
> *Scilicet vt fuluum spectatur in ignibus aurum:*
> *Tempore sic duro est inspicienda fides.*"

> "*Loues triall.*
>
> As gold is by the fyre, and by the fournace tryde,
> And thereby rightly known if it be bad or good,
> Hard fortune and distresse do make it vnderstood,
> Where true loue doth remayn, and fayned loue resyde."

> "Come l'oro nel foco.
>
> *Sù la pietra, e nel foco l'or si proua,*
> *E nel bisogno, come l'or nel foco,*
> *Si dee mostrar leale in ogni loco*
> *l'Amante; e alhor si vee d'Amor la proua.*"

The same metaphor of attesting characters, as gold is proved by the touchstone or by the furnace, is of frequent occurrence in Shakespeare's undoubted plays; and sometimes the turn of the thought is so like Whitney's as to give good warrant for the supposition, either of a common original, or that Shakespeare had read the Emblems of our Cheshire poet and made use of them.

King Richard III. says to Buckingham (act iv. sc. 2, l. 8, vol. v. p. 580),—

> "O Buckingham, now do I play the touch,
> To try if thou be current gold indeed."

And in *Timon of Athens* (act iii. sc. 3, l. 1, vol. vii. p. 245), when Sempronius observes to a servant of Timon's,—

> "Must he needs trouble me in't,—hum!—'bove all others?
> He might have tried Lord Lucius and Lucullus;
> And now Ventidius is wealthy too,
> Whom he redeem'd from prison: all these
> Owe their estates unto him."

The servant immediately replies,—

> "My lord,
> They have all been touch'd and found base metal, for
> They have all denied him."

Isabella, too, in *Measure for Measure* (act ii. sc. 2, l. 149, vol. i. p. 324), most movingly declares her purpose to bribe Angelo, the lord-deputy,—

> "Not with fond shekels of the tested gold,
> Or stones whose rates are either rich or poor
> As fancy values them; but with true prayers
> That shall be up at heaven and enter there
> Ere sun-rise, prayers from preserved souls,
> From fasting maids whose minds are dedicate
> To nothing temporal."

In the dialogue from *King John* (act iii. sc. 1, l. 96, vol. iv. p. 37) between Philip of France and Constance, the same testing is alluded to. King Philip says,—

"By heaven, lady, you shall have no cause
To curse the fair proceedings of this day:
Have I not pawn'd to you my majesty?"

But Constance answers with great severity,—

"You have beguiled me with a counterfeit
Resembling majesty, which being touch'd and tried,
Proves valueless: you are forsworn, forsworn."

One instance more shall close the subject;—it is from the *Coriolanus* (act iv. sc. 1, l. 44, vol. vi. p. 369), and contains a very fine allusion to the testing of true metal; the noble traitor is addressing his mother Volumnia, his wife Virgilia, and others of his kindred,—

"Fare ye well:
Thou hast years upon thee; and thou art too full
Of the wars' surfeits, to go rove with one
That's yet unbruised: bring me but out at gate.
Come, my sweet wife, my dearest mother, and
My friends of noble touch, when I am forth,
Bid me farewell, and smile."

So beautifully and so variously does the great dramatist carry out that one thought of making trial of men's hearts and characters to learn the metal of which they are made.

To finish our notices and illustrations of the Triumph Scene in *Pericles*, there remain to be considered the device and the motto of the sixth—the stranger knight—who "with such a graceful courtesy delivered,"—

"A wither'd branch, that's only green at top,*
The motto, *In hac spe vivo;*" (Act ii. sc. 2, lines 43, 44.)

and on which the remark is made by Simonides,—

"A pretty moral:
From the dejected state wherein he is,
He hopes by you his fortune yet may flourish."

* The phrase is matched by another in *Much Ado about Nothing* (act ii. sc. 1, l. 214, vol. ii. p. 22), when Benedict said of the Lady Beatrice, "O, she misused me past endurance of a block! an oak but with one green leaf on it would have answered her."

With these I have found nothing identical in any of the various books of Emblems which I have examined; indeed, I cannot say that I have met with anything similar. The sixth knight's emblem is very simple, natural, and appropriate; and I am most of all disposed to regard it as invented by Shakespeare himself to complete a scene, the greater part of which had been accommodated from other writers.

Yet the sixth device and motto need not remain without illustration. Hope is a theme which Emblematists could not possibly omit. Alciatus gives a series of four Emblems on this virtue,—Emblems 43, 44, 45, and 46; Sambucus, three, with the mottoes "Spes certa," "In spe fortitudo," and "Spes aulica;" and Whitney, three from Alciatus (pp. 53, 137, and 139); but none of these can be accepted as a proper illustration of the *In hac spe vivo.* Their inapplicability may be judged of from Alciat's 46th Emblem, very closely followed by Whitney (p. 139).

Illicitum non sperandum.

Whitney, 1586.

"SPES *simul & Nemesis nostris altaribus adsunt,*
Scilicet vt speres non nisi quod liceat."

The unlawful thing not to be hoped for.

"HERE NEMESIS, and Hope: our deedes doe rightlie trie,
Which warnes vs, not to hope for that, which iustice doth denie."

In the spirit, however, if not in the words of the sixth knight's device, the Emblem writers have fashioned their thoughts. From Paradin's "DEVISES HEROIQVES," so often quoted, we select two devices (fol. 30 and 152) illustrative of our subject. The one, an arrow issuing from a tomb, on which is the sign of the cross, and having verdant shoots twined around it, was the emblem which Madame Diana of Poitiers adopted to express her strong hope of a resurrection from the dead; and the same hope is also shadowed forth by ears of corn growing out of a collection of dry bones, and ripening and shedding their seed.

The first, *Sola viuit in illo,*—"Alone on that," *i.e.*, on the cross, "she lives,"—we now offer with Paradin's explanation; "*L'esperance que Madame Diane de Poitiers Illustre Duchesse de Valentinois, a de la resurrection, & que son noble esprit, contemplant les cieus en cette vie, paruiendra en l'autre après la mort: est possible signifié par sa Deuise, qui est d'vn Sercueil, ou tombeau, duquel sort vn trait, acompagné de certains syons verdoyans.*" *i.e.*,—"The hope which Madame Diana of Poitiers, the illustrious Duchess de Valentinois, has of the resurrection, and which her noble spirit, contemplating the heavens in this life, will arrive at in the other, after death: it is really signified by her Device, which is a Sepulchre or tomb, from which issues an arrow, accompanied by certain verdant shoots."

The motto of the second is more directly to the purpose, *Spes altera vitæ,*—"Another hope of life," or "The hope of another

[1] "The sixth device," say the *Illustrations of Shakespeare*, by Francis Douce, vol. ii. p. 127, "from its peculiar reference to the situation of Pericles, may, perhaps, have been altered from one in the same collection (Paradin's), used by Diana of Poictiers. It is a green branch springing from a tomb, with the motto, 'SOLA VIVIT IN ILLO,'"—*Alone on that she lives.*

life,"—and its application is thus explained by Paradin (leaf 151 *reverso*),—"*Les grains des Bleds, & autres herbages, semées & mortifiées en terre, se reuerdoyent, & prennent nouuel accroissement: aussi les corps humains tombãs par Mort, seront releués en gloire, par generale resurrection.*"—*i.e.*, "The seeds of wheat, and other herbs, sown and dying in the ground, become green again, and take new growth: so human bodies cast down by Death will be raised again in glory, by the general resurrection."

We omit the woodcut which Paradin gives, and substitute for it the 100th Emblem, part i. p. 102, from Joachim Camerarius, edition, 1595, which bears the very same motto and device.

SPES ALTERA VITÆ.

Camerarius, 1595.

"*Securus moritur, qui scit se morte renasci:*
Non ea mors dici, sed noua vita potest."

"Fearless doth that man die, who knows
From death he again shall be born;
We never can name it as death,—
'Tis new life on eternity's morn."

A sentence or two from the comment may serve for explanation; "The seeds and grains of fruits and herbs are thrown upon the earth, and as it were entrusted to it; after a certain time they spring up again and produce manifold. So also our bodies, although already dead, and destined to burial in the earth, yet at the last day shall arise, the good to life, the wicked to judgment." . . . "Elsewhere it is said, ONE HOPE SURVIVES, doubtless beyond the grave." *

"MORT VIVIFIANTE," of Messin, *In Morte Vita*, of Boissard, edition 1588, pp. 38, 39, also receive their emblematical representation, from wheat growing among the signs of death.

> "En vain nous attendons la moisson, si le grain
> Ne se pourrit au creux de la terre beschée.
> Sans la corruption, la nature empeschée
> Retient toute semence au ventre soubterrain."

At present we must be content to say that the source of the motto and device of the sixth knight has not been discovered. It remains for us to conjecture, what is very far from being an improbability, that Shakespeare had read Spenser's *Shepherd's Calendar*, published in 1579, and from the line, on page 364 of Moxon's edition, for January (l. 54),—

> "Ah, God! that love should breed both ioy and paine!"—

and from the Emblem, as Spenser names it, *Anchora speme*,—"Hope is my anchor,"—did invent for himself the sixth knight's device, and its motto, *In hac spe vivo*,—"In this hope I live." The step from applying so suitably the Emblems of other writers to the construction of new ones would not be great; and

* "FRVMENTORVM *ac leguminum semina ac grana in terram projecta, ac illi quasi concredita, certo tempore renascuntur, atque multiplices fructus producunt. Sic nostra etiam corpora, quamvis jam mortua, ac terrestri sepulturæ destinata, in die tamen ultima resurgent, & piorum quidem ad vitam, impiorum vero ad judicium.*" "*Alibi legitur*, SPES VNA SVPERSTES, *nimirum post funus.*"

from what he has actually done in the invention of Emblems in the *Merchant of Venice* he would experience very little trouble in contriving any Emblem that he needed for the completion of his dramatic plans.

The *Casket* Scene and the *Triumph* Scene then justify our conclusion that the correspondencies between Shakespeare and the Emblem writers which preceded him are very direct and complete. It is to be accepted as a fact that he was acquainted with their works, and profited so much from them, as to be able, whenever the occasion demanded, to invent and most fittingly illustrate devices of his own. The spirit of Alciat was upon him, and in the power of that spirit he pictured forth the ideas to which his fancy had given birth.

Horapollo, ed. 1551.

CHAPTER VI.

CLASSIFICATION OF THE CORRESPONDENCIES AND PARALLELISMS OF SHAKESPEARE WITH EMBLEM WRITERS.

AVING established the facts that Shakespeare invented and described Emblems of his own, and that he plainly and palpably adopted several which had been designed by earlier authors, we may now, with more consistency, enter on the further labour of endeavouring to trace to their original sources the various hints and allusions, be they more or less express, which his sonnets and dramas contain in reference to Emblem literature. And we may bear in mind that we are not now proceeding on mere conjecture: we have dug into the virgin soil and have found gold that can bear every test, and may reasonably expect, as we continue our industry, to find a nugget here and a nugget there to reward our toil.

But the correspondencies and parallelisms existing in Shakespeare between himself and the earlier Emblematists are so numerous, that it becomes requisite to adopt some system of arrangement, or of classification, lest a mere chaos of confusion and not the symmetry of order should reign over our enterprise. And as "all Emblemes for the most part," says Whitney to his readers, "maie be reduced into these three kindes, which is *Historicall, Naturall, & Morall,*" we shall make that division of his our foundation, and considering the various instances of imitation or of adaptation to be met with in Shakespeare, shall arrange them under the *eight* heads of—1, Historical Emblems; 2, Heraldic Emblems; 3, Emblems of Mythological Characters; 4, Emblems illustrative of Fables; 5, Emblems in connexion with Proverbs; 6, Emblems from Facts in Nature, and from the Properties of Animals; 7, Emblems for Poetic Ideas; and 8, Moral and Æsthetic, and Miscellaneous Emblems.

SECTION I.

HISTORICAL EMBLEMS.

S SOON as learning revived in Europe, the great models of ancient times were again set up on their pedestals for admiration and for guidance. Nearly all the Elizabethan authors, certainly those of highest fame, very frequently introduce, or expatiate upon, the worthies of Greece and Rome,—both those which are named in the epic poems of Homer and Virgil, and those which are within the limits of authentic history. It seemed enough to awaken interest, "to point a moral, or adorn a tale," that there existed a record of old.

Shakespeare, though cultivating, it may be, little direct acquaintance with the classical writers, followed the general practice. He has built up some of the finest of his Tragedies, if not with chorus, and semi-chorus, strophe, antistrophe, and epode, like the Athenian models, yet with a wonderfully exact appreciation of the characters of antiquity, and with a delineating power surprisingly true to history and to the leading events and circumstances in the lives of the personages whom he introduces. From possessing full and adequate scholarship, Giovio, Domenichi, Claude Mignault, Whitney, and others of the Emblem schools, went immediately to the original sources of information. Shakespeare, we may admit, could do this only in a limited degree, and generally availed himself of assistance from the learned translators of ancient authors. Most marvellously does he transcend them in the creative attributes of high genius: they supplied the rough marble, blocks of Parian perchance, and a few tools more or less suited to the work; but it was himself, his soul and intellect and good right arm, which have produced almost living and moving forms,—

> "See, my lord,
> Would you not deem it breath'd? and that those veins
> Did verily bear blood?"
>
> *Winter's Tale*, act v. sc. 3, l. 63.

For Medeia, one of the heroines of Euripides, and for Æneas and Anchises in their escape from Troy, Alciat (Emblem 54), and his close imitator Whitney (p. 33), give each an emblem.

To the first the motto is,—

"*Ei qui semel sua prodegerit, aliena credi non oportere,*"

"To that man who has once squandered his own, another person's ought not to be entrusted,"—

similar, as a counterpart, to the Saviour's words (*Luke* xvi. 12), "If ye have not been faithful in that which is another man's, who shall give you that which is your own."

The device is,—

Alciat, 1581.

with the following Latin elegiacs,—

> COLCHIDOS *in gremio nidum quid congeris? eheu*
> *Nescia cur pullos tam malè credis auis?*
> *Dira parens Medea suos sæuissima natos*
> *Perdidit; & speras parcat vt illa tuis?*

Which Whitney (p. 33) considerably amplifies,—

"MEDEA loe with infante in her arme,
Whoe kil'de her babes, shee shoulde haue loued beste:
The swallowe yet, whoe did suspect no harme,
Hir Image likes, and hatch'd vppon her breste: *
And lifte her younge, vnto this tirauntes guide,
Whoe, peecemeale did her proper fruicte deuide.

Oh foolishe birde, think'ste thow, shee will haue care,
Vppon thy yonge? Whoe hathe her owne destroy'de,
And maie it bee, that shee thie birdes should spare?
Whoe slue her owne, in whome shee shoulde haue ioy'd.
Thow arte deceau'de, and arte a warninge good,
To put no truste, in them that hate theire blood."

* "Swallows have built
In Cleopatra's sails their nests: the augurers
Say they know not, they cannot tell; look grimly
And dare not speak their knowledge."
Ant. & Cleop., act 4, sc. 12, l. 3.

And to the same purport, from Alciat's 193rd Emblem, are Whitney's lines (p. 29),—

> "MEDEA nowe, and PROGNE, blusshe for shame:
> By whome, are ment yow dames of cruell kinde
> Whose infantes yonge, vnto your endlesse blame,
> For mothers deare, do tyrauntes of yow finde:
> Oh serpentes seede, each birde, and sauage brute,
> Will those condempne, that tender not theire frute."

The stanza of his 194th Emblem is adapted by Alciat, and by Whitney after him (p. 163), to the motto,—

Pietas filiorum in parentes,—
"The reverence of sons towards their parents."

Alciat, 1581.

> PER *medios hosteis patriæ cùm ferret ab igne*
> *Aeneas humeris dulce parentis onus:*
> *Parcite, dicebat: vobis sene adorea rapto*
> *Nulla erit, erepto sed patre summa mihi.*

> "AENEAS beares his father, out of Troye,
> When that the Greekes, the same did spoile, and sacke:
> His father might of suche a sonne haue ioye,
> Who throughe his foes, did beare him on his backe:
> No fier, nor sworde, his valiaunt harte coulde feare,
> To flee awaye, without his father deare.

Which showes, that sonnes must carefull bee, and kinde,
For to releeue their parentes in distresse :
And duringe life, that dutie shoulde them binde,
To reuerence them, that God their daies maie blesse :
And reprehendes tenne thowsande to their shame,
Who ofte dispise the stocke whereof they came."

The two emblems of Medeia and of Æneas and Anchises, Shakespeare, in 2 *Henry VI.* (act. v. sc. 2, l. 45, vol. v. p. 218), brings into close juxta-position, and unites by a single description; it is, when young Clifford comes upon the dead body of his valiant father, stretched on the field of St. Albans, and bears it lovingly on his shoulders. With strong filial affection he addresses the mangled corpse,—

"Wast thou ordain'd, dear father,
To lose thy youth in peace, and to atchieve
The silver livery of advised age :
And, in thy reverence, and thy chair-days, thus
To die in ruffian battle?"

On the instant the purpose of vengeance enters his mind, and fiercely he declares,—

"Even at this sight,
My heart is turn'd to stone ; and, while 'tis mine,
It shall be stony. York not our old men spares ;
No more will I their babes : tears virginal
Shall be to me even as the dew to fire ;
And beauty, that the tyrant oft reclaims,
Shall to my flaming wrath be oil and flax.
Henceforth I will not have to do with pity :
Meet I an infant of the house of York,
Into as many gobbets will I cut it,
As wild Medea young Absyrtus did :
In cruelty will I seek out my fame."

Then suddenly there comes a gush of feeling, and with most exquisite tenderness he adds,—

"Come, thou new ruin of old Clifford's house :
As did Æneas old Anchises bear,

> So bear I thee upon my manly shoulders :
> But then Æneas bare a living load,
> Nothing so heavy as these woes of mine."

The same allusion, in *Julius Cæsar* (act. i. sc. 2, l. 107, vol. vii. p. 326), is also made by Cassius, when he compares his own natural powers with those of Cæsar, and describes their stout contest in stemming "the troubled Tyber,"—

> "The torrent roar'd, and we did buffet it
> With lusty sinews, throwing it aside
> And stemming it with hearts of controversy ;
> But ere he could arrive the point proposed,
> Cæsar cried, 'Help me, Cassius, or I sink !'
> I, as Æneas our great ancestor
> Did from the flames of Troy upon his shoulder
> The old Anchises bear, so from the waves of Tiber
> Did I the tired Cæsar : and this man
> Is now become a god, and Cassius is
> A wretched creature, and must bend his body
> If Cæsar carelessly but nod on him."

Progne, or Procne, Medeia's counterpart for cruelty, who placed the flesh of her own son Itys before his father Tereus, is represented in Aneau's "PICTA POESIS," ed. 1552, p. 73, with a Latin stanza of ten lines, and the motto, "IMPOTENTIS VINDICTÆ FOEMINA,"—*The Woman of furious Vengeance.* In the *Titus Andronicus* (act. v. sc. 2, l. 192, vol. vi. p. 522) the fearful tale of Progne enters into the plot, and a similar revenge is repeated. The two sons of the empress, Chiron and Demetrius, who had committed atrocious crimes against Lavinia the daughter of Titus, are

Aneau, 1552.

bound, and preparations are made to inflict such punishment as the world's history had but once before heard of. Titus declares he will bid their empress mother, "like to the earth swallow her own increase."

> "This is the feast that I have bid her to,
> And this the banquet she shall surfeit on;
> For worse than Philomel you used my daughter,
> And worse than Progne I will be revenged."

'Tis a fearful scene, and the father calls,—

> "And now prepare your throats. Lavinia, come,
> [*He cuts their throats.*
> Receive the blood: and when that they are dead,
> Let me go grind their bones to powder small,
> And with this hateful liquor temper it;
> And in that paste let their vile heads be baked.
> Come, come, be every one officious
> To make this banquet; which I wish may prove
> More stern and bloody than the Centaurs' feast."

A character from Virgil's *Æneid* (bk. ii. lines 79-80; 195-8; 257-9),* frequently introduced both by Whitney and Shakespeare, is that of the traitor Sinon, who, with his false tears and lying words, obtained for the wooden horse and its armed men admission through the walls and within the city of Troy. Asia, he averred, would thus secure supremacy over Greece, and Troy find a perfect deliverance. It is from the "PICTA POESIS" of Anulus (p. 18), that Whitney (p. 141) on one occasion adopts the Emblem of treachery, the untrustworthy shield of Brasidas,—

---

* "Nec, si miserum fortuna Sinonem
Finxit, vanum etiam mendacemque improba finget."
"Talibus insidiis, perjurique arte Sinonis,
Credita res: captique dolis, lachrymisque coactis,
Quos neque Tydides, nec Larissæus Achilles,
Non anni domuere decem, non mille carinæ."
"fatisque Deûm defensus iniquis,
Inclusos utero Danaos et pinea furtim
Laxat claustra Sinon."

Perfidus familiaris,—
"The faithless friend."

Aneau, 1552.

PER *medium Brasidas clypeum traiectus ab hoste:*
Quóque foret læsus ciue rogante modum.
Cui fidebam (inquit) penetrabilis vmbo fefellit.
SIC CVI *sæpe fides credita: proditor est.*

Thus rendered in the *Choice of Emblemes*,—

"WHILE throughe his foes, did boulde BRASIDAS thruste,
And thought with force, their courage to confounde:
Throughe targat faire, wherein he put his truste,
His manlie corpes receau'd a mortall wounde.
Beinge ask'd the cause, before he yeelded ghoste:
Quoth hee, my shielde, wherein I trusted moste.

Euen so it happes, wee ofte our bayne doe brue,
When ere wee trie, wee trust the gallante showe:
When frendes suppoas'd, do prooue them selues vntrue,
When SINON false, in DAMONS shape dothe goe:
Then gulfes of griefe, doe swallowe vp our mirthe,
And thoughtes ofte times, doe shrow'd vs in the earthe.

* * * * *

But, if thou doe inioye a faithfull frende,
See that with care, thou keepe him as thy life:
And if perhappes he doe, that may offende,
Yet waye thy frende: and shunne the cause of strife,
Remembringe still, there is no greater crosse;
Then of a frende, for, to sustaine the losse.

Yet, if this knotte of frendship be to knitte,
And SCIPIO yet, his LELIVS can not finde?
Content thy selfe, till some occasion fitte,
Allot thee one, according to thy minde:
  Then trie, and truste: so maiste thou liue in rest,
  But chieflie see, thou truste thy selfe the beste?"

Sambucus, 1564.

And again, adopting the Emblem of John Sambucus, edition Antwerp, 1564, p. 184,* and the motto,

Nusquam tuta fides,—
"Trustfulness is never sure,"

with the exemplification of the Elephant and the undermined tree, Whitney writes (p. 150),—

"NO state so sure, no seate within this life
  But that maie fall, thoughe longe the same haue stoode:
Here fauninge foes, here fained frendes are rife.
With pickthankes, blabbes, and subtill Sinons broode,
  Who when wee truste, they worke our ouerthrowe,
  And vndermine the grounde, wheron wee goe.

The Olephant so huge, and stronge to see,
No perill fear'd: but thought a sleepe to gaine
But foes before had vndermin'de the tree,
And downe he falles, and so by them was slaine:

* The text of Sambucus is dedicated to his father, Peter Sambukins.

"DUM *rigidos artus elephas, dum membra quiete*
  Sublevat, assuetis nititur arboribus:
Quas ubi venator didicit, succidit ab imo,
  Paulatim et recubans belua mole ruit.
Tam leviter capitur duri qui in prælia Martis
  Arma, viros, turrim, tergore vectat opes.
Nusquam tuta fides, nimium ne crede quieti,
  Sæpius & tutis decipiere locis.
Hippomenes pomis Schœneida vicit amatam,
  Sic Peliam natis Colchis acerba necat.
Sic nos decipiunt dedimus quibus omnia nostra:
  Saltem conantur deficiente fide."

First trye, then truste : like goulde, the copper showes :
And NERO ofte, in NVMAS clothinge goes."

Freitag's "MYTHOLOGIA ETHICA," pp. 176, 177, sets forth the well-known fable of the Countryman and the Viper, which after receiving warmth and nourishment attempted to wound its benefactor. The motto is,—

Maleficio beneficium compensatum,—
"A good deed recompensed by maliciousness."

Freitag, 1579.

"*Qui reddit mala pro bonis, non recedet malum de domo eius.*"—*Prouerb.* 17, 13.
"Whoso rewardeth evil for good, evil shall not depart from his house."

Nicolas Reusner, also, edition Francfort, 1581, bk. ii. p. 81, has an Emblem on this subject, and narrates the whole fable,—

Merces anguina,—"Reward from a serpent."

"Frigore confectum quem rusticus inuenit anguem
  Imprudens fotum recreat ecce sinu.
Immemor hic miserum lethale sauciat ictu :
  Reddidit hic vitam ; reddidit ille necem.
Si benefacta locis malè, simplex mente, bonusq. :
  Non benefacta quidem, sed malefacta puta.
Ingratis seruire nefas, gratisq. nocere :
  Quod benè fit gratis, hoc solet esse lucro." *

In several instances in his historical plays, Shakespeare very expressly refers to this fable. On hearing that some of his nobles had made peace with Bolingbroke, in *Richard II.* (act. iii. sc. 2, l. 129, vol. iv. p. 168), the king exclaims,—

"O villains, vipers, damn'd without redemption!
Dogs, easily won to fawn on any man!
Snakes, in my heart blood warm'd that sting my heart!"

In the same drama (act. v. sc. 3, l. 57, vol. iv. p. 210) York urges Bolingbroke,—

"Forget to pity him, lest thy pity prove,
A serpent that will sting thee to the heart."

And another, bearing the name of York, in 2 *Henry VI.* (act. iii. sc. 1, l. 343, vol. v. p. 162), declares to the nobles,—

"I fear me, you but warm the starved snake,
Who, cherish'd in your breasts, will sting your hearts."

Also Hermia, *Midsummer Night's Dream* (act. ii. sc. 2, l. 145,

* "A snake worn out with cold a rustic found,
  And cherished in his breast doth rashly warm ;
Thankless the snake inflicts a fatal wound,
  And life restored requites with deadly harm.
If badly benefits thou dost intend,
  Simple of heart and good within thy mind,
No benefits suppose them in their end,
  But deeds of evil and of evil kind.
To serve the thankless is a sinful thing,
  And wicked they who wilfully give pain ;
Whatever with free soul of good thou bring,
  This rightfully thou may'st account true gain."

vol. ii. p. 225), when awakened from her trance-like sleep, calls on her beloved,—

> "Help me, Lysander, help me! do thy best
> To pluck this crawling serpent from my breast."

Whitney combines Freitag's and Reusner's Emblems under one motto (p. 189), *In sinu alere serpentem*,—"To nourish a serpent in the bosom,"—but applies them to the siege of Antwerp in 1585 in a way which Schiller's famous history fully confirms: * — "The government of the citizens was shared among too many hands, and too strongly influenced by a disorderly populace to allow any one to consider with calmness, to decide with judgment, or to execute with firmness."

The typical Sinon is here introduced by Whitney,—

> "THOVGHE, cittie stronge the cannons shotte dispise,
> And deadlie foes, beseege the same in vaine:
> Yet, in the walles if pining famine rise,
> Or else some impe of SINON, there remaine.
> What can preuaile your bulwarkes? and your towers,
> When, all your force, your inwarde foe deuoures."

In fact, Sinon seems to have been the accepted representative of treachery in every form; for when Camillus, at the siege of Faleria, rewarded the Schoolmaster as he deserved for attempting to give up his scholars into captivity, the occurence is thus described in the *Choice of Emblemes*, p. 113,—

> "With that, hee caus'de this SINON to bee stripte,
> And whippes, and roddes, vnto the schollers gaue:
> Whome, backe againe, into the toune they whipte."

---

* *Schiller's Werke*, band 8, pp. 426-7. "Die Regierung dieser Stadt war in allzu viele Hände vortheilt, und der stürmischen Menge ein viel zu grossen Antheil daran gegeben, als dasz man mit Ruhe hätte überlegen mit Einsicht wählen und mit Festigkeit ausführenkonnen."

Shakespeare is even more frequent in his allusions to this same Sinon. The *Rape of Lucrece*, published in 1594, speaks of him as "the perjured Sinon," "the false Sinon," "the subtle Sinon," and avers (vol. ix. p. 537, l. 1513),—

> "Like a constant and confirmed devil,
> He entertain'd a show so seeming just,
> And therein so ensconc'd his secret evil,—
> That jealousy itself could not mistrust,
> False creeping craft and perjury should thrust
> Into so bright a day such black-faced storms,
> Or blot with hell-born sin such saint-like forms."

Also in 3 *Henry VI.* (act. iii. sc. 2, l. 188, vol. v. p. 285), and in *Titus Andronicus* (act. v. sc. 3, l. 85, vol. vi. p. 527), we read,—

> "I'll play the orator as well as Nestor,
> Deceive more slyly than Ulysses could,
> And like a Sinon, take another Troy;"

and,—

> "Tell us what Sinon hath bewitch'd our ears,
> Or who hath brought the fatal engine in
> That gives our Troy, our Rome, the civil wound."

But in *Cymbeline* (act. iii. sc. 4, l. 57, vol. ix. p. 226), Æneas is joined in almost the same condemnation with Sinon. Pisano expostulates with Imogen,—

> "*Pis.* Good madam, hear me.
> *Imo.* True honest men being heard, like false Æneas,
> Were in his time thought false; and Sinon's weeping
> Did scandal many a holy tear, took pity
> From most true wretchedness: so thou, Posthumus,
> Wilt lay the leaven on all proper men;
> Goodly and gallant shall be false and perjured
> From thy great fail."

Doubtless it will be said that such allusions to the characters in classical history are the common property of the whole modern race of literary men, and that to make them implies no actual copying by later writers of those who preceded them in point of time; still in the examples just given there are such coincidences of expression, not merely of idea, as justify the opinion that Shakespeare both availed himself of the usual sources of information, and had read and taken into his mind the very colour of thought which Whitney had lately spread over the same subject.

The great Roman names, Curtius, Cocles, Manlius and Fabius gave Whitney the opportunity for saying (p. 109),—

"With these, by righte comes *Coriolanus* in,
Whose cruell minde did make his countrie smarte;
Till mothers teares, and wiues, did pittie winne."

And these few lines, in fact, are a summary of the plot and chief incidents of Shakespeare's play of *Coriolanus*, so that it is far from being unlikely that they may have been the germ, the very seed-bed of that vigorous offset of his genius. Almost the exact blame which Whitney imputes is also attributed to Coriolanus by his mother Volumnia (act. v. sc. 3, l. 101, vol. vi. p. 407), who charges him with,—

"Making the mother, wife and child, to see
The son, the husband and the father, tearing
His country's bowels out."

And when wife and mother have conquered his strong hatred against his native land (act. v. sc. 3, l. 206, vol. vi. p. 411), Coriolanus observes to them,—

"Ladies, you deserve
To have a temple built you: all the swords
In Italy, and her confederate arms,
Could not have made this peace."

The subject of Alciat's 119th Emblem, edition 1581, p. 430, is the *Death of Brutus*, with the motto,—

Fortuna virtutem superans,—

"Fortune overcoming valour."

Alciat, 1581.

CÆSAREO *poſtquàm ſuperatus milite, vidit*
Ciuili vndantem ſanguine Pharſaliam :
Jam iam ſtricturus moribunda in pectora ferrum,
Audaci hos Brutus protulit ore ſonos :
Infelix virtus ; & ſolis prouida verbis,
Fortunam in rebus cur ſequeris dominam ?

On the ideas here suggested Whitney enlarges, p. 70, and writes,—

"WHEN BRVTVS knewe, AVGVSTVS parte preuail'de,
And sawe his frendes, lie bleedinge on the grounde,
Such deadlie griefe, his noble harte assail'de,
That with his sworde, hee did him selfe confounde :
But firste, his frendes perswaded him to flee,
Whoe aunswer'd thus, my flighte with handes shalbee.

And bending then to blade, his bared breste,
Hee did pronounce, theise wordes with courage great :
Oh Prowes vaine, I longe did loue thee beste,
But nowe I see, thou doest on fortune waite.
Wherefore with paine, I nowe doe prouue it true,
That fortunes force, maie valiant hartes subdue."

So, in the *Julius Cæsar* (act. v. sc. 5, l. 25, vol. vii. p. 413), the battle of Philippi being irretrievably lost to the party of the Republic, and Marcus Cato slain, Brutus, meditating self-destruction, desires aid from one of his friends that he may accomplish his purpose,—

> "Good Volumnius,
> Thou know'st that we two went to school together:
> Even for that our love of old, I prithee,
> Hold thou my sword-hilts, whilst I run on it.
> *Vol.* That's not an office for a friend, my lord."

The alarum continues,—the friends of Brutus again remonstrate, and Clitus urges him to escape (l. 30),—

> "*Cli.* Fly, fly, my lord; there is no tarrying here.
> *Bru.* Farewell to you; and you; and you, Volumnius.
> Strato, thou hast been all this while asleep;
> Farewell to thee, too, Strato. Countrymen,
> My heart doth joy that yet in all my life
> I found no man but he was true to me.
> I shall have glory by this losing day,
> More than Octavius and Mark Antony
> By this vile contest shall attain unto.
> So, fare you well at once; for Brutus' tongue
> Hath almost ended his life's history:
> Night hangs upon mine eyes; my bones would rest,
> That have but labour'd to attain this hour."

Once more is the alarum raised,—"Fly, fly, fly." "Hence, I will follow thee," is the hero's answer; but when friends are gone, he turns to one of his few attendants, and entreats (l. 44),—

> "I prithee, Strato, stay thou by thy lord:
> Thou art a fellow of a good respect;
> Thy life hath had some smatch of honour in it:
> Hold then my sword, and turn away thy face,
> While I do run upon it. Wilt thou, Strato?
> *Stra.* Give me your hand first: fare you well, my lord.
> *Bru.* Farewell, good Strato. [*Runs on his sword.*] Cæsar, now be still:
> I kill'd not thee with half so good a will. [*Dies.*]"

In the presence of the conquerors Strato then declares,—

> "The conquerors can but make a fire of him;
> For Brutus only overcame himself,
> And no man else hath honour by his death.
> *Lucil.* So Brutus should be found. I thank thee, Brutus,
> That thou hast proved Lucilius' saying true."

And we must mark how finely the dramatist represents the victors at Philippi testifying to the virtues of their foe (l. 68),—

> "*Antony.* This was the noblest Roman of them all:
> All the conspirators, save only he,
> Did that they did in envy of great Cæsar;
> He only, in a general honest thought
> And common good to all, made one of them.
> * * * *
> *Octavius.** According to his virtue let us use him,
> With all respect and rites of burial.
> Within my tent his bones to-night shall lie,
> Most like a soldier, order'd honourably."

The mode of the catastrophe differs slightly in the two writers; and undoubtedly, in this as in most other instances, there is a very wide difference between the life and spiritedness of the dramatist, and the comparative tameness of the Emblem writers,—the former instinct with the fire of genius, the latter seldom rising above an earth-bound mediocrity; yet the references or allusions by the later poet to the earlier can scarcely be questioned; they are too decided to be the results of pure accident.

In one instance Whitney (p. 110, l. 32) hits off the characteristics of Brutus and Cassius in a single line,—

> "With *Brutus* boulde, and *Cassius*, pale and wan."

* As Whitney describes him (p. 110, l. 27),—

> "*Augustus* eeke, that happie most did raigne,
> The scourge to them, that had his vnkle slaine."

It is remarkable how Shakespeare amplifies these two epithets, "pale and wan" into a full description of the personal manner and appearance of Cassius. Cæsar and his train have re-entered upon the scene, and (act. i. sc. 2, l. 192, vol. vii. p. 329) the dictator haughtily and satirically gives order,—

> "*Cæs.* Let me have men about me that are fat,
> Sleek-headed men, and such as sleep o' nights :
> Yond Cassius has a lean and hungry look ;
> He thinks too much : such men are dangerous.
> *Ant.* Fear him not, Cæsar ; he's not dangerous ;
> He is a noble Roman, and well given.
> *Cæs.* Would he were fatter ! but I fear him not :
> Yet if my name were liable to fear,
> I do not know the man I should avoid
> So soon as that spare Cassius. He reads much ;
> He is a great observer, and he looks
> Quite through the deeds of men : he loves no plays,
> As thou dost, Antony ; he hears no music ;
> Seldom he smiles, and smiles in such a sort
> As if he mock'd himself and scorn'd his spirit
> That could be moved to smile at any thing.
> Such men as he be never at heart's ease
> Whiles they behold a greater than themselves,
> And therefore are they very dangerous."

"Pale and wan,"—two most fruitful words, certainly, to bring forth so graphic a description of men that are "very dangerous."

Of names historic the Emblem writers give a great many examples, but only a few, within the prescribed boundaries of our subject, that are at the same time historic and Shakespearean.

Vel post mortem formidolosi,—"Even after death to be dreaded,"—is the sentiment with which Alciatus (Emblem 170), and Whitney after him (p. 194), associate the noisy drum and the shrill-sounding horn; and thus the Emblem-classic illustrates his device,—

"CÆTERA *mutescent, coriumq. silebit ouillum,*
Si confecta lupi tympana pelle sonent.
Hanc membrana ouium sic exhorrescit, vt hostem
Exanimis quamuis non ferat exanimem.
Sic cute detracta Ziscas, in tympana versus,
Boëmos potuit vincere Pontifices."

Literally rendered the Latin elegiacs declare,—

"Other things will grow dumb, and the sheep-skin be silent,
If drums made from the hide of a wolf should sound.
Of this so sore afraid is the membrane of sheep,
That though dead it could not bear its dead foe.
So Zisca's skin torn off, he, changed to a drum,
The Bohemian chief priests was able to conquer."

These curious ideas Whitney adopts, and most lovingly enlarges,—

"A Secret cause, that none can comprehende,
In natures workes is often to bee seene;
As, deathe can not the ancient discorde ende,
That raigneth still, the wolfe and sheepe betweene;
The like, beside in many thinges are knowne,
The cause reueal'd, to none, but GOD alone.

For, as the wolfe, the sillye sheepe did feare,
And make him still to tremble, at his barke:
So beinge dead, which is most straunge to heare,
This feare remaynes, as learned men did marke;
For with their skinnes, if that two drommes bee bounde,
That, clad with sheepe, doth iarre; and hathe no sounde.

And, if that stringes bee of their intrailes wroughte,
And ioyned both, to make a siluer sounde:
No cunninge care can tune them as they oughte,
But one is harde, the other still is droun'de:
Or discordes foule, the harmonie doe marre;
And nothinge can appease this inward warre.

So, ZISCA thoughte when deathe did shorte his daies,
As with his voice, hee erste did daunte his foes;
That after deathe hee shoulde new terror raise,
And make them flee, as when they felte his bloes.
Wherefore, hee charg'd that they his skinne shoulde frame,
To fitte a dromme, and marche forth with the same.

> So, HECTORS sighte greate feare in Greekes did worke,
> When hee was showed on horsebacke, beeinge dead:
> HVNIADES, the terrour of the Turke,
> Thoughe layed in graue, yet at his name they fled:
> And cryinge babes, they ceased with the same,
> The like in FRANCE, sometime did TALBOTS name."

The cry[1] "A Talbot! a Talbot!" is represented by Shakespeare as sufficient in itself to make the French soldiers flee and leave their clothes behind; 1 *Henry VI.* (act ii. sc. 1, l. 78, vol. v. p. 29),—

> "*Sold.* I'll be so bold to take what they have left.
> The cry of Talbot serves me for a sword;
> For I have loaden me with many spoils
> Using no other weapon but his name."

And in the same play (act ii. sc. 3, l. 11, vol. v. p. 32), when the Countess of Auvergne is visited by the dreaded Englishman, the announcement is made,—

> "*Mess.* Madam,
> According as your ladyship desired,
> By message craved, so is Lord Talbot come.
> *Count.* And he is welcome. What! is this the man?
> *Mess.* Madam, it is.
> *Count.* Is this the scourge of France?
> Is this the Talbot, so much fear'd abroad
> That with his name the mothers still their babes?

Five or six instances may be found in which Shakespeare introduces the word "lottery;" and, historically, the word is deserving of notice,—for it was in his boyhood that the first public lottery was set on foot in England; and judging from the nature of the prizes, he appears to have made allusion to them. There were 40,000 chances,—according to Bohn's *Standard Library Cyclopædia*, vol. iii. p. 279,—sold at ten shillings each: "The prizes consisted of articles of plate, and the profit was

---

[1] "His soldiers spying his undaunted spirit,
A Talbot! a Talbot! cried out amain,
And rush'd into the bowels of the battle."
1 *Henry VI.*, act i. sc. 1, l. 127.

employed for the repair of certain harbours." The drawing took place at the west door of St. Paul's Cathedral; it began "23rd January, 1569, and continued incessantly drawing, *day and night*, till the 6th of May following."[*] How such an event should find its record in a Book of Emblems may at first be accounted strange; but in addition to her other mottoes, Queen Elizabeth had, on this occasion of the lottery, chosen a special motto, which Whitney (p. 61) attaches to the device,—

Whitney, 1586.

Silentium,—"Silence,"—

which, after six stanzas, he closes with the lines,—

"Th' Ægyptians wise, and other nations farre,
Vnto this ende, HARPOCRATES deuis'de,
Whose finger, still did seeme his mouthe to barre,
To bid them speake, no more than that suffis'de,
Which signe thoughe oulde, wee may not yet detest,
But marke it well, if wee will liue in reste."

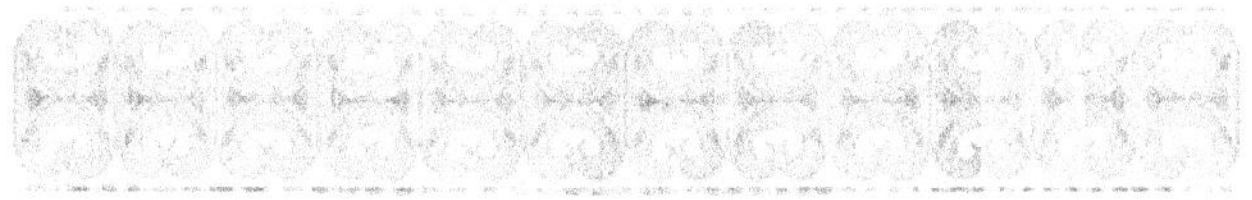

Written to the like effecte, vppon
Video, & taceo.
Her Maieſties poëſie, at the great Lotterie in LONDON,
begon M.D.LXVIII. *and ended* M.D.LXIX.

I See, and houlde my peace: a Princelie Poëſie righte,
For euerie faulte, ſhoulde not prouoke, a Prince, or man of mighte.
For if that IOVE ſhoulde ſhoote, ſo ofte as men offende,
The Poëttes ſaie, his thunderboltes ſhoulde ſoone bee at an ende.

[*] See *Gentleman's Magazine*, 1778, p. 470; 1821, pt. 1, p. 531; and *Archæologia*, vol. xix. pt. 1, art. x. Also, Blomfield's *Norfolk*, vol. v. p. 1600.

Then happie wee that haue, a Princeſſe ſo inclin'de.
That when as iuſtice drawes hir ſworde, hath mercie in her minde,
And to declare the ſame, howe prone ſhee is to ſaue:
Her Maieſtie did make her choice, this Poëſie for to haue.

Sed piger ad pœnas princeps, ad præmia velox:
*Cuique dolet, quoties cogitur eſſe ferox.**

Lines from Ovid, 2 *Trist.*, are in the margin,—

"*Si quoties peccāt homines sua fulmina mittat*
Jupiter, exiguo tempore inermis erit." †

Silence, also, was represented by the image of the goddess Ageniora. In an Emblem-book by Peter Costalius, *Pegma*, edition Lyons, 1555, p. 109, he refers to her example, and concludes his stanza with the words, *Si sapis à nostra disce tacere dea*,—"If thou art wise, learn from our goddess to be silent."

That Casket Scene in the *Merchant of Venice* (act i. sc. 2, l. 24), —from which we have already made long extracts,—contains a reference to lotteries quite in character with the prizes, "articles of plate and rich jewelry." Portia is deeming it hard, that according to her father's will, she "may neither choose whom she would, nor refuse whom she disliked." "Is it not hard, Nerissa, that I cannot choose one, nor refuse none?"

"*Ner.* Your father was ever virtuous; and holy men, at their death, have good inspirations: therefore, the lottery, that he hath devised in these three chests of gold, silver, and lead,—whereof who chooses his meaning chooses you—will, no doubt, never be chosen by any rightly, but one who shall rightly love."

The Prince of Morocco (act ii. sc. 1, l. 11) affirms to Portia,—

"I would not change this hue,
Except to steal your thoughts, my gentle queen;"

* "But a prince slow for punishments, swift for rewards:
To whomsoever he grieves, how often is he forced to be severe."

† "If as often as men sin his thunderbolts he should send,
Jupiter, in very brief time, without arms will be."

and Portia answers,—

> "In terms of choice I am not solely led
> By nice direction of a maiden's eyes;
> Besides the lottery of my destiny
> Bars me the right of voluntary choosing."

The prevalence of lotteries, too, seems to be intimated by the Clown in *All's Well that Ends Well* (act i. sc. 3, l. 73, vol. iii. p. 123), when he repeats the song,—

> "Among nine bad if one be good,
> Among nine bad if one be good,
> There's yet one good in ten;"

and the Countess reproving him says,—

> "What, one good in ten? you corrupt the song, sirrah.
>
> *Clo.* One good woman in ten, madam; which is a purifying o' the song: would God would serve the world so all the year! we'd find no fault with the tithe-woman, if I were the parson: one in ten, quoth a'! an' we might have a good woman born but one every blazing star, or at an earthquake, 'twould mend the lottery well: a man may draw his heart out, ere a' pluck one."

Shakespeare's words will receive a not inapt illustration from the sermon of a contemporary prelate, Dr. Chatterton, Bishop of Chester from 1579 to 1595, and to whom Whitney dedicated the Emblem on p. 120, *Vigilantia et custodia*,—"Watchfulness and guardianship."* He was preaching a wedding sermon in

---

"THE Heraulte, that proclaimes the daie at hande,
The Cocke I meane, that wakés vs out of sleepe,
On steeple highe, doth like a watchman stande:
The gate beneath, a Lion still doth keepe.
And why? theise two, did alder time decree,
That at the Churche, theire places still should bee.

That pastors, shoulde like watchman still be preste,
To wake the worlde, that sleepeth in his sinne,
And rouse them vp, that longe are rock'd in reste,
And showe the daie of Christe, will straighte beginne:
And to foretell, and preache, that light deuine,
Euen as the Cocke doth singe, ere daie doth shine.

The Lion shewes, they shoulde of courage bee
And able to defende, their flocke from foes:
If rauening wolfes, to lie in waite they see:
They shoulde be stronge, and boulde, with them to close:
And so be arm'de with learning, and with life,
As they might keepe, their charge, from either strife."

Cambridge, and Ormerod, i. p. 146, quoting King's *Vale Royal*, tells us,—

"He used this merry comparison. The choice of a wife is full of hazard, not unlike to a man groping for one fish in a barrel full of serpents: if he escape harm of the snakes, and light on the fish, he may be thought fortunate; yet let him not boast, for perhaps it may be but an eel."

That "good woman" "to mend the lottery well," that "one fish in a barrel full of serpents," came, however, to the chance of one of Cæsar's friends. Even when Antony (*Antony and Cleopatra*, act ii. sc. 2, l. 245, vol. ix. p. 40) was under the witchery of the "rare Egyptian queen," that "did make defect, perfection," the dramatist says,—

"If beauty, wisdom, modesty, can settle
The heart of Antony, Octavia is
A blessed lottery to him."

The Emblems applicable to Shakespeare's historical characters are only a few among the numbers that occur in the Emblem writers, as Alciat, Cousteau, Giovio, Symeoni, &c.: but our choice is limited, and there would be no pertinency in selecting devices to which in the dramas of our author there are no corresponding expressions of thought, though there may be parallelisms of subject.

Alciat's Arms (Giovio, ed. 1562).

SECTION II.

HERALDIC EMBLEMS, OR EMBLEMS APPLIED TO HERALDRY.

KNOTTED together as are Emblems and the very language of Heraldry, we must expect to find Emblem writers devoting some at least of their inventions to heraldic purposes. This has been done to a very considerable extent by the Italians, especially by Paolo Giovio, Domenichi, Ruscelli, and Symeoni; but in several other authors also there occur heraldic devices among their more general emblems. These are not full coats of arms and the complete emblazonnes of "the gentleman's science," but rather cognizances, or badges, by which persons and families of note may be distinguished. In this respect Shakespeare entirely agrees with the Emblem writers; neither he nor they give us the quarterings complete, but they single out for honourable mention some prominent mark or sign.

I attempt not to arrange the subject according to the Rules of the Art, but to exhibit instances in which Shakespeare and the Emblematists agree, of Poetic Heraldry, the Heraldry of Reward for Heroic Achievements, and the Heraldry of Imaginative Devices.

Of Poetic Heraldry the chief type is that bird of renown,

which was a favourite with Shakespeare, and from which he has been named by general consent, "the Swan of Avon." A white swan upon a shield occurs both in Alciat and in Whitney, and is expressly named *Insignia Poetarum*,—"The poets' ensigns."

The swan, in fact, was sacred to Apollo and the Muses; and hence was supposed to be musical. Æschylus, in his *Agamemnon*, makes Cassandra speak of the fable, when the Chorus bewail her sad destiny (vv. 1322, 3),—

> "Ἅπαξ ἔτ' εἰπεῖν ῥῆσιν ἢ θρῆνον θέλω
> ἐμὸν τὸν αὐτῆς."

i.e.,—"Yet once again I wish for her to speak forth prophecy or lamentation, even my own,"—and Clytæmnēstra mentions the singing of the swan at the point of death (vv. 1444-7),—

> "Ὁ μὲν γὰρ οὕτως· ἡ δέ τοι κύκνου δίκην
> τὸν ὕστατον μέλψασα θανάσιμον γόον
> κεῖται φιλήτωρ, τοῦδ', ἐμοὶ δ' ἐπήγαγεν
> εὐνῆς παροψώνημα τῆς ἐμῆς χλιδῆς."

Which is to this effect: that when she has sung the last mortal lamentation, according to the custom of the swan, she lies down as a lover, and offers to me the solace of the bed of my joy.

Horapollo, ed. 1551.

This notion of the singing of the swan is to be traced even to the hieroglyphics of Egypt. In answer to the question, "Πῶς γέροντα μουσικόν;"—how to represent "an old man musical?"—Horapollo, edition Paris, 1551, p. 136, replies,—

> "Γέροντα μουσικὸν βουλόμενοι σημῆναι, κύκνον ζωγραφοῦσιν. οὗτος γαρ ἥδυτατον μέλος ᾄδει γηράσκων."

i.e.—"Wishing to signify an old man musical, they paint a swan; for this bird sings its sweetest melody when growing old."

Virgil frequently speaks of swans, both as melodious and as shrill voiced. Thus in the *Æneid*, vii. 700-3: xi. 457,—

> "Cum sese è pastu referunt, et longa canoros
> Dant per colla modos: sonat amnis et Asia longè
> Pulsa palus."

i.e.—"When they return from feeding, and through their long necks give forth melodious measures; the river resounds and the Asian marsh from far."

> "Piscosóve amne Padusæ
> Dant sonitum rauci per stagna loquacia cycni."*

i.e.—"Or on the fish-abounding river Po the hoarse swans give forth a sound through the murmuring pools."

Horace, *Carm.* iv. 2. 25, names Pindar *Dircæum cycnum*,—"the Dircæan swan;" and *Carm.* ii. 20. 10, likens himself to an *album alitem*,—"a white-winged creature;" which a few lines further on he terms a *canorus ales*,—"a melodious bird,"—and speaks of his apotheosis to immortal fame.†

Anacreon is called by Antipater of Sidon, *Anthol. Græc. Carm.* 76, κύκνος Τήϊος,—"the Teian swan."

Poets, too, after death, were fancifully supposed to assume the form of swans. It was believed also that swans foresaw their own death, and previously sang their own elegy. Thus in Ovid, *Metam.* xiv. 430,—

> "Carmina jam moriens canit exequialia Cygnus,"—
> "Now dying the Swan chants its funereal songs."

Very beautifully does Plato advert to this fiction in his account of the conversation of Socrates with his friends on the day of his execution. (See *Phædon*, Francfort edition, 1602, p. 77, 64A.) They were fearful of causing him trouble and vexation; but he reminds them they should not think him inferior in foresight to the swans; for these,—

* See also *Ecl.* ix. 29, 36.

† See also *Carm.* ii. 3. 20.

"Fall a singing, as soon as they perceive that they are about to die, and sing far more sweetly than at any former time, being glad that they are about to go away to the God whose servants they are. . . . They possess the power of prophesying, and foreseeing the blessings of Hades they sing and rejoice exceedingly. Now I imagine that I am also a fellow-servant with the Swans and sacred to the same God, and that I have received from the same Master a power of foresight not inferior to theirs, so that I could depart from life itself with a mind no more cast down."

Thus the melodious dirge of the swan was attributed to the same kind of prescience which enables good men to look forward with delight to that time "when this mortal shall put on immortality."

The "PICTA POESIS," p. 28, adopts the same fancy of the swan singing at the end of life, but makes it the emblem of "old age eloquent." Thus,—

"FACVNDA SENECTVS.

"CANDIDA Cygnus auis suprema ætate canora est :
Inquam verti homines tabula picta docet,
Nam sunt canitie Cygni dulciq. canore,
Virtute illustres, eloquioque senes.
Dulce vetus vinum : senis est oratio dulcis,
Dulcior hoc ipso quò sapientior est."

i.e.—"At the end of life tuneful is the bird, the white swan, into which the painted tablet teaches that men are changed, for swans are illustrious from hoariness and the sweet singing, old men illustrious for virtue and for eloquence. Old wine is sweet; of an old man sweet is the speech; sweeter, for this very cause, the wiser it is."

Shakespeare himself adopts this notion in the *Merchant of Venice* (act i. sc. 2, l. 24, vol. ii. p. 286), when he says, "Holy men at their death have good inspirations."

Reusner, however, luxuriating in every variety of silvery and snowy whiteness, represents the swan as especially the symbol of the *pure simplicity of truth.* (*Emblemata,* lib. ii. 31, pp. 91, 92, ed. 1581.)

Simplicitas veri ſana.

Reusner, 1581.

EMBLEMA XXXI.

"*Albo candidius quid est olore,*
Argento, niue, lilio, ligustro?
Fides candida, candidiq' mores,
Et mens candida, candidi sodalis.
Te Schedi niueam fidem Melisse,
Moratum benè, candidamq' mentem
Possidere sodalis integelli:
Ligustro niueo nitentiorem:
Argento niueo beatiorem:
Albis liliolis fragrantiorem:
Cygnis candidulis decentiorem:
Armorum niueus docet tuorum
Cygnus: liliolis decorus albis:
Phœbea redimitus ora lauro.
Albo candidior cygnus ligustro:
Argento preciosior beato:
Cui nec par eboris decus, nec auri,
Nec gemmæ valor est, nitorq' pulcræ:
Et si pulcrius est in orbe quicquam."

i.e.—"Than a white swan what is brighter,—than silver, snow, the lily, the privet? Bright faith and bright morals,—and the bright mind of a bright companion. That thou of good morals, O Schedius Melissus, dost possess snow-like faith, and the bright mind of an uncorrupted companion;—that (thou art) more fair than the snowy privet,—more blessed than the snowy silver,—more fragrant than the white lilies,—more comely than the little bright swans,—the snowy swan on thy arms doth teach: a swan handsome with white lilies, encircled as to its features with the laurel of Phœbus; a swan brighter than the white privet,—more precious than the blessed silver; to which cannot be equalled the comeliness of ivory, or of gold; nor the worth and the splendour of a beautiful gem: and if in the world there is any thing more beautiful still."

To a short, but very learned dissertation on the subject, and to the device of a swan on a tomb, in his work, *De Volatilibus*, edition 1595, Emb. 23, Joachim Camerarius affixes the motto, "SIBI CANIT ET ORBI,"—*It sings for itself and for the world,*—

> "*Ipsa suam celebrat sibi mens bene conscia mortem,*
> *Vt solet herbiferum Cygnus ad Eridanum.*"

i.e.—"The mind conscious of good celebrates its own death for itself; as the swan is accustomed to do on the banks of the grassy Eridanus." *

Shakespeare's expressions, however, as to the swan, correspond more closely with the stanzas of Alciat (edition Lyons, 1551, p. 197) which are contained in the woodcut on next page.

Whitney (p. 126) adopts the same ideas, but enlarges upon them, and brings out a clearer moral interpretation, fortifying himself with quotations from Ovid, Reusner, and Horace,—

> "THE Martiall Captaines ofte, do marche into the fielde,
> With Egles, or with Griphins fierce, or Dragons, in theire shielde.
> But Phœbus sacred birde, let Poettes moste commende.
> Who, as it were by skill deuine, with songe forshowes his ende.
> And as his tune delightes: for rarenes of the same.
> So they with sweetenes of theire verse, shoulde winne a lasting name.
> And as his colour white: Sincerenes doth declare.
> So Poëttes must bee cleane, and pure, and must of crime beware.
> For which respectes the Swanne, should in their Ensigne stande.
> No forren fowle, and once suppos'de kinge of LIGVRIA Lande."

* The same author speaks also of the soft Zephyr moderating the sweet sounding song of the swan, and of sweet honour exciting the breasts of poets; and presents the swan as saying, "I fear not lightnings, for the branches of the laurel ward them off; so integrity despises the insults of fortune."—*Emb.* 24 and 25.

Alciat, Lugd 1551, p. 193.

In the very spirit of these Emblems of the Swan, the great dramatist fashions some of his poetical images and most tender descriptions. Thus in *King John* (act v. sc. 7, lines 1—24, vol. iv. p. 91), in the Orchard Scene at Swinstead Abbey, the king being in his mortal sickness, Prince Henry demands, "Doth he still rage?" And Pembroke replies,—

> "He is more patient
> Than when you left him; even now he sung.
> *P. Hen.* O vanity of sickness! fierce extremes
> In their continuance will not feel themselves.
> Death, having prey'd upon the outward parts,
> Leaves them invisible, and his siege is now
> Against the mind, the which he pricks and wounds
> With many legions of strange fantasies,
> Which in their throng and press to that last hold,
> Confound themselves. 'Tis strange that death should sing.
> I am the cygnet to this pale faint swan,
> Who chants a doleful hymn to his own death,
> And from the organ pipe of frailty sings
> His soul and body to their lasting rest."

To the same purport, in *Henry VIII.* (act iv. sc. 2, l. 77, vol. vi. p. 88), are the words of Queen Katharine, though she does not name the poet's bird,—

> "I have not long to trouble thee. Good Griffith,
> Cause the musicians play me that sad note
> I named my knell, whilst I sit meditating
> On that celestial harmony I go to."

And in the Casket Scene, so often alluded to (*Merchant of Venice*, act iii. sc. 2, l. 41, vol. ii. p. 325), when Bassanio is about to try his fortune, Portia thus addresses him,—

> "If you do love me, you will find me out.
> Nerissa and the rest, stand all aloof.
> Let music sound while he doth make his choice;
> Then, if he lose, he makes a swan-like end,
> Fading in music: that the comparison
> May stand more proper, my eye shall be the stream,
> And watery death-bed for him. He may win;

And what is music then? Then music is
Even as the flourish when true subjects bow
To a new-crowned monarch: such it is
As are those dulcet sounds in break of day
That creep into the dreaming bridegroom's ear
And summon him to marriage."

In the sad ending, too, of the *Moor of Venice* (act v. sc. 2, l. 146, vol. viii. p. 581), after Othello had said of Desdemona,—

"Nay, had she been true,
If heaven would make me such another world
Of one entire and perfect chrysolite,
I'd not have sold her for it:"

and the full proof of innocence having been brought forward, Emilia desires to be laid by her dead "Mistress' side," and inquires mournfully (l. 249, p. 586),—

"What did thy song bode, lady?
Hark, canst thou hear me? I will play the swan,
And die in music. [*Singing.*] Willow, willow, willow.
Moor, she was chaste; she loved thee, cruel Moor,
So come my soul to bliss, as I speak true;
So speaking as I think, I die, I die. [*Dies.*]"

After this long dissertation *anent* swans, there may be readers who will press hard upon me with the couplet from Coleridge,—

"Swans sing before they die: 'twere no bad thing,
Should certain persons die before they sing."

From Heraldry itself the *Midsummer Night's Dream* (act iii. sc. 2, l. 201, vol. ii. p. 239) borrows one of its most beautiful comparisons; it is in the passage where Helena so passionately reproaches Hermia for supposed treachery,—

"O, is all forgot?
All school-days' friendship, childhood innocence?
We, Hermia, like two artificial gods,

Have with our needles created both one flower,
Both on one sampler, sitting on one cushion,
Both warbling of one song, both in one key;
As if our hands, our sides, voices, and minds,
Had been incorporate. So we grew together,
Like to a double cherry, seeming parted;
But yet an union in partition,
Two lovely berries moulded on one stem;
So, with two seeming bodies, but one heart;
Two of the first, like coats in heraldry,
Due but to one, and crowned with one crest."

In speaking of the Heraldry of Heroic Achievements, we may refer to the "wreath of chivalry" (p. 168), already described from the *Pericles.* There were, however, other wreaths which the Romans bestowed as the rewards of great and noble exploits. Several of these are set forth by the Emblem writers; we will select one from Whitney (p. 115), *Fortiter & feliciter*,—"Bravely and happily."

Whitney, 1586

To this device of an armed hand grasping a spear, on which are hanging four garlands or crowns of victory, the stanzas are,—

"MARC SERGIVS nowe, I maye recorde by righte,
A Romane boulde, whome foes coulde not dismaye:
Gainste HANNIBAL hee often shewde his mighte,
Whose righte hande loste, his lefte hee did assaye
Vntill at lengthe an iron hande hee proou'd:
And after that CREMONA siege remoou'd.

Then, did defende PLACENTIA in distresse,
And wanne twelue houldes, by dinte of sworde in France,
What triumphes great? were made for his successe,
Vnto what state did fortune him aduance?
What speares? what crounes? what garlandes hee possest;
The honours due for them, that did the beste."

Of such honours, like poets generally, Shakespeare often tells. After the triumph at Barnet (3 *Henry VI.*, act v. sc. 3, l. 1, vol. v. p. 324), King Edward says to his friends,—

"Thus far our fortune keeps an upward course,
And we are grac'd with wreaths of victory."

Wreaths of honour and of victory are figured by Joachim Camerarius, "EX RE HERBARIA," edition 1590, in the 99th Emblem. The laurel, the oak, and the olive garlands are ringed together; the motto being, "HIS ORNARI AVT MORI,"—*With these to be adorned or to die,*—

"*Fronde oleæ, lauri, quercus contexta corolla*
Me decoret, sine qua viuere triste mihi,"—

i.e. "From bough of olive, laurel, oak, a woven crown
Adorns me, without which to live is sadness to me."

Among other illustrations are quoted the words of the *Iliad*, which are applied to Hector, τεθνάτω, οὔ οἱ ἀεικὲς ἀμυνομένῳ περὶ πάτρης,—"Let death come, it is not unbecoming to him who dies defending his country."

Of the three crowns two are named (3 *Henry VI.*, act iv. sc. 6, l. 32, vol. v. p. 309), when Warwick rather blames the king for preferring him to Clarence, and Clarence replies,—

> "No, Warwick, thou art worthy of the sway,
> To whom the heavens in thy nativity
> Adjudged an olive branch and laurel crown,
> As likely to be blest in peace and war,
> And therefore I yield thee my free consent."

The introduction to *King Richard III.* (act i. sc. 1, l. 1, vol. v. p. 473) opens suddenly with Gloster's declaration,—

> "Now is the winter of our discontent
> Made glorious summer by this sun of York;
> And all the clouds, that lour'd upon our house,
> In the deep bosom of the ocean bury'd."

"Sun of York" is a direct allusion to the heraldic cognizance which Edward IV. adopted, "in memory," we are told, "of the *three suns*," which are said to have appeared at the battle which he gained over the Lancastrians at Mortimer's Cross. Richard then adds,—

> "Now are our brows bound with victorious wreaths,
> Our bruised arms hung up for monuments;
> Our stern alarums changed to merry meetings,
> Our dreadful marches to delightful measures."

We meet, too, in the *Pericles* (act ii. sc. 3, l. 9, vol. ix. p. 345) with the words of Thaisa to the victor,—

> "But you, my knight and guest;
> To whom this wreath of victory I give,
> And crown you king of this day's happiness."

But in the pure Roman manner, and according to the usage of Emblematists, Shakespeare also tells of "victors' crowns;" following, as would appear, "LES DEVISES HEROIQVES" of Paradin, edition Anvers, 1562, f. 147 *verso*, which contains several instances of garlands for noble brows. Of these, one is entitled, *Seruati gratia ciuis,*—"For sake of a citizen saved."

The garland is thus described in Paradin's French,—

"*La Courõne, apellee Ciuique, estoit dõnee par le Citoyẽ, au Citoyẽ qu'il auoit sauué en guerre: en representatiõ de vie sauuee. Et estoit cete Courõne, tissue de fueilles, ou petis rameaus de Chesne: pour autãt qu'au Chesne, la vielle antiquité, souloit prẽdre sa substãce, sõ mãger, ou sa nourriture.*"

i.e.—"The crown called Civic was given by the Citizen to the Citizen* whom he had saved in war; in testimony of life saved. And this Crown was an inweaving of leaves or small branches of Oak; inasmuch as from the Oak, old antiquity was accustomed to take its subsistence, its food, or its nourishment."

"Among the rewards" for the Roman soldiery, remarks Eschenburg (*Manual of Classical Literature,* p. 274), "golden or gilded crowns were particularly common; as, the *corona castrensis,* or *vallaris,* to him who first entered the enemy's entrenchments; *corona muralis,* to him who first scaled the enemy's walls; and *corona navalis,* for seizing a vessel of the enemy in a sea-fight; also wreaths and crowns formed of leaves and blossoms; as the *corona civica,* of oak leaves, conferred for freeing a citizen from death or captivity at the hands of the enemy; the *corona obsidionalis,* of grass, for delivering a besieged city; and the *corona triumphalis,* of laurel, worn by a triumphing general."

* Paradin's words and his meaning differ; the Civic crown was bestowed, not on the citizen saved, but on the citizen who delivered him from danger.

Shakespeare's acquaintance with these Roman customs we find, where we should expect it to be, in the *Coriolanus* and in the *Julius Cæsar.* Let us take the instances; first, from the *Coriolanus,* act i. sc. 9, l. 58, vol. vi. p. 304; act i. sc. 3, l. 7, p. 287; act ii. sc. 2, l. 84, p. 323; and act ii. sc. 1, l. 109, p. 312. Cominius thanks the gods that "our Rome hath such a soldier" as Caius Marcius, and declares (act i. sc. 9, l. 58),—

> "Therefore, be it known,
> As to us, to all the world, that Caius Marcius
> Wears this war's garland: in token of the which,
> My noble steed, known to the camp, I give him,
> With all his trim belonging; and from this time,
> For what he did before Corioli, call him,
> With all the applause and clamour of the host,
> CAIUS MARCIUS CORIOLANUS. Bear
> The addition nobly ever!"

With most motherly pride Volumnia rehearses the brave deed to Virgilia, her son's wife (act i. sc. 3, l. 7),—

> "When, for a day of kings' entreaties, a mother should not sell him an hour from her beholding; I, considering how honour would become such a person; that it was no better than picture-like to hang by the wall, if renown made it not stir, was pleased to let him seek danger where he was like to find fame. To a cruel war I sent him; from whence he returned, his brows bound with oak. I tell thee, daughter, I sprang not more in joy at first hearing he was a man-child than now in first seeing he had proved himself a man."

And the gaining of that early renown is most graphically drawn by Cominius, the consul (act ii. sc. 2, l. 84),—

> "At sixteen years,
> When Tarquin made a head for Rome, he fought
> Beyond the mark of others: our then dictator,
> Whom with all praise I point at, saw him fight,
> When with his Amazonian chin he drove
> The bristled lips before him: he bestrid
> An o'er press'd Roman, and i' the consul's view
> Slew three opposers: Tarquin's self he met,
> And struck him on his knee: in that day's feats,

When he might act the woman in the scene,
He proved best man i' the field, and for his meed
Was brow-bound with the oak. His pupil age
Man-enter'd thus, he waxed like a sea;
And, in the brunt of seventeen battles since,
He lurch'd all swords of the garland."

The successful general is expected in Rome, and this dialogue is held between Menenius, Virgilia, and Volumnia (act ii. sc. 1, l. 109, p. 312),—

"*Men.* Is he not wounded? he was wont to come home wounded.
Vir. O, no, no, no.
Vol. O, he is wounded; I thank the gods for't.
Men. So do I too, if it be not too much: brings a' victory in his pocket? The wounds become him.
Vol. On's brows: Menenius, he comes the third time home with the oaken garland."

Next, we have an instance from the *Julius Cæsar* (act v. sc. 3, l. 80, vol. vii. p. 409), on the field of Philippi, when "in his red blood Cassius' day is set," Titanius asks,—

"Why didst thou send me forth, brave Cassius?
Did I not meet thy friends? and did not they
Put on my brows this wreath of victory,
And bid me give it thee? Didst thou not hear their shouts?
Alas, thou hast misconstrued every thing!
But, hold thee, take this garland on thy brow;
Thy Brutus bid me give it thee, and I
Will do his bidding."

The heraldry of honours from sovereign princes, as testified to, both by Paradin in his "DEVISES HEROIQVES," edition Antwerp, 1562, folio 12*v*, and 25, 26, and by Shakespeare, embraces but two or three instances, and is comprised in the magniloquent lines (1 *Henry VI.*, act iv. sc. 7, l. 60, vol. v. p. 80) in which Sir William Lucy inquires,—

"But where's the great Alcides of the field,
Valiant Lord Talbot, Earl of Shrewsbury,

Created, for his rare success in arms,
Great Earl of Washford, Waterford and Valence;
Lord Talbot of Goodrig and Urchinfield,
Lord Strange of Blackmere, Lord Verdun of Alton,
Lord Cromwell of Wingfield, Lord Furnival of Sheffield,
The thrice-victorious Lord of Falconbridge:
Knight of the noble order of Saint George,
Worthy Saint Michael and the Golden Fleece;
Great marshal to Henry the Sixth
Of all his wars within the realm of France?"

From Paradin we learn that the Order of St. Michael had for its motto *Immensi tremor Oceani*,—"The trembling of the immeasurable ocean,"—and for its badge the adjoining collar.—

Paradin, ed. 1562, p. 100.

"This order was instituted by Louis XI., King of France, in the year 1469.* He directed for its ensign and device a collar of gold, made with shells laced together in a double row, held firm upon little chains or meshes of gold; in the middle of which collar on a rock was a gold-image of Saint Michael, appearing in the front. And this the king did (with respect to the Archangel) in imitation of King Charles VII. his father; who had formerly borne that image as his ensign, even at his entry into Rouen. By reason always (it is said) of the apparition, on the bridge of Orleans, of Saint Michael defending the city against the English in a famous attack. This collar then of the royal order and device of the Knights of the same is the sign or true ensign of their nobleness, virtue, concord, fidelity and friendship; Pledge, reward and remuneration of their valour and prowess. By the richness and purity of the gold are pointed out their high rank and grandeur;

* Consequently there is an anachronism by Shakespeare in assigning the order of St. Michael to "valiant Lord Talbot, Earl of Shrewsbury," who was slain in 1453.

by the similarity or likeness of its shells, their equality, or the equal fraternity of the Order (following the Roman senators, who also bore shells on their arms for an ensign and a device): by the double lacing of them together, their invincible and indissoluble union; and by the image of Saint Michael, victory over the most dangerous enemy. A device then instituted for the solace, protection and assurance of this so noble a kingdom; and, on the contrary, for the terror, dread and confusion of the enemies of the same."

Paradin (f. 25) is also our authority with respect to the Order of the Golden Fleece, its motto and device being thus presented:—

Precium non vile laborum,—
"No mean reward of labours."

Paradin, 1562.

"The order of the Golden Fleece," says Paradin, "was instituted by Philip, Duke of Burgundy, styled the Good, in the year 1429, for which he named* twenty-four Knights without reproach, besides himself, as chief and founder, and gave to each one of them for ensign of the said Order a Collar of gold composed of his device of the Fusil, with the Fleece of gold appearing in front; and this (as people say) was in imitation of that which Jason acquired in Colchis, taken customarily for Virtue, long so much loved by this good Duke, that he merited this surname of Goodness, and other praises contained on his Epitaph, where there is mention made of this Order of the Fleece, in the person of the Duke saying,—

'Pour maintenir l'Eglise, qui est de Dieu maison,
J'ai mis sus le noble Ordre, qu'on nomme la Toison.'"

* The name of Lord Talbot, Earl of Shrewsbury, does not occur in the list which Paradin gives of the twenty-four Knights Companions of the Golden Fleece.

The expedition of the Argonauts, and Jason's carrying off of the Golden Fleece may here be appropriately mentioned; they are referred to by the Emblem writers, as well as the exploit of Phrixus, the brother of Helle, in swimming across the Hellespont on the golden-fleeced ram. The *former* Whitney introduces when describing the then new and wonderful circumnavigation of the globe by Sir Francis Drake (p. 203),—

> "Let GRÆCIA then forbeare, to praise her IASON boulde?
> Who throughe the watchfull dragons pass'd, to win the fleece of goulde.
> Since by MEDEAS helpe, they weare inchaunted all,
> And IASON without perrilles, pass'de: the conqueste therfore small?
> But, hee, of whome I write, this noble minded DRAKE,
> Did bringe away his goulden fleece, when thousand eies did wake."

The *latter* forms the subject of one of Alciat's Emblems, edition Antwerp, 1581, Emb. 189, in which, seated on the precious fleece, Phrixus crosses the waters, and fearless in the midst of the sea mounts the tawny sheep, the type of "the rich man unlearned." Whitney (p. 214) substitutes *In diuitem, indoctum*, — "To the rich man, unlearned," — and thus paraphrases the original,—

Diues indoctus.

Alciat, 1551

Tranat aquas resides precioso in vellere Phrixus,
Et flauam impauidus per mare scandit ouem.
Ecquid id est? vir sensu hebeti, sed diuite gaza,
Coniugis aut serui quem regit arbitrium.

"ON goulden fleece, did Phryxus passe the waue,
And landed safe, within the wished baie :
By which is ment, the fooles that riches haue,
Supported are, and borne throughe Lande, and Sea :
And those enrich'de by wife, or seruauntes goodds,
Are borne by them like Phryxus through the floodds."

In a similar emblem, Beza, edition Geneva, 1580, Emb. 3, alludes to the daring deed of Phrixus,—

"*Aurea mendaci vates non vnicus ore*
Vellera phrixeæ commemorauit ouis.
Nos, te, Christe, agnum canimus. Nam diuite gestas
Tu verè veras vellere solus opes."

Thus rendered in the French version,—

"*Maint poete discourt de sa bouche menteuse*
Sur vne toison d'or. Nous, à iuste raison,
Te chantons, Christ, agneau, dont la riche toison
Est l'vnique thresor qui rend l'Eglise heureuse."

The *Merchant of Venice* (act. i. sc. 1, l. 161, vol. ii. p. 284) presents Shakespeare's counterpart to the Emblematists ; it is in Bassanio's laudatory description of Portia, as herself the golden fleece,—

"In Belmont is a lady richly left ;
And she is fair, and, fairer than that word,
Of wondrous virtues : sometimes from her eyes
I did receive fair speechless messages :
Her name is Portia ; nothing undervalued
To Cato's daughter, Brutus' Portia :
Nor is the wide world ignorant of her worth ;
For the four winds blow in from every coast
Renowned suitors : and her sunny locks
Hang on her temples like a golden fleece :
Which makes her seat of Belmont Colchos strand,
And many Jasons come in quest of her."

To this may be added a line or two by Gratiano, l. 241, p. 332,—

"How doth that royal merchant, good Antonio ?
I know he will be glad of our success ;
We are the Jasons, we have won the fleece."

The heraldry of Imaginative Devices in its very nature offers a wide field where the fancy may disport itself. Here things the most incongruous may meet, and the very contrariety only justify their being placed side by side.

Let us begin with the device, as given in the "TETRASTICHI MORALI," p. 56, edition Lyons, 1561, by Giovio and Symeoni, used between 1498 and 1515; it is the device

DI LVIGI XII. RE
DI FRANCIA.

Giovio and Symeoni, 1561

to the motto, "Hand to hand and afar off,"—

Cominus & eminus.

Di lontano & da presso il Re Luigi,
Ferì'l nimico, & lo ridusse à tale,
Che dall' Indico al lito Occidentale
Di sua virtù si veggiono i vestigi.

A Porcupine is the badge, and the stanza declares,—

"From far and from near the King Louis,
Smites the enemy and so reduces him,
That from the Indian to the Western shore,
Of his valour the traces are seen."

Camerarius with the same motto and the like device testifies that this was the badge of Louis XI., king of France, to whose praise he also devotes a stanza,—

"*Cominus ut pugnat jaculis, atq. eminus histrix,*
Rex bonus esto armis consiliisque potens."

i.e. "As close at hand and far off the porcupine fights with its spines,
Let a good king be powerful in arms and in counsels."

It was this Louis who laid claim to Milan, and carried Ludovic Sforza prisoner to France. He defeated the Genoese after their revolt, and by great personal bravery gained the victory of Agnadel over the Venetians in 1509. At the same time he made war on Spain, England, Rome, and Switzerland, and was in very deed the porcupine darting quills on every side.

The well known application in *Hamlet* (act. i. sc. 5, l. 13, vol. viii. p. 35) of the chief characteristic of this vexing creature is part of the declaration which the Ghost makes to the Prince of Denmark,—

"But that I am forbid
To tell the secrets of my prison-house,
I could a tale unfold whose lightest word
Would harrow up thy soul, freeze thy young blood,
Make thy two eyes, like stars, start from their spheres,
Thy knotted and combined locks to part
And each particular hair to stand an end,
Like quills upon the fretful porpentine."

And of "John Cade of Ashford," in 2 *Henry VI.* (act. iii. sc. 1, l. 360, vol. v. p. 162), the Duke of York avers,—

"In Ireland I have seen this stubborn Cade
Oppose himself against a troop of kernes;
And fought so long, 'till that his thighs with darts
Were almost like a sharp-quill'd porcupine."

From the same source, Giovio's and Symeoni's "SENTENTIOSE IMPRESE," Lyons, 1561, p. 115, we also derive the cognizance,—

DEL CAPITANO GIROLAMO
MATTEI ROMANO.

Giovio and Symeoni, 1561.

Diuora il struzzo con ingorda furia
Il ferro, & lo smaltisce poi pian piano,
Così (come dipinge il buon Romano)
Smaltir fa il tempo ogni maggiore ingiuria.

Spiritus durissima coquit.

To this Ostrich, with a large iron nail in its mouth, and with a scroll inscribed, "Courage digests the hardest things," the stanza is devoted which means,—

"Devour does the ostrich with eager greediness
The iron, and then very easily digests it,
So (as the good Romano represents)
Time causes every injury to be digested."

Camerarius, to the same motto, *Ex Volatilibus* (ed. 1595, p. 19), treats us to a similar couplet,—

> "*Magno animo fortis perferre pericula suevit,*
> *Vllo nec facile frangitur ille metu.*"

i.e. "With mighty mind the brave grows accustomed to bear dangers,
Nor easily is that man broken by any fear."

Shakespeare's description of the ostrich, as given by Jack Cade, 2 *Henry VI.* (act iv. sc. 10, l. 23, vol. v. p. 206), is in close agreement with the ostrich device,—

"Here's the lord of the soil," he says, "come to seize me for a stray, for entering his fee-simple without leave. Ah, villain, thou wilt betray me, and get a thousand crowns of the king for carrying my head to him; but I'll make thee eat iron like an ostrich, and swallow my sword like a great pin, ere thou and I part."

Note the iron pin in the ostrich's mouth.

Sola facta solum Deum sequor.

Paradin, 1562.

"My Lady Bona of Savoy," as Paradin (ed. 1562, fol. 165) names her, "the mother of Ian Galeaz, Duke of Milan, finding herself a widow, made a device on her small coins of a Phœnix in the midst of a fire, with these words, 'Being made lonely, I follow God alone.' Wishing to signify that, as there is in the world but one Phœnix, even so being left by herself, she wished only to love conformably to the only God, in order to live eternally."*

* Paradin's text:—"*Ma Dame Bone de Sauoye mere de Ian Galeaz, Duc de Milan, se trouuant veufe feit faire vne Deuise en ses Testons d'vne Fenix au milieu d'vn feu auec ces paroles:* Sola facta, solum Deum sequor. *Voulant signifier que comme il n'y a au monde qu'vne Fenix, tout ainsi estant demeuree seulette, ne vouloit aymer selon le seul Dieu, pour viure eternellement.*"

The "TETRASTICHI MORALI" presents the same Emblem, as indeed do Giovio's "DIALOGO DELL' IMPRESE," &c., ed. Lyons, 1574, and "DIALOGVE DES DEVISES," &c., ed. Lyons, 1561;

DI MADAMA BONA
DI SAVOIA.

Giovio, 1574, diminished.

with the same motto, and the invariable Italian Quatrain,—

Sola facta solū
Deū sequor.

Perduto ch' hebbe il fido suo conforte
La nobil Donna, qual Fenice sola,
A Dio volse ogni priego, ogni parola,
Dando vita al pensier con l' altrui morte.

In English,—

"Lost had she her faithful consort,
The noble Lady, as a Phœnix lonely.
To God wills every prayer, every word
Giving life to consider death with others."

The full description and characteristics of the Phœnix we reserve for the section which treats of Emblems for Poetic Ideas; but the loneliness, or if I may use the term, the oneliness of this fabulous bird Shakespeare occasionally dwells upon.

In the *Cymbeline* (act i. sc. 6, l. 12, vol. ix. p. 183), Posthumus and Iachimo had made a wager as to the superior qualities and beauties of their respective ladies, and Iachimo takes from Leonatus an introduction to Imogen; the Dialogue thus proceeds,—

> "*Iach.* The worthy Leonatus is in safety,
> And greets your highness dearly. [*Presents a letter.*
> *Imo.* Thanks, good sir:
> You're kindly welcome.
> *Iach.* [*Aside.*] All of her that is out of door most rich!
> If she be furnish'd with a mind so rare,
> She is alone the Arabian bird, and I
> Have lost the wager."

Rosalind, in *As You Like It* (act iv. sc. 3, l. 15, vol. ii. p. 442), thus speaks of the letter which Phebe, the shepherdess, had sent her,—

> "She says I am not fair, that I lack manners;
> She calls me proud, and that she could not love me,
> Were man as rare as phœnix."

The oneliness of the bird is, too, well set forth in the *Tempest* (act iii. sc. 3, l. 22, vol. i. p. 50),—

> "In Arabia
> There is one tree, the phœnix' throne; one phœnix
> At this hour reigning there."

To the Heraldry of Imaginative Devices might be referred the greater part of the coats of arms, badges and cognizances by which noble and gentle families are distinguished. To conclude this branch of our subject, I will name a woodcut which was probably peculiar to Geffrey Whitney at the time when Shakespeare wrote, though accessible to the dramatist from other sources; it is the fine frontispiece to the *Choice of Emblemes*, setting forth the heraldic honours and arms of Robert, Earl of Leycester, and in part of his brother, Ambrose, Earl of Warwick. Each of these noblemen bore the same crest, and it was, what

Shakespeare, 2 *Henry VI.* (act v. sc. 1, l. 203, vol. v. p. 215), terms "the rampant bear chained to the ragged staff."

How long this had been the cognizance of the Earls of Warwick, and whether it was borne by all the various families of the Saxon and Norman races who held the title,—by the Beauchamps, the Nevilles, and the Dudleys, admits of doubt; but it is certain that such was the cognizance in the reign of Henry VI. and in that of Elizabeth.

Whitney, 1586.

According to Dugdale's *Antiquities of Warwickshire*, edition 1730, p. 398, the monument of Thomas Beauchamp, Earl of Warwick in Edward III.'s time, has a lion, not a bear; and a lamb for his Countess, the Lady Katherine Mortimer. Also on the monument of another Earl (p. 404), who died in 1401, the bear does not appear; but on the monument of Richard Beauchamp, who died "the last day of Aprill, the year of our lord god 1434," the inscriptions are crowded with bears, instead of commas and colons; and the recumbent figure of the Earl has a muzzled bear at his feet (p. 410). The Nevilles now succeeded to the title, and a limner's or designer's very curious bill, of the fifteenth year of Henry VI., 1438, shows that the bear and ragged staff were then both in use and in honour,—

"First CCCC Pencels bete with the Raggidde staffe of silver pris the pece v d	08*l.* 06*s.* 00
Item for a grete Stremour for the Ship of XI yerdis length and IIII yerdis in brede, with a grete Bere and Gryfon holding a Raggid staffe, poudrid full of raggid staves; and for a grate Crosse of S. George for the lymmynge and portraying	01 . 06 . 08
Item XVIII Standardes of worsted, entretailled with the Bere and a Chayne, pris the pece xii d.	00 . 18 . 00"

Among the monuments in the Lady Chapel at Warwick is a full length figure of "Ambrose Duddeley," who died in 1589, and of a muzzled bear crouching at his feet. Robert Dudley, Earl of Leycester, his brother, died in 1588; and on his magnificent tomb, in the same chapel, is seen the same cognizance of the bear and ragged staff. The armorial bearings, however, are a little different from those which Whitney figures.

If, according to the Cambridge edition of Shakespeare's works, 1863-1866, vol. v. p. vii., "the play upon which the Second part of Henry the Sixth was founded was first printed in quarto, in 1594;" or if, as some with as much reason have supposed,* it existed even previous to 1591, it is not likely that these monuments of elaborate design and costly and skilled workmanship could have been completed, so that from them Shakespeare had taken his description of "old Nevil's crest." Nathan Drake's *Shakspeare and his Times* (vol. i. pp. 410, 416) tells us that he left Stratford for London "about the year 1586, or 1587;" yet "the *family residence* of Shakspeare was *always* at Stratford: that he himself originally went *alone* to London, and that he spent the greater part of every year there *alone*, annually, however, and probably for some months, returning to the bosom of his family, and that this alternation continued until he finally left the capital."

Of course, had the monuments in question existed before the composition of the *Henry VI.*, his annual visits to his native Warwickshire would have made them known to him, and he would thus have noted the family cognizance of the brother Earls; but reason favours the conjecture that these monuments in the Lady Chapel were not the sources of his knowledge.

Common rumour, indeed, may have supplied the information;

---

* See *Penny Cyclopædia*, vol. xxi. p. 343: "We have no doubt that the three plays in their original form, which we now call the three Parts of *Henry VI.*, were his," *i. e.* Shakespeare's, "and they also belong to this epoch," *i. e.* previous to 1591.

but as Geffrey Whitney's book appeared in 1586, its first novelty would be around it about the time at which Shakespeare was engaged in producing his *Henry VI.* That Emblem-book was dedicated to "ROBERT Earle of LEYCESTER;" and, as we have said, contains a drawing, remarkably graphic, of a bear grasping a ragged staff, having a collar and chain around him, and standing erect on the helmet's burgonet. There is also a less elaborate sketch of the same badge on the title-page to the second part of Whitney's *Emblemes*, p. 105.

Most exactly, most artistically, does the dramatist ascribe the same crest, in the same attitude, and in the same standing place, to Richard Nevil, Earl of Warwick, the king-setter-up and putter-down of History. In the fields between Dartford and Blackheath, in Kent, the two armies of Lancaster and York are encamped; in the Dialogue, there is almost a direct challenge from Lord Clifford to Warwick to meet upon the battle-field. York is charged as a traitor by Clifford (2 *Henry VI.*, act v. sc. 1, l. 143, vol. v. p. 213), but replies,—

> "I am the king, and thou a false-heart traitor.
> Call hither to the stake my two brave bears,
> That with the very shaking of their chains
> They may astonish these fell-lurking curs:
> Bid Salisbury and Warwick come to me.
>
> *Enter the* EARLS OF WARWICK *and* SALISBURY.
>
> *Clif.* Are these thy bears? we'll bait thy bears to death,
> And manacle the bear-ward in their chains,
> If thou darest bring them to the baiting place.
> *Rich.* Oft have I seen a hot o'erweening cur
> Run back and bite, because he was withheld;
> Who, being suffer'd with the bear's fell paw,
> Hath clapp'd his tail between his legs and cried:
> And such a piece of service will you do,
> If you oppose yourselves to match Lord Warwick."

The Dialogue continues until just afterwards Warwick makes this taunting remark to Clifford (l. 196),—

"*War.* You were best to go to bed and dream again,
To keep thee from the tempest of the field.
Clif. I am resolved to bear a greater storm
Than any thou canst conjure up to-day;
And that I'll write upon thy burgonet,
Might I but know thee by thy household badge.
War. Now, by my father's badge, old Nevil's crest,
The rampant bear chain'd to the ragged staff,
This day I'll wear aloft my burgonet,
As on a mountain top the cedar shows
That keeps his leaves in spite of any storm,
Even to affright thee with the view thereof.
Clif. And from thy burgonet I'll rend thy bear
And tread it underfoot with all contempt,
Despite the bear-ward that protects the bear."

A closer correspondence between a picture and a description of it cannot be desired: Shakespeare's lines and Whitney's frontispiece exactly coincide;

"Like coats in heraldry
Due but to one, and crowned with one crest."

By Euclid's axiom, "magnitudes which coincide are equal;" and though the reasonings in geometry and those in heraldry are by no means of forces identical, it may be a just conclusion; therefore, the coincidences and parallelisms of Shakespeare, with respect to Heraldic Emblems, have their original lines and sources in such writers as Giovio, Paradin, and Whitney. It was not he who set up the ancient fortifications, but he has drawn circumvallations around them, and his towers nod over against theirs, though with no hostile rivalry.

Horapollo, ed. 1551.

Section III.

EMBLEMS FOR MYTHOLOGICAL CHARACTERS.

CHO has not more voices than Mythology has transmutations, eccentricities, and cunningly devised fancies,—and every one of them has its tale or its narrative—its poetic tissues woven of such an exquisite thinness that they leave no shadows where they pass. The mythologies of Egypt and of Greece, of Etruria and of Rome, in all their varying phases of absolute fiction and substantial truth, perverted by an unguarded imagination, were the richest mines that the Emblem writers attempted to work; they delighted in the freedom with which the fancy seemed invited to rove from gem to gem, and luxuriated in the many forms into which their fables might diverge. Now they touched upon Jove's thunder, or on the laurel for poets' brows, which the lightning's flash could not harm—then on the beauty and gracefulness of Venus, or on the doves that fluttered near her car;—Dian's severe strictness supplied them with a theme, or Juno with her queenly birds; and they did not disdain to tell of Bacchus and the vine, of Circe, and Ulysses, and the Sirens. The slaying of Niobe's children, Actæon seized by his hounds, and Prometheus chained to the rock, Arion rescued by the dolphin, and Thetis at the tomb of Achilles,—these and many other myths and tales of antiquity grew up in the minds of Emblematists, self-sown—ornaments, if not utilities.

Though the great epic poems are inwrought throughout with the mosaic work of fables that passed for divine, and of exploits that were almost more than human, Ovid's *Metamorphoses*, printed as early as 1471, and of which an early French edition, in 1484, bears the title **La Bible des poetes**, may be regarded as the chief storehouse of mythological adventure and misadventure. The revival of literature poured forth the work in various forms and languages. Spain had her translation in 1494, and Italy in 1497; and as Brunet informs us (vol. iv. c. 277), to another of Ovid's books, printed in Piedmont before 1473, there was this singularly incongruous subscription, "*Laus Deo et Virgini Mariæ Gloriosissimæ Johannes Glim.*" Caxton, in England, led the way by printing Ovid's *Metamorphoses* in 1480, which Arthur Golding may be said to have completed in 1567 by his *English Metrical Version.*

Thus everywhere was the storehouse of mythology open: and of the Roman fabulist the Emblem writers, as far as they could, made a Book of Emblems, and often into their own works transported freely what they had found in his.

And for a poet of no great depth of pure learning, but of unsurpassed natural power and genius, like Shakespeare, no class of books would attract his attention and furnish him with ideas and suggestions so readily as the Emblem writers of the Latin and Teutonic races. "The eye," which he describes, "in a fine phrensy rolling," would suffice to take in at a single glance many of the pictorial illustrations which others of duller sensibilities would only master by laborious study; and though undoubtedly, from the accuracy with which Shakespeare has depicted ancient ideas and characters, and shown his familiarity with ancient customs, usages, and events, he must have read much and thought much, or else have thought intuitively, it is a most reasonable conjecture that the popular literature of his times—the illustrated Emblem-books, which made their way of welcome among the chief nations of middle, western, and southern Europe—should have been one of the fountains at which he gained knowledge. Nature, indeed, forms the poet, and his storehouses of materials on which to work are the inner and outer worlds, first of his own consciousness, and next of heaven and earth spread before him. But as a portion of this latter world we may name the appliances and results of artistic skill in its delineations of outward forms, and in the fixedness which it gives to many of the conceptions of the mind. To the artist himself, and to the poet not less than to the artist, the pictured shapes and groupings of mythological or fabulous beings are most suggestive, both of thoughts already embodied there, and also of other thoughts to be afterwards combined and expressed.

Hence would the Emblem-books, on some of which the foremost painters and engravers had not disdained to bestow their powers, become to poets especially fruitful in instruction. A proverb, a fable, an old world deity is set forth by the pencil and the graving tool, and the combination supplies additional elements of reflection. Thus, doubtless, did Shakespeare use such works; and not merely are some of his thoughts and expressions in unison with them, but moulded and modified by them.

For much indeed of his mythological lore he was indebted to Ovid's *Metamorphoses*, or, rather, I should say, to "*Ovid's Metamorphoses* translated out of Latin in English metre by Arthur Golding, gent. A worke very pleasaunt and delectable: 4to London 1565." That he did attend to Golding's couplet,—

> "With skill, heed, and judgment, thys work must be red,
> For els too the reader it stands in small stead,"—

will appear from some few instances: as,—

> "Thy promises are like Adonis' gardens
> That one day bloom'd, and fruitful were the next."
>
> 1 *Hen. VI.*, act i. sc. 6, l. 6

"Apollo flies and Daphne holds the chase,
The dove pursues the griffin; the mild hind
Makes speed to catch the tiger."

Midsummer Night's Dream, act ii. sc. 1, l. 231.

"We still have slept together,
Rose at an instant, learn'd, play'd, eat together,
And wheresoe'er we went, like Juno's swans,
Still we went coupled and inseparable."

As You Like It, act i. sc. 3, l. 69.

"Approach the chamber and destroy your sight
With a new Gorgon."

Macbeth, act ii. sc. 3, l. 67.

"I'll have no worse a name than Jove's own page;
And therefore look you call me Ganymede."

As You Like It, act i. sc. 3, l. 120.

and,—

"O Proserpina,
For the flowers now, that frighted thou let'st fall
From Dis's waggon! daffodils,
That come before the swallow dares, and take
The winds of March with beauty; violets dim
But sweeter than the lids of Juno's eyes
Or Cytherea's breath; pale primroses,
That die unmarried, ere they can behold
Bright Phœbus in his strength, a malady
Most incident to maids; bold oxlips and
The crown imperial; lilies of all kinds,
The flower-de-luce being one! O, these I lack
To make you garlands of; and my sweet friend
To strew him o'er and o'er!"

Winter's Tale, act iv. sc. 4, l. 116.

Yet from the Emblem writers as well he appears to have derived many of his mythological allusions and expressions; we may trace this generally, and with respect to some of the Heathen Divinities,—to several of the ancient Heroes and Heroines, we may note that they supply him with most beautiful personifications.

Generally, as in *Troilus and Cressida* (act ii. sc. 3, l. 240), the expression "bull-bearing Milo" finds its device in the *Emblemata* of Lebeus Batillius, edition Francfort, 1596, where we are told that "Milo by long custom in carrying the calf could also carry it when it had grown to be a bull." In *Romeo and Juliet* (act ii. sc. 5, l. 8) the lines,—

> "Therefore do nimble-pinion'd doves draw love
> And therefore hath the wind swift Cupid wings."

We have the scene pictured in Corrozet's *Hecatomgraphie*, Paris, 1540, leaf 70, with, however, a very grand profession of regard for the public good,—

> "Ce n'est pas cy Cupido ieune enfant
> Que vous voier au carre triumphant,
> Mais c'est amour lequel tiẽt en sa corde
> Tous les estatz en grãd paix & cõcorde."

In *Richard II.* (act iii. sc. 2, l. 24) Shakespeare seems to have in view the act of Cadmus, when he sowed the serpent's teeth,—

> "This earth shall have a feeling and these stones
> Prove armed soldiers, ere her native king
> Shall falter under foul rebellion's arms."

And the device which emblematizes the fact occurs in Symeoni's abbreviation of the *Metamorphoses* into the form of Italian Epigrams (edition Lyons, 1559, device 41, p. 52).

And lastly, in 3 *Henry VI.* (act v. sc. 1, l. 34), from a few lines of dialogue between Warwick and King Edward, we read,—

> "*War.* 'Twas I that gave the kingdom to thy brother.
> *K. Edw.* Why then 'tis mine, if but by Warwick's gift.
> *War.* Thou art no Atlas for so great a weight:
> And weakling, Warwick takes his gift again."

But a better comment cannot be than is found in Giovio's "DIALOGVE," edition Lyons, 1561, p. 129, with Atlas carrying the Globe of the Heavens, and with the motto, "SVSTINET NEC FATISCIT,"—*He bears nor grows weary.*

The story of Jupiter and Io is presented in the Emblem-books by Symeoni, 1561, and by the Plantinian edition of

Ovid's *Metamorphoses*, Antwerp, 1591, p. 35. From the latter, were it needed, we could easily have added a pictorial illustration to the *Taming of the Shrew* (Induction, sc. 2, l. 52),—

> "We'll show thee Io as she was a maid
> And how she was beguiled and surprised,
> As lively painted as the deed was done."

The *Antony and Cleopatra* (act ii. sc. 7, l. 101, vol. ix. p. 60), in one part, presents the banquet, or, rather, the drinking bout, between Cæsar, Antony, Pompey, and Lepidus, "the third part of the world." Enobarbus addresses Antony,—

> "*Eno.* [*To Antony.*] Ha, my brave emperor!
> Shall we dance now the Egyptian Bacchanals,
> And celebrate our drink?
> *Pom.* Let's ha't, good soldier.
> *Ant.* Come, let's all take hands,
> Till that the conquering wine hath steep'd our sense
> In soft and delicate Lethe.
> *Eno.* All take hands.
> Make battery to our ears with the loud music:
> The while I'll place you: then the boy shall sing;
> The holding every man shall bear as loud
> As his strong sides can volley.
> [*Music plays*, ENOBARBUS *places them hand in hand.*
>
> THE SONG.
>
> "Come, thou monarch of the vine,
> Plumpy Bacchus with pink eyne!
> In thy fats our cares be drown'd,
> With thy grapes our hairs be crown'd:
> Cup us, till the world go round,
> Cup us, till the world go round!"

Now, the figures in Alciat, in Whitney, in the *Microcosmos*,* and especially in Boissard's "THEATRVM VITÆ HUMANÆ," ed. Metz, 1596, p. 213, of a certainty suggest the epithets "plumpy Bacchus" "with pink eyne," a very chieftain of "Egyptian Bac-

* Or *Parvus Mundus*, ed. 1579, where the figure of Bacchus by Gerard de Jode has wings on the head, and a swift Pegasus by its side, just striking the earth for flight.

chanals." This last depicts the "monarch of the vine" approaching to mellowness.

Boissard, 1596.

The Latin stanzas subjoined would, however, not have suited Enobarbus and the roistering triumvirs of the world,—

> "*Suave Dei munus vinum est: hominumque saluti*
> *Conducit: præsit dummodò sobrietas.*
> *Immodico sed si tibi proluat ora Lyæo,*
> *Pro dulci potas tetra aconita mero.*"

i.e.
> "Wine is God's pleasant gift, and for men's health
> Conduces, when sobriety presides;
> But if excessive drained Lyæan wealth,
> For liquor sweet black aconite abides."

The phrase, "rempli de vin dont son visage est teint," in "LE MICROCOSME," Lyons, 1562, suggests the placing the stanzas in which it occurs, in illustration of Shakespeare's song; they are,—

> "Le Dieu Bacchus d'ordinaire on depeint
> Ayant en main vn chapelet de lierre,
> Tenant aussi vne couppe ou vn verre
> Rempli de vin dont son visage est teint.

Des deux costes son chef on void aislé.
Et pres de luy d'vne pasture belle
Le genereux Pegasus à double aisle
Se veut guinder vers le ciel estoilé."

In ſtatuam Bacchi.
Dialogismvs.
XXV.

Alciat, 1581

It may give completion to this sketch if we subjoin the figured Bacchus of Alciat (edition Antwerp, 1581, p. 113), and present the introductory lines,—

"Bacche *pater quis te mortali lumine nouit,*
Et docta effinxit quis tua membra manu?
Praxiteles, qui me rapientem Gnossida vidit,
Atque illo pinxit tempore, qualis eram."

Of Alciat's 36 lines, Whitney, p. 187, gives the brief yet paraphrastic translation,—

"The timelie birthe that Semele did beare,
See heere, in time howe monstêrous he grewe:
With drinkinge muche, and dailie bellie cheare,
His eies weare dimme, and fierie was his hue.
His cuppe, still full: his head, with grapes was croun'de:
Thus time he spent with pipe, and tabret sounde.*

Which carpes all those, that loue to much the canne,
And dothe describe theire personage, and theire guise:
For like a beaste, this doth transforme a man,
And makes him speake that moste in secret lies;
Then, shunne the sorte that bragge of drinking muche,
Seeke other frendes, and ioyne not handes with suche."

* It is curious to observe how in the margin Whitney supports his theme by a reference to Ovid, and by quotations from Anacreon, John Chrysostom, Sambucus, and Propertius.

On the same subject we may refer to *Love's Labour's Lost* (act iv. sc. 3, l. 308, vol. ii. p. 151), to the long discourse or argument by Biron, in which he asks,—

> "For where is any author in the world
> Teaches such beauty as a woman's eye?"

The offensiveness of excess in wine is then well set forth (l. 333),—

> "Love's feeling is more soft and sensible,
> Than are the tender horns of cockled snails;
> Love's tongue proves dainty Bacchus gross in taste."

On these words the best comment are two couplets from Whitney (p. 133), to the sentiment, *Prudentes vino abstinent,*—"The wise abstain from wine."

Whitney, 133.

LOE here the vine dothe claſpe, to prudent Pallas tree,
The league is nought, for virgines wiſe, doe Bacchus frendſhip flee.

Alciat. *Quid me vexatis rami? Sum Palladis arbor,*
Auferte hinc botros, virgo fugit Bromium.

Engliſhed ſo.

Why vexe yee mee yee boughes? ſince I am Pallas tree:
Remoue awaie your cluſters hence, the virgin wine doth flee.

K K

Not less degrading and brutalising than the goblets of Bacchus are the poisoned cups of the goddess Circe. Her fearful power and enchantments form episodes in the 10th book of the *Odyssey*, in the 7th of the *Æneid*, and in the 14th of the *Metamorphoses*. So suitable a theme for their art is not neglected by the Emblem writers. Alciat adopts it as a warning against meretricious allurements (edition 1581, p. 184),—

ANDREAE ALCIATI

Cauendum à meretricibus.

EMBLEMA LXXVI.

Alciat, 1581.

SOLE *satæ Circes tam magna potentia fertur,*
Verterit vt multos in noua monstra viros.
Testis equûm domitor Picus, tum Scylla biformis,
Atque Ithaci postquàm vina bibere sues.
Indicat illustri meretricem nomine Circe,
Et rationem animi perdere, quisquis amat.

Adopting another motto, *Homines voluptatibus transformantur*, —"Men are transformed by pleasures,"—Whitney (p. 82) yet gives expression to Alciat's idea,—

"SEE here VLISSES men, transformed straunge to heare :
Some had the shape of Goates, and Hogges, some Apes, and Asses weare.
Who, when they might haue had their former shape againe,
They did refuse, and rather wish'd, still brutishe to remaine.
Which showes those foolishe sorte, whome wicked loue dothe thrall,
Like brutishe beastes do passe theire time, and haue no sence at all.
And thoughe that wisedome woulde, they shoulde againe retire,
Yet, they had rather CIRCES serue, and burne in theire desire.
Then, loue the onelie crosse, that clogges the worlde with care,
Oh stoppe your eares, and shutte your eies, of CIRCES cuppes beware."

The striking lines from Horace (*Epist.* i. 2) are added,—

"*Sirenum voces, & Circes pocula nosti :*
Quæ si cum sociis stultus, cupidusq' bibisset,
Sub domina meretrice fuisset turpis, & excors,
Vixisset canis immundus, vel amica luto sus."

i.e. "Of Sirens the voices, and of Circe the cups thou hast known :
Which if, with companions, anyone foolish and eager had drunk,
Under a shameless mistress he has become base and witless,
Has lived as a dog unclean, or a sow in friendship with mire."

Circe and Ulysses are also briefly treated of in *The Golden Emblems* of Nicholas Reusner, with Stimmer's plates, 1591, sign C. v.

Bellua dira libido
Pulcra facit Circe meretrix excordia corda :
Fortis Vlyſseâ, qui ſapit, arte domat.
Ins Vieh verzaubert Circe vil,
Schlägt Hurn von sich, wer weiß sein will.

Reusner (edition 1581, p. 134), assuming that "Slothfulness is the wicked Siren," builds much upon Virgil and Horace, as may be seen from the epithets he employs. We give only a portion of his Elegiacs, and the English of them first,—

"Through various chances, through so many dangerous things,
While again and again the Ithacan pursues the long ways :
The voices of Sirens, and of Circe the kingdoms he forsakes :
Nor does the bland Atlantis his journey retard.
But as Circe to his companions supplies the potations foul,
Witless and shameless this becomes a sow and that a dog."

Improba Siren deſidia.

EMBLEMA XXIV.

Ad Vuolfgangum, & Carolum Rechlingeros, Patr. Auguſtanos.

Reusner, 1581.

PEr varios caſus, per tot diſcrimina rerum,
Dum longas Ithacus itq́, reditq́, vias:
Sirenum voces, & Circes regna relinquit:
Blanda nec Atlantis tunc remoratur iter.
At ſocijs Circe dum pocula fœda miniſtrat:
Excors, & turpis ſus fit hic, ille canis.

Now, Shakespeare's allusions to Circe are only two. The *first*, in the *Comedy of Errors* (act v. sc. 1, l. 269, vol. i. p. 455), when all appears in inextricable confusion, and Antipholus of Ephesus demands justice because of his supposed wrongs. The Duke Solinus in his perplexity says,—

"Why what an intricate impeach is this!
I think you all have drunk of Circe's cup."

The *second*, in 1 *Henry VI.* (act v. sc. 3, l. 30, vol. v. p. 86). On fighting hand to hand with the Maid of Orleans, and taking her prisoner, the Duke of York, almost like a dastard, reproaches and exults over her noble nature,—

> "Damsel of France I think, I have you fast:
> Unchain your spirits now with spelling charms
> And try if they can gain you liberty.
> A goodly prize, fit for the devil's grace!
> See, how the ugly witch doth bend her brows,
> As if, with Circe, she would change my shape!"

So closely connected with Circe are the Sirens of fable that it is almost impossible to treat of them separately. As usual, Alciat's is the Emblem-book (edition 1551) from which we obtain the illustrative print and the Latin stanzas.

Sirenes.

Alciat, 1551

> *Absque alis volucres, & cruribus absque puellas,*
> *Rostro absque, & pisces, qui tamen ore canant:*
> *Quis putet esse vllos? iungi hæc natura negauit*
> *Sirenes fieri sed potuisse docent.*
> *Illicitum est mulier, quæ in piscem desinit atrum,*
> *Plurima quòd secum monstra libido vehit.*
> *Aspectu, verbis, animi candore, trahuntur,*
> *Parthenope, Ligia, Leucosiaque viri.*
> *Has musæ explumant, has atque illudit Vlysses.*
> *Scilicet est doctis cum meretrice nihil.*

It is Whitney who provides the poetic comment (p. 10),—

"WITHE pleasaunte tunes, the SYRENES did allure
Vlisses wise, to listen to theire songe:
But nothinge could his manlie harte procure,
Hee sailde awaie, and scap'd their charming stronge,
The face, he lik'de, the nether parte, did loathe:
For womans shape, and fishes had they bothe.

Which shewes to vs, when Bewtie seekes to snare
The carelesse man, whoe dothe no daunger dreede,
That he shoulde flie, and shoulde in time beware,
And not on lookes, his fickle fancie feede:
Such Mairemaides liue, that promise onelie ioyes:
But hee that yeldes, at lengthe him selffe distroies."

The Dialogue, from the *Comedy of Errors* (act iii. sc. 2, lines 27 and 45, vol. i. pp. 425, 6), between Luciana and Antipholus of Syracuse, maintains,—

"'Tis holy sport, to be a little vain,
When the sweet breath of flattery conquers strife;"

and the remonstrance urges,—

"O train me not, sweet mermaid, with thy note,
To drown me in thy sister flood of tears:
Sing, siren, for thyself, and I will dote:
Spread o'er the silver waves thy golden hairs,
And, as a bed I'll take them, and there lie;
And, in that glorious supposition, think
He gains by death that hath such means to die."

And in the *Titus Andronicus* (act ii. sc. 1, l. 18, vol. vi. p. 451), Aaron, the Moor, resolves, when speaking of Tamora his imperial mistress,—

"Away with slavish weeds and servile thoughts!
I will be bright, and shine in pearl and gold,
To wait upon this new-made empress.
To wait, said I? to wanton with this queen,
This goddess, this Semiramis, this nymph,

This siren, that will charm Rome's Saturnine,
And see his shipwreck and his commonweal's." *

To recommend the sentiment that "Art is a help to nature," Alciatus (edition 1551, p. 107) introduces the god Mercury and the goddess Fortune,—

Ars Naturam adiuuans.

Alciat, 1551.

Vt sphæræ Fortuna, cubo sic insidet Hermes :
Artibus hic, varijs casibus illa præest.
Aduersus vim Fortunæ est ars facta : sed artis
Cùm fortuna mala est, sæpe requirit opem.
Disce bonas artes igitur studiosa iuuentus,
Quæ certæ secum commoda sortis habent.

i.e. "As on a globe Fortune rests, so on a cube Mercury :
In various arts this one excells, that in mischances.
Against the force of Fortune art is used ; but of art,
When Fortune is bad, she often demands the aid.
Learn good arts then ye studious youth,
Which being sure have with themselves the advantages of destiny."

* To the device of the Sirens, Camerarius, *Ex Aquatilibus* (ed. 1604, leaf 64), affixes the motto, "MORTEM DABIT IPSA VOLVPTAS,"—*Pleasure itself will give death*, —and with several references to ancient authors adds the couplet,—

"*Dulcisono mulcent Sirenes æthera cantu :*
Tu fuge, ne pereas, callida monstra maris."

i.e. "With sweet sounding song the Sirens smooth the breeze :
Flee, lest thou perish, the crafty monsters of the seas."

Sambucus takes up the lyre of some Emblem Muse and causes Mercury to strike a similar strain to the saying, "Industry corrects nature."

Induſtria naturam corrigit.

Sambucus, 1564.

TAM *rude & incultum nihil eſt, induſtria poſſit*
Naturæ vitium quin poliiſſe, labor.
Inuentam caſu cochleam, temereque iacentem
Inſtruxit neruis nuntius ille Deûm.
Informem citharam excoluit: nunc gaudia mille,
Et reddit dulces pectine mota ſonos.
Cur igitur quereris, naturam & fingis ineptam?
Nónne tibi ratio eſt? muta loquuntur, abi.
Ritè fit è concha teſtudo, ſeruit vtrinque:
In venerem hæc digitis, ſæpiùs illa gula.

The god is mending a broken or an imperfect musical instrument, a lyrist is playing, and a maiden dancing before him. Whitney thus performs the part of interpreter (p. 92),—

"THE Lute, whose sounde doth most delighte the eare
Was caste aside, and lack'de bothe striges, and frettes:
Whereby, no worthe within it did appeare,
MERCVRIVS came, and it in order settes:
Which being tun'de, such Harmonie did lende,
That Poëttes write, the trees theire toppes did bende.

Euen so, the man on whome dothe Nature froune,
Wereby, he liues dispis'd of euerie wighte,
Industrie yet, maie bringe him to renoume,
And diligence, maie make the crooked righte :
Then haue no doubt, for arte maie nature helpe.
Thinke howe the beare doth forme her vgly whelpe."

The cap with wings, and the rod of power with serpents entwined, are almost the only outward signs of which Shakespeare avails himself in his descriptions of Mercury, so that in this instance there is very little correspondence of idea or of expression between him and our Emblem authors. Nevertheless, we produce it for what it is worth.

In *King John* (act iv. sc. 2, l. 170, vol. iv. p. 67), the monarch urges Falconbridge's brother Philip to inquire respecting the rumours that the French had landed,—

"Nay, but make haste ; the better foot before.
O, let me have no subject enemies,
When adverse foreigners affright my towns
With dreadful pomp of stout invasion !
Be Mercury, set feathers to thy heels
And fly like thought from them to me again."

One of Shakespeare's gems is the description which Sir Richard Vernon gives to Hotspur of the gallant appearance of "The nimble-footed madcap Prince of Wales" (1 *Henry IV.*, act iv. sc. 1, l. 104, vol. iv. p. 318),—

"I saw young Harry, with his beaver on,
His cuisses on his thighs, gallantly arm'd,
Rise from the ground like feather'd Mercury,
And vaulted with such ease into his seat,
As if an angel dropp'd down from the clouds,
To turn and wind a fiery Pegasus
And witch the world with noble horsemanship."

The railer Thersites (*Troilus and Cressida*, act ii. sc. 3, l. 9, vol. vi. p. 168) thus mentions our Hermes,—

O thou great thunder-darter of Olympus, forget that thou art Jove the king of gods ; and Mercury, lose all the serpentine craft of thy caduceus."

And centering the good qualities of many into one, Hamlet (act iii. sc. 4, l. 55, vol. viii. p. 111) sums up to his mother the perfections of his murdered father,—

> "See what a grace was seated on this brow:
> Hyperion's curls, the front of Jove himself,
> An eye like Mars, to threaten and command;
> A station like the herald Mercury
> New lighted on a heaven-kissing hill;
> A combination and a form indeed,
> Where every god did seem to set his seal
> To give the world assurance of a man."

Personifications, or, rather, deifications of the powers and properties of the natural world, and of the influences which presided over them, belong especially to the ancient Mythology. Of these, there is one from the Emblem writers decidedly claiming our notice, I may say, our admiration, because of its essential truth and beauty;—it is the Personification of Fortune, or, as some writers name the goddess, Occasion and Opportunity; and it is highly poetical in all its attributes.

From at least four distinct sources in the Emblem-books of the sixteenth century, Shakespeare might have derived the characteristics of the goddess; from Alciat, Perriere, Corrozet, and Whitney.

Perriere's "THEATRE DES BONS ENGINS," Paris, 1539, presents the figure with the stanzas of old French here subjoined,—

> "Qvel est le nō de la presentę image?
> Occasion ce nôme pour certain.
> Qui fut l'autheur? Lysipus fist l'ouurage:
> Et que tient ellę? vng rasoir en sa main.
> Pourquoi? pourtãtque tout trãche souldain.
> Ellę a cheueulx deuãt & non derriere?
> Cest pour mõstrer quelle tourne ẽ arriere
> Sõ fault le coup quãd on la doibt tenir
> Aulx talons a dis esles? car barriere
> (Quellesque soit) ne la peult retenir."

These French verses may be accepted as a translation of the Latin of Alciat, on the goddess Opportunity: as may be seen, she is portrayed standing on a wheel that is floating upon the waves; and as the tide rises, there are apparently ships or boats making for the shore. The figure holds a razor in the right hand, has wings upon the feet, and abundance of hair streaming from the forehead.

In occaſionem.

Διαλογιστικῶς.

Alciat, 1551.

Lyſippi hoc opus eſt, Sycion cui patria. Tu quis?
Cuncta domans capti temporis articulus.
Cur pinnis ſtas? vſque rotor. Talaria plantis
Cur retines? Paſſim me leuis aura rapit.
In dextra eſt tenuis dic vnde nouacula? Acutum
Omni acie hoc ſignum me magis eſſe docet.
Cur in frõte coma? Occurrẽs vt prẽdar. At heus tu
Dic cur pars calua eſt poſterior capitis?
Ne ſemel alipedem ſi quis permittat abire,
Ne poſſim apprehenſo poſtmodò crine capi.
Tali opifex nos arte, tui cauſa, edidit hoſpes.
Vtq; omnes moneam: pergula aperta tenet.

Whitney's English lines (p. 181) sufficiently express the meaning, both of the French and of the Latin stanzas,—

"WHAT creature thou? *Occasion I doe showe.*
On whirling wheele declare why doste thou stande?
Bicause, I still am tossed too, and froe.
Why doest thou houlde a rasor in thy hande?
That men maie knowe I cut on euerie side,
And when I come, I armies can deuide.

But wherefore hast thou winges vppon thy feete?
To showe, how lighte I flie with little winde.
What meanes longe lockes before? *that suche as meete,*
Maye houlde at firste, when they occasion finde.
Thy head behinde all balde, what telles it more?
That none shoulde houlde, that let me slippe before.

Why doest thou stande within an open place?
That I maye warne all people not to staye,
But at the firste, occasion to imbrace,
And when shee comes, to meete her by the waye.
Lysippus so did thinke it best to bee,
Who did deuise mine image, as you see.

The correspondent part to the thought contained in these three writers occurs in the *Julius Cæsar* (act iv. sc. 3, l. 213, vol. vii. p. 396), where Brutus and Cassius are discussing the question of proceeding to Philippi and offering battle to "young Octavius and Marc Antony;" it is decided by the argument which Brutus urges with much force,—

"Our legions are brim-full, our cause is ripe:
The enemy increaseth every day;
We, at the height, are ready to decline.
There is a tide in the affairs of men
Which taken at the flood leads on to fortune;
Omitted, all the voyage of their life
Is bound in shallows and in miseries.
On such a full sea are we now afloat,
And we must take the current when it serves,
Or lose our ventures."

These lines, we may observe, are an exact comment on Whitney's text; there is the "full sea," on which Fortune is "now afloat;" and people are all warned, "at the first occasion to embrace," or "take the current when it serves."

The "images," too, of Fortune and of Occasion in Corrozet's "HECATOMGRAPHIE," Embs. 41 and 84, are very suggestive of the characteristics of the "fickle goddess."

Corrozet, 1540.

Fortune is standing upright upon the sea; one foot is on a fish, the other on a globe; and in the right hand is a broken mast. Occasion is in a boat and standing on a wheel; she has wings to her feet, and with her hands she holds out a swelling sail; she has streaming hair, and behind her in the stern of the boat Penitence is seated, lamenting for opportunities lost. The stanzas to "Occasion" are very similar to those of other Emblem writers; and we add, therefore, only the English of the verses to "Fortune,"—*The Image of Fortune.*

> "A strange event our Fortune is,
> Unlook'd for, sudden as a shower;
> Never then, worldling! give to her
> Right over thee to wield her power."

A series of questions follow,—

> "Tell me, O fortune, for what end thou art holding the broken mast wherewith thou supportest thyself? And why also is it that thou art painted upon the sea, encircled with so long a veil? Tell me too why under thy feet are the ball and the dolphin?"

As in the answers given by Whitney, there is abundant plainness in Corrozet,—

> "It is to show my instability, and that in me there is no security. Thou seest this mast broken all across,—this veil also puffed out by various winds,—beneath one foot, the dolphin amid the waves; below the other foot, the round unstable ball;—I am thus on the sea at a venture. He who has made my portraiture wishes no other thing to be understood than this, that distrust is enclosed beneath me and that I am uncertain of reaching a safe haven;—near am I to danger, from safety ever distant: in perplexity whether to weep or to laugh,—doubtful of good or of evil, as the ship which is upon the seas tossed by the waves, is doubtful in itself where it will be borne. This then is what you see in my true image, hither and thither turned without security."

A description, very similar to this, occurs in the dialogue between Fluellen, a Welsh captain, and "an aunchient lieutenant" Pistol (*Henry V.*, act iii. sc. 6, l. 20, vol. iv. p. 543),—

> "*Pist.* Captain, I thee beseech to do me favours:
> The Duke of Exeter doth love thee well.
> *Flu.* Ay, I praise God; and I have merited some love at his hands.
> *Pist.* Bardolph, a soldier, firm and sound of heart,
> And of buxom valour, hath, by cruel fate,
> And giddy Fortune's furious fickle wheel,

That goddess blind,*
That stands upon the rolling, restless stone—

Flu. By your patience, Aunchient Pistol, Fortune is painted blind, with a muffler afore her eyes, to signify to you that fortune is blind; and she is painted also with a wheel, to signify to you, which is the moral of it, that she is turning, and inconstant, and mutability, and variation: and her foot, look you, is fixed upon a spherical stone, which rolls, and rolls, and rolls: in good truth, the poet makes a most excellent description of it: Fortune is an excellent moral."

Fortune on the sphere, or "rolling, restless stone," is also well pictured in the "ΜΙΚΡΟΚΟΣΜΟΣ," editions 1579 and 1584. The whole device is described in the French version,—

"L'oiseau de Paradis est de telle nature
Qu'en nul endroit qui soit on ne le void iucher,
Car il n'a point de pieds, & ne peut se rucher
Ailleurs qu'en l'air serein dont il prend nourriture.

En cest oiseau se void de Fortune l'image,
En laquelle n'y a sinon legreté:
Iamais son cours ne fut egal & arresté,
Mais tousiours incertain inconstant & volage.

Pour la quelle raison on souloit la pourtraire,
Tenant vn voile afin d'aller au gré du vent,
Des aisles aux costez pour voler bien auant,
Ayant les pieds coupez, estant sur vne sphære;

Et pourtant cestuy la qui se fie en Fortune,
Au lieu de fier au grand Dieu souuerain,
Est bien maladuisé, & se monstre aussi vain
Que celuy qui bastit sur le dos de Neptune."

The ideas of the Emblematists respecting the goddess "OCCASION" are also embodied by Shakespeare two or three

* Shakespeare's "goddess blind" and his representation of blind Love have their exact correspondence in the motto of Otho Vænius, "Blynd fortune blyndeth loue;" which is preceded by Cicero's declaration, "Non solùm ipsa fortuna cæca est: sed etiam plerumque cæcos efficit quos complexa est: adeò vt spernant amores veteres, ac indulgeant nouis,"—

"Sometyme blynd fortune can make loue bee also blynd,
And with her on her globe to turne & wheel about,
When cold preuailes to put light loues faint feruor out,
But ferwent loyall loue may no such fortune fynde."

times. Thus on receiving the evil tidings of his mother's death and of the dauphin's invasion, King John (act iv. sc. 2, l. 125, vol. iv. p. 65) exclaims,—

> "Withhold thy speed, dreadful Occasion!
> O make a league with me, till I have pleased
> My discontented peers!"

In 2 *Henry IV.* (act iv. sc. 1, l. 70, vol. iv. p. 431) the Archbishop of York also says,—

> "We see which way the stream of time doth run,
> And are enforced from our most quiet there
> By the rough torrent of occasion."

Most beautiful too, and forcible are the stanzas on *Occasion*, or *Opportunity* from *Lucrece* (lines 869—882, vol. ix. p. 515),—

> "Unruly blasts wait on the tender spring;
> Unwholesome weeds take root with precious flowers;
> The adder hisses where the sweet birds sing;
> What virtue breeds iniquity devours:
> We have no good that we can say is ours
> But ill-annexed Opportunity
> Or kills his life or else his quality.
>
> O Opportunity, thy guilt is great!
> 'Tis thou that executest the traitor's treason;
> Thou set'st the wolf where he the lamb may get;
> Whoever plots the sin, thou point'st the season;
> 'Tis thou that spurn'st at right, at law, at reason,
> And in thy shady cell, where none may spy him,
> Sits Sin, to seize the souls that wander by him." *

Very appropriately in illustration of these and other passages in Shakespeare may we refer to John David's work, "OCCASIO

---

* Well shown in Whitney's device to the motto, *Veritas inuicta*,—"Unconquered truth" (p. 166),—where the Spirits of Evil are sitting in "shady cell" to catch the souls of men, while the Great Enemy is striving—

> "with all his maine and mighte
> To hide the truthe, and dimme the lawe deuine."

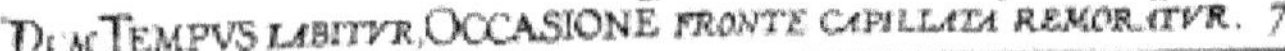

DUM TEMPUS LABITUR, OCCASIONEM FRONTE CAPILLATA REMORATUR. 7.

A. Nunc opus est alios Terrarum inuisere tractus,
Et Iuuenes alios Monstrs vos ergo valete.
B. Quis subitæ calor iste fugæ? C. Quum sit fuga tandem
Certa tibi est; pennas saltem Dea calua fugaces
Sistat adhuc. D. Cur tot nequidquam verba per auras
Perditis? hinc alio, mora nulla, recedo; valete.
E. Aufugiat? sparsosq; potius pro fronte capillos
Arripite. D. At sine, sponte sequar; vestrisq; morabor
Ædibus, ad iustam donec perduxero metam.
F. Laudo animos, nam vi cogi DEA gaudet amicâ.

From Darius [illegible]

ARREPTA NEGLECTA" (4to, Antwerp, 1605),—*Opportunity seized or neglected.* It contains twelve curiously beautiful plates by Theodore Galle, showing the advantages of seizing the Occasion, the disadvantages of neglecting it. We choose an example, it is Schema 7, cap. 1, p. 117. (See Plate XII.)

> "While Time is passing onward men keep Occasion back by seizing the hair on her forehead."

Various speakers are introduced,—

> "*Time.* Now the need is to visit other climes of earth
> And other youths. Ye warned then, bid farewell.
> *B.* What this heat of sudden flight?
> *C.* If flight indeed at length
> For thee is fix'd, her swift wings let the bald goddess
> At least rest here.
> *Occasion.* Why to no purpose words in air
> Waste ye? hence elsewhere, no delay, I go; farewell.
> *E.* Should she flee? rather her scattered locks in front
> Seize hold of.
> *Occasion.* Alas! freely I follow, at your own homes
> Will tarry, till in just measure I prolong my stay.
> *Faith.* I praise your spirit, for by friendly force the goddess
> Rejoices to be compelled."

The line, "her scattered locks in front seize hold of," has its parallel in *Othello* (act iii. sc. 1, l. 47, vol. viii. p. 505),—

> "he protests he loves you,
> And needs no other suitor but his likings
> To take the safest occasion by the front
> To bring you in again."

Classical celebrities, whether hero or heroine, wrapt round with mystery, or half-developed into historical reality, may also form portion of our Mythological Series.

The grand character in Æschylus, *Prometheus Bound*, is depicted by at least four of the Emblematists. The hero of suffering is reclining against the rock on Caucasus, to which he had been chained; a vulture is seated on his broad chest and feeding there. Alciat's Emblem, from the Lyons edition of 1551, or Antwerp, 1581, number 102, has the motto which reproves men for seeking the knowledge which is beyond them: *Things which are above us, are nothing to us,*—they are not our concern. The whole fable is a warning.

Quæ ſupra nos, nihil ad nos.

Alciat, 1551

Caucaſi a æternùm pendens in rupe Prometheus
Diripitur ſacri præpetis vngue iecur.
Et nollet feciſſe hominem: figulosq́; peroſus
Accenſam rapto damnat ab igne facem.
Roduntur variis prudentum pectora curis,
Qui cæli affectant ſcire, deûmque vices.

"On the Caucasian rock Prometheus eternally suspended,
Has his liver torn in pieces by talons of an accursed bird.
And unwilling would he be to have made man; and hating the potters
Dooms to destruction the torch lighted from stolen fire.
Devoured by various cares are the bosoms of the wise,
Who affect to know secrets of heaven, and courses of gods."

Similarly as a dissuasive from vain curiosity, Anulus, in his "Picta Poesis" (Lyons, 1555, p. 90), sets up the notice,—

CVRIOSITAS FVGIENDA.

"Curiosity must be shunned."

Anton, 1555.

MITTE *arcana Dei cœlumq; inquirere quid sit.*
Nec sapias plusquàm debet homo sapere.
Caucaseo vinctus monet hoc in rupe Prometheus
Scrutator cœli, fur & in igne Iouis.
Cui cor edax Aquila in rediuiuo vulnere rodit.
Materia pœnis sufficiente suis.
Ἡ δὲ προμηθεῖ' ἄχος δάπτει κέαρ ἔντερον ἔνδον
Καρδιοβόρος ὅπως αἰετὸς ἐστὶν ἄχος.

The device is almost the same with Alciat's,—the stanzas, however, are a little different,—

"Forbear to inquire the secrets of God, and what heaven may be.
Nor be wise more than man ought to be wise.
Bound on Caucasian rock this does Prometheus warn,
Scrutator of heaven and thief in the fire of Jove.
His heart the voracious Eagle gnaws in ever reviving wound,
Material sufficient this for all his penalties."

"As for Prometheus pain gnaws his heart the bosom within,
So is pain the eagle that consumes the heart."

The "MICROCOSME," first published in 1579, fol. 5, celebrates in French stanzas Prometheus and his cruel destiny; a fine device accompanies the emblem, representing him bound not to Caucasus, but to the cross.

"Promethee s' estant guindé iusques aux cieux
Pour desrober le feu des redoubables Dieux,
Pour retribution de ceste outrecuidance
Fut par eux poursuiui d'une rude vengeance.

> Il fut par leur decret à la croix attaché,
> La ou pour expier deuenant son peché,
> L'Aigle de Iupiter le becquetoit sans cesse,
> Si que ce patient estoit en grand oppressé."

But Reusner's *Emblems* (bk. i. Emb. 27, p. 37, edition 1581), and Whitney's (p. 75), adopt the same motto, *O vita misero longa*,—"O life, how long for the wretched." The stanzas of the latter may be accepted as being in some degree representative of those of the former,—

> "TO Caucasus, behoulde PROMETHEVS chain'de,
> Whose liuer still, a greedie gripe dothe rente:
> He neuer dies, and yet is alwaies pain'de,
> With tortures dire, by which the Poëttes ment,
> That hee, that still amid misfortunes standes,
> Is sorrowes slaue, and bounde in lastinge bandes.
>
> For, when that griefe doth grate vppon our gall,
> Or surging seas, of sorrowes moste doe swell,
> That life is deathe, and is no life at all,
> The liuer rente, it dothe the conscience tell:
> Which being launch'de, and prick'd, with inward care,
> Although wee liue, yet still wee dyinge are."

How Shakespeare applies this mythic story appears in the *Titus Andronicus* (act ii. sc. 1, l. 14, vol. vi. p. 451), where Aaron, speaking of his queen, Tamora, affirms of himself,—

> "Whom thou in triumph long
> Hast prisoner held, fetter'd in amorous chains,
> And faster bound to Aaron's charming eyes
> Than is Prometheus tied to Caucasus."

And still more clearly is the application made, 1 *Henry VI.* (act iv. sc. 3, l. 17, vol. v. p. 71), when Sir William Lucy thus urges York,—

> "Thou princely leader of our English strength,
> Never so needful on the earth of France,
> Spur to the rescue of the noble Talbot,
> Who now is girdled with a waist of iron
> And hemm'd about with grim destruction:"

and at York's inability, through "the vile traitor Somerset," to render aid, Lucy laments (l. 47, p. 72),—

> "Thus, while the vulture of sedition
> Feeds in the bosoms of such great commanders,
> Sleeping neglection doth betray to loss
> The conquest of our scarce cold conqueror,
> That ever living man of memory,
> Henry the Fifth."

It may readily be supposed that in writing these passages Shakespeare had in memory, or even before him, the delineations which are given of Prometheus, for the vulture feeding on the heart belongs to them all, and the allusion is exactly one of those which arises from a casual glance at a scene or picture without dwelling on details.

This casual glance indeed seems to have been the way in which our Dramatist appropriated others of the Emblem sketches. In the well-known quarrel scene between Brutus and Cassius, in *Julius Cæsar* (act iv. sc. 3, l. 21, vol. vii. p. 389), Brutus demands,—

> "What, shall one of us,
> That struck the foremost man of all this world
> But for supporting robbers, shall we now
> Contaminate our fingers with base bribes,
> And sell the mighty space of our large honours
> For so much trash as may be grasped thus?
> I had rather be a dog, and bay the moon,
> Than such a Roman."

The expression is the perfect counterpart of Alciat's 164th Emblem (p. 571, edition Antwerp, 1581); the motto, copied by Whitney (p. 213), is, *Inanis impetus*,—"A vain attack."

> "By night, as at a mirror, the dog looks at the lunar orb:
> And seeing himself, believes another dog to be on high.

And barks : but in vain is his angry voice driven by winds,
The silent Diana ever onward goes in her course." *

The device engraved on Alciat's and Whitney's pages depicts the full moon surrounded by stars, and a large dog baying. Whitney's stanzas give the meaning of Alciat's, and also of Beza's, which follow below,—

"BY shininge lighte, of wannishe CYNTHIAS raies,
The dogge behouldes his shaddowe to appeare :
Wherefore, in vaine aloude he barkes, and baies,
And alwaies thoughte, an other dogge was there :
But yet the Moone, who did not heare his queste,
Hir woonted course, did keep vnto the weste.

This reprehendes, those fooles which baule, and barke,
At learned men, that shine aboue the reste :
With due regarde, that they their deedes should marke,
And reuerence them, that are with wisedome bleste :
But if they striue, in vaine their winde they spende,
For woorthie men, the Lorde doth still defende."

The same device to a different motto, "DESPICIT ALTA CANIS," —*The dog despises high things,*—is adopted by Camerarius, *Ex Anim. quadrup.*, p. 63, edition 1595,—

Beza, ed. 1580.

"Why carest thou for the angry thorns of a vain speaking tongue?
Diana on high cares not for the loud-barking dog." †

We will conclude our "baying" with Beza's 22nd Emblem.

* "LVNAREM noctu, et speculum, canis inspicit orbem :
Seq. videns, alium credit inesse canem,
Et latrat : sed frustra agitur vox irrita ventis,
Et peragit cursus surda Diana suos."

† "Irrita vaniloquæ quid curas spicula linguæ?
Latrantem curatne alta Diana canem."

The Latin stanza is sufficiently severe,—

> "*Luna velut toto collustrans lumine terras,*
> *Frustra allatrantes despicit alta canes :*
> *Sic quisquis Christum allatrat Christive ministros,*
> *Index stultitiæ spernitor usque suæ.*"

i.e. "As the moon with full light shining over the lands,
From on high doth despise dogs barking in vain :
So whoso is barking at Christ or Christ's ministers,
The scorner is the pointer out even of his own folly."

In connection with the power of music Orpheus is named by many writers of the sixteenth century; and among the Emblematists the lead may be assigned to Pierre Coustau in "Le Pegme" (Lyons, 1560, p. 389),—

Sur la harpe d'Orpheus.

La force d'Eloquence.

Coustau, 1560.

> *De son gentil & fort melodieux*
> *D'vn instrument, Orpheus feit mouuoir*
> *Rocs & patitz de leur places & lieux.*
> *C'est eloquence ayant force & pouuoir*
> *D'ēbler les cueurs de tous part son sçauoir :*
> *C'est l'orateur qui au fort d'eloquence,*
> *Premierement soux méme demourance*
> *Gens bestiaulx, & par ferocité, &c.*

"*On the Harp of Orpheus.*

The Power of Eloquence.

"With sound gentle and very melodious
Of an instrumeut Orpheus caused to move
Rocks and pastures from their place and home.
It is eloquence having force and power
To steal the hearts of all his learning shows,
It is the orator who by strength of eloquence
First brings even under influence
Brutal people, and from fierceness
Gathers them ; and who to benevolence
From fierceness then reclaims."

A *Narration Philosophique* follows for three pages, discoursing on the power of eloquence.

Musicæ, & Poeticæ vis,—"The force of Music and Poetry,"—occupies Reusner's 21st Emblem (bk. iii. p. 129), oddly enough dedicated to a mathematician, David Nephelite. Whitney's stanzas (p. 186), *Orphei Musica,*—"The Music of Orpheus,"—bear considerable resemblance to those of Reusner, and are sufficient for establishing the parallelism of Shakespeare and themselves.

"LO, ORPHEVS with his harpe, that sauage kinde did tame :
The Lions fierce, and Leopardes wilde, and birdes about him came.
For, with his musicke sweete, their natures hee subdu'de :
But if wee thinke his playe so wroughte, our selues wee doe delude.
For why ? besides his skill, hee learned was, and wise :
And coulde with sweetenes of his tonge, all sortes of men suffice.
And those that weare most rude, and knewe no good at all :
And weare of fierce, and cruell mindes, the worlde did brutishe call.
Yet with persuasions sounde, hee made their hartes relente,
That meeke, and milde they did become, and followed where he wente.
Lo, these, the Lions fierce, these, Beares, and Tigers weare :
The trees, and rockes, that lefte their roomes, his musicke for to heare.
But, you are happie most, who in suche place doe staye :
You neede not THRACIA seeke, to heare some impe of ORPHEVS playe.
Since, that so neare your home, Apollos darlinge dwelles ;
Who LINVS, & AMPHION staynes, and ORPHEVS farre excelles.
For, hartes like marble harde, his harmonie dothe pierce :
And makes them yeelding passions feele, that are by nature fierce.

But, if his musicke faile : his curtesie is suche,
That none so rude, and base of minde, but hee reclaimes them muche.
Nowe since you, by deserte, for both, commended are :
I choose you, for a Iudge herein, if truthe I doe declare.
And if you finde I doe, then ofte therefore reioyce :
And thinke, I woulde suche neighbour haue, if I might make my choice."

In a similar strain, from the *Merchant of Venice* (act v. sc. 1, l. 70, vol. ii. p. 361), we are told of the deep influence which music possesses over—

"a wild and wanton herd
Or race of youthful and unhandled colts."

The poet declares,—

"If they but hear perchance a trumpet sound,
Or any air of music touch their ears,
You shall perceive them make a mutual stand,
Their savage eyes turn'd to a modest gaze
By the sweet power of music : therefore the poet *
Did feign that Orpheus drew trees, stones and floods ;
Since nought so stockish, hard and full of rage,
But music for the time doth change his nature.
The man that hath no music in himself,
Nor is not moved with concord of sweet sounds,
Is fit for treasons, stratagems and spoils :
The motions of his spirit are dull as night,
And his affections dark as Erebus :
Let no such man be trusted."

And in the *Two Gentlemen of Verona* (act iii. sc. 2, l. 68, vol. i. p. 129), the method is developed by which Silvia, through the conversation of Proteus, may be tempered "to hate young Valentine" and Thurio love. Proteus says,—

"You must lay lime to tangle her desires
By wailful sonnets, whose composed rhymes
Should be full-fraught with serviceable vows.
Duke. Ay,
Much is the force of heaven-bred poesy.
Pro. Say that upon the altar of her beauty
You sacrifice your tears, your sighs, your heart :

* See Ovid's *Metamorphoses*, bk. x. fab. 1, 2.

> Write till your ink be dry, and with your tears
> Moist it again ; and frame some feeling line
> That may discover such integrity :
> For Orpheus' lute was strung with poets' sinews ;
> Whose golden touch could soften steel and stones,
> Make tigers tame, and huge leviathans
> Forsake unsounded deeps to dance on sands."*

Again, in proof of Music's power, consult *Henry VIII.* (act iii. sc. 1, l. 1, vol. vi. p. 56), when Queen Katharine, in her sorrowfulness, says to one of her women who were at work around her,—

> "Take thy lute, wench : my soul grows sad with troubles ;
> Sing and disperse 'em if thou canst : leave working."

The sweet simple song is raised,—

> "Orpheus with his lute made trees,
> And the mountain tops that freeze,
> Bow themselves when he did sing :
> To his music plants and flowers
> Ever sprung, as sun and showers
> There had made a lasting spring.
>
> Everything that heard him play,
> Even the billows of the sea,
> Hung their heads, and then lay by.
> In sweet music is such art,
> Killing care and grief of heart
> Fall asleep, or hearing die."

How splendidly does the dramatic poet's genius here shine forth! It pours light upon each Emblem, and calls into day the hidden glories. His spirit breathes upon a dead picture, and rivalling Orpheus himself, he makes the images breathe and glance and live.

The mythic tale of Actæon transformed into a stag, and hunted by hounds because of his rudeness to Diana and her

---

* For pictorial representations of the wonders which Orpheus wrought, see the Plantinian edition of "P. OVIDII NASONIS METAMORPHOSES," Antwerp, 1591, pp. 238—243.

nymphs, was used to point the moral of widely different subjects. Alciatus (Emb. 52, ed. 1551, p. 60) applies it "*to the harbourers of assassins,*" and makes it the occasion of a very true but very severe reflection.

Alciat, 155

"Of thieves and robbers evil-omen'd bands the city through
 Go thy companions; and a cohort girded with dreadful swords.
And so, O prodigal, thou thinkest thyself of generous mind,
 Because thy cooking pot allures very many of the bad ones.
Lo, a new Actæon, who after he assumed the horns,
 Himself gave himself a prey to his own dogs."

The device is graphically drawn: Actæon is in part embruted; he is fleeing with the dogs close upon him. Supposing Shakespeare to have seen this print, it represents to the life Pistol's words in the *Merry Wives of Windsor* (act ii. sc. 1, l. 106, vol. i. p. 186),—

"Prevent, or go thou,
Like Sir Actæon he, with Ringwood at thy heels."

"EX DOMINO SERVUS,"—*The slave out of the master*,—is another saying which the tale of Actæon has illustrated. The application is from Aneau's "PICTA POESIS," fol. 41. On the left hand of the tiny drawing are Diana and her nymphs, busied in the bath, beneath the shelter of an overhanging cliff,—on the right is Actæon, motionless, with a stag's head; dogs are around him. The verses translated read thus,—

"Horns being bestowed upon Actæon when changed to a stag,
 Member by member his own dogs tore him to pieces.
Alas! wretched the Master who feeds wasteful parasites;
 A ready prepared prey he is for his fawning dogs!
It suggests, he is mocked by them and devoured,
 And out of a master is made a slave, bearing horns."

But Sambucus in his *Emblems* (edition 1564, p. 128), and Whitney after him (p. 15)—making use of the same woodcut, only with a different border—adapt the Actæon-tragedy to another subject and moral, and take the words, *Pleasure purchased by anguish.*

Voluptas ærumnoſa.

Sambucus, 1564.

QVI *nimis exercet venatus, ac ſine fine*
Haurit opes patrias, prodigit inque canes:
Tantus amor vani, tantus furor vſque recurſat,
Induat vt celeris cornua bina feræ.
Accidit Actæon tibi, qui cornutus ab ortu,
A' canibus propriis dilaceratus eras.
Quàm multos hodie, quos paſcit odora canum vis,
Venandi ſtudium conficit, atque vorat.
Seria ne ludis poſtponas, commoda damnis,
Quod ſupereſt rerum ſic vt egenus habe.
Sæpe etiam propria qui interdum vxore relicta
Deperit externas corniger iſta luit.

Stanzas which may thus be rendered,—

"Whoever too eagerly hunting pursues, and without moderation
Drains paternal treasures and lavishes them on dogs:
So great the love of the folly, so strong does the passion return
That it clothes him in the twin horns of the swift stag.
It happen'd, Actæon, to thee, who though horned from thy birth,
By thy own dogs into pieces wast torn.
At this day how many, whom the dogs' quick scent delights,
The strong passion for hunting wastes and devours.
Put not off serious things for sports,—advantages for losses:
As one in need so hold fast whatever things remain:
Often even the horn bearer, his own wife forsaken,
Loves desperately strangers, and pays penalties for crimes."

We here see that Sambucus has adopted the theory of the old grammarian or historian of Alexandria, Palæphatus, who informs us,—

"Actæon by race was an Arcadian, very fond of dogs. Many of them he kept, and hunted in the mountains. But he neglected his own affairs, for men then were all self-workers; they had no servants, but themselves tilled the earth; and that man was the richest, who tilled the earth and was the most diligent workman. But Actæon being careless of domestic affairs, and rather going about hunting with his dogs, his substance was wasted. And when he had nothing left, people kept saying: the wretched Actæon was eaten up by his own dogs."

A very instructive tale this for some of our Nimrods, mighty hunters and racers in the land; but it is not to be pressed too strictly into the service of the parsimonious.

From the same motto Whitney (p. 15) keeps much closer to the mythological narrative,—

"ACTÆON heare, vnhappie man behoulde,
When in the well, hee sawe Diana brighte,
With greedie lookes, hee waxed ouer boulde,
That to a stagge hee was transformed righte,
Whereat amasde, hee thought to runne awaie,
But straighte his howndes did rente hym, for their praie.

By which is ment, That those whoe do pursue
Theire fancies fonde, and thinges vnlawfull craue,
Like brutishe beastes appeare vnto the viewe,
And shall at lengthe, Actæons guerdon haue:
And as his houndes, soe theire affections base,
Shall them deuowre, and all their deedes deface."

Very beautifully, in *Twelfth Night* (act i. sc. 1, l. 9, vol. iii. p. 223), is this idea applied by Orsino, duke of Illyria,—

"O spirit of love, how quick and fresh art thou!

* See Ovid's *Metamorphoses*, bk. iii. fab. 2; or the Plantinian Devices to Ovid, edition 1591, pp. 85, 87.

That, notwithstanding thy capacity
Receiveth as the sea, nought enters there,
Of what validity and pitch soe'er,
But falls into abatement and low price,
Even in a minute! so full of shapes is fancy
That it alone is high fantastical.
Cur. Will you go hunt, my lord?
Duke. What, Curio?
Cur. The hart.
Duke. Why, so I do, the noblest that I have:
O, when mine eyes did see Olivia first,
Methought she purged the air of pestilence!
That instant was I turn'd into a hart;
And my desires, like fell and cruel hounds,
E'er since pursue me."

The full force and meaning of the mythological tale is, however, brought out in the *Titus Andronicus* (act ii. sc. 3, l. 55, vol. vi. p. 459), that fearful history of passion and revenge. Tamora is in the forest, and Bassianus and Lavinia make their appearance,—

"*Bass.* Who have we here? Rome's royal empress,
Unfurnish'd of her well-beseeming troop?
Or is it Dian, habited like her,
Who hath abandoned her holy groves,
To see the general hunting in this forest?
Tam. Saucy controller of my private steps!
Had I the power that some say Dian had,
Thy temples should be planted presently
With horns, as was Actæon's, and the hounds
Should drive upon thy new-transformed limbs,
Unmannerly intruder as thou art!"

Arion rescued by the Dolphin is another mythic tale in which poets may well delight. Alciatus (Emblem 89, edition 1581), directs the moral, "*against the avaricious, or those to whom a better condition is offered by strangers.*" Contrary to the French writers of time and place, the emblem presents in the same device the harpist both cast out of the ship and riding triumphantly to the shore.

In auaros, vel quibus melior conditio ab extraneis offertur.

EMBLEMA LXXXIX.

Alciat. 1581

DELPHINI *insidens vada cærula sulcat Arion,*
Hocq; aures mulcet, frenat & ora sono.
Quàm sit auari hominis, non tam mens dira ferarũ est;
Quiq; viris rapimur, piscibus eripimur.

i.e. "On the dolphin sitting Arion ploughs cerulean seas,
With a sound he soothes the ears, with a sound curbs the mouth.
Of wild creatures not so dreadful is the mind, as of greedy man;
We who by men are pillaged, are by fishes rescued."

With this thought before him Whitney (p. 144) at the head of his stanzas has placed the strong expression, "Man is a wolf to man."* *Cave canem,*—"Beware of the dog,"—is certainly a far more kindly warning; but the motto,

* In the beautiful Silverdale, on Morecambe Bay, at Lindow Tower, there is the same hospitable assurance over the doorway, "*Homo homini lupus.*"

Homo homini lupus, tallies exactly with the conduct of the mariners.

> "No mortall foe so full of poysoned spite,
> As man, to man, when mischiefe he pretendes:
> The monsters huge, as diuers aucthors write,
> Yea Lions wilde, and fishes weare his frendes:
> And when their deathe, by frendes suppos'd was sought,
> They kindnesse shew'd, and them from daunger brought.
>
> ARION lo, who gained store of goulde,
> In countries farre: with harpe, and pleasant voice:
> Did shipping take, and to CORINTHVS woulde,
> And to his wishe, of pilottes made his choise:
> Who rob'd the man, and threwe him to the sea,
> A Dolphin, lo, did beare him safe awaie."

A comment from St. Chrysostom, *super Matth.* xxii., is added,—

"As a king is honoured in his image, so God is loved and hated in man. He cannot hate man, who loves God, nor can he, who hates God, love men."

Reference is also made to Aulus Gellius (bk. v. c. 14, vol. i. p. 408), where the delightful story is narrated of the slave Androclus and the huge lion whose wounded foot he had cured, and with whom he lived familiarly for three years in the same cave and on the same food. After a time the slave was taken and condemned to furnish sport in the circus to the degraded Romans. That same lion also had been taken, a beast of vast size, and power and fierceness. The two were confronted in the arena.

"When the lion saw the man at a distance," says the narrator, "suddenly, as if wondering, he stood still; and then gently and placidly as if recognising drew near. With the manner and observance of fawning dogs, softly and blandly he wagged his tail and placed himself close to the man's body, and lightly with his tongue licked the legs and hands of the slave almost lifeless from fear. The man Androclus during these blandishments of the fierce wild creature recovered his lost spirits; by degrees he directed his eyes to behold the lion. Then, as if mutual recognition had been made, man and lion appeared glad and rejoicing one with the other."

Was it now, from having this tale in mind that, in the *Troilus and Cressida* (act v. sc. 3, l. 37, vol. vi. p. 247), these words were spoken to Hector?—

> "Brother, you have a vice of mercy in you,
> Which better fits a lion than a man."

Arion sauué par vn Dauphin, is also the subject of a well executed device in the "ΜΙΚΡΟΚΟΣΜΟΣ" (edition Antwerp, 1592),* of which we give the French version (p. 64),—

> "Arion retournant par mer en sa patrie
> Chargé de quelque argẽt, vid que les mariniers
> Animéz contre luy d'une auare furie
> Pretendoyent luy oster sa vie & ses deniers.
>
> Pour eschapper leurs mains & changer leur courage,
> Sur la harpe il chanta vn chant melodieux
> Mais il ne peut fleschir la nature sauuage
> De ces cruels larrons & meurtriers furieux.
>
> Estant par eux ietté deans la mere profonde,
> Vn Dauphin attiré au son de l'instrument,
> Le chargea sur son dos, & au trauers de l'onde
> Le portant, le sauua miraculeusement.
>
> Maintes fois l'innocent à qui on fait offense
> Trouue plus de faueur es bestes qu'es humains:
> Dieu qui aime les bons les prend en sa defense,
> Les gardant de l'effort des hommes inhumains."

To the Emblems we have under consideration we meet with this coincidence in *Twelfth Night* (act i. sc. 2, l. 10, vol. iii. p. 225); it is the Captain's assurance to Viola,—

* The device by Gerard de Jode, in the edition of 1579, is a very fine representation of the scene here described.

"When you and those poor number saved with you
Hung on our driving boat, I saw your brother,
Most provident in peril, bind himself,
Courage and hope both teaching him the practice,
To a strong mast that lived upon the sea;
Where, like Arion on the dolphin's back,
I saw him hold acquaintance with the waves
So long as I could see."

As examples of a sentiment directly opposite, we will briefly refer to Coustau's *Pegma* (p. 323, edition Lyons, 1555), where to the device of a Camel and his driver, the noble motto is recorded and exemplified from Plutarch, *Homo homini Deus*,—"Man is a God to man;" the reason being assigned,—

"As the world was created for sake of gods and men, so man was created for man's sake;" and, "that the grace we receive from the immortal God is to be bestowed on man by man."

Reusner, too, in his *Emblemata* (p. 142, Francfort, 1581), though commenting on the contrary saying, *Homo homini lupus*, declares,—

"*Aut homini Deus est homo; si bonus: aut lupus hercle,*
Si malus: ô quantum est esse hominem, atq. Deum."

i.e. "Or man to man is God; if good: or a wolf in truth,
If bad: O how great it is to be man and God!"*

Was it in reference to these sentiments that Hamlet and Cerimon speak? The one says (*Hamlet*, act iv. sc. 4, l. 33, vol. viii. p. 127),—

* May we not in one instance illustrate the thought from a poet of the last century?—

"Who, who would live, my Nana, just to breathe
This idle air, and indolently run,
Day after day, the still returning round
Of life's mean offices, and sickly joys?
But in the service of mankind to be
A guardian god below; still to employ
The mind's brave ardour in heroic aims,
Such as may raise us o'er the grovelling herd,
And make us shine for ever—that is life." *Thomson*

> "What is a man,
> If his chief good and market of his time
> Be but to sleep and feed? a beast, no more.
> Sure, he that made us with such large discourse,
> Looking before and after, gave us not
> That capability and god-like reason
> To fust in us unused."

And again (act ii. sc. 2, l. 295, vol. viii. p. 63),—

> "What a piece of work is a man! how noble in reason! how infinite in faculty! in form and moving how express and admirable! in action how like an angel! in apprehension how like a god!"

So in the *Pericles* (act iii. sc. 2, l. 26, vol. ix. p. 366), the fine thought is uttered,—

> "I hold it ever,
> Virtue and cunning were endowments greater
> Than nobleness and riches: careless heirs
> May the two latter darken and expend,
> But immortality attends the former,
> Making a man a god."

The horses and chariot of Phœbus, and the presumptuous charioteer Phaëton, who attempted to drive them, are celebrated with great splendour of description in Ovid's *Metamorphoses* (bk. ii. fab. 1), that rich storehouse of Mythology. The palace of the god has lofty columns bright with glittering gold; the roof is covered with pure shining ivory; and the double gates are of silver. Here Phœbus was throned, and clothed in purple;—the days and months and years,—the seasons and the ages were seated around him; Phaëton appears, claims to be his son, and demands for one day to guide the glorious steeds. At this point we take up the narrative which Alciat has written (Emb. 56), and inscribed, "*To the rash.*"*

* For other pictorial illustrations of Phaeton's charioteership and fall, see Plantin's *Ovid* (pp. 46—49), and De Passe (16 and 17); also Symeoni's *Vita, &c., d'Ovidio* (edition 1559, pp. 32—34).

In temerarios.

Aſpicis aurigam currus Phaëtonta paterni
Ignivomos auſum flectere Solis equos.
Maxima qui poſtquam terris incendia ſparſit:
Eſt temerè inſeſſo lapſus ab axe miſer.
Sic plerique rotis Fortunæ ad ſydera Reges
Evecti; ambitio quos iuvenilis agit.
Poſt magnam humani generis cladémque, ſuamq;
Cunctorum pœnas denique dant ſcelerum.

Alciat, 1551.

"You behold Phaeton the driver of his father's chariot,—
Who dared to guide the fire breathing horses of the sun.
After over the lands mightiest burnings he scattered,
Wretched he fell from the chariot where rashly he sat.

So many kings, whom youthful ambition excites,
On the wheels of Fortune are borne to the stars.
After great slaughter of the human race and their own,
For all their crimes at last the penalties they pay."

Shakespeare's notices of the attempted feat and its failure are frequent. First, in the *Two Gentlemen of Verona* (act iii. sc. 1, l. 153, vol. i. p. 121), the Duke of Milan discovers the letter addressed to his daughter Silvia, with the promise,—

"Silvia, this night will I enfranchise thee,"—

and with true classic force denounces the folly of the attempt,—

"Why, Phaethon,—for thou art Merops' son,—
Wilt thou aspire to guide the heavenly car,
And with thy daring folly burn the world?
Wilt thou reach stars because they shine on thee?"

In her impatience for the meeting with Romeo (*Romeo and Juliet*, act iii. sc. 2, l. 1, vol. vii. p. 72), Juliet exclaims,—

"Gallop apace, you fiery-footed steeds,
Towards Phœbus' lodging: such a waggoner
As Phaethon would whip you to the west
And bring in cloudy night immediately."

The unfortunate Richard II. (act iii. sc. 3, l. 178, vol. iv. p. 179), when desired by Northumberland to meet Bolingbroke in the courtyard ("may't please you to come down"), replies,—

"Down, down, I come; like glistering Phaeton
Wanting the manage of unruly jades."

And he too, in 3 *Henry VI.* (act i. sc. 4, l. 16, vol. v. p. 244), Richard, Duke of York, whose son cried,—

"A crown, or else a glorious tomb!
A sceptre or an earthly sepulchre!"—

when urged by Northumberland (l. 30),—

"Yield to our mercy, proud Plantagenet;"

had this answer given for him by the faithful Clifford,—

> "Ay, to such mercy, as his ruthless arm,
> With downright payment, shew'd unto my father.
> Now Phaethon hath tumbled from his car,
> And made an evening at the noontide prick."

That same Clifford (act ii. sc. 6, l. 10, vol. v. p. 271), when wounded and about to die for the Lancastrian cause, makes use of the allusion,—

> "And who shines now but Henry's enemy?
> O Phœbus! hadst thou never given consent
> That Phaëthon should check thy fiery steeds,
> Thy burning car had never scorch'd the earth!
> And, Henry, hadst thou sway'd as kings should do,
> Or as thy father and his father did,
> Giving no ground unto the house of York,
> They never then had sprung like summer flies;
> I and ten thousand in this luckless realm
> Had left no mourning widows for our death;
> And thou this day hadst kept thy chair in peace."

In the early heroic age, when Minos reigned in Crete and Theseus at Athens, just as Mythology was ripening into history, the most celebrated for mechanical contrivance and for excellence in the arts of sculpture and architecture were Dædalus and his sons Talus and Icarus. To them is attributed the invention of the saw, the axe, the plumb-line, the auger, the gimlet, and glue; they contrived masts and sailyards for ships; and they discovered various methods of giving to statues expression and the appearance of life. Chiefly, however, are Dædalus and Icarus now known for fitting wings to the human arms, and for attempting to fly across the sea from Crete to the shore of Greece. Dædalus, hovering just above the waves, accomplished the aërial voyage in safety; but Icarus, too ambitiously soaring aloft, had his wings injured by the heat of the sun, and fell into the waters, which from his death there were named the Icarian sea.

From the edition of Alciat's *Emblems*, 1581, we select a drawing which represents the fall of Icarus; it is dedicated "To Astrologers," or fortune tellers. The warning in the last two lines is all we need to translate,—

> "Let the Astrologer take heed what he foretells; for headlong
> The impostor will fall though he fly the stars above."

In aſtrologos.

EMBLEMA CIII.

Alciat, 1581.

> ICARE, *per ſuperos qui raptus & aëra, donec*
> *In mare præcipitem cera liquata daret,*
> *Nunc te cera eadem, feruensq; reſuſcitat ignis,*
> *Exemplo vt doceas dogmata certa tuo.*
> *Aſtrologus caueat quicquam prædicere: præceps*
> *Nam cadet impoſtor dum ſuper aſtra volat.*

Whitney, however (p. 28), will supply the whole,—

> "HEARE, ICARVS with mountinge vp alofte,
> Came headlonge downe, and fell into the Sea:
> His waxed winges, the sonne did make so softe,
> They melted straighte, and feathers fell awaie:
> So, whilste he flewe, and of no dowbte did care,
> He mouu'de his armes, but loe, the same were bare.

Let suche beware, which paste theire reache doe mounte,
Whoe seeke the thinges, to mortall men deny'de,
And searche the Heauens, and all the starres accoumpte,
And tell therebie, what after shall betyde :
  With blusshinge nowe, theire weakenesse rightlie weye,
  Least as they clime, they fall to theire decaye."

We use this opportunity to present two consecutive pages of Corrozet's "HECATOMGRAPHIE" (Emb. 67), that the nature of his

Faire tout par moyen.

Qui trop ſ' exalte trop ſe priſe,
Qui trop ſ'abaiſſe il ſe deſpriſe,
Mais celluy qui veult faire bien
Il ſe gouuerne par moyen.

O! Icarus que t'eſt il aduenu?
Tu as treſmal le conſeil retenu
De Dedalus ton pere qui t'apprint
L'art de voler, lequel il entreprint
Pour eſchapper de Minos la priſon
Ou vous eſtiez enfermez, pour raiſon
Qu'il auoit faict & baſty vne vache
D'ung boys leger ou Paſiphe ſe cache.
Ce Dedalus nature ſurmonta
A toy & luy des ælles adiouſta
Aux bras & piedz, tant que pouiez voler
Et en volant il ſe print à parler
A toy diſant: mon filz qui veulx pretendre
De te ſauluer, vng cas tu doibs entendre
Que ſi tu veulx à bon port arriuer
Il ne te fault vers le ciel eſleuer.
Car le Soleil la cire fonderoit,
Et par ainſi ta plume tomberoit,
Sy tu vas bas l'humidité des eaulx
Te priuera du pouoir des oyſeaulx,
Mais ſi tu vas ne hault ne bas, adoncques
La voyé eſt ſeure & ſans dangers quelzconques:
O pauure ſot le hault chemin tu prins
Trop hault pour toy car mal il t'en eſt prins
La cire fond, & ton plumage tumbe
Et toy auſſi preſt à mettre ſoubz tumbe.

devices, and of their explanations may be seen. There is a motto,—"To take the middle way,"—and these lines follow—

"Who too much exalts himself too much values himself,
Who too much abases himself, he undervalues himself,
But that man who wills to do well,
He governs himself the medium way."

In the page of metrical explanation subjoined, the usual mythic narrative is closely followed.

The full idea is carried out in 3 *Henry VI.* (act v. sc. 6, l. 18, vol. v. p. 332), Gloucester and King Henry being the speakers,—

"*Glou.* Why, what a peevish fool was that of Crete,
That taught his son the office of a fowl!
And yet for all his wings, the fool was drown'd.
K. Hen. I, Dædalus; my poor boy, Icarus;
Thy father, Minos, that denied our course;
The sun that sear'd the wings of my sweet boy
Thy brother Edward, and thyself the sea
Whose envious gulf did swallow up his life.
Ah, kill me with thy weapon, not with words!
My breast can better brook thy dagger's point
Than can my ears that tragic history."

In the 1st part also of the same dramatic series (act iv. sc. 6, l. 46, vol. v. p. 78), John Talbot, the son, is hemmed about in the battle near Bourdeaux. Rescued by his father, he is urged to escape, but the young hero replies,—

"Before young Talbot from old Talbot fly,
The coward horse that bears me fall and die!
And like me to the peasant boys of France,
To be shame's scorn and subject of mischance!
Surely, by all the glory you have won,
An if I fly, I am not Talbot's son:
Then talk no more of flight, it is no boot;
If son to Talbot, die at Talbot's foot.
Tal. Then follow thou thy desperate sire of Crete,
Thou Icarus; thy life to me is sweet:
If thou wilt fight, fight by thy father's side;
And, commendable proved, let's die in pride."

The tearful tale of Niobe, who that has read Ovid's *Metamorphoses* (bk. vi. fab. 5) could not weep over it! Seven stalwart sons and seven fair daughters clustered round the haughty dame, and she gloried in their attendance upon her; but at an evil hour she dared to match herself with Latona, and at a public festival in honour of the goddess to be the only one refusing to offer incense and prayers. The goddess called her own children to avenge the affront and the impiety; and Apollo and Diana, from the clouds, slew the seven sons as they were exercising on the plain near Thebes. Yet the pride of Niobe did not abate, and Diana in like manner slew also the seven daughters. The mother's heart was utterly broken; she wept herself to death, and was changed to stone. Yet, says the poet, *Flet tamen,*—"Yet she weeps,"—

> *Liquitur, et lacrymas etiam nunc marmora manant,*—

i.e. "It melts, and even now the marble trickles down tears."

Alciat adopts the tale as a warning; *Pride* he names his 67th Emblem.

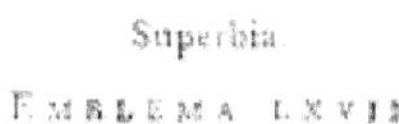
Superbia.

EMBLEMA LXVII.

Alciat, 1551.

En statuæ statua, & ductum de marmore marmor,
Se conferre Deis ausa procax Niobe.
Est vitium muliebre superbia, & arguit oris
Duritiem, ac sensus, qualis inest lapidi.

As we look at the device we are sensible to a singular incongruity between the subject and the droll, *Punch*-like figures, which make up the border. The sentiment, too, is as incongruous, that "Pride is a woman's vice and argues hardness of look and of feeling such as there is in stone."

Making a slight change in the motto, Whitney (p. 13) writes, *Superbiæ vltio*,—"Vengeance upon pride,"—

"OF NIOBE, behoulde the ruthefull plighte,
Bicause shee did dispise the powers deuine :
Her children all, weare slaine within her sighte,
And, while her selfe with tricklinge teares did pine,
Shee was transform'de, into a marble stone,
Which, yet with teares, dothe seeme to waile, and mone.

This tragedie, thoughe Poëtts first did frame,
Yet maie it bee, to euerie one applide :
That mortall men, shoulde thinke from whence they came,
And not presume, nor puffe them vp with pride,
Leste that the Lorde, whoe haughty hartes doth hate,
Doth throwe them downe, when sure they thinke theyr state.

Shakespeare's notices of Niobe are little more than allusions : the mode in which Apollo and Diana executed the cruel vengeance may be glanced at in *All's Well* (act v. sc. 3, l. 5, vol. iii. p. 201), when the Countess of Rousillon pleads for her son to the King of France,—

"*Count.* 'Tis past, my liege ;
And I beseech your majesty to make it
Natural rebellion, done i' the blaze of youth :
When oil and fire, too strong for reason's force,
O'erbears it and burns on.
King. My honour'd lady,
I have forgiven and forgotten all ;
Though my revenges were high bent upon him,
And watch'd the time to shoot."

Troilus (act v. sc. 10, l. 16, vol. vi. p. 261), anticipating Priam's and Hecuba's mighty grief over the slain Hector, speaks thus of the fact,—

"Let him that will a screech-owl aye be call'd
Go into Troy, and say there, 'Hector's dead:'
There is a word will Priam turn to stone,
Make wells and Niobes of the maids and wives,
Cold statues of the youth, and in a word,
Scare Troy out of itself."

Hamlet, too (act i. sc. 2, l. 147, vol. viii. p. 17), in his bitter expressions respecting his mother's marriage, speaks thus severely of the brevity of her widowhood,—

"A little month, or ere those shoes were old
With which she follow'd my poor father's body,
Like Niobe, all tears:—why she, even she,—
O God! a beast that wants discourse of reason,
Would have mourn'd longer;—within a month;
Ere yet the salt of most unrighteous tears
Had left the flushing in her galled eyes,
She married."

Tiresias, the blind soothsayer of Thebes, had foretold that the comely Narcissus would live as long as he could refrain from the sight of his own countenance,—

"But he, ignorant of his destiny," says Claude Mignault, "grew so desperately in love with his own image seen in a fountain, that he miserably wasted away, and was changed into the flower of his own name, which is called *Narce*, and means drowsiness or infatuation, because the smell of the Narcissus affects the head."

However that may be, Alciatus, edition Antwerp, 1581, exhibits the youth surveying his features in a running stream; the flower is behind him, and in the distance is Tiresias pronouncing his doom. "Self love" is the motto.

Φιλαυτία.

EMBLEMA LXIX.

Alciat, 1581.

QVOD *nimium tua forma tibi Narciſſe placebat,*
In florem, & noti eſt verſa ſtuporis olus.
Ingenij eſt marcor, cladeſq; φιλαυτία, doctos
Quæ peſſum plures datq; deditq; viros:
Qui veterum abiecta methodo, noua dogmata quærunt,
Nilq; ſuas præter tradere phantaſias.

Anulus also, in the "PICTA POESIS" (p. 48), mentions his foolish and vain passion,—

Contemnens alios, arsit amore sui,—

i.e. "Despising others, inflamed he was with love of himself."

From Alciat and Anulus, Whitney takes up the fable (p. 149), his printer Rapheleng using the same wood-block as Plantyn did in 1581. Of the three stanzas we subjoin one,—

"NARCISSVS lou'de, and liked so his shape,
He died at lengthe with gazinge there vppon :
Which shewes selfe loue, from which there fewe can scape,
A plague too rife : bewitcheth manie a one.
The ritche, the pore, the learned, and the sotte,
Offende therein : and yet they see it not."

It is only in one instance, *Antony and Cleopatra* (act ii. sc. 5, l. 95, vol. ix. p. 48), and very briefly, that Shakespeare names Narcissus ; he does this when the Messenger repeats to Cleopatra that Antony is married, and she replies,—

"The Gods confound thee !
. . . . . . Go, get thee hence :
Hadst thou Narcissus in thy face, to me
Thou wouldst appear most ugly."

The most beautiful of the maidens of Thessaly, Daphne, the daughter of the river-god Peneus, was Apollo's earliest love. He sought her in marriage, and being refused by her, prepared to force consent. The maiden fled, and was pursued, and, at the very moment of her need invoked her father's aid, and was transformed into a laurel. At this instant the device of Anulus represents her, in the "PICTA POESIS" (p. 47).*

[illegible], 1551

Ille amat, hæc odit, fugit hæc : ſectatur at ille
Dúmque fugit : Laurus facta repente ſtetit.
Sic amat, & fruſtra, nec Apollo potitus amore eſt.
Vltus Apollinis eſt, ſic Amor opprobrium.
HAECINE *doctorum ſors eſt inimica virorum,*
Vt iuuenes quamuis non redamentur ament?
Exoſoſque habeat prudentes ſtulta iuuentus
His ne iungatur ſtipes vt eſſe velit.

* Ovid's *Metamorphoses*, by Crispin de Passe (editions 1602 and 1607, p. 10), presents the fable well by a very good device.

"He loves, she hates; she flees, but he pursues,
And while she flees, stopped suddenly, to laurel changed.
So loves Apollo, and in vain; nor enjoys his love.
So love has avenged the reproach of Apollo.
This very judgment of learned men is it not hostile,
That youths should love though not again be loved?
Hated should foolish youth account the wise
Lest by these the log be not joined as it wishes to be."

The *Midsummer Night's Dream* (act ii. sc. 1, l. 227, vol. ii. p. 218) reverses the fable; Demetrius flees and Helena pursues,—

"*Dem.* I'll run from thee and hide me in the brakes,
And leave thee to the mercy of wild beasts.
Hel. The wildest hath not such a heart as you.
Run when you will, the story shall be changed:
Apollo flies, and Daphne holds the chase:
The dove pursues the griffin; the mild hind
Makes speed to catch the tiger; bootless speed,
When cowardice pursues, and valour flies."

There is, too, the quotation already made for another purpose (p. 115) from the *Taming of the Shrew* (Introd. sc. 2, l. 55),—

"Or Daphne roaming through a thorny wood,
Scratching her legs that one shall swear she bleeds,
And at that sight shall sad Apollo weep,
So workmanly the blood and tears are drawn."

And Troilus (act i. sc. 1, l. 94, vol. vi. p. 130) makes the invocation,—

"Tell me, Apollo, for thy Daphne's love
What Cressid is, what Pandar, and what we?"

Among Mythological Characters we may rank Milo, "of force unparalleled;" to whom with crafty words of flattery Ulysses likened Diomed; *Troilus and Cressida* (act ii. sc. 3, l. 237),—

"But he that disciplined thine arms to fight,
Let Mars divide eternity in twain,
And give him half: and for thy vigour,

> Bull-bearing Milo his addition yield
> To sinewy Ajax."

Milo's prowess is the subject of a fine device by Gerard de Jode, in the "ΜΙΚΡΟΚΟΣΜΟΣ" (p. 61), first published in 1579, with Latin verses. Respecting Milo the French verses say,—

> " La force de Milon a esté nompareille,
> Et de ses grands efforts on raconte meruellle :
> S'il se tenoit debout, il ne se trouuoit pas
> Homme aucun qui le peust faire bouger d'un pas.
>
> A frapper il estoit si fort & si adestre
> Que d'un seul coup de poing il tua de sa dextre
> Vn robuste taureau, & des ses membres forts
> Vne lieue le porta sans se greuer le corps.
>
> Mais se fiant par trop en ceste grande force,
> Il fut en fin saisi d'une mortelle entorce :
> Car il se vid manger des bestes, estant pris
> A l'arbre qu'il auoit de desioindre entrepris.
>
> Qui de sa force abuse en chase non faisable
> Se rend par son effort bien souuent miserable,
> Le fol entrepreneur tombe en confusion
> Et s'expose à chacun en grand derision.

The famous winged horse, Pegasus, heroic, though not a hero, has a right to close in our array of mythic characters. Sprung from the blood of Medusa when Perseus cut off her head, Pegasus is regarded sometimes as the thundering steed of Jove, at other times as the war-horse of Bellerophon; and in more modern times, under a third aspect, as the horse of the Muses. Already (at p. 142) we have spoken of some of the merits attributed to him, and have presented Emblems in which he is introduced. It will be sufficient now to bring forward the device and stanza of Alciat, in which he shows us how "by prudence and valour to overcome the Chimæra, that is, the stronger and those using stratagems."

Consilio & virtute Chimæram superari, id est, fortiores & deceptores.

EMBLEMA XIIII.

Alciat. 1581.

BELLEROPHON *ut fortis eques superare Chimæram,*
Et Lycij potuit sternere monstra soli:
Sic tu Pegaseis vectus petis æthera pennis,
Consilioq; animi monstra superba domas.

i.e. "As the brave knight Bellerophon could conquer Chimæra,
And the monsters of the Lycian shore stretch on the ground:
So thou borne on the wings of Pegasus seekest the sky,
And by prudence dost subdue proud monsters of the soul."

Shakespeare recognises neither Bellerophon nor the Chimæra, but Pegasus, the wonderful creature, and Perseus its owner.

The dauphin Lewis (see p. 141) likens his own horse to Pegasus, "with nostrils of fire,"—

"It is a beast for Perseus: he is pure air and fire . . . . he is indeed a horse.

In the Grecian camp (see *Troilus and Cressida*, act i. sc. 3, l. 33, vol. vi. p. 142), Nestor is urging the worth of dauntless valour, and uses the apt comparison,—

"In the reproof of chance
Lies the true proof of men: the sea being smooth,
How many shallow bauble boats dare sail
Upon her patient breast, making their way
With those of nobler bulk!
But let the ruffian Boreas once enrage
The gentle Thetis, and anon behold
The strong-ribb'd bark through liquid mountains cut,
Bounding between the two moist elements,
Like Perseus' horse."

The last lines are descriptive of Alciat's device, on p. 299.

It is the same Nestor (act iv. sc. 5, l. 183), who so freely and generously compliments Hector, though his enemy,—

"I have, thou gallant Trojan, seen thee oft,
Labouring for destiny, make cruel way
Through ranks of Greekish youth; and I have seen thee,
As hot as Perseus, spur thy Phrygian steed,
Despising many forfeits and subduements,
When thou hast hung thy advanced sword i' the air,
Nor letting it decline on the declined,
That I have said to some my standers by,
'Lo, Jupiter is yonder, dealing life!'"

Young Harry's praise, too, in 1 *Henry IV.*, act iv. sc. 1, l. 109, vol. iv. p. 318, is thus celebrated by Vernon,—

"As if an angel dropp'd down from the clouds
To turn and wind a fiery Pegasus,
And witch the world with noble horsemanship."

For nearly all the personages and the tales contained in this section, authority may be found in Ovid, and in the various pictorially illustrated editions of the *Metamorphoses* or of portions of them, which were numerous during the actively literary life of Shakespeare. It is, I confess, very questionable, whether for his classically mythic tales he was indeed indebted to the Emblematists; yet the many parallels in mythology between him and them justify the pleasant labour of setting both side by side, and, by this means, of facilitating to the reader the forming for himself an independent judgment.

SECTION IV.

EMBLEMS ILLUSTRATIVE OF FABLES.

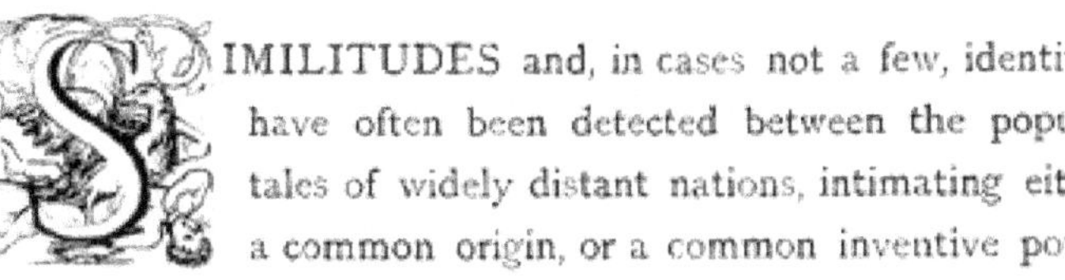

SIMILITUDES and, in cases not a few, identities have often been detected between the popular tales of widely distant nations, intimating either a common origin, or a common inventive power to work out like results. Fables have ever been a floating literature,—borne hither and thither on the current of Time,—used by any one, and properly belonging to no one. How they have circulated from land to land, and from age to age, we cannot tell: whence they first arose it is impossible to divine. There exist, we are told, fables collected by Bidpai in Sanscrit, by Lokman in Arabic, by Æsop in Greek, and by Phædrus in Latin: and they seem to have been interchanged and borrowed one from the other as if they were the property of the world,—handed down from the ancestorial times of a remote antiquity.

Shakespeare's general estimation of fables, and of those of Æsop in particular, may be gathered from certain expressions in two of the plays,—in the *Midsummer Night's Dream* (act v. sc. 1, l. 1, vol. ii. p. 258) and in 3 *Henry VI.* (act v. sc. 5, l. 25, vol. v. p. 329). In the *former* the speakers are Hippolyta and Theseus,—

> "*Hip.* 'Tis strange, my Theseus, that these lovers speak of.
> *The.* More strange than true: I never may believe
> These antique fables, nor these fairy toys.
> Lovers and madmen have such seething brains

> Such shaping fantasies, that apprehend
> More than cool reason ever comprehends."

In the *latter* Queen Margaret's son in reproof of Gloucester, declares,—

> "Let Æsop fable in a winter's night;
> His currish riddles sort not with this place."

The year of Shakespeare's birth, 1564, saw the publication, at Rome, of the Latin Fables of Gabriel Faerni; they had been written at the request of Pope Pius IV., and possess a high degree of excellence, both for their correct Latinity and for the power of invention which they display. Roscoe, in his *Life of Leo X.* (Bohn's ed. ii. p. 172), even avers that they "are written with such classical purity, as to have given rise to an opinion that he had discovered and fraudulently availed himself of some of the unpublished works of Phædrus." This opinion, however, is without any foundation.

The *Dialogues of Creatures moralised* preceded, however, the *Fables* of Faerni by above eighty years. "In the Latin and Dutch only there were not less than fifteen known editions before 1511."* An edition in Dutch is named as early as 1480, and one in French in 1482; and the English version appeared, it is likely, at nearly as early a date. These and other books of fables, though by a contested claim, are often regarded as books of Emblems. The best Emblem writers, even the purest, introduce fables and little tales of various kinds; as *Alciat*, Emb. 7, The Image of Isis, the Ass and the Driver; Emb. 15, The Cock, the Lion, and the Church; Emb. 59, The Blackamoor washed White, &c.: *Hadrian Junius*, Emb. 4, The caged Cat and the Rats; Emb. 19, The Crocodile and her Eggs: *Perriere*, Emb. 101, Diligence, Idleness, and the Ants. They all, in fact, adopted without scruple the illustrations which suited

* See the reprint of The Dialoges of Creatures Moralysed, by Joseph Haslewood, 4to, London, 1816 (Introd., pp. viij and ix).

their particular purpose: and Whitney, in one part of his *Emblemes*, uses twelve of Faerni's fables in succession.

Of the fables to which Shakespeare alludes some have been quoted in the former part of this work;—as The Fly and the Candle; The Sun, the Wind, and the Traveller; The Elephant and the undermined Tree; The Countryman and the Serpent. Of others we now proceed to give examples.

The Hares biting the dead Lion had, perhaps, one of its earliest applications, if not its origin, in the conduct of Achilles and his coward Greeks to the dead body of Hector, which Homer thus records (*Iliad*, xxii. 37),—

> "The other sons of the Greeks crowded around:
> And admired Hector's stature and splendid form:
> Nor was there one standing by who did not inflict a wound.

Claude Mignault, in his notes to Alciatus (Emb. 153), quotes an epigram, from an unknown Greek author, which Hector is supposed to have uttered as he was dragged by the Grecian chariot.—

> "Now after my death ye pierce my body;
> The very hares are bold to insult a dead lion."

The *Troilus and Cressida* (act v. sc. 8, l. 21, vol. vi. p. 259) exhibits the big, brutal Achilles exulting over his slain enemy, and giving the infamous order,—

> "Come, tie his body to my horse's tail;
> Along the field I will the Trojan trail."

And afterwards (act v. sc. 10, l. 4, vol. vi. p. 260) the atrocities are recounted to which Hector's body was exposed,—

> "He's dead, and at the murderer's horse's tail
> In beastly sort dragg'd through the shameful field."

The description thus given accords with that of Alciatus, Reusner, and Whitney, in reference to the saying, "We must not struggle with phantoms." Alciat's stanzas (Emb. 153) are,—

Cum laruis non luctandum.

ÆACIDÆ moriens percussu cuspidis Hector
Qui toties hosteis vicerat ante suos;
Comprimere haud potuit vocem, insultantibus illis,
Dum curru & pedibus nectere vincla parant.
Distrahite vt libitum est: sic cassi luce leonis
Conuellunt barbam vel timidi lepores.

Thus rendered by Whitney (p. 127), with the same device,—

Cùm laruis non luctandum.

Whitney, 1586.

"WHEN Hectors force, throughe mortall wounde did faile,
And life beganne, to dreadefull deathe to yeelde:
The Greekes moste gladde, his dyinge corpes assaile,
Who late did flee before him in the fielde:
Which when he sawe, quothe hee nowe worke your spite,
For so, the hares the Lion dead doe byte.

Looke here vpon, you that doe wounde the dead,
With slaunders vile, and speeches of defame:
Or bookes procure, and libelles to be spread,
When they bee gone, for to deface theire name:
Who while they liu'de, did feare you with theire lookes,
And for theire skill, you might not beare their bookes."

Reusner's lines, which have considerable beauty, may thus be rendered,—

> "Since man is mortal, the dead it becomes us
> Neither by word nor reproachful writing to mock at.
> Theseus, mindful of mortal destiny, the bones of his friends
> Both laves, and stores up in the tomb, and covers with earth.
> 'Tis the mark of a weak mind, to wage war with phantoms,
> And after death to good men insult to offer.
> So when overcome by the strength of Achilles
> The scullions of the camp struck Hector with darts.
> So whelps bite the lion laid prostrate by death;
> So his weapon any one bloods in the boar that is slain.
> Better 'tis, ye gods, well to speak, of those deserving well;
> And wickedness great indeed, to violate sacred tombs."

The device itself, in these three authors, is a representation of Hares biting a dead Lion; and in this we find an origin for the words used in *King John* (act ii. sc. 1, l. 134, vol. iv. p. 17), to reprove the Archduke of Austria. Austria demands of Philip Faulconbridge, "What the devil art thou?" and Philip replies,—

> "One that will play the devil, sir, with you,
> An a' may catch your hide and you alone:
> You are the hare of whom the proverb goes,
> Whose valour plucks dead lions by the beard."

Immediately references follow to other fables, or to their pictorial representations,—

> "I'll smoke your skin-coat, an I catch you right:"

in allusion to the fable of the fox or the ass hunting in a lion's skin. Again (l. 141),—

> "*Blanch.* O, well did he become that lion's robe
> That did disrobe the lion of that robe.
> *Bast.* It lies as sightly on the back of him
> As great Alcides' shows upon an ass:"

a sentiment evidently suggested to the poet's mind by some device or emblem in which the incongruity had found a place. Farther research might clear up this and other unexplained allusions in Shakespeare to fables or proverbs; but there is no necessity for attempting this in every instance that occurs.

"*Friendship enduring even after death,*" might receive a variety of illustrations. The conjugal relation of life frequently exemplifies its truth; and occasionally there are friends who show still more strongly how death hallows the memory of the departed, and makes survivors all the more faithful in their love. As the emblem of such fidelity and affection Alciat (Emb. 159) selects the figures of the elm and the vine.*

Amicitia etiam poſt mortem durans.

EMBLEMA CLIX.

Alciat, 1581.

* With the addition of two friends in conversation seated beneath the elm and vine, Boissard and Messin (1588, pp. 64, 65) give the same device, to the mottoes, "AMICITIÆ IMMORTALI,"—*To immortal friendship*: "Parfaite est l'Amitié qui vit après la mort."

The consociation in life is not forgotten; and though the supporting tree should die, the twining plant still grasps it round and adorns it with leaves and fruit.

> ARENTEM *ſenio, nudam quoque frondibus vlmum,*
> *Complexa eſt viridi vitis opaca coma:*
> *Agnoſcitq́; vices naturæ, & grata parenti*
> *Officij reddit mutua iura ſuo.*
> *Exemploq́; monet, tales nos quærere amicos,*
> *Quos neque diſiungat fœdere ſumma dies.*

To which lines Whitney (p. 62) gives for interpretation the two stanzas,—

> "A Withered Elme, whose boughes weare bare of leaues
> And sappe, was sunke with age into the roote:
> A fruictefull vine, vnto her bodie cleaues,
> Whose grapes did hange, from toppe vnto the foote:
> And when the Elme, was rotten, drie, and dead,
> His braunches still, the vine abowt it spread.
>
> Which showes, wee shoulde be linck'de with such a frende,
> That might reuiue, and helpe when wee bee oulde:
> And when wee stoope, and drawe vnto our ende,
> Our staggering state, to helpe for to vphoulde:
> Yea, when wee shall be like a sencelesse block,
> That for our sakes, will still imbrace our stock."

The Emblems of Joachim Camerarius,—*Ex Re Herbaria* (edition 1590, p. 36),—have a similar device and motto,—

> "*Quamlibet arenti vitis tamen hæret in ulmo,*
> *Sic quoque post mortem verus amicus amat.*"

i.e. "Yet as it pleases the vine clings to the withered elm,
So also after death the true friend loves."

And in the Emblems of Otho Vænius (Antwerp, 1608, p. 244), four lines of Alciat being quoted, there are both English and Italian versions, to—

"*Loue after death.*"

"The vyne doth still embrace the elme by age ore-past,
Which did in former tyme those feeble stalks vphold,
And constantly remaynes with it now beeing old,
Loue is not kil'd by death, that after death doth last."

And,—

"Ne per morte muore."

"*s'Auiticchia la vite, e l'olmo abbraccia,*
Anchor che il tempo secchi le sue piante;
Nopo morte l'Amor tiensi constante.
Non teme morte Amore, anzi la scaccia."

It is in the *Comedy of Errors* (act ii. sc. 2, l. 167, vol. i. p. 417) that Shakespeare refers to this fable, when Adriana addresses Antipholus of Syracuse,—

"How ill agrees it with your gravity
To counterfeit thus grossly with your slave,
Abetting him to thwart me in my mood!
Be it my wrong, you are from me exempt,
But wrong not that wrong with a more contempt.
Come, I will fasten on this sleeve of thine:
Thou art an elm, my husband, I a vine,
Whose weakness, married to thy stronger state,
Makes me with thy strength to communicate."

With a change from the vine to the ivy a very similar comparison occurs in the *Midsummer Night's Dream* (act iv. sc. 1, l. 37, vol. ii. p. 250). The infatuated Titania addresses Bottom the weaver as her dearest joy,—

"Sleep thou, and I will wind thee in my arms.
Fairies begone, and be all ways away.
So doth the woodbine the sweet honeysuckle
Gently entwist; the female ivy so
Enrings the barky fingers of the elm.
O, how I love thee! how I dote on thee!"

The fable of the Fox and the Grapes is admirably represented in Freitag's *Mythologia Ethica* (p. 127), to the motto, "Feigned is the refusal of that which cannot be had,"—

Ficta eius quod haberi nequit recusatio.

Freitag, 1579.

Fatuus statim indicat iram suam: qui autem dissimulat iniuriam, callidus est.
Prouerb. 12, 16.

"A fool's wrath is presently known: but a prudent man covereth shame."

The fable itself belongs to an earlier work by Gabriel Faerni, and there exemplifies the thought, "to glut oneself with one's own folly,"—

"*Stultitia sua seipsum saginare.*"

"Vulpes esuriens, alta de vite racemos
Pendentes nulla quum prensare arte valeret,
Nec pedibus tantum, aut agili se tollere saltu,

Re infecta abscedens, hæc secum, Age, desine, dixit.
Immatura vva est, gustuque insuavis acerbo.
Consueuere homines, eventu si qua sinistro
Vota cadunt, iis sese alienos velle videri."

Whitney takes possession of Faerni's fable, and gives the following translation (p. 98), though by no means a literal one,—

"THE Foxe, that longe for grapes did leape in vayne,
With wearie limmes, at lengthe did sad departe :
And to him selfe quoth hee, I doe disdayne
These grapes I see, bicause their taste is tarte :
So thou, that hunt'st for that thou longe hast mist,
Still makes thy boast, thou maist if that thou list."

Plantin, the famed printer of Antwerp, had, in 1583, put forth an edition of Faerni's fables,* and thus undoubtedly it was that Whitney became acquainted with them ; and from the intercourse then existing between Antwerp and London it would be strange if a copy had not fallen into Shakespeare's hands.

Owing to some malady, the King of France, in *All's Well that Ends Well* (act ii. sc. 1, l. 59, vol. iii. p. 133), is unable to go forth to the Florentine war with those whom he charges to be "the sons of worthy Frenchmen." Lafeu, an old lord, has learned from Helena some method of cure, and brings the tidings to the king, and kneeling before him is bidden to rise,—

"*King.* I'll fee thee to stand up.
Laf. Then here's a man stands, that has brought his pardon.
I would you had kneel'd, my lord, to ask me mercy ;
And that at my bidding you could so stand up.
King. I would I had ; so I had broke thy pate,
And ask'd thee mercy for't.

* "Centvm Fabvlæ ex Antiqvis delectæ, et a Gabriele Faerno Cremonense carminibus explicatæ. Antuerpiæ ex officina Christoph. Plantini, M.D.LXXXIII." 16mo. pp. 1—171.

> *Laf.* Good faith, across: but, my good lord, 'tis thus;
> Will you be cured of your infirmity?
> *King.* No.
> *Laf.* O, will you eat no grapes, my royal fox?
> Yes, but you will my noble grapes, an if
> My royal fox could reach them: I have seen a medicine
> That's able to breathe life into a stone,
> Quicken a rock, and make you dance canary
> With spritely fire and motion."

The fox, indeed, has always been a popular animal, and is the subject of many fables which are glanced at by Shakespeare;—as in the *Two Gentlemen of Verona* (act iv. sc. 4, l. 87, vol. i. p. 143), when Julia exclaims,—

> "Alas, poor Proteus! thou hast entertained
> A fox to be the shepherd of thy lambs."

Or in 2 *Henry VI.* (act iii. sc. 1, l. 55, vol. v. p. 153), where Suffolk warns the king of "the bedlam brain-sick duchess" of Gloucester,—

> "Smooth runs the water where the brook is deep."
> "The fox barks not when he would steal the lamb."

And again, in 3 *Henry VI.* (act iv. sc. 7, l. 24, vol. v. p. 312), the cunning creature is praised by Gloucester in an "*aside*,"—

> "But when the fox hath once got in his nose,
> He'll soon find means to make the body follow."

The bird in borrowed plumes, or the Jackdaw dressed out in Peacock's feathers, was presented, in 1596, on a simple device, not necessary to be produced, with the motto, "QVOD SIS ESSE VELIS"—*Be willing to be what thou art.*

> "*Mutatis de te narratur fabula verbis,*
> *Qui ferre alterius parta labore studes.*"

i.e. "By a change in the words of thyself the fable is told,
Who by labour of others dost seek to bear off the gold."

It is in the *Third* Century of the Symbols and Emblems of Joachim Camerarius (No. 81), and by him is referred to Æsop,* Horace, &c.; and the recently published *Microcosm*, the 1579 edition of which contains Gerard de Jode's fine representation of the scene.

Shakespeare was familiar with the fable. In 2 *Henry VI.* (act iii. sc. 1, l. 69, vol. v. p. 153), out of his simplicity the king affirms,—

> "Our kinsman Gloucester is as innocent
> From meaning treason to our royal person
> As is the sucking lamb or harmless dove."

But Margaret, his strong-willed queen, remarks (l. 75),—

> "Seems he a dove? his feathers are but borrow'd,
> For he's disposed as the hateful raven.
> Is he a lamb? his skin is surely lent him,
> For he's inclined as is the ravenous wolf."

In *Julius Cæsar* (act i. sc. 1, l. 68, vol. vii. p. 322), Flavius, the tribune, gives the order,—

> "Let no images
> Be hung with Cæsar's trophies;"

and immediately adds (l. 72),—

> "These growing feathers pluck'd from Cæsar's wing
> Will make him fly an ordinary pitch,
> Who else would soar above the view of men
> And keep us all in servile fearfulness."

But more forcibly is the spirit of the fable expressed, when of Timon of Athens (act ii. sc. 1, l. 28, vol. vii. p. 228)

---

* See the French version of Æsop, with 150 beautiful vignettes, "LES FABLES ET LA VIE D'ESOPE:" "A Anvers En l'imprimerie Plantiniéne Chez la Vefue, & Jean Mourentorf, M.D.XCIII." Here the bird is a jay (see p. 117, *Du Gay*, xxxi); and the peacocks are the avengers upon the base pretender to glories not his own.

a Senator, who was one of his importunate creditors, declares,—

"I do fear,
When every feather sticks in his own wing,
Lord Timon will be left a naked gull,
Which flashes now a phœnix."

The fable of the Oak and the Reed, or, the Oak and the Osier, has an early representation in the Emblems of Hadrian Junius, Antwerp, 1565, though by him it is applied to the ash. "Εἴξας νικᾷ," or, *Victrix animi æquitas*,—"By yielding conquer," or, "Evenness of mind the victrix,"—are the sentiments to be pictured forth and commented on. The device we shall take from Whitney; but the comment of Junius runs thus (p. 49),—

"*Ad Victorem Giselinum.*"

"Vis Boreæ obnixas violento turbine sternit
Ornos: Arundo infracta eandem despicit.
Fit victor patiens animus cedendo furori:
Insiste, Victor, hanc viam & re, & nomine."

i.e. "The stout ash trees, with violent whirl
The North-wind's force is stretching low;
The reeds unbroken rise again
And still in full vigour grow.
Yielding to rage, the patient mind
Victor becomes with added fame;
That course, my Victor, thou pursue
Reality, as well as name."

Whitney adopts the same motto (p. 220), "He conquers who endures;" but while retaining from Junius the ash-tree in the pictorial illustration, he introduces into his stanzas "the mightie oke," instead of the "stout ash." From Erasmus (*in Epist.*) he introduces an excellent quotation, that "it is truly the mark of a great mind to pass over some injuries, nor to have either ears or tongue ready for certain revilings."

Vincit qui patitur.

Whitney, 1586.

"THE mightie oke, that shrinkes not with a blaste,
But stiflie standes, when Boreas moste doth blowe,
With rage thereof, is broken downe at laste,
When bending reedes, that couche in tempestes lowe
With yeelding still, doe safe, and sounde appeare :
And looke alofte, when that the cloudes be cleare.

When Enuie, Hate, Contempte, and Slaunder, rage :
Which are the stormes, and tempestes, of this life ;
With patience then, wee must the combat wage,
And not with force resist their deadlie strife :
But suffer still, and then wee shall in fine,
Our foes subdue, when they with shame shall pine."

On several occasions Shakespeare introduces this fable, and once moralises on it quite in Whitney's spirit, if not in his manner. It is in the song of Guiderius and Arviragus from the *Cymbeline* (act iv. sc. 2, l. 259, vol. ix. p. 257),—

"*Gui.* Fear no more the heat o' the sun,
Nor the furious winter's rages ;
Thou thy worldly task hast done,
Home art gone and ta'en thy wages :
Golden lads and girls all must,
As chimney-sweepers, come to dust.

Arv. Fear no more the frown o' the great ;
Thou art past the tyrant's stroke ;
Care no more to clothe and eat ;
To thee the reed is as the oak :
The sceptre, learning, physic, must
All follow this and come to dust."

Less direct is the reference in the phrase from *Troilus and Cressida* (act i. sc. 3, l. 49, vol. vi. p. 143),—

"when the splitting wind
Makes flexible the knees of knotted oaks."

To the same purport are Cæsar's words (*Julius Cæsar*, act i. sc. 3, l. 5, vol. vii. p. 334),—

"I have seen tempests, when the scolding wings
Have rived the knotty oaks."

In *Love's Labour's Lost* (act iv. sc. 2, l. 100, vol. ii. p. 138), the Canzonet, which Nathaniel reads, recognises the fable itself,—

"If love make me forsworn, how shall I swear to love?
Ah, never faith could hold, if not to beauty vow'd !
Though to myself forsworn, to thee I'll faithful prove ;
Those thoughts to me were oaks, to thee like osiers bow'd."

We have, too, in *Coriolanus* (act v. sc. 2, l. 102, vol. vi. p. 403) the lines, "The worthy fellow is our general : He is the rock ; the oak not to be wind shaken."

This phrase is to be exampled from Otho Vænius (p. 116), where occur the English motto and stanza, "Strengthened by trauaile,"—

"Eu'n as the stately oke whome forcefull wyndes do moue,
Doth fasten more his root the more the tempest blowes,
Against disastres loue or firmness greater growes,
And makes each aduers change a witness to his loue."

In several instances it is difficult to determine whether expressions which have the appearance of glancing at fables really do refer to them, or whether they are current sayings, passing to and fro without any defined ownership. Also it is difficult to make an exact classification of what belongs to the fabulous and what to the proverbial. Of both we might collect many more examples than those which we bring forward; but the limits of our subject remind us that we must, as a general rule, confine our researches and illustrations to the Emblem writers themselves. We take this opportunity of saying that we may have arranged our instances in an order which some may be disposed to question; but mythology, fable, and proverb often run one into the other, and the knots cannot easily be disentangled. Take a sword and cut them; but the sword though sharp is not convincing.

Horapollo, ed. 1551.

SECTION V.

EMBLEMS IN CONNEXION WITH PROVERBS.

PROVERBS are nearly always suggestive of a little narrative, or of a picture, by which the sentiment might be more fully developed. The brief moral reflections appended to many fables partake very much of the nature of proverbs. Inasmuch, then, as there is this close alliance between them, we might consider the Proverbial Philosophy of Shakespeare only as a branch of the Philosophy of Fable; still, as there are in his dramas many instances of the use of the pure proverb, and instances too of the same kind in the Emblem writers, we prefer making a separate Section for the proverbs or wise sayings.

Occasionally, like the Sancho Panza of his renowned contemporary, Michael de Cervantes Saavedra, 1549—1616,* Shakespeare launches "a leash of proverbial philosophies at once;" but with this difference, that the dramatist's application of them is usually suggestive either of an Emblem-book origin, or of an Emblem-book destination. The example immediately in view is from the scene (3 *Henry VI.*, act i. sc. 4, l. 39, vol. v. p. 245) in which Clifford and Northumberland lay hands of violence on

* Cervantes and Shakespeare died about the same time,—it may be, on the same day; for the *former* received the sacrament of extreme unction at Madrid 18th of April, 1616, and died soon after; and the *latter* died the 23rd of April, 1616.

Richard Plantagenet, duke of York; the dialogue proceeds in the following way, York exclaiming,—

> "Why come you not? what! multitudes, and fear?
> *Clif.* So cowards fight, when they can fly no further.
> So doves do peck the falcon's piercing talons."

The queen entreats Clifford, "for a thousand causes," to withhold his arm, and Northumberland joins in the entreaty,—

> "*North.* Hold, Clifford! do not honour him so much,
> To prick thy finger, though to wound his heart:
> What valour were it, when a cur doth grin,
> For one to thrust his hand between his teeth,
> When he might spurn him with his foot away?"

Clifford and Northumberland seize York, who struggles against them (l. 61),—

> "*Clif.* Ay, ay, so strives the woodcock with the gin.
> *North.* So doth the cony struggle in the net."

York is taken prisoner, as he says (l. 63),—

> "So triumph thieves upon their conquer'd booty;
> So true men yield, with robbers so o'ermatch'd."

The four or five notions or sayings here enunciated a designer or engraver could easily translate into as many Emblematical devices, and the mind which uses them, as naturally as if he had invented them, must surely have had some familiarity with the kind of writing of which proverbs are the main source and foundation.

In this connection we will quote the proverb which "Clifford of Cumberland" (2 *Henry VI.*, act v. sc. 2, l. 28, vol. vi. p. 217) utters in French at the very moment of death, and which agrees

---

* Paralleled in Æsop's *Fables*, Antwerp, 1593: by Fab. xxxviii., *De l Esprivier & du Rossignol*; lii., *De l Oyseleur & du Merle*; and lxxvii., *Du Laboureur & de la Cigoigne.*

very closely with similar sayings in Emblem-books by French authors,—Perriere and Corrozet,—and still more in suitableness to the occasion on which it was spoken, the end of life.

York and Clifford,—it is the elder of that name,—engage in mortal combat (l. 26),—

> "*Clif.* My soul and body on the action both:
> *York.* A dreadful lay! address thee instantly."
>
> (*They fight, and* CLIFFORD *falls.*

At the point of death Clifford uses the words (l. 28), *La fin couronne les œuvres,*—"The end crowns the work." It was, no doubt, a common proverb; but it is one which would suggest to the Emblem writer his artistic illustration, and, with a little change, from some such illustration it appears to have been borrowed. Whitney (p. 130) records a resemblance to it among the sayings of the Seven Sages, dedicated "*to Sir* HVGHE CHOLMELEY *Knight,*"—

> "And SOLON said, *Remember still thy ende.*"

Perriere, 1539.

The two French Emblems alluded to above are illustrative of the proverb, "The end makes us all equal," and both use a very appropriate and curious device from the game of chess. Take, first, Emb. 27 from Perriere's *Theatre des Bons Engins:* Paris, 1539,—

* Identical almost with "La fin covronne l'oevvre" in Messin's version of Boissard's *Emblematum Liber* (4to, 1588), where (p. 20) we have the device of the letter Y as emblematical of human life; and at the end of the stanzas the lines,—

> "L'estroit est de vertu le sentier espineux,
> Qui couronne de vie en fin le vertueux:
> C'est ce que considere en ce lieu Pythagore."

XXVII.

LE Roy d'eschez, pendant que le ieu dure,
Sur ses subiectz ha grande preference,
Sy l'on le mattę, il conuiẽt qu'il endure
Que l'on le mettę au sac sans difference.
Cecy nous faict notable demonstrance,
Qu' apres le ieu de vie transitoire,
Quãd mort nous a mis en sõ repertoire,
Les roys ne sũt plusgrãs que les vassaulx;
Car dans le sac (cõmę à tous est notoire),
Roys & pyons en hõneur sont esgaulx.

The other, from Corrozet, is in his "Hecatomgraphie:" Paris, 1540,—

Corrozet, 1540.

SVr l'eſchiquier ſont les eſchez aſſis,
Tous en leur rēg par ordre biē raſſis,
Les roys en hault pour duyre les combatz,
Les roynes pres, les cheualiers plus bas,
Les folz deſſoubz, puis apres les pions,
Les rocz auſſy de ce ieu champions.
Et quand le tout eſt aſſis en ſon lieu
Subtilement on commence le ieu.
* Or vault le roy au ieu de l'eſchiquier,
Mieulx que la royne & moins le cheualier.
Chaſcun pion de tous ceulx la moins vault,
Mais quand c'eſt faict & que le ieu deffault
Il n'ya roy, ne royne, ne le roc,
Qu' enſemblement tout ne ſoit à vng bloc,
Mis dans vng ſac, ſans ordre ne degré,
Et ſans auoir l'ung plus que l'aultre à gré.
Ainſi eſt il de nous pauures humains,
Aulcuns ſont grands Empereurs des Romains,
Les aultres roys, les aultres ducz & comtes,
Aultres petis dont on ne faict grandz comptes.
Nous iouons tous aux eſchez en ce monde,
Entre les biens ou l'ung pluſqu' aultre abonde,
Mais quand le iour de la vie eſt paſſe,
Tout corps humain eſt en terre muſſé,
Autant les grands que petis terre cœuure,
Tant ſeulement nous reſte la bonne œuure.

Corrozet's descriptive verses conclude with thoughts to which old Clifford's dying words might well be appended: "When the game of life is over, every human body is hidden in the earth; as well great as little the earth covers; what alone remains to us is the good deed." "LA FIN COURONNE LES ŒUVRES."

But Shakespeare uses the expression, "the end crowns all," almost as Whitney (p. 230) does the allied proverb, "Time terminates all,"—

* In the Emblems of Lebeus-Batillius (4to, Francfort, 1596), human life is compared to a game with dice. The engraving by which it is illustrated represents three men at play with a backgammon-board before them.

Tempus omnia terminat.

Whitney, 1586

THE *longest daye, in time resignes to nighte.*
The greatest oke, in time to duste doth turne:
The Rauen dies, the Egle failes of flighte.
The Phœnix rare, in time her selfe doth burne.
The princelie stagge at lengthe his race doth ronne
And all must ende, that euer was begonne.

A sentiment this corresponding nearly with Hector's words, in the *Troilus and Cressida* (act iv. sc. 5, l. 223, vol. vi. p. 230),—

"The fall of every Phrygian stone will cost
A drop of Grecian blood: the end crowns all,
And that old common arbitrator, Time.
Will one day end it."

Prince Henry (2 *Henry IV.*, act ii. sc. 2, l. 41, vol. iv. p. 392), in reply to Poins, gives yet another turn to the proverb: "By this hand, thou thinkest me as far in the devil's books as thou and Falstaff for obduracy and persistency; let the end try the man."

In Whitney's address "to the Reader," he speaks of having collected "sondrie deuises" against several great faults which he names, "bycause they are growē so mightie that one bloe will not beate them downe, but newe headdes springe vp like *Hydra*, that *Hercules* weare not able to subdue them." "But," he adds, using an old saying, "manie droppes pierce the stone, and with manie blowes the oke is ouerthrowen."

Near Mortimer's Cross, in Herefordshire, a messenger relates how "the noble Duke of York was slain" (3 *Henry VI.*, act ii. sc. 1, l. 50, vol. v. p. 252), and employs a similar, almost an identical, proverb,—

> "Environed he was with many foes,
> And stood against them, as the hope of Troy
> Against the Greeks that would have enter'd Troy.
> But Hercules himself must yield to odds;
> And many strokes, though with a little axe,
> Hew down and fell the hardest-timber'd oak."

This is almost the coincidence of the copyist, and but for the necessities of the metre, Whitney's words might have been literally quoted.

"Manie droppes pierce the stone," has its parallel in the half-bantering, half-serious, conversation between King Edward and Lady Grey (3 *Henry VI.*, act iii. sc. 2, l. 48, vol. v. p. 280). The lady prays the restoration of her children's lands, and the king intimates he has a boon to ask in return,—

> "*King Edw.* Ay, but thou canst do what I mean to ask.
> *Grey.* Why then I will do what your grace commands.
> *Glou.* [*Aside to* CLAR.] He plies her hard; and much rain wears the marble.
> *Clar.* [*Aside to* GLOU.] As red as fire! nay, then her wax must melt."

In Otho Vænius (p. 210), where Cupid is bravely working at felling a tree, to the motto, "By continuance," we find the stanza,—

"Not with one stroke at first the great tree goes to grownd,
But it by manie strokes is made to fall at last,
The drop doth pierce the stone by falling long and fast,
So by enduring long long sought-for loue is found."

"To clip the anvil of my sword," is an expression in the *Coriolanus* (act iv. sc. 5, lines 100—112, vol. vi. p. 380) very difficult to be explained, unless we regard it as a proverb, denoting the breaking of the weapon and the laying aside of enmity. Aufidius makes use of it in his welcome to the banished Coriolanus,—

"O Marcius, Marcius!
Each word thou hast spoke hath weeded from my heart
A root of ancient envy. If Jupiter
Should from yond cloud speak divine things,
And say ''Tis true,' I'd not believe them more
Than thee, all noble Marcius. Let me twine
Mine arms about that body, where against
My grained ash an hundred times hath broke,
And scarr'd the moon with splinters: here I clip
The anvil of my sword, and do contest
As hotly and as nobly with thy love
As ever in ambitious strength I did
Contend against thy valour."

To clip, or cut, *i.e.*, strike the anvil with a sword, is exhibited by more than one of the Emblem writers, whose stanzas are indeed to the same effect as those of Massinger in his play, *The Duke of Florence* (act ii. sc. 3),—

"Allegiance
Tempted too far is like the trial of
A good sword on an anvil; as that often
Flies in pieces without service to the owner;
So trust enforced too far proves treachery,
And is too late repented."

In his 31st Emblem, Perriere gives the device, and stanzas which follow,—

Perrière, 1539

XXXI.

EN danger eſt de rompre ſon eſpée
    Qui ſur l'enclumę en frappe rudement.
Auſſi l'amour eſt bien toſt ſincoppée,
Quand ſon amy on preſſe follement.
Qui le fera, perdra ſubitement
Ce qu'il deburoit bien cheremẽt garder.
De tel abus, ſe fault contregarder,
Cũmę en ce lieu auõs doctrinę expreſſe.
A tel effort, ne te fault hazarder
De perdre amy, quãd ſouuẽt tu le preſſe.

But the meaning is, the putting of friendship to too severe a trial: "As he is in danger of breaking his sword who strikes it upon an anvil, so is love very soon cut in pieces when foolishly a man presses upon his friend." So Whitney (p. 192), to the motto, *Importunitas euitanda*,—"Want of consideration to be avoided,"—

> "WHO that with force, his burnish'd blade doth trie
> On anuill harde, to prooue if it be sure:
> Doth Hazarde muche, it shoulde in peeces flie,
> Aduentring that, which else mighte well indure:
> For, there with strengthe he strikes vppon the stithe,
> That men maye knowe, his youthfull armes haue pithe.
>
> Which warneth those, that louinge frendes inioye,
> With care, to keepe, and frendlie them to treate,
> And not to trye them still, with euerie toye,
> Nor presse them doune, when causes be too greate,
> Nor in requests importunate to bee:
> For ouermuche, dothe tier the courser free?"

Touchstone, the clown, in *As You Like It* (act ii. sc. 4, l. 43, vol. ii. p. 400), names the various tokens of his affections for Jane Smile, and declares, "I remember, when I was in love I broke my sword upon a stone and bid him take that for coming a-night to Jane Smile: and I remember the kissing of her batlet and the cow's-dugs that her pretty chopt hands had milked."

It may, however, from the general inaccuracy of spelling in the early editions of Shakespeare, be allowed to suppose a typographical error, and that the phrase in question should read, not "anvil of my sword," but "handle;"—I clip, or embrace the handle, grasp it firmly in token of affection.

The innocence of broken love-vows is intimated in *Romeo and Juliet* (act ii. sc. 2, l. 90, vol. vii. p. 42),—

> "Dost thou love me? I know thou wilt say 'Ay,'

And I will take thy word: yet if thou swear'st,
Thou mayst prove false: at lovers' perjuries,
They say, Jove laughs."

And most closely is the sentiment represented in the design by Otho van Veen (p. 140), of Venus dispensing Cupid from his oaths, and of Jupiter in the clouds smiling benignantly on the two. The mottoes are, "AMORIS IVSIVRANDVM PŒNAM NON HABET,"—*Love excused from periurie,*—and "Giuramento sparso al vento."

In Callimachus occurs Juliet's very expression, "at lovers' perjuries Jove laughs,"—

"*Nulla fides inerit: periuria ridet amantum*
Juppiter, & ventis irrita ferre iubet:"

and from Tibullus we learn, that whatever silly love may have eagerly sworn, Jupiter has forbidden to hold good,—

"*Gratia magna Ioui: vetuit pater ipse valere,*
Iurasset cupidè quidquid ineptus Amor."

The English lines in Otho van Veen are,—

"The louer freedome hath to take a louers oth,
Whith if it proue vntrue hee is to be excused,
For venus doth dispence in louers othes abused,
And loue no fault comitts in swearing more than troth."

The thoughts are, as expressed in Italian,—

"*Se ben l'amante assai promette, e giura,*
Non si da pena à le sue voci infide,
Anzi Venere, e Gioue se ne ride.
l'Amoroso spergiuro non si cura."

To such unsound morality, however, Shakespeare offers strong objections in the Friar's words (*Romeo and Juliet*, act iii. sc. 3, l. 126),—

"Thy noble shape is but a form of wax,
Digressing from the valour of a man;

> Thy dear love sworn, but hollow perjury,
> Killing that love which thou hast vow'd to cherish."

"Labour in vain,"—pouring water into a sieve, is shown by Perriere in his 77th Emblem,

Perriere, 15[illegible]

where however it is a blind Cupid that holds the sieve, and lovers' gifts are the waters with which the attempt is made to fill the vessel.

LXXVII.

QVi plus mettra dans le crible d'amours,
Plus y perdra, car chose n'y profitte:
Le temps si pert, biens, bagues & atours,
Sa douleur est en tout amer confitte.
Folle ieunesse & franc vouloir incite
A tel desduict despendre grosse somme:
Sur ce pẽser doibuent biẽ ieunes hõmes,
Que de ce fait meilleurs n'ẽ peuuẽt estre:
Et quãd naurõt le vaillãt de deux põmes,
Ne fera temps leur erreur recognoistre.

We have endeavoured to interpret the old French stanza into English rhyme,—

"Who in love's tempting sieve shall place his store,
Since nothing profits there, will lose the more:
Lost are his time, goods, rings and rich array,
Till grief in bitterness complete his day.
Folly of youth and free desire incite
Great sums to lavish on each brief delight.
Surely young men on this ought well to ponder,
That better cannot be, if thus they wander;
And when remains two apples' worth alone,
'Twill not the time be their mistake to own."

Shakespeare presents the very same thought and almost the identical expressions. To the Countess of Rousillon, Bertram's mother, Helena confesses love for her son, *All's Well that Ends Well* (act i. sc. 3, l. 182, vol. iii. p. 127),—

"Then, I confess,
Here on my knee, before high heaven and you,
That before you, and next unto high heaven,
I love your son.
My friends were poor, but honest; so's my love:
Be not offended; for it hurts not him
That he is loved of me: I follow him not
By any token of presumptuous suit;
Nor would I have him till I do deserve him;
Yet never know how that desert should be.

I know I love in vain, strive against hope ;
Yet, in this captious and intenible sieve,
I still pour in the waters of my love,
And lack not to lose still : thus, Indian-like,
Religious in my error, I adore
The sun, that looks upon his worshipper,
But knows of him no more."

How probable do the turns of thought, "captious and intenible sieve," "the waters of my love," render the supposition that Perriere's Emblem of Love and the Sieve had been seen by our dramatist. Cupid appears patient and passive, but the Lover in very evident surprise sees "the rings and rich array" flow through "le crible d'amours." Cupid's eyes, in the device, are bound, and the method of binding them corresponds with the lines, *Romeo and Juliet* (act i. sc. 4, l. 4, vol. vii. p. 23),—

"We'll have no Cupid hoodwink'd with a scarf,
Bearing a Tartar's painted bow of lath,
Scaring the ladies like a crow-keeper."

Again, though not in reference to the same subject, there is in *Much Ado About Nothing* (act v. sc. 1, l. 1, vol. ii. p. 69), the comparison of the sieve to labour in vain. Antonio is giving advice to Leonato when overwhelmed with sorrows,—

"*Ant.* If you go on thus you will kill yourself ;
And 'tis not wisdom thus to second grief
Against yourself.
Leon. I pray thee, cease thy counsel,
Which falls into mine ears as profitless
As water in a sieve : give not me counsel ;
Nor let no comforter delight mine ear
But such a one whose wrongs do suit with mine."

By way of variation we consult Paradin's treatment of the same thought (fol. 88*v*), in which he is followed by Whitney (p. 12), with the motto *Frustrà.*

Hac illac perfluo

Paradin, 156.

"THE Poëtes faine, that DANAVS daughters deare,
Inioyned are to fill the fatall tonne :
Where, thowghe they toile, yet are they not the neare,
But as they powre, the water forthe dothe runne :
No paine will serue, to fill it to the toppe,
For, still at holes the same doth runne, and droppe."

"Every rose has its thorn," or "No pleasure without pain," receives exemplification from several sources. Perriere (Emb. 30) and Whitney (p. 165) present us with a motto implying *No bitter without its sweet*, but giving the gathering of a rose in illustration ; thus the former writer,—

"*Post amara dulcia.*"

"QVI veult la rose au vert buysson saisir
Esmerueiller ne se doibt s'il se poinct.
Grād biē na'uōs, sās quelque desplaisir,
Plaisir ne vient sans douleur, si apoint.
Conclusion sommaire, c'est le point,
Qu' apres douleur, on ha plaisir : souuēt
Beau tēps se voit, tost apres le grāt vēt,
Grād biē suruiēt apres quelque maleur.

Parquoy pēser doibt tout hōme scauāt,
Que volupté n'est iamais sans douleur."

So Whitney (p. 165),—

Whitney, 1586.

"SHARPE prickes preserue the Rose, on euerie parte,
That who in haste to pull the same intendes,
Is like to pricke his fingers, till they smarte?
But being gotte, it makes him straight amendes
It is so freshe, and pleasant to the smell,
Thoughe he was prick'd, he thinkes he ventur'd well.

And he that faine woulde get the gallant rose,
And will not reache, for feare his fingers bleede;
A nettle, is more fitter for his nose?
Or hemblocke meete his appetite to feede?
None merites sweete, who tasted not the sower,
Who feares to climbe, deserues no fruicte, nor flower."

In the Emblems of Otho Vænius (p. 160), Cupid is plucking a rose, to the motto from Claudian, "ARMAT SPINA ROSAS, MELLA TEGUNT APES,"—Englished, "*No pleasure without payn.*"

"In plucking of the rose is pricking of the thorne,
In the attayning sweet, is tasting of the sowre,
With ioy of loue is mixt the sharp of manie a showre,
But at the last obtayned, no labor is forlorne."

The pretty song from *Love's Labour's Lost* (act iv. sc. 3, l. 97, vol. ii. p. 144), alludes to the thorny rose,—

"On a day—alack the day!
Love, whose month is ever May,
Spied a blossom passing fair
Playing in the wanton air:
Through the velvet leaves the wind,
All unseen, can passage find;
That the lover, sick to death,
Wish himself the heaven's breath.
Air, quoth he, thy cheeks may blow;
Air, would I might triumph so!
But, alack, my hand is sworn
Ne'er to pluck thee from thy thorn."

The scene in the Temple-garden; the contest in plucking roses between Richard Plantagenet and the Earls of Somerset, Suffolk, and Warwick (1 *Henry VI.*, act ii. sc. 4, lines 30—75, vol. v. pp. 36, 37), continually alludes to the thorns that may be found. We may sum the whole "brawl," as it is termed, into a brief space (l. 68),—

"*Plan.* Hath not thy rose a canker, Somerset?
Som. Hath not thy rose a thorn, Plantagenet?
Plan. Ay, sharp and piercing, to maintain his truth;
Whiles thy consuming canker eats his falsehood."

"True as the needle to the pole," is a saying which of course must have originated since the invention of the mariner's compass. Sambucus, in his *Emblems* (edition 1584, p. 84, or 1599, p. 79), makes the property of the loadstone his emblem for the motto, *The mind remains unmoved.*

Mens immota manet.

Sambucus, 1564.

Dicitvr *interna vi Magnes ferra mouere:*
Perpetuò nautas dirigere inq; viam.
Semper enim stellam firmè aspicit ille polarem.
Indicat hac horas, nos variéque monet.
Mens vtinam in cælum nobis immota maneret,
Nec subitò dubiis fluctuet illa malis.
Pax coëat tandem, Christe, vnum claudat ouile,
Lisque tui verbi iam dirimatur ope.
Da, sitiens anima excelsas sic appetat arces:
Fontis vt ertiui ceruus anhelus aquas.

In the latter part of his elegiacs Sambucus introduces another subject, and gives a truly religious turn to the device,—

"Gather'd one fold, O Christ, let peace abound,
Be vanquish'd by thy word, our jarring strife;
Then thirsting souls seek towers on heavenly ground,
As pants the stag for gushing streams of life."

The magnet's power alone is kept in view by Whitney (p. 43),—

"By vertue hidde, behoulde, the Iron harde,
The loadestone drawes, to poynte vnto the starre:
Whereby, wee knowe the Seaman keepes his carde,
And rightlie shapes, his course to countries farre:
And on the pole, dothe euer keepe his eie,
And withe the same, his compasse makes agree.

> Which shewes to vs, our inward vertues shoulde,
> Still drawe our hartes, althoughe the iron weare:
> The hauenlie starre, at all times to behoulde,
> To shape our course, so right while wee bee heare:
> That Scylla, and Charybdis, wee maie misse,
> And winne at lengthe, the porte of endlesse blisse."

The pole of heaven itself, rather than the magnetic needle, is in Shakespeare's dramas the emblem of constancy. Thus in the *Julius Cæsar* (act iii. sc. 1, l. 58, vol. vii. p. 363), Metellus, Brutus, and Cassius are entreating pardon for Publius Cimber, but Cæsar replies, in words almost every one of which is an enforcement of the saying, "Mens immota manet,"—

> "I could be well moved, if I were as you;
> If I could pray to move, prayers would move me:
> But I am constant as the northern star,
> Of whose true-fix'd and resting quality
> There is no fellow in the firmament.
> The skies are painted with unnumber'd sparks;
> They are all fire and every one doth shine;
> But there's but one in all doth hold his place:
> So in the world; 'tis furnish'd well with men,
> And men are flesh and blood, and apprehensive;
> Yet in the number I do know but one
> That unassailable holds on his rank,
> Unshak'd of motion: and that I am he,
> Let me a little show it, even in this;
> That I was constant Cimber should be banish'd,
> And constant do remain to keep him so."

The *Midsummer Night's Dream* (act i. sc. 1, l. 180, vol. ii. p. 205), introduces Hermia greeting her rival Helena,—

> "*Her.* God speed fair Helena! whither away?
> *Hel.* Call you me fair? that fair again unsay.
> Demetrius loves you fair: O happy fair!
> Your eyes are lode-stars."

The scene changes, Helena is following Demetrius, but he turns to her and says (act ii. sc. 1, l. 194, vol. ii. p. 217),—

"Hence, get thee gone, and follow me no more.
Hel. You draw me, you hard-hearted adamant;
But yet you draw not iron, for my heart
Is true as steel: leave but your power to draw,
And I shall have no power to follow you.

The averment of his fidelity is thus made by Troilus to Cressida (act iii. sc. 2, l. 169, vol. vi. p. 191),—

"As true as steel, as plantage to the moon,
As sun to day, as turtle to her mate,
As iron to adamant, as earth to the centre.
Yet after all comparisons of truth,
As truth's authentic author to be cited,
'As true as Troilus' shall crown up the verse
And sanctify the numbers."

So Romeo avers of one of his followers (act ii. sc. 4, l. 187, vol. vii. p. 58),—

"I warrant thee, my man's as true as steel."

"EX MAXIMO MINIMVM,"—*Out of the greatest the least,*—is a saying adopted by Whitney (p. 229), from the "PICTA POESIS" (p. 55) of Anulus,—

EX MAXIMO MINIMVM

Anulus, 1555

HAE *Sunt Relliquiæ Sacrarij, in quo*
Fertur viua Dei fuisse imago.
Hæc est illius, & domus ruina,
In qua olim Ratio tenebat arcem.
At nunc horribilis figura Mortis.
Ventosum caput, haud habens cerebrum.

X X

Both writers make the proverb the groundwork of reflexions on a human skull. According to Anulus, "the relics of the charnel house were once the living images of God,"—"that ruin of a dome was formerly the citadel of reason." Whitney thus moralizes,—

> "WHERE liuely once, GODS image was expreste,
> Wherin, sometime was sacred reason plac'de,
> The head, I meane, that is so ritchly bleste,
> With sighte, with smell, with hearinge, and with taste.
> Lo, nowe a skull, both rotten, bare, and drye,
> A relike meete in charnell house to lye."

The device and explanatory lines may well have given suggestion to the half-serious, half-cynical remarks by Hamlet in the celebrated grave-yard scene (*Hamlet*, act v. sc. 1, l. 73, vol. viii. p. 153). A skull is noticed which one of the callous grave-diggers had just thrown up upon the sod, and Hamlet says (l. 86),—

> "That skull had a tongue in it, and could sing once: how the knave jowls it to the ground, as if it were Cain's jaw-bone, that did the first murder!"

And a little further on,—

> "Here's a fine revolution, an we had the trick to see't. Did these bones cost no more the breeding, but to play at loggats with 'em? mine ache to think on't." *

And when Yorick's skull is placed in his hand, how the Prince moralizes! (l. 177),—

> "Here hung those lips, that I have kissed I know not how oft. Where be your gibes now? your gambols? your songs? your flashes of merriment, that were wont to set the table on a roar? Not one now, to mock your own

* The skeleton head on the shield in Death's escutcheon by Holbein, may supply another pictorial illustration, but it is not sufficiently distinctive to be dwelt on at any length. The fac-simile reprints by Pickering, Bohn, Quaritch, or Brothers, render direct reference to the plate very easy.

grinning? quite chap-fallen? Now get you to my lady's chamber, and tell her, let her paint an inch thick, to this favour she must come; make her laugh at that."

And again (lines 191 and 200),—

> "To what base uses we may return, Horatio!
>
> . . . .
>
> Imperial Cæsar, dead, and turn'd to clay,
> Might stop a hole to keep the wind away."

Of the skull Anulus says, "Here reason held her citadel;" and the expression has its parallel in Edward's lament (3 *Henry VI.*, act ii. sc. 1, l. 68, vol. v. p. 252),—

> "Sweet Duke of York, our prop to lean upon;"

when he adds (l. 74),—

> "Now my soul's palace is become a prison;"

to which the more modern description corresponds,—

> "The dome of thought, the palace of the soul."

A far nobler emblem could be made, and I believe has been made, though I cannot remember where, from those lines in *Richard II.* (act ii. sc. 1, l. 267, vol. iv. p. 145), which allude to the death's head and the light of life within. Northumberland, Ross and Willoughby are discoursing respecting the sad state of the king's affairs, when Ross remarks,—

> "We see the very wreck that we must suffer:
> And unavoided is the danger now,
> For suffering so the causes of our wreck."

And Northumberland replies in words of hope (l. 270),—

> "Not so: even through the hollow eyes of death
> I spy life peering."

It is a noble comparison, and most suggestive,—but of a flight higher than the usual conceptions of the Emblem writers. Supplied to them they could easily enough work it out into device and picture, but possess scarcely power enough to give it origin.*

"A snake lies hidden in the grass," is no unfrequent proverb; and Paradin's "Devises Heroiqves" (41) set forth both the fact and the application.

Latet anguis in herba.

Paradin, 1562.

En cueillant les Fleurs, & les Fraizes des champs, ſe faut d'autant garder du dangereus Serpent, qu'il nous peut enuenimer, & faire mourir nos corps. Et auſsi en colligeant les belles autoritez, & graues ſentences des liures, faut euiter d'autant les mauuaiſes opinions, qu'elles nous peuuent peruertir, damner, & perdre nos ames.

From the same motto and device Whitney (p. 24) makes the application to flatterers,—

> "Of flattringe speeche, with sugred wordes beware,
> Suspect the harte, whose face doth fawne, and smile,

* A note of inquiry, from Mr. W. Aldis Wright, of Trinity College, Cambridge, asking me if Shakespeare's thought may not have been derived from an emblematical picture, informs me that he has an impression of having "somewhere seen an allegorical picture of a child looking through the eyeholes of a skull."

> With trusting theise, the worlde is clog'de with care,
> And fewe there bee can scape theise vipers vile :
> With pleasinge speeche they promise, and proteste,
> When hatefull hartes lie hidd within their brest."

According to the 2nd part of *Henry VI.* (act iii. sc. 1, l. 224, vol. v. p. 158), the king speaks favourably of Humphrey, Duke of Gloucester, and Margaret the queen declares to the attendant nobles,—

> "Henry my lord is cold in great affairs,
> Too full of foolish pity, and Gloucester's show
> Beguiles him as the mournful crocodile
> With sorrow snares relenting passengers,
> Or as the snake roll'd in a flowering bank,
> With shining checker'd slough, doth sting a child,
> That for the beauty thinks it excellent."

In Lady Macbeth's unscrupulous advice to her husband (*Macbeth*, act i. sc. 5, l. 61, vol. vii. p. 438), the expressions occur,—

> "Your face, my thane, is as a book where men
> May read strange matters. To beguile the time,
> Look like the time; bear welcome in your eye,
> Your hand, your tongue : look like the innocent flower,
> But be the serpent under't."

Romeo slays Tybalt, kinsman to Julia, and the nurse announces the deed to her (*Romeo and Juliet*, act iii. sc. 2, l. 69, vol. vii. p. 75),—

> "*Nurse.* Tybalt is gone, and Romeo banished ;
> Romeo that kill'd him, he is banished.
> *Jul.* O God ! did Romeo's hand shed Tybalt's blood ?
> *Nurse.* It did, it did ; alas the day, it did !
> *Jul.* O serpent heart, hid with a flowering face !
> Did ever dragon keep so fair a cave ?
> Beautiful tyrant ! fiend angelical !
> Dove-feather'd raven ! wolvish-ravening lamb !"

Though not illustrative of a Proverb, we will here conclude what has to be remarked respecting Serpents. An Emblem in

Paradin's "DEVISES HEROIQVES" (112) and in Whitney (p. 166), represents a serpent that has fastened on a man's finger, and that is being shaken off into a fire, while the man remains unharmed; the motto, "Who against us?"—

Quis contra nos?

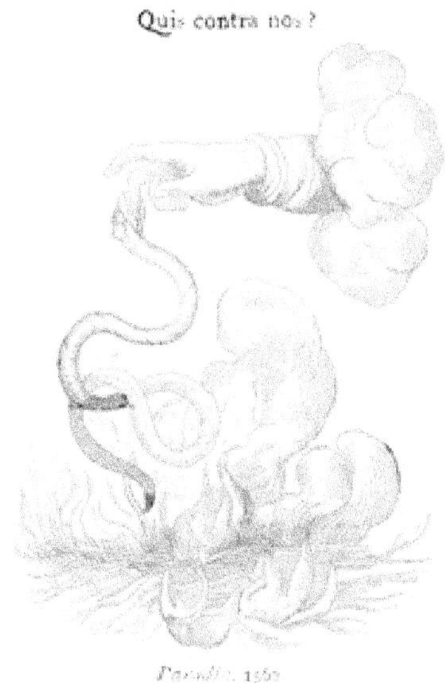

Paradin, 1562.

The scene described in the *Acts of the Apostles*, chap. xxviii. v. 3—6, Paradin thus narrates,—

"*Saint Paul, en l'isle de Malte fut mordu d'vne Vipere : ce neantmoins (quoi que les Barbares du lieu le cuidassent autrement) ne valut pis de la morsure, secouant de sa main la Beste dans le feu : car veritablement à qui Dieu veut aider, il n'y a rien que puisse nuire.*"

Whitney, along with exactly the same device, gives the full motto,—

"*Si Deus nobiscum, quis contra nos?*"

"HIS seruantes GOD preserues, thoughe they in danger fall:
Euen as from vipers deadlie bite, he kept th' Appostle Paule."

The action figured in this Emblem is spoken of in the *Midsummer Night's Dream* (act iii. sc. 2, l. 254, vol. ii. p. 241).

Puck has laid the "love-juice" on the wrong eyes, and in consequence Lysander avows his love for Helen instead of for Hermia; and the dialogue then proceeds,—

> "*Dem.* I say I love thee more than he can do.
> *Lys.* If thou say so, withdraw, and prove it too.
> *Dem.* Quick, come!
> *Her.* Lysander, whereto tends all this?
> *Lys.* Away, you Ethiope!
> *Dem.* No, no; he'll . . .
> Seem to break loose; take on as you would follow,
> But yet come not: you are a tame man, go!
> *Lys.* Hang off, thou cat, thou burr! vile thing, let loose,
> Or I will shake thee from me like a serpent!"

Cardinal Pandulph, the Pope's legate, in *King John* (act iii. sc. 1, l. 258, vol. iv. p. 42), urges King Philip to be champion of the Church, and says to him,—

> "France, thou mayst hold a serpent by the tongue,
> A chafed lion by the mortal paw,
> A fasting tiger safer by the tooth,
> Than keep in peace that hand which thou dost hold."

King Richard's address to the "gentle earth," when he landed in Wales (*Richard II.*, act iii. sc. 2, l. 12, vol. iv. p. 164), calls us to the Emblem of the snake entwined about the flower,—

> "Feed not thy sovereign's foe, my gentle earth,
> Nor with thy sweets comfort his ravenous sense;
> But let thy spiders, that suck up thy venom,
> And heavy-gaited toads lie in their way,
> Doing annoyance to the treacherous feet
> Which with usurping steps do trample thee:
> Yield stinging nettles to mine enemies;
> And when they from thy bosom pluck a flower,
> Guard it, I pray thee, with a lurking adder
> Whose double tongue may with a mortal touch
> Throw death upon thy sovereign's enemies."

"The Engineer hoist with his own petar" may justly be regarded as a proverbial saying. It finds its exact correspondence in Beza's 8th Emblem (edition 1580), in which for device is a cannon bursting, and with one of its fragments killing the cannonier.

Beza, 1580.

> "*Cernis ut in cœlum fuerat quæ machina torta,*
> *Fit iaculatori mors properata suo:*
> *In sanctos quicunque Dei ruis impie seruos,*
> *Conatus merces hæc manet vna tuas.*"

Thus rendered into French in 1581,—

> "Vois tu pas le canon braqué contre les cieux,
> En se creuant creuer celui la qui le tire?
> Le mesme t'aduiendra, cruel malicieux,
> Qui lasches sur les bons les balles de ton ire."

The sentiment is the same as that of the proverb in the motto which Lebeus-Batillius prefixes to his 18th Emblem (edition 1596), "QVIBVS REBVS CONFIDIMVS, IIS MAXIME EVERTIMVS,"—*To whatever things we trust, by them chiefly are we overthrown.* The subject is Milo caught in the cleft of the tree which he had riven by his immense strength; he is held fast, and devoured by wolves.

The application of Beza's Emblem is made by Hamlet (act iii. sc. 4, l. 205, vol. viii. p. 117), during the long interview with his mother, just after he had said,—

"No, in despite of sense and secrecy,
Unpeg the basket on the house's top,*
Let the birds fly, and like the famous ape,
To try conclusions, in the basket creep,
And break your own neck down."

Then speaking of his plot and of the necessity which marshals him to knavery, he adds,—

"Let it work;
For 'tis the sport to have the enginer
Hoist with his own petar: and 't shall go hard
But I will delve one yard below their mines,
And blow them at the moon: O, 'tis most sweet
When in one line two crafts directly meet."

* In Johnson's and Steeven's *Shakespeare* (edition 1785, vol. x. p. 434) the passage is thus explained, "Sir John Suckling, in one of his letters, may possibly allude to this same story. 'It is the story of the *jackanapes* and the partridges; thou starest after a beauty till it is lost to thee, and then let'st out another, and starest after that till it is gone too.'"

Horapollo, ed. 1551.

Section VI.

EMBLEMS FROM FACTS IN NATURE, AND FROM THE PROPERTIES OF ANIMALS.

EMBLEM writers make the *Natural*, one of the divisions of their subject, and understand by it, in Whitney's words, the expressing of the natures of creatures, for example, "the loue of the yonge Storkes to the oulde, or of such like." We shall extend a little the application of the term, taking in some facts of nature, as well as the natural properties and qualities of animals, but reserving in a great degree the Poetry, with which certain natural things are invested, for the next general heading, "Emblems for Poetic Ideas."

There is no need to reproduce the Device of Prometheus bound, but simply to refer to it, and to note the allusions which Shakespeare makes to the mountain where the dire penalty was inflicted, "the frosty Caucasus." From the *Titus Andronicus* we have already (p. 268) spoken of Tamora's infatuated love,—

> "faster bound to Aaron's charming eyes
> Than is Prometheus ty'd on Caucasus."

John of Gaunt, Duke of Lancaster, endeavours, in *Richard II.* (act i. sc. 3, lines 275, 294, vol. iv. pp. 130, 131), to reconcile his son Henry Bolingbroke to the banishment which was decreed against him, and urges,—

"All places that the eye of heaven visits
Are to a wise man ports and happy havens.
Teach thy necessity to reason thus;
There is no virtue like necessity.
Think not the king did banish thee,
But thou the king."

Bolingbroke, however, replies,—

"O, who can hold a fire in his hand
By thinking on the frosty Caucasus?

The indestructibility of adamant by force or fire had for ages been a received truth.

QVEM NVLLA PERICVLA, TERRENT.

Le Bey de Batilly 1596

"Whom no dangers terrify," is a fitting motto for the Emblem that pertains to such as fear nor force nor fire.

Speaking of the precious gem that figures forth their character, it is the remark of Lebeus-Batillius (Emb. 29), "Duritia inenarrabilis est, simulque ignium victrix naturâ & nunquam incalescens,"—for which we obtain a good English expression from Holland's *Pliny* (bk. xxxvii. c. 4): "Wonderfull and inenarrable is the *hardnesse* of a *diamant;* besides it hath a nature to conquer the fury of fire, nay, you shall never make it hote."

The Latin stanzas in illustration close with the lines,—

> "*Qualis, non Adamas ullo contunditur ictu,*
> *Vique sua ferri duritiem superat.*"

i.e. "As by no blow the Adamant is crushed,
And by its own force overcomes the hardness of iron."

When the great Talbot was released from imprisonment (1 *Henry VI.*, act i. sc. 4, l. 49, vol. v. p. 20), his companions-in-arms on welcoming him back, inquired, "How wert thou entertained?" (l. 39)—

> "With scoffs and scorns and contumelious taunts.
>
> In iron walls they deem'd me not secure;
> So great fear of my name 'mongst them was spread
> That they supposed I could rend bars of steel
> And spurn in pieces posts of adamant."

The strong natural affection of the bear for its young obtained record nearly three thousand years ago (2 *Samuel* xvii. 8),—"mighty men, chafed in their minds" are spoken of "as a bear robbed of her whelps in the field."* Emblems delineated by Boissard and engraved by Theodore De Bry in 1596, at Emb. 43 present the bear licking her whelp, in sign that the inborn force of nature is to be brought into form and comeliness by instruction and good learning. At a little later period, the "TRONVS CVPIDINIS," or "EMBLEMATA AMATORIA" (fol. 2), so beautifully adorned by Crispin de Passe, adopts the sentiment, *Perpolit incultum paulatim tempus amorem,*—that "by degrees

* See a most touching account of a she-bear and her whelps in the *Voyage of Discovery to the North Seas* in 1772, under Captain C. J. Phipps, afterwards Lord Mulgrave.

time puts the finish, or perfectness to uncultivated love." The device by which this is shown introduces a Cupid as well as the bear and her young one,—

De Passe, 1596.

and is accompanied by Latin and French stanzas,—

> "*Vrsa novum fertur lambendo fingere fœtum*
> *Paulatim & formam, quæ decet, ore dare;*
> *Sic dominam, vt valde sic cruda sit aspera Amator*
> *Blanditiis sensim mollet & obsequio.*"

Peu à peu.

> "Ceste masse de chair, que toute ourse faonne
> En la leschant se forme à son commencement.
> Par seruir: par flatter, par complaire en aymant,
> L'amour rude à l'abord, à la fin se façonne."

The sentiment of these lines finds a parallel in the *Midsummer Night's Dream* (act i. sc. 1, l. 232, vol. ii. p. 206),—

> "Things base and vile, holding no quantity,
> Love can transpose to form and dignity:
> Love looks not with the eyes, but with the mind;
> And therefore is wing'd Cupid painted blind."

Perchance, too, it receives illustration from the praise accorded to the young Dumain by Katharine, in *Love's Labour's Lost* (act ii. sc. 1, l. 56, vol. ii. p. 114),—

> "A well accomplish'd youth,
> Of all that virtue love for virtue loved :
> Most power to do most harm, least knowing ill;
> For he hath wit to make an ill shape good,
> And shape to win grace, though he had no wit."

To the denial of natural affection towards himself Gloucester (3 *Henry VI.*, act iii. sc. 2, l. 153, vol. v. p. 284) deemed it almost a thing impossible for him to "make his heaven in a lady's lap,"—

> "Why, love forswore me in my mother's womb :
> And, for I should not deal in her soft laws,
> She did corrupt frail nature with some bribe,
> To shrink mine arm up like a wither'd shrub;
> To make an envious mountain on my back,
> Where sits deformity to mock my body;
> To shape my legs of an unequal size;
> To disproportion me in every part,
> Like to a chaos, or an unlick'd bear-whelp
> That carries no impression like the dam."

Curious it is to note how slowly the continent which Columbus discovered became fully recognised as an integral portion of what had been denominated, ἡ οἰκουμένη, —"the inhabited world." The rotundity of the earth and of the water was acknowledged, but Brucioli's "TRATTATO DELLA SPHERA," published at Venice, D.M.XLIII., maintains that the earth is immovable and the centre of the universe; and in dividing the globe into climates, it does not take a single instance except from what is named the old world; in fact, the new world of America is never mentioned.

Somewhat later, in 1564, when Sambucus published his

Emblems, and presented *Symbols of the parts of the Inhabited Earth,* he gave only three; thus (p. 113).—

Partium τῆς οἰκουμένης symbola.

Sambucus, 1564.

EST *regio quæuis climate certo*
Aëre distincta, & commoditate.
Quælibet haud quiduis terra feretque.
Africa monstrosa est semper habendo
Antea quod nemo viderat usquam.
Fert Asia immanes frigidiore
Nempe solo apros, & nimbigera ursos:
Sed reliquas vincit viribus omnes
Belua, quam Europæ temperat aër.
Taurus ut est fortis, bufalus una.
Ergo sit Europæ taurus alumnus,
Africæ at insigne sitque Chimæra.
Sint Asiæ immites ursus, aperque.

The Bull is thus set forth as the *alumnus,* or nursling of Europe; of Africa the Chimæra is the ensign; and to Asia belong the untamed Bear and Boar; America and the broad

Pacific, from Peru to China, have neither token nor locality assigned.

Shakespeare's geography, however, though at times very defective, extended further than its "symbols" by Sambucus. In the humorous mapping out, by Dromio of Syracuse, of the features of the kitchen-wench, who was determined to be his wife (*Comedy of Errors*, act iii. sc. 2, l. 131, vol. i. p. 429), the question is asked,—

> "*Ant. S.* Where America, the Indies?
> *Dro. S.* Oh, sir, upon her nose, all o'er embellished with rubies, carbuncles, sapphires, declining their rich aspect to the hot breath of Spain."

In *Twelfth Night* (act iii. sc. 2, l. 73, vol. iii. p. 271) Maria thus describes the love-demented steward,—

> "He does smile his face into more lines than is in the new map with the augmentation of the Indies; you have not seen such a thing as 'tis."

And in the *Merry Wives of Windsor* (act i. sc. 3, l. 64, vol. i. p. 177), Sir John Falstaff avers respecting Mistress Page and Mistress Ford,—

> "I will be cheaters to them both, and they shall be exchequers to me: they shall be my East and West Indies, and I will trade to them both."

Yet in agreement with the map of Sambucus, with the three capes prominent upon it, of Gibraltar Rock, the Cape of Good Hope, and that of Malacca, Shakespeare on other occasions ignores America and all its western neighbours. At the consultation by Octavius, Antony, and Lepidus, about the division of the Roman Empire (*Julius Cæsar*, act iv. sc. 1, l. 12, vol. vii. p. 384), Antony, on the exit of Lepidus, remarks,—

> "This is a slight unmeritable man,
> Meet to be sent on errands: is it fit,
> The three-fold world divided, he should stand
> One of the three to share it?"

Plate 13

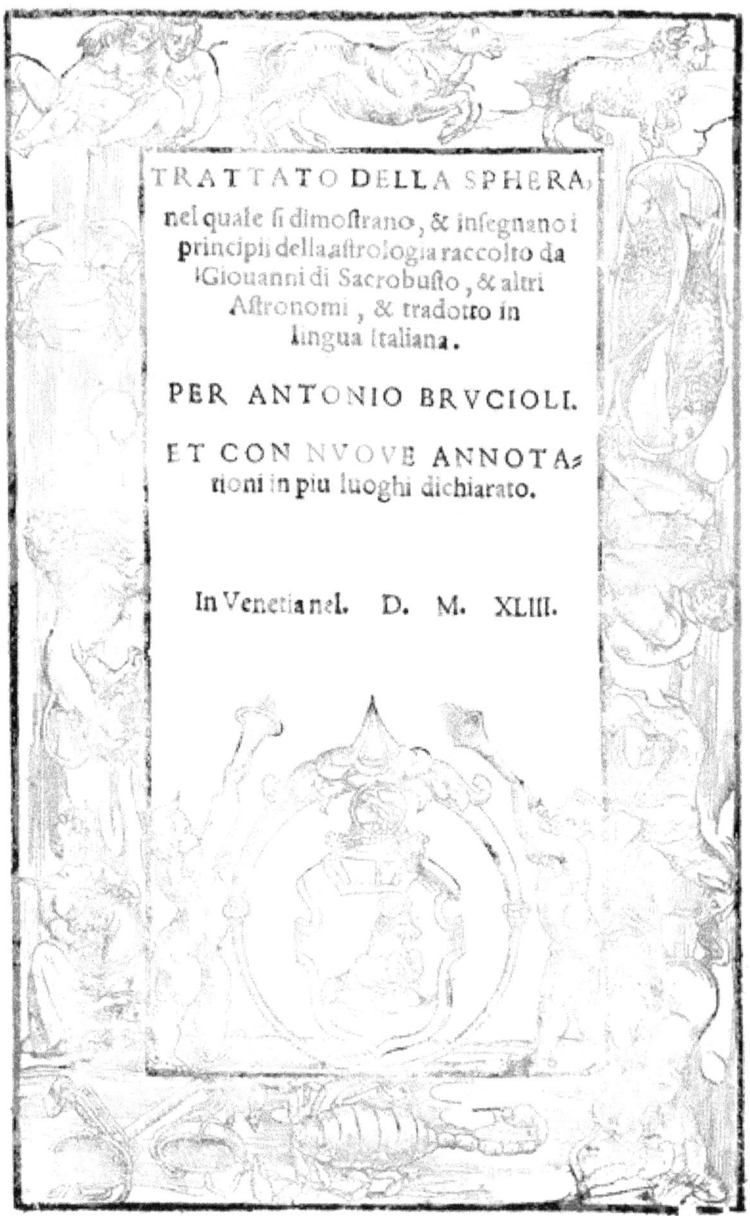

TRATTATO DELLA SPHERA,
neI quale ſi dimoſtrano, & inſegnano i
principii della aſtrologia raccolto da
Giouanni di Sacrobuſto, & altri
Aſtronomi, & tradotto in
lingua italiana.

PER ANTONIO BRVCIOLI.

ET CON NVOVE ANNOTA=
tioni in piu luoghi dichiarato.

In Venetia nel. D. M. XLIII.

The Zodiac from a Title page Brucioli 1543

And when the camp of Octavius is near Alexandria (*Antony and Cleopatra*, act iv. sc. 6, l. 5, vol. ix. p. 109), and orders are issued to take Antony alive, Cæsar declares,—

> "The time of universal peace is near:
> Prove this a prosperous day, the three-nook'd world
> Shall bear the olive freely."

The Signs of the Zodiac, or, rather, the figures of the animals of which the zodiac is composed, were well known in Shakespeare's time from various sources; and though they are Emblems, and have given name to at least one book of Emblems that was published in 1618,* —almost within the limits to which our inquiries are confined,—some may doubt whether they strictly belong to Emblem writers. Frequently, however, are they referred to in the dramas of which we are speaking; and, therefore, it is not out of place to exhibit a representation of them. This we do from the frontispiece or title page of an old Italian astronomical work by Antonio Brucioli (see Plate XIII.), who was banished from Florence for his opposition to the Medici, and whose brothers, in 1532, were printers in Venice. It is not pretended that Shakespeare was acquainted with this title page, but it supplies an appropriate illustration of several astronomical phenomena to which he alludes.

The zodiac enters into the description of the advancing day in *Titus Andronicus* (act ii. sc. 1, l. 5, vol. vi. p. 450),—

> "As when the golden sun salutes the morn,
> And, having gilt the ocean with his beams,
> Gallops the zodiac in his glistering coach,
> And overlooks the highest-peering hills:
> So Tamora.
> Upon her wit doth earthly honour wait,
> And virtue stoops and trembles at her frown."

* "Zodiacvs Christianvs, seu signa 12, *diuinæ Prædestinationis, &c., à Raphaele Sadelero*, 12mo, p. 126, Monaci CD. DCXVIII."

It also occupies a place in a homely comparison in *Measure for Measure* (act i. sc. 2, l. 158, vol. i. p. 303), to point out the duration of nineteen years, or the moon's cycle,—

> "This new governor
> Awakes me all the enrolled penalties
> Which have, like unscour'd armour, hung by the wall
> So long, that nineteen zodiacs have gone round.
> And none of them been worn; and for a name
> Now puts the drowsy and neglected act
> Freshly on me: 'tis surely for a name."

The archery scene in *Titus Andronicus* (act iv. sc. 3, l. 52, vol. vi. p. 501) mentions several of the constellations and the figures by which they were known. The dialogue is between Titus and Marcus,—

> "*Tit.* You are a good archer, Marcus;
> [*He gives them the arrows.*
> 'Ad Jovem,' that's for you: here, 'Ad Apollinem:'
> 'Ad Martem,' that's for myself:
> Here, boy, to Pallas: here, to Mercury:
> To Saturn, Caius, not to Saturnine;
> You were as good to shoot against the wind.
> To it, boy! Marcus, loose when I bid.
> Of my word, I have written to effect;
> There's not a god left unsolicited.
> *Marc.* Kinsmen, shoot all your shafts into the court:
> We will afflict the emperor in his pride.
> *Tit.* Now, masters, draw. [*They shoot.*] O, well said, Lucius!
> Good boy, in Virgo's lap; give it Pallas.
> *Marc.* My Lord, I aim a mile beyond the moon;
> Your letter is with Jupiter by this.
> *Tit.* Ha, ha!
> Publius, Publius, what hast thou done?
> See, see, thou hast shot off one of Taurus' horns.
> *Marc.* This was the sport, my lord: when Publius shot,
> The Bull, being gall'd, gave Aries such a knock
> That down fell both the Ram's horns in the court."

In allusion to the old medico-astrological idea that the

different members of the human body were under the influence of their proper or peculiar constellations, the following dialogue occurs in the *Twelfth Night* (act i. sc. 3, l. 127, vol. iii. p. 231),—

> "*Sir And.* Shall we not set about some revels?
> *Sir Toby.* What shall we do else? were we not born under Taurus?
> *Sir And.* Taurus! That's sides and heart.
> *Sir Toby.* No sir; it is legs and thighs. Let me see thee caper: ha! higher: ha, ha! excellent!"

Falstaff, in the *Merry Wives of Windsor* (act ii. sc. 2, l. 5, vol. i. p. 190), vaunts of the good services which he had rendered to his companions: "I have grated upon my good friends for three reprieves for you and your coach-fellow Nym: or else you had looked through the grate, like a geminy of baboons."

In telling of the folly of waiting on Achilles (*Troilus and Cressida*, act ii. sc. 3, l. 189, vol. vi. p. 175), Ulysses declares,—

> "That were to enlard his fat-already pride,
> And add more coals to Cancer when he burns
> With entertaining great Hyperion."

The figure of the ninth of the zodiacal constellations, Sagittarius, is named in *Troilus and Cressida* (act v. sc. 5, l. 11, vol. vi. p. 253),—

> "Polixenes is slain,
> Amphimachus and Thaos deadly hurt;
> Patroclus ta'en or slain; and Palamedes
> Sore hurt and bruised: the dreadful sagittary
> Appals our number."

If it be demanded why we do not give a fuller account of these constellations, we may almost remark as the fool does in *King Lear* (act i. sc. 5, l. 33, vol. viii. p. 295),—" The reason why the seven stars are no more than seven, is a pretty reason.

> *Lear.* Because they are not eight?
> *Fool.* Yes, indeed: thou wouldst make a good fool."

How soon the American bird, which we name a Turkey, was known in England, is in some degree a subject of conjecture. It has been supposed that its introduction into this country is to be ascribed to Sebastian Cabot, who died in 1557, and that the year 1528 is the exact time; but if so, it is strange that the bird in question should not have been called by some other name than that which indicates a European or an Asiatic origin. Coq d'Inde, or Poule d'Inde, Gallo d'India, or Gallina d'India, the French and Italian names, point out the direct American origin, as far as France and Italy are concerned: for we must remember that the term India, at the early period of Spanish discovery, was applied to the western world. But most probably the Turkey fleet brought the bird into England, by way of Cadiz and Lisbon, and hence the name; and hence also the reasonableness of supposing that its permanent introduction into this country was not so early as the time of Cabot. A general knowledge of the bird was at any rate spread abroad in Europe soon after the middle of the sixteenth century, for we find it figured in the Emblem-books; one of which, Freitag's *Mythologia Ethica*, in 1579, p. 237, furnishes a most lively and exact representation to illustrate "the violated right of hospitality." [a]

---

[a] See also the Emblems of Camerarius (pt. iii. edition 1596, Emb. 47), where the turkey is figured to illustrate "RABIE SVCCENSA TVMESCIT,"—*Being angered it swells with rage.*

> "*Quam deforme malum feruentis accensa furore*
> *Ira sit, iratis Indica monstrat auis.*"—

> "How odious an evil to the violent anger may be
> Inflamed to fury,—the Indian bird shows to the angry."

Ius hoſpitalitatis violatum.

Freitag, 1579.

Si habitauerit aduena in terra veſtra, & moratus fuerit inter vos, non exprobretis ei.
Leu. 19. 33.

"And if a stranger sojourn with thee in your land, ye shall not vex him."

Shakespeare, no doubt, was familiarly acquainted with the figure and habits of the Turkey, and yet may have seized for description some of the expressive delineations and engravings which occur in the Emblem writers. Freitag's turkey he characterises with much exactness, though the sentiment advanced is more consistent with the lines from Camerarius. In the *Twelfth Night* (act ii. sc. 5, lines 15, 27, vol. iii. p. 257), Malvolio, as his arch-tormenter Maria narrates the circumstance, "has been yonder i' the sun practising behaviour to his own shadow this half hour;" he enters on the scene, and Sir Toby says to Fabian, "Here's an overweening rogue!" to which the reply is made, "O peace! Contemplation makes a rare turkey-cock of him; how he jets under his advancing plumes!"

The same action is well hit off in showing the bearing of the "pragging knave, Pistol," as Fluellen terms him (*Henry V.*, act v. sc. 1, l. 13, vol. iv. p. 591),—

> "*Gow.* Why here he comes, swelling like a turkey-cock.
> *Flu.* 'Tis no matter for his swellings, nor his turkey-cocks. God pless you, Aunchient Pistol! you scurvy, lousy knave, God pless you!"

Referring again to the "Prometheus ty'd on Caucasus," the Vulture may be accepted as the Emblem of cruel retribution. So when Falstaff expresses his satisfaction at the death of Henry IV. (2nd part, act v. sc. 3, l. 134, vol. iv. p. 474), "Blessed are they that have been my friends; and woe to my lord chief-justice;" Pistol adds,—

> "Let vultures vile seize on his lungs also!"

And Lear, telling of the ingratitude of one of his daughters (*King Lear*, act ii. sc. 4, l. 129, vol. viii. p. 320), says,—

> "Beloved Regan,
> Thy sister's naught: O Regan, she hath tied
> Sharp-tooth'd unkindness, like a vulture, here."

A remarkable instance of similarity between Whitney and Shakespeare occurs in the descriptions which they both give of the Commonwealth of Bees. Whitney, it may be, borrowed his device (p. 200) from the "HIEROGLYPHICA" of Horus Apollo (edition 1551, p. 87), where the question is asked, Πῶς λαὸν πειθήνιον βασιλεῖ;—

Horapollo, 1551.

"How to represent a people obedient to their king? They depict a BEE, for of all animals bees alone have a king, whom the crowd of bees follow, and to whom as to a king they yield obedience. It is intimated also, as well from the remarkable usefulness of honey as from the force which the animal has in its sting, that a king is both useful and powerful for carrying on their affairs."

It is worthy of remark that several, if not all, of the Greek and Roman authors name the head of a hive not a queen but a king. Plato, in his *Politics* (Francfort edition, 1602, p. 557A), writes,—

"Νῦν δέ γε ὅτε οὐκ ἔστι γιγνόμενος, ὡς δὴ φαμὲν, ἐν ταῖς πόλεσι βασιλεὺς, οἷος ἐν σμήνεσιν, ἐμφυέται, τό, τε σῶμα εὐθὺς καὶ τὴν ψυχὴν διαφέρων," κ. τ. λ.

"There is not born, as we say, in cities a king such as is naturally produced in hives, decidedly differing both in body and soul."

Xenophon's *Cyropædia* (bk. v. c. 1, § 23) declares of his hero,—

"Βασιλεὺς μὲν γὰρ ἔμοιγε δοκεῖς σὺ φυσεὶ πεφυκέναι, οὐδὲν ἧττον ἢ ὁ ἐν τῳ σμήνει φυόμενος τῶν μελιττῶν ἡγεμών."

"Thou seemest to me to have been formed a king by nature, no less than he who in the hive is formed general of the bees."

In his *Georgics* Virgil always considers the chief bee to be a king, as iv. 75,—

"Et circa regem atque ipsa ad prætoria densæ
Miscentur, magnisque vocant clamoribus hostem." *

* See also other passages from the *Georgics*,—

"Ut, cum prima novi ducent examina reges
Vere suo." iv. 21.

"Sin autem ad pugnam exierint, nam sæpe duobus
Regibus incessit magno discordia motu." iv. 67.

Description of the kings (iv. 87—99),—

"tu regibus alas
Eripe." iv. 106.

And,—

"ipsæ regem parvosque Quirites
Sufficiunt, aulasque et cerea regna refingunt." iv. 201.

"And thick around the king, and before the royal tent
They crowd, and with mighty din call forth the foe."

Alciat's 148th Emblem (edition 1581, p. 528, or edition 1551, p. 161) sets forth the clemency of a prince; but the description relates to wasps, not bees.—

Principis clementia.

Alciat, 1551.

Vesparũ quòd nulla vnquam Rex spicula figet:
Quodq́ aliis duplo corpore maior erit.
Arguet imperium clemens, moderataq́ regna,
Sanctaq́ iudicibus credita iura bonis.

"That the king of the wasps will never his sting infix;
And that by double the size of body he is larger than others,
This argues a merciful empire and well-ordered rule,
And sacred laws to good judges entrusted."

Whitney's stanzas (p. 200), dedicated to "Richard Cotton, Esquier," of Combermere, Cheshire, are original writing, not a translation.

We will take the chief part of them; the motto being, "To every one his native land is dear."

Patria cuique chara.

To RICHARDE COTTON *Esquier.*

Whitney, 1586.

"THE bees at lengthe retourne into their hiue,
When they haue suck'd the sweete of FLORAS bloomes ;
And with one minde their worke they doe contriue,
And laden come with honie to their roomes :
A worke of arte ; and yet no arte of man,
Can worke, this worke ; these little creatures can.

The maister bee, within the midst dothe liue,
In fairest roome, and most of stature is ;
And euerie one to him dothe reuerence giue,
And in the hiue with him doe liue in blisse :
Hee hath no stinge, yet none can doe him harme,
For with their strengthe, the rest about him swarme.

Lo, natures force within these creatures small,
Some, all the daye the honie home doe beare.
And some, farre off on flowers freshe doe fall,
Yet all at nighte vnto their home repaire :
And euerie one, her proper hiue doth knowe
Althoughe there stande a thousande on a rowe.

3 A

A Common-wealthe, by this, is right expreste :
Bothe him, that rules, and those, that doe obaye :
Or suche, as are the heads aboue the rest,
Whome here, the Lorde in highe estate dothe staye :
By whose supporte, the meaner sorte doe liue,
And vnto them all reuerence dulie giue.

Which when I waied : I call'd vnto my minde
Your CVMBERMAIRE, that fame so farre commendes :
A stately seate, whose like is harde to finde,
Where mightie IOVE the horne of plentie lendes :
With fishe, and foule, and cattaile sondrie flockes,
Where christall springes doe gushe out of the rockes.

There, fertile fieldes ; there, meadowes large extende :
There, store of grayne : with water, and with wood.
And, in this place, your goulden time you spende,
Vnto your praise, and to your countries good :
This is the hiue ; your tennaunts, are the bees :
And in the same, haue places by degrees."

By the side of these stanzas let us place for comparison what Shakespeare wrote on the same subject,—the Commonwealth of Bees,—and I am persuaded we shall perceive much similarity of thought, if not of expression. In *Henry V.* (act i. sc. 2, l. 178, vol. iv. p. 502), the Duke of Exeter and the Archbishop of Canterbury enter upon an argument respecting a well-governed state,—

"*Exe.* While that the armed hand doth fight abroad,
The advised head defends itself at home ;
For government, though high and low and lower,
Put into parts, doth keep in one consent,
Congreeing in a full and natural close,
Like music.
Cant. Therefore doth heaven divide
The state of man in divers functions,
Setting endeavour in continual motion :
To which is fixed, as an aim or butt,
Obedience : for so work the honey-bees,
Creatures that by a rule in nature teach
The act of order to a peopled kingdom.

They have a king * and officers of sorts;
Where some, like magistrates, correct at home,
Others, like merchants, venture trade abroad,
Others, like soldiers, armed in their stings,
Make boot upon the summer's velvet buds,
Which pillage they with merry march bring home
To the tent-royal of their emperor;
Who, busied in his majesty, surveys
The singing masons building roofs of gold,
The civil citizens kneading up the honey,
The poor mechanic porters crowding in
Their heavy burdens at his narrow gate,
The sad-eyed justice, with his surly hum,
Delivering o'er to executors pale
The lazy yawning drone."

Again, in the *Troilus and Cressida* (act i. sc. 3, l. 75, vol. vi. p. 144), Ulysses draws from the unsuitableness of a general, as he terms the ruling bee, over a hive, an explanation of the mischiefs from an incompetent commander,—

"Troy, yet upon his basis, had been down,
And the great Hector's sword had lack'd a master,
But for these instances.
The specialty of rule hath been neglected:
And, look, how many Grecian tents do stand
Hollow upon this plain, so many hollow factions.
When that the general is not like the hive
To whom the foragers shall all repair,
What honey is expected?"

The Dramatist's knowledge of bee-life appears also in the metaphor used by Warwick (2 *Henry VI.*, act iii. sc. 2, l. 125, vol. v. p. 168),—

* At a time even later than Shakespeare's the idea of a king-bee prevailed; Waller, the poet of the Commonwealth, adopted it, as in the lines to Zelinda,—

"Should you no honey vow to taste
But what the master-bees have placed
In compass of their cells, how small
A portion to your share will fall."

In Le Moine's *Devises Heroiqves et Morales* (4to, Paris, 1649, p. 8) we read, "Du courage & du conseil au Roy des abeilles,"—and the creature is spoken of as a male.

> "The commons, like an angry hive of bees,
> That want their leader, scatter up and down,
> And care not who they sting in his revenge."

In an earlier play, 2 *Henry IV.* (act iv. sc. 5, l. 75, vol. iv. p. 454), the comparison is taken from the bee-hive,—

> "When, like the bee, culling from every flower
> The virtuous sweets,
> Our thighs pack'd with wax, our mouths with honey,
> We bring it to the hive ; and like the bees,
> Are murdered for our pains."

In the foregoing extracts on the bee-king, the plea is inadmissible that Shakespeare and Whitney went to the same fountain ; for neither of them follows Alciatus. The two accounts of the economy and policy of these "creatures small" are almost equally excellent, and present several points of resemblance, not to name them imitations by the more recent writer. Whitney speaks of the "Master bee," Shakespeare of the king, or "emperor,"—both regarding the head of the hive not as a queen, but a "born king," and holding forth the polity of the busy community as an admirable example of a well-ordered kingdom or government.

The conclusion of Whitney's reflections on those "that suck the sweete of FLORA'S bloomes," conducts to another parallelism ; and to show it we have only to follow out his idea of returning home after "absence manie a yeare," "when happe some goulden honie bringes." Here is the whole passage (p. 201),—

> "And as the bees, that farre and neare doe straye,
> And yet come home, when honie they haue founde :
> So, thoughe some men doe linger longe awaye,
> Yet loue they best their natiue countries grounde.
> And from the same, the more they absent bee,
> With more desire, they wishe the same to see.

Euen so my selfe ; throughe absence manie a yeare,
A straunger meere, where I did spend my prime.
Nowe, parentes loue dothe hale mee by the eare,
And sayeth, come home, deferre no longer time :
  Wherefore, when happe, some goulden honie bringes ?
  I will retorne, and rest my wearie winges.

Ouid. I. Pont. 4.

Quid melius Roma? Scythico quid frigore peius?
Huc tamen ex illa barbarus vrbe fugit."

The parallel is from *All's Well that Ends Well* (act i. sc. 2, l. 58, vol. iii. p. 119), when the King of France speaks the praise of Bertram's father,—

"'Let me not live,' quoth he,
'After my flame lacks oil, to be the snuff
Of younger spirits, whose apprehensive senses
All but new things disdain ; whose judgments are
Mere fathers of their garments ; whose constancies
Expire before their fashions.' This he wish'd :
I after him do after him wish too,
Since I nor wax nor honey can bring home,
I quickly were dissolved from my hive,
To give some labourers room."

The noble art and sport of Falconry were long the recreation, and, at times, the eager pursuit of men of high birth or position. Various notices, collected by Dr. Nathan Drake, in *Shakespeare and his Times* (vol. i. pp. 255—272), show that Falconry was—

"During the reigns of Elizabeth and James, the most prevalent and fashionable of all amusements ; . . . . it descended from the nobility to the gentry and wealthy yeomanry, and no man could then have the smallest pretension to the character of a gentleman who kept not a cast of hawks."

From joining in this amusement, or from frequently witnessing it, Shakespeare gained his knowledge of the sport and of the technical terms employed in it. We do not even suppose that our pictorial illustration supplied him with suggestions, and we offer it merely to show that Emblem writers, as well as others, found in falconry the source of many a poetical expression.* The Italian we quote from, Giovio's "SENTENTIOSE IMPRESE" (Lyons, 1562, p. 41), makes it a mark "of the true nobility;" but by adding, "So more important things give place," implies that it was wrong to let mere amusement occupy the time for serious affairs.

DELLA VERA.
NOBILTA'.

Giovio, 1562.

Lo ſparbier ſol tra piu falcon portato,
Franchi gli fa paſſar per ogni loco,
Et par che dica all' huom triſto & da poco,
Nobil' è quel, ch' è di virtù dotato.

---

* To mention only Joachim Camerarius, edition 1596, *Ex Volatilibus* (Emb. 29–34); here are no less than five separate devices connected with Hawking or Falconry.

Thus we interpret the motto and the stanza,—

> "Many falcons the falconer carries so proud
> Through every place he makes them pass free;
> And says to men sorrowing and of low degree,
> Noble is he, who with virtue's endowed."

Falconers form part of the retinue of the drama (2 *Henry VI.*, act ii. sc. 1, l. 1, vol. v. p. 132), and the dialogue at St. Albans even illustrates the expression, "Nobil' è quel, ch' è di virtù dotato,"—

> "*Q. Marg.* Believe me, lords, for flying at the brook,
> I saw not better sport these seven years' day:
> Yet, by your leave, the wind was very high:
> And, ten to one, old Joan had not gone out.
> *K. Henry.* But what a point, my lord, your falcon made,
> And what a pitch she flew above the rest!
> To see how God in all his creatures works!
> Yea, man and birds are fain of climbing high.
> *Suf.* No marvel, an it like your majesty,
> My lord protector's hawks do tower so well;
> They know their master likes to be aloft,
> And bears his thoughts above his falcon's pitch.
> *Glo.* My lord, 'tis but a base ignoble mind
> That mounts no higher than a bird can soar."

On many other occasions Shakespeare shows his familiarity with the whole art and mysteries of hawking. Thus Christophero Sly is asked (*Taming of the Shrew*, Introduction, sc. 2, l. 41, vol. iii. p. 10),—

> "Dost thou love hawking? Thou hast hawks will soar
> Above the morning lark."

And Petruchio, after the supper scene, when he had thrown about the meat and beaten the servants, quietly congratulates himself on having "politicly began his reign" (act iv. sc. 1, l. 174, vol. iii. p. 67),—

"My falcon now is sharp and passing empty,
And till she stoop she must not be full-gorged:
For then she never looks upon her lure.
Another way I have to man my haggard,
To make her come and know her keeper's call,
That is, to watch her, as we watch these kites
That bate and beat and will not be obedient."

Touchstone, too, in *As You Like It* (act iii. sc. 3, l. 67, vol. ii. p. 427), hooking several comparisons together, introduces hawking among them: "As the ox hath his bow, sir, the horse his curb, and the falcon her bells, so man hath his desires; and as pigeons bill, so wedlock will be nibbling."

Also in *Macbeth* (act ii. sc. 4, l. 10, vol. vii. p. 459), after "hours dreadful and things strange," so "that darkness does the face of earth entomb, when living light should kiss it," the Old Man declares,—

"'Tis unnatural,
Even like the deed that's done. On Tuesday last
A falcon towering in her pride of place
Was by a mousing owl hawk'd at and kill'd."

To renew our youth, like the eagle's, is an old scriptural expression (*Psalms*, ciii. 5): and various are the legends and interpretations belonging to the phrase.* We must not wander among these,—but may mention one which is given by Joachim Camerarius, *Ex Volatilibus* (Emb. 34), for which he quotes Gesner as authority, how in the solar rays, hawks or falcons, throwing off their old feathers, are accustomed to set right their defects, and so to renew their youth.

---

* Take an example from the Paraphrase in an old Psalter: "The arne," *i.e.* the eagle, "when he is greved with grete elde, his neb waxis so gretely, that he may nogt open his mouth and take mete: bot then he smytes his neb to the stane, and bas away the slogh, and then he gaes til mete, and he commes yong a gayne. Swa Crist duse a way fra us oure elde of syn and mortalite, that settes us to ete oure brede in hevene, and newes us in hym."

RENOVATA

IVVENTVS.

Camerarius, 1596.

Exuviis vitii abjectis, decus indue recti,
Ad ſolem ut plumas accipiter renovat.

i.e. "Sin's spoils cast off, man righteousness assumes,
As in the sun the hawk renews its plumes."

The thought of the sun's influence in renovating what is decayed is unintentionally advanced by the jealousy of Adriana in the *Comedy of Errors* (act ii. sc. 1, l. 97, vol. i. p. 411), when to her sister Luciana she blames her husband Antipholus of Ephesus,—

"What ruins are in me that can be found
By him not ruin'd? then is he the ground
Of my defeatures. My decayed fair
A sunny look of his would soon repair."

In the *Cymbeline* (act i. sc. 1, l. 130, vol. ix. p. 167), Posthumus Leonatus, the husband of Imogen, is banished with great fierceness by her father, Cymbeline, King of Britain. A passage between daughter and father contains the same notion as that in the Emblem of Camerarius,—

> "*Imo.* There cannot be a pinch in death
> More sharp than this is.
> *Cym.* O disloyal thing,
> That shouldst repair my youth, thou heap'st
> A year's age on me!"

Nil penna, sed vsus.

Paradin, 1562.

The action of the ostrich in spreading out its feathers and beating the wind while it runs, furnished a device for Paradin (fol. 23), which, with the motto, *The feather nothing but the use,* he employs against hypocrisy.

Whitney (p. 51) adopts motto, device, and meaning,—

> "THE Hippocrites, that make so great a showe,
> Of Sanctitie, and of Religion sounde,
> Are shaddowes meere, and with out substance goe,
> And beinge tri'de, are but dissemblers founde.
> Theise are compar'de, vnto the Ostriche faire,
> Whoe spreades her winges, yet sealdome tries the aire."

A different application is made in 1 *Henry IV.* (act iv. sc. 1, l. 97, vol. iv. p. 317), yet the figure of the bird with outstretching wings would readily supply the comparison employed by Vernon while speaking to Hotspur of "the nimbled-footed madcap Prince of Wales, and his comrades,"—

> "All furnish'd, all in arms;

> All plumed like estridges that with the wind
> Baited like eagles having lately bathed."

It must, however, be conceded, according to Douce's clear annotation (vol. i. p. 435), that "it is by no means certain that this bird (the ostrich) is meant in the present instance." A line probably is lost from the passage, and if supplied would only the more clearly show that the falcon was intended,—"estrich," in the old books of falconry, denoting that bird, or, rather, the goshawk. In this sense the word is used in *Antony and Cleopatra* (act iii. sc. 13, l. 195, vol. ix. p. 100),—

> "To be furious
> Is to be frighted out of fear; and in that mood
> The dove will peck the *estridge*."

Though a fabulous animal, the Unicorn has properties and qualities attributed to it which endear it to writers on Heraldry and on Emblems. These are well, it may with truth be said, finely set forth in Reusner's *Emblems* (edition 1581, p. 60), where the creature is made the ensign for the motto, *Faith undefiled victorious.*

Victrix casta fides.

EMBLEMA IV.

Reusner, 1581.

Casta pudicitiæ defenstrix bellua: cornu
Vnum quæ media fronte, nigrumq; gerit:
Thesauros ornans regum, preciumq; rependens:
(Nam cornu præsens hoc leuat omne malum)
Fraude capi nulla, nulla valet arte virorum
Callida: nec gladios, nec fera tela pauet:
Solius in gremio requiescens sponte puellæ:
Fœminea capitur, victa sopore, manu.

i.e. "This creature of maiden modesty protectress pure,
In the mid-forehead bears one dark black horn,
Kings' treasures to ornament, and equalling in worth:
(For where the horn abides, no evil can be born).
Captured nor by guile, nor by crafty art of man,
Trembling nor at swords nor iron arms, firm doth it stand:
Of choice reposing in the lap of a maiden alone,*
Should sleep overpower, it is caught by woman's hand."

A volume of tales and wonders might be collected respecting the unicorn; for a sketch of these the article on the subject in the *Penny Cyclopædia* (vol. xxvi. p. 2) may be consulted. There are the particulars given which Reusner mentions, and the medical virtues of the horn extolled,† which, at one time, it is said, made it so estimated that it was worth ten times its weight in gold. It is remarkable that Shakespeare, disposed as he was, occasionally at least, to magnify nature's marvels, does not dwell on the properties of the unicorn, but rather discredits its existence; for when the strange shapes which Prospero conjures up to serve the banquet for Alonso make their appearance (*Tempest*, act iii. sc. 3, l. 21, vol. i. p. 50), Sebastian avers,—

* The Virgin, in Brucioli's *Signs of the Zodiac*, as given in our Plate XIII., has a unicorn kneeling by her side, to be fondled.

† The wonderful curative and other powers of the horn are set forth in his *Emblems* by Joachim Camerarius, *Ex Animalibus Quadrupedibus* (Emb. 12, 13 and 14). He informs us that "Bartholomew Alvianus, a Venetian general, caused to be inscribed on his banner, *I drive away poisons*, intimating that himself, like a unicorn putting to flight noxious and poisonous animals, would by his own warlike valour extirpate his enemies of the contrary factions."

"Now I will believe
That there are unicorns; that in Arabia
There is one tree, the phœnix' throne; one phœnix
At this hour reigning there."

Timon of Athens (act iv. sc. 3, l. 331, vol. vii. p. 281) just hints at the animal's disposition: "Wert thou the unicorn, pride and wrath would confound thee, and make thine own self the conquest of thy fury."

Decius Brutus, in *Julius Cæsar* (act ii. sc. 1, l. 203, vol. vii. p. 347), vaunts of his power to influence Cæsar, and among other things names the unicorn as a wonder to bring him to the Capitol. The conspirators doubt whether Cæsar will come forth;—

"Never fear that: if he be so resolved,
I can o'ersway him; for he loves to hear
That unicorns may be betray'd with trees,
And bears with glasses, elephants with holes,
Lions with toils, and men with flatterers."

The humorous ballad in the *Percy Reliques* (vol. iv. p. 198), written it is supposed close upon Shakespeare's times, declares,—

"Old stories tell, how Hercules
A dragon slew at Lerna,
With seven heads and fourteen eyes
To see and well discern-a:
But he had a club, this dragon to drub
Or he had ne'er done it. I warrant ye.

It is curious that the device in Corrozet's *Hecatomgraphie* of the Dragon of Lerna should figure forth, in the multiplication of processes or forms, what Hamlet terms "the law's delay."

That is the very subject against which even Hercules,—"qu' aqerre honneur par ses nobles conquestes,"—is called into requisition to rid men of the nuisance. We need not quote in full so familiar a narrative, and which Corrozet embellishes with

Multiplication de proces.

Tout hommé en proces tant ſoit fin,
Alors qu'il penſe eſtre à la fin,
Il luy en ſuruient troys ou quatre
Pour leſquelz il ſe fault debatre.

Corrozet, 1540.

twenty-four lines of French verses,—but content ourselves with a free rendering of his quatrain,—

> "All clever though a man may be in various tricks of law,
> Though he may think unto the end, his suit contains no flaw,
> Yet up there spring forms three or four with which he hardly copes,
> And lawyers' talk and lawyers' fees dash down his fondest hopes."

It is not, however, with such speciality that Shakespeare uses this tale respecting Hercules and the Hydra. On the occasion serving, the questions may be asked, as in *Hamlet* (act v. sc. 1, l. 93, vol. viii. p. 154), "Why may not that be the skull of a lawyer? Where be his quiddities now, his quillets, his cases, his tenures, and his tricks? why does he suffer this rude knave now to knock him about the sconce with a dirty shovel, and will not tell him of his action of battery?"

But simply by way of allusion the Hydra is introduced; as in the account of the battle of Shrewsbury (1 *Henry IV.* act v. sc. 4, l. 25, vol. iv. p. 342), Douglas had been fighting with one whom he thought the king, and comes upon "another king:" "they grow," he declares, "like Hydra's heads."

In *Othello* (act ii. sc. 3, l. 290, vol. vii. p. 498), some time after the general had said to him (l. 238),—

> "Cassio, I love thee;
> But never more be officer of mine,"

Cassio says to Iago,—

> "I will ask him for my place again; he shall tell me I am a drunkard! Had I as many mouths as Hydra, such an answer would stop them all."

So of the change which suddenly came over the Prince of Wales (*Henry V.*, act i sc. 1, l. 35, vol. iv. p. 493), on his father's death, it is said,—

> "Never Hydra-headed wilfulness
> So soon did lose his seat and all at once
> As in this king."

This section of our subject is sufficiently ample, or we might press into our service a passage from *Timon of Athens* (act iv. sc. 3, l. 317, vol. vii. p. 281), in which the question is asked, "What wouldst thou do with the world, Apemantus, if it lay in thy power?" and the answer is, "Give it the beasts, to be rid of the men."

In the wide range of the pre-Shakespearean Emblematists and Fabulists we might peradventure find a parallel to each animal that is named (l. 324),—

"If thou wert the lion, the fox would beguile thee: if thou wert the lamb, the fox would eat thee: if thou wert the fox, the lion would suspect thee when peradventure thou wert accused by the ass: if thou wert the ass, thy dulness would torment thee, and still thou livedst but as a breakfast to the wolf: if thou wert the wolf, thy greediness would afflict thee, and oft thou shouldst hazard thy life for thy dinner* . . . . . wert thou a bear, thou wouldst be killed by the horse: wert thou a horse, thou wouldst be seized by the leopard: wert thou a leopard, thou wert german to the lion, and the spots of thy kindred were jurors on thy life: all thy safety were remotion, and thy defence absence."

And so may we take warning, and make our defence for writing so much,—it is the absence of far more that might be gathered,—

> "Letting 'I dare not' wait upon 'I would,'
> Like the poor cat i' the adage."
>
> *Macbeth*, act i. sc. 7, l. 44.

* See the fable of the Wolf and the Ass from the *Dialogues of Creatures* (pp. 53—55 of this volume).

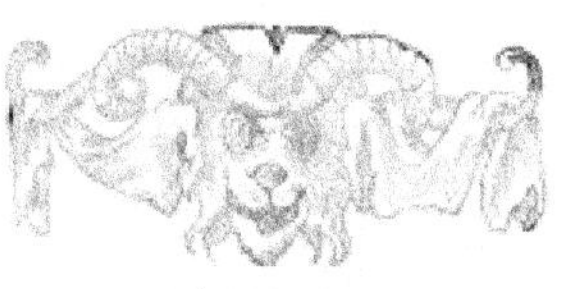

Aneau, 1552

Section VII.

EMBLEMS FOR POETIC IDEAS.

LTHOUGH many persons may maintain that the last two or three examples from the Naturalist's division of our subject ought to be reserved as Emblems to illustrate Poetic Ideas, the animals themselves may be inventions of the imagination, but the properties assigned to them appear less poetic than in the instances which are now to follow. The question, however, is of no great importance, as this is not a work on Natural History, and a strictly scientific arrangement is not possible when poets' fancies are the guiding powers.

How finely and often how splendidly Shakespeare makes use of the symbolical imagery of his art, a thousand instances might be brought to show. Three or four only are required to make plain our meaning. One, from *All's Well that Ends Well* (act i. sc. 1, l. 76, vol. iii. p. 112), is Helena's avowal to herself of her absorbing love for Bertram,—

> "My imagination
> Carries no favour in't but Bertram's.
> I am undone: there is no living, none,
> If Bertram be away. 'Twere all one
> That I should love a bright particular star
> And think to wed it, he is so above me:
> In his bright radiance and collateral light
> Might I be comforted, not in his sphere.
> The ambition in my love thus plagues itself:

> The hind that would be mated by the lion
> Must die of love. 'Twas pretty, though a plague,
> To see him every hour; to sit and draw
> His arched brows, his hawking eye, his curls,
> In our heart's table; heart too capable
> Of every line and trick of his sweet favour:
> But now he's gone, and my idolatrous fancy
> Must sanctify his reliques."

Another instance shall be from *Troilus and Cressida* (act iii. sc. 3, l. 145, vol. vi. p. 198). Neglected by his allies, Achilles demands, "What, are my deeds forgot?" and Ulysses pours forth upon him the great argument, that to preserve fame and honour active exertion is continually demanded,—

> "Time hath, my lord, a wallet at his back
> Wherein he puts alms for oblivion,
> A great-sized monster of ingratitudes:
> Those scraps are good deeds past, which are devour'd
> As fast as they are made, forgot as soon
> As done: perseverance, dear my lord,
> Keeps honour bright: to have done, is to hang
> Quite out of fashion, like a rusty mail
> In monumental mockery."

And so on, with inimitable force and beauty, until the crowning thoughts come (l. 165),—

> "Time is like a fashionable host
> That slightly shakes his parting guest by the hand,
> And with his arms outstretch'd, as he would fly,
> Grasps in the comer: welcome ever smiles,
> And farewell goes out sighing. O, let not virtue seek
> Remuneration for the thing it was;
> For beauty, wit,
> High birth, vigour of bone, desert in service,
> Love, friendship, charity, are subjects all
> To envious and calumniating time.
> One touch of nature makes the whole world kin;
> That all with one consent praise new-born gawds,
> Though they are made and moulded of things past,
> And give to dust that is a little gilt
> More laud than gilt o'er-dusted."

As a last instance, from the *Winter's Tale* (act iv. sc. 4, l. 135, vol. iii. p. 383), take Florizel's commendation of his beloved Perdita,—

> "What you do
> Still betters what is done. When you speak, sweet,
> I'ld have you do it ever: when you sing,
> I'ld have you buy and sell so, so give alms,
> Pray so; and, for the ordering your affairs,
> To sing them too: when you do dance, I wish you
> A wave o' the sea, that you might ever do
> Nothing but that; move still, still so,
> And own no other function: each your doing,
> So singular in each particular,
> Crowns what you are doing in the present deeds,
> That all your acts are queens."

Our Prelude we may take from Le Bey de Batilly's *Emblems* (*Francofurti* 1596, Emb. 51), in which with no slight zeal he celebrates "The Glory of Poets." For subject he takes "The Christian Muse" of his Jurisconsult friend, Peter Poppæus of Barraux, near Chambery.

POETARVM GLORIA.

De Batilly, 1596.

With the sad fate of Icarus, Le Bey contrasts the far different condition of Poets,—

"*Quos Phœbus ad aurea cœli*
Limina sublimis Iouis omnipotentis in aula
Sistit, & ætherei monstrat commercia cœtus;
Et sacri vates & Diuûm cura vocantur.
Quos etiam sunt qui numen habere putent."

i.e.

"Whom at heaven's golden threshold,
Within the halls of lofty Jove omnipotent
Phœbus doth place, and to them clearly shows
The intercourses of ethereal companies.
Both holy prophets and the care of gods
Are poets named; and those there are who think
That they possess the force of power divine."

In vigorous prose Le Bey declares "their home of glory is the world itself, and for them honour without death abides." Then personally to his friend Poppæus he says,—

"Onward, and things not to be feared fear not thou, who speakest nothing little or of humble measure, nothing mortal. While the pure priest of the Muses and of Phœbus with no weak nor unpractised wing through the liquid air as prophet stretches to the lofty regions of the clouds. Onward, and let father Phœbus himself bear thee to heaven."

Now by the side of Le Bey's laudatory sentences, may be placed the Poet's glory as sung in the *Midsummer Night's Dream* (act v. sc. 1, l. 12, vol. ii. p. 258),—

"The poet's eye, in a fine frenzy rolling,
Doth glance from heaven to earth, from earth to heaven;
And as imagination bodies forth
The forms of things unknown, the poet's pen
Turns them to shapes, and gives to airy nothing
A local habitation and a name."

The Swan of silvery whiteness may have been the heraldic badge of the Poets, but that "bird of wonder," the Phœnix, which,—

"Left sweete Arabie:
And on a Cædar in this coast
Built vp her tombe of spicerie," *—

* See p. 11 of J. Payne Collier's admirably executed Reprint of "THE PHŒNIX NEST," from the original edition of 1593.

is the source of many more Poetic ideas. To the Emblem writers as well as to the Poets, who preceded and followed the time of Shakespeare, it really was a constant theme of admiration.

One of the best pictures of what the bird was supposed to be occurs in Freitag's "MYTHOLOGIA ETHICA" (Antwerp, 1579). The drawing and execution of the device are remarkably fine: and the motto enjoins that "youthful studies should be changed with advancing age,"—

Iuuenilia ſtudia cum prouectiori
ætate permutata.

"*Deponite vos, ſecundum priſtinam conuerſationem, veterem hominem, qui corrumpitur ſecundum deſideria erroris.*"—*Epheſ.* 4. 22.

After describing the bird, Freitag applies it as a type of the resurrection from the dead; but its special moral is,—

"That ye put off concerning the former conversation the old man, which is corrupt according to the deceitful lusts."

Ancient authors, as well as the comparatively modern, very gravely testify to the lengthened life, and self-renovating power, and splendid beauty of the Phœnix. In the "EUTERPE" of Herodotus (bk. ii. 73) we meet with the following narrative, —

"Ἔστι δὲ καὶ ἄλλος ὄρνις," κ. τ. λ. "There is another sacred bird, named the Phœnix, which I myself never saw except in picture; for according to the people of Heliopolis, it seldom makes its appearance among them, only once in every 500 years. They state that he comes on the death of his sire. If at all like the picture, this bird may be thus described both in size and shape. Some of his feathers are of the colour of gold; others are red. In outline he is exceedingly similar to the Eagle, and in size also. This bird is said to display an ingenuity of contrivance which to me does not seem credible: he is represented as coming out of Arabia and bringing with him his father, embalmed in myrrh, to the temple of the Sun, and there burying him. The following is the manner in which this is done. First of all he sticks together an egg of myrrh, as much as he can carry, and then if he can bear the burden, this experiment being achieved, he scoops out the egg sufficiently to deposit his sire within; next he fills with fresh myrrh the opening in the egg, by which the body was enclosed; thus the whole mass containing the carcase is still of the same weight. The embalming being completed, he transports him into Egypt and to the temple of the Sun."

Pliny's account is brief (bk. xiii. ch. iv.), —

"The bird Phœnix is supposed to have taken that name from the date tree, which in Greek is called φοῖνιξ; for the assurance was made me that the said bird died with the tree, and of itself revived when the tree again sprouted forth."

Numerous indeed are the authorities of old to the same or a similar purport. They are nearly all comprised in the introductory dissertation of Joachim Camerarius to his device of the Phœnix, and include about eighteen classic writers, ten of the Greek and Latin Fathers, and three modern writers of the sixteenth century.

Appended to the works of Lactantius, an eloquent Christian Father of the latter part of the third century, there is a *Carmen De Phœnice*,—"Song concerning the Phœnix,"—in elegiac verse, which contains very many of the old tales and legends of "the Arabian bird," and describes it as,—

> "*Ipsa sibi proles, suus est pater, & suus hæres:*
> *Nutrix ipsa sui, semper alumna sibi.*"

> "She to herself offspring is, and her own father, and her own heir:
> Nurse is she of herself, and ever her own foster daughter."

(See *Lactantii Opera, studio Gallæi*, Leyden, 8vo. 1660, pp. 904—923.)

Besides Camerarius, there are at least five Emblematists from whom Shakespeare might have borrowed respecting the Phœnix. Horapollo, whose *Hieroglyphics* were edited in 1551: Claude Paradin and Gabriel Symeoni, whose *Heroic Devises* appeared in 1562; Arnold Freitag, in 1579: Nicholas Reusner, in 1581; Geffrey Whitney, in 1586, and Boissard, in 1588,—these all take the Phœnix for one of their emblems, and give a drawing of it in the act of self-sacrifice and self-renovation. They make it typical of many truths and doctrines,—of long duration for the soul, of devoted love to God, of special rarity of character, of Christ's resurrection from the dead, and of the resurrection of all mankind.

There is a singular application of the Phœnix emblem which existed before and during Shakespeare's time, but of which I find no pictorial representation until 1633. It is in Henry Hawkins' rare volume, "Η ΠΑΡΘΕΝΟΣ,"—*The Virgin*,—"Symbolically set forth and enriched with piovs devises and emblemes for the entertainement of Devovt Sovles." This peculiar emblem bestows upon the bird two hearts, which are united in closest sympathy and in entire oneness of affection and purpose; they are the hearts of the Virgin-Mother and her Son.

Hawkins' Parthenos, 1633.

"BEhold, how Death aymes with his mortal dart,
And wounds a Phœnix with a twin-like hart.
These are the harts of Jesus and his Mother
So linkt in one, that one without the other
Is not entire. They (sure) each others smart
Must needs sustaine, though two, yet as one hart.
One Virgin-Mother, Phenix of her kind,
And we her Sonne without a father find.
The Sonne's and Mothers paines in one are mixt,
His side, a Launce, her soule a Sword transfixt.
Two harts in one, one Phenix loue contriues : *
One wound in two, and two in one reuiues."

Whitney's and Shakespeare's uses of the device resemble each other, as we shall see, more closely than the rest do,—and present a singular coincidence of thought, or else show that the later writer had consulted the earlier.

"*The Bird always alone,*" is the motto which Paradin, Reusner, and Whitney adopt. Paradin (fol. 53), informs us,—

* There are similar thoughts in Shakespeare's *Phœnix and Turtle* (Works, lines 25 and 37, vol. ix. p. 671),—

"So they loved, as love in twain
Had the essence but in one ;
Two distincts, division none,
Number there in love was slain."

And,—

"Property was thus appalled,
That the self was not the same ;
Single nature's double name
Neither two nor one was called."

Vnica ſemper auis.

Paradin, 1562.

Comme le Phenix eſt à jamais ſeul, & vnique Oiſeau au monde de ſon eſpece. Auſſi ſont les tresbonnes choſes de merueilleuſe rarité, & bien cler ſemees. Deuiſe que porte Madame Alienor d' Auſtriche, Roine Douairiere de France. Theophraſte.

i.e. "As the Phœnix is always alone, and the only bird of its kind in the world, so are very good things of marvellous rarity and very thinly sown. It is the device which Madam Elinor of Austria bears, Queen Dowager of France."

The Phœnix is Reusner's 36th Emblem (bk. ii. p. 98),—

Vnica ſemper auis.
EMBLEMA XXXVI.

Reusner, 1581.

*Quæ thuris lacrymis, & ſucco viuit amomi:**
Fert cunas Phœnix, buſta paterna, ſuas.

* Reusner adopts this first line from Ovid's *Fable of the Phœnix* (*Metam.*, bk. xv. 37. l. 3),—
"Sed thuris lacrymis, & succo vivit amomi."

Sixteen elegiac lines of Latin are devoted to its praise and typical signification, mixed with some curious theological conjectures,—

> "On tears of frankincense, and on the juice of balsam lives
> The Phœnix, and bears its cradle, the coffin of its sire.
> Always alone is this bird;—itself its own father and son,
> By death alone does it give to itself a new life.
> For oft as on earth it has lived the ten ages through,
> Dying at last, in the fire it is born of its own funeral pile.
> So to himself and to his, Christ gives life by his death,
> Life to his servants, whom in equal love he joins to himself.
> True Man is he, the one true God, arbiter of ages,
> Who illumines with light, with his spirit cherishes all.
> Happy, who by holy baptisms in Christ is reborn,
> In the sacred stream he takes hold of life,—in the stream he obtains it."

And again, in reference to the birth unto life eternal,—

> "If men report true, death over again forms the Phœnix,
> To this bird both life and death the same funeral pile may prove.
> Onward, executioners! of the saints burn ye the sainted bodies;
> For whom ye desire perdition, to them brings the flame new birth."

Whitney, borrowing his woodcut and motto from Plantin's edition of "LES DEVISES HEROIQVES," 1562, to a very considerable degree makes the explanatory stanzas his own both in the conception and in the expression. The chief town near to his birth-place had on December 10, 1583, been almost totally destroyed by fire, but through the munificence of the Queen and many friends, by 1586, "the whole site and frame of the town, so suddenly ruined, was with great speed re-edified in that beautifull manner," says the chronicler, "that now it is." The Phœnix (p. 177) is standing in the midst of the flames, and with outspreading wings is prepared for another flight in renewed youth and vigour.

Vnica semper auis.

To my countrimen of the Namptwiche *in Chefshire.*

Whitney, 1586.

"THE Phœnix rare, with fethers freshe of hewe,
ARABIAS righte, and sacred to the Sonne :
Whome, other birdes with wonder seeme to vewe,
Dothe liue vntill a thousande yeares bee ronne :
Then makes a pile : which, when with Sonne it burnes,
Shee flies therein, and so to ashes turnes.

Whereof, behoulde, an other Phœnix rare,
With speede dothe rise most beautifull and faire :
And thoughe for truthe, this manie doe declare,
Yet thereunto, I meane not for to sweare :
Althoughe I knowe that Aucthors witnes true,
What here I write, bothe of the oulde, and newe.

Which when I wayed, the newe, and eke the oulde,
I thought vppon your towne destroyed with fire :
And did in minde, the newe NAMPWICHE behoulde,
A spectacle for anie mans desire :
Whose buildinges braue, where cinders weare but late,
Did represente (me thought) the Phœnix fate.

And as the oulde, was manie hundreth yeares,
A towne of fame, before it felt that crosse :
Euen so, (I hope) this WICHE, that nowe appeares,
A Phœnix age shall laste, and knowe no losse :
Which GOD vouchsafe, who make you thankfull, all :
That see this rise, and sawe the other fall."

The *Concordance to Shakespeare*, by Mrs. Cowden Clarke, for thoroughness hitherto unmatched,* notes down eleven instances in which the Phœnix is named, and in most of them, with some epithet expressive of its nature. It is spoken of as the Arabian bird, the bird of wonder; its nest of spicery is mentioned; it is made an emblem of death, and employed in metaphor to flatter both Elizabeth and James.

Besides the instances already given (p. 236), we here select others of a general nature; as:—When on the renowned Talbot's death in battle, Sir William Lucy, in presence of Charles, the Dauphin, exclaims over the slain (1 *Hen. VI.*, act iv. sc. 7, l. 92),—

> "O that I could but call these dead to life!
> It were enough to fright the realm of France:"

his request for leave to give their bodies burial is thus met,—

> "*Pucelle.* I think this upstart is old Talbot's ghost,
> He speaks with such a proud commanding spirit.
> For God's sake, let him have 'em.
> *Charles.* Go, take their bodies hence.
> *Lucy.* I'll bear them hence; but from their ashes shall be rear'd
> A phœnix, that shall make all France afeard."

And York, on the haughty summons of Northumberland and Clifford, declares (3 *Hen. VI.*, act i. sc. 4, l. 35),—

> "My ashes, as the Phœnix, may bring forth
> A bird that will revenge upon you all."

In the *Phœnix and the Turtle* (lines 21 and 49, vol. ix. p. 671), are the lines,—

> "Here the anthem doth commence:
> Love and constancy is dead;
> Phœnix and the turtle fled
> In a mutual flame from hence.
>
> Whereupon it made this threne
> To the phœnix and the dove,
> Co-supremes and stars of love,
> As chorus to their tragic scene."

* To render it still more useful, the words should receive something of classification, as in Cruden's *Concordance to the English Bible*, and the *number* of the *line* should be given as well as of the *Act* and *Scene*.

The "threne," or *Lamentation* (l. 53, vol. ix. p. 672), then follows,—

> "Beauty, truth and rarity
> Grace in all simplicity,
> Here enclosed in cinders lie.
>
> Death is now the phœnix' nest;
> And the turtle's loyal breast
> To eternity doth rest."

The Maiden in *The Lover's Complaint* (l. 92, vol. ix. p. 638) thus speaks of her early love,—

> "Small show of man was yet upon his chin;
> His phœnix down began but to appear,
> Like unshorn velvet, on that termless skin,
> Whose bare out-bragg'd the web it seem'd to wear."

Some of the characteristics of the Phœnix are adduced in the dialogue, *Richard III.* (act iv. sc. 4, l. 418, vol. v. p. 606), between Richard III. and the queen or widow of Edward IV. The king is proposing to marry her daughter,—

> "*Q. Eliz.* Shall I be tempted of the devil thus?
> *K. Rich.* Ay, if the devil tempt thee to do good.
> *Queen.* Shall I forget myself, to be myself?
> *K. Rich.* Ay, if yourself's remembrance wrong yourself.
> *Queen.* But thou didst kill my children.
> *K. Rich.* But in your daughter's womb I bury them:
> Where in that nest of spicery, they shall breed
> Selves of themselves, to your recomforture."

Another instance is from *Antony and Cleopatra* (act iii. sc. 2, l. 7, vol. ix. p. 64). Agrippa and Enobarbus meet in Cæsar's ante-chamber, and of Lepidus Enobarbus declares,—

> "O how he loves Cæsar!
> *Agrip.* Nay, but how dearly he adores Marc Antony!
> *Enob.* Cæsar? Why, he's the Jupiter of men.
> *Agrip.* What's Antony? The god of Jupiter.
> *Enob.* Speak you of Cæsar? How? the nonpareil!
> *Agrip.* O Antony! O thou Arabian bird!"

And in *Cymbeline* (act i. sc. 6, l. 15, vol. ix. p. 183), on being welcomed by Imogen, Iachimo says, *aside*,—

> "All of her that is out of door most rich!
> If she be furnish'd with a mind so rare,
> She is alone th' Arabian Bird, and I
> Have lost the wager."

But the fullest and most remarkable example is from *Henry VIII.* (act v. sc. 5, l. 28, vol. vi. p. 114). Cranmer assumes the gift of inspiration, and prophesies of the new-born child of the king and of Anne Bullen an increase of blessings and of all princely graces,—

> "Truth shall nurse her,
> Holy and heavenly thoughts still counsel her:
> She shall be loved and fear'd: her own shall bless her;
> Her foes shake like a field of beaten corn,
> And hang their heads with sorrow. Good grows with her:
> In her days every man shall eat in safety,
> Under his own vine, what he plants, and sing
> The merry songs of peace to all his neighbours:
> God shall be truly known; and those about her
> From her shall read the perfect ways of honour,
> And by these claim their greatness, not by blood.
> Nor shall this peace sleep with her; but, as when
> The bird of wonder dies, the maiden phœnix,
> Her ashes new create another heir,
> As great in admiration as herself,
> So shall she leave her blessedness to one—
> When heaven shall call her from this cloud of darkness—
> Who from the sacred ashes of her honour
> Shall star-like rise, as great in fame as she was,
> And so stand fix'd."

There is another bird, the emblem of tranquillity and of peaceful and happy days; it is the KING-FISHER, which the poets have described with the utmost embellishment of the fancy. Aristotle and Pliny tell even more marvellous tales about it than Herodotus and Horapollo do about the Phœnix.

The fable, on which the poetic idea rests, is two-fold; one that Alcyone, a daughter of the wind-god Æolus, had been married to Ceyx; and so happily did they live that they gave one another the appellations of the gods, and by Jupiter in anger were changed into birds; the other narrates, that Ceyx perished from shipwreck, and that in a passion of grief Alcyone threw herself into the sea. Out of pity the gods bestowed on the two the shape and habit of birds. Ovid has greatly enlarged the fable, and has devoted to it, in his *Metamorphoses* (xi. 10), between three and four hundred lines. We have only to do with the conclusion,—

> "The gods at length taking compassion
> The pair are transformed into birds; tried by one destiny
> Their love remained firm; nor is the conjugal bond
> Loosened although they are birds; parents they become,
> And through a seven days' quietness in midwinter
> In nests upborne by the sea the King-fishers breed.
> Safe then is the sea-road; the winds Æolus guards,
> Debarring from egress; and ocean's plain favours his children."

According to Aristotle's description (*Hist. Anim.* ix. 14),—

"The nest of the Alcyon is globular, with a very narrow entrance, so that if it should be upset the water would not enter. A blow from iron has no effect upon it, but the human hand soon crushes it and reduces it to powder. The eggs are five."

"The *halcyones*," Pliny avers, "are of great name and much marked. The very seas, and they that saile thereupon, know well when they sit and breed. This bird, so notable, is little bigger than a sparrow; for the more part of her pennage, blew, intermingled yet among with white and purple feathers; having a thin small neck and long withal they lay and sit about mid-winter, when daies be shortest; and the times while they are broodie, is called the *halcyon* daies; for during that season the sea is calm and navigable, especially on the coast of Sicilie."—*Philemon Holland's Plinie*, x. 32.

We are thus prepared for the device which Paolo Giovio sets before his readers, with an Italian four-lined stanza to a French motto, *We know well the weather.* The drawing suggests that the two Alcyons in one nest are sailing "on the coast of Sicilie," in the straits of Messina, with Scylla and Charybdis on each hand—but in perfect calmness and security,—

DE I MEDESIMI.

San gl' Alcionij augei il tempo eletto,
Ch' al nido, e all' oua lor non nuoca il mare.
Infelice quell' huom, ch'el di aspettare
Non sa, per dare al suo disegno effetto.

Nous sauons bien le temps.

" Happy the Alcyons, whom choice times defend.
Nor in the nest nor egg the sea can harm ;
But luckless man knows not to meet alarm,
Nor to his purpose gives the wished for end."

The festival of Saint Martin, or Martlemas, is held November 11th, at the approach of winter, and was a season of merriment and good cheer. It is in connection with this festival that Shakespeare first introduces a mention of the Alcyon (1 *Henry VI.*, act i. sc. 2, l. 129, vol. v. p. 14). The Maid of Orleans is propounding her mission for the deliverance of France to Reignier, Duke of Anjou,—

" Assign'd I am to be the English scourge.
This night the siege assuredly I'll raise :
Expect Saint Martin's summer, halcyon days,
Since I have enter'd into these wars."

It was, and I believe still is, an opinion prevalent in some parts of England, that a King-fisher, suspended by the tail or beak, will turn round as the wind changes. To this fancy, allusion is made in *King Lear* (act ii. sc. 2, l. 73, vol. viii. p. 307),—

> "Renege, affirm and turn their halcyon beaks
> With every gale and vary of their masters,
> Knowing nought, like dogs, but following."

The Poet delights to tell of self-sacrificing love; and hence the celebrity which the PELICAN has acquired for the strong natural affection which impels it, so the tale runs, to pour forth the very fountain of its life in nourishment to its young. From Epiphanius, bishop of Constantia in the island of Cyprus, whose *Physiologus* was printed by Plantin in 1588, we have the supposed natural history of the Pelicans and their young, which he symbolizes in the Saviour. His account is accompanied by a pictorial representation, "ΠΕΡΙ ΤΗΣ ΠΕΛΕΚΑΝΟΣ,"—*Concerning the Pelican* (p. 30).

Epiphanius, 1588.

The good bishop narrates as physiological history the following,—

"Beyond all birds the Pelican is fond of her young. The female sits on the nest, guarding her offspring, and cherishes and caresses them and wounds them with loving; and pierces their sides and they die. After three days the male pelican comes and finds them dead, and very much his heart is pained. Driven by grief he smites his own side, and as he stands over the wounds of the dead young ones, the blood trickles down, and thus are they made alive again."

Reusner and Camerarius both adopt the Pelican as the emblem of a good king who devotes himself to the people's welfare. *For Law and for Flock*, is the very appropriate motto they prefix; Camerarius simply saying (ed. 1596, p. 87),—

> "*Sanguine vivificat Pelicanus pignora, sic rex*
> *Pro populi vitæ est prodigus ipse suæ.*"

> "By blood the Pelican his young revives; and so a king
> For his people's sake himself of life is prodigal."

Reusner (bk. ii. p. 73) gives the following device,—

Pro lege, & grege.

EMBLEMA XIV.

Reusner, 1581.

And tells how,—

"Alphonsus the wise and good king of Naples, with his own honoured hand painted a Pelican which with its sharp beak was laying open its breast so as with its own blood to save the lives of its young. Thus for people, for law, it is right that a king should die and by his own death restore life to the nations. As by his own death Christ did restore life to the just, and with life peace and righteousness."

He adds this personification of the Pelican,—

"For people and for sanctioned law heart's life a king will pour ;
So from this blood of mine do I life to my young restore."

The other motto, which Hadrian Junius and Geffrey Whitney select, opens out another idea, *Quod in te est, prome,*—"Bring forth what is in thee." It suggests that of the soul's wealth we should impart to others.

Junius (Emb. 7) thus addresses the bird he has chosen,—

"By often striking, O Pelican, thou layest open the deep recesses of thy breast and givest life to thy offspring. Search into thine own mind (my friend), seek what is hidden within, and bring forth into the light the seeds of thine inner powers."

And very admirably does Whitney (p. 87) apply the sentiment to one of the most eminent of divines in the reign of Queen Elizabeth,—namely, to Dr. Alexander Nowell, the celebrated Dean of St. Paul's, illustrious both for his learning and his example,—

"THE Pellican, for to reuiue her younge,
Doth peirce her brest, and geue them of her blood :
Then searche your breste, and as yow haue with tonge,
With penne proceede to doe our countrie good :
Your zeale is great, your learning is profounde,
Then helpe our wantes, with that you doe abounde."

The full poetry of the thoughts thus connected with the Pelican is taken in, though but briefly expressed by Shakespeare. In *Hamlet* (act iv. sc. 5, l. 135, vol. viii. p. 135), on Laertes determining to seek revenge for his father's death, the king adds fuel to the flame,—

> "*King.* Good Laertes,
> If you desire to know the certainty
> Of your dear father's death, is't writ in your revenge,
> That, swoopstake, you will draw both friend and foe,
> Winner and loser?
> *Laer.* None but his enemies.
> *King.* Will you know them then?
> *Laer.* To his good friends thus wide I'll ope my arms;
> And like the kind life-rendering pelican,
> Repast them with my blood." *

From *Richard II.* (act ii. sc. 1, l. 120, vol. iv. p. 140) we learn how in zeal and true loyalty John of Gaunt counsels his headstrong nephew, and how rudely the young king replies,—

> "Now, by my seat's right royal majesty,
> Wert thou not brother to great Edward's son,
> This tongue that runs so roundly in thy head
> Should run thy head from thy unreverent shoulders.
> *Gaunt.* O, spare me not, my brother Edward's son,
> For that I was his father Edward's son;
> That blood already, like the pelican,
> Hast thou tapp'd out and drunkenly caroused."

The idea, indeed, almost supposes that the young pelicans strike at the breasts of the old ones, and forcibly or thoughtlessly drain their life out. So it is in *King Lear* (act iii. sc. 4, l. 68, vol. viii. p. 342), when the old king exclaims,—

* The whole stanza as given on the last page, beginning with the line,—

"The Pellican, for to reuiue her younge,"

is quoted in Knight's "PICTORIAL SHAKSPERE" (vol. i p. 154), in illustration of these lines from *Hamlet* concerning "the kind life-rendering pelican." The woodcut which Knight gives is also copied from Whitney, and the following remark added,—"Amongst old books of emblems there is one on which Shakspere himself might have looked, containing the subjoined representation. It is entitled 'A Choice of Emblemes and other Devices by Geffrey Whitney, 1586.'" Knight thus appears prepared to recognise what we contend for, that Emblem writers were known to Shakespeare.

"Death, traitor! nothing could have subdued nature
To such a lowness but his unkind daughters.
Is it the fashion that discarded fathers
Should have thus little mercy on their flesh?
Judicious punishment! 'twas this flesh begot
Those pelican daughters."

And again (2 *Henry VI.*, act iv. sc. 1, l. 83, vol. v. p. 182), in the words addressed to Suffolk,—

"By devilish policy art thou grown great,
And, like ambitious Sylla, over-gorged
With gobbets of thy mother's bleeding heart."

The description of the wounded stag, rehearsed to the banished duke by one of his attendants, is as touching a narrative, as full of tenderness, as any which show the Poet's wonderful power over our feelings; it is from *As You Like It* (act ii. sc. 1, l. 29, vol. ii. p. 394).—

"To-day my Lord of Amiens and myself
Did steal behind him [*Jaques*] as he lay along
Under an oak whose antique root peeps out
Upon the brook that brawls along this wood:
To the which place a poor sequester'd stag,
That from the hunter's aim had ta'en a hurt,
Did come to languish, and indeed, my lord,
The wretched animal heaved forth such groans,
That their discharge did stretch his leathern coat
Almost to bursting, and the big round tears
Coursed one another down his innocent nose
In piteous chase; and thus the hairy fool,
Much marked of the melancholy Jacques,
Stood on the extremest verge of the swift brook,
Augmenting it with tears."

Graphic and highly ornamented though this description may be, it is really the counterpart of Gabriel Symeoni's Emblem of love incurable. The poor stag lies wounded and helpless,—the mortal dart in his flank, and the life-stream gushing out. The scroll above bears a Spanish motto, *This holds their Remedy and not I;* and it serves to introduce the usual quatrain.

D'VN AMORE.

INCVRABILE.

Giovio and Symeoni, 1562.

Troua il ceruio ferito al ſuo gran male	Eſto tiene
Nel dittamo Creteo fido ricorſo,	ſu reme-
Ma laſſo (io'l sò) rimedio ne ſoccorſo	dio, y non
All' amoroſo colpo alcun non vale.	yo.

"The smitten stag hath found sad pains to feel,
No trusted Cretan dittany* is near,
Wearied, for succour there is only fear,—
The wounds of love no remedy can heal."

---

* Virgil's *Æneid* (bk. xii. 412—414), thus expressed in Dryden's rendering, will explain the passage; he is speaking of Venus,—

"A branch of healing dittany she brought:
Which in the Cretan fields with care she sought:
Rough is the stem, which wooly leafs surround;
The leafs with flow'rs, the flow'rs with purple crown'd."

See also Joachim Camerarius, *Ex Animalibus Quadrup.* (ed. 1595, Emb. 69, p. 71).

To the same motto and the same device Paradin (fol. 168) furnishes an explanation,—

"*The device of love incurable*," he says, "*may be a stag wounded by an arrow, having a branch of Dittany in its mouth, which is a herb that grows abundantly in the island of Crete. By eating this the wounded stag heals all its injuries. The motto*, 'Esto tienne su remedio, y no yo,' *follows those verses of Ovid in the Metamorphoses, where Phœbus, complaining of the love for Daphne, says*, 'Hei mihi, quòd nullis amor est medicabilis herbis.'"

The connected lines in Ovid's *Metamorphoses* (bk. i. fab. 9), show that even Apollo, the god of healing, whose skill does good to all others, does no good to himself. The *Emblems* of Otho Vænius (p. 154) gives a very similar account to that of Symeoni,—

> "*Cerua venenato venantûm saucia ferro*
> *Dyctamno quærit vulneris auxilium.*
> *Hei mihi, quod nullis sit Amor medicabilis herbis,*
> *Et nequeat medicâ pellier arte malum.*"

The following is the English version of that date,—

"*No help for the louer.*"

> "The hert that wounded is, knowes how to fynd relief,
> And makes by dictamon the arrow out to fall,
> And with the self-same herb hee cures his wound withall,
> But love no herb can fynd to cure his inward grief."

In the presence of those who had slain Cæsar, and over his dead body at the foot of Pompey's statue, "which all the while ran blood," Marc Antony poured forth his fine avowal of continued fidelity to his friend (*Julius Cæsar*, act iii. sc. 1, l. 205, vol. vii. p. 368),—

> "Pardon me, Julius! Here wast thou bay'd, brave hart;
> Here didst thou fall, and here thy hunters stand,
> Sign'd in thy spoil and crimson'd in thy lethe.
> O world! thou wast the forest to this hart;
> And this, indeed, O world, the heart of thee.
> How like a deer strucken by many princes
> Dost thou here lie!"

The same metaphor from the wounded deer is introduced in *Hamlet* (act iii. sc. 2, l. 259, vol. viii. p. 97). The acting of the play has had on the king's mind the influence which Hamlet hoped for; and as in haste and confusion the royal party disperse, he recites the stanza,—

> "Why, let the stricken deer go weep,
> The hart ungalled play;
> For some must watch, whilst some must sleep:
> Thus runs the world away."

The very briefest allusion to the subject of our Emblem is also contained in the *Winter's Tale* (act i. sc. 2, l. 115, vol. iii. p. 323). Leontes is discoursing with his queen Hermione,—

> "But to be paddling palms and pinching fingers,
> As now they are, and making practised smiles,
> As in a looking glass, and then to sigh, as 'twere
> The mort o' the deer; O, that is entertainment
> My bosom likes not, nor my brows!"

The poetical epithet "golden," so frequently expressive of excellence and perfection, and applied even to qualities of the mind, is declared by Douce (vol. i. p. 84) to have been derived by Shakespeare either from Sidney's *Arcadia* (bk. ii.), or from Arthur Golding's translation of Ovid's *Metamorphoses* (4to, fol. 8), where speaking of Cupid's arrows, he says,—

> "*That causeth love* is all of *golde* with point full sharp and bright.
> That chaseth love, is blunt, whose steele with leaden head is dight."

This borrowing and using of the epithet "golden" might equally well, and with as much probability, have taken place through the influence of Alciat, or by adoption from Whitney's very beautiful translation and paraphrase of Joachim Bellay's *Fable of Cupid and Death*. The two were lodging together at an inn,[1] and unintentionally exchanged quivers: death's darts were made of bone, Cupid's were "dartes of goulde."

[1] In Haechtan's *Parvus Mundus* (ed. 1579), Gerard de Jode represents the sleeping place as "sub tegmine fagi,"—but the results of the mistake as equally unfortunate with those in Bellay and Whitney.

The conception of the tale is admirable, and the narrative itself full of taste and beauty. Premising that the same device is employed by Whitney as by Alciat, we will first give almost a literal version from the 154th and 155th Emblems of the latter author (edition 1581),—

"Wandering about was Death along with Cupid as companion,
 With himself Death was bearing quivers; little Love his weapons;
Together at an inn they lodged; one night together one bed they shared;
 Love was blind, and on this occasion Death also was blind.
Unforeseeing the evil, one took the darts of the other,
 Death the golden weapons,—those of bone the boy rashly seizes.
Hence an old man who ought now to be near upon Acheron,
 Behold him loving,—and for his brow flower-fillets preparing.
But I, since Love smote me with the dart that was changed,
 I am fainting, and their hand the fates upon me are laying.
Spare, O boy; spare, O Death, holding the ensigns victorious,—
 Make me the lover, the old man make him sink beneath Acheron."

And carrying on the idea into the next Emblem (155),—

"Why, O Death, with thy wiles darest thou deceive Love the boy,
 That thy weapons he should hurl, while he thinks them his own?"

Whitney's "sportive tale, concerning death and love," possesses sufficient merit to be given in full (p. 132),—

De morte, & amore: Iocosum.
To EDWARD DYER, *Esquier.*

Whitney, 1586.

"WHILE furious Mors, from place, to place did flie,
And here, and there, her fatall dartes did throwe :
At lengthe shee mette, with Cupid passing by,
Who likewise had, bene busie with his bowe :
Within one Inne, they bothe togeather stay'd,
And for one nighte, awaie theire shooting lay'd.

The morrowe next, they bothe awaie doe haste,
And eache by chaunce, the others quiuer takes :
The frozen dartes, on Cupiddes backe weare plac'd,
The fierie dartes, the leane virago shakes :
Whereby ensued, suche alteration straunge,
As all the worlde, did wonder at the chaunge.

For gallant youthes, whome Cupid thoughte to wounde,
Of loue, and life, did make an ende at once.
And aged men, whome deathe woulde bringe to grounde :
Beganne againe to loue, with sighes, and grones ;
Thus natures lawes, this chaunce infringed soe :
That age did loue, and youthe to graue did goe.

Till at the laste, as Cupid drewe his bowe,
Before he shotte : a younglinge thus did crye,
Oh Venus sonne, thy dartes thou doste not knowe,
They pierce too deepe : for all thou hittes, doe die :
Oh spare our age, who honored thee of oulde,
Theise dartes are bone, take thou the dartes of goulde.

Which beinge saide, a while did Cupid staye,
And sawe, how youthe was almoste cleane extinct :
And age did doate, with garlandes freshe, and gaye,
And heades all balde, weare newe in wedlocke linckt :
Wherefore he shewed, this error vnto Mors,
Who miscontent, did chaunge againe perforce.

Yet so, as bothe some dartes awaie conuay'd,
Which weare not theirs : yet vnto neither knowne,
Some bonie dartes, in Cupiddes quiuer stay'd,
Some goulden dartes, had Mors amongst her owne.
Then, when wee see, vntimelie deathe appeare :
Or wanton age : it was this chaunce you heare."

For an interlude to our remarks on the "golden," we must mention that the pretty tale *Concerning Death and Cupid* was attributed to Whitney by one of Shakespeare's contemporaries; and, if known to other literary men of the age, very reasonably may be supposed not unknown to the dramatist. Henry Peacham, in 1612, p. 172 of his *Emblems*, acknowledges that it was from Whitney that he derived his own tale,—

"*De Morte, et Cupidine.*"

"DEATH meeting once, with *CVPID* in an Inne,
Where roome was scant, togeither both they lay.
Both wearié, (for they roving both had beene,)
Now on the morrow when they should away,
CVPID Death's quiver at his back had throwne,
And *DEATH* tooke *CVPIDS*, thinking it his owne.

By this o're-sight, it shortly came to passe,
That young men died, who readie were to wed:
And age did revell with his bonny-lasse,
Composing girlonds for his hoarie head:
Invert not Nature, oh ye Powers twaine,
Giue *CVPID'S* dartes, and *DEATH* take thine againe."

Whitney luxuriates in this epithet "golden;"—golden fleece, golden hour, golden pen, golden sentence, golden book, golden palm are found recorded in his pages. At p. 214 we have the lines,—

"A Leaden sworde, within a goulden sheathe,
Is like a foole of natures finest moulde,
To whome, shee did her rarest giftes bequethe,
Or like a sheepe, within a fleece of goulde."

We may indeed regard Whitney as the prototype of Hood's world-famous "Miss Kilmansegg, with her golden leg,"—

"And a pair of Golden Crutches." (vol. i. p. 189.)

Shakespeare is scarcely more sparing in this respect than the Cheshire Emblematist; he mentions for us "golden tresses of the dead," "golden oars and a silver stream," "the glory, that in gold clasps locks in the golden story," "a golden casket," "a golden bed," and "a golden mind." *Merchant of Venice* (act ii. sc. 7, lines 20 and 58, vol. ii. p. 312),—

> "A golden mind stoops not to shows of dross.
>
> But here an angel in a golden bed
> Lies all within."

And applied direct to Cupid's artillery in *Midsummer Night's Dream* (act i. sc. 1, l. 168, vol. ii. p. 204), Hermia makes fine use of the epithet golden,—

> "My good Lysander!
> I swear to thee by Cupid's strongest bow,
> By his best arrow with the golden head."

So in *Twelfth Night* (act i. sc. 1, l. 33, vol. iii. p. 224), Orsino, Duke of Milan, speaks of Olivia,—

> "O, she that hath a heart of that fine frame
> To pay the debt of love but to a brother,
> How will she love, when the rich golden shaft
> Hath kill'd the flock of all affections else
> That live in her; when liver, brain and heart
> These sovereign thrones, are all supplied, and fill'd
> Her sweet perfections with one self king!"

And when Helen praised the complexion or comeliness of Troilus above that of Paris, Cressida avers (*Troilus and Cressida*, act i. sc. 2, l. 100, vol. vi. p. 134),—

> "I had as lief Helen's golden tongue had commended Troilus for a copper nose."

As Whitney's pictorial illustration represents them, Death and Cupid are flying in mid-air, and discharging their arrows from the clouds. Confining the description to Cupid, this is exactly the action in one of the scenes of the *Midsummer Night's Dream* (act ii. sc. 1, l. 155, vol. ii. p. 216). The passage was intended to flatter Queen Elizabeth; it is Oberon who speaks,—

> "That very time I saw, but thou couldst not,
> Flying between the cold moon and the earth,

Plate 14

THEATRVM VITÆ HVMANÆ.

CAPVT I.

VITA HVMANA EST TANQVAM Theatrum omnium miseriarum.

Vita hominis tanquam circus, vel grande theatrum est:
Quod tragici oſtentat cuncta referta metus.
Hic laſciva caro, peccatum, morſque, Satanque
Triſti hominem vexant, exagitantque modo.

1596

Cupid all arm'd: a certain aim he took
At a fair vestal throned by the west,
And loosed his love-shaft smartly from his bow,
As it should pierce a hundred thousand hearts:
But I might see young Cupid's fiery shaft
Quench'd in the chaste beams of the watery moon,
And the imperial votaress passed on,
In maiden meditation, fancy free.
Yet mark'd I where the bolt of Cupid fell:
It fell upon a little western flower,
Before milk-white, now purple with love's wound,
And maidens call it love-in-idleness.'

Scarcely by possibility could a dramatist, who was also an actor, avoid the imagery of poetic ideas with which his own profession made him familiar. I am not sure if Sheridan Knowles did not escape the temptation; but if Shakespeare had done so, it would have deprived the world of some of the most forcible passages in our language. The theatre for which he wrote, and the stage on which he acted, supplied materials for his imagination to work into lines of surpassing beauty.

Boissard's "THEATRVM VITÆ HUMANÆ" (edition Metz, 4to, 1596) presents its first Emblem with the title,—*Human life is as a Theatre of all Miseries.* (See Plate XIV.)

" The life of man a circus is, or theatre so grand:
Which every thing shows forth filled full of tragic fear;
Here wanton sense, and sin, and death, and Satan's hand
Molest mankind and persecute with penalties severe."

The picture of human life which Boissard draws in his "Address to the Reader" is gloomy and dispiriting; there are in it, he declares, the various miseries and calamities to which man is subject while he lives,—and the conflicts to which he is exposed from the sharpest and cruellest enemies, the devil, the flesh, and the world; and from their violence and oppression there is no possibility of escape, except by the favour and help of God's mercy.

Very similar ideas prevail in some of Shakespeare's lines; as "the thousand natural shocks that flesh is heir to" (*Hamlet*, act iii. sc. 1, l. 62, vol. viii. p. 79); "my heart all mad with misery beats in this hollow prison of my flesh" (*Titus Andronicus*, act iii. sc. 2, l. 9, vol. vi. p. 483); and, "shake the yoke of inauspicious stars from this world-wearied flesh" (*Romeo and Juliet*, act v. sc. 3, l. 111, vol. vii. p. 126).

But more particularly in *As You Like It* (act ii. sc. 7, l. 136, vol. ii. p. 409),—

> "Thou seest we are not all alone unhappy :
> This wide and universal theatre
> Presents more woeful pageants than the scene
> Wherein we play in."

Also in *Macbeth* (act v. sc. 5, l. 22, vol. vii. p. 512),—

> "And all our yesterdays have lighted fools
> The way to dusty death. Out, out, brief candle !
> Life's but a walking shadow, a poor player
> That struts and frets his hour upon the stage
> And then is heard no more : it is a tale
> Told by an idiot, full of sound and fury
> Signifying nothing."

And when the citizens of Angiers haughtily closed their gates against both King Philip and King John, the taunt is raised (*King John*, act ii. sc. 1, l. 373, vol. iv. p. 26),—

> "By heaven, these scroyles of Angiers flout you, kings,
> And stand securely on their battlements,
> As in a theatre, whence they gape and point
> At your industrious scenes and acts of death."

The stages or ages of man have been variously divided. In the Arundel MS., and in a Dutch work printed at Antwerp in 1820, there are ten of these divisions of Man's Life.* The celebrated physician Hippocrates (B.C. 460—357), and Proclus,

* See "ARCHÆOLOGIA," vol. xxxv. 1853, pp. 167—189; "Observations on the Origin of the Division of Man's Life into Stages. By John Winter Jones, Esq."

Seven Ages of Life, from an early Block Print in the British Museum

the Platonist (A.D. 412—485), are said to have divided human life, as Shakespeare has done, into *seven* ages. And a mosaic on the pavement of the cathedral at Siena gives exactly the same division. This mosaic is very curious, and is supposed to have been executed by Antonio Federighi in the year 1476. Martin's "SHAKSPERE'S SEVEN AGES," published in 1848, contains a little narrative about it, furnished by Lady Calcott, who shortly before that time had been travelling in Italy,—

> "We found," she says, "in the cathedral of Sienna a curious proof that the division of human life into seven periods, from infancy to extreme old age with a view to draw a moral inference, was common before Shakspeare's time: the person who was showing us that fine church directed our attention to the large and bold designs of Beccafumi, which are inlaid in black and white in the pavement, entirely neglecting some works of a much older date which appeared to us to be still more interesting on account of the simplicity and elegance with which they are designed. Several of these represent Sibyls and other figures of a mixed moral and religious character; but in one of the side chapels we were both suprised and pleased to find seven figures, each in a separate compartment, inlaid in the pavement, representing the Seven Ages of Man."

Lord Lindsay notices the same work, and in his "CHRISTIAN ART," vol. iii. p. 112, speaking of the Pavement of the Duomo at Siena, says,—"Seven ages of life in the Southern Nave, near the Capella del Voto."

Of as old a date, even if not more ancient, is the Representation of the Seven Ages from a Block-Print belonging to the British Museum, and of which we present a diminished facsimile (Plate XV.), the original measuring 15½ in. by 10½ in.

The inscription on the centre of the wheel, *Rota vite que septima notatur,*—"The wheel of life which seven times is noted;" on the outer rim,—*Est velut aqua labuntur deficiens ita. Sic ornati nascuntur in hac mortali vita,*—"It is as water so failing, they pass away. So furished are they born in this mortal life." The figures for the seven ages are inscribed, *Infans ad vii.*

annos,—"An infant for vii. years." *Pueritia* * *ad xv. años*,—"Childhood up to xv. years." *Adolescētia ad xxv. años*,—"Youthhood to xxv. years." *Iuvētus ad xxxv. annos*,—"Young manhood to xxxv. years." *Virilitas ad l. annos*,—"Mature manhood to 50 years." *Senatus ad lxx. annos*,—"Age to 70 years." *Decrepitus usque ad mortem*,—"Decrepitude up to death." The angel with the scrolls holds in her right hand that on which is written *Beuerano*, in her left, *Corruptio*,—"Corruption:" below her left, *clav*, for *clavis*, "a key."

Some parts of the Latin stanzas are difficult to decipher; they appear, however, to be the following, read downward,—

"Est hominis status in flore significatus
Situ sentires quis esses et unde venisses
Sunt triaque vere quæ faciunt me sæpe dicere.
Secundum timeo quia hoc nescio quando

Flos cadit et periit sic homo cinis erit
Nunquam rideres sed olim sæpe fleres
Est primo durum quare scio me moriturum
Hinc ternum flebo quare nescio ut manebo."

The lines, however, are to be read across the page,—

"Est hominis status in flore significatus, Flos cadit et periit sic homo cinis erit.
Situ sentires quis esses et unde venisses, Nunquam rideres sed olim sæpe fleres.
Sunt triaque vere quæ faciunt me sæpe dicere, Est primo durum quare scio me moriturum.
Secundum timeo quia hoc nescio quando, Hinc ternum flebo quare nescio ut manebo."

They are only doggerel Latin, and in doggerel English may be expressed,—

"Lo here is man's state—in flowers significate:
The flower fades and perishes,—so man but ashes is;
Who mayst be thou feelest,—whence com'st thou revealest;

* It may be noted that the Romans understood by *Pueritia* the period from infancy up to the 17th year; by *Adolescentia*, the period from the age of 15 to 30; by *Juventus*, the season of life from the 20th to the 40th year. *Virilitas*, manhood, began when in the 16th year a youth assumed the *virilis toga*, "the manly gown."

Laugh shouldst thou never,—but be weeping for ever;
Three things there are truly,—which make me say duly,
The first hard thing 'tis to know,—that to death I must go;
The second I fear then,—since I know not the when;—
The third again will I weep,—for I know not in life to keep."

The celebrated speech of Jaques to his dethroned master, "All the world's a stage," from *As You Like It* (act ii. sc. 7, lines 139—165, vol. ii. p. 409), is closely constructed on the model of the Emblematical Devices in the foregoing Block-print. The simple quoting of the passage will be sufficient to show the parallelism and correspondence of the thoughts, if not of the expressions,—

"*Jaques.* All the world's a stage,
And all the men and women merely players:
They have their exits and their entrances;
And one man in his time plays many parts,
His acts being seven ages. At first the infant,
Mewling and puking in the nurse's arms.
Then the whining school-boy, with his satchel
And shining morning face, creeping like snail
Unwillingly to school. And then the lover,
Sighing like furnace, with a woeful ballad
Made to his mistress' eyebrow. Then a soldier,
Full of strange oaths, and bearded like the pard,
Jealous in honour, sudden and quick in quarrel,
Seeking the bubble reputation
Even in the cannon's mouth. And then the justice,
In fair round belly with good capon lined,
With eyes severe and beard of formal cut,
Full of wise saws and modern instances;
And so he plays his part. The sixth age shifts
Into the lean and slipper'd pantaloon,
With spectacles on nose and pouch on side,
His youthful hose, well saved, a world too wide
For his shrunk shank; and his big manly voice,
Turning again toward childish treble, pipes
And whistles in his sound. Last scene of all,
That ends this strange eventful history,
Is second childishness and mere oblivion,
Sans teeth, sans eyes, sans taste, sans every thing."

In far briefer phrase, but with a similar comparison, in reply to the charge of having "too much respect upon the world," Antonia (*Merchant of Venice*, act i. sc. 1, l. 77, vol. ii. p. 281) remarked,—

> I hold the world but as the world, Gratiano :
> A stage, where every man must play a part,
> And mine a sad one.

The pencil and the skill alone are wanting to multiply the Emblems for the Poetic Ideas which abound in Shakespeare's dramas. His thoughts and their combinations are in general so clothed with life and with other elements of beauty, that materials for pictures exist in all parts of his writings. Our office, however, is not to exercise the inventive faculty, nor, even when the invention has been perfected for us by the poet's fancy, to give it a visible form and to portray its outward graces. We have simply to gather up the scattered records of the past, and to show what correspondencies there really are between Shakespeare and the elder Emblem artists, and, when we can, to point out where to him they have been models, imitated and thus approved. Though, therefore, we might draw many a sketch, and finish many a picture from ideas to be supplied from this unexhausted fountain, we are mindful of the humbler task belonging to him who collects, and on his shelf of literary antiquities places, only what has the stamp of nearly three centuries upon them.

Boissard, 1596.

Section VIII.

MORAL AND ÆSTHETIC EMBLEMS.

REJOICING much if the end should crown the earlier portions of our work, we enter now on the last and most welcome section of this chapter,—on the Emblems which depict moral qualities and æsthetical properties,—the Emblems which concern the judgments and perceptions of the mind, and the conduct of the heart, the conscience, and the life.

Quæ ante pedes.

Whitney, 1586.

We will initiate this division by the motto and device which Whitney (p. 64) adopts from Sambucus (edition 1564, p. 30),—"Things lying at our feet,"—that is, of immediate importance and urgency. The Emblems are warnings from the hen which is eating her own eggs, and from the cow which is drinking her own milk.

The Hungarian poet thus sets forth his theme,—

"The hen which had seen the eggs to her care entrusted,
Is here sucking them, and hope she holds forth by no pledge.
It is herself she serves and not others,—of future days heedless,
No sense of feeling has she for the good of posterity.

This a fault is in many,—things gained without labour
  Thoughtless they waste, unmindful of times that are coming.
So cows suck their own udders,—the milk proper for milk pails
  They pilfer away,—and why bear to them the rich fodder?
Not alone for ourselves do we live,—we live from the birth hour
  For our friends and our country, and whom the ages shall bring."

The sentiment is admirable, and well placed by Whitney in the foremost ground,—

"NOT for our selues, alone wee are create,
  But for our frendes, and for our countries good:
And those, that are vnto theire frendes ingrate,
And not regarde theire ofspringe, and theire blood,
Or hee, that wastes his substance till he begges,
Or selles his landes, which seru'de his parentes well:
Is like the henne, when shee hathe lay'de her egges,
That suckes them vp and leaues the emptie shell,
  Euen so theire spoile, to theire reproche, and shame,
  Vndoeth theire heire, and quite decayeth theire name."

These two, Sambucus and Whitney, are the types, affirming that our powers and gifts and opportunities were all bestowed, not for mere selfish enjoyments, but to be improved for the general welfare; Shakespeare is the antitype: he amplifies, and exalts, and finishes; he carries out the thought to its completion, and thus attains absolute perfection; for in *Measure for Measure* (act i. sc. 1, l. 28, vol. i. p. 296), Vincentio, the duke, addresses Angelo,—

"There is a kind of character in thy life,
That to th' observer doth thy history
Fully unfold. Thyself and thy belongings
Are not thine own so proper, as to waste
Thyself upon thy virtues, they on thee.
Heaven doth with us as we with torches do,
Not light them for ourselves; for if our virtues
Did not go forth of us, 'twere all alike
As if we had them not. Spirits are not finely touch'd
But to fine issues; nor Nature never lends
The smallest scruple of her excellence,

> But, like a thrifty goddess, she determines
> Herself the glory of a creditor,
> Both thanks and use."

Now, there is beauty in the types, brief though they be, and on a very lowly subject: but how admirable is the antitype! It entirely redeems the thought from any associated meanness, carries it out to its full excellence, and clothes it with vestments of inspiration. Such, in truth, is Shakespeare's great praise;—he can lift another man's thought out of the dust, and make it a fitting ornament even for an archangel's diadem.

One of Whitney's finest Emblems, in point of conception and treatment, and, I believe, peculiar to himself, one of those "newly devised," is founded on the sentiment, "By help of God" (p. 203).

Auxilio diuino.

To RICHARDE DRAKE, *Esquier, in praise of Sir* FRANCIS DRAKE *Knight.*

Whitney, 1586.

The representation is that of the hand of Divine Providence issuing from a cloud and holding the girdle which encompasses the earth. With that girdle Sir Francis Drake's ship, "the Golden Hind," was drawn and guided round the globe.

The whole Emblem possesses considerable interest,—for it relates to the great national event of Shakespeare's youth,—the first accomplishment by Englishmen of the earth's circumnavigation. With no more than 164 able-bodied men, in five small ships, little superior to boats with a deck, the adventurous commander set sail 13th December, 1577;

he went by the Straits of Magellan, and on his return doubled the Cape of Good Hope, the 15th of March, 1580, having then only fifty-seven men and three casks of water. The perilous voyage was ended at Plymouth, September the 26th, 1580, after an absence of two years and ten months.

These few particulars give more meaning to the Poet's description,—

"THROVGHE scorchinge heate, throughe coulde, in stormes, and tempests force,
By ragged rocks, by shelfes, & sandes: this Knighte did keepe his course.
By gapinge gulfes hee pass'd, by monsters of the flood,
By pirattes, theeues, and cruell foes, that long'd to spill his blood.
That wonder greate to scape: but, GOD was on his side,
And throughe them all, in spite of all, his shaken shippe did guide.
And, to requite his paines: *By helpe of power deuine.*
His happe, at lengthe did aunswere hope, to finde the goulden mine.
Let GRÆCIA then forbeare, to praise her IASON boulde?
Who throughe the watchfull dragons pass'd, to win the fleece of goulde.
Since by MEDEAS helpe, they weare inchaunted all,
And IASON without perrilles, pass'de: the conqueste therefore small?
But, hee, of whome I write, this noble minded DRAKE,
Did bringe away his goulden fleece, when thousand eies did wake.
Wherefore, yee woorthie wightes, that seeke for forreine landes:
Yf that you can, come alwaise home, by GANGES goulden sandes.
And you, that liue at home, and can not brooke the flood,
Geue praise to them, that passe the waues, to doe their countrie good.
Before which sorte, as chiefe: in tempeste, and in calme,
Sir FRANCIS DRAKE, by due deserte, may weare the goulden palme."

How similar, in part at least, is the sentiment in *Hamlet* (act v. sc. 2, l. 8, vol. viii. p. 164),—

"Our indiscretion sometimes serves us well
When our deep plots do pall; and that should learn us
There's a divinity that shapes our ends,
Rough-hew them how we will."

In the Emblem we may note the girdle by which Drake's ship is guided; may it not have been the origin of Puck's fancy in the *Midsummer Night's Dream* (act ii. sc. 1, l. 173, vol. ii. p. 216), when he answers Oberon's strict command,—

> "And be thou here again
> Ere the Leviathan can swim a league.
> *Puck.* I'll put a girdle round about the earth
> In forty minutes."

Besides, may it not have been from this voyage of Sir Francis Drake, and the accounts which were published respecting it, that the correct knowledge of physical geography was derived which Richard II. displays (act iii. sc. 2, l. 37, &c. vol. iv. p. 165)? as in the lines,—

> "when the searching eye of heaven is hid,
> Behind the globe, that lights the lower world.
> . . . .
> when from under this terrestrial ball
> He fires the proud tops of the eastern pines
> And darts his light through every guilty hole.
> . . . .
> revell'd in the night
> Whilst we were wandering with the antipodes."

A mere passing allusion to the same sentiment, a hint respecting it, a single line expressing it, or only a word or two relating to it, may sometimes very decidedly indicate an acquaintance with the author by whom the sentiment has been enunciated in all its fulness. Thus, Shakespeare, in speaking of Benedick, in *Much Ado about Nothing* (act v. sc. 1, l. 170, vol. ii. p. 75), makes Don Pedro say,—

> "An if she did not hate him deadly, she would love him dearly: the old man's daughter told us all."

To which Claudius replies,—

> "All, all; and, moreover, God saw him when he was hid in the garden."

Now, Whitney (p. 229) has an Emblem on this very subject; the motto, "God lives and sees." It depicts Adam concealing himself, and a divine light circling the words, "VBI ES?"—*Where art thou?*

Dominus viuit & videt.

Whitney, 1586.

" BEHINDE a figtree great, him selfe did ADAM hide :
And thought from GOD hee there might lurke, and should not bee espide.
Oh foole, no corners seeke, thoughe thou a sinner bee ;
For none but GOD can thee forgiue, who all thy waies doth see." *

With the same motto, "VBI ES?" and a similar device, Georgette de Montenay (editions 1584 and 1620) carries out the same thought,—

* Soon after Whitney's time this emblem was repeated in that very odd and curious volume ; "Stamm Buch, Darinnen Christliche Tugenden Beyspiel Einhundert ausserlesener *Emblemata*, mit schönen Kupffer-stucke gezierer:" Franckfurt-am-Mayn, Anno MDCXIX. 8vo, pp. 447. At p. 290, Emb. 65, with the words "UBI ES?" there is the figure of Adam hiding behind a tree, and among descriptive stanzas in seven or eight languages, are some intended to be specimens of the language at that day spoken and written in Britain :—

" Adam did breake God's commandement,
In Paradise against his dissent,
Therefore he hyde him vnder a tree
Because *his* Lorde, him *should* not see.
But (alas) to God is all *thing* euident
Than *he* faunde *him* in a moment
And will alwayes such wicked men
Feind, if they doo from *him* runn."

"*Adam pensoit estre fort bien caché,*
Quand il se meit ainsi sous le figuier.
Mais il n'y a cachette où le peché
Aux yeux de Dieu se puisse desnier.
Se vante donc, qui voudra s'oublier,
Que Dieu ne void des hommes la meschance,
Je croy qu' à rien ne sert tout ce mestier
Qu' à se donner à tout peché licence."

The similarity is too great to be named on Shakespeare's part an accidental coincidence; it may surely be set down as a direct allusion, not indeed of the mere copyist, but of the writer, who, having in his mind another's thought, does not quote it literally, but gives no uncertain indication that he gathered it up he cannot tell where, yet has incorporated it among his own treasures, and makes use of it as entirely his own.

From Corrozet, Georgette de Montenay, Le Bey de Batilly, and others their contemporaries, we might adduce various Moral and Æsthetical Emblems to which there are similarities of thought or of expression in Shakespeare's Dramas, but too slight to deserve special notice. For instance, there are ingratitude, the instability of the world, faith and charity and hope, calumny, adversity, friendship, fearlessness,—but to dwell upon them would lengthen our statements and remarks more than is necessary.

We will, however, make one more extract from Corrozet's "HECATOMGRAPHIE" (Emb. 83); to the motto, *Beauty the companion of goodness;* which might have been in Duke Vincentio's mind (*Measure for Measure*, act iii. sc. 1, l. 175, vol. i. p. 340) when he addressed Isabel,—

"The hand that hath made you fair hath made you good; the goodness that is cheap in beauty makes beauty brief in goodness; but grace, being the soul of your complexion, shall keep the body of it ever fair."

Beaulté compaigne de bonté.

Comme la pierre precieuse
Est à l'anneau d'or bien conioincte,
Ainsi la beaulté gracieuse
Doibt estre auecq la bonté ioincte.

[illegible], 1540.

LA pierre bonne
A l'homme donne
Ioyeuseté,
Quand la personne
A voir l'adonne
Sa grand clarté,
Mais sa beaulté
Et dignité
Augmente quand l'or l'enuironne
Que ie compare à la bonté
Pour sa tresgrande vtilité
Qui à telle vertu consonne.

Forme elegante
Beaulté patente
De personnage
Du tout augmente
Se rend luysante
Quand il est sage
Non au visage,
Mais au courage
Reluyst la bonté excellente
Et alors c'est vng chef d'ouurage
Quand on est tresbeau de corsage
Et qu'au cueur est vertu latente.

The French verse which immediately follows the Emblem well describes it,—

> "As, for the precious stone
> The ring of gold is coin'd;
> So, beauty in its grace
> Should be to goodness join'd."

The dramas we have liberty to select from furnish several instances of the same thought. First, from the *Two Gentlemen of Verona* (act iv. sc. 2, l. 38, vol. i. p. 135), in that exquisitely beautiful little song which answers the question, "Who is Silvia?"—

> "Who is Silvia? what is she,
> That all our swains commend her?
> Holy, fair, and wise is she;
> The heaven such grace did lend her,
> That she might admired be.
>
> Is she kind as she is fair?
> For beauty lives with kindness.
> Love doth to her eyes repair,
> To help him of his blindness,
> And, being help'd, inhabits there.
>
> Then to Silvia let us sing,
> That Silvia is excelling;
> She excels each mortal thing
> Upon the dull earth dwelling:
> To her let us garlands bring."

But a closer parallelism to Corrozet's Emblem of beauty joined to goodness occurs in *Henry VIII.* (act ii. sc. 3, lines 60 and 75, vol. vi. pp. 45, 46): it is in the soliloquy or *aside* speech of the Lord Chamberlain, who had been saying to Anne Bullen,—

> "The king's majesty
> Commends his good opinion of you, and
> Does purpose honour to you no less flowing
> Than Marchioness of Pembroke."

With perfect tact Anne meets the flowing honours, and says,—

"Vouchsafe to speak my thanks and my obedience,
As from a blushing handmaid to his highness,
Whose health and royalty I pray for."

In an *aside* the Chamberlain owns,—

"I have perused her well:
Beauty and honour in her are so mingled
That they have caught the king: and who knows yet
But from this lady may proceed a gem
To lighten all this isle?"

So on Romeo's first sight of Juliet (*Romeo and Juliet,* act i. sc. 5, l. 41, vol. vii. p. 30), her beauty and inner worth called forth the confession,—

"O, she doth teach the torches to burn bright!
It seems she hangs upon the cheek of night
Like a rich jewel in an Ethiope's ear;
Beauty too rich for use, for earth too dear."

And the Sonnet (CV. vol. ix. p. 603, l. 4) that represents love,—

"Still constant in a wondrous excellence;"

also tells us of the abiding beauty of the soul,—

"'Fair, kind, and true,' is all my argument,
'Fair, kind, and true,' varying to other words;
And in this change is my invention spent,
Three themes in one, which wondrous scope affords.
'Fair, kind, and true,' have often lived alone,
Which three till now never kept seat in one."

The power of Conscience, as the soul's bulwark against adversities, has been sung from the time when Horace wrote (*Epist.* i. 1. 60),—

"Hic murus aëneus esto,
Nil conscire sibi, nulla pallescere culpa,"—

"This be thy wall of brass, to be conscious to thyself of no shame, to become pale at no crime."

Or, in the still more popular ode (*Carm.* i. 22), which being of old recited in the palaces of Mæcenas and Augustus at Rome, has, after the flow of nearly nineteen centuries, been revived in the drawing rooms of Paris and London, and of the whole civilized world ;—

> " Integer vitæ, scelerisque purus,
> Non eget Mauris jaculis, neque arcu,
> Non venenatis gravida sagittis,
> Fusce, pharetra,"—

> " He, sound in his life, from all transgression free,
> Doth need no Moorish javelins, nor bended bow,
> Nor of arrows winged with poisons a quiver-tree,
> Fuscus, to strike his foe." *

Both these sentiments of the lyric poet have been imitated or adapted by the dramatic; as in 2 *Henry VI.* (act iii. sc. 2, l. 232, vol. v. p. 171), where the good king exclaims,—

> " What stronger breast-plate than a heart untainted !
> Thrice is he arm'd, that hath his quarrel just,
> And he but naked, though lock'd up in steel,
> Whose conscience with injustice is corrupted."

And again, in *Titus Andronicus* (act iv. sc. 2, l. 18, vol. vi. p. 492), in the words of the original, on the scroll which Demetrius picks up,—

> " *Dem.* What's here ? A scroll, and written round about !
> Let's see :
> [*Reads.*] ' Integer vitæ, scelerisque purus,
> Non eget Mauri jaculis, nec arcu.'
>
> *Chi.* O, 'tis a verse in Horace ; I know it well :
> I read it in the grammar long ago.
> *Aar.* Ay, just ; a verse in Horace ; right, you have it.
> [*Aside.*] Now, what a thing it is to be an ass !
> Here's no sound jest : the old man hath found their guilt,
> And sends them weapons wrapp'd about with lines,
> That wound, beyond their feeling, to the quick."

* For a fine Emblem to illustrate this passage, see "HORATII EMBLEMATA," by Otho Vænius, pp. 58, 59, edit. Antwerp, 4to, 1612 ; also pp. 70 and 71, to give artistic force to the idea of the "just man firm to his purpose."

Several of the Emblem writers, however, propound a sentiment not so generally known, in which Apollo's favourite tree, the Laurel, is the token of a soul unalarmed by threatening evils. Sambucus and Whitney so consider it, and illustrate it with the motto,—*The pure conscience is man's laurel tree.*

Conſcientia integra, laurus.

Sambucus, 1564.

The saying rests on the ancient persuasion that the laurel is the sign of joy, victory and safety, and that it is never struck even by the bolts of Jove. Sambucus, personifying the laurel, celebrates its praise in sixteen elegiac lines beginning,—

> "PRONA *virens cœlum ſpecto, nec fulmina terrent,*
> *Ob ſcelus excelſa quæ iacit arce pater,*" &c.

"Spread out flourishing heaven I survey, nor do lightnings terrify,
  Though for crime's sake the father hurls them from citadels on high,
Yea even with my leaves I crackle, and although burnt
  Daphne I name, whom the master's love so importuned.
So conscious virtue strengthens, and placed far from destruction
  Pleasing my state is to powers above, and long time is flourishing.
Men's voices he never fears, nor the weapons of fire,
  Who hath girded his mind round with snow-bright love.
This mind the raging Eumenides will not distress, nor the home
  For the sad and the guiltless overturn'd without cause.
Even the hoary swan worn out in inactive old age
  Gives forth admonitions, as it sings from a stifling throat;

Pure of heart with its mate conversing, it washes in water,
And morals of clearest hue in due form rehearses.
Who repents of unlawful life, and whom conscious errors
Do not oppress,—that man sings forth hymns everlasting."

These thoughts in briefer and more nervous style Whitney rehearses to the old theme, *A brazen wall, a sound conscience* (p. 67),—

Murus æneus, ſana conſcientia.

To Miles Hobart *Eſquier.*

"Bothe freshe, and greene, the Laurell standeth sounde,
Thoughe lightninges flasshe, and thunderboltes do flie:
Where, other trees are blasted to the grounde.
Yet, not one leafe of it, is withered drie:
Euen so, the man that hathe a conscience cleare.
When wicked men, doe quake at euerie blaste,
Doth constant stande, and dothe no perrilles feare,
When tempestes rage, doe make the worlde agaste:
Suche men are like vnto the Laurell tree,
The others, like the blasted boughes that die."

But a much fuller agreement with the above motto does Whitney express in the last stanza of Emblem 32,—

"A conscience cleare, is like a wall of brasse,
That dothe not shake, with euerie shotte that hittes;
Eauen soe there by, our liues wee quiet passe,
When guiltie mindes, are rack'de with fearful fittes:
Then keepe thee pure, and soile thee not with sinne,
For after guilte, thine inwarde greifes beginne."

The same property is assigned to the Laurel by Joachim Camerarius ("Ex Re Herbaria," p. 35, edition 1590). He quotes several authorities, or opinions for supposing that the laurel was not injured by lightning. Pliny, he says, supported the notion; the Emperor Tiberius in thunder storms betook himself to the shelter of the laurel; and Augustus before him did the same thing, adding as a further protection a girdle made from the skin of a sea-calf. Our modern authorities give no countenance to either of these fancies.

Now, combining the thoughts on Conscience presented by the Emblems on the subject which have been quoted, can we fail to perceive in Shakespeare, when he speaks of Conscience and its qualities, a general agreement with Sambucus, and more especially with Whitney?

How finely, in *Henry VIII.* (act iii. sc. 2, l. 372, vol. vi. p. 76), do the old Cardinal and his faithful Cromwell converse,—

"*Enter* CROMWELL, *and stands amazed.*

Wol. Why, how now, Cromwell?
Crom. I have no power to speak, sir.
Wol. What, amazed
At my misfortunes? can thy spirit wonder
A great man should decline? Nay, an you weep,
I am fall'n indeed.
Crom. How does your grace?
Wol. Why, well:
Never so truly happy, my good Cromwell.
I know myself now; and I feel within me
A peace above all earthly dignities,
A still and quiet conscience.

I am able now, methinks,
Out of a fortitude of soul I feel,
To endure more miseries and greater far
Than my weak-hearted enemies dare offer."

And, on the other hand, the stings of Conscience, the deep remorse for iniquities, the self-condemnation which lights upon the sinful, never had expounder so forcible and true to nature. When Alonso, as portrayed in the *Tempest* (act iii. sc. 3, l. 95, vol. i. p. 53), thought of his cruel treachery to his brother Prospero, he says,—

"O, it is monstrous, monstrous!
Methought the billows spoke, and told me of it;
The winds did sing it to me; and the thunder,

That deep and dreadful organ-pipe, pronounced
The name of Prosper: it did bass my trespass."

And the King's dream, on the eve of Bosworth battle (*Richard III.*, act v. sc. 3, lines 179, 193, and 200, vol. v. p. 625), what a picture it gives of the tumult of his soul!—

"O coward conscience, how dost thou affright me!

My conscience hath a thousand several tongues,
And every tongue brings in a several tale,
And every tale condemns me for a villain.

There is no creature loves me;
And, if I die, no soul shall pity me:—
Nay, wherefore should they? since that I myself,
Find in myself no pity to myself.
Methought, the souls of all that I had murder'd
Came to my tent; and everyone did threat
To-morrow's vengeance on the head of Richard."

Various expressions of the dramatist may end this notice of the Judge within us,—

"The worm of conscience still begnaw thy soul."

"Every man's conscience is a thousand swords
To fight against that bloody homicide."

"I'll haunt thee, like a wicked conscience still,
That mouldeth goblins swift as frenzy thought."

"Thus conscience doth make cowards of us all."

In some degree allied to the power of conscience is the retribution for sin ordained by the Divine Wisdom. We have not an Emblem to present in illustration, but the lines from *King Lear* (act v. sc. 3, l. 171, vol. viii. p. 416),—

"The gods are just, and of our pleasant vices
Make instruments to plague us,"—

are so co-incident with a sentiment in the *Confessions* (bk. i. c. 12, § 19) of the great Augustine that they deserve at least to be set in juxta-position. The Bishop is addressing the Supreme in prayer, and naming the sins and follies of his youth, says,—

> "*De peccanti meipso justè retribuebas mihi.* JUSISTI *enim, & sic est, ut pœna sua sibi sit omnis inordinatus animus.*"

> *i.e.* "By my own sin Thou didst justly punish me. For thou hast commanded, and so it is, that every inordinate affection should bear its own punishment."*

"*Timon of Athens*," we are informed by Dr. Drake (vol. ii. p. 447), "is an admirable satire on the folly and ingratitude of mankind; the former exemplified in the thoughtless profusion of Timon, the latter in the conduct of his pretended friends; it is, as Dr. Johnson observes,—

> "'A very powerful warning against that ostentatious liberality, which scatters bounty, but confers no benefits, and buys flattery but not friendship.'"

There is some doubt whether Shakespeare derived his idea of this play from the notices of Timon which appear in Lucian, or from those given by Plutarch. The fact, however, that the very excellent work by Sir Thomas North, Knight, *The Lives of the Noble Grecians and Romaines, &c.*, was published in 1579, —and that Shakespeare copies it very closely in the account of Timon's sepulchre and epitaph, show, I think, Plutarch to have been the source of his knowledge of Timon's character and life.

One of the Emblem writers, Sambucus, treated of the same subject in eighteen Latin elegiacs, and expressly named it, *Timon the Misanthrope.* The scene, too, which the device represents, is in a garden, and we can very readily fancy that

---

* Shakespeare illustrated by parallelisms from the Fathers of the Church might, I doubt not, be rendered very interesting and instructive by a writer of competent learning and enthusiasm, not to name it *furore*, in behalf of his subject.

the figure on the left is the old steward Flavius come to reason with his master,—

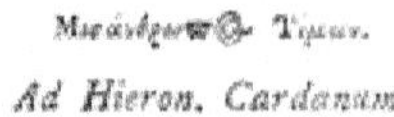

Μισάνθρωπος Τίμων.

Ad Hieron. Cardanum.

Sambucus, 1584.

ODERAT *hic cunctos, nec ſe, nec amabat amicos,*
Μισῶν ἀνθρώπους nomina digna gerens.
Hoc vitium, & morbus de bili naſcitur atra,
Anxiat hæc, curas ſuppeditatq; graues.
Quapropter cecidiſſe piro, fregiſſeq; crura
Fertur, & auxilium non petiiſſe malo.
Suauibus à ſociis, & conſuetudine dulci
Qui ſe ſubducunt, vulnera ſæua ferunt.
Conditio hæc miſera eſt, triſtes ſuſpiria ducunt,
Cumq; nihil cauſæ eſt, occubuiſſe velint.
At tu dum poteris, noto ſociere ſodali,
Subleuet vt preſſum, cordq; dolore vacet.
Quos nulla attingunt prorſus commercia grato
Atque ſodalitio, ſubſidiisq; carent:
Aut Dij ſunt proprij, aut falſus peruertit inanes
Senſus, vt hos ſtolidos, vanaq; corda putes.
Tu verò tandem nobis dialectica ſponte
Donata, in lucem mittito, ſi memor es.

In this case we have given the Latin of Sambucus in full, and append a nearly literal translation,—

"All men did he hate, nor loved himself, nor his kindred,—
One hating mankind was the name, worthy of him, he bore.
This faultiness and disease from the black bile arise,
When freely it flows heavy cares it increases.
Wherefore from a pear tree he is said to have fallen,
To have broken his legs, nor help to have sought for the evil.
From pleasant companions, and sweet conversation
They who withdraw themselves, cruel wounds have to bear.
Wretched this state of theirs, sorrowful what sighs they draw,
And though never a cause arise, 'tis their wish to have died.
But thou, while the power remains, join thy well-known companion,
Thee overwhelmed he strengthens, and free sets the heart from its grief.
Whom, with a friend that is pleasing, never intercourse touches,
Without companionship, long without assistance they remain.
Either the gods are our own, or false feeling perverteth the soul,
And you fancy men stupid, and their hearts all are vain.
To us at length reasoning power freely being granted,
Into light do thou send them, if of light thou art mindful."

The character here sketched is deficient in the thorough heartiness of hatred for which Shakespeare's Timon is distinguished, yet may it have served him for the primal material out of which to create the drama. In Sambucus there is a mistiness of thought and language which might be said almost to prefigure the doubtful utterances of some of our modern philosophers, but in Shakespeare the master himself takes in hand the pencil of true genius, and by the contrasts and harmonies, the unmistakeable delineations and portraitures, lays on the canvas a picture as rich in its colouring as it is constant in its fidelity to nature, and as perfect in its finish as it is bold in its conceptions.

The extravagance of Timon's hatred may be gathered from only a few of his expressions,—

"Burn, house! sink, Athens! henceforth hated be
Of Timon man and all humanity."

Timon of Athens, act iii. sc. 6, l. 103.

"Timon will to the woods, where he shall find
The unkindest beast more kinder than mankind.

The gods confound—hear me, you good gods all!—
The Athenians both within and out that wall!
And grant, as Timon grows, his hate may grow
To the whole race of mankind, high and low!
Amen."

Act iv. sc. 1, l. 35.

"All is oblique;
There's nothing level in our cursed natures
But direct villany. Therefore be abhorr'd
All feasts, societies and throngs of men."

Act iv. sc. 3, l. 18.

"I am misanthropos, and hate mankind.
For thy part, I do wish thou wert a dog,
That I might love thee something."

Act iv. sc. 3, l. 51.

"I never had honest man about me, I; all
I kept were knaves, to serve in meat to villains."

Act iv. sc. 3, l. 475.

And so his ungoverned passion of hatred goes on until it culminates in the epitaph placed on his tomb, which he names his "everlasting mansion,"—

"Upon the beached verge of the salt flood."

That epitaph as given by Shakespeare, from North's *Plutarch* (edition 1579, p. 1003), is almost a literal rendering from the real epitaph recorded in the Greek Anthology (Jacobs, vol. i. p. 86),—

"Ἐνθάδ' ἀποῤῥήξας ψυχὴν βαρυδαίμονα κεῖμαι,
Τοὔνομα δ' οὐ πεύσεσθε, κακοὶ δὲ κακῶς ἀπόλοισθε."

Of which a very close translation will be,—

"Here, having rent asunder a dæmon oppressed soul, I lie;
The name ye shall not inquire, but ye bad ones badly shall perish."

The epitaph of the drama (*Timon of Athens*, act v. sc. 4, l. 69, vol. vii. p. 305) is thus read by Alcibiades from the wax impression taken at the tomb,—

> "Here lies a wretched corse, of wretched soul bereft.
> Seek not my name: a plague consume you wicked caitiffs left!
> Here lie I, Timon; who, alive, all living men did hate:
> Pass by and curse thy fill: but pass and stay not here thy gait."

Plutarch * introduces a mention of Timon into the life of Marc Antony, whom he compares in some respects to the misanthrope of Athens. He gives the same epitaph as that of the Anthology above quoted, except a letter or two,—

> "Ἐνθαδ' ἀποῤῥήξας ψυχὴν βαρυδαίμονα κεῖμαι,
> Τοὔνομα δ' οὐ πεύσεσθε, κακοὶ δὲ κακῶς ἀπόλοισθε."

Plutarch avers, "*καὶ τοῦτο μὲν αὐτὸν ἔτι ζῶντα πεποιηκέναι λέγουσι,*"—"And people say that during his life he himself made this epitaph." The narrator then adds, "*τοῦτο δε περιφερόμενον, Καλλιμάχου εστι,*"—"But this round the margin is by Callimachus,"—

> "Τιμων μισάνθρωπος ἐνοικέω· ἀλλα πάρελθε
> Οἰμώζειν εἴπας πολλά, πάρελθε μόνον."

> "I, Timon the manhater dwell within: but pass by,
> To bewail *me* thou hast spoken many things;—only pass by."

The two epitaphs Shakespeare has combined into one, showing indeed his acquaintance with the above passage through North's *Plutarch*, but not discriminating the authorship of the two parts. North's translation of the epitaphs is simple and expressive, but the Langhornes, in 1770, vulgarise the lines into,—

> "At last I've bid the knaves farewell
> Ask not my name, but go to hell."

* *Opera*, vol. i. p. 649 B, Francofurti, 1620.

> "My name is Timon: knaves begone,
> Curse me, but come not near my stone."

How Wrangham, in his edition of the Langhornes, 1826, could without notice let this pass for a translation, is altogether unaccountable!

Shakespeare's, adapted as it is by Sir Thomas North in 1612, may certainly be regarded as a direct version from the Greek, and might reasonably be adduced to prove that he possessed some knowledge of that language. Probably, however, he collected, as he could, the general particulars respecting the veritable and historical Timon, and obtained the help of some man of learning so as to give the very epitaph which in the time of the Peloponnesian war had been placed on the thorn-surrounded sepulchre of the Athenian misanthrope.

To conclude this notice we may observe that [*] the breaking of the legs, which Sambucus mentions, is said to have been the actual cause of the real Timon's death; for that in his hatred of mankind he even hated himself, and would not allow a surgeon to attempt his cure.

Envy and Hatred may be considered as nearly allied, the latter too often springing from the former. Alciat, in his 71st Emblem, gives a brief description of Envy,—

> "SQVALLIDA *vipereas manducans femina carnes,*
> *Cuiq. dolent oculi, quæq. suum cor edit,*
> *Quam macies & pallor habent, spinosaq. gestat*
> *Tela manu: talis pingitur Inuidia.*"

Thus amplified with considerable force of expression by Whitney (p. 94). —

[*] Reference might be made also to Whitney's fine tale, *Concerning Envy and Avarice*, which immediately follows the *Description of Envy*.

Inuidiæ descriptio.

Whitney, 1586.

"WHAT hideous hagge with visage sterne appeares?
 Whose feeble limmes, can scarce the bodie staie:
This, Enuie is: leane, pale, and full of yeares,
Who with the blisse of other pines awaie.
 And what declares, her eating vipers broode?
 That poysoned thoughtes, bee euermore her foode.

What meanes her eies? so bleared, sore, and redd:
Her mourninge still, to see an others gaine.
And what is mente by snakes vpon her head?
The fruite that springes, of such a venomed braine.
 But whie, her harte shee rentes within her brest?
 It shewes her selfe, doth worke her owne vnrest.

Whie lookes shee wronge? bicause shee woulde not see,
An happie wight, which is to her a hell:
What other partes within this furie bee?
Her harte, with gall: her tonge, with stinges doth swell.
 And laste of all, her staffe with prickes aboundes:
 Which showes her wordes, wherewith the good shee woundes."

The dramatist speaks of the horrid creature with equal power. Among his phrases are,—

"Thou makest thy knife keen; but no metal can,

No, not the hangman's axe, bear half the keenness
Of thy sharp envy."

Merchant of Venice, act iv. sc. 1, l. 124.

"And for we think the eagle-winged pride
Of sky-aspiring and ambitious thoughts,
With rival-hating envy, set on you
To wake our peace."

Richard II., act i. sc. 3, l. 129.

"Would curses kill, as doth the mandrake's groan,
I would invent as bitter-searching terms,
As curst, as harsh and horrible to hear,
Deliver'd strongly through my fixed teeth,
With full as many signs of deadly hate,
As lean-faced Envy in her loathsome cave."

2 *Hen. VI.*, act iii. sc. 2, l. 310.

"'tis greater skill
In a true hate, to pray they have their will:
The very devils cannot plague them better."

Cymbeline, act ii. sc. 5, l. 33.

"Men that make
Envy and crooked malice nourishment
Dare bite the best."

Hen. VIII., act v. sc. 3, l. 43.

"That monster envy."

Pericles, act iv. *Introd.*, l. 12.

The ill-famed Thersites, that railer of the Grecian camp, may close the array against "the hideous hagge with visage sterne" (*Troilus and Cressida*, act ii. sc. 3, l. 18, vol. vi. p. 169),—

"I have said my prayers; and devil Envy say Amen."

The wrong done to the soul, through denying it at the last hour the consolations of religion, or through negligence in not informing it of its danger when severe illness arises, is set forth with true Shakespearean power in Holbein's

Simulachres & Historiees faces de la Mort (Lyons, 1538), on sign. Nij,—

"O si ceulx, qui font telles choses, scauoient le mal qu'ilz font, ilz ne comettroient iamais vne si grande faulte. Car de me oster mes biens, persecuter ma personne, denigrer ma renommée, ruyner ma maison, destruire mõ parẽtaige, scãdalizer ma famille, criminer ma vie, ces ouures sõt dũg cruel ennemy. Mais d'estre occasion, q̃ ie perde mõ ame, pour nõ la cõseiller au besoing, c'est vne oeuure dũg diable d'Enfer. Car pire est q̃ vng diable l'hõme, qui trompe le malade."

It is in a similar strain that Shakespeare in *Othello* (act iii. sc. 3, lines 145 and 159, vol. viii. pp. 512, 513) speaks of the wrong done by keeping back confidence, and by countenancing calumny,—

"*Oth.* Thou dost conspire against thy friend, Iago,
If thou but think'st him wrong'd and mak'st his ear
A stranger to thy thoughts.

Iago. It were not for your quiet nor your good,
Nor for my manhood, honesty, or wisdom,
To let you know my thoughts.
Oth. What dost thou mean?
Iago. Good name in man and woman, dear my lord,
Is the immediate jewel of their souls:
Who steals my purse steals trash; 'tis something, nothing;
'Twas mine, 'tis his, and has been slave to thousands;
But he that filches from me my good name
Robs me of that which not enriches him
And makes me poor indeed."

The gallant ship, courageously handled and with high soul of perseverance and fearlessness guided through adverse waves, has for long ages been the type of brave men and brave women struggling against difficulties, or of states and nations amid opposing influences battling for deliverance and victory. Even if that gallant ship fails in her voyage she becomes a fitting type, how "human affairs may decline at their highest." So Sambucus, and Whitney after him (p. 11), adapt their device and stanzas to the motto,—

Res humanæ in ſummo declinant.

Sambucus, 1564.

In medio librat Phœbus dum lumina cælo,
Diſſoluit radiis, quæ cecidere, niues.
Cùm res humanæ in ſummo ſtant, ſæpe liqueſcunt:
Et nihil æternum, quod rapit atra dies.
Nil iuuat ingentes habitare palatia Reges,
Conditio miſeros hæc eadémque manet.
Mors æquat cunctos, opibus nec parcit in horam,
Verbáque dum Volitant, ocyus illa venit.
Heu, leuiter ventus pellit nos omnis inermes,
Concidimus citiùs quàm leuat aura roſas.

"THE gallante Shipp, that cutts the azure surge,
And hathe both tide, and wisshed windes, at will:
Her tackle sure, with shotte her foes to vrge,
With Captaines boulde, and marriners of skill,
With streamers, flagges, topgallantes, pendantes braue,
When Seas do rage, is swallowed in the waue.

The snowe, that falles vppon the mountaines greate,
Though on the Alpes, which seeme the clowdes to reache,
Can not indure the force of Phœbus heate,
But wastes awaie, Experience doth vs teache:
Which warneth all, on Fortunes wheele that clime
To beare in minde how they haue but a time."

But with brighter auguries, though from a similar device, Alciat (Emb. 43) shadows forth hope for a commonwealth when dangers are threatening. A noble vessel with its sails set is tossing upon the billows, the winds, however, wafting it forward; then it is he gives utterance to the thought, *Constancy the Companion of Victory;* and thus illustrates his meaning,*—

> " By storms that are numberless our Commonwealth is shaken,
> And hope for safety in the future, hope alone is present :
> So a ship with the ocean about her, when the winds seize her,
> Gapes with wide fissures 'mid the treacherous waters.
> What of help, the shining stars, brothers of Helen, can bring :
> To spirits cast down good hope soon doth restore."

Whitney (p. 37), from the same motto and device, almost with a clarion's sound, re-echoes the thought,—

Conſtantia comes victoriæ.

To MILES CORBET *Eſquier.*

Whitney, 1586.

> "THE shippe, that longe vppon the sea dothe saile,
> And here, and there, with varrijng windes is toste :
> On rockes, and sandes, in daunger ofte to quaile,
> Yet at the lengthe, obtaines the wished coaste :
> Which beinge wonne, the trompetts ratlinge blaste,
> Dothe teare the skie, for ioye of perills paste.

* The original lines are,—

> " INNVMERIS *agitur Respublica nostra procellis,*
> *Et spes venturæ sola salutis adest :*
> *Non secus ac navis medio circum æquore, venti,*
> *Quam rapiunt; salsis iamq. fatiscit aquis.*
> *Quod si Helenæ adveniant lucentia sidera fratres:*
> *Amissos animos spes bona restituit."*

Thoughe master reste, thoughe Pilotte take his ease,
Yet nighte, and day, the ship her course dothe keepe :
So, whilst that man dothe saile theise worldlie seas,
His voyage shortes : althoughe he wake, or sleepe.
And if he keepe his course directe, he winnes
That wished porte, where lastinge ioye beginnes."

To a similar purport is the "FINIS CORONAT OPVS,"—*The end crowns the work*,—of Otho Vænius (p. 108), if perchance Shakespeare may have seen it. Cupid is watching a sea-tossed ship, and appears to say,—

"*Ni ratis optatum varijs iactata procellis*
Obtineat portum, tum perijsse puta.
Futilis est diuturnus amor, ni in fine triumphet,
Nam benè cœpit opus, qui benè finit opus."

i.e. "Unless the raft though tossed by various storms
The port desired obtains, think that it perishes ;
Vain is the daily love if it no triumph forms,
For well he work begins, who well work finishes."

Thus, however, rendered at the time into English and Italian,—

"*Where the end is good all is good.*"

"The ship toste by the waues doth to no purpose saile,
Vnlesse the porte shee gayn whereto her cours doth tend.
Right so th' euent of loue appeereth in the end,
For losse it is to loue and neuer to preuaile."

"Il fine corona l'opere."

"*Inutile è la naue, che in mar vaga*
Senza prender giamai l'amato porto :
Impiagato d'Amor quel cor' è à torto,
Che con vano sperar mai non s'appaga."

Messin in his translation of Boissard's *Emblems* (edition 1588, p. 24), takes the motto, "AV NAVIRE AGITÉ *semble le jour de l'homme*," and dilates into four stanzas the neatly expressed single stanza of the original.

"*Vita hæc est tanquam pelago commissa carina,*
Instanti semper proxima naufragio.
Optima res homini est non nasci: proxima, si te
Nasci fata velent, quàm citò posse mori."

i.e. "This life is as a keel entrusted to the sea,
Ever to threatening shipwreck nearest.
Not to be born for man is best; next, if to thee
The fates give birth, quick death is dearest."

Shakespeare takes up these various ideas of which the ship in storm and in calm is typical, and to some of them undoubtedly gives utterance from the lips of the dauntless Margaret of Anjou (3 *Henry VI.*, act v. sc. 4, l. 1, vol. v. p. 325),—

"Great lords, wise men ne'er sit and wail their loss,
But cheerly seek how to redress their harms.
What though the mast be now blown overboard,
The cable broke, our holding-anchor lost,
And half our sailors swallow'd in the flood?
Yet lives our pilot still: Is't meet that he
Should leave the helm and like a fearful lad
With tearful eyes add water to the sea
And give more strength to that which hath too much:
Whiles, in his moan, the ship splits on the rock,
Which industry and courage might have saved?
Ah, what a shame! ah, what a fault were this!
Say, Warwick was our anchor; what of that?
And Montague our top-mast; what of him?
Our slaughter'd friends the tackles; what of these?
Why, is not Oxford here another anchor?
And Somerset another goodly mast?
The friends of France our shrouds and tacklings?
And, though unskilful, why not Ned and I
For once allow'd the skilful pilot's charge?
We will not from the helm to sit and weep,
But keep our course, though the rough wind say,—no,
From shelves and rocks that threaten us with wreck.
As good to chide the waves as speak them fair.
And what is Edward but a ruthless sea?
What Clarence but a quicksand of deceit?
And Richard but a rugged fatal rock?

All these the enemies to our poor bark.
Say, you can swim; alas, 'tis but a while:
Tread on the sand; why, there you quickly sink:
Bestride the rock; the tide will wash you off,
Or else you famish; that's a threefold death.
This speak I, lords, to let you understand,
If case some one of you would fly from us,
That there's no hoped-for mercy with the brothers
More than with ruthless waves, with sands and rocks.
Why, courage then! what cannot be avoided
'Twere childish weakness to lament or fear."

Well did the bold queen merit the outspoken praises of her son,—

"Methinks, a woman of this valiant spirit
Should, if a coward heard her speak these words,
Infuse his breast with magnanimity,
And make him, naked, foil a man at arms."

And in a like strain, when Agamemnon would show that the difficulties of the ten years' siege of Troy were (l. 20),—

"But the protractive trials of great Jove
To find persistive constancy in men;"

the venerable Nestor, in *Troilus and Cressida* (act i. sc. 3, l. 33, vol. vi. p. 142), enforces the thought by adding,—

"In the reproof of chance
Lies the true proof of men: the sea being smooth,
How many shallow bauble boats dare sail
Upon her patient breast, making their way
With those of nobler bulk!
But let the ruffian Boreas once enrage
The gentle Thetis, and anon behold
The strong-ribb'd bark through liquid mountains cut,
Bounding between the two moist elements
Like Perseus' horse.

Even so
Doth valour's show and valour's worth divide

In storms of fortune: for in her ray and brightness
The herd hath more annoyance by the breese
Than by the tiger; but when the splitting wind
Makes flexible the knees of knotted oaks,
And flies fled under shade, why then the thing of courage
As roused with rage with rage doth sympathize,
And with an accent tuned in selfsame key
Retorts to chiding fortune."

To the same great sentiments Georgette Montenay's "EMBLEMES CHRESTIENNES" (Rochelle edition, p. 11) supplies a very suitable illustration; it is to the motto, *Quem timebo?*—"Whom shall I fear?"—

"*Du grand peril des vens & de la mer,*
C'est homme a bien cognoissance très claire,
Et ne craind point de se voir abismer
Rusque son Dieu l'adresse et luy esclaire."

The device itself is excellent,—a single mariner on a tempestuous sea, undaunted in his little skiff; and the hand of Providence, issuing from a cloud, holds out to him a beacon light.

"On a student entangled in love," is the subject of Alciat's 108th Emblem. The lover appears to have been a jurisconsult, whom Alciat, himself a jurisconsult, represents,—

"Immersed in studies, in oratory and right well skilled,
And great especially in all the processes of law,
Haliarina he loves; as much as ever loved
The Thracian prince his sister's beauteous maid.
Why in Cyprus dost thou overcome Pallas by another judge?
Sufficient is it not to conquer at Mount Ida?"

The unfinished thoughts of Alciat are brought out more completely by Whitney, who thus illustrates his subject (p. 135),—

In studiosum captum amore.

Whitney, 1586.

> "A Reuerend sage, of wisedome most profounde,
> Beganne to doate, and laye awaye his bookes :
> For CVPID then, his tender harte did wounde,
> That onlie nowe, he lik'de his ladies lookes ?
> Oh VENVS staie ? since once the price was thine,
> Thou ought'st not still, at PALLAS thus repine."

Note, now, how the thoughts of the Emblematists, though greatly excelled in the language which clothes them, are matched by the avowals which the severe and grave Angelo made to himself in *Measure for Measure* (act ii. sc. 4, l. 1, vol. i. p. 327). He had been disposed to carry out against another the full severity of the law, which he now felt himself inclined to infringe, but confesses,—

> "When I would pray and think, I think and pray
> To several subjects. Heaven hath my empty words :
> Whilst my invention, hearing not my tongue,
> Anchors on Isabel : Heaven in my mouth,
> As if I did but only chew his name ;
> And in my heart the strong and swelling evil
> Of my conception. The state, whereon I studied,
> Is like a good thing, being often read,
> Grown fear'd and tedious ; yea, my gravity,
> Wherein—let no man hear me—I take pride,

Could I with boot change for an idle plume,
Which the air beats for vain. O place, O form,
How often dost thou with thy case, thy habit,
Wrench awe from fools, and tie the wiser souls
To thy false seeming! Blood, thou art blood:
Let's write good angel on the devil's horn;
'Tis not the devil's crest."

But the entire force of this parallelism in thought is scarcely to be apprehended, unless we mark Angelo's previous conflict of desire and judgment. Isabel utters the wish, "Heaven keep your honour safe!" And after a hearty "Amen," the old man confesses to himself (p. 324),—

"For I am that way going to temptation,
Where prayers cross."

Act ii. sc. 2, l. 158.

"What's this, what's this? Is this her fault or mine?
The tempter or the tempted, who sins most?
Ha!
Not she; nor doth she tempt: but it is I
That, lying by the violet in the sun,
Do as the carrion does, not as the flower,
Corrupt with virtuous season. Can it be
That modesty may more betray our sense
Than woman's lightness."

Act ii. sc. 2, l. 162.

"What, do I love her,
That I desire to hear her speak again,
And feast upon her eyes? What is't I dream on?
O cunning enemy, that, to catch a saint,
With saints dost bait thy hook! Most dangerous
Is that temptation that doth goad us on
To sin in loving virtue."

Act ii. sc. 2, l. 177.

There is an Emblem by Whitney (p. 131), which, though in some respects similar to one at p. 178 of the "Pegma" by Costalius, 1555, entitled "Iron," "on the misery of the human lot," is to a very great degree his own, and which makes it appear in a stronger light than usual, that a close resemblance exists between his ideas and even expressions and those of Shakespeare. The subject is "Writings remain," and the device the overthrow of stately buildings, while books continue unharmed.

Scripta manent.

To Sir ARTHVRE MANWARINGE *Knight.*

Whitney, 1586.

"IF mightie TROIE, with gates of steele, and brasse,
Bee worne awaie, with tracte of stealinge time:
If CARTHAGE, raste: if THEBES be growne with grasse.
If BABEL stoope: that to the cloudes did clime:
If ATHENS, and NVMANTIA suffered spoile:
If ÆGYPT spires, be euened with the soile.

Then, what maye laste, which time dothe not impeache.
Since that wee see, theise monumentes are gone:
Nothinge at all, but time doth ouer reache,
It eates the steele, and weares the marble stone:
But writinges laste, thoughe yt doe what it can,
And are preseru'd, euen since the worlde began.

And so they shall, while that they same dothe laste,
Which haue declar'd, and shall to future age:
What thinges before three thousande yeares haue paste,
What martiall knightes, haue march'd vppon this stage:
Whose actes, in bookes if writers did not saue,
Their fame had ceaste, and gone with them to graue.

Of SAMSONS strengthe, of worthie IOSVAS might.
Of DAVIDS actes, of ALEXANDERS force.
Of CÆSAR greate ; and SCIPIO noble knight,
Howe shoulde we speake, but bookes thereof discourse :
Then fauour them, that learne within their youthe :
But loue them beste, that learne, and write the truthe."

La vie de Memoire, and *Viue ut viuas*,—"Live that you may live,"—emblematically set forth by pen, and book, and obelisk, and ruined towers, in Boissard's *Emblems* by Messin (1588, pp. 40, 41), give the same sentiment, and in the Latin by a few brief lines,—

"*Non omnis vivit, vitâ qui spirat in istâ :*
Sed qui post fati funera vivit adhuc :
Et cui posteritas famæ præconia servat
Æternum is, calamo vindice, nomen habet."

Thus having the main idea taken up in the last of the four French stanzas,—

" Mais qui de ses vertus la plume a pour garand :
Celuy contre le temps invincible se rend :
Car elle vainc du temps & l'effort, & l'injure."

In various instances, only with greater strength and beauty, Shakespeare gives utterance to the same sequences of thought. When, in *Love's Labour's Lost* (act i. sc. 1, l. 1, vol. ii. p. 97), fashioning his court to be,—

"A little Academe,
Still and contemplative in living art,"

Ferdinand, king of Navarre, proclaims,—

"Let Fame, that all hunt after in their lives,
Live register'd upon our brazen tombs,
And then grace us in the disgrace of death ;
When, spite of cormorant devouring Time,
The endeavour of this present breath may buy
That honour which shall bate his scythe's keen edge,
And make us heirs of all eternity."

In his Sonnets, more especially, Shakespeare celebrates the enduring glory of the mind's treasures. Thus, the 55th Sonnet (*Works*, vol. ix. p. 578) is written almost as Whitney wrote,—

> "Not marble, nor the gilded monuments
> Of princes, shall outlive this powerful rhyme;
> But you shall shine more bright in these contents,
> Than unswept stone, besmear'd with sluttish lime.
> When wasteful war shall statues overturn,
> And broils root out the work of masonry,
> Nor Mars his sword, nor war's quick fire shall burn
> The living record of your memory.
> 'Gainst death and all-oblivious enmity,
> Shall you pace forth; your praise shall still find room,
> Even in the eyes of all posterity
> That wear this world out to the ending doom.
> So, till the judgment that yourself arise,
> You live in this, and dwell in lovers' eyes."

But the 65th Sonnet (p. 583) is still more in accordance with Whitney's ideas,—not a transcript of them, but an appropriation,—

> "Since brass, nor stone, nor earth, nor boundless sea,
> But sad mortality o'ersways their power,
> How with this rage shall beauty hold a plea,
> Whose action is no stronger than a flower?
> O how shall summer's honey breath hold out
> Against the wreckful siege of battering days,
> When rocks impregnable are not so stout,
> Nor gates of steel so strong, but Time decays?
> O fearful meditation! where, alack!
> Shall Time's best jewel from Time's chest lie hid?
> Or what strong hand can hold his swift foot back?
> Or who his spoil of beauty can forbid?
> No one, unless this miracle have might,
> That in black ink my love may still shine bright."

How closely, too, are these thoughts allied to some in that Emblem (p. 197) in which Whitney, following Hadrian Junius, so well celebrates "the eternal glory of the pen."

Pennæ gloria immortalis.

Ad Iacobum Blondelium.

Junius, 1565.*

He has been telling of Sidney's praise, and in a well-turned compliment to him and to his other friend, "EDWARDE DIER," makes the award,—

"This Embleme lo, I did present, vnto this woorthie Knight.
Who, did the same refuse, as not his proper due :
And at the first, his sentence was, it did belonge to you.
Wherefore, lo, fame with trompe, that mountes vnto the skye :
And, farre aboue the highest spire, from pole, to pole dothe flye,
Heere houereth at your will, with pen adorn'd with baies :
Which for you bothe, shee hath prepar'd, vnto your endlesse praise.
The laurell leafe for you, for him, the goulden pen ;
The honours that the Muses giue, vnto the rarest men.
Wherefore, proceede I praye, vnto your lasting fame ;
For writinges last when wee bee gonne, and doe preserue our name.
And whilst wee tarrye heere, no treasure can procure,
The palme that waites vpon the pen, which euer doth indure.

* The original lines by Hadrian Junius are,—

"*Oculata, pennis fulta, sublimem vehens*
Calamum aurea inter astra Fama collocat.
Illustre claris surgit è scriptis decus,
Feritque perpes vertice alta sidera."

Two thousand yeares, and more, HOMERVS wrat his booke ;
And yet, the same doth still remayne, and keepes his former looke.
Wheare Ægypte spires bee gonne, and ROME doth ruine feele,
Yet, both begonne since he was borne, thus time doth turne the wheele.
Yea, thoughe some Monarche greate some worke should take in hand,
Of marble, or of Adamant, that manie worldes shoulde stande,
Yet, should one only man, with labour of the braine,
Bequeathe the world a monument, that longer shoulde remaine,
And when that marble waules, with force of time should waste ;
It should indure from age, to age, and yet no age should taste."

"EX MALO BONUM,"—*Good out of evil*,—contains a sentiment which Shakespeare not unfrequently expresses. An instance occurs in the *Midsummer Night's Dream* (act i. sc. 1, l. 232, vol. ii. p. 206),—

"Things base and vile, holding no quantity,
Love can transpose to form and dignity."

Also more plainly in *Henry V.* (act iv. sc. 1, l. 3, vol. iv. p. 555),—

"God Almighty !
There is some soul of goodness in things evil,
Would men observingly distil it out.
For our bad neighbour makes us early stirrers,
Which is both healthful and good husbandry :
Besides they are our outward consciences,
And preachers to us all, admonishing
That we should dress us fairly for our end.
Thus we may gather honey from the weed,
And make a moral of the devil himself !"

So in Georgette Montenay's *Christian Emblems* we find the stanzas,—

"*On tire bien des epines poignantes*
Rose tres bonnę & pleine de beauté.
Des reprouuer & leurs œuures meschantes
Dieu tirę aussi du bien par sa bonté,
Faisant seruir leur fausse volonté
A sa grand' gloirę & salut des esleuz,
Et par iusticę, ainsi qu' a decreté,
Dieu fait tout bien ; que nul n'en doute plus."

As we have mentioned before (pp. 242, 3), Ovid's *Metamorphoses* are the chief source to which, from his time downwards, poets in general have applied for their most imaginative and popular mythic illustrations; and to him especially have Emblem writers been indebted. For a fact so well known a single instance will suffice; it is the description of Chaos and of the Creation of the World (bk. i. fab. 1),—

> "Ante mare et terras, et quod tegit omnia, cœlum,
> Unus erat toto naturæ vultus in orbe,
> Quem dixère Chaos: rudis indigestaque moles."

An early Italian Emblematist, Gabriel Symeoni, in 1559, presents on this subject the following very simple device in his *Vita et Metamorfosco d'Ovidio* (p. 12), accompanied on the next page by "The creation and confusion of the world,"—

Il Caos.

Symeoni, 1559.

> "*Prima fuit rerum confusa sine ordine moles,*
> *Vnaq. erat facies sydera, terra, fretum.*"

i.e. "First was there a confused mass of things without order,
And one appearance was stars, earth, sea."

But Ovid's lines are applied in a highly figurative sense, to show the many evils and disorders of injustice. A wild state where wrong triumphs and right is unknown,—that is the Chaos which Anulus sets forth in his "PICTA POESIS" (p. 49); *Without justice, confusion.*

SINE IVSTITIA, CONFVSIO.

Aneau, 1555.

SI TERRAE *Cœlum ſemiſceat: & mare cælo.*
Sol Erebo. Tenebris lumina, Terra Polo.
Quattuor & Mundi mixtim primordia pugnent.
Arida cum ſiccis, algida cum calidis.
In Chaos antiquum omnia denique confundantur:
Vt cùm ignotus adhuc mens Deus orbis erat.
Eſt Mundanarum talis confuſio rerum.
Quo Regina latet Tempore Iuſtitia.

i.e. "If with earth heaven should mingle and the sea with heaven,
The sun with Erebus, light with darkness, the earth with the pole,
Should the four elements of the world in commixture fight,
Dry things with the moist and cold things with the hot,
Into ancient chaos at last all things would be confounded
As when God as yet unknown was the soul of the globe.
Such is the confusion of all mundane affairs,
At what time soever Justice the queen lies concealed."

Whitney (p. 122), borrowing this idea and extending it, works it out with more than his usual force and skill, and dedicates his stanzas to Windham and Flowerdewe, two eminent judges of Elizabeth's reign,—but his amplification of the thought is to a great degree peculiar to himself. Ovid, indeed, is his authority for representing the elements in wild disorder, and the peace and the beauty which ensued,—

"When they weare dispos'd, eache one into his roome."

The motto, dedication, and device, are these,—

Sine iustitia, confusio.

Ad eosdem Iudices.

Whitney, 1566.

"WHEN Fire, and Aire, and Earthe, and Water, all weare one :
Before that worke deuine was wroughte, which nowe wee looke vppon.
There was no forme of thinges, but a confused masse :
A lumpe, which CHAOS men did call : wherein no order was.
The Coulde, and Heate, did striue : the Heauie thinges, and Lighte.
The Harde, and Softe. the Wette, and Drye. for none had shape arighte.
But when they weare dispos'd, eache one into his roome :
The Fire, had Heate : the Aire, had Lighte : the Earthe, with fruites did bloome.
The Sea, had his increase : which thinges, to passe thus broughte :
Behoulde, of this vnperfecte masse, the goodly worlde was wroughte."

Whitney then celebrates "The goulden worlde that Poettes praised moste ;" next, "the siluer age :" and afterwards, "the age of brasse."

"The Iron age was laste, a fearefull cursed tyme :
Then, armies came of mischiefes in : and fil'd the worlde with cryme.
Then rigor, and reuenge, did springe in euell hower :
And men of mighte, did manadge all, and poore opprest with power.

And hee, that mightie was, his worde, did stand for lawe :
And what the poore did ploughe, and sowe : the ritch away did drawe.
None mighte their wiues inioye, their daughters, or their goodes,
No, not their liues : such tyraunts broode, did seeke to spill their bloodes.
Then vertues weare defac'd, and dim'd with vices vile,
Then wronge, did maske in cloke of righte : then bad, did good exile.
Then falshood, shadowed truthe : and hate, laugh'd loue to skorne :
Then pitie, and compassion died : and bloodshed fowle was borne.
So that no vertues then, their proper shapes did beare :
Nor coulde from vices bee decern'd, so straunge they mixed weare.
That nowe, into the worlde, an other CHAOS came :
But GOD, that of the former heape : the heauen and earthe did frame.
And all thinges plac'd therein, his glorye to declare :
Sente IVSTICE downe vnto the earthe : such loue to man hee bare.
Who, so suruay'd the world, with such an heauenly vewe :
That quickley vertues shee aduanc'd : and vices did subdue.
And, of that worlde did make, a paradice, of blisse :
By which wee doo inferre : That where this sacred Goddes is.
That land doth florishe still, and gladnes, their doth growe :
Bicause that all, to God, and Prince, by her their dewties knowe.
And where her presence wantes, there ruine raignes, and wracke :
And kingdomes can not longe indure, that doe this ladie lacke.
Then happie England most, where IVSTICE is embrac'd :
And eeke so many famous men, within her chaire are plac'd."

With the description thus given we may with utmost appropriateness compare Shakespeare's noble commendation of order and good government, into which, by way of contrast, he introduces the evils and miseries of lawless power. The argument is assigned to Ulysses, in the *Troilus and Cressida* (act i. sc. 3, l. 75, vol. vi. p. 144), when the great chieftains, Agamemnon, Nestor, Menelaus, and others are discussing the state and prospects of their Grecian confederacy against Troy. With great force of reasoning, as of eloquence, he contends,—

"Troy, yet upon his basis, had been down,
And the great Hector's sword had lack'd a master,
But for these instances.

The specialty of rule hath been neglected :
And, look, how many Grecian tents do stand
Hollow upon this plain, so many hollow factions.
When that the general is not like the hive,
To whom the foragers shall all repair,
What honey is expected? Degree being vizarded,
The unworthiest shows as fairly in the mask.
The heavens themselves, the planets and this centre,
Observe degree, priority and place,
Insisture, course, proportion, season, form,
Office and custom, in all line of order :
And therefore is the glorious planet Sol
In noble eminence enthroned and sphered
Amidst the other ;

. .

but when the planets
In evil mixture to disorder wander,
What plagues and what portents, what mutiny,
What raging of the sea, shaking of earth,
Commotion in the winds, frights, changes, horrors,
Divert and crack, rend and deracinate
The unity and married calm of states
Quite from their fixure! O, when degree is shaked,
Which is the ladder to all high designs,
Then enterprise is sick! How could communities,
Degrees in schools and brotherhoods in cities,
Peaceful commerce from dividable shores,
The primogenitive and due of birth,
Prerogative of age, crowns, sceptres, laurels,
But by degree, stand in authentic place?
Take but degree away, untune that string,
And, hark, what discord follows! each thing meets
In mere oppugnancy : The bounded waters
Should lift their bosoms higher than the shores,
And make a sop of all this solid globe :
Strength should be lord of imbecility,
And the rude son should strike his father dead :
Force should be right ; or rather, right and wrong,
Between whose endless jar justice resides,
Should lose their names, and so should justice too.
Then everything includes itself in power,
Power into will, will into appetite ;
And appetite, an universal wolf,

So doubly seconded with will and power,
Must make perforce an universal prey,
And last eat up himself. Great Agamemnon,
This chaos, when degree is suffocate,
Follows the choking.
And this neglection of degree it is
That by a pace goes backward, with a purpose
It hath to climb. The general's disdain'd
By him one step below; he, by the next;
That next by him beneath: so every step,
Exampled by the first pace that is sick
Of his superior, grows to an envious fever
Of pale and bloodless emulation:
And 'tis this fever that keeps Troy on foot,
Not her own sinews. To end a tale of length,
Troy in our weakness stands, not in her strength."

At a hasty glance the two passages may appear to have little more connection than that of similarity of subject, leading to several coincidences of expression; but the Emblem of Chaos, given by Whitney, represents the winds, the waters, the stars of heaven, all in confusion mingling, and certainly is very suggestive of the exact words which the dramatic poet uses,—

"What raging of the sea? shaking of earth?
Commotion in the winds?
. . . .
The bounded waters
Should lift their bosoms higher than the shores,
And make a sop of all this solid globe."

Discord as one of the great causes of confusion is also spoken of with much force (1 *Henry VI.*, act iv. sc. 1, l. 188, vol. v. p. 68),—

"No simple man that sees
This jarring discord of nobility,
This should'ring of each other in the court,
This factious bandying of their favourites,

> But that he doth presage some ill event.
> 'Tis much, when sceptres are in children's hands;
> But more when envy breeds unkind division;
> There comes the ruin, there begins confusion."

The Paris edition of Horapollo's *Hieroglyphics*, 1551, subjoins several to which there is no Greek text (pp. 217—223). Among them (at p. 219) is one that figures, *The thread of life*, a common poetic idea.

Horapollo, ed. 1551.

Quo pacto mortem seu hominis exitum.

Hominis exitum innuentes, fusum pingebant, & fili extremum resectum, quasi à colo diuulsum, finguntur siquidem à poetis Parcæ hominis vitam nere: Clotho quidem colum gestans: Lachesis quæ Sors exponitur, nens: Atropos verò inconuertibilis seu inexorabilis Latinè redditur, filum abrumpens.

The question is asked, "How do they represent the death or end of man?" Thus answered,—"To intimate the end of man they paint a spindle, and the end of the thread cut off, as if broken from the distaff: so indeed by the poets the Fates are feigned to spin the life of man: Clotho indeed bearing the distaff; Lachesis spinning whatever lot is declared; but

Atropos, breaking the thread, is rendered unchangeable and inexorable."

This thread of life Prospero names when he speaks to Ferdinand (*Tempest*, act iv. sc. 1, l. 1, vol. i. p. 54) about his daughter,—

> "If I have too austerely punish'd you,
> Your compensation makes amends; for I
> Have given you here a thread* of mine own life
> Or that for which I live."

"Their thread of life is spun," occurs in 2 *Henry VI.* (act iv. sc. 2, l. 27).

So the "aunchient Pistol," entreating Fluellen to ask a pardon for Bardolph (*Henry V.*, act iii. sc. 6, l. 44, vol. iv. p. 544), says,—

> "The duke will hear thy voice;
> And let not Bardolph's vital thread be cut
> With edge of penny cord and vile reproach.
> Speak, captain, for his life, and I will thee requite.

The full application of the term, however, is given by Helena in the *Pericles* (act i. sc. 2, l. 102, vol. ix. p. 325), when she says to the Prince of Tyre,—

> "Antiochus you fear,
> And justly too, I think, you fear the tyrant,
> Who either by public war or private treason
> Will take away your life.
> Therefore, my lord, go travel for a while,
> Till that his rage and anger be forgot,
> Or till the Destinies do cut his thread of life."

The same appendix to Horapollo's *Hieroglyphics* (p. 220) assigns a burning lamp as the emblem of life; thus,—

* "A third," in the modern sense of the word, is just nonsense, and therefore we leave the reading of the Cambridge edition, and abide by those critics who tell us that thread was formerly spelt thrid or third. See Johnson and Steevens' *Shakspeare*, vol. i. ed. 1785, p. 92.

Horapollo, ed. 1551.

Quo modo vitam.

Vitam innuentes ardentem lampada pingebant: quòd tantisper dum accensa lampas est, luceat, extincta verò tenebras offundat. ita & anima corpore soluta, & aspectu & luce caremus.

"To intimate life they paint a burning lamp; because so long as the lamp is kindled it gives forth light, but being extinguished spreads darkness; so also the soul being freed from the body we are without seeing and light."

This Egyptian symbol Cleopatra names just after Antony's death (*Antony and Cleopatra*, act iv. sc. 15, l. 84, vol. ix. p. 132),—

> "Ah, women, women, look
> Our lamp is spent, it's out."

Similar the meaning when Antony said (act iv. sc. 14, l. 46, vol. ix. p. 123),—

> "Since the torch is out,
> Lie down and stray no farther."

Of the Emblems which depict moral qualities and æsthetical principles, scarcely any are more expressive than that which denotes an abiding sense of injury. This we can trace through Whitney (p. 183) to the French of Claude Paradin (fol. 160), and to the Italian of Gabriel Symeoni (p. 24). It is a sculptor, with mallet and chisel, cutting a memorial of his wrongs into a block of marble; the title, *Of offended Poverty*, and the motto, "Being wronged he writes on marble."

DI POVERTA
OFFESA.

Giovio and Symeoni, 1562.

Scribit in marmore læsus.

Tempri l' ira veloce ogniun, che viue.
Et per esser potente non ha cura,
Di far' altrui talhor danno o paura,
Che l' offeso l'ingiuria in marmo scriue.

Like the other "Imprese" of the "TETRASTICHI MORALI," the woodcut is surrounded by a curiously ornamented border, and manifests much artistic skill. The stanza is,—

"Each one that lives may be swift passion's slave,
And through a powerful will at times delight
In causing others harm and terror's fright:
The injured doth those wrongs on marble grave."

The "DEVISES HEROIQVES" adds to the device a simple prose description of the meaning of the Emblem,—

Scribit in marmore lesus.

Paradin, 1562.

Certains fols euentés s' asseurans trop sus leur credit & richesses, ne font point cas d'iniurier ou gourmander de faict & de paroles vne pauure personne, estimans que a faute de biens, de faueur, de parens, ou d'amis elle n'aura jamais le moyen de se venger, ou leur rēdre la pareille, ains qu'elle doiue bien tost oublier le mal qu'elle a receu. Or combien ces Tirans (c'est leur propre nom) soyent abusez de leur grande folie & ignorance, l'occasion & le temps le leur fera a la fin connoistre, apres les auoir admonestez par ceste Deuise d'vn homme assis, qui graue en vn tableau de marbre ce qu'il a en memoire auec ces parolles : Scribit in marmore læsus. (f. 160.)

The word here propounded is of very high antiquity. The prophet Jeremiah (xvii. 1 and 13) set forth most forcibly what Shakespeare names "men's evil manners living in brass;" and Whitney, "harms graven in marble hard." "The sin of Judah is written with a pen of iron, and with the point of a diamond: it is graven upon the table of their heart, and upon the horns of your altars." And the writing in water, or in the dust, is in the very spirit of the declaration, "They that depart from me shall be written in the earth,"—*i.e.*, the first wind that blows over them shall efface their names,—"because they have forsaken the LORD, the fountain of living waters."

Some of Shakespeare's expressions,—some of the turns of thought, when he is speaking of injuries,—are so similar to those used by the Emblem writers in treating of the same subject, that we reasonably conclude "the famous Scenicke Poet, Master W. Shakespeare," was intimate with their works, or with the work of some one out of their number; and, as will appear in a page or two, very probably those expressions and turns of thought had their origin in the reading of Whitney's *Choice of Emblemes* rather than in the study of the French and Italian authors.

Of the same cast of idea with the lines illustrative of *Scribit in marmore læsus*, are the words of Marc Antony's oration over Cæsar (*Julius Cæsar*, act iii. sc. 2, l. 73, vol. vii. p. 375),—

> "I come to bury Cæsar, not to praise him.
> The evil that men do lives after them;
> The good is oft interred with their bones;
> So let it be with Cæsar."

A sentiment, almost the converse of this, and of higher moral excellence, crops out where certainly we should not expect to find it—in the *Timon of Athens* (act iii. sc. 5, l. 31, vol. vii. p. 254),—

> "He's truly valiant that can wisely suffer
> The worst that man can breathe, and make his wrongs
> His outsides, to wear them like his raiment, carelessly,
> And ne'er prefer his injuries to his heart,
> To bring it into danger.
> If wrongs be evils and enforce us kill,
> What folly 'tis to hazard life for ill!"

In that scene of unparalleled beauty, tenderness, and simplicity, in which there is related to Queen Katharine the death of "the great child of honour," as she terms him, Cardinal Wolsey (*Henry VIII.*, act iv. sc. 2, l. 27, vol. vi. p. 87), Griffith describes him as,—

> "Full of repentance,
> Continual meditations, tears and sorrows,
> He gave his honours to the world again,
> His blessed part to heaven, and slept in peace."

And just afterwards (l. 44), when the Queen had been speaking with some asperity of the Cardinal's greater faults, Griffith remonstrates,—

> "Noble Madam,
> Men's evil manners live in brass; their virtues
> We write in water. May it please your highness
> To hear me speak his good now?"

How very like to the sentiment here enunciated is that of Whitney (p. 183),—

> "In marble harde our harmes wee alwayes graue,
> Bicause, wee still will beare the same in minde :
> In duste wee write the benifittes wee haue,
> Where they are soone defaced with the winde.
> So, wronges wee houlde, and neuer will forgiue,
> And soone forget, that still with vs shoulde liue."

Lavinia's deep wrongs (*Titus Andronicus*, act iv. sc. 1, l. 85, vol. vi. p. 490) were written by her on the sand, to inform Marcus and Titus what they were and who had inflicted them ; and Marcus declares,—

> "There is enough written upon this earth
> To stir a mutiny in the mildest thoughts
> And arm the minds of infants to exclaims."

Marcus is for instant revenge, but Titus knows the power and cruel nature of their enemies, and counsels (l. 102),—

> "You are a young huntsman, Marcus ; let alone ;
> And, come, I will go get a leaf of brass,
> And with a gad of steel will write these words,
> And lay it by : the angry northern wind
> Will blow these sands, like Sibyl's leaves, abroad,
> And where's your lesson then ?"

The Italian and French Emblems as pictures to be looked at would readily supply Shakespeare with thoughts respecting the record of "men's evil manners," and of "their virtues," but there is a closer correspondence between him and Whitney ; and allowing for the easy substitution of "brass" and of "water" for "marble" and "dust," the parallelism of the ideas and words is so exact as to be only just short of being complete.

We must not, however, conceal what may have been a common origin of the sentiment for all the four writers,—for the three Emblematists and for the dramatist, namely, a sentence written by Sir Thomas More, about the year 1516, before even Alciatus had published his book of Emblems. Dr. Percy, as quoted by Ayscough (p. 695), remarks that, "This reflection bears a great resemblance to a passage in Sir Thomas More's *History of Richard III.*, where, speaking of the ungrateful turns which Jane Shore experienced from those whom she had served in her prosperity, More adds, 'Men use, if they have an evil turne, to write it in marble, and whoso doth us a good turne, we write it in duste.'"

But the thought is recorded as passing through the mind of Columbus, when, during mutiny, sickness, and cruel tidings from home, he had, on the coast of Panama, the vision which Irving describes and records. A voice had been reproving him, but ended by saying, "Fear not, Columbus, all these tribulations are written in marble, and are not without cause."

"To write in dust," however, has sometimes a simple literal meaning in Shakespeare; as when King Edward (3 *Henry VI.*, act v. sc. 1, l. 54, vol. v. p. 319), uses the threat,—

> "This hand, fast wound about thy coal-black hair,
> Shall, while thy head is warm and new cut off,
> Write in the dust this sentence with thy blood,—
> Wind-changing Warwick now can change no more."

But in the *Titus Andronicus* (act iii. sc. 1, l. 12, vol. vi. p. 472), the phrase is of doubtful meaning: it may denote the oblivion of injuries or the deepest of sorrows,—

> "In the dust I write
> My heart's deep languor, and my soul's sad tears."

Whitney also has the lines to the praise of Stephen Limbert, Master of Norwich School (p. 173),—

> "Our writing in the duste, can not indure a blaste;
> But that which is in marble wroughte, from age to age, doth laste."

It is but justice to Shakespeare to testify that at times his judgment respecting injuries rises to the full height of Christian morals. The spirit Ariel avows, that, were he human, his "affections would become tender" towards the shipwrecked captives on whom his charms had been working (*Tempest*, act v. sc. 1, l. 21, vol. i. p. 64); and Prospero enters into his thought with strong conviction,—

> "Hast thou, which art but air, a touch, a feeling
> Of their afflictions, and shall not myself,
> One of their kind, that relish all as sharply,
> Passion as they, be kindlier moved than thou art?
> Though with their high wrongs I am struck to the quick,
> Yet with my nobler reason 'gainst my fury
> Do I take part: the rarer action is
> In virtue than in vengeance: they being penitent,
> The sole drift of my purpose doth extend
> Not a frown further."

The subject in this connection finds a fitting conclusion from the words of a later writer, communicated to me by the Rev. T. Walker, M.A., formerly of Nether Tabley, in which a free forgiveness of injuries is ascribed to the world's great and blessed Saviour,—

> "Some write their wrongs on marble, He more just
> Stoop'd down serene, and wrote them in the dust,
> Trod under foot, the sport of every wind,
> Swept from the earth, quite banished from his mind,
> There secret in the grave He bade them lie,
> And grieved, they could not 'scape the Almighty's eye."

Whitney. Reprint, 1866, p. 43.

CHAPTER VII.

MISCELLANEOUS EMBLEMS; RECAPITULATION, AND CONCLUSION.

EMBLEMS Miscellaneous will include some which have been omitted, or which remain unclassified from not belonging to any of the foregoing divisions. They are placed here without any attempt to bring them into any special order.

Several words and forms of thought employed by the Emblem writers, and especially by Whitney, have counterparts, if not direct imitations, in Shakespeare's dramas; he often treats of the same heroes in the same way.

Thus, in reference to Paris and Helen, Whitney utters his opinion respecting them (p. 79),—

> "Thoughe PARIS, had his HELEN at his will,
> Thinke howe his faite, was ILIONS foule deface."

And Shakespeare sets forth Troilus (*Troilus and Cressida*, act ii. sc. 2, l. 81, vol. vi. p. 164) as saying of Helen,—

> "Why, she is a pearl,
> Whose price hath launch'd above a thousand ships,
> And turn'd crown'd kings to merchants."

And then, as adding (l. 92),—

> " O, theft most base,
> That we have stol'n what we do fear to keep!

But thieves unworthy of a thing so stol'n,
That in their country did them that disgrace,
We fear to warrant in our native place!"

Whitney inscribes a frontispiece or dedication of his work with the letters, D. O. M.,—*i.e.*, *Deo, Optimo, Maximo*,—"To God, best, greatest,"—and writes,—

D. O. M.

SINCE *man is fraile, and all his thoughtes are finne,*
And of him felfe he can no good inuent,
Then euerie one, before they oughte beginne,
Should call on GOD, *from whome all grace is fent:*
So, I befeeche, that he the fame will fende,
That, to his praife I maie beginne, and ende.

Very similar sentiments are enunciated in several of the dramas; as in *Twelfth Night* (act iii. sc. 4, l. 340, vol. iii. p. 285),—

"Taint of vice, whose strong corruption
Inhabits our frail blood."

In *Henry VIII.* (act v. sc. 3, l. 10, vol. vi. p. 103), the Lord Chancellor says to Cranmer,—

"But we all are men,
In our own nature frail and capable
Of our flesh; few are angels."

Even Banquo (*Macbeth*, act ii. sc. 1, l. 7, vol. vii. p. 444) can utter the prayer,—

"Merciful powers,
Restrain in me the cursed thoughts that nature
Gives way to in repose!"

And very graphically does Richard III. (act iv. sc. 2, l. 65, vol. v. p. 583) describe our sinfulness as prompting sin,—

"But I am in
So far in blood that sin will pluck on sin."

Or as Romeo puts the case (*Romeo and Juliet*, act v. sc. 3, l. 61, vol. vii. p. 124),—

> "I beseech thee, youth,
> Put not another sin upon my head,
> By urging me to fury."

Coriolanus thus speaks of man's "unstable lightness" (*Coriolanus*, act iii. sc. 1, l. 160, vol. vi. p. 344),—

> "Not having the power to do the good it would,
> For the ill which doth control 't."

Human dependence upon God's blessing is well expressed by the conqueror at Agincourt (*Henry V.*, act iv. sc. 7, l. 82, vol. iv. p. 582),—"Praised be God, and not our strength, for it;" and (act iv. sc. 8, l. 100),—

> "O God, thy arm was here!
> And not to us, but to thy arm alone
> Ascribe we all."

And simply yet truly does the Bishop of Carlisle point out that dependence to Richard II. (act iii. sc. 2, l. 29, vol. iv. p. 164),—

> "The means that heaven yields must be embraced,
> And not neglected; else, if heaven would,
> And we will not, heaven's offer we refuse,
> The proffer'd means of succour and redress."

The closing thought of Whitney's whole passage is embodied in Wolsey's earnest charge to Cromwell (*Henry VIII.*, act iii. sc. 2, l. 446, vol. vi. p. 79),—

> "Be just, and fear not:
> Let all the ends thou aim'st at be thy country's,
> Thy God's, and truth's: then if thou fall'st, O Cromwell,
> Thou fall'st a blessed martyr!"

The various methods of treating the very same subject by the professed Emblem writers will prove that, even with a full knowledge of their works, a later author may yet allow scarcely a hint to escape him, that he was acquainted, in some particular instance, with the sentiments and expressions of his predecessors;

indeed, that knowledge itself may give birth to thoughts widely different in their general character. To establish this position we offer a certain proverb which both Sambucus and Whitney adopt, the almost paradoxical saying, *We flee the things which we follow, and they flee us,*—

Quæ ſequimur fugimus, noſque fugiunt.

Ad Philip. Apianum.

Sambucus, 1564.

QVID *ſemper querimur deeſſe nobis?*
Cur nunquam ſatiat fames perennis?
Haud res nos fugiunt, loco ſolemus
Ipſi cedere ſed fugaciore.
Mors nos arripit antè quàm lucremur
Tantum quod cupimus, Deum & precamur,
Vel ſi rem fateare confitendam,
Res, & nos fugimus ſimul fugaces.
Ne ſint diuitiæ tibi dolori:
At veram ſtatuas beatitatem
Firmis rebus, in aſperaque vita.

In both instances there is exactly the same pictorial illustration, indeed the wood-block which was engraved for the Emblems of Sambucus, in 1564, with simply a change of border, did service for Whitney's Emblems in 1586. The device contains Time, winged and flying and holding forward a scythe; a man and woman walking before him, the scythe being held over their heads threateningly,—the man as he advances turning half round and pointing to a treasure-box left behind. Sambucus thus moralizes,—

"What do we querulous always deem our want?
Why never to hunger sense of fulness grant?
Wealth flees us not,—but we accustomed are
By our own haste its benefits to mar.
Death takes us off before we reach the gain
Great as our wish; and vows to God we feign
For wealth which fleeing at the time we flee,
Even when wealth around we own to be.
O let not riches prove thy spirit's bane!
Nor shalt thou seek for happiness in vain,—
Though rough thy paths of life on every hand,
Firm on its base thy truest bliss shall stand."

Now Whitney adopts, in part at least, a much more literal interpretation; he follows out what the figure of Time and the accessory figures suggest, and so improves his proverb-text as to found upon it what appears pretty plainly to have been the groundwork of the ancient song,—"The old English gentleman, one of the olden time." The type of that truly venerable character was "THOMAS WILBRAHAM *Esquier*," an early patron of Lord Chancellor Egerton. Whitney's lines are (p. 199),—

"WEE flee, from that wee seeke; & followe, that wee leaue:
And, whilst wee thinke our webbe to skante, & larger still would weaue,
Lo, Time dothe cut vs of, amid our carke: and care.
Which warneth all, that haue enoughe, and not contented are.
For to inioye their goodes, their howses, and their landes:
Bicause the Lorde vnto that end, commits them to their handes.

Yet, those whose greedie mindes : enoughe, doe thinke too small :
Whilst that with care they seeke for more, oft times are reu'd of all,
Wherefore all such (I wishe) that spare, where is no neede :
To vse their goodes whilst that they may, for time apace doth speede.
And since, by proofe I knowe, you hourde not vp your store ;
Whose gate, is open to your frende : and purce, vnto the pore :
And spend vnto your praise, what God dothe largely lende :
I chiefly made my choice of this, which I to you commende.
In hope, all those that see your name, aboue the head :
Will at your lampe, their owne come light, within your steppes to tread.
Whose daily studie is, your countrie to adorne :
And for to keepe a worthie house, in place where you weare borne."

In the spirit of one part of these stanzas is a question in Philemon Holland's *Plutarch* (p. 5). "What meane you, my masters, and whither run you headlong, carking and caring all that ever you can to gather goods and rake riches together ?"

Similar in its meaning to the two Emblems just considered is another by Whitney (p. 218), *Mulier vmbra viri,*—"Woman the shadow of man,"—

"Ovr shadowe flies, if wee the same pursue :
But if wee flie, it followeth at the heele.
So, he throughe loue that moste dothe serue, and sue,
Is furthest off his mistresse harte is steele.
But if hee flie, and turne awaie his face,
Shee followeth straight, and grones to him for grace."

This Emblem is very closely followed in the *Merry Wives of Windsor* (act ii. sc. 2, l. 187, vol. i. p. 196), when Ford, in disguise as "Master Brook," protests to Falstaff that he had followed Mrs. Ford "with a doting observance ;" "briefly," he says, "I have pursued her as love hath pursued me ; which hath been on the wing of all occasions,"—

"Love like a shadow flies when substance love pursues ;
Pursuing that that flies, and flying what pursues."

Death in most of its aspects is described and spoken of by the great Dramatist, and possibly we might hunt out some expressions of his which coincide with those of the Emblem writers on the same subject, but generally his mention of death is peculiarly his own,—as when Mortimer says (1 *Henry VI.*, act ii. sc. 5, l. 28, vol. v. p. 40),—

> "The arbitrator of despairs,
> Just death, kind umpire of men's miseries,
> With sweet enlargement doth dismiss me hence."

In his beautiful edition of Holbein's *Dance of Death*, Noel Humphreys (p. 81), in describing the CANONESS, thus conjectures,—"May not Shakespeare have had this device in his mind when penning the passage in which Othello" (act v. sc. 2, l. 7, vol. viii. p. 574), "determining to kill Desdemona, exclaims, 'Put out the light—and then—put out the light?'"

Holbein's Simulachres, 1538.

The way, however, in which Shakespeare sometimes speaks of Death and Sleep induces the supposition that he was acquainted with those passages in Holbein's *Simulachres de la Mort* (Lyons, 1538) which treat of the same subjects by the same method. Thus,—

"Cicero disoit bien: Tu as le sommeil pour imaige de la Mort, & tous les iours tu ten reuestz. Et si doubtes, sil y à nul sentiment a la Mort, combien que tu voyes qu' en son simulachre il n'y à nul sentimēt." Sign. Liij *verso*. And again, sign. Liiij *verso*, "La Mort est le veritable reffuge, la santé parfaicte, le port asseure, la victoire entiere, la chair sans os, le poisson sans espine, le grain sans paille. . . . La Mort est vng eternel sommeil, vne dissolution du Corps, vng espouuētement des riches, vng desir des poures, vng cas ineuitable, vng pelerinaige incertain, vng larron des hõmes, vne Mere du dormir, vne vmbre de vie, vng separement des viuans, vne compaignie des Mortz."

Thus the Prince Henry by his father's couch, thinking him dead, says (2 *Hen. IV.*, act iv. sc. 5, l. 35, vol. iv. p. 453),—

> "This sleep is sound indeed ; this is a sleep,
> That from this golden rigol hath divorced
> So many English kings."

And still more pertinently speaks the Duke (*Measure for Measure*, act iii. sc. 1, l. 17, vol. i. p. 334),—

> "Thy best of rest is sleep,
> And that thou oft provokest ; yet grossly fear'st
> Thy death, which is no more."

Again, before Hermione, as a statue (*Winter's Tale*, act v. sc. 3. l. 18, vol. iii. p. 423),—

> "prepare
> To see the life as lively mock'd as ever
> Still sleep mock'd death."

Or in *Macbeth* (act ii. sc. 3, l. 71, vol. vii. p. 454), when Macduff raises the alarm,—

> "Malcolm ! awake !
> Shake off this downy sleep, death's counterfeit,
> And look on death itself ! up, up, and see
> The great doom's image." *

Finally, in that noble soliloquy of Hamlet (act iii. sc. 1, lines 60—69, vol. viii. p. 79),—

> "To die : to sleep ;
> No more ; and by a sleep to say we end
> The heart-ache, and the thousand natural shocks
> That flesh is heir to ; 'tis a consummation
> Devoutly to be wished. To die, to sleep :
> To sleep : perchance to dream : ay, there's the rub ;
> For in that sleep of death what dreams may come,

* Can this be an allusion to Holbein's *Last Judgment* and *Escutcheon of Death* in his *Simulachres de la Mort*, ed. 1538 ?

When we have shuffled off this mortal coil,
Must give us pause: there's the respect
That makes calamity of so long life."

So the *Evils of Human Life* and the *Eulogy on Death*, ascribed in Holbein's *Simulachres de la Mort* to Alcidamus, sign. Liij *verso*,* may have been suggestive of the lines in continuation of the above soliloquy in *Hamlet*, namely (lines 70—76),—

"For who would bear the whips and scorns of time,
The oppressor's wrong, the proud man's contumely,
The pangs of despised love, the law's delay,
The insolence of office, and the spurns
That patient merit of the unworthy takes,
When he himself might his quietus make
With a bare bodkin?"

To another of the devices of the *Images of Death* (Lyons, 1547), attributed to Holbein, we may also refer as the source of one of the Dramatist's descriptions, in Douce's *Dance of Death*, (London, 1833, and Bohn's, 1858); the device in question is numbered XLIII. and bears the title of the IDIOT FOOL. Woltmann's *Holbein and his Time* (Leipzig, 1868, vol. ii. p. 121), names the figure "Narr des Todes,"—*Death's Fool*,—and thus discourses respecting it. "Among the supplemental Figures,"—that is to say, in the edition of 1545, supplemental to the *forty-one* Figures in the edition of 1538,—"is found that of the Fool, which formerly in the Spectacle-plays of the *Dance of Death* represented by living persons played an important part. Also as these were no longer wont to be exhibited, the Episode of the contest of Death with the Fool was kept separate, and for the diversion of the people became a pantomimic representation.

* "Cicero dict que Alcidamus vng Rheteur antique escripuit les louanges de la Mort, en les quelles estoient cōtenuz les nombres des maulx des humains, & ce pour leur faire desirer la Mort. Car si le dernier iour n'amaine extinction, mais commutation de lieu, Quest il plus a desirer? Et s'il estainct & efface tout, Quest il rien meilleur, que de s' endormir au milieu des labeurs de ceste vie & ainsi reposer en vng sempiternel sommeil."

From England expressly have we information that this usage maintained itself down to the former century. The Fool's efforts

Holbein's Imagines, Cologne, 1566.

and evasions in order to escape from Death, who in the end became his master, form the subject of the particular figures. On such representations Shakespeare thought in his verses in *Measure for Measure*" (act iii. sc. 1, lines 6—13, vol. i. p. 334). Though Woltmann gives only three lines, we add the whole passage better to bring out the sense,—

> "Reason thus with life :
> If I do lose thee, I do lose a thing
> That none but fools would keep : a breath thou art,
> Servile to all the skyey influences,
> That dost this habitation, where thou keep'st,
> Hourly afflict : merely, thou art death's fool :
> For him thou labour'st by thy flight to shun,
> And yet runn'st toward him still."

The action described by Shakespeare is so conformable to Holbein's Figures of Death and the Idiot Fool that, without doing violence to the probability, we may conclude that the two portraits had been in the Poet's eye as well as in his mind.

Woltmann's remarks in continuation uphold this idea. He says (vol. ii. p. 122),—

"Also in the Holbein picture the Fool is foolish enough to think that he can slip away from Death. He springs aside, seeks through his movements to delude him, and brandishes the leather-club, in order unseen to plant a blow on his adversary; and this adversary seems in sport to give in, skips near him, playing on the bag-pipe, but unobserved has him fast by the garment, in order not again to let him loose."

Old Time is a character introduced by way of Chorus into the *Winter's Tale* (act iv. sc. 1, l. 7, vol. iii. p. 371), and he takes upon himself "to use his wings," as he says,—

"It is in my power
To o'erthrow law and in one self-born hour
To plant and o'erwhelm custom. Let me pass
The same I am, ere ancient'st order was
Or what is now received: I witness to
The times that brought them in; so shall I do
To the freshest things now reigning, and make stale
The glistering of this present."

Something of the same paradox which appears in the Emblematist's motto, "What we follow we flee," also distinguishes the quibbling dialogue about time between Dromio of Syracuse and Adriana (*Comedy of Errors*, act iv. sc. 2, l. 53, vol. i. p. 437),—

"*Dro. S.* 'Tis time that I were gone:
It was two ere I left him, and now the clock strikes one.
Adr. The hours come back! that did I never hear.
Dro. S. O, yes; if any hour meet a sergeant, a' turns back for very fear.
Adr. As if Time were in debt! how fondly dost thou reason!
Dro. S. Time is a very bankrupt, and owes more than he's worth to season.
Nay, he's a thief too: have you not heard men say,
That Time comes stealing on by night and day?
If Time be in debt and theft, and a sergeant in the way,
Hath he not reason to turn back an hour in a day?"

Almost of the same complexion are some of the other strong contrasts of epithets which Shakespeare applies. Iachimo, in *Cymbeline* (act i. sc. 6, l. 46, vol. ix. p. 185), uses the expressions,—

> "The cloyed will,
> That satiate yet unsatisfied desire, that tub
> Both fill'd and running, ravening first the lamb,
> Longs after for the garbage."

But "old fond paradoxes, to make fools laugh i' the alehouse," are also given forth from the storehouse of his conceits. Desdemona and Emilia and Iago play at these follies (*Othello*, act ii. sc. 1, l. 129, vol. viii. p. 477), and thus some of them are uttered,—

> "*Iago.* If she be fair and wise, fairness and wit,
> The one's for use, the other useth it.
> *Des.* Well praised! How if she be black and witty?
> *Iago.* If she be black, and thereto have a wit,
> She'll find a white that shall her blackness fit.
>
> . . . .
>
> *Des.* But what praise couldst thou bestow on a deserving woman indeed? one that, on the authority of her merit, did justly put on the vouch of very malice itself?
> *Iago.* She that was ever fair, and never proud,
> Had tongue at will, and yet was never loud,
> Never lack'd gold, and yet went never gay,
> Fled from her wish, and yet said, now I may;
>
> . . . . .
>
> She was a wight, if ever such wight were,—
> *Des.* To do what?
> *Iago.* To suckle fools, and chronicle small beer."

We thus return, by a wandering path indeed, to the paradoxical saying with which we set out,—concerning "fleeing what we follow;" for Iago's paragon of a woman,—

> "Fled from her wish, and yet said, now I may."

Taken by itself, the coincidence of a few words in the dedications of works by different authors is of trifling importance;

but when we notice how brief are the lines in which Shakespeare commends his "VENUS AND ADONIS" to the patronage of the Earl of Southampton, it is remarkable that he has adopted an expression almost singular, which Whitney had beforehand employed in the long dedication of his Emblems to the Earl of Leycester. "Being abashed," says Whitney, "that my habillitie can not affoorde them such, as are fit to be offred vp to so honorable a suruaighe" (p. xi); and Shakespeare, "I leave it to your honourable survey, and your Honour to your heart's content." Whitney then declares, "yet if it shall like your honour to allowe of anie of them, I shall thinke my pen set to the booke in happie hour; and it shall incourage mee, to assay some matter of more momente, as soon as leasure will further my desire in that behalfe;" and Shakespeare, adopting the same idea, also affirms, "only if your Honour seem but pleased, I account myself highly praised and vow to take advantage of all idle hours, till I have honoured you with some graver labour." Comparing these passages together, the inference appears not unwarranted, that Whitney's dedication had been read by Shakespeare, and that the tenor of it abided in his memory, and so was made use of by him.

From the well-known lines of *Horace* (Ode ii. 10),—

> "Sæpius ventis agitatur ingens
> Pinus; et celsæ graviore casu
> Decidunt turres; feriuntque summos
> Fulgura montes,"

several of the Emblem writers, and Shakespeare after them, tell of the huge pine and of its contests with the tempests; and how lofty towers fall with a heavier crash, and how the lightnings smite the highest mountains. Sambucus (edition 1569, p. 279) and Whitney (p. 59) do this, as a comment for the injunction, *Nimium rebus ne fide secundis*,—"Be not too confident in prosperity." In this instance the stanzas of Whitney serve well to express the verses of Sambucus,—

Nimium rebus ne fide secundis.

Whitney, 1586.

"THE loftie Pine, that on the mountaine growes,
And spreades her armes, with braunches freshe, & greene,
The raginge windes, on sodaine ouerthrowes,
And makes her stoope, that longe a farre was seene:
So they, that truste to muche in fortunes smiles,
Thoughe worlde do laughe, and wealthe doe moste abounde,
When leste they thinke, are often snar'de with wyles,
And from alofte, doo hedlonge fall to grounde:
Then put no truste, in anie worldlie thinges,
For frowninge fate, throwes downe the mightie kinges."

Antonio, in the *Merchant of Venice* (act iv. sc. 1, l. 75, vol. ii. p. 345), applies the thought to the fruitlessness of Bassanio's endeavour to soften Shylock's stern purpose of revenge,—

"You may as well forbid the mountain pines
To wag their high tops, and to make no noise
When they are fretten with the gusts of heaven."

And when "dame Eleanor Cobham, Gloster's wife," is banished, and her noble husband called on to give up the Lord

Protector's staff of office (2 *Henry VI.*, act ii. sc. 3, l. 45, vol. v. p. 145), Suffolk makes the comparison,—

> "Thus droops this lofty pine, and hangs his sprays;
> Thus Eleanor's pride dies in her youngest days."

So, following almost literally the words of Horace, the exiled Belarius, in *Cymbeline* (act iv. sc. 2, l. 172, vol. ix. p. 253), declares of the "two princely boys," that passed for his sons,—

> "They are as gentle
> As zephyrs blowing below the violet,
> Not wagging his sweet head; and yet as rough,
> Their royal blood enchafed, as the rudest wind
> That by the top doth take the mountain pine
> And make him stoop to the vale."

Words, which, though now obsolete, were in current use in the days of Surrey, Sidney, Spenser, and Shakespeare, cannot of themselves be adduced in evidence of any interchange of ideas; but when the form of the sentence and the application of some peculiar term agree, we may reasonably presume that it has been more than the simple use of the same common tongue which has caused the agreement. When, indeed, one author writes in English, and the others in Latin, or Italian, or French, we cannot expect much more than similarity of idea in treating of the same subject, and a mutual intercommunion of thought; but, in the case of authors employing the same mother tongue, there are certain correspondencies in the use of the same terms and turns of expression which betoken imitation.

Such correspondencies exist between Whitney and Shakespeare, as may be seen from the following among many other instances. I adopt the old spelling of the folio edition of Shakespeare, 1632,—

Abroach .	Whitney, p. 7	And bluddie broiles at home are set *abroache.*
	Rom. and J. i. 1. l. 102	Who set this ancient quarrell new *abroach?*
	2 *Hen. IV.* iv. 2, 14 .	Alacke, what Mischeifes might be set *abroach.*
a-worke	Whitney, p. vi. . . .	They set them selues *a worke.*
	2 *Hen. IV.* iv. 3, 107 .	Skill in the Weapon is nothing, without Sacke (for that sets it *a-worke*).
	K. Lear, iii. 5, 5	— a provoking merit set *a-worke* by a reprovable badnesse in himselfe.
Banne .	Whitney, p. 189	The maide her pacience quite forgot And in a rage, the brutishe beaste did *banne.*
	Hamlet, iii. 2, 246 .	With Hecats *ban,* thrice blasted, thrice infected.
	1 *Hen. VI.* v. 3, 42	Fell *banning* Hagge, Inchantresse hold thy tongue.
	2 *Hen. VI.* ii. 4, 25	And *banne* thine Enemies, both mine and thine.
Cates	Whitney, p. 18 . .	Whose backe is fraughte with *cates* and daintie cheere.
	C. Errors, iii. 1, 28 .	But though my *cates* be meane, take them in good part.
	1 *Hen. IV.* iii. 1, 163 .	I had rather live With Cheese and Garlike in a Windmill far Then feed on *Cates,* and have him talke to me In any Summer House in Christendome.
create	Whitney, p. 64 . .	Not for our selues alone wee are *create.*
	M. N. Dr. v. 1, 394	And the issue there *create* Ever shall be fortunate.
	K. John, iv. 1, 106	The fire is dead with griefe Being *create* for comfort.
	Hen. V. ii. 2, 31	With hearts *create* of duty and of zeal.
Erksome .	Whitney, p. 118	With *erksome* noise and eke with poison fell.
	T. of Shrew, i. 2, 182 .	I know she is an *irkesome* brawling scold.
	2 *Hen. VI.* ii. 1, 56	How *irkesome* is this Musicke to my heart!

Ingrate .	Whitney, p. 64 . . .	And those that are vnto theire frendes *ingrate*.
	T. of Shrew, i. 2, 266 .	Will not so gracelesse be, to be *ingrate*.
	Coriol. v. 2, 80 . . .	*Ingrate* forgetfulness shall poison rather.
Prejudicate	Whitney, xiii.	The enuious, who are alwaies readie with a *prejudicate* opinion to condempe.
	All's Well, i. 2, 7 .	wherein our deerest friend *Prejudicates* the businesse.
Ripes . .	Whitney, p. 23 .	When autumne *ripes* the frutefull fieldes of grane.
	K. John, ii. 1, 472 .	— yon greene Boy shall haue no Sunne to *ripe* The bloome that promiseth a mighty fruit.
Vnrest . .	Whitney, p. 94 .	It shewes her selfe doth worke her own *vnrest*.
	Rich. II. ii. 4, 22	Witnessing Stormes to come, Woe and *Vnrest*.
	T. An. ii. 3, 8	And so repose sweet Gold for their *unrest*.
vnsure . .	Whitney, p. 191	So, manie men do stoope to sightes *vnsure*.
	Hamlet, iv. 4, 51 . .	Exposing what is mortal and *unsure*.
	Macbeth, v. 4, 19	Thoughts speculative their *unsure* hopes relate.
vnthrifte	Whitney, p. 17 .	And wisdome still, against such *vnthriftes* cries.
	Rich. II. ii. 3, 120 .	my Rights and Royalties Pluckt from my armes perforce, and giuen away To upstart *Vnthriftes*.
	Timon, iv. 3, 307 . .	What man didd'st thou euer knowe *unthrifte* that was beloved after his meanes?
	M. Venice, v. 1, 16. .	And with an *unthrift* love did run from Venice As far as Belmont.*

* For many other instances of similarities in the use of old words, see the APPENDIX, I. p. 497.

So close are some of these correspondencies that they can scarcely be accounted for except on the theory that Shakespeare had been an observant reader of Whitney's Emblems.

There are also various expressions, or epithets, which the Emblem-books may be employed to illustrate, and which receive their most natural explanation from this same theory that Shakespeare was one of the very numerous host of Emblem students or readers. Perriere's account of a man attempting to swim with a load of iron on his back (Emb. 70), is applied by Whitney with direct reference to the lines in Horace, "O cursed lust of gold, to what dost thou not compel mortal bosoms?" He sets off the thought by the device of a man swimming with "a fardle," or heavy burden (p. 179),—

Auri sacra fames quid non!

Whitney, 1586.

"DESIRE to haue, dothe make vs muche indure,
In trauaile, toile, and labour voide of reste:
The marchant man is caried with this lure,
Throughe scorching heate, to regions of the Easte:
Oh thirste of goulde, what not? but thou canst do:
And make mens hartes for to consent thereto.

The trauailer poore, when shippe doth suffer wracke,
Who hopes to swimme vnto the wished lande,
Dothe venture life, with fardle on his backe,
That if he scape, the same in steede maye stande.
Thus, hope of life, and loue vnto his goods,
Houldes vp his chinne, with burthen in the floods."

In the *Winter's Tale*, the word "fardel" occurs several times; we will, however, take a familiar quotation from *Hamlet* (act iii. sc. 1, l. 76, vol. viii. p. 80),—

"Who would fardels bear,
To grunt and sweat under a weary life,
But that the dread of something after death,
The undiscover'd country from whose bourn
No traveller returns, puzzles the will,
And makes us rather bear those ills we have
Than fly to others that we know not of?"

The Bandogs, which Sir Thomas More and Spenser describe, appear to have been different from those of Sambucus and Whitney, or, rather, they were employed for a different purpose. "We must," writes the worthy Chancellor (p. 586), "haue bande dogges to dryue them (the swine) out of the corne with byting, and leade them out by the ears;" and Spenser, in *Virgil's Gnat* (l. 539), speaks of—

"greedie Scilla, under whom there lay
Manie great bandogs, which her gird about."

These dogs were mastiffs, and their banning was barking or braying; but the dogs entitled bandogs in Whitney, though also mastiffs, were fastened by a band to a small cart, and trained to draw it. A large species of dog may be seen at this day in the towns of Belgium performing the very same service to which their ancestors had been accustomed above three centuries ago. Sambucus heads his description of the bandog's strength and labours with the sentence,—"The dog complains that he is greatly wronged."

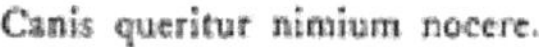

Canis queritur nimium nocere.

Sambucus, 1584.

NON *ego furaces nec apros insector & vrsos,*
Applaudit nec hero blandula cauda dolo:
Sub iuga sed mittor validus, traho & essedа collo,
Quaeq; leuant alios viribus vsque premor.
Per vicos ductum me alij latratibus vrgent,
Miratur casus libera turba meos.
Quàm fueram charus dominae, si paruulus essem,
Non mensa, lecto nec caruisse velim.
Sic multis vires, & opes nocuere superbae:
Contentum modico & profuit esse statu.

Seated near the toiling mastiff is a lady with two or three pet curs, and the large dog complains,—

"Were I a little whelp, to my lady how dear I should be;
Of board and of bed I never the want should see." *

---

* Were it only for the elegance and neat turn of the lines, we insert an epigram on a dog, by Joachim du Bellay, given in his Latin Poems, printed at Paris in 1569,—

"Latratu fures excepi;—mutus amantes;
Sic placui domino, sic placui dominae."

"With barking the thieves I awaited,—in silence the lovers;
So pleased I the master,—so pleased I the mistress."

Whitney, using the woodcut which adorns the editions of Sambucus both in 1564 and 1599, prefixes a loftier motto (p. 140),—*Feriunt summos fulmina montes*,—"Thunderbolts strike highest mountains;" and thus expatiates he,—

"THE bandogge, fitte to matche the bull, or beare,
With burthens greate, is loden euery daye:
Or drawes the carte, and forc'd the yoke to weare:
Where littell dogges doe passe their time in playe:
And ofte, are bould to barke, and eeke to bite,
When as before, they trembled at his sighte.

Yet, when in bondes they see his thrauled state,
Eache braggинge curre, beginnes to square, and brall:
The freër sorte, doe wonder at his fate,
And thinke them beste, that are of stature small:
For they maie sleepe vppon their mistris bedde,
And on their lappes, with daynties still bee fedde.

The loftie pine, with axe is ouerthrowne,
And is prepar'd, to serue the shipmans turne:
When bushes stande, till stormes bee ouerblowne,
And lightninges flashe, the mountaine toppes doth burne.
All which doe shewe that pompe, and worldlie power,
Makes monarches, markes: when varrijnge fate doth lower."

The mastiff is almost the only dog to which Shakespeare assigns any epithet of praise. In *Henry V.* (act iii. sc. 7, l. 130, vol. iv. p. 552), one of the French lords, Rambures, acknowleges "that island of England breeds very valiant creatures; their mastiffs are of unmatchable courage." It is the same quality in Achilles and Ajax on which Ulysses and Nestor count when "the old man eloquent," in *Troilus and Cressida* (act i. sc. 3, l. 391, vol. vi. p. 155), says of the two warriors,—

"Two curs shall tame each other: pride alone
Must tarre * the mastiffs on, as 'twere their bone."

* "Tarre," *i.e.* provoke or urge; see Johnson and Steevens' *Shakspeare*, vol. ix. p. 48, note.

It is, however, only in a passing allusion that Shakespeare introduces any mention of the bandog. He is describing the night "when Troy was set on fire" (2 *Henry VI.*, act i. sc. 4, l. 16, vol. v. p. 129), and thus speaks of it,—

> "The time when scritch-owls cry, and ban-dogs howl,
> When spirits walk, and ghosts break up their graves."

We are all familiar with the expression "motley's the only wear," and probably we are disposed simply to refer it to the way in which that important personage was arrayed who exercised his fun and nonsense and shrewd wit in the courts of the kings and in the mansions of the nobles of the middle ages. The pictorial type exists in the Emblems both of Sambucus and of his copyist Whitney (p. 81), by whom the sage advice is imparted,—"Give trifles in charge to fools."

Fatuis levia committito.

Whitney, 1586.

> "THE little childe, is pleas'de with cockhorse gaie,
> Althoughe he aske a courser of the beste:
> The ideot likes, with bables for to plaie,
> And is disgrac'de, when he is brauelie dreste:
> A motley coate, a cockescombe, or a bell,
> Hee better likes, then Iewelles that excell.

So fondelinges vaine, that doe for honor sue,
And seeke for roomes, that worthie men deserue :
The prudent Prince, dothe giue hem ofte their due,
Whiche is faire wordes, that right their humors serue :
For infantes hande, the rasor is vnfitte,
And fooles vnmeete, in wisedomes seate to sitte."

The word "motley" is often made use of in Shakespeare's plays. Jaques, in *As You Like It* (act ii. sc. 7, lines 12 and 42, vol. ii. pp. 405, 406), describes the "motley fool" "in a motley coat,"—

"I met a fool i' the forest,
A motley fool ; a miserable world !
As I do live by food, I met a fool ;
Who laid him down and bask'd him in the sun,
And rail'd on Lady Fortune in good terms,
In good set terms, and yet a motley fool.

O that I were a fool !
I am ambitious for a motley coat."

The Prologue to *Henry VIII.* (l. 15) alludes to the dress of the buffoons that were often introduced into the plays of the time,—

"a fellow
In a long motley coat, guarded with yellow."

The fool in *King Lear* (act i. sc. 4, l. 93, vol. viii. p. 280) seems to have been dressed according to Whitney's pattern, for, on giving his cap to Kent, he says,—

"Sirrah, you were best take my coxcomb.
Kent. Why, fool ?
Fool. Why, for taking one's part that's out of favour : nay, an thou canst not smile as the wind sits, thou'lt catch cold shortly : there, take my coxcomb : why, this fellow hath banished two on's daughters, and done the third a blessing against his will ; if thou follow him, thou must needs wear my coxcomb."

Drant's translations* from Horace, published in 1567, convey to us a pretty accurate idea of the fool's attire,—

> "Well geue him cloth and let the fool
> Goe like a cockescome still."

Perchance we know the lines in the "FAERIE QUEENE" (vi. c. 7, 49, l. 6),—

> "And other whiles with bitter mockes and mowes
> He would him scorne, that to his gentle mynd
> Was much more grievous then the others blowes:
> Words sharpely wound, but greatest griefe of scorning growes."

But probably we are not prepared to trace some of the expressions in these lines to an Emblem-book origin. The graphic "mockes and mowes," indeed, no Latin nor French can express; but our old friend Paradin, in the "DEVISES HEROIQVES" (leaf 174), names an occasion on which very amusing "mockes and mowes" were exhibited: it was, moreover, an example that,—

"*Things badly obtained are badly scattered.*" As he narrates the tale,—"One day it happened that a huge ape, nourished in the house of a miser who found pleasure only in his crowns, after seeing through a hole his master playing with his crowns upon a table, obtained means of entering within by an open window, while the miser was at dinner. The ape took a stool, as his master did, but soon began to throw the silver out of the window into the street. How much the passers by kept laughing and the miser was vexed, I shall not attempt to say. I will not mock him among his neighbours who were picking up his bright crowns either for a nestegg, or for a son or a brother,—for a gamester, a driveller or a drunkard,—for I cannot but remember that fine and true saying which affirms, '*Things badly gained are badly scattered.*'"

This tale, derived by Paradin from Gabriel Symeoni's *Imprese Heroiche et Morali*, is assumed by Whitney as the groundwork of his very lively narrative (p. 169), *Against Userers*, of which we venture to give the whole.

* See "Horace his Arte of Poetrie, pistles, and satyres, englished" by Thomas Drant, 4to, 1567.

Malè parta malè dilabuntur.

In fœneratores.

Whitney, 1586.

"AN vserer, whose Idol was his goulde,
Within his house, a peeuishe ape retain'd:
A seruaunt fitte, for suche a miser oulde,
Of whome both mockes, and apishe mowes, he gain'd.
Thus, euerie daie he made his master sporte,
And to his clogge, was chained in the courte.

At lengthe it hap'd? while greedie graundsir din'de?
The ape got loose, and founde a windowe ope:
Where in he leap'de, and all about did finde,
The GOD, wherein the Miser put his hope?
Which soone he broch'd, and forthe with speede did flinge,
And did delighte on stones to heare it ringe?

The sighte, righte well the passers by did please,
Who did reioyce to finde these goulden crommes:
That all their life, their pouertie did ease.
Of goodes ill got, loe heere the fruicte that commes.
Looke herevppon, you that haue MIDAS minte,
And bee posseste with hartes as harde as flinte.

Shut windowes close, leste apes doe enter in,
And doe disperse your goulde, you doe adore.
But woulde you learne to keepe, that you do winne?
Then get it well, and hourde it not in store.
If not: no boultes, nor brasen barres will serue,
For GOD will waste your stocke, and make you sterue."

Poor Caliban, in the *Tempest* (act ii. sc. 2, l. 7, vol. i. p. 36), complains of Prospero's spirits that,—

> "For every trifle are they set upon me;
> Sometimes like apes, that mow and chatter at me,
> And after bite me."

And Helena, to her rival Hermia (*Midsummer Night's Dream*, act iii. sc. 2, l. 237, vol. ii. p. 240), urges a very similar charge,—

> "Ay, do, persever, counterfeit sad looks,
> Make mouths upon me when I turn my back;
> Wink each at other; hold the sweet jest up."

There is not, indeed, any imitation of the jocose tale about the ape * and the miser's gold, and it is simply in "the mockes and apishe mowes" that any similarity exists. These, however, enter into the dialogue between Imogen and Iachimo (*Cymbeline*, act i. sc. 6, l. 30, vol. ix. p. 184); she bids him welcome, and he replies,—

> "*Iach.* Thanks, fairest lady.
> What, are men mad? Hath nature given them eyes
> To see this vaulted arch and the rich crop
> Of sea and land, which can distinguish 'twixt
> The fiery orbs above and the twinn'd stones
> Upon the number'd beach, and can we not
> Partition make with spectacles so precious
> 'Twixt fair and foul?
> *Imo.* What makes your admiration?
> *Iach.* It cannot be i' the eye; for apes and monkeys,
> 'Twixt two such shes, would chatter this way and
> Contemn with mows the other."

There is a fine thought in Furmer's *Use and Abuse of Wealth*, first published in Latin in 1575, and afterwards, in 1585, translated into Dutch by Coornhert; it is respecting the distribution of poverty and riches by the Supreme wisdom. The subject (at

* The character, however, of the animal is named in *Midsummer Night's Dream* (act ii. sc. 1, l. 181), where Titania may look—

> "On meddling monkey, or on busy ape"

IIII.

PAVPERTAS IMMERITA.

Dominus pauperem facit & ditat.
1. *Regum* 2, 7.

Vt Deus auctor opum quas olim Iobus habebat,
Sic paupertatis tum Deus auctor erat.
Qui bonum vtrumq; putat, Dominus quia donat vtrumque,
In animo forti semper vtrumque feret.

Providence making Rich and making Poor — *Coornhert, 1585*

p. 6) is *Undeserved Poverty*,—"The Lord maketh poor, and enriches." (See Plate XVI.)

> "The riches which Job had as God bestows,
>   So giver of poverty doth God appear.
> Who thinks each good because from God each flows,
>   Shall always each with bravest spirit bear."

In the device, the clouds are opened to bestow fulness upon the poor man, and emptiness upon the rich. By brief allusion chiefly does Shakespeare express either of these acts; but in the *Tempest* (act iii. sc. 2, l. 135, vol. i. p. 48), Caliban, after informing Stephano that "the isle is full of noises," and that "sometimes a thousand twangling instruments will hum about mine ears," adds,—

> "And then, in dreaming,
> The clouds methought would open, and show riches
> Ready to drop upon me; that when I waked,
> I cried to dream again."

A very similar picture and sentiment to those in Coornhert are presented by Gloucester's words in *King Lear* (act iv. sc. 1, l. 64, vol. viii. p. 366),—

> "Here, take this purse, thou whom the heavens' plagues
> Have humbled to all strokes: that I am wretched
> Makes thee the happier. Heavens, deal so still!
> Let the superfluous and lust-dieted man,
> That slaves your ordinance, that will not see
> Because he doth not feel, feel your power quickly;
> So distribution should undo excess,
> And each man have enough."

Coornhert's title, "**Recht Ghebruyck ende Misbruyck van-tydlycke have,**"—*The right use and misuse of worldly wealth*,—and, indeed, his work, have their purport well carried out by the king in 2 *Henry IV.* (act iv. sc. 4, l. 103, vol iv. p. 450),—

> "Will Fortune never come with both hands full,
> But write her fair words still in foulest letters?
> She either gives a stomach and no food;
> Such are the poor, in health; or else a feast
> And takes away the stomach; such are the rich,
> That have abundance and enjoy it not."

The fine thoughts of Ulysses, too, in *Troilus and Cressida* (act iii. sc. 3, l. 196, vol. vi. p. 201), have right and propriety here to be quoted,—

"The providence that's in a watchful state
Knows almost every grain of Plutus' gold,
Finds bottom in the uncomprehensive deeps,
Keeps place with thought and almost like the gods
Does thoughts unveil in their dumb cradles.
There is a mystery, with whom relation
Durst never meddle, in the soul of state;
Which hath an operation more divine
Than breath or pen can give expressure to."

Petruchio's thought, perchance, may be mentioned in this connection (*Taming of the Shrew*, act iv. sc. 3, l. 165, vol. iii. p. 78), when he declares his will to go to Kate's father,—

"Even in these honest mean habiliments:
Our purses shall be proud, our garments poor;
For 'tis the mind that makes the body rich:
And as the sun breaks through the darkest clouds,
So honour peereth in the meanest habit."

The Horatian thought, "Time flies irrevocable," so well depicted by Otho Vænius in his *Emblemata* (edition 1612, p. 206), has only general parallels in Shakespeare; and yet it is a thought with which our various dissertations on Shakespeare and the Emblematists may find no unfitting end. The Christian artist far excels the Heathen poet. Horace, in his *Odes* (bk. iv. carmen 7), declares,—

"*Immortalia ne speres, monet annus & almum*
Quæ rapit hora diem:
Frigora mitescunt Zephyris: Ver proterit Æstas
Interitura, simul
Pomifer Autumnus fruges effuderit: & mox
Bruma recurrit iners."

i.e. "Not to hope immortal things, the year admonishes, and the hour which steals the genial day. By western winds the frosts grow mild; the summer soon to perish supplants the spring, then fruitful autumn pours forth his stores, and soon sluggish winter comes again."

Time Flying from "Emblemata" by Otho Vænius p. 206 ed. 1612

These, however, the artist makes (*Henry V.*, act iv. sc. 1, l. 9, vol. v. p. 555),—

> "Preachers to us all, admonishing
> That we should dress us fairly for our end."

Youthful Time (see Plate XVII.) is leading on the seasons,—a childlike spring, a matured summer wreathed with corn, an autumn crowned with vines, and a decrepid winter,—and yet the emblem of immortality lies at their feet; and the lesson is taught, as our Dramatist expresses it (*Hamlet*, act i. sc. 2, l. 71, vol. viii. p. 14),—

> "All that lives must die
> Passing through nature to eternity."

The irrevocable time flies on, and surely it has its comment in *Macbeth* (act v. sc. 5, l. 19, vol. vii. p. 512),—

> "To-morrow, and to-morrow, and to-morrow,
> Creeps in this petty pace from day to day
> To the last syllable of recorded time;
> And all our yesterdays have lighted fools
> The way to dusty death."

Or, in Hotspur's words (1 *Henry IV.*, act v. sc. 2, l. 82, vol. iv. p. 337),—

> "O gentlemen, the time of life is short!
> To spend that shortness basely were too long,
> If life did ride upon a dial's point,
> Still ending at the arrival of an hour."

And for eternity's Emblem, the Egyptians, we are told (Horapollo, i. 1), made golden figures of the Basilisk, with its tail covered by the rest of its body; so Otho Vænius presents the device to us. But Shakespeare, without symbol, names the desire, the feeling, the fact itself; he makes Cleopatra exclaim (*Antony and Cleopatra*, act v. sc. 2, l. 277, vol. ix. p. 150), "I have immortal longings in me," "I am fire and air; my other elements I give to baser life."

When Romeo asks (*Romeo and Juliet*, act v. sc. 1, l. 15, vol. vii. p. 117),—

---

* See woodcut in this volume, p. 37.

> "How fares my Juliet? that I ask again:
> For nothing can be ill, if she be well;"

with the force of entire faith the answer is conceived which Balthasar returns,

> "Then she is well, and nothing can be ill:
> Her body sleeps in Capel's monument,
> And her immortal part with angels lives."

We thus know in what sense to understand the words from *Macbeth* (act iii. sc. 2, l. 22, vol. vii. p. 467),—

> "Duncan is in his grave;
> After life's fitful fever he sleeps well;
> Treason has done his worst: nor steel, nor poison,
> Malice domestic, foreign levy, nothing,
> Can touch him further."

Therefore, in spite of quickly fading years, in spite of age irrevocable, and (*Love's Labour's Lost*, act i. sc. 1, l. 4, vol. ii. p. 97),—

> "In spite of cormorant devouring Time,
> The endeavour of this present breath may buy
> That honour which shall bate his scythe's keen edge,
> And make us heirs of all eternity."

A brief *resumé*, or recapitulation, will now place the nature of our argument more clearly in review.

When writing and its kindred arts of designing and colouring were the only means in use for the making and illustrating of books, drawings of an emblematical character were frequently executed both for the ornamenting and for the fuller explanation of various works.

From the origin of printing, books of an emblematical character, as the *Bibles of the Poor* and other block-books, were generally known in the civilised portions of Europe; they constituted, to a considerable degree, the illustrated literature of their age, and enjoyed wide fame and popularity.

Not many years after printing with moveable types had been invented, Emblem works as a distinct species of literature appeared; and of these some of the earliest were soon translated into English.

It is on undoubted record that the use of Emblems, derived from German, Latin, French, and Italian sources, prevailed in England for purposes of ornamentation of various kinds; that the works of Brandt, Giovio, Symeoni, and Paradin were translated into English; and that there were several English writers or collectors of Emblems within Shakespeare's lifetime,—as Daniell, Whitney, Willet, Combe, and Peacham.

Shakespeare possessed great artistic powers, so as to appreciate and graphically describe the beauties and qualities of excellence in painting, sculpture, and music. His attainments, too, in the languages enabled him to make use of the Emblem-books that had been published in Latin, Italian, and French, and possibly in Spanish.

In everything, except in the actual pictorial device, Shakespeare exhibited himself as a skilled designer,—indeed, a writer of Emblems: he followed the very methods on which this species of literary composition was conducted, and needed only the engraver's aid to make perfect designs.

Freest among mortals were the Emblem writers in borrowing one from the other, and from any source which might serve the construction of their ingenious devices; and they generally did this without acknowledgment. An Emblem once launched into the world of letters was treated as a fable or a proverb,—it became for the time and the occasion the property of whoever chose to take it. In using Emblems, therefore, Shakespeare is no more to be regarded as a copyist than his contemporaries are, but simply as one who exercised a recognised right to appropriate what he needed of the general stock of Emblem notions.

There are several direct References in Shakespeare, at least six, in which, by the closest description and by express quotation, he identifies himself with the Emblem writers who preceded him.

But besides these direct References, there are several collateral ones, in which ideas and expressions are employed similar to those of Emblematists, and which indicate a knowledge of Emblem art.

And, finally, the parallelisms and correspondencies are very numerous between devices and turns of thought, and even between the words of the Emblem writers and passages in Shakespeare's Sonnets and Dramas; and these receive their most appropriate *rationale* on the supposition that they were suggested to his mind through reading the Emblem-books, or through familiarity with the Emblem literature.

Now, such References and Coincidences are not to be regarded as purely accidental, neither can all of them be urged with entire confidence. Some persons even may be disposed to class them among the similarities which of necessity arise when writers of genius and learning take up the same themes, and call to their aid all the resources of their memory and research.

I presume not, however, to say that my arguments and statements are absolute proofs, except in a few instances. What I maintain is this: that the Emblem writers, and our own Whitney especially, do supply many curious and highly interesting illustrations of the Shakespearean dramas, and that several of them, probably, were in the mind of the Dramatist as he wrote.

To show that the theory carried out in these pages is neither singular nor unsupported by high authorities, it should not be forgotten that the very celebrated critic, Francis Douce, in his *Illustrations of Shakespeare* (pp. 302, 392), maintains that Paradin was the source of the torch-emblem in the *Pericles* (act ii. sc. 2, l. 32): the "wreath of victory," and "gold on the touchstone," have also the same source. To Holbein's *Simulachres* Noel Humphreys assigns the origin of the expression in *Othello*, "Put out the light—and then, put out the light;" and in the same work, Dr. Alfred Woltmann, in *Holbein and his Times* (vol. ii.

p. 121), finds the origin of Death's fool in *Measure for Measure:* and Shakespeare's comparisons of "Death and Sleep" may be traced to Jean de Vauzelle, who wrote the Dissertations for *Les Simulachres.* Charles Knight, also, in his *Pictorial Shakspere* (vol. i. p. 154), to illustrate the lines in *Hamlet* (act iv. sc. 5, l. 142) respecting "the kind life-rendering pelican," quotes Whitney's stanza, and copies his woodcut, as stated *ante*, p. 396, note.

Though not a learned man, as Erasmus or Beza was, Shakespeare, as every page of his wonderful writings shows, must have been a reading man, and well acquainted with the current literature of his age and country. Whitney's *Emblemes* were well known in 1612 to the author of "MINERVA BRITANNA," and boasted of in 1598 by Thomas Meres, in his *Wit's Commonwealth,* as fit to be compared with any of the most eminent Latin writers of Emblems, and dedicated to many of the distinguished men of Elizabeth's reign; and they could scarcely have been unknown to Shakespeare even had there been no similarities of thought and expression established between the two writers.

Nor after the testimonies which have been adduced, and comparing the picture-emblems submitted for consideration with the passages from Shakespeare which are their parallels, as far as words can be to drawings, are we required to treat it as nothing but a conjecture that Shakespeare, like others of his countrymen, possessed at least a general acquaintance with the popular Emblem-books of his own generation and of that which went before.

The study of the old Emblem-books certainly possesses little of the charm which the unsurpassed natural power of Shakespeare has infused into his dramas, and which time does not diminish; yet that study is no barren pursuit for such as will seek for "virtue's fair form and graces excellent," or who desire to note how the learning of the age disported itself at its hours of recreation, and how, with few exceptions, it held firm its allegiance to purity of thought, and reverenced the spirit of religion. Should there be any whom these pages incite to gain a fuller knowledge of the Emblem literature, I would say in the words of Arthur Bourchier, Whitney's steady friend,—

> "*Goe forwarde then in happie time, and thou shalt surely finde,*
> *With coste, and labour well set out, a banquet for thy minde,*
> *A storehouse for thy wise conceiptes, a whetstone for thy witte:*
> *Where, eache man maye with daintie choice his fancies finely fitte.*"

So much for the early cultivators of Emblematical mottoes, devices, and poesies, and for him whom Hugh Holland, and Ben Jonson, and "The friendly Admirer of his Endowments," salute as "The Famous Scenicke Poet," "The Sweet Swan of Avon," "The Starre of Poets,"—

> "*Soule of the Age!*
> The applause! delight! the wonder of our stage!"

"To the memory of my beloved, the Author, **Mr. William Shakespeare**: *and what he has left us*;"—such the dedication when Jonson declared,—

> "*Thou art a Moniment without a tombe.*
> . . . .
> *And art aliue still, while thy Booke doth liue*
> And we haue wits to read, and praise to giue."

[illegible], ed. 1556.

Appendix.

I.

COINCIDENCES BETWEEN SHAKESPEARE AND WHITNEY IN THE USE AND APPLICATION OF WORDS NOW OBSOLETE, OR OF OLD FORM.

N.B. After the words the References are to the pages and lines of Whitney's Emblems; in the Dramas to the act, scene, and line, according to the Cambridge Edition, 8vo, in 9 vols. 1866.

WORD.	REFERENCE.	PASSAGE.
Accidentes .	p. vi. line 2	yet they set them selues a worke in handlinge suche accidentes, as haue bin done in times paste.
	p. vii. l. 21	this present time behouldeth the accidentes of former times.
	Tempest, v. 1, 305	And the particular accidents gone by.
	1 *Hen. IV.* i. 2, 199.	And nothing pleaseth but rare accidents.
	W. Tale, iv. 4, 527	As the unthought-on accident is guilty.
affectioned .	p. vi. l. 5	one too much affectioned, can scarce finde an ende of the praises of Hector.
	Twelfth N. ii. 3, 139	An affectioned ass.
	L. L. Lost, i. 2, 158.	I do affect the very ground.
aie, or aye	p. 21, l. 7 .	With theise hee liues, and doth reioice for aie.
	p. 111, l. 12	Thy fame doth liue, and eeke, for aye shall laste.
	M. N. Dr. i. 1, 71	For aye to be in shady cloister mew'd.
	Pericles, v. 3, 95 .	The worth that learned charity aye wears.
	Tr. and Cr. iii. 2, 152	To feed for aye her lamp and flames of love.
alder, or elder	p. 120, l. 5	And why? theise two did alder time decree.
	2 *Hen. VI.* i. 1, 28 .	With you my alder, liefest sovereign.
	Tr. and Cr. ii. 2, 104	Virgins and boys, mid-age and wrinkled eld.
	Rich. II. ii. 3, 43 .	— which elder days shall ripen.

WORD.	REFERENCE.	PASSAGE.
amisse	p. 211, l. 16	That all too late shee mourn'd, for her amisse.
	Hamlet, iv. 5, 18	Each toy seems prologue to some great amiss.
	Sonnet cli. 3	Then gentle cheater urge not my amiss.
	Sonnet xxxv. 7	Myself corrupting, salving thy amiss.
annoyes	p. 219, l. 9	His pleasures shalbee mated with annoyes.
	Rich. III. v. 3, 156	Guard thee from the boar's annoy!
	Tit. An. iv. 1, 50	— root of thine annoy.
	3 *Hen. VI.* v. 7, 45	— farewell, sour annoy!
assaie	p. 34, l. 13	But when the froste, and coulde, shall thee assaie.
	p. 40, l. 3	With reasons firste, did vertue him assaie.
	1 *Hen. IV.* v. 4, 34	I will assay thee; so defend thyself.
	Hamlet, ii. 2, 71	Never more to give the assay of arms against your majesty.
a worke	p. vi. l. 2	They set them selues a worke in handlinge.
	2 *Hen. IV.* iv. 3, 108	for that sets it a-work.
	K. Lear, iii. 5, 6	set a-work by a reproveable badness.
Baie, *or* baye	p. 213, l. 3	Wherefore, in vaine aloude he barkes and baies.
	p. 191, l. 4	And curteous speeche, dothe keepe them at the baye.
	Cymb. v. 5, 222	— set the dogs o' the street to bay me.
	J. Cæs. iv. 3, 27	I had rather be a dog, and bay the moon.
	T. of Shrew, v. 2, 56	Your deer does hold you at a bay.
	2 *Hen. IV.* i. 3, 80	— baying him at the heels.
bale	p. 180, l. 7	A worde once spoke, it can retourne no more, But flies awaie, and ofte thy bale doth breede.
	p. 219, l. 16	Lo this their bale, which was her blisse you heare.
	1 *Hen. VI.* v. 4, 122	By sight of these our baleful enemies.
	Coriol. i. 4, 155	Rome and her rats are at the point of battle; The one side must have bale.
bane *or* bayne	p. 141, l. 7	Euen so it happes, wee ofte our bayne doe brue.
	p. 211, l. 14	Did breede her bane, who mighte haue bath'de in blisse.
	Tit. An. v. 3, 73	Lest Rome herself be bane unto herself.
	M. for M. i. 2, 123	Like rats that ravin down their proper bane.
	Macbeth, v. 3, 59	I will not be afraid of death and bane.
banne	p. 189, l. 10	And in a rage, the brutishe beaste did banne.
	Hamlet, iii. 2, 246	With Hecate's ban thrice blasted.
	1 *Hen. VI.* v. 4, 42	Fell, banning hag, enchantress, hold thy tongue!
	2 *Hen. VI.* iii. 2, 319	Every joint should seem to curse and ban.

WORD.	REFERENCE.	PASSAGE.
betide . . .	p. 9, l. 2 .	Woulde vnderstande what weather shoulde betide.
	3 *Hen. VI.* iv. 6, 88.	A salve for any sore that may betide.
	T. G. Ver. iv. 3, 40 .	Recking as little what betideth me.
betime . . .	p. 50, l. 1 .	Betime when sleepe is sweete, the chattringe swallowe cries.
	Hamlet, iv. 5, 47 . .	All in the morning betime.
	2 *Hen. VI.* iii. 3, 285	And stop the rage betime.
bewraye . . .	p. v. l. 30 .	bewrayeth it selfe as the smoke bewrayeth the fire.
	p. 124, l. 5	Theire foxes coate, theire fained harte bewraies.
	1 *Hen. VI.* iv. 1, 107	Bewray'd the faintness of my master's heart.
	K. Lear, ii. 1, 107 .	He bewray his practice.
	3 *Hen. VI.* i. 1, 211 .	Whose looks bewray her anger.
bleared . . .	p. 94, l. 7 .	What meanes her eies ? so bleared, sore, and redd.
	T. of Shrew, v. 1, 103	While counterfeit supposes blear'd thine eyne.
	M. Venice, iii. 2, 58 .	Dardanian wives with blear'd visages.
bloodes . . .	p. 99, l. 18	Can not be free, from guilte of childrens bloodes.
	Cymb. i. 1, 1 .	Our bloods no more obey the heavens than our courtiers.
broache . . .	p. 7, l. 2	And bluddie broiles, at home are set a broache.
	Rom. and J. i. 1, 102	Who set this ancient quarrel new abroach?
	2 *Hen. IV.* iv. 2, 14 .	Alack what mischiefs might he set a broach.
budgettes .	p. 209, l. 10 .	The quicke Phisition did commaunde that tables should be set About the misers bed, and budgettes forth to bring.
	W. Tale, iv. 3, 18	If tinkers may have leave to live, And bear the sow-skin budget.
Carle	p. 209, l. 5	At lengthe, this greedie carle the Lythergie posseste.
	Cymb. v. 2, 4 . . .	— this carl, a very drudge of nature's.
	As Like it, iii. 5, 106	And he hath bought the cottage and the bounds That the old carlot once was master of.

WORD.	REFERENCE.	PASSAGE.
carpes	p. 50, l. 3	Which carpes the pratinge crewe, who like of bablinge beste.
	K. Lear, i. 4, 194	— your insolent retinue do hourly carp and quarrel.
	1 *Hen. VI.* iv. 1, 90.	This fellow here, with envious carping tongue.
catch'de . .	p. 77, l. 6	Yet, with figge leaues at lengthe was catch'de, & made the fisshers praie.
	Rom. and J. iv. 5, 47	But one thing to rejoice and solace in, And cruel death hath catch'd it from my sight!
cates	p. 18, l. 9	Whose backe is fraighte with cates and daintie cheare.
	p. 202, l. 12 .	And for to liue with CODRVS cates: a roote and barly bonne.
	T. of Shrew, ii. 1, 187	My super-dainty Kate, for dainties are all Kates.
	1 *Hen. VI.* ii. 3, 78.	That we may taste of your wine, and see what cates you have.
	C. Errors, iii. 1, 28.	But though my cates be mean, take them in good part.
caytiffe .	p. 95, l. 19	See heare how vile, theise caytiffes doe appeare.
	Rom. and J. v. 1, 52	Here lives a caitiff wretch.
	Rich. II. i. 2, 53.	A caitiff recreant to my cousin Hereford.
clogges . . .	p. 82, l. 9	Then, loue the onelie crosse, that clogges the worlde with care.
	Macbeth, iii. 6, 42	You'll rue the time that clogs me with this answer.
	Rich. II. i. 3, 200	Bear not along the clogging burden of a guilty soul.
cockescombe	p. 81, l. 5	A motley coate, a cockescombe, or a bell.
	M. Wives, v. 5, 133	Shall I have a coxcomb of frize?
	K. Lear, ii. 4, 119	She knapped 'em o' the coxcombs with a stick.
consummation.	p. xi. l. 23	wee maie behoulde the consummatiō of happie ould age.
	Cymb. iv. 2, 281	Quiet consummation have.
	Hamlet, iii. 1, 63.	'Tis a consummation devoutly to be wish'd.
corrupte . .	p. xiv. l. 19	too much corrupte with curiousnes and newfanglenes.
	1 *Hen. VI.* v. 4, 45.	Corrupt and tainted with a thousand vices.
	Hen. VIII. i. 2, 116	the mind growing once corrupt, They turn to vicious forms.

WORD.	REFERENCE.	PASSAGE.
corse . . .	p. 109, l. 30	But fortie fiue before, did carue his corse.
	W. Tale, iv. 4, 130 .	Like a bank, for love to lie and play on; not like a corse.
	Rom. and J. v. 2, 30	Poor living corse, clos'd in a dead man's tomb.
create . . .	p. 64, l. 1 .	Not for our selues alone wee are create.
	Hen. V. ii. 2, 31 . .	With hearts create of duty and of zeal.
	K. John, iv. 1, 107 .	Being create for comfort.
Deceaste .	p. 87, l. 13	Throughe Aschalon, the place where he deceaste.
	Cymb. i. 1, 38	His gentle lady—deceas'd as he was born.
delight .	p. xiii. l. 37	Lastlie, if anie deuise herein shall delight thee.
	Hamlet, ii. 2, 300 .	Man delights not me.
	Much Ado, ii. 1, 122	None but libertines delight him.
dernell .	p. 68, l. 2 .	The hurtfull tares, and dernell ofte doe growe.
	1 *Hen. VI.* iii. 2, 44.	'Twas full of darnel; do you like the taste?
	K. Lear, iv. 4, 4 .	Darnel, and all the idle weeds that grow.
determine .	p. x. l. 9	healthe and wealthe—determine with the bodie.
	Coriol. iii. 3, 43 .	Must all determine here?
	Coriol. v. 3, 119 .	I purpose not to wait,—till these wars determine.
distracte . .	p. 102, l. 17	Which when hee sawe, as one distracte with care.
	K. Lear, iv. 6, 281 .	Better I were distract: so should my thoughts be severed from my griefs.
	2 *Hen. VI.* iii. 3, 318	My hair be fix'd on end as one distract.
doombe . .	p. 30, l. 4 .	Wronge sentence paste by AGAMEMNONS doombe.
	As Like it, i. 3, 79 .	Firm and irrevocable is my doom, which I have pass'd upon her.
	Rom. and J. iii. 2, 67	Then, dreadful trumpet, sound the general doom.
doubt	p. 148, l. 3	The boye no harme did doubt, vntill he felt the stinge.
	Rich. II. iii. 4, 69	'Tis doubt he will be.
	Coriol. iii. 1, 152.	More than you doubt the change on't.

WORD.	REFERENCE.	PASSAGE.
dulcet . . .	p. 128, l. 11	And biddes them feare, their sweet and dulcet meates.
	As Like it, v. 4, 61 .	According to the fool's bolt, Sir, and such dulcet diseases.
	Twelfth N. ii. 3, 55 .	To hear by the nose is a dulcet in contagion.
dull	p. 103, l. 12	For ouermuch, dothe dull the finest wittes
	Hen. V. ii. 4, 16 .	For peace itself should not so dull a kingdom.
	Sonnet ciii. l. 8	Dulling my lines and doing me disgrace.
Eeke, *or* eke.	p. 2, l. 8 .	Before whose face, and eeke on euerye side.
	p. 45, l. 10	And eke this verse was grauen on the brasse.
	M. N. Dr. iii. 1, 85.	Most brisky juvenal, and eke most lovely Jew.
	All's Well, ii. 5, 73 .	With true observance seek to eeke out that.
	M. Wives, ii. 3, 67 .	And eke Cavaleiro Slender.
englished .	Title, l. 5 .	Englished and Moralized.
	M. Wives, i. 3, 44	— to be English'd rightly, is, I am Sir John Falstaff's.
ercksome .	p. 118, l. 4	With ercksome noise, and eke with poison fell.
	T. of Shrew, i. 2, 181	I know she is an irksome brawling scold.
	2 Hen. VI. ii. 1, 56 .	Irksome is this music to my heart.
erste . . .	p. 194, l. 20	As with his voice hee erste did daunte his foes.
	As Like it, iii. 5, 94 .	Thy company, which erst was irksome to me.
	2 Hen. VI. ii. 4, 13 .	That erst did follow thy proud chariot wheels.
eschewed .	p. vii. l. 19	examples—eyther to bee imitated, or eschewed.
	M. Wives, v. 5, 225 .	What cannot be eschew'd, must be embraced.
eternised . .	p. ii. l. 32 .	— learned men haue eternised to all posterities.
	2 Hen. VI. v. 3, 30 .	Saint Alban's battle won by famous York Shall be eterniz'd in all age to come.
euened .	p. 131, l. 6	If ÆGYPT spires, be euened with the soile.
	K. Lear, iv. 7, 80	To make him even o'er the time he has lost.
	Hamlet, v. 1, 27 .	Their even Christian.
extincte . .	p. iv. l. 32 .	deathe—coulde not extincte nor burie their memories.
	Othello, ii. 1, 81	Give renew'd fire to our extincted spirits.
	Rich. II. i. 3. 222	— be extinct with age.

WORD.	REFERENCE.	PASSAGE.
Facte . . .	p. 79, l. 22	Thinke howe his facte, was ILIONS foule deface.
	M. for M. v. 1, 432 .	Should she kneel down in mercy of this fact.
	2 *Hen. VI.* i. 3, 171 .	A fouler fact did never traitor in the land commit.
fardle . . .	p. 179, l. 9	Dothe venture life, with fardle on his backe.
	Hamlet, iii. 1, 76 .	Who would fardels bear, to groan and sweat under a weary life?
	W. Tale, v. 2, 2 .	I was by at the opening of the fardel.
falls . . .	p. 176, l. 7	Euen so, it falles, while carelesse times wee spende.
	J. Cæs. iii. 1, 244	I know not what may fall; I like it not.
feare . . .	p. 127, l. 11	Who while they liu'de did feare you with theire lookes.
	Ant. and C. ii. 6, 24	Thou canst not fear us, Pompey, with thy sails.
	M. for M. ii. 1, 2	Setting it up to fear the birds of prey.
fell. . . .	p. 3, l. 12 .	Hath Nature lente vnto this Serpent fell.
	M. N. Dr. v. 1, 221	A lion-fell, nor else no lion's dam.
	2 *Hen. VI.* iii. 1, 351	This fell tempest shall not cease to rage.
filed . . .	p. 30, l. 5 .	But howe? declare, Vlysses filed tonge Allur'de the Iudge, to giue a Iudgement wronge.
	Macbeth, iii. 1, 63	If't be so, for Banquo's issue have I fil'd my mind.
fittes . . .	p. 103, l. 11	Sometime the Lute, the Chesse, or Bowe by fittes.
	Tr. and Cr. iii. 1, 54	Well, you say so in fits.
floate . . .	p. 7, l. 10	This, robbes the good, and setts the theeues a floate.
	J. Cæs. iv. 3, 220	On such a full sea are we now afloat.
	Macbeth, iv. 2, 21	But float upon a wild and violent sea.
foile . . .	p. 4, l. 10 .	And breake her bandes, and bring her foes to foile.
	Tempest, iii. 1, 45	Did quarrel with the noblest grace she ow'd, And put it to the foil.
fonde . . .	p. 223, l. 7	Oh worldlinges fonde, that ioyne these two so ill.
	M. for M. v. 1, 105 .	Fond wretch, thou know'st not what thou speak'st.
	M. N. Dr. iii. 2, 317	How simple and how fond I am.

WORD.	REFERENCE.	PASSAGE.
forgotte	p. 5, l. 7	Yet time and tune, and neighbourhood forgotte.
	Othello, ii. 3, 178	How comes it, Michael, you are thus forgot?
	Rich. II. ii. 3, 37	That is not forgot which ne'er I did remember.
foyles	p. xvii. l. 18	PERFECTION needes no other foyles, suche helpes comme out of place.
	1 *Hen. IV.* iv. 2, 207	That which hath no foil to set it off.
fraies	p. 51, l. 6	Unto the good, a shieide in ghostlie fraies.
	1 *Hen. IV.* i. 2, 74	To the latter end of a fray, and the beginning of a feast.
	M. Venice, iii. 4, 68	And speak of frays, like a fine bragging youth.
frende	p. 172, l. 14	As bothe your Towne, and countrie, you maye frende.
	Macbeth, iv. 3, 10	As I shall find the time to friend.
	Hen. VIII. i. 2, 140.	Not friended by his wish.
frettes	p. 92, l. 1	The Lute...lack'de bothe stringes, and frettes.
	T. of Shrew, ii. 1, 148	She mistook her frets.
fustie	p. 80, l. 6	Or fill the sacke, with fustie mixed meale.
	Tr. and Cr. i. 3, 161	at this fusty stuff, The large Achilles...laughs out a loud applause.
Gan	p. 156, l. 3	At lengthe when all was gone, the pacient gan to see.
	Macbeth, i. 2, 54	The thane of Cawdor began a dismal conflict.
	Coriol. ii. 2, 112	— the din of war gan pierce his ready sense.
ghoste.	p. 141, l. 5	Beinge ask'd the cause, before he yeelded ghoste.
	1 *Hen. VI.* i. 1, 67	— cause him once more yield the ghost.
	Rich. III. i. 4, 36	— often did I strive to yield the ghost.
ginnes.	p. 97, l. 3	For to escape the fishers ginnes and trickes.
	Twelfth N. ii. 5, 77	Now is the woodcock near the gin.
	2 *Hen. VI.* iii. 1	Be it by gins, by snares.
gladde	p. 198, l. 10	And CODRVS had small cates, his harte to gladde.
	3 *Hen. VI.* iv. 6, 93.	— did glad my heart with hope.
	Tit. An. i. 2, 166	The cordial of mine age to glad my heart!

WORD.	REFERENCE.	PASSAGE.
glasse . . .	p. 113, l. 6 . . .	An acte moste rare, and glasse of true renoume.
	Twelfth N. iii. 4, 363	I my brother know yet liuing in my glasse.
	C. Errors, v. 1, 416.	Methinks you are my glass, and not my brother.
	J. Cæs. i. 2, 68 . .	So well as by reflection, I, your glass.
	Rich. II. i. 3, 208 .	Even in the glasses of thine eyes I see thy grieved heart.
glosse . . .	p. 219, l. 17 .	O loue, a plague, thoughe grac'd with gallant glosse.
	L. L. Lost, ii. 1, 47 .	The only soil of his fair virtue's gloss.
	Hen. VIII. v. 3, 71 .	Your painted gloss discovers,—words and weakness.
gripe . . .	p. 75, l. 2 .	Whose liuer still, a greedie gripe dothe rente.
	p. 199, l. 1, 2 .	If then, content the chiefest riches bee, And greedie gripes, that doe abounde be pore.
	Cymb. i. 6, 105 .	Join gripes with hands made hard with hourly falshood.
	Hen. VIII. v. 3, 100	Out of the gripes of cruel men.
guerdon . .	p. 15, l. 10	And shall at lenghte Actæons guerdon haue.
	Much Ado, v. 3, 5 .	Death in guerdon of her wrongs.
	1 *Hen. VI.* iii. 1, 170	— in reguerdon of that duty done.
guide . . .	p. 33, l. 5 .	And lefte her younge, vnto this tirauntes guide.
	Timon, i. 1, 244 .	Pray entertain them ; give them guide to us.
	Othello, ii. 3, 195 .	My blood begins my safer guides to rule.
guise . . .	p. 159, l. 9	Inquired what in sommer was her guise.
	Macbeth, v. 1, 16 . .	This is her very guise ; and, upon my life, fast asleep.
	Cymb. v. 1, 32 . .	To shame the guise o' the world.
Hale, hal'de	p. 71, l. 2 .	In hope at lengthe, an happie hale to haue.
	p. 37, l. 10	And AJAX gifte, hal'de HECTOR throughe the fielde.
	1 *Hen. VI.* v. 4, 64 .	Although ye hale me to a violent death.
	Tit. An. v. 3, 143 .	Hither hale that misbelieving Moor.
	1 *Hen. VI.* ii. 5, 3 .	Even like a man new haled from the rack.
happe . . .	p. 147, l. 13 .	So ofte it happes, when wee our fancies feede.
	p. 201, l. 29 . .	Wherefore, when happe, some goulden honie bringes?
	T. of Shrew, iv. 4, 102	Hap what hap may, I'll roundly go about her.
	Rom. and J. ii. 2, 190	His help to crave, and my dear hap to tell.

WORD.	REFERENCE.	PASSAGE.
harmes	p. 183, l. 7	In marble harde our harmes wee always graue.
	1 *Hen. VI.* iv. 7, 30.	My spirit can no longer bear these harms.
	Rich. III. ii. 2, 103	None can cure their harms by wailing.
hatche	p. 180, l. 9	A wise man then, settes hatche before the dore.
	K. John, i. 1, 171	In at the window, or else o'er the hatch.
	K. Lear, iii. 6, 71	Dogs leap the hatch and all are fled.
haughtie	p. 53, l. 7	In craggie rockes, and haughtie mountaines toppe.
	1 *Hen. VI.* iv. 1, 35.	Valiant and virtuous, full of haughty courage.
hauocke	p. 6, l. 6	Till all they breake, and vnto hauocke bringe.
	J. Cæs. iii. 1, 274	Cry "Havock," and let slip the dogs of war.
	K. John, ii. 1, 220	Wide havock made for bloody power.
heste	p. 87, l. 10	And life resigne, to tyme, and natures heste.
	Tempest, i. 2, 274	Refusing her grand hests.
	Tempest, iii. 1, 37	I have broke your hest to say so.
hidde	p. 43, l. 1	By vertue hidde, behoulde, the Iron harde.
	Much Ado, v. 1, 172	Adam, when he was hid in the garden.
	M. Venice, i. 1, 115	Two grains of wheat hid in two bushels of chaff.
Impe	p. 186, l. 14	You neede not THRACIA seeke, to heare some impe of ORPHEVS playe.
	p. 19, l. 9	But wicked Impes, that lewdlie runne their race.
	2 *Hen. IV.* v. 5, 43	The heavens thee guard and keep, most royal imp of fame.
	L. L. Lost, v. 2, 581	Great Hercules is presented by this imp.
indifferencie.	p. xiv. l. 29	those that are of good iudgemente, with indifferencie will reade.
	K. John, ii. 1, 579	Makes it take head from all indifferency.
	2 *Hen. IV.* iv. 3, 20.	An I had but a belly of any indifferency.
ingrate	p. 64, l. 3	And those, that are vnto theire frendes ingrate.
	T. of Shrew, i. 2, 266	— will not so graceless be, to be ingrate.
	1 *Hen. IV.* i. 3, 137.	As this ingrate and canker'd Bolinbroke.
ioye	p. 5, l. 5	And bothe, did ioye theire iarringe notes to sounde.
	T. of Shrew, Ind. 2, 76	Oh, how we joy to see your wit restored.
	2 *Hen. VI.* iii. 2, 364	Live thou to joy thy life.

WORD.	REFERENCE.	PASSAGE.
Kinde	p. 49, l. 16	And spend theire goodes, in hope to alter kinde.
	p. 178, l. 8	And where as malice is by kinde, no absence helpes at all.
	Ant. and C. v. 2, 259	Look you, that the worm will do his kind.
	J. Cæs. i. 3, 64	Why birds and beasts, from quality and kind.
	As Like it, iii. 2, 93	If the cat will after kind, So, be sure, will Rosalind.
knitte	p. 76, l. 2	And knittes theire subiectes hartes in one.
	M. N. Dr. iv. 1, 178	These couples shall eternally be knit.
	Macbeth, ii. 2, 37	Sleep that knits up the ravell'd sleave of care.
knotte	p. 142, l. 10	Yet, if this knotte of frendship be to knitte.
	Cymb. ii. 3, 116	To knit their souls...in self-figur'd knot.
	M. Wives, iii. 2, 64	He shall not knit a knot in his fortune.
Launch'de	p. 75, l. 11	Which being launch'de and prick'd with inward care.
	Rich. III. iv. 4, 224.	Whose hand soever lanced their tender hearts.
	Ant. and C. v. 1, 36.	We do lance diseases in our bodies.
leaue	p. 80, l. 5	For noe complaintes, coulde make him leaue to steale.
	Tr. and Cr. iii. 3, 132	What some men do, while some men leave to do!
let	p. 89, l. 8	But Riuers swifte, their passage still do let.
	p. 209, l. 9	But, when that nothinge coulde OPIMIVS sleepinge let.
	Hamlet, i. 4, 85	By heaven, I'll make a ghost of him that lets me.
	T. G. Ver. iii. 1, 113	What lets, but one may enter at her window.
like	p. xi. l. 14	if it shall like your honour to allowe of anie of them.
	K. Lear, ii. 2, 85	His countenance likes me not.
	T. G. Ver. iv. 2, 54	The music likes you not.
linke, linckt	p. 226, l. 8	Take heede betime: and linke thee not with theise.
	p. 133, l. 4	And heades all balde, weare newe in wedlocke linckt.
	1 *Hen. VI.* v. 5, 76	Margaret, he be link'd in love.
	Hamlet, i. 5, 55	though to a radiant angel linked.

WORD.	REFERENCE.	PASSAGE.
liste . . .	p. 63, l. 3	And with one hande, he guydes them where he liste.
	T. of Shrew, iii. 2, 159	Now take them up, quoth he, if any list.
lobbe . .	p. 145, l. 6	Let Grimme haue coales : and lobbe his whippe to lashe.
	M. N. Dr. ii. 1, 16 .	Farewell, thou lob of spirits ; I'll be gone.
lotterie	p. 61	Her Maiesties poesie, at the great Lotterie in London.
	M. Venice, i. 2, 25	The lottery—in these three chests of gold, silver and lead.
	All's Well, i. 3, 83	— 'twould mend the lottery well.
lustie . .	p. 9, l. 1	A YOUTHEFVLL Prince, in prime of lustie yeares.
	As Like it, ii. 3, 52 .	Therefore my age is as a lusty winter.
	T. G. Ver. iv. 2, 25 .	Let's tune, and to it lustily a while.
Meane .	p. 23, l. 12	The meane preferre, before immoderate gaine.
	M. Venice, i. 2, 6	It is no mean happiness, therefore, to be seated in the mean.
mid .	p. 160, l. 1	A Satyre, and his hoste, in mid of winter's rage.
	Rich. III. v. 3, 77	About the mid of night come to my tent.
misliked . .	p. xiv. l. 22	Some gallant coulours are misliked.
	2 *Hen. VI.* i. 1, 135.	'Tis not my speeches that you do mislike.
	3 *Hen. VI.* iv. 1, 24.	Setting your scorns and your mislike aside.
misse . .	p. 149, l. 15 . .	Or can we see so soone an others misse.
	1 *Hen. IV.* v. 4, 105	O, I should have a heavy miss of thee.
mockes and mowes.	p. 169, l. 4	Of whome both mockes, and apishe mowes he gain'd.
	Othello, v. 2, 154.	O mistress, villainy hath made mocks of love!
	Cymb. i. 7, 40.	— contemn with mows.
motley . . .	p. 81, l. 5 .	A motley coate, a cockes combe, or a bell.
	Hen. VIII. Prol. 15.	A fellow in a long motley coat, guarded with yellow.
	As Like it, ii. 7, 43 .	I am ambitious for a motley coat.

WORD.	REFERENCE.	PASSAGE.
muskecattes.	p. 79, l. 1, 2 . .	Heare LAIS fine, doth braue it on the stage, With muskecattes sweete, and all shee coulde desire.
	All's Well, v. 2, 18 .	fortune's cat,—but not a musk-cat.
Neare .	p. 12, l. 3 .	Where, thowghe they toile, yet are they not the neare.
	Rich. II. v. 1, 88	Better far off, than—near, be ne'er the near.
newfanglenes	p. xiv. l. 19	too much corrupte with curiousnes and newfanglenes.
	L. L. Lost, i. 1, 106.	Than wish a snow in May's new fangled shows.
	As Like it, iv. 1, 135	— more new-fangled than an ape.
nones . . .	p. 103, l. 10	And studentes muste haue pastimes for the nones.
	Hamlet, iv. 7, 159 .	I'll have prepared him a chalice for the nonce.
	1 *Hen. IV.* i. 2, 172.	I have cases of buckram for the nonce.
Occasion .	p. 181, l. 1	What creature thou? Occasion I doe showe.
	K. John, iv. 2, 125 .	Withhold thy speed, dreadful occasion.
	2 *Hen. IV.* iv. 1, 71.	And are enforced from our most quiet there, By the rough torrent of occasion.
ope .	p. 71, l. 9 .	Let Christians then, the eies of faithe houlde ope.
	C. Errors, iii. 1, 73.	I'll break ope the gate.
	2 *Hen. VI.* iv. 9, 13.	Then, heaven, set ope thy everlasting gates.
Packe. . .	p. 42, l. 9 .	Driue VENVS hence, let BACCHVS further packe.
	C. Errors, iii. 2, 151	'Tis time, I think, to trudge, pack and be gone.
	T. of Shrew, ii. 1, 176	If she do bid me pack, I'll give her thanks.
paine . . .	p. 85, l. 8 .	The Florentines made banishement theire paine.
	M. for M. ii. 4, 86 .	Accountant to the law upon that pain.
	Rich. II. i. 3, 153	— against thee upon pain of life.
pelfe . . .	p. 198, l. 8	No choice of place, nor store of pelfe he had.
	Timon, i. 2	Immortal gods, I crave no pelf, I pray for no man but myself.
personage .	p. 187, l. 8	And dothe describe theire personage, and theire guise.
	Twelfth N. i. 5, 146.	Of what personage and years is he?
	M. N. Dr. iii. 2, 292	And with her personage, her tall personage.

WORD.	REFERENCE.	PASSAGE.
pickthankes.	p. 150, l. 4 .	With pickthankes, blabbes, and subtill Sinons broode.
	1 *Hen. IV.* iii. 2, 24.	By smiling pick-thanks, and base news mongers.
pikes . . .	p. 41, l. 17	And thoughe long time, they doe escape the pikes.
	Much Ado, v. 2, 18 .	You must put in the pikes with a vice.
	3 *Hen. VI.* i. 1, 244.	The soldiers should have toss'd me on their pikes.
pill .	p. 151, l. 4	His subiectes poore, to shaue, to pill, and poll.
	Timon, iv. 1, 11	Large handed robbers your grave masters are And pill by law.
pithie .	p. x. l. 31	a worke both pleasaunte and pithie.
	T. of Shrew, iii. 1, 65	To teach you gamut in a briefer sort, More pleasant, pithy, and effectual.
poastes . .	p. 39, l. 7	And he that poastes, to make awaie his landes.
	Tr. and Cr. i. 3, 93.	And posts, like the commandment of a king.
preiudicate .	p. xiii. l. 44	with a preiudicate opinion to condempne.
	All's Well, i. 2, 7	Wherein our dearest friend prejudicates the business.
proper	p. iv. l. 7	that which hee desired to haue proper to him selfe.
	M. for M. v. 1, 110.	Faults proper to himself: if he had so offended.
purge .	p. 68, l. 5 .	When graine is ripe, with siue to purge the seede.
	M. N. Dr. iii. 1, 146	I will purge thy mortal grossness so.
	Rom. and J. v. 3, 225	And here I stand, both to impeach and purge Myself condemned and myself excused.
Quaile . . .	p. 111, l. 5	No paine, had power his courage highe to quaile.
	Ant. and C. v. 2, 85.	But when he meant to quail and shake the orb.
	3 *Hen. VI.* ii. 3, 54 .	This may plant courage in their quailing breasts.
queste . . .	p. 213, l. 5	But yet the Moone, who did not heare his queste.
	M. for M. iv. 1, 60 .	Run with these false and most contrarious quests.
	C. Errors, i. 1, 130 .	Might bear him company in the quest of him.
Reaue .	p. 25, l. 3 .	Or straunge conceiptes, doe reaue thee of thie rest.
	All's Well, v. 3, 86 .	To reave her of what should stead her most.
	2 *Hen. VI.* v. 1, 187.	To reave the orphan of his patrimony.

WORD.	REFERENCE.	PASSAGE.
rente	p. 30, l. 3	What is the cause, shee rentes her goulden haire?
	Tit. An. iii. 1, 261	Rent off thy silver hair (*note*).
	2 *Hen. VI.* i. 1, 121	torn and rent my very heart.
ripes	p. 23, l. 1	When autumne ripes, the frutefull fieldes of graine.
	As Like it, ii. 7, 26	We ripe and ripe and then.
	2 *Hen. IV.* iv. 1, 13	He is retired, to ripe his growing fortunes.
roomes	p. 186, l. 12	the trees, and rockes, that lefte their roomes, his musicke for to heare.
	3 *Hen. VI.* iii. 2, 131	the unlook'd for issue—take their rooms, ere I can place myself.
	Rom. and J. i. 5, 24.	— give room! and foot it, girls.
ruthe	p. 4, l. 1	Three furies fell which turne the worlde to ruthe.
	Rich. II. iii. 4, 106	Rue even for ruth.
	Coriol. i. 1, 190	Would the nobility lay aside their ruth.
ruthefull	p. 13, l. 1	Of NIOBE, behoulde the ruthefull plighte.
	3 *Hen. VI.* ii. 5, 95	O, that my death would stay these ruthful deeds.
	Tr. and Cr. v. 3, 48	Spur them to ruthful work, rein them from ruth!
Sauced	p. 147, l. 4	He founde that sweete, was sauced with the sower.
	Tr. and Cr. i. 2, 23.	His folly sauced with discretion.
	Coriol. i. 9, 52	— dieted in praises sauced with lies.
scanne	p. 95, l. 6	Theise weare the two, that of this case did scanne.
	Othello, iii. 3, 248	I might entreat your honour to scan this thing no further.
	Hamlet, iii. 3, 75	That would be scann'd; a villain kills my father.
scape	p. 24, l. 4	And fewe there be can scape theise vipers vile.
	K. Lear, ii. 1, 80	the villain shall not scape.
sillye	p. 194, l. 7	For, as the wolfe, the sillye sheep did feare.
	3 *Hen. VI.* ii. 5, 43	— looking on their silly sheep.
	Cymb. v. 3, 86	there was a fourth man in a silly habit.
sith	p. 109, l. 3	And sithe, the worlde might not their matches finde.
	3 *Hen. VI.* i. 1, 110.	Talk not of France, sith thou hast lost it all.
	Othello, iii. 3, 415	But, sith I am enter'd in this cause so far.

WORD.	REFERENCE.	PASSAGE.
sithe . . .	p. 225, l. 6	For, time attendes with shredding sithe for all.
	L. L. Lost, i. 1, 6 .	That honour which shall bate his scythe's keen edge.
	Ant. and C. iii. 13, 193	I'll make death love me, for I will contend Even with his pestilent scythe.
skante .	p. 199, l. 8	And, whilst wee thinke our webbe to skante.
	Ant. and C. iv. 2, 21	Scant not my cups.
	K. Lear, iii. 2, 66	Return, and force their scanted courtesy.
skap'd .	p. 153, l. 1	The stagge, that hardly skap'd the hunters in the chase.
	3 *Hen. VI.* ii. 1, 1	I wonder how our princely father scap'd.
	Hamlet, i. 3, 38 .	Virtue itself 'scapes not calumnious strokes.
soueraigne .	p. 161, l. 8	But that your tonge is soueraigne, as I heare.
	Coriol. ii. 1, 107 .	The most sovereign prescription in Galen is but empyric.
spare . . .	p. 60, l. 5 .	VLVSSES wordes weare spare, but rightlie plac'd.
	As Like it, iii. 2, 18 .	As it is a spare life look you.
	2 *Hen. IV.* iii. 2, 255	O give me the spare men, and spare me.
square . .	p. 140, l. 8	Each bragginge curre, beginnes to square, and brall.
	Ant. & C. iii. 13, 41	Mine honesty and I begin to square.
	Tit. An. ii. 1, 99. .	And are you such fools to square for this?
stall'd . . .	p. 38, l. 10	And to be stall'd, on sacred iustice cheare.
	All's Well, i. 3, 116 .	Leave me; stall this in your bosom.
	Rich. III. i. 3, 206 .	Deck'd in thy rights, as thou art stall'd in mine.
starke . . .	p. ix. l. 31 .	whose frendship is frozen, and starke towarde them.
	1 *Hen. IV.* v. 3, 40 .	Many a nobleman lies stark and stiff.
	Rom. and J. iv. 1, 103	Shall stiff, and stark and cold, appear like death.
stithe . . .	p. 192, l. 5	For there with strengthe he strikes vppon the stithe.
	Hamlet, iii. 2, 78. .	And my imaginations are as foul as Vulcan's stithy.
	Tr. and Cr. iv. 5, 255	By the forge that stithied Mars his helm.

WORD.	REFERENCE.	PASSAGE.
swashe . .	p. 145, l. 5	Giue PAN, the pipe; giue bilbowe blade, to swashe.
	Rom. and J. i. 1, 60.	Gregory, remember thy swashing blow.
	As Like it, i. 3, 116 .	We'll have a swashing and a martial outside.
Teene . .	p. 138, l. 14 .	Not vertue hurtes, but turnes her foes to teene.
	L. L. Lost, iv. 3, 160	Of sighs, of groans, of sorrow, and of teene.
	Rom. and J. i. 3, 14.	To my teen be it spoken.
threate .	p. 85, l. 11	And eke Sainct Paule, the slothful thus doth threate.
	Rich. III. i. 3, 113	What threat you me with telling of the king?
	Tit. An. ii. 1, 39.	Are you so desperate grown to threat your friends?
Vndergoe .	p. 223, l. 3	First, vndergoes the worlde with might, and maine.
	Much Ado, v. 2, 50 .	Claudio undergoes my challenge.
	Cymb. iii. 5, 110 .	— undergo those employments.
vnmeete . .	p. 81, l. 12	And fooles vnmeete, in wisedomes seate to sitte.
	M. for M. iv. 3, 63 .	A creature unprepar'd, unmeet for death.
	Much Ado, iv. 1, 181	Prove you that any man convers'd with me at hours unmeet.
vnneth .	p. 209, l. 5, 6 .	At lengthe, this greedie carle the Lethergie posseste: That vnneth hee could stere a foote.
	2 Hen. VI. ii. 4, 8 .	Uneath may she endure the flinty streets.
vnperfecte .	p. 122, l. 10 .	Behoulde, of this vnperfecte masse, the goodly worlde was wroughte.
	Othello, ii. 3, 284.	One unperfectness shews me another.
vnrest .	p. 94, l. 12	It shewes her selfe, doth worke her owne vnrest.
	Rich. III. iv. 4, 29 .	Rest thy unrest on England's lawful earth.
	Rich. II. ii. 4, 22	Witnessing storms to come, woe and unrest.
vnsure . . .	p. 191, l. 3	So, manie men do stoope to sightes vnsure.
	Macbeth, v. 4, 19. .	Thoughts speculative their unsure hopes relate.
	Hamlet, iv. 4, 51 .	Exposing what is mortal and unsure.

WORD.	REFERENCE.	PASSAGE.
vnthriftes .	p. 17, l. 18	And wisedome still, againste such vnthriftes cries.
	Rich. II. ii. 3, 120 .	My rights and royalties—given away to upstart unthrifts.
	M. Venice, v. 1, 16 .	And with an unthrift love did run from Venice.
Wagge . .	p. 148, l. 14	The wanton wagge with poysoned stinge assay'd.
	L. L. Lost, v. 2, 108	Making the bold wag by their praises bolder.
	W. Tale, i. 2, 65.	Was not my lord the verier wag of the two.
weakelinges.	p. 16, l. 10	Wee weakelinges proove, and fainte before the ende.
	3 *Hen. VI.* v. 1, 37	And, weakling, Warwick takes his gift again.
wighte .	p. 24, l. 7 .	The faithfull wighte, dothe neede no collours brave.
	M. Wives, i. 3, 35	I ken the wight: he is of substance good.
	Othello, ii. 1, 157.	She was a wight, if ever such wight were.
Yerke . . .	p. 6, l. 5	They praunce, and yerke, and out of order flinge.
	Hen. V. iv. 7, 74	With wild rage, yerk out their armed heels.
	Othello, i. 2, 5.	I had thought to have yerked him here under the ribs.
younglinge .	p. 132, l. 20	Before he shotte: a younglinge thus did crye.
	T. of Shrew, ii. 1, 329	Youngling! thou canst not love so dear as I.
	Tit. An. iv. 2. 93	I tell you, younglings, not Enceladus.

Sambucus, 1564, *p.* 15.

II.

SUBJECTS OF THE EMBLEM · IMPRESE AND ILLUSTRATIONS, WITH THEIR MOTTOES AND SOURCES.

The * denotes there is no device given in our volume.

DEVICE.	PAGE.	MOTTO.	SOURCE.
Actæon and Hounds .	275	*In receptatores sicariorum*	Alciat, *Emb.* 52, Ed. 1551, p. 60.
	276	*Ex domino servus*	Aneau's *Picta Poesis*, Ed. 1552, f. 41.
	277	*Voluptas ærumnosa* .	Sambucus, Ed. 1564, p. 128.
	278	,, ,,	Whitney's *Emb.* Ed. 1586, p. 15.
Adam hiding in the Garden.	416	*Dominus vivit & videt* .	Whitney's *Emb.* Ed. 1586, p. 229.
	416	*Vbi es?*	Montenay's *Emb.* Ed. 1584.
	416	*Vbi es?*	*Stamm Buch*, Emb. 65, Ed. 1619, p. 290.
Adam's Apple. Pl. X.	132	*Vijt Adams Appel Sproot Ellende Zonde en Doodt.* .	Vander Veen's *Zinne-beelden*, Ed. 1642.
Adamant on the Anvil	347	*Quem nulla pericula terrent* .	Le Bey de Batilly's *Emb.* 29, Ed. 1596.
Æneas bearing Anchises.	191	*Pietas filiorum in parentes* .	Alciat, *Emb.* 194, Ed. 1581.
	191	,, ,,	Whitney's *Emb.* Ed. 1586, p. 163.
Alciat's Device . .	211	*Virtuti fortuna comes* . .	Giovio, *Dev. &c.* Ed. 1561.
*Annunciation of the Virgin Mary.	124	*Fortitudo ejus Rhodum tenuit*	Drummond's *Scotland*, Ed. 1665.
Ants and Grasshopper	149	*Contraria industriæ ac desidiæ præmia.*	Freitag's *Myth. Eth.* Ed. 1579, p. 29.
	148	*Dum ætatis ver agitur: consule brumæ.*	Whitney's *Emb.* Ed. 1586, p. 159.
Ape and Miser's Gold,	128, 487	*Malè parta malè dilabuntur*	Whitney's *Emb.* Ed. 1586, p. 169.
	486	,, ,,	Paradin's *Dev. Her.* Ed. 1562, f. 174.

DEVICE.	PAGE.	MOTTO.	SOURCE.
Ape and Miser's Gold	128	*Ut parta labuntur*	Cullum's *Hawsted*, Ed. 1813, p. 159.
	486	. . . .	Symeoni's *Imprese, &c.*
Apollo receiving the Christian Muse.	379	*Poetarum gloria* .	Le Bey de Batilly's *Emb.* 51, Ed. 1596.
*Apple - tree on a Thorn.	123	*Per vincula crescit*	Drummond's *Scotland*, Ed. 1665.
Arion and the Dolphin	280	*In avaros, vel quibus melior conditio ab extraneis offertur.*	Alciat, *Emb.* 89, Ed. 1581, p. 323.
	280, 281	*Homo homini lupus*	Whitney's *Emb.* Ed. 1586, p. 144.
*Arrow through three Birds.	123	*Dederit ne viam Casusve Deusve.*	Drummond's *Scotland*, Ed. 1655.
Arrow wreathed on a Tomb.	183	*Sola vivit in illo*	Paradin's *Dev. Her.* Ed. 1562, f. 30.
	126	,, ,,	*Gent. Mag.* Nov. 1811, p. 410.
Ass and Wolf .	53		*Dyalogus Creaturarum*, Ed. 1480.
	54	*Scelesti hominis imago, et exitus.*	*Apologi Creat.* Ed. 1584, f. 54.
Astronomer, Magnet, and Pole-star.	335	*Mens immota manet* .	Sambucus' *Emb.* Ed. 1584, p. 84.
	335	,, ,,	Whitney's *Emb.* Ed. 1586, p. 43.
Athenian Coin .	8	ΑΘΕ . .	Eschenburg's *Man.* Ed. 1844, p. 351.
*Atlas .	245	*Sustinet nec fatiscit*	Giovio's *Dialogue*, Ed. 1561, p. 129.
Bacchus .	247	*Ebrietas*	Boissard's *Theat. V. H.* Ed. 1596, p. 213.
	247, 248	. . . . . .	*Le Microcosme*, Ed. 1562.
	248	*In statuam Bacchi* .	Alciat, *Emb.* Ed. 1581, p. 113.
	248	,, ,,	Whitney's *Emb.* Ed. 1586, p. 187.
Ban-dog . .	482	*Canis queritur nimium nocere.*	Sambucus' *Emb.* Ed. 1599, p. 172.
	483	*Feriunt summos fulmina montes.*	Whitney's *Emb.* Ed. 1586, p. 140.
Barrel full of Holes .	332	*Hac illac perfluo*	Paradin's *Dev. Her.* Ed. 1562, f. 88.
	331	*Frustrà*	Whitney's *Emb.* Ed. 1586, p. 12.
Bear and Ragged Staff	236		Whitney's *Emb.* Ed. 1586, Frontispiece.
Bear, Cub, and Cupid	348	*Perpolet incultum paulatim tempus amorem.*	*Tronus Cupid.* Ed. *about* 1598, f. 2.

DEVICE.	PAGE.	MOTTO.	SOURCE.
Bear, Cub, and Cupid	349	. . . .	Boissard's *Emb.* 43, Ed. 1596.
Bees types of a well-governed People.	358	Πῶς λαοῦ πειθήνιου βασιλεῖ .	Horapollo, Ed. 1551, p. 87.
	360	*Principis clementia*	Alciat, *Emb.* 148, Ed. 1551, p. 161.
Bees types of Love for our Native Land.	361	*Patria cuique chara* . .	Whitney's *Emb.* Ed. 1586, p. 200.
Bellerophon and Chimæra.	299	*Consilio et virtute Chimæram superare, id est, fortiores et deceptores.*	Alciat, *Emb.* 14, Ed. 1581.
Bible of the Poor. Pl. VI.	46	*Ecce virgo concipiet et pariet filium, &c.*	Humphrey's Fac-simile from Pl. 2, *Block-book*, 1410-20.
Bird caught by an Oyster (*see* Mouse).	130	*Speravi et perii* .	Cullum's *Hawsted*, Ed. 1813.
*Bird in Cage and Hawk.	124	*Il mal me preme et me spaventa a Peggio.*	Drummond's *Scotland*, Ed. 1665.
Block Book, specimens. Pl. VI.	46	*Ecce virgo concipiet et pariet filium, &c.*	Humphrey's Fac-simile from Pl. 2, *Block-book*, 1410-20.
Pl. VII.	49	*Conversi ab idolis, &c.*	Tracings photo-lithed from *Hist. S. Joan. Euang.* About 1430.
Pl. VIII.	49	*Datæ sunt mulieri duæ alæ aquilæ, &c.*	Tracings photo-lithed from *Hist. S. Joan. Euang.* About 1430.
Block Print. Pl. XV.	407	*Seven ages of man*	*Archæologia*, vol. xxxv., 1853, p. 167, a print from original in *Brit. Museum.*
Brasidas and his Shield	195	*Perfidus familiaris*	Aneau's *Picta Poesis*, Ed. 1552, p. 18.
	195		Whitney's *Emb.* Ed. 1586, p. 141.
Brutus, Death of .	202	*Fortuna virtutem superans* .	Alciat, *Emb.* 119, Ed. 1581, p. 430.
	202	,, ,,	Whitney's *Emb.* Ed. 1586, p. 70.
Butterfly and Candle .	151	*Cosi vivo piacer conduce à morte.*	Paradin's *Dev. Her.* Ed. 1562.
	152	*La guerre doulce aux inexperimentes.*	Corrozet's *Hecatomg.* Ed. 1540.
	152	*Brevis et damnosa voluptas* .	Camerarius, Ed. 1596.
	152	,, ,,	Vænius' *Emb. of Love*, Ed. 1608, p. 102.
	152	*Breue gioia*	Vænius' *Emb. of Love*, Ed. 1608, p. 102.
	153	*D'amor soverchio*	Symeoni's *Imprese*, Ed. 1561.
*Camel and his Driver.	283	*Homo homini Deus* .	Cousteau's *Pegma*, Ed. 1555, p. 323.

DEVICE.	PAGE.	MOTTO.	SOURCE.
*Camomile trodden down.	124	*Fructus calcata dat amplos* .	Drummond's *Scotland*, Ed. 1665.
Cannon bursting .	344	. .	Beza's *Emb.* 8; Ed. 1580.
Canoness (*see* Nun) .	469		
Cebes, Tablet of .	12	*Picture of Human Life*	Ed. "Francphordio," anno 1507.
Pl. I. . .	13	,, ,,	Ed. Berkeli, 1670, De Hooghe.
Pl. I.*b* .	68	,, ,,	Old Woodcut.
Chaos .	448	*Il Caos*	Symeoni's *Ovid*, Ed. 1559, p. 12.
ΧΑΟΣ	449	*Sine iustitia confusio* .	Aneau's *Picta Poesis*, Ed. 1551, p. 49.
	450	,, ,,	Whitney's *Emb.* Ed. 1586, p. 122.
Chess an Emblem of Life.	320	*La fin nous faict tous egaulx*	Perriere's *Th. Bons Engins*, 27; Ed. 1539.
	321	,, ,,	Corrozet's *Hecatomg.* Ed. 1540
Child and motley Fool	484	*Fatuis leuia committito.*	Whitney's *Emb.* Ed. 1586, p. 81.
	484	,, ,,	Sambucus.
Chivalry, Wreath of (*see* Wreath).	169		
Christian Love presenting the Soul to Christ. Pl. II.	32		Vænius' *Amoris Div. Emb.* Ed. 1615.
Circe transforming Ulysses' men.	250	*Cauendum à meretricibus*	Alciat, *Emb.* 76, Ed. 1581, p. 184.
	250	*Homines voluptatibus transformantur.*	Whitney's *Emb.* Ed. 1586, p. 82.
	252	*Improba Siren desidia*	Reusner's *Emb.* Ed. 1581, p. 634.
*Cleopatra applying the Asps.	131		*Chimneypiece*, Lower Tabley Hall.
*Conscience, Power of	420	*Hic murus aheneus esto* .	*Emb. of Horace*, Ed. 1612, pp. 58 and 70.
Countryman and Viper	197	*Maleficio beneficium compensatum.*	Freitag's *Myth. Eth.* Ed. 1579.
	198	*Merces anguina* .	Reusner's *Emb.* Ed. 1581, p. 81.
	199	*In sinu alere serpentem* .	Whitney's *Emb.* Ed. 1586, p. 189.
Crab and Butterfly	15	*Festina lente*	Symeoni's *Dev.* Ed. 1561, p. 218.
Creation and Confusion. Pl. III.	35	*La creatione & confusione del mondo.*	Symeoni's *Ovid*, Ed. 1559, p. 13.
Crescent Moon . .	127	*Donec totum impleat orbem* .	Iovio's *Dial. des Dev.* Ed. 1561, p. 25.
	123	,, ,,	Drummond's *Scotland*, Ed. 1655.

DEVICE.	PAGE.	MOTTO.	SOURCE.
*Crossbow at full stretch.	126	*Ingenio superat vires* .	*Gent. Mag.* Nov. 1811, p. 416.
Crowns of Victory (*see* Wreaths, Four).	221		
*Crowns, Three, one on the Sea.	124	*Aliamque moratur*	Drummond's *Scotland*, Ed. 1655.
*Crucifix and kneeling Queen.	123	*Undique*	Drummond's *Scotland*, Ed. 1655.
Cupid and Bear (*see* Bear, Cub, and Cupid).	348		
Cupid and Death .	401	*De morte et amore: Iocosum*	Whitney's *Emb.* Ed. 1586, p. 132.
	401	,, ,,	Alciat, *Emb.* Ed. 1581.
	403	*De Morte et Cupidine* .	Peacham's *Min.* Ed. 1612, p. 172.
Cupid blinded, holding a Sieve.	329		Perriere's *Th. Bons Engins*, 1539, p. 77.
*Cupid felling a Tree .	324	"*By continuance*"	Vænius, Ed. 1608, p. 210.
Daphne changed to a Laurel.	296		Aneau's *Picta Poesis*, Ed. 1551, p. 47.
Dedication page	v		Alciat's *Emb.* Ed. 1661, Title-page.
Diana	3	*Quodcunque petit, consequitur*	Symeoni's *Ovid*, Ed. 1559, p. 2.
Diligence and Idleness	145		Perriere's *Th. Bons Engins*, Ed. 1539, Emb. 101.
	146	*Otiosi semper egentes* .	Whitney's *Emb.* Ed. 1586, p. 175.
Dog baying at the Moon.	270		Beza's *Emb.* Ed. 1580, Emb. 22.
	269	*Inanis ineptis*	Alciat, *Emb.* 164, Ed. 1581, p. 571.
	269	,, ,,	Whitney's *Emb.* Ed. 1586, p. 213.
	270	*Despicit alta Canis*	Camerarius, Ed. 1595, p. 63.
Dolphin and Anchor .	16	*Propera tarde*	Symeoni's *Imprese*, Ed. 1574, p. 175.
	16	.	Giovio's *Dialogo*, Ed. 1574, p. 10.
D. O. M. . .	464	*Domino Optimo Maximo*	Whitney's *Emb.* Ed. 1586, Frontispiece.
*Doves and winged Cupid.	245		Corrozet's *Hecatomg.* Ed. 1540, f. 70.
Drake's Ship	413	*Auxilio diuino* .	Whitney's *Emb.* Ed. 1586, p. 203.

DEVICE.	PAGE.	MOTTO.	SOURCE.
Eagle renewing its Feathers.	368	*Renouata iuuentus*	Camerarius, *Emb.* 34, Ed. 1596.
*Eclipses of Sun and Moon.	124	*Ipsa sibi lumen quod inuidet aufert.*	Drummond's *Scotland*, Ed. 1665.
Elephant and under-mined Tree.	196	*Nusquam tuta fides*	Sambucus' *Emb.* Ed. 1564, p. 184.
	196	,, ,,	Whitney's *Emb.* Ed. 1586, p. 150.
Elm and Vine . .	307	*Amicitia etiam post mortem durans.*	Alciat, *Emb.* 159, Ed. 1581, p. 556.
	307	,, ,,	Whitney's *Emb.* Ed. 1586, p. 62.
	308	,, ,,	Camerarius, Ed. 1590, p. 36.
Envy.	432	*Inuidiæ descriptio*	Whitney's *Emb.* Ed. 1586, p. 94.
	431	,, ,,	Alciat, *Emb.* 71, Ed. 1581.
Falconry .	366	*Sic maiora cedunt*	Giovio's *Sent. Imprese*, Ed. 1562, p. 41.
Fame armed with a Pen.	446	*Pennæ gloria immortalis*	Whitney's *Emb.* Ed. 1586, p. 197.
	446	,, ,,	Junius, Ed. 1565.
Fardel on a Swimmer	480	*Auri sacra fames quid non?*	Whitney's *Emb.* Ed. 1586, p. 179.
	481	.	Perriere's *Th. Bons Engins*, Ed. 1539, p. 70.
February .	135	*Iddio, perche è uecchio, Fa suoi al suo essempio.*	Spenser's *Works*, Ed. 1616.
Fleece, Golden, and Phryxus.	229	*Diues indoctus*	Alciat, *Emb.* 189, Ed. 1581.
	229	*In diuitem indoctum*	Whitney's *Emb.* Ed. 1586, p. 214.
Fleece, Golden, Order of.	228	*Precium non vile laborum* .	Paradin's *Dev. Her.* Ed. 1562, f. 25.
*Flourishes of Arms, &c.	124	*Dabit Deus his quoque finem*	Drummond's *Scotland*, Ed. 1665.
*Forehead measured by Compasses.	129	*Fronte nulla fides*	Cullum's *Hawsted*, Ed. 1813.
	129	,, ,,	Whitney's *Emb.* Ed. 1586, p. 100.
	129	,, ,,	Sambucus, *Emb.* Ed. 1564, p. 177.
Forehead shows the Man.	129	*Frons hominem præfert*	Symeoni's *Dev. Her.* Ed. 1561, p. 246.
Fortune	261	*L'ymage de fortune*	Corrozet's *Hecatomg.* Ed. 1540, Emb. 41.
Fox and Grapes	310	*Ficta eius quod haberi nequit recusatio.*	Freitag's *Myth. Eth.* Ed. 1579, p. 127.
	310	*Stultitia sua seipsum saginari*	Faerni's *Fables*, Ed. 1583.
	311	,, ,,	Whitney's *Emb.* Ed. 1586, p. 98.

DEVICE.	PAGE.	MOTTO.	SOURCE.
Gem in a Ring of Gold	418	*Beaulté compaigne de bonté* .	Corrozet's *Hecatomg.* Ed. 1540, p. 83.
Gemini . . .	355	*Tratta della Sphera*	Brucioli, Ed. Venice, 1543.
Gold on the Touch-stone.	175	*Sic spectanda fides*	Paradin's *Dev. Her.* Ed. 1562, f. 100.
	178	,, ,,	Whitney's *Emb.* Ed. 1586, p. 139.
	177	*Pecunia sanguis et anima mortalium.*	Crispin de Passe, about 1589.
Good out of Evil	447	*Ex malo bonum*	Montenay, Ed. 1574.
Halcyon days (*see* King-fisher).	391		
Hands of Providence. Pl. XVI.	489	*Dominus pauperem facit, et ditat.*	Coornhert, Ed. 1585, p. 6.
Hares biting a dead Lion.	305	*Cum larvis non luctandum* .	Whitney's *Emb.* Ed. 1586, p. 127.
	305	,, ,,	Alciat, *Emb.* 153, Ed. 1581.
	306	,, ,,	Reusner's *Emb.* Ed. 1581.
Harpocrates guarding his Mouth.	208	*Silentium* .	Whitney's *Emb.* Ed. 1586, p. 61.
	209	*The Goddess Angeronа*	*Pegma*, Ed. 1555, p. 109.
Hawk on Mummy-case	26	Πῶς δηλοῦσι ψυχήν	Cory's *Horapollo*, Ed. 1840, p. 15.
Hen eating her own Eggs.	411	*Quæ ante pedes* .	Whitney's *Emb.* Ed. 1586, p. 64.
	411	,, ,,	Sambucus, *Emb.* Ed. 1564, p. 30.
Hives of Bees (*see* Bees).	358, &c.		
Hope and Nemesis .	182	*Illicitum non sperandum*	Whitney's *Emb.* Ed. 1586, p. 139.
Hydra slain by Hercules.	374	*Multiplication de proces*	Corrozet's *Hecatomg.* Ed. 1540.
Icarus and his ill Fortune.	288	*In astrologos*	Alciat, *Emb.* 103, Ed. 1581.
	288	,, ,,	Whitney's *Emb.* Ed. 1586, p. 28.
	289	*Faire tout par moyen* .	Corrozet's *Hecatomg.* Ed. 1540, Emb. 67.
Idiot-Fool, and Death	472		Holbein's *Imag. Mortis*, Lyons, 1547.
*Introductory Lines (*see* D. O. M.).	464		Whitney.
Inverted Torch .	171	*Qui me alit me extinguit*	Symeoni's *Sent. Imprese*, 1561, p. 35.

DEVICE.	PAGE.	MOTTO.	SOURCE.
Inverted Torch .	173	*Qui me alit me extinguit*	Paradin's *Dev. Her.* Ed. 1562, f. 169.
	173	,, ,,	Whitney's *Emb.* Ed. 1586, p. 183.
*Jackdaw in Peacock's Feathers.	313	*Quod sis esse velis*	Camerarius, Ed. 1596, Emb. 81.
Janus, Double-headed	139	*Prudentes* .	Alciat, Ed. 1581, p. 92.
	139	*Respice, et prospice*	Whitney's *Emb.* Ed. 1586, p. 108.
	140		Perriere's *Th. Bons Engins,* Ed. 1539.
John, St. (Apocalypse). Pl. VIII.	49		*Block-book*, about 1430.
John, St., the Evangelist, History of. Pl. VII.	49		*Block-book*, about 1430.
June .	136		Spenser's *Works*, Ed. 1616.
King-fisher, Emblem of Tranquillity.	392	*Nous scavons bien le temps* .	Giovio's *Sent. Imprese*, Ed. 1561, p. 107.
	125	*Mediis tranquillus in undis.*	Drummond's *Scotland*, Ed. 1665.
Lamp burning	456	*Quo modo vitam* .	Horapollo, Ed. 1551, p. 220.
Laurel, Safety against Thunderbolts.	422	*Conscientia integra, laurus* .	Sambucus, *Emb.* Ed. 1564, p. 14.
	423	*Murus æneus, sana conscientia.*	Whitney's *Emb.* Ed. 1586, p. 67.
	423	. .	Camerarius, Ed. 1590, p. 35.
*Leafless Trees and Rainbow.	128	*Jam satis* .	Paradin's *Dev. Her.* Ed. 1562, f. 38.
	128	. . .	Cullum's *Hawsted*, Ed. 1813.
*Lion and Whelp .	124	*Unum quidem, sed leonem* .	Drummond's *Scotland*, Ed. 1665.
*Lion in a Net, and Hares.	124	*Et lepores devicto insultant leone.*	Drummond's *Scotland*, Ed. 1665.
Loadstone (*see* Astronomer).	335		
*Loadstone towards the Pole.	123	*Maria Stuart, sa virtu m'attire.*	Drummond's *Scotland*, Ed. 1665.
*Lotterie in London, 1568.	208	*Video, et taceo*	Whitney's *Emb.* Ed. 1586, p. 62.
*Lucrece	131		*Lower Tabley Old Hall*, 1619.

DEVICE.	PAGE.	MOTTO.	SOURCE.
Macaber, Dance of (*see* Brunet's *Manuel*, vol. v. c. 1559-60).	39	.	MS. of the 14th century.
*Man measuring his Forehead.	129	*Fronte nulla fides*	Cullum's *Hawsted*, Ed. 1813.
Man swimming with a Burden (*see* Fardel on a Swimmer).	480		
Map of inhabited World.	351	*Partium τῆς οἰκουμένης symbola.*	Sambucus' *Emb.* Ed. 1564, p. 113.
Medeia and the Swallows.	189	*Ei qui semel sua prodegerit, aliena credi non oportere.*	Alciat, *Emb.* 54, Ed. 1581.
	190	,, ,,	Whitney's *Emb.* Ed. 1586, p. 33.
Mercury and Fortune.	255	*Ars Naturam adiuuans* .	Alciat, *Emb.* Ed. 1551, p. 107.
Mercury charming Argus.	123	*Eloquium tot lumina clausit.*	Drummond's *Scotland*, Ed. 1665.
Mercury mending a Lute.	256	*Industria naturam corrigit* .	Sambucus' *Emb.* Ed. 1564, p. 57.
	256	,, ,,	Whitney's *Emb.* Ed. 1586, p. 92.
Michael, St., Order of	227	*Immensi tremor Oceani* .	Paradin's *Dev. Her.* Ed. 1562, p. 12.
*Milo caught in a Tree	344	*Quibus rebus confidimus, iis maxime evertimur.*	Le Bey de Batilly, Ed. 1596, Emb. 18.
Moth and Candle (*see* Butterfly).	151		
Motley Fool (*see* Child).	484		
Mouse caught by an Oyster.	130	*Captiuus ob gulam*	Alciat, *Emb.* 94, Ed. Paris, 1602, p. 437.
	130	,, ,,	Whitney's *Emb.* Ed. 1586, p. 128.
	130		Freitag's *Myth. Eth.* Ed. 1579, p. 169.
Narcissus viewing himself.	294	Φιλαυτία .	Alciat, *Emb.* 69, Ed. 1581, p. 261.
	295	*Amor sui* .	Whitney's *Emb.* Ed. 1586, p. 149.
	295	*Contemnens alios, arsit amore sui.*	Aneau's *Picta Poesis*, Ed. 1552, p. 48.
Nemesis and Hope (*see* Hope).	182		
Niobe's Children slain	292	*Superbia*	Alciat, *Emb.* 67, Ed. 1581, p. 255.
	293	*Superbiæ ultio*	Whitney's *Emb.* Ed. 1586, p. 13.

DEVICE.	PAGE.	MOTTO.	SOURCE.
Nun or Canoness	469		Holbein's *Simulachra, &c.,* Sign. Liiij. 1538.
Oak and Reed, or Osier.	315	*Vincit qui patitur*	Whitney's *Emb.* Ed. 1586, p. 220.
	314	Εἴξας νικᾷ, or *victrix animi equitas.*	Junius' *Emb.* Ed. 1565.
Occasion. Pl. XII.	265	*Dum Tempus labitur, Occasionem fronte capillatam remorantur.*	David's *Occasio,* Ed. 1605, p. 117.
Occasion, or Opportunity.	259	*In occasionem.* Διαλογιστικῶν.	Alciat, *Emb.* Ed. 1551, p. 133.
	260	,, ,,	Whitney's *Emb.* Ed. 1586, p. 181.
	258		Perriere's *Th. Bons Engins,* Ed. 1539.
	261	*L'image d'occasion*	Corrozet's *Hecatomg.* Ed. 1540, p. 84.
Olive and Vine (*see* Vine).	249		
Order, &c. (*see* Fleece, Golden, *and* Michael, St., Order of).	228 227		
Orpheus and Harp	271	*La force d'eloquence*	Cousteau's *Pegme,* Ed. 1560, p. 389.
	272	*Musicæ, et poetica vis*	Reusner's *Emb.* Ed. 1581, p. 129.
	272	*Orphei musica*	Whitney's *Emb.* Ed. 1586, p. 186.
Ostrich eating Iron	233	*Spiritus durissima coquit*	Giovio's *Sent. Imprese,* Ed. 1561, p. 115.
	234	,, ,,	Camerarius, *Emb.* Ed. 1595, p. 19.
	126	,, ,,	*Gent. Mag.* Nov. 1811, p. 416.
Ostrich with outspread Wings.	370	*Nil penna, sed usus*	Paradin's *Dev. Her.* Ed. 1562, f. 23.
	370	,, ,,	Whitney's *Emb.* Ed. 1586, p. 51.
Palm Tree	124	*Ponderibus virtus innata resistit.*	Drummond's *Scotland,* Ed. 1665.
Pegasus	141	*Ars rhetor, triplex movet, &c.*	Bocchius, *Symb.* 137, Ed. 1555, p. 314.
	143	*Non absque Theseo*	Reusner's *Emb.* Ed. 1581, p. 1.

DEVICE.	PAGE.	MOTTO.	SOURCE.
Pegasus (*see* Bellerophon).	299		
Pelican and Young .	393	ΠΕΡΙ ΤΗΣ ΠΕΛΕΚΑΝΟΣ .	Epiphanius, S., Ed. 1588, p. 30.
	394	*Pro lege et grege* .	Reusner's *Emb.* Ed. 1581, p. 73.
	394	,, ,,	Camerarius, Ed. 1596, p. 87.
	395	*Quod in te est, prome* .	Junius' *Emb.* 7, Ed. 1565.
	395	,, ,,	Whitney's *Emb.* Ed. 1586, p. 87.
Phaeton and the Sun's Chariot.	285	*In temerarios*	Alciat, *Emb.* 56, Ed. 1551.
	284	*Phaethontis casus*	Plantinian *Ovid*, Ed. 1591, pp. 46-9.
	281	*Fetonte fulminato da Gioue* .	Symeoni's *Ovid*, Ed. 1559, p. 34.
Phœnix, Emblem of New Birth, &c.	381	*Juuenilia studia cum prouectiori ætate permutata.*	Freitag's *Myth. Eth.* Ed. 1579, p. 249.
	123	*En ma fin gît mon commencement.*	Drummond's *Scotland*, Ed. 1665.
Phœnix, Emblem of Duration.	23	Πῶς ψυχὴν ἐνταῦθα πολὺν χρόνον διαβέβουσαν.	Horapollo, Ed. 1551, p. 52.
Phœnix, Emblem of Loneliness.	234	*Sola facta solum Deum sequor*	Paradin's *Dev. Her.* Ed. 1562, f. 165.
	235	*Sola facta solum Deum sequor*	Giovio's *Sent. Imprese*, Ed. 1561.
Phœnix, Emblem of Oneliness.	385	*Unica semper auis*	Paradin's *Dev. Her.* Ed. 1562, f. 53.
	385	,, ,,	Reusner's *Emb.* Ed. 1581, p. 98.
	387	,, ,,	Whitney's *Emb.* Ed. 1586, p. 177.
Phœnix with two Hearts.	384	*Eadem inter se. Sunt eadem vni tertia.*	Hawkin's ΠΑΡΘΕΝΟΣ, Ed. 1633.
Phryxus (*see* Fleece, Golden).	229		
*Pilgrim travelling .	128	*Dum transis, time* . .	Cullum's *Hawsted*, Ed. 1813.
Pine-trees in a Storm.	476	*Nimium rebus ne fide secundis.*	Whitney's *Emb.* Ed. 1586, p. 59.
	475	,, ,,	Sambucus' *Emb.* Ed. 1569 p. 279.
Poets, Insignia of (*see* Swan).	218		
Porcupine .	231	*Cominus et eminus*	Giovio's *Sent. Imprese*, Ed. 1561, p. 56.
	124	*Ne volutetur*	Drummond's *Scotland*, Ed. 1665.
*Portcullis .	124	*Altera securitas* .	Drummond's *Scotland*, Ed. 1665.

DEVICE.	PAGE.	MOTTO.	SOURCE.
Progne, or Procne	193	*Impotentis Vindictæ Fæmina*	Aneau's *Picta Poesis*, Ed. 1552, p. 73.
Prometheus chained	266	*Quæ supra nos, nihil ad nos.*	Alciat, *Emb.* 102, Ed. 1551.
	267	*Curiositas Fugienda*	Aneau's *Picta Poesis*, Ed. 1552, p. 90.
	267	. . . . .	*Microcosme*, Ed. 1579, p. 5.
	268	*O vita, misero longa*	Reusner's *Emb.* Ed. 1581, p. 37.
	268	,, ,,	Whitney's *Emb.* Ed. 1586, p. 75.
Providence and Girdle (*see* Drake's Ship).	413		
*Pyramid and Ivy	124	*Te stante virebo*	Drummond's *Scotland*, Ed. 1665.
			Various Authors.
Quivers of Cupid and Death (*see* Cupid and Death).	401		
*Rock in Waves	125	*Rompe ch'il percote*	Drummond's *Scotland*, Ed. 1665.
Rose and Thorn	333	*Post amara dulcia*	Whitney's *Emb.* Ed. 1586, p. 165.
	332	,, ,,	Perriere's *Th. Bons Engins*, Ed. 1539, Emb. 30.
	333	*Armat spina rosas, mella tegunt apes.*	Otho Vænius, Ed. 1608, p. 160.
Ruins and Writings	443	*Scripta manent*	Whitney's *Emb.* Ed. 1586, p. 131.
	442		Costalius' *Pegma*, Ed. 1555, p. 178.
Salamander	126	*Nutrisco et extinguo*	Jovio's *Dialogue*, Ed. 1561, p. 24.
	123	,, ,,	Drummond's *Scotland*, Ed. 1665.
Satan, Fall of. Pl. XI.	133	*Lapsus Satanæ*	Boissard's *Theatrum*, Ed. 1596, p. 19.
Sepulchre and Cross (*see* Arrow wreathed).	183 & 126		
Serpent and Countryman (*see* Countryman).	197	*Maleficio beneficium compensatum.*	Freitag's *Myth. Eth.* Ed. 1579, p. 177.

DEVICE.	PAGE.	MOTTO.	SOURCE.
*Serpent and Country-man.	198	*Merces anguina* .	Reusner's *Emb.* Ed. 1581, p. 81.
*Serpent in the Bosom	199	*In sinu alere serpentem*	Whitney's *Emb.* Ed. 1586, p. 189.
Seven Ages of Man. Pl. XV.	407	*Rota vitæ quæ septima notatur.*	*Archæologia*, vol. xxxv. 1853, p. 167.
*Shadows Fled and Pursued.	468	*Mulier umbra viri*	Whitney's *Emb.* Ed. 1586, p. 218.
Shield, Untrustworthy (*see* Brasidas and his Shield).	195		
Ship on the Sea. .	125	*Durate*	Drummond's *Scotland*, Ed. 1665.
Ship tossed by the Waves.	435	*Res humanæ in summo declinans.*	Sambucus' *Emb.* Ed. 1564, p. 46.
	435	,, ,,	Whitney's *Emb.* Ed. 1586, p. 11.
Ship sailing forward .	436	*Constantia comes victoriæ*	Whitney's *Emb.* Ed. 1586, p. 137.
	436	,, ,,	Alciat, *Emb.* 43, Ed. 1581.
*Ship with Mast over-board.	124	*Nusquam nisi rectum* .	Drummond's *Scotland*, Ed. 1665.
Sieve held by Cupid (*see* Cupid).	329		
Sirens and Ulysses	253	*Sirenes*	Alciat, *Emb.* Ed. 1551.
	254	,, ,,	Whitney's *Emb.* Ed. 1586, p. 10.
Skull, human	337	*Ex Maximo Minimum*	Aneau's *Picta Poesis*, Ed. 1552, p. 55.
	338	,, ,,	Whitney's *Emb.* Ed. 1586, p. 229.
Snake fastened on the Finger.	342	*Quis contra nos ?*	Paradin's *Dev. Her.* Ed. 1562, f. 112.
	342	*Si Deus nobiscum, quis contra nos ?*	Whitney's *Emb.* Ed. 1586, p. 166.
	126	*Quis contra nos ?*	*Gent. Mag.* Nov. 1811, p. 416.
Snake in the Grass .	340	*Latet anguis in herba*	Paradin's *Dev. Her.* Ed. 1562, f. 41.
	340	,, ,,	Whitney's *Emb.* Ed. 1586, p. 24.
Speculum,—*Photoliths in small size.* Pl. IV. and V.	44	*Speculum humanæ salvationis.*	An exact MS. copy in the collection of H. Yates Thompson, Esq.
Stag wounded . .	398	*Esto tiene su remedio y non yo.*	Giovio and Symeoni's *Sent. Imprese*, Ed. 1561.
	398	*Esto tienne su remedio, y non yo.*	Paradin's *Dev. Her.* Ed. 1562, f. 168.
	399	*Vulnus, salus et umbra*	Camerarius, Ed. 1595, Emb. 69, p. 71.

DEVICE.	PAGE.	MOTTO.	SOURCE.
Star, Hieroglyphic .	25	Τί ἀστέρα γράφοντες δηλοῦσι.	Leeman's *Horapollo*, Ed. 1835, Fig. 31.
	25	,, ,,	Cory's *Horapollo*, Ed. 1840, p. 30.
Storks, their Purity and Love.	28	.	Epiphanius, S., Ed. 1588, p. 106.
Student entangled in Love.	441	*In studiosum captum amore.*	Whitney's *Emb.* Ed. 1586, p. 135.
	441	,, ,,	Alciat, *Emb.* 108, Ed. 1581.
Sun and Moon .	52	*De sole et luna*	*Dyal. Creat.* Lyons Ed. 1511.
*Sun in Eclipse .	124	*Medio occidet die*	Drummond's *Scotland*, Ed. 1665.
Sun Setting	323	*Tempus omnia terminat*	Whitney's *Emb.* Ed. 1586, p. 230.
Sun, Wind, and Traveller.	165	*Plus par douleeur que par force.*	Corrozet's *Hecatomg.* Ed. 1540, Emb. 28.
	166	*Moderata vis impotenti violentia potior.*	Freitag's *Myth. Eth.* Ed. 1579, p. 27.
Swan, Insignia of Poets.	218	*Insignia poetarum*	Alciat, *Emb.* Ed. 1551, p. 197.
	217	,, ,,	Whitney's *Emb.* Ed. 1586, p. 126.
Swan (Old Age eloquent).	215	*Facunda senectus*	Aneau's *Picta Poesis*, Ed. 1552, p. 28.
Swan (Pure Truth) .	216	*Simplicitas veri sana* .	Reusner's *Emb.* Ed. 1581, p. 91.
	217	*Sibi canit et orbi*	Camerarius, Ed. 1595, Emb. 23.
Swan singing at Death	213	Παῖς γέροντα μουσικόν .	Horapollo, Ed. 1551, p. 136.
Sword broken on an Anvil.	326		Perriere's *Th. Bons Engins*, Ed. 1539, p. 31.
	327	*Importunitas euitanda*	Whitney's *Emb.* Ed. 1586, p. 192.
*Sword to weigh Gold	124	*Quid nisi victis dolor* .	Drummond's *Scotland*, Ed. 1665.
Sword with a Motto .	138	*Si Fortune me tourmente L'Esperance me contente.*	Douce's *Illustr.* vol. i. p. 452.
Testing of Gold (*see* Gold on Touchstone).	173		
Theatre of Human Life. Pl. XIV.	405	*Theatrum omnium miserorum.*	Boissard's *Theatrum*, 1596.
Things at our Feet (*see* Hen eating her Eggs).	411		

DEVICE.	PAGE.	MOTTO.	SOURCE.
Thread of Life .	454	*Quo pacto mortem seu hominis exitum.*	Horapollo, Ed. 1551, p. 219.
Time flying, &c.	466	*Quæ sequimur fugimus, nosque fugiunt.*	Sambucus, Ed. 1564.
	467	. . .	Whitney's *Emb.* Ed. 1586, p. 199.
Time leading the Seasons, and of Eternity a Symbol. Pl. XVII.	491	*Tempus irrevocabile*	Vænius, *Emb. Hor.* Ed. 1612, p. 206.
Timon . . .	427	**Μισάνθρωπος Τίμων**	Sambucus, Ed. 1564.
Title-page, *Photolith fac-simile.* Pl. IX.	57	*Navis stultorum*	Brant's and Locher's *Navis stultifera*, Ed. 1497.
*Tongue with Bats' Wings.	128	*Quò tendis?*	Cullum's *Hawsted*, Ed. 1813.
	128	,, ,,	Paradin's *Dev. Her.* Ed. 1562, f. 65.
Torch (*see* Inverted Torch).	171		
Tree of Life (*see* Arrow wreathed).	183		
*Tree planted in a Churchyard.	124	*Pietas revocabit ob orco*	Drummond's *Scotland*, Ed. 1665.
*Triangle, Sun, Circle	124	*Trino non convenit orbis*	Drummond's *Scotland*, Ed. 1665.
*Trophy on a Tree, &c.	124	*Ut casus dederet* .	Drummond's *Scotland*, Ed. 1665.
Turkey and Cock .	357	*Jus hospitalitatis violatum*	Freitag's *Myth. Eth.* Ed. 1579, p. 237.
	357	*Rabie succensa tumescit*	Camerarius, Ed. 1596, Emb. 47.
Unicorn, Type of Faith undefiled.	371	*Victrix casta fides*	Reusner's *Emb.* Ed. 1581, p. 60.
	372	*Nil inexplorato* .	Camerarius, Ed. 1595, Emb. 12.
	372	*Hoc virtutis amor*	Camerarius, Ed. 1595, Emb. 13.
	372	*Pretiosum quod utile*	Camerarius, Ed. 1595, Emb. 14, pp. 14—16.
*Venus dispensing Cupid from his Oaths.	328	*Amoris iusiurandum pœnam non habet.*	Van Veen's *Emb. of Love*, p. 140.
Vine and Olive .	249	*Prudentes vino abstinent*	Whitney's *Emb.* Ed. 1586, p. 133.
	249	,, ,,	Alciat, *Emb.* 24, Ed. 1602, p. 164.

DEVICE.	PAGE.	MOTTO.	SOURCE.
*Vine watered with Wine.	124	*Mea sic mihi prosunt*	Drummond's *Scotland*, Ed. 1665.
*Waves and Siren	125	*Bella Maria*	Drummond's *Scotland*, Ed. 1665.
*Waves, with Sun over	125	*Nunquam siccabitur æstu*	Drummond's *Scotland*, Ed. 1665.
Wheat among Bones	184	*Spes altera vitæ*	Camerarius, Ed. 1595, p. 102.
	184	,, ,,	Paradin's *Dev. Her.* Ed. 1562.
Wheel rolling into the Sea	124	*Pena di dolor venda de Speranza.*	Drummond's *Scotland*, Ed. 1665.
Wings and Feathers scattered	124	*Magnatum vicinitas*	Drummond's *Scotland*, Ed. 1665.
World, Three-cornered (see Map, &c.).	351		
Wreath of Chivalry	169	*Ut tempore proveniat apto*	Paradin's *Dev. Her.* Ed. 1562, f. 146.
Wreath of Oak	224	*Servati gratia civis*	Paradin's *Dev. Her.* Ed. 1562, f. 147.
Wreaths, Four on a Spear.	221	*Fortiter et feliciter*	Whitney's *Emb.* Ed. 1586, p. 115.
	222	*Hic ornari aut mori*	Camerarius, Ed. 1590, Emb. 99.
Wrongs engraved on Marble.	457	*Scribit in marmore læsus*	Giovio and Symeoni's *Sent. Imprese*, Ed. 1562, p. 24.
	458	,, ,,	Paradin's *Dev. Her.* Ed. 1562, f. 160.
	460	,, ,,	Whitney's *Emb.* Ed. 1586, p. 183.
Zodiac, Signs of. Pl. XIII.	353	*Trattato della sphera*	Brucioli, Ed. Venetia, 1543, Title.

Durand, ed. [illegible]

III.

EFERENCES TO PASSAGES FROM SHAKESPEARE, IN THE ORDER OF THE PLAYS AND POEMS OF MACMILLAN'S EDITION, 1866, AND TO THE CORRESPONDING DEVICES AND SUBJECTS OF THE EMBLEMS TREATED OF IN THIS WORK.

N.B. The subjects printed in *italics* have no corresponding device.

THE TEMPEST.

VOL.	PAGE.	ACT.	SC.	LINE.	DEVICE OR SUBJECT.	PAGES.
I.	20	I.	2	387	*Appreciation of music*	116
	36	II.	2	7	Ape and miser's gold . . .	438
	48	III.	2	135	Hands of Providence. Plate XVI.	489
	50	III.	3	21	Unicorn .	. 373
	50	III.	3	21	Phœnix . . .	373, 385
	50	III.	3	22	Phœnix, type of oneliness	234, 236
	53	III.	3	95	Laurel, type of conscience	422, 424
	54	IV.	1	1	Thread of life . .	454, 455
	57	IV.	1	110	Diligence and idleness .	145, 146
	64	V.	1	21	*rarer action in virtue*	. 462

THE TWO GENTLEMEN OF VERONA.

VOL.	PAGE.	ACT.	SC.	LINE.	DEVICE OR SUBJECT.	PAGES.
I.	112	II.	6	24	*a swarthy Ethiope* .	. 162
	121	III.	1	153	Phaeton . .	285, 286
	129	III.	2	68	Orpheus and harp	273, 274
	135	IV.	2	38	Gem in ring of gold	418, 419
	143	IV.	4	87	The Fox and Grapes	310, 312

THE MERRY WIVES OF WINDSOR.

VOL.	PAGE.	ACT.	SC.	LINE.	DEVICE OR SUBJECT.	PAGES.
I.	177	I.	3	64	*East and West Indies*	351, 352
	186	II.	1	106	Actæon and hounds . .	275, 276
	190	II.	2	5	Gemini,—Zodiac. Plate XIII.	353, 355
	196	II.	2	187	Shadows fled and followed	466, 468

MEASURE FOR MEASURE.

VOL.	PAGE.	ACT.	SC.	LINE.	DEVICE OR SUBJECT.	PAGES.
I.	296	I.	1	28	Hen eating her own eggs .	411, 412
	303	I.	2	158	Zodiac, signs of. Plate XIII.	353, 354
	324	II.	2	149	Gold on the touchstone	175, 180
	327	II.	4	1	Student entangled in love . . .	. 441
	334	III.	1	6	Idiot-fool, and death, Holbein's *Simulachres* .	. 472
	334	III.	1	17	Sleep and death, Holbein's *Simulachres*	469, 470
	340	III.	1	175	Gem in ring of gold	417, 418

THE COMEDY OF ERRORS.

VOL.	PAGE.	ACT.	SC.	LINE.	DEVICE OR SUBJECT.	PAGES.
I.	411	II.	1	97	Eagle renewing its feathers	. 369
	417	II.	2	167	Elm and vine .	307, 309
	425	III.	2	27	Sirens and Ulysses	253, 254
	429	III.	2	131	*America* . .	351, 352
	437	IV.	2	53	*Time turning back*	473
	455	V.	1	210	Circe transforming men	252

MUCH ADO ABOUT NOTHING.

VOL.	PAGE.	ACT.	SC.	LINE.	DEVICE OR SUBJECT.	PAGES.
II.	22	II.	1	214	*Withered branch* .	. 181
	69	V.	1	4	*Water through a sieve*	329, 331
	75	V.	1	170	Adam hiding	415, 416

LOVE'S LABOUR'S LOST.

VOL.	PAGE.	ACT.	SC.	LINE.	DEVICE OR SUBJECT.	PAGES.
II.	97	I.	1	1	Ruins and writings	443, 444
	97	I.	1	4	Time leading the Seasons. Plate XVII.	. 491
	114	II.	1	56	Bear, cub, and Cupid . .	349, 350
	138	IV.	2	100	Oak and reed, or osier .	315, 316
	144	IV.	3	97	Rose and thorn .	333, 334
	144	IV.	3	111	*Juno but an Ethiope were*	. 162
	151	IV.	3	308	Bacchus .	247, 249

MIDSUMMER NIGHT'S DREAM.

VOL.	PAGE.	ACT.	SC.	LINE.	DEVICE OR SUBJECT.	PAGES.
II.	204	I.	1	168	*arrow with a golden head*	. 404
	205	I.	1	180	Astronomer and magnet	335, 336
	206	I.	1	232	Bear, cub, and Cupid .	. 349
	215	II.	1	148	*Appreciation of melody* .	. 116
	216	II.	1	155	Cupid and Death .	401, 404
	216	II.	1	173	Drake's ship . . .	413, 415
	216	II.	1	181	Ape and miser's gold . . .	488
	217	II.	1	194	Astronomer and magnet . .	335, 336
	218	II.	1	227	Daphne changed to a laurel . .	296, 297
	218	II.	1	231	*Golding's Ovid used* . . .	244
	225	II.	2	145	Countryman and serpent	197, 198
	239	III.	2	200	*Coats in heraldry* . .	218, 220
	240	III.	2	237	Ape and miser's gold	. 488
	241	III.	2	260	Snake on the finger	342, 343

MIDSUMMER NIGHT'S DREAM—*continued.*

VOL.	PAGE.	ACT.	SC.	LINE.	DEVICE OR SUBJECT.	PAGES.
II.	250	IV.	I	37	Vine and elm	307, 309
	258	V.	I	I	*Æsop* .	. 302
	258	V.	I	12	The poet's glory	379, 380

MERCHANT OF VENICE.

VOL.	PAGE.	ACT.	SC.	LINE.	DEVICE OR SUBJECT.	PAGES.
II.	280	I.	I	50	The two-headed Janus .	139, 140
	281	I.	I	77	The world a stage	. 133
	281	I.	I	77	The world a stage. Plate XV.	407, 410
	284	I.	I	161	Golden fleece and Phryxus	229, 230
	286	I.	2	24	*The old man prophesying*	213, 215
	286	I.	2	4	Lottery .	208, 209
	296	II.	I	11	Lottery .	208, 209
	312	II.	7	4	*A casket scene*	150
	312	II.	7	20	*"golden mind," "golden bed"*	404
	313	II.	7	62	*Casket scene* .	150
	318	II.	9	63	*Casket scene* .	. 151
	319	II.	9	79	Moth and candle	151, 153
	325	III.	2	41	Insignia of Poets .	218, 219
	328	III.	2	115	*A painter's power* .	112
	345	IV.	I	75	The mountain pine	. 476
	347	IV.	I	124	Envy, description of	432, 433
	360	V.	I	54	*Appreciation of melody*	. 116
	361	V.	I	70	Power of music	271, 273

AS YOU LIKE IT.

VOL.	PAGE.	ACT.	SC.	LINE.	DEVICE OR SUBJECT.	PAGES.
II.	391	I.	3	69	*Juno's swans*, Golding's *Ovid*	244
	393	I.	3	120	*Ganymede*, Golding's *Ovid*	. 244
	394	II.	I	29	The wounded stag .	397, 398
	400	II.	4	43	Sword broken on an anvil	326, 327
	405	II.	7	13	A motley fool	485
	406	II.	7	42	*"A motley coat"* . . .	. 485
	409	II.	7	136	Theatre of human life. Plate XIV.	405, 406
	409	II.	7	137	Theatre of human life . . .	133, 405
	409	II.	7	139	The seven ages of man. Plate XV.	407, 409
	427	III.	3	67	Hawking . .	366, 368
	442	IV.	3	15	The Phœnix	234, 236

THE TAMING OF THE SHREW.

VOL.	PAGE.	ACT.	SC.	LINE.	DEVICE OR SUBJECT.	PAGES.
III.	10	Ind.	2	41	Hawking . . .	366, 367
	10	Ind.	2	47	*Mythological pictures by Titian*	114
	10	Ind.	2	47	*Cytherea, Io, Daphne, Apollo*	115
	10	Ind.	2	52	*Jupiter and Io* .	. 246
	10	Ind.	2	55	Daphne and Apollo	296, 297
	23	I.	2	24	*Two Italian sentences* . .	. 163
	45	II.	I	338	*Beautiful furniture described* . .	. 112
	67	IV.	I	174	Falconry	. 366, 367
	78	IV.	3	165	*"honour peereth in the meanest habit."* Plate XVI.	490

ALL'S WELL THAT ENDS WELL.

VOL.	PAGE.	ACT.	SC.	LINE.	DEVICE OR SUBJECT.	PAGES.
III.	112	I.	1	76	*Symbolical imagery* .	377
	119	I.	2	58	Bees,—and native land .	361, 365
	123	I.	3	73	A lottery	208, 210
	127	I.	3	182	Cupid and the sieve	329, 330
	132	II.	1	40	"*cicatrice an emblem of war*"	9
	133	II.	1	59	The Fox and the Grapes	310, 311
	201	V.	3	5	Niobe's children slain	292, 293
					TWELFTH NIGHT.	
III.	223	I.	1	9	Actæon and the hounds	277, 278
	224	I.	1	33	"*The rich golden shaft*"	404
	225	I.	2	10	Arion and the dolphin .	280, 282
	231	I.	3	127	Zodiac,—Taurus. Plate XIII.	353, 355
	234	I.	5	50	*Mottoes,—Latin, &c.* .	138
	240	I.	5	214	*Power of judging artistic skill*	113
	257	II.	5	15	A turkey-cock	357
	257	II.	5	27	A turkey-cock .	357
	265	III.	1	68	*Snatches of French*	163
	271	III.	2	73	*New map with the Indies*	352
	285	III.	4	340	Whitney's Introduction	464
					THE WINTER'S TALE.	
III.	323	I.	2	115	The wounded deer	398, 400
	371	IV.	1	7	*Old Time, power of* .	473
	382	IV.	4	116	*Proserpina,*—see *Ovid* .	244
	383	IV.	4	135	*Poetic ideas,* or symbolical imagery	379
	420	V.	2	8	"*Julio Romano*" .	110
	422	V.	3	14	*Description of statuary*	109
	423	V.	3	18	Sleep and death, Holbein's *Simulachres*	469, 470
	424	V.	3	63	*Description of statuary* . .	189
					KING JOHN.	
IV.	17	II.	1	134	Hares biting a dead lion . .	305, 306
	26	II.	1	373	Theatre of human life. Plate XIV. .	405, 406
	37	III.	1	96	Gold on the touchstone	177, 180
	42	III.	1	258	Snake on the finger	342, 343
	65	IV.	2	125	Occasion, 259; or Fortune . .	261, 264
	67	IV.	2	170	Mercury mending a lute .	256, 257
	76	IV.	3	155	Wind, sun, and traveller . .	166
	91	V.	7	1	The swan, the Poet's badge . .	218, 219
					RICHARD II.	
IV.	116	I.	1	202	Wreath of chivalry	169, 170
	125	I.	3	129	Envy	432, 433
	130	I.	3	275	"*no virtue like necessity*"	347
	131	I.	3	294	"*the frosty Caucasus*"	. 347

RICHARD II.—*continued.*

VOL.	PAGE.	ACT.	SC.	LINE.	DEVICE OR SUBJECT.	PAGES.
IV.	137	II.	1	53	Wreath of chivalry . .	169, 170
	140	II.	1	120	The Pelican	393, 396
	145	II.	1	270	*hollow eyes of death* . . .	. 339
	164	III.	2	12	Snake in the grass . . .	340, 343
	164	III.	2	24	*Cadmus and the serpent's teeth* .	. 245
	164	III.	2	29	Human dependence . .	. 465
	165	III.	2	37	Drake's ship . . .	413, 415
	168	III.	2	129	Countryman and serpent . . .	197, 198
	179	III.	3	178	Phaeton and the Sun-chariot . .	285, 286
	210	V.	3	57	Countryman and serpent . .	197, 198

FIRST PART HENRY IV.

VOL.	PAGE.	ACT.	SC.	LINE.	DEVICE OR SUBJECT.	PAGES.
IV.	317	IV.	1	97	Ostrich with spreading wings	. 370
	318	IV.	1	104	Mercury . .	255, 257
	323	IV.	3	30	*Sir Walter Blount* . . .	160
	337	V.	2	82	Time leading the Seasons. Plate XVII.	. 491
	342	V.	4	25	Hydra slain by Hercules	374, 375

SECOND PART HENRY IV.

VOL.	PAGE.	ACT.	SC.	LINE.	DEVICE OR SUBJECT.	PAGES.
IV.	392	II.	2	41	Time terminates all .	323
	405	II.	4	165	Sword with Spanish motto	137, 138
	431	IV.	1	70	Occasion, 259 ; Fortune .	261, 264
	450	IV.	4	103	Hands of Providence. Plate XVI.	. 489
	453	IV.	5	35	Sleep and Death, Holbein's *Simulachres*	469, 470
	454	IV.	5	75	Bees . . .	361, 364
	474	V.	3	136	Prometheus chained	266, 358

KING HENRY V.

VOL.	PAGE.	ACT.	SC.	LINE.	DEVICE OR SUBJECT.	PAGES.
IV.	491	I.	Chor.	5	Diligence and idleness .	145, 146
	493	I.	1	35	Hydra slain by Hercules	374, 375
	502	I.	2	178	Bees . . .	360, 362
	538	III.	4	1	*Snatches of French*	. 163
	543	III.	6	20	Image of Fortune .	261, 262
	544	III.	6	44	Thread of life	454, 455
	549	III.	7	10	Pegasus . . .	141, 142
	550	III.	7	54	*French and Latin proverb*	144
	552	III.	7	130	*The mastiff praised* .	483
	555	IV.	1	3	"goodness out of evil" .	447
	555	IV.	1	9	Time irrevocable. Plate XVII.	491
	564	IV.	1	256	*Sound sleep of the slave* .	147
	574	IV.	4	2	*Snatches of French*	163
	582	IV.	7	82	*Human dependence*	465
	588	IV.	8	100	*Human dependence*	. 465
	591	V.	1	13	Turkey-cock	357, 358
	596	V.	2	48	*Evils of war* . .	147
	598	V.	2	107	*Snatches of French*	163

FIRST PART HENRY VI.

VOL.	PAGE.	ACT.	SC.	LINE.	DEVICE OR SUBJECT.	PAGES.
V.	8	I.	1	127	*"A Talbot! a Talbot!"*	207
	14	I.	2	129	Halcyon days	392
	20	I.	4	49	Adamant on the anvil	347, 348
	25	I.	6	6	*Adonis' gardens*, Golding's *Ovid*	243
	29	II.	1	78	The cry, "A Talbot! a Talbot!"	207
	32	II.	3	11	The cry, "A Talbot! a Talbot!"	207
	33	II.	3	36	*A picture gallery named*	114
	36	II.	4	30	Rose and thorn	333, 334
	40	II.	5	28	*Death*	469
	68	IV.	1	188	Chaos,—*discord*	450, 453
	71	IV.	3	17	Prometheus bound	266, 268
	72	IV.	3	47	Prometheus bound	267, 268
	78	IV.	6	46	Icarus and his ill fortune	288, 291
	80	IV.	7	60	Order of St. Michael	227
	80	IV.	7	60	Order of the Golden Fleece	227, 228
	82	IV.	7	92	Phœnix	386, 388
	86	V.	3	30	Circe	252

SECOND PART HENRY VI.

VOL.	PAGE.	ACT.	SC.	LINE.	DEVICE OR SUBJECT.	PAGES.
V.	129	I.	4	16	Ban-dog	484
	132	II.	1	1	Falconry	366, 367
	145	II.	3	45	Pine-trees in a storm	477
	153	III.	1	55	Fox and Grapes	310, 312
	153	III.	1	69	*Jackdaw in peacock's feathers*	312
	158	III.	1	224	Snake in the grass	340, 341
	162	III.	1	343	Countryman and serpent	197, 198
	162	III.	1	360	The porcupine	231, 232
	168	III.	2	125	Bees	361, 363
	171	III.	2	232	Conscience	421, 422
	174	III.	2	310	Envy	432, 433
	182	IV.	1	83	The pelican	393, 394, 397
	185	IV.	2	27	Thread of life	454, 455
	197	IV.	7	49	*Latin proverb, "bona terra," &c.*	139
	206	IV.	10	23	Ostrich eating iron	233, 234
	213	V.	1	143	Bear and ragged staff	237, 239
	215	V.	1	196	Bear and ragged staff	237, 240
	217	V.	2	28	The game of chess	320
	217	V.	2	28	French proverb, "*La fin couronne*," *&c.*	320
	218	V.	2	45	Æneas and Anchises	191, 192

THIRD PART HENRY VI.

VOL.	PAGE.	ACT.	SC.	LINE.	DEVICE OR SUBJECT.	PAGES.
V.	244	I.	4	16	Phaeton	285, 286
	245	I.	4	35	Phœnix	385, 387, 388
	245	I.	4	39	*Leash of proverbs*	318
	252	II.	1	50	*Cupid felling a tree*	324
	252	II.	1	68	Human skull	337, 339

THIRD PART HENRY VI.—*continued.*

VOL.	PAGE.	ACT.	SC.	LINE.	DEVICE OR SUBJECT.	PAGES.
V.	271	II.	6	10	Phaeton . . .	285, 287
	280	III.	2	48	*Many drops pierce the stone*	. . 324
	281	III.	2	51	Inverted torch .	171, 173, 174
	284	III.	2	153	Bear, cub, and Cupid . .	349, 350
	285	III.	2	188	Countryman and serpent, *Sinon*	197, 200
	309	IV.	4	32	*Olive branch and laurel crown*	. 223
	312	IV.	7	24	Fox and Grapes	310, 312
	319	V.	1	34	*Atlas* . .	. 245
	319	V.	1	54	Wrongs on marble .	458, 461
	324	V.	3	1	Four wreaths on a spear	221, 222
	325	V.	4	1	Ships sailing	435, 436, 438
	329	V.	5	25	*Æsop* .	. 303
	332	V.	6	18	Icarus .	288, 290

KING RICHARD III.

VOL.	PAGE.	ACT.	SC.	LINE.	DEVICE OR SUBJECT.	PAGES.
V.	473	I.	1	1	"*Sun of York*"	223
	580	IV.	2	8	Gold on the touchstone	177, 180
	583	IV.	2	65	D. O. M. .	. 464
	606	IV.	4	418	The phœnix . .	385, 389
	615	V.	2		*Sir James Blount* .	. 160
	617	V.	3	30	*Sir James Blount* . .	160
	625	V.	3	181	Laurel, type of conscience	422, 425

KING HENRY VIII.

VOL.	PAGE.	ACT.	SC.	LINE.	DEVICE OR SUBJECT.	PAGES.
VI.	3	Prol.		15	A motley coat .	. 485
	45	II.	3	60	Gem in a ring of gold	418, 419
	46	II.	3	75	Gem in a ring of gold	418, 420
	56	III.	1	1	Orpheus and his harp .	271, 274
	76	III.	2	372	Laurel, type of conscience	422, 424
	79	III.	2	446	D. O. M. .	465
	84	IV.	1	81	*Emblems literally* .	. 9
	87	IV.	2	27	Wrongs on marble .	458, 459
	88	IV.	2	77	Swan, the Poet's badge	218, 219
	103	V.	3	10	D. O. M. .	. 464
	104	V.	3	43	Envy	432, 433
	114	V.	5	28	Phœnix	385, 390

TROILUS AND CRESSIDA.

VOL.	PAGE.	ACT.	SC.	LINE.	DEVICE OR SUBJECT.	PAGES.
VI.	130	I.	1	94	Daphne .	295, 296
	134	I.	2	100	*Epithet golden* .	403, 404
	142	I.	3	33	Ship sailing forward	436, 439
	142	I.	3	33	Perseus' horse	299, 300
	142	I.	3	39	Pegasus . .	. 143
	143	I.	3	49	Oak and reed, or osier .	. 315, 316
	144	I.	3	75	Bees	360, 361, 363

TROILUS AND CRESSIDA—*continued.*

VOL.	PAGE.	ACT.	SC.	LINE.	DEVICE OR SUBJECT.	PAGES.
VI.	144	I.	3	75	Chaos	449, 451
	155	I.	3	391	Ban-dog, or Mastiff	483
	164	II.	2	81	*Paris and Helen*	463
	164	II.	2	92	*Paris and Helen*	463
	168	II.	3	9	Mercury	255, 257
	169	II.	3	18	Envy	432, 433
	175	II.	3	189	*Cancer*,—Zodiac. Plate XIII.	353, 355
	177	II.	3	237	*Milo*	297
	178	II.	3	240	*Milo*	244, 344
	191	III.	2	169	Astronomer, magnet, polestar	335, 337
	198	III.	3	145	*Active exertion demanded*	378
	201	III.	3	196	Hand of Providence	489
	228	IV.	5	183	Pegasus	299, 300
	230	IV.	5	223	Setting sun	323
	247	V.	3	37	"*kindness befitting a lion*"	282
	253	V.	5	11	*Sagittary*,—Zodiac. Plate XIII.	353, 355
	259	V.	9	21	Hares biting a dead lion	304, 305
	261	V.	11	16	Niobe and her children	292, 294

CORIOLANUS.

VOL.	PAGE.	ACT.	SC.	LINE.	DEVICE OR SUBJECT.	PAGES.
VI.	287	I.	3	7	Wreath of oak	224, 225
	304	I.	9	58	Wreaths of victory	221, 225
	312	II.	1	109	Wreath of oak	224, 226
	323	II.	2	84	Wreath of oak	224, 225
	344	III.	1	161	D. O. M.	465
	369	IV.	1	44	Gold on the touchstone	175, 177, 181
	380	IV.	5	100	Sword on an anvil	325, 326
	403	V.	2	102	Oak and reed, or osier	315, 316
	407	V.	3	101	*Great Roman names*	201
	411	V.	3	206	*Great Roman names*	201

TITUS ANDRONICUS.

VOL.	PAGE.	ACT.	SC.	LINE.	DEVICE OR SUBJECT.	PAGES.
VI.	450	II.	1	5	The zodiac. Plate XIII.	353
	451	II.	1	14	Prometheus chained	266, 268
	451	II.	1	18	Sirenes	253, 254
	456	II.	2	1	*Tabley Old Hall, chimneypiece*	131
	459	II.	3	55	Actæon and hounds	277, 279
	472	III.	1	12	"*to write in the dust*"	461
	483	III.	2	9	Theatre of human life. Plate XIV.	405, 406
	490	IV.	1	85	Wrongs on marble	458, 460
	490	IV.	1	102	Wrongs on marble	458, 460
	492	IV.	2	18	*Conscience, power*	420
	501	IV.	3	52	The zodiac. Plate XIII.	353, 354
	522	V.	2	192	Progne	193
	527	V.	3	85	Countryman and serpent, 197 ; *Sinon*	200

ROMEO AND JULIET.

VOL.	PAGE.	ACT.	SC.	LINE.	DEVICE OR SUBJECT.	PAGES.
VII.	23	I.	4	4	Cupid hoodwinked	329, 331
	30	I.	5	41	Gem set in gold	418, 420
	42	II.	3	90	*Venus dispensing Cupid from his oaths*	327
	58	II.	4	187	Astronomer and magnet	187, 335
	59	II.	5	8	*Doves and winged Cupid*	245
	72	III.	2	1	Phaeton	285, 286
	75	III.	2	69	Snake in the grass	340, 341
	84	III.	3	126	*Dispensing from oaths*	327, 328
	117	V.	1	15	Time and eternity, symbol. Plate XVII.	492
	124	V.	3	61	D. O. M.	464
	126	V.	3	111	Theatre of human life. Plate XIV.	405, 406

TIMON OF ATHENS.

VOL.	PAGE.	ACT.	SC.	LINE.	DEVICE OR SUBJECT.	PAGES.
VII.	228	II.	1	28	*Jackdaw in borrowed plumes*	312, 314
	245	III.	3	1	Gold on the touchstone	175, 177, 180
	254	III.	5	31	Wrongs on marble	458, 459
	263	III.	6	103	*Timon's intense hatred*	427, 428
	265	IV.	1	35	The extravagance of Timon's hatred	429
	269	IV.	3	18	The extravagance of Timon's hatred	429
	270	IV.	3	51	The extravagance of Timon's hatred	429
	288	IV.	3	473	The extravagance of Timon's hatred	429
	269	IV.	3	25	Gold on the touchstone	175, 177, 178
	281	IV.	3	317	*Mention of many animals*	375
	281	IV.	3	324	*Mention of many animals*	376
	281	IV.	3	331	The unicorn	371, 373
	283	IV.	3	377	Gold on the touchstone	177, 178
	305	V.	4	69	*Timon's epitaph*	430

JULIUS CÆSAR.

VOL.	PAGE.	ACT.	SC.	LINE.	DEVICE OR SUBJECT.	PAGES.
VII.	322	I.	1	68	*Jackdaw in borrowed plumes*	312, 313
	326	I.	2	107	Æneas and Anchises	191, 193
	329	I.	2	192	*Characteristics of Brutus and Cassius*	205
	334	I.	3	5	Oak and reed, or osier	315, 316
	347	II.	1	203	Unicorn	371, 372
	363	III.	1	58	Astronomer and magnet	335, 336
	368	III.	1	205	The wounded stag	398, 399
	375	III.	2	73	Wrongs on marble	458, 459
	384	IV.	1	12	Three-cornered world	351, 352
	389	IV.	3	21	Dog baying at the moon	269, 270
	396	IV.	3	213	Occasion. Plate XII.	259, 260
	409	V.	3	80	Wreath of victory	221, 224, 226
	413	V.	5	25	Death of Brutus	202, 203

MACBETH.

VOL.	PAGE.	ACT.	SC.	LINE.	DEVICE OR SUBJECT.	PAGES.
VII.	438	I.	5	61	Snake in the strawberry	340, 341
	442	I.	7	44	*"I dare not," "I would"*	376

MACBETH—*continued.*

VOL.	PAGE.	ACT.	SC.	LINE.	DEVICE OR SUBJECT.	PAGES.
VII.	444	II.	1	7	D. O. M.	464
	454	II.	2	71	Sleep and death, Holbein's *Simulachres*	469, 470
	454	II.	3	67	*Gorgon*, Golding's *Ovid*	244
	459	II.	4	10	Falconry	366, 368
	467	III.	2	22	"*After life's fretful fever he sleeps well*"	492
	512	V.	5	19	Theatre of life. Plate XIV.	405, 406
	512	V.	5	24	Time leading on the Seasons. Plate XVII.	491

HAMLET.

VOL.	PAGE.	ACT.	SC.	LINE.	DEVICE OR SUBJECT.	PAGES.
VIII.	14	I.	2	71	Time leading the Seasons. Plate XVII.	491
	35	I.	5	13	The porcupine	231, 232
	63	II.	2	295	"*Man a God to man*"	283, 284
	79	III.	1	62	Theatre of life. Plate XIV.	405, 406
	79	III.	1	60	Sleep and death, Holbein's *Simulachres*	469, 470
	79	III.	1	70	*Death's praises, life's evils*	471
	80	III.	1	76	Fardel on a swimmer	481
	97	III.	2	259	The wounded stag	398, 399
	111	III.	4	53	The herald Mercury	255, 256, 258
	111	III.	4	55	*A poet's artistic description*	112
	117	III.	4	205	Cannon bursting	344, 345
	127	IV.	4	33	*The camel and his driver*	283
	135	IV.	5	135	The pelican	393, 394, 396
	145	IV.	7	84	Pegasus	143, 144
	153	V.	1	73	Human skull	337, 338
	154	V.	1	86	Human skull	337, 338
	158	V.	1	191	Human skull	337, 339
	164	V.	2	8	Drake's ship	413, 414

KING LEAR.

VOL.	PAGE.	ACT.	SC.	LINE.	DEVICE OR SUBJECT.	PAGES.
VIII.	280	I.	4	93	Child and motley fool	485
	295	I.	5	33	"*why seven stars*"	356
	307	II.	2	73	King-fishers	392, 393
	317	II.	4	61	Ants and grasshopper	148, 149
	320	II.	4	129	Prometheus and the vulture	266, 358
	342	III.	4	68	Pelican	393, 394, 396
	366	IV.	1	64	Hands of Providence. Plate XVI.	489
	416	V.	3	171	*our pleasant vices, &c.*	425

OTHELLO.

VOL.	PAGE.	ACT.	SC.	LINE.	DEVICE OR SUBJECT.	PAGES.
VIII.	477	II.	1	129	"*Old fond paradoxes*"	474
	498	II.	3	290	Hydra slain by Hercules	374, 375
	500	II.	3	326	*Symbols*	2
	505	III.	1	47	Occasion. Plate XII.	259, 261, 265
	512	III.	3	145	*Confidence kept back*	434
	513	III.	3	159	*Calumny*	434

OTHELLO—*continued.*

VOL.	PAGE.	ACT.	SC.	LINE.	DEVICE OR SUBJECT.	PAGES.
VIII.	574	V.	2	7	Light; the Canoness	469
	581	V.	2	146	Swan . . .	218
	586	V.	2	249	Swan	213, 216, 218, 220

ANTONY AND CLEOPATRA.

VOL.	PAGE.	ACT.	SC.	LINE.	DEVICE OR SUBJECT.	PAGES.
IX.	38	II.	2	201	*Appreciation of art* .	113
	40	II.	2	245	The lottery .	208, 211
	48	II.	5	95	Narcissus at the stream .	205, 206
	60	II.	7	101	Bacchus	246, 247
	64	III.	2	7	The Phœnix .	381, 387, 389
	100	III.	13	195	Ostrich, or estridge	371, 372
	109	IV.	6	5	Map, "three-nooked world"	351, 353
	118	IV.	12	3	Medeia, swallows on her breast	190
	123	IV.	14	46	Lamp, or torch of life	456
	132	IV.	15	84	Lamp of life	456
	150	V.	2	277	Time's and eternity's emblems. Plate XVII.	491
	151	V.	2	305	*Chimney-piece at the Old Hall, Tabley*	131

CYMBELINE.

VOL.	PAGE.	ACT.	SC.	LINE.	DEVICE OR SUBJECT.	PAGES.
IX.	167	I.	1	130	The eagle renewing its feathers	369
	183	I.	6	12	The phœnix .	234, 235, 236
	183	I.	6	15	The phœnix, "Arabian bird"	387, 390
	184	I.	6	30	Ape and miser's gold	488
	185	I.	6	46	*Contrasts of epithets*	474
	191	I.	6	188	*Jewels and ornaments of rare device*	8
	207	II.	4	68	*Adornments of Imogen's chamber*	111
	212	II.	5	33	Envy	432, 433
	226	III.	4	57	Countryman and serpent, *Sinon*	197, 208
	240	III.	6	31	Diligence and idleness	145, 147
	253	IV.	2	172	Pine-trees in a storm	477
	257	IV.	2	259	The oak and reed, or osier .	315

PERICLES PRINCE OF TYRE.

VOL.	PAGE.	ACT.	SC.	LINE.	DEVICE OR SUBJECT.	PAGES.
IX.	325	I.	2	102	Thread of life .	454, 455
	343	II.	2	17	*The Triumph Scene*	158, 159
	343	II.	2	19	*A black Ethiop:*	160
	343	II.	2	27	*Spanish motto*	162
	343	II.	2	30	Wreath of chivalry	168, 169
	343	II.	2	32	Inverted torch	170, 171, 173
	343	II.	2	33	*Quod* or *qui me alit*	170, 174
	344	II.	2	36	Gold on the touchstone	175, 177
	344	II.	2	43	*Withered branch* .	181, 183
	345	II.	3	9	Wreath of victory .	223, 224
	366	III.	2	26	*Man a God to man*	283, 284
	375	IV.	Intr.	12	Envy	432, 433

POEMS.

VENUS AND ADONIS.

VOL.	PAGE.	LINE.	SONNET.	DEVICE OR SUBJECT.	PAGES.
IX.	436			*Dedication* . . .	475

RAPE OF LUCRECE.

VOL.	PAGE.	LINE.	SONNET.	DEVICE OR SUBJECT.	PAGES.
IX.	544	1723		*The chimney-piece, Tabley Old Hall*	. 133
	515	869		Occasion or opportunity. Plate XII.	259, 264
	537	1513		Countryman and serpent, *Sinon* .	197, 200

SONNETS.

VOL.	PAGE.	LINE.	SONNET.	DEVICE OR SUBJECT.	PAGES.
IX.	578	1	55	Ruins and writings	443, 445
	583	1	65	Ruins and writings	443, 445

A LOVER'S COMPLAINT.

VOL.	PAGE.	LINE.	SONNET.	DEVICE OR SUBJECT.	PAGES.
IX.	638	92		Phœnix	381, 385, 389

THE PHŒNIX AND THE TURTLE.

VOL.	PAGE.	LINE.	SONNET.	DEVICE OR SUBJECT.	PAGES.
IX.	671	21		Phœnix	381, 385, 388
	671	25		Phœnix with two hearts	. 384
	671	37		Phœnix with two hearts	. . 384
	672	53		Phœnix' nest	23, 381, 389

Hesius, 1536.

Per cæcum videt omnia punctum.

ENERAL INDEX,

ARRANGED ACCORDING TO *FOUR* SUBJECTS:

1. EMBLEM WRITERS PREVIOUS TO A.D. 1616.
2. PROVERBS, SAYINGS, AND MOTTOES.
3. WORKS QUOTED OR REFERRED TO.
4. MISCELLANEOUS REFERENCES.

A.

B.

C.

D.

E.

F.

G.

H.

K.

L.

M.

N.

O.

P.

Q.

R.

S.

COLOPHON.

Ex literarum studiis immortalitatem acquiri.

Alciat, ed. 1534, *p.* 45.

BRADBURY, EVANS, AND CO., PRINTERS, WHITEFRIARS.

www.ingramcontent.com/pod-product-compliance
Lightning Source LLC
Chambersburg PA
CBHW022124020426
42334CB00015B/749

* 9 7 8 3 7 4 2 8 5 8 7 5 7 *